Introduction
to American
Constitutional Law

Introduction to American Constitutional Law

A SELECTION OF CASES
AND MATERIALS

BY

Francis H. Heller

UNIVERSITY OF KANSAS

Harper & Brothers . Publishers . New York

Library of Congress catalog card number: 51–11922

CONTENTS

Contents

P R E F A C E

The study of Constitutional Law is normally required of all hopeful aspirants to the legal profession. It is also customarily included in the curriculum of college departments of political science. To find two entries of the same name in the academic sweepstakes invites the assumption that identity of title reflects sameness of substance as well. In some instances this may indeed be the case. But, as Chief Justice Vanderbilt recently observed, there is a "wide gap in methods of thinking and in point of view between the practicing lawyer and the political scientist." The distinguished Chief Justice of New Jersey suggests in his stimulating lectures on *Man and Measures in the Law* that the difference in approach can best be perceived by intermingling with the fraternity of the other calling at their annual conclaves. To this one might add that, with increasing frequency and intensity, the difference might also be noted by attending a course in Constitutional Law, first in a law school and then as a political science offering, or vice versa.

Because legal education must concern itself primarily with the preparation of the student for his future vocation, the subject matter of Constitutional Law can, in a law curriculum, be only one of the several disciplines which it may be well to master in order, eventually, to be able to advise clients and win cases. It may be symptomatic that one recent casebook by an eminent law teacher in the field should virtually ignore dissenting opinions—an altogether reasonable procedure if one concedes the purpose to be vocational training. Nor is it surprising to discover that considerable emphasis is placed by another casebook editor on problems of jurisdiction and of approach to the Court *arguendo*. For the preparation of practicing lawyers this is undoubtedly the most suitable introduction to the field of Constitutional Law.

The student of political science comes to Constitutional Law with considerably different ends in mind. The pronouncements of the Supreme Court become, for him, integral parts of the process of government in the United States. The nine men on that highest tribunal in the land head one of the three branches of our government; to examine into their work is to study a—peculiarly American—technique of political decision-making, to appraise and to assess a paramount method of social and political adjustment in our society.

That is not to say that lawyers and law teachers are not quite as fully cognizant of the role of the Court in our political system. On the contrary, the rise of "realist" philosophies of law has given much impetus to the interpretation of Constitutional Law in terms of social context rather than of legal formalism. What is suggested here is that the ends of legal education make it requisite and, perhaps, desirable to stress *what* the Court does and may do, while the nonvocational course can devote time and attention to the question of *why* the Court acts as it does.

The present collection of materials has been prepared with the needs of the general, non-law student in mind. The emphasis, it will be found, is not on the rendering of rules of law but on the raising of questions and issues.

It may be well, at the outset, to indicate what this volume is not. I have not attempted to offer a clause-by-clause annotation of the Constitution. Thus some topics dear to individual instructors' hearts may be found missing. It is my hope that these omissions will not be deemed disrupting, especially since their subject matter may be found more or less adequately noted in most textbooks in American Government. For ready reference to the current meaning read into any particular phrase of the Constitution, Professor Corwin's *The Constitution and What It Means Today* is of such standing and competence that it seemed superfluous to attempt a duplication.

By contrast, this volume contains some materials not previously offered in standard collections. Indeed, I would venture to suggest that this departure from the tradition of Constitutional Law books is peculiarly adapted to the needs of political science instruction. The first and last chapters fall, in their entireties, into this class and, as I conceive them, may be used as the broad framework into which the case content of the other chapters can be fitted. Thus the opening sections offer summary considerations on the content and methods of Constitutional Law in the United States, including an introduction of the student to the terminology of legal cases. The closing chapter invites reflection on the place of the Supreme Court and of judicial review in our democracy; each reading here mirrors a different approach or emphasis while addressing itself to the same basic problems, to the themes of which the preceding cases have been the variations and concretions.

As to the selection of cases, I have consoled myself with the well-known adage that no textbook ever meets the demands of any teacher in full unless it be the author's, and he usually can think of improvements by the time his copy is in print. The present collection offers a goodly share of recent material, to include notes on cases decided at the end of the 1950–1951 session of the Court. On the other hand, the inevitable classics have not been omitted. Some of them are here because, without them, modern decisions and the problems they represent would lose much of their meaning; others have been retained because they display in especially sharp profile the characteristics of American Constitutional Law. Throughout, dissenting and concurring opinions will be found amply represented. In some instances, contemporary or historical comment has been added to highlight the significance of given decisions. Summaries of constitutional developments have been resorted to, especially where the issues are no longer as keenly acute as some others. That my own estimate and value-judgment in that respect is weighted in favor of the problems of civil liberties today will be readily evident from even a cursory perusal of the Table of Contents.

All case material used is identified in the body of the volume by reference to the official (U.S.) reports only. The Table of Cases, however, gives full citations to the unofficial (L. ed. and S. Ct.) reports as well. In the editing of materials, spelling and punctuation of the originals have normally been followed except that, for clarity's sake, I have elected to capitalize "Constitution" whenever and only where it refers to the Constitution of the United States, and similarly the word "Court" with a capital pertains to the Supreme Court of the United States only whereas "court" is used for all other judicial tribunals and for courts in general. Footnotes of the original have been omitted as a rule and, unless otherwise identified, all such notes are editorial addenda.

Material not accompanied by a reference to the source has been prepared by me for this edition. The same is true of occasional notes that may be found contained within brackets. All other non-case material will be found to carry acknowledgments to the source and to the copyright holder with whose permission it is reprinted.

My debts to individuals are so numerous that I can only indicate their general range without according tribute by name. My grateful sentiments encompass a long list, extending to two continents, of challenging and inspiring teachers in the fields of law and political science. My erstwhile fellow-graduate students at the University of Virginia have contributed perhaps more than they could know. My teaching colleagues have given me the benefit of their encouragement, their criticism, and their indulgence in my preoccupation with this project. A number of young ladies have, at one time or another, applied their stenographic skill to the manuscript in the making. Lastly, of course, the publisher's staff has done yeoman work in its expedition. To all of them, I am sincerely thankful.

FRANCIS H. HELLER

Lawrence, Kansas
September, 1951

*Introduction
to American
Constitutional Law*

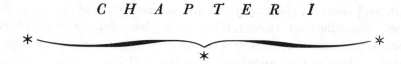

CHAPTER I

Concepts and Methods

1. CONSTITUTION

THE FUNDAMENTAL LAW

It appears to be an integral part of American popular thinking that a *constitution* in the political sense, and particularly *the* Constitution, is a concept the meaning and import of which is rather generally accepted. Thus, a standard dictionary of considerable authority says that a constitution is "the fundamental organic law or principles of government of a nation, state, society, or other organized body of men, embodied in written documents, or implied in institutions and customs; also, a written instrument embodying such organic law."[1] The definition seems fairly descriptive of the term as it may be applied to American and British institutions. But does it convey a correct picture of, say, the Stalin constitution of 1936? Could one, from reading that document, acquire a knowledge of the basic principles of the Soviet government? Similarly, neither the German nor the Italian constitutions were formally discarded, yet who would claim that Hitler or Mussolini were guided by the fundamental law or the principles of government which those documents embodied?

One may further inquire whether the "fundamental organic law" always and necessarily coincides with the "principles of government"? In any case, just what is or is not "fundamental," what is or is not a "principle"?

Merely to pose these questions is to illustrate the difficulty of

[1] *Webster's Collegiate Dictionary*, 5th ed., p. 218.

1

arriving at any one satisfactory definition of the term "constitution." Yet, of course, nation-states commonly possess instruments or institutions which they denominate constitutions. The differences of form and content, the variations in permanence and stability, and other dissimilarities may render definition difficult but cannot obscure the fact that almost everywhere "constitutions" occupy a singular place in the organization of the political community.

Much is usually made of the distinction between written and unwritten constitutions, especially by American authors. The first observation that seems appropriate in this connection is to point out that the nomenclature is anything but felicitous. A "written" constitution, to be sure, usually consists of a single document in writing, with or without subsequent emendations, as the case may be. But it is hardly to be expected that all of the "fundamental law" or all the "principles of government" of the nation should be found in this document and there alone. Political reality will not be fettered by the written word; the needs and demands of peoples are not static; the boundaries between the "fundamental" and the ephemeral are rarely clear-cut. Customs arise and attain acceptance and observance fully as much as if they had been solemnly agreed upon by conventions or "founding fathers." Conversely, provisions placed on record by the constitution-makers may be sapped of meaning and significance through prolonged nonenforcement. American experience furnishes examples for both developments: note the extraconstitutional, yet no less commanding, traditions surrounding the election of the President, and, on the other hand, the quiet burial given the penalty provision of the Fourteenth Amendment.

In speaking of "unwritten" constitutions it is similarly necessary to understand that, of course, there is no lack of written, recorded materials in such constitutions. Rather what the term seeks to connote is that the instrument was not set down in writing by a deliberate "constituent" act, but that, as has been signally the case in England, it has grown from custom and tradition, some recorded, some literally unwritten.

Thus the principal point of distinction between so-called written and unwritten constitutions devolves in effect upon the mode of their adoption. There are no known instances of a people deliberately choosing to live under an unwritten constitution, but such instruments have in every case been the result of an evolutionary process from absolute or autocratic governments. It is, of course, entirely feasible for small groups to seize power and maintain themselves in power without committing themselves in writing on matters pertaining to its exercise. But large groups cannot operate in such a fashion; their very size requires recourse to representation, and the representative device, if it is to endure, necessitates deliberate agreement and decision.

To assume that a people is free to choose between a "written" or "unwritten" constitution is to neglect basic facts of political development. Constitutional arrangements are not entered into because of altruistic attachments to theoretical concepts; they arise to a large extent from the necessities of the situation and the political exigencies of the day. Whether they be reduced to writing at a given moment or evolve through custom and accretion, constitutions are never elaborated in a vacuum.

The same is true about the subsequent evolution of constitutions. Here some scholars, notably the late Lord Bryce, have sought to establish a classification of constitutions into "rigid" and "flexible" ones. Historical analysis seems to indicate, however, that whether or not a constitution should prove itself malleable is not necessarily dependent upon the stringency or laxity of its amending provisions. Neither immutability nor complete looseness could be assured by verbal enactments alone. For, as the story of the American Constitution reveals, if the amending process is encumbered with difficulties, ways will be found for the attainment of modifications by other methods; and Great Britain's constitutional history indicates that even where institutionalized obstacles are completely lacking changes may be slow in coming.

What has been suggested here with regard to formal criteria of constitutions applies, probably with equal force, to the acceptance of constitutions as the fundamental law of the land. To one raised under the American Constitution that document's declaration that it is "the supreme law of the land" may appear as a commonplace assertion. It needs to be recognized, however, that the prevailing acceptance of the Constitution as the fundamental law represents the extreme range when placed alongside the political mores of other nations. The practice in many another country acknowledges, in differing degrees, that the problems to which a constitution addresses itself are predominantly political in nature. To enshrine political objectives in the permanence of the law is, of course, always the hope and aim of the dominant forces. But that only those features of a constitution are addressed as possessing legal character which have passed beyond the realm of partisan contest is the rule in most countries and as such exemplifies again that the definition of a constitution as "the fundamental organic law" is conceived with perhaps excessive emphasis upon familiar arrangements. Even within the United States, however, the general obeisance toward the Constitution commonly stops short of complete submission where political differences prevail. The argumentative lay usage of the term "unconstitutional" is not infrequently another way of saying, not "illegal," but "politically distasteful."

Of necessity, any constitution must be framed in general terms which permit of interpretation. Law, however, is predicated upon acceptance of norms. A constitution may thus well be defined as "law" or "supreme law," provided it is not forgotten that as such the constitution represents an aim which may be approximated but that to the extent that it remains open to dispute and discussion its nature is essentially political. It is the fundamental *law* thus in so far and only in so far as it represents fundamental consensus on political arrangements.

POWER AND RESTRAINT

To repeat what has already been suggested above, no one definition of the word "constitution" has as yet been generally accepted. The late Professor Edward McChesney Sait reported in his *Political Institutions*[2] that he had collected more than forty definitions of the word. C. J. Friedrich has suggested that most of the definitions thus far attempted fall into one of five broad categories. In three of these, "constitution" is defined broadly enough to be applicable to every form of state. These are: the Aristotelian concept (paralleled in modern days by Hegel) that the whole order of things in a *polis* (city-state) is to be known as its constitution; the notion that a constitution is a description in broad outline of the actual organization of the government; and the idea, found in Coke as well as Rousseau, that a constitution represents the basic legal conceptions of a community. Friedrich says that "it is obvious that these three descriptive, general concepts of what a constitution is apply to all political communities, to a Fascist and Communist dictatorship just as much as to the United States or England."[3] The two other types of usages are

[2] New York: D. Appleton-Century Co., 1938, p. 311 n.
[3] *Constitutional Government and Democracy*, Boston: Little, Brown & Co., 1941, p. 120.

more restrictive in nature: one is the purely formal definition of a constitution as a written document, and the other hinges on procedural aspects and assumes a need of popular participation in the amending process. Neither of these latter categories of definitions appears too useful. As Lord Bryce observed, written constitutions become "developed by interpretation, fringed with decisions, and enlarged by custom, so that after a time the letter of their text no longer conveys their full effect,"[4] and thus the criterion of a written, assembled record is of no great utility. To exclude from the area of "constitutions" such an arrangement as the working basis of British government before 1911 because of the determining influence of a nonrepresentative body (the House of Lords) in its amending process is equally incongruous.

Professor Friedrich suggests therefore that a constitution be defined by reference to its function. What is it that a constitution is expected to accomplish? The answer, we are told, is that it is to provide *regularized restraint of power*. To be sure, prevailing usage in Anglo-American thought tends to contrast "constitutional" and "arbitrary," to equate "constitutional government" and "limited government." While a dictatorship may constrain its own exercise of power, if only by provisions for the transmission of power through a line of succession, such self-limitations provide no more assurance of permanence and certainty than any other act of arbitrary power. Under such circumstances to speak of a "constitutional" basis of government may be agreeable to the broad definitions adduced by some of the scholars but fails to conform to the common understanding of that term in our society. Prevalent notions as to the meaning of the word "constitution" consist most frequently, it is suggested, of some blending of the three elements contained in Professor Friedrich's phrase—regularization, restraint, power.

It should be noted that each of these three elements is essential to any useful application of this functional definition. *Power* must be restrained, but it must also be provided for and its structural allocation determined. Professor Edward S. Corwin has analyzed the functions of the Constitution of the United States as being "instrumental" and "symbolic," meaning that it was designed as an instrument for the exercise of positive political power and as a symbolic

---

[4] *Studies in History and Jurisprudence*, New York: Oxford University Press, 1901, vol. I, p. 128.

expression of the limitations on that same power.[5] To varying degrees and in different methods, all constitutions in the Western world would appear to encompass these two functions. *Restraint,* of course, presupposes the existence of power to be restrained. The recognition of both elements suggests that neither can be absolute and their adjustment thus must be one of degrees. For just as unrestrained power is the rule of the despot so restraints which defeat all power spell the advent of social disorganization and anarchy.

Lastly, the restraints on power as well as the provision for power should be *regularized.* The citizen as well as the government needs to know which exercises of power are permissible and which will not be allowed. It is inherent in the nature of man that he should seek certainty, that he should insist on knowing, with reasonable assurance, what conduct is expected of him. The significant rule of conduct is thus not necessarily that which is formally established and exalted, but rather that rule, whatever its source or form, which can be taken as a reasonable guideline for future action. Whether such a certain directive is found in a document called a constitution or in a formal legislative pronouncement or merely in the customs and usages of a people or its officialdom, in every case, if its function is to establish regularized restraint of governmental power, it operates as a constitutional rule within the meaning of the definition employed by Friedrich.

2. LAW

Crucial among all problems of political organization is that of the reconciliation of liberty and authority, or, differently expressed, the adjustment of individual and community interests. No aggregation of humans (or animals, for that matter) can persist long without arriving at some rules for the conduct of its members. Modern man, living in an urban or at least increasingly nonagrarian society, largely takes it for granted that his conduct shall be restrained by multitudes of customs and of *laws.* He is perhaps less cognizant that his liberty, being the freedom from restraining rules, is consequently dependent upon the existence of *some* restraint. Robinson Crusoe did not rejoice in his absolute freedom, for liberty has meaning only

[5] "The Constitution as Instrument and as Symbol," *American Political Science Review,* XXX (1936), 1071; see also Robert K. Carr, *The Supreme Court and Judicial Review,* pp. 54–98, and Carl B. Swisher, *The Growth of Constitutional Power in The United States,* pp. 3–5 and passim.

in relation to organized society and its rules. The nature and function of these rules are therefore of central significance to the analysis and interpretation of that society.

Political theorists from the earliest known days have addressed themselves to the problem of assessing the proper scope of the state's authority and the correlative obligation of the individual to accept that authority. Because the peaceful state exercises its authority through law, the inquiry tends to resolve into an argument over the nature and meaning of law.

It would be entirely feasible to reproduce an imposing list of attempted definitions of law. One recent textbook[6] offers no less than forty-seven, without making any claim to completeness. Public acceptance and veneration of the law is, of course, very succinctly expressed in the lines from Gilbert and Sullivan's *Iolanthe*: "The Law is the true embodiment of everything that's excellent," but such universal submission merely accentuates the need for an answer to the what and why. Yet the contest of the jurists remains at a stage where one can do little but list their answers, without declaring any one to be conclusive and final.

Customarily and broadly speaking, most modern theorists of the law may be grouped into four schools of thought:

1. *The analytical school,* also called Austinian, after the English jurist John Austin whose *Lectures on Jurisprudence* are the classic exposition of its views. Derived from the analyses of Jeremy Bentham, this theory had its most eminent exponents in America in John W. Burgess, for many years the chairman of the School of Political Science, the first of its kind, at Columbia University, and W. W. Willoughby, whose teachings influenced three generations of students. Although developing his own conclusions in his "Pure Theory of Law," Hans Kelsen in our day builds heavily on Austinian foundations. The analytical jurists' definition declares law to be "a command given by a political superior to a political inferior and enforced by material sanctions." It will be noted that this on its face is an uncomplicated description which accords with the citizen's experience. Common parlance personalizes "the law," endowing it with an "arm," a "hand," "reach," all implying an active agent which bids the citizen obey or suffer the consequences.

2. *The historical school* received its primary impetus from the

---

[6] Kenneth Redden, *An Introductory Survey of The Place of Law in Our Civilization,* Charlottesville, Va.: The Michie Co., 1946, pp. 11–15.

writings of the German Friedrich von Savigny. Sir Henry Maine was the most prominent English name in its ranks and James C. Carter its principal American exponent. These scholars, and others who belong to their school of thought, reject the idea of law as a command and assert that law springs from the customs of society, from the *Volksgeist* of a people. "No government," said Carter, "ever made law in the sense of creating substantive legal rights and correlative legal duties . . . it is the acceptance of the rules by society that makes laws and government." Law making by legislation is at best only reinforcement of custom, and unless the custom has received the acceptance of society no valid law can result. Carter wrote before the establishment of National Prohibition, the "noble experiment" which seemed to confirm his conceptions.

3. *The idealistic* or *philosophical school* has found more adherents in Europe, particularly in Germany, than in the common-law countries. Kant and Hegel laid the foundations while Rudolf Stammler is the outstanding representative of this school in more recent years. The substance of the views of this school is based on the assumption of the existence of a metaphysical ideal "law," law which is intrinsically just and of which real laws are mere manifestations, more or less valid, depending upon the degree of their approximation to the abstract ideal.

4. *The sociological school,* while by no means unanimous in its conclusion, seeks to define law in terms of its application to society. The German Rudolf von Jhering, the Frenchman Leon Duguit, and the American Roscoe Pound have produced the principal formulations of this concept. Pound entitled a highly significant series of lectures *Social Control Through Law,* indicating that he conceived of law as an instrument for social control, a method of adjusting social conflict.

Even these extremely cursory summaries of juristic theories should permit the conclusion that each view in turn remains open to criticism. The most contentious point, by and large, is the evaluation of the place held in a given theoretical conception by the common law, that is, of the body of rules of English (and American) law derived from the decision of the judges.[7] If, as the philosophical school would hold, there exists an abstraction of "law," or, as the historical

[7] The English law came to be known as "common," i.e., common to all England, after royal judges provided a degree of uniformity of justice unknown in pre-Norman days. Common law is distinguished from "civil" law, the Roman system, where uniformity is aimed at by the promulgation of presumably all-inclusive codes.

school argues, law presupposes acceptance of customs by society, then judges are but the discoverers of a pre-existing rule. Analytical as well as sociological jurists view the judge as a lawmaker himself, at least potentially so. The follower of Austin would address the judge as the "political superior" of his analysis, or as the agent of that superior. The sociological school, with varying degrees of candor, is inclined to place the judge on the same level with the legislator as determinant of policy and manipulator of control. Oliver Wendell Holmes, who himself might have disdained the label of any particular school of thought, offered a test of pragmatic simplicity: "The prophecies of what the courts will do in fact, and nothing more pretentious, are what I mean by law."[8] The skeptical implication of this formula has more recently been spelled out in varying degrees of bluntness by such writers as Karl Llewellyn *(Bramble Bush)*, Jerome Frank *(Law and The Modern Mind, Courts on Trial)*, and others, who are usually referred to as *realists* and who emphasize the uncertainty of the law and the personal element in adjudication.

While realism and sociology are the most recent formulations of juristic theory they have not by any means displaced the earlier schools. Nurtured on such ideas of natural rights as are expressed, for instance, in the Declaration of Independence, the concept of law as a pre-existing norm retains vitality in this country in particular. The jurists' debate thus continues inconclusive.

3. CONSTITUTIONAL LAW

To offer a definition of the term "constitutional law" that might be found of general applicability seems to present insurmountable difficulties if one considers the lack of agreement on the meaning of the two component parts of the phrase. Indeed, a recent panel of prominent scholars of "public law," a field which, by definition, embraces constitutional law, could agree only to disagree on the specific boundaries of the subject matter.[9]

Professional and academic practice has, however, diminished the range of useful definitions. In its narrowest application, the term "constitutional law" in the United States includes those decisions of the federal Supreme Court which apply and interpret the written

[8] *Collected Legal Papers,* New York: Harcourt, Brace & Co., 1920, p. 173.
[9] Ernest S. Griffith, ed.: *Research in Political Science,* Chapel Hill: University of North Carolina Press, 1948, pp. 54 ff.

language of the national Constitution. In a broader sense, it can be held to cover all those rules which, to revert to Friedrich's terminology, regularize restraints ᴏf power. In the latter case, not only Supreme Court decisions but Acts of Congress, Presidential orders, rulings of the Attorney General and of administrative boards, decisions of lower courts, etc., are part of the "constitutional law" of the United States.

The minimum content of American constitutional law consists thus of judicial material. Even if the scope of the definition is expanded, the preponderance of material would still be found in the court reports.

The "American doctrine of judicial supremacy" (a term coined by Charles G. Haines and the title of his classic volume on the subject) [10] has placed the judiciary in a uniquely dominant position. It is, of course, axiomatic that the determination of the breadth and extent of power in a state is an essentially *political* question, but the Constitution of the United States proclaims itself as the supreme *law* of the land. It follows that American usage has vested with legal character, and treated as legal, issues which are in fact political in nature. "American constitutional law is primarily political theory dressed in lawyers' language, and . . . the justices of the United States Supreme Court, when they act in constitutional law cases, deal with juristic theories of politics."[11]

Not all of the business of the Supreme Court, of course, falls into the category of constitutional law. Indeed, in the Court's first century in particular, it heard more cases of general, nonconstitutional impression than constitutional ones. In all cases, though, the technique of the Court is that of the law.

The student of politics, who seeks to grasp the varying import of the Constitution, is thus confronted with a specialized method which must be assimilated and penetrated if he is to reach his goal. The technique of the law is as fully of the warp and woof of constitutional law as are the political elements of the issues, their historical

[10] Berkeley: University of California Press, 1914; 2nd rev. ed., 1932.

[11] Earl Latham, "The Supreme Court as a Political Institution," 31 *Minnesota Law Review* 205 (1947). Similar insight was revealed by James M. Beck: " . . . The Supreme Court is not only a court of justice but in a qualified sense a continuous constitutional convention. It continues the work of the convention of 1787 by adapting through interpretation the great charter of government, *and thus its duties become political,* in the highest sense of the word, as well as judicial." *The Constitution of the United States,* New York: George H. Doran Co., 1924, p. 221; italics added. Beck was Solicitor General under Harding and Coolidge.

significance, and, last but not least, the judges whose task it is to decide them.

4. THE TECHNIQUE OF LAW

Not so many centuries ago, if one Englishman claimed to have been injured or wronged by another, the issue of innocence or guilt was decided by recourse to various quaint forms of procedure collectively known as the ordeal. The essence of this method was an appeal or challenge to the Deity to announce on which side justice was to be found. Whatever the decision, the individual, whether accuser or accused, was not presumed to affect its course.

In our day the individual who seeks redress for injury or loss of property or freedom is no more expected, nor any more likely, to help himself. Although the priestly interpretations of a divine oracle have been replaced by the findings of "twelve men, true and sworn" or by the ratiocinations of specialists in the settlement of controversies (called judges), the procedures employed to appeal to these arbiters are so largely removed from lay conceptions that it is normally necessary to employ a man trained in this special technique to champion one's cause in the courts of law.

Yet the barrier that seemingly separates the layman from the lawyer consists of no more than words and a (frequently acquired) adeptness in their use. The tools of the law are verbal symbols, the technique of the law primarily manipulation of these symbols. Holmes' immortal phrase that "the life of the law is not logic, but experience" might perhaps be paraphrased: the life of the law is experience, the *way* of the law emulates logic.

For, whatever philosophy of law one may choose to adopt or follow, the central element of law is that it provides rules of conduct for the members of a given community. The idea of a *rule* connotes certainty and constancy. But the decision of a given controversy does not become a rule unless it is followed in subsequent like situations, unless it is accorded the strength of a *precedent*. The lawyers speak of the principle of *stare decisis* (meaning "to stand by that which has been decided") which demands that prior decisions should be followed in like cases.

On the face of it, that appears to be a fairly simple proposition. It would only be necessary for a lawyer to find the applicable precedent and the entire issue would be settled. In fact, however, no two situations are ever entirely alike. To drive a car at sixty miles per hour might be appropriate on a four-lane concrete highway, but it is not on a single-lane dirt road. What then of the man who proceeds at such a speed on a two-lane, black-top road? Is that more like the situation on the four-lane turnpike or on the narrow dirt road? Obviously, if the speed of the car is going to determine guilt and liability, one party will argue one way and one the other; each will urge that the case fits this or that line of precedents, rule A or rule B. You are, in effect, dealing with competing analogies. Even though formal logic decries the use of imperfect syllogisms, the matching process frequently takes this form:

a. Major premise: "60 m.p.h. is a reasonable speed on wide, hard-sur-
                     faced roads."

   Minor premise: "A two-lane, black-top highway is a wide, hard-sur-
                     faced road."

   Conclusion: "60 m.p.h. is a reasonable speed on a two-lane, black-
                     top highway."

b. Major premise: "60 m.p.h. is too fast for narrow roads."

   Minor premise: "A two-lane road is a narrow road."

   Conclusion: "60 m.p.h. is too fast on a two-lane road."

The major premise in each instance is, we assume, an established rule of law, buttressed by decisions that can be adduced as precedents. They limit, as it were, the range within which the new rule is to be found.

Now let us assume that the court decides that sixty miles per hour is a safe driving speed on a two-lane, black-top road. Presumably that sets a rule for the conduct of motorists on such roads. A little later an accident occurs and once again the question is one of safe driving speeds. Let us assume that all the facts are the same; but in the first case the vehicle involved was a passenger car and in the second case it was a truck. Does the rule apply? We know, of course, that in practice highway traffic is closely governed by statutes, i.e., rules established by the legislature. Our illustration aims, however, not at the content of any particular rule, but at the methods courts use when confronted with a case. The example could be continued without end: the condition of the road, of the car, the driver's experience or lack thereof, the weather, the time of the day, the density of the traffic, etc., etc., all may yield bases for distinguishing one situation from another apparently identical case, thus permitting an escape from the rule of that case. To be sure, in a multitude of cases the courts are content to follow what seems to be the nearest applicable rule. In every instance, however, the question is: Does this (or that) rule fit the facts? (Or, conversely, do the facts fit the rule?) [12]

A distinction needs to be made here between trial courts and appellate courts. It is in the trial court (the court of "first instance") that disputed facts are brought to settlement. The jury, or in its absence the judge, decides what happened and whether, within a given rule of the law (on which the judge *instructs* the jury), these facts constitute guilt or innocence of the accused. If the judge has erred, either in the conduct of the trial or in the choice of the rule of law on which he instructed the jury, the way may be open to appeal the case. (Almost everywhere the grounds for appeal are now specified by statute.)

An appellate court does not concern itself with questions of fact. No witnesses appear to testify, no jury is present to decide what took place. The court accepts there what has already been settled in the trial court. The appellate court deals with questions of law. Did the trial judge properly exclude such and such testimony? Did he act correctly when he overruled that objection? Did he properly instruct the jury? Was the rule he followed in keeping with principles of higher order (e.g., the Constitution)? Of course, these and the host of other questions that could be raised are not all opened up; appellate courts examine only those points on which it is alleged that an error has been committed in the lower court.

Frequently the parties to a dispute will not even be present in the appellate court. And properly so; for what goes on here is strictly lawyers' work. It is a matter of using words which former decisions of the courts have endowed with authority to fashion an argument that would accomplish one's ends. Lawyers customarily gather the precedents on which they expect to rely in written *briefs* which are submitted in advance of oral argument. When the judges of an appellate court hear the lawyers for each side in verbal exchange, they have thus already been acquainted with their respective lines of reasoning. In effect, each side has told them: "We want you to decide for us and here is why!" Some judges have been known to lean very

[12] Edward H. Levi's brief *Introduction to Legal Reasoning*, Chicago: University of Chicago Press, 1949, has most helpfully sharpened my formulation of these paragraphs.

heavily on the reasons furnished by counsel while others have hewn their own paths to their own solutions.

How, then, do the judges arrive at their choice? Because one's conception of the function of the judge is intricately interwoven with one's notion of what law is, there has been little if any agreement on the answer to this question. The late Justice Cardozo, whose lectures on *The Nature of the Judicial Process*[13] are as stimulating as they are illuminating, formulated four methods by which judicial choices may be materialized: "The directive force of a principle may be exerted along the lines of logical progression; this I will call the rule of analogy or the method of philosophy; along the line of historical development; this I will call the method of evolution; along the line of the customs of the community; this I will call the method of tradition; along the line of justice, morals and social welfare, the mores of the day; and this I will call the method of sociology."[14] It should be noted that Cardozo's first method, what he designates as the method of philosophy, coincides with the normal techniques of the law. It is thus the method most easily resorted to, though its use in the articulation of a judicial choice should not obscure the possibility that the inarticulate premises upon which the decision is founded may have been motivated by elements of any one or more of the other methods.

What appears in the recorded statement of a court's reasoning is, of course, not necessarily conclusive proof of either the methods or the causes by which the decision was reached. Yet in the absence of adequate biographical, and even psychoanalytical, data it is usually necessary to accept the record as it stands.

Appellate courts habitually reduce their decisions and reasons to writing. In these *opinions* they customarily state as much of the facts as appears pertinent and then state the reasoning by which they have reached their decision. The *decision* is the adjudication by the court of the particular controversy at the bar; the judgment of the lower court is affirmed or reversed or the case sent back (remanded) with instructions (other formulae may be used): the court determines "who gets the money."

The process of reasoning will, of course, hardly ever be stated in the form of naked syllogisms. Indeed, while expounding his reasons, the judge may even enunciate rules on points that are not necessary

[13] New Haven: Yale University Press, 1921.
[14] *Op. cit.*, pp. 30–31.

to the decision of the particular case. In legal language such judicial "asides" are called *obiter dicta,* or simply *dicta* (singular: *dictum*). Because they are not really the result of the determination of controversies they are not accorded the same standing as rules derived from the *decision* of a case. A dictum, and even more so a series of dicta, may indicate a trend of judicial thinking, but it does not establish a principle in law.

If the judges of an appellate court do not reach unanimity on a decision or on the reasons therefor, more than one opinion may be delivered in a case. Those who disagree with the decision reached by the court's majority will *dissent* and may state their reasons in a *dissenting opinion.* A judge (or judges) who joins in the result of the case but disagrees with the majority reasoning may *concur* and may state his views in a *concurring opinion.*

The full opinions of the appellate courts, sometimes accompanied by excerpts from counsel's argument, are printed in the *law reports* of the respective jurisdiction. The official reports of the United States Supreme Court are the *United States Reports* (abbreviated U.S.) of which between two and three volumes usually comprise the work of one term (October till June). The first ninety volumes of the series are known by the name of the reporter and cited this way:

Volume 1–4   (1789–1800):   1–4 Dallas *(Dall.)*

Volume 5–13 (1801–1815):   1–9 Cranch *(Cr.)*

Volume 14–25 (1816–1827): 1–12 Wheaton *(Wheat.)*

Volume 26–41 (1828–1842): 1–16 Peters *(Pet.)*

Volume 42–65 (1843–1860): 1–24 Howard *(How.)*

Volume 66–67 (1861–1862): 1–2 Black *(Bl.)*

Volume 68–90 (1863–1874): 1–23 Wallace *(Wall.)*

Beginning with Volume 91 the official reports are cited as 91 U.S., etc. (In all legal work the volume number is cited first, followed by the title, and then the page number: 4 Blackstone, *Commentaries* 1370: page 1370 in volume 4 of that work.) The opinions of the United States Supreme Court are also privately reprinted, usually one volume containing the decisions of one term, in the Lawyer's Edition (cited as *L. ed.*) and in the Supreme Court Reporter *(S. Ct.).* References to *Fed.* or *F.* are to the Federal Reporter, containing the decisions of the lower federal courts to 1924. Thereafter these decisions are collected in *Fed.* (2d) or *F.* (2d) (Federal Reporter, second series) except that since 1933 the federal district-court decisions are published separately in the Federal Supplement *(F. Supp.)*. Abbreviations of the state's name are used for citations to the reports of the various state supreme courts.

The student may consult the full text of opinions in the official reports but he is more likely to be using selections arranged especially for instructional purposes. It is important to bear in mind that so-called casebooks (and inasmuch as it uses cases the present volume is to be included in this caveat) are the results of eclectic sampling. This process begins in the trial court, the record of which, of necessity, mirrors the facts as seen through the eyes of the jury or the judge. The opinion of the appellate court renders that tribunal's understanding of the trial court record; and the casebook extract adds, of course, the (intentional or unintentional) emphasis of the editor. With these limitations in mind, the student's first task must be to find out what happened, what the *facts* of the case are.

The next step is to ascertain what *legal question* was raised by the facts. Inasmuch as all cases considered in this volume pertain to constitutional powers and limitations, it can be said for present purposes that the student should find out in what respects these powers and limitations are in dispute. Thus, for instance, where a landlord seeks to evict a tenant we are not particularly concerned here if the tenant claims a right under a private agreement of lease; but if the tenant resists eviction because Congress has by legislation extended the duration of his lease the question becomes one of whether or not Congress possesses the power to enact such legislation.

The court's determination of the legal question is called the *holding*. Thus, in the landlord-tenant controversy just referred to, the United States Supreme Court *held* that the emergency created by the wartime housing shortage in the District of Columbia justified Congressional action in this case.[15] Note that the verb "to hold" has a very specific meaning in the law. Also distinguish between *holding* and *decision*: the latter refers to the adjudication of the particular controversy (the tenant may remain), the former to the determination of the legal question (Congress had power to pass this rent control law).

[15] *Block* v. *Hirsh,* 256 U.S. 135, decided in 1921.

An outline of the court's *reasoning* will normally be necessary for a proper appreciation of the results. As was shown above, the methods of a court of law are essentially founded in logic. The most common difficulty in the analysis of judicial opinions arises from the fact that in most controversies more than one question of law is presented to the court. The lawyer who can muster support for his position from a number of legal principles is, of course, more likely to hit upon the one acceptable to the court than the attorney who bases his claim on only one accepted proposition of law. The court in its reasoning will more than likely dispose of most of the several points urged by counsel. Since lawyers' arguments are only occasionally reprinted in the reports, the need for the likely ambivalence of the judicial opinion may not always be apparent. The student should seek, at this point, to grasp that line of reasoning that will lead to the decision of the case. The refutations of counsel (or dissenting judges on the court) may serve to clarify the issues but they do not necessarily decide the case.

Separate (dissenting or concurring) opinions may be of significance because of the critical light they cast on the majority's position or because they spell or foreshadow trends in judicial attitudes. Read together, majority and minority opinions in constitutional cases reflect the conflicts of political, economic, or social interests which the Court is called upon to adjust and decide. Analysis of such separate opinions is therefore a necessary part of the study of cases.

The novice in the field, who has not previously been confronted with legal materials, will undoubtedly feel that the *language* of the cases presents an added obstacle to understanding. Part of this difficulty arises not from the subject matter but rather from the customary display of erudition in judicial pronouncements. The standard dictionary will be found a useful auxiliary tool. In addition, however, there will be encountered a number of terms and expressions which bear all the earmarks of hallowed tradition. The use of Latin phrases has only recently fallen off; a number of technical terms of the law have changed but little since the days of the Tudors or even the Norman kings. An effort has been made in this volume to furnish parenthetical explanations for specifically legal words. Where these notations are not found or are insufficient in nature, recourse should be had to a law dictionary, available in the reference collection of most general libraries and, of course, in all law libraries.

5. THE COURTS

Constitution of the United States, Article III:

Section 1. The judicial power of the United States shall be vested in one Supreme Court, and in such inferior courts as the Congress may from time to time ordain and establish . . . .

Section 2. The judicial power shall extend to all cases, in law and equity, arising under this Constitution, the laws of the United States, and treaties made, or which shall be made, under their authority; –to all cases affecting ambassadors, other public ministers and consuls; –to all cases of admiralty and maritime jurisdiction; –to controversies between two or more states; –between a state and citizens of another state;[16] –between citizens of different states; –between citizens of the same state claiming lands under grants of different states, and between a state, or the citizens thereof, and foreign states, citizens or subjects.

In all cases affecting ambassadors, other public ministers and consuls, and those in which a state shall be party, the Supreme Court shall have original jurisdiction. In all the other cases before mentioned, the Supreme Court shall have appellate jurisdiction, both as to law and fact, with such exceptions, and under such regulations as the Congress shall make.

. . . . .

The Judiciary Article of the Constitution, the pertinent portions of which are set forth above, did not in itself set up a system of courts for the United States. It refers to *one* Supreme Court but does not specify its composition. It authorizes Congress to set up lower courts but leaves their number, place, and function to be determined.

In the Judiciary Act of 1789, Congress in its first session proceeded to fill in the blanks. The better part of this act is still on the statute books while multiple changes and additions have reflected altered conditions. The Supreme Court was originally set up to consist of a Chief Justice and five Associate Justices, making a bench of six judges. The present number, nine, dates from 1869. Previously, Congress at one time or another set the number at five (1801), six again (1802), seven (1807), nine (1837), ten (1863), and seven again (1866). The figure nine is thus of no particular significance although the defeat of President Roosevelt's court reform plan in 1937 may indicate that the public may have come to consider it as fixed.

Until 1891, the justices of the Supreme Court were required to attend not only the sessions of that court but also to sit in the Circuit

[16] Modified by the Eleventh Amendment.

Court, to "ride the circuit." From 1802 on, each justice was given one circuit, or rather it was customary to select the judges so that each circuit would be represented on the bench. With the increase of business in the federal courts, particularly after the Civil War, the burden on the individual court members threatened to interfere with the effective administration of justice. After much delay, Congress finally revamped the lower court system, relieved the Supreme Court justices of their circuit duties, and curtailed the stream of cases to the Supreme Court.

Flow of Cases to U. S. Supreme Court

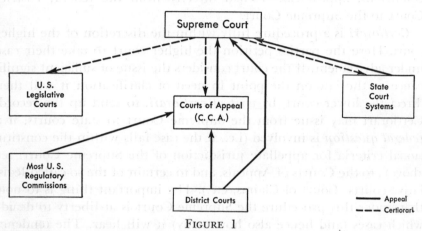

FIGURE 1

Today the lowest federal court is the District Court. The territory of the forty-eight states is divided into 84 districts, each of which constitutes the jurisdiction of one District Court. Similarly, Washington, D.C., forms a judicial district. To expedite the business of these courts, several judges may be assigned to one court, each with authority to hear cases separately (except for a few instances when three judges are required to make up the court, district judges sit alone). Above the districts are circuits, of which there are now ten. In each circuit sits a Court of Appeals (CCA). The District of Columbia, analogous to circuits, also has a Court of Appeals. The number of judges on each of these courts varies at present from three to seven.

At the apex of the judicial hierarchy stands the Supreme Court. Its nine justices have, since 1891, been freed of circuit-riding duties and, by a law of 1925, have been relieved of the danger of an excessively large docket of cases. Inasmuch as the Court's original jurisdiction is narrowly circumscribed by the Constitution, the bulk of the High Court's business comes to it from the lower courts.

A case may reach the Supreme Court today by two principal methods, *appeal* and *certiorari*.[17] In the first method there is a right to be heard. Generally, appeal will be available where, in a conflict between state law and federal Constitution, the lower court has held in favor of its political unit, i.e., a federal court for, a state court against, supremacy of the federal Constitution, laws, or treaties, or where the validity of a federal statute or treaty is in question. Acts of Congress provide for other instances too. Under certain specified conditions, appeal can be had directly from the federal District Court to the Supreme Court.

Certiorari is a procedure fully within the discretion of the higher court. Here the parties petition the higher court to take their case under advisement. If the court considers the issue of sufficient significance or the law on the point in need of clarification it will then direct the lower court, by *writ of certiorari,* to send up the record. Certiorari may issue from the Supreme Court to state courts, if a *federal question* is involved (i.e., if the case falls within the constitutional criteria for appellate jurisdiction of the Supreme Court; see above) , to the Courts of Appeals, and to certain of the so-called legislative courts (Court of Claims, etc.). The important thing is to note that under this procedure the Supreme Court is at liberty to decide which cases (and hence also how many) it will hear. The tendency over the years has been to restrict the right of appeal and to enlarge the area of discretion through certiorari. (Courts of Appeals may also *certify* cases to the Supreme Court, meaning that the CCA may request the higher court's decision or instructions for a decision. This procedure, while available, is used too infrequently to affect the Supreme Court's agenda materially.)

What, then, about the lawyer who tells you that he will take your case "all the way to the United States Supreme Court"? In the first place, unless your case involves a federal question, that is, unless it fits into one of the categories enumerated in the jurisdictional clause of the Judiciary Article of the federal Constitution, there is no access to the federal courts. Let us assume, however, that a federal question is present. Under these circumstances, should the lower court's

---

[17] A third method, the *writ of error,* may be encountered in some older cases. Not dissimilar in use and application from the writ of certiorari, it was abolished (for the federal court system) in 1928. 42 *U.S. Stat. at L.* 54.

decision on the subject matter of the controversy place the case within the respective category set off by the Congress, there may be a right to appeal. It is more likely, however, that once the case has reached the highest state court or the federal Court of Appeals, the only further recourse open will be in the nature of a petition to the Supreme Court of the United States for a writ of certiorari. The granting of this writ, it will be remembered, is a purely discretionary matter. While the Court has announced rules according to which it would grant certiorari, their observance has not been consistent. It has indeed been suggested that these rules are rapidly turning into "legal fictions"—another way of saying that the Court will not be bound by conditions, not even self-imposed ones.[18] Denial of certiorari by the Supreme Court has become so frequent that, even from among the Justices themselves, it has at times been intimated that such a denial was an approval *sub silentio* of the lower court's decision.[19] In a rather unprecedented separate opinion accompanying the routine announcement of a denial of certiorari by the Court, Mr. Justice Frankfurter stated his views as to the significance of such denials.

MARYLAND v. BALTIMORE RADIO SHOW
338 U.S. 912 (1950)

Opinion of Mr. Justice FRANKFURTER respecting the denial of the petition for writ of certiorari.

. . . . . .

A variety of considerations underlie denials of the writ, and as to the same petition different reasons may lead different Justices to the same result. This is especially true of petitions for review on writ of certiorari to a State court. Narrowly technical reasons may lead to denials. Review may be sought too late; the judgment of the lower court may not be final; it may not be the judgment of a State court of last resort; the decision may be supportable as a matter of State law, not subject to review by this Court, even though the State court also passed on issues of federal law. A decision may

[18] John P. Frank, "The United States Supreme Court: 1948–49." 17 *University of Chicago Law Review* 1, 36–39 (1949), (Note) "The Supreme Court, 1948 Term," 63 *Harvard Law Review* 119, 120 (1949).

[19] In *Christoffel* v. *United States*, 338 U.S. 84, 94 n. (1949), Mr. Justice Jackson thus hints that denial of certiorari in an earlier, similar case could not be squared with the decision in the principal case.

satisfy all these technical requirements and yet may commend itself for review to fewer than four members of the Court. Pertinent considerations of judicial policy here come into play. A case may raise an important question but the record may be cloudy. It may be desirable to have different aspects of an issue further illumined by the lower courts. Wise adjudication has its own time for ripening.

Since there are these conflicting and, to the uninformed, even confusing reasons for denying petitions for certiorari, it has been suggested from time to time that the Court indicate its reasons for denial. Practical considerations preclude. In order that the Court may be enabled to discharge its indispensable duties, Congress has placed the control of the Court's business, in effect, within the Court's discretion. During the last three terms the Court disposed of 260, 217, 224 cases, respectively, on their merits. For the same three terms the Court denied, respectively, 1,260, 1,105, 1,189 petitions calling for discretionary review. If the Court is to do its work it would not be feasible to give reasons, however brief, for refusing to take these cases. The time that would be required is prohibitive, apart from the fact as already indicated that different reasons not infrequently move different members of the Court in concluding that a particular case at a particular time makes review undesirable. It becomes relevant here to note that failure to record a dissent from a denial of a petition for writ of certiorari in nowise implies that only the member of the Court who notes his dissent thought the petition should be granted.

Inasmuch, therefore, as all that a denial of a petition for a writ of certiorari means is that fewer than four members of the Court thought it should be granted, this Court has rigorously insisted that such a denial carries with it no implication whatever regarding the Court's views on the merits of a case which it has declined to review. The Court has said this again and again; again and again the admonition has to be repeated.

. . . .

It is worthy of note that at the same terms of court for which Justice Frankfurter cites certiorari figures the number of cases heard under the appeal procedure averaged forty a year. Thus, even though a party may possess the time, perseverance, and money to have his case pushed to the very threshold of the highest court in the land, he may, and nine times out of ten will, be denied the use of the Court's time and authority.

The Supreme Court is plainly not a court of appeals in the usual sense; it has become primarily an adjudicator of issues of public policy in the presentation of which the individual litigant tends to turn into an illustrative figure rather than a principal actor. It is the Court which occupies the center of the stage and dominates the action. That it should be so appears to have become an accepted part of the American scene. For, if the American nation possesses a symbol to equal the emotive and cohesive value of the Crown in England, the Constitution is that symbol—and in the American mythology the Supreme Court personifies the symbol of the Constitution with nearly the same effect as George VI gives substance to the abstract idea of the Crown.

THE RITUAL AND THE WORK OF THE COURT
By Wesley McCune[20]

There are many reasons for the hush which automatically comes over visitors to the Greek temple, Corinthian order, that houses the Supreme Court of the United States of America. Of course reverence is due any institution that has survived 157 years of national wear and tear, and the domicile of any institution is the physical catchall for whatever bows, genuflections and burnt offering are intended for the spirits that inhabit it.

However, Americans not being a nation of ancestor worshipers—in the usual sense at least—there must be more earthy reasons for their respect to the High Tribunal, the Court of Last Resort.

For one thing, the nine mortals on exhibit there put on one of the best shows in Washington, a city of highly specialized shows. There is nothing in the capital city to compare with the drama enacted about eighty times each year in the magnificent Court chamber when the gavel raps, the chief justice of the United States parts the rich red drapes behind the long mahogany bar, the eight black-robed associate justices appear from their hiding places, and all nine take positions carefully governed by years of custom.

"Oyez, Oyez, Oyez! All persons having business before the Honorable, the Supreme Court of the United States are admonished to draw near and give their attention, for the Court is now sitting. God save the United States and this Honorable Court," intones the marshall in carefully groomed syllables.

As the gavel falls again and knickered page boys scamper to

adjust the chair for each justice, one is tempted to borrow a min-strel show phrase to make the ceremony complete: "Gentlemen, be seated!" It's a good show. One quarter of a million people, many of whom have waited in long queues in the severe white corridors outside, come to see it each year, even in wartime.

But if the Court is not in session visitors huddle around the open chamber door in the same hushed reverence. With the actors gone they look over the stage, the more historically minded of them recalling famous lines of the judicial theater, the others merely ohing and ahing.

There is enough in the theater building alone to make the pil-grimage worth while. The $3,000,000 worth of marble that was brought from Vermont, Alabama, Italy and Spain for the Court's new $10,000,000 home has been arranged in dignity but with as much warmth as marble offers.

As a symbol of "the national ideal of justice in the highest sphere of activity," it stands across a beautiful park from the Capitol, where for seventy-five years, up to 1935, the Court occupied a dingy room smaller than some congressional committees now have to themselves. The planners who wanted a building that would sym-bolize the independence of the judiciary certainly got it.

And those who wanted permanence built into the Court's home need only describe its roof: cream-colored Roman tile set in bronze strips over lead-coated copper and all resting on a slab of watertight concrete. The Court might succumb to a political storm, but it will never be driven out by any other kind of inclement weather.

This same deliberate massiveness is affected at the entrance by thirty-two tall columns and numerous wide steps of gleaming white marble. That lowly starlings, unschooled in the laws, insist on living high in the columns and fouling the pristine entrance or that the gleaming steps are dangerous when icy do not interfere materially with the Court's functions. Worldly board steps and rails are dragged out in the winter and the starlings are frightened away daily or—during the stress of war—left to their own devices.

It also seems unimportant that the chamber in which the nine justices convene to hear arguments and announce decisions is too small to seat much of the public. When the Court moved across the street from its sardine can in the Capitol to its Taj Mahal, the chamber space was increased only 60 per cent, making room on churchlike benches and extra chairs for a total of 316 people.

But small matter—the chamber is beautiful. One notices first the great yardage of rich red velour drapes, then the massive mahogany bar and the forty-four foot ceiling with its modern indirect lighting.

Visitors who have no interest in the legalism of the proceedings cannot write letters or doze off—a roving bailiff enforces Court rules against both. However, there is no rule against admiring panels of art on the four walls above the twenty-four columns, including "Divine Inspiration," "Powers of Evil," "Defense of Virtue" and "Harmony." Or visitors may study a muralist's conception of ancient law-makers, such as Mohammed and Confucius; but most prefer to study their nine contemporaries and watch the quick page boys fetch water or documents for Their Honors.

The building blends artfully the old and the new. A medallion of Hammurabi, promulgator in 2000 B.C. of the oldest known written code, is balanced with air conditioning and metal Venetian shades. The two library rooms upstairs—one resembling a room in an old castle, the other a room in an old cathedral—are offset by a pneumatic tube system for dispatching press copy from the chamber. The archaic system of introducing applicants for admission to practice before the Court is in sharp contrast to the basement traffic light system for the justices' cars.

The only place science fell down in designing the building was in the acoustics department. Spectators can hardly pick up the weighty pronouncements that fall from bench and bar a few feet away.[21]

It is in oak-paneled offices arranged in a U-shape around the formal chamber that the wheels of justice actually do their grinding. Along this private corridor each member of the Court has a suite of three comfortable rooms: one for his own meditation, one for his female secretary and her records and one for his clerk, traditionally an honor graduate of the previous year's class from each justice's favored law school. Each suite includes a fireplace and ultramodern bath with glass-doored shower stall, yet the tone of each is dignified simplicity.

A typical day for a justice starts in midmorning, usually after some reading has been done at home, both after breakfast and into the night before. There are no liveried chauffeurs in the Court's ritual or expense account; the justices drive ordinary cars, walk or ride streetcars to work. The routine from October through May is divided into fortnightly periods. For two weeks the Court sits to hear oral arguments, then for two weeks it drafts and re-

[21] A public address system was installed in 1950.

drafts opinions. Results are announced only on three Monday noons of each month, dubbed "judgment days."

When the Court is in public session, the official work day starts a few minutes before noon, when the justices gather in their inner sanctum, formally known as the "conference room." Here they chat until time to pass into the adjoining robing room, an over-sized closet where a Negro attendant helps each jurist with the black faille robe which he had tailored when he was appointed. Nowhere is the Court's system of seniority better symbolized than here. Along one of the oak-paneled walls are nine oak lockers for as many robes, the door of each labeled with a brass name plate in the order of service on the Court.

By exactly high noon—and that means *exactly* high noon—the nine justices have crossed a white marble corridor, where they stand in place behind dark red curtains until the chief justice parts the center curtains dramatically and each takes his place to stand until the Oyez ritual is finished. Before each robed justice is a reading light, a small calendar, a black leather loose-leaf copy of the official docket and assorted pencils. Beside most of them is an old-fashioned spittoon, should nature interfere with justice momentarily, and each is seated in a chair of his own selection— high backed, black leather swivel chairs which can and do lean far back. Each party to the dispute at hand distributes its legal briefs, printed in large type by order of previous eye-weary justices.

If it is an opinion Monday, or judgment day, the Court's decision is read or given orally in essence, followed by any dissents. No matter what day it may be, if the Court is in session at all it adjourns promptly at two o'clock for a thirty-minute lunch period in the justices' private dining room upstairs. There they have a refrigerator large enough to hold a horse, but more than likely it will be harboring a lonely can of beans. Some of the justices bring their own lunches from home.

From two-thirty until four oral arguments are resumed, with questions freely hurled or needled in from the high bench. Rare is the lawyer who has been given much more than sixty minutes for his case, which allows him time to do little more than refer to important sections of the printed brief that each justice will have to read anyway.

Saturdays are also oral argument days, but of a different kind— the nine justices argue among themselves in the privacy of their conference room. Here they sit more comfortably, around a huge table covered with black felt, and enjoy freedom from the ban on smoking which prevails on the bench. Beside each is a small table for books and other paraphernalia; in front of each is a small drawer for which he has his own key. The inevitable brass name plate is on each high black chair, and a dazzling crystal chandelier hangs over the table's center. Other light streams through three floor-to-ceiling windows, hung with blue-and-gold figured drapes. A short stepladder is handy for any justice who wants a tome from the uppermost of many shelves around the room.

As he presides, from one end of the table, the chief justice faces an old-fashioned gold clock on the mantel opposite him, above which is the only picture in the room, that of Salmon P. Chase, chief justice from 1864 to 1873.

When each justice arrives in this setting he has studied the week's grist of cases and is ready to hash over each until it appears that the time is ripe for the final vote. The freshman member is put on the hot spot by being required to vote first, followed by his less green colleagues and on up to the chief justice, who frequently is also on a hot spot by having to break a tie. Later, the chief justice assigns the job of writing majority opinions. Old-timers usually get the most important opinions, while the thankless, highly technical tax opinions are tossed to the freshman to bore himself with. The minority opinion is assigned by the senior dissenter.

Each justice returns to his office to give his law clerk the bad news and start him gathering material and technical citations. Drafts of opinions are passed up and down the corridors for comment and approval before printing.

From oral argument to announcement may have taken two weeks or it may have taken two years, but the wheels of justice have ground. The grindings fill [as of 1946] 328 volumes of official reports on lawyers' and librarians' shelves all over the country.[22]

[22] The internal working of the Court has been authoritatively described by two men who subsequently rose to the Chief Justiceship. See Charles Evans Hughes, *The Supreme Court of the United States* (1928), especially pp. 26–28, and Harlan F. Stone, "Fifty Years' Work of the United States Supreme Court," 14 *American Bar Association Journal* 428, at 435–436 (1928), also in 8 *Oregon Law Review* 248, 266–268 (1929). Hughes' law clerk, Edwin McElwain, gives one of the most revealing accounts in an article on "The Business of the Supreme Court as Conducted by Chief Justice Hughes," in 63 *Harvard Law Review* 5 (1949).

✳ ⌣⌣⌣⌣⌣⌣⌣⌣⌣⌣⌣⌣⌣⌣⌣⌣⌣⌣⌣⌣⌣⌣⌣⌣ ✳
✳

Judicial Review[1]

1. JOHN MARSHALL'S DECISION

MARBURY v. MADISON
1 Cr. 137 (1803)

The following opinion of the Court was delivered by the Chief Justice:

Opinion of the Court.

At the last term of the affidavits then read and filed with the clerk, a rule was granted in this case, requiring the Secretary of State to show cause why a mandamus [a court order directing a public official to perform a lawful duty] should not issue, directing him to deliver to William Marbury his commission as a justice of the peace for the county of Washington, in the District of Columbia.

No cause has been shown, and the present motion is for a mandamus. The peculiar delicacy of this case, the novelty of some of its circumstances, and the real difficulty attending the points which occur in it, require a complete exposition of the principles on which the opinion to be given by the Court is founded.

These principles have been, on the side of the applicant, very ably argued at the bar. In rendering the opinion of the Court, there will be some departure in form, though not in substance, from the points stated in that argument.

---

[1] "Judicial review is the power of a court to pass upon the validity of the acts of a legislature in relation to a 'higher law' which is regarded as binding on both." Edward S. Corwin, "Judicial Review in Action," 74 *Pennsylvania Law Review* 639 (1926).

In the order in which the Court has viewed this subject, the following questions have been considered and decided.

1st. Has the applicant a right to the commission he demands?

2d. If he has a right, and that right has been violated, do the laws of this country afford him a remedy?

3d. If they do afford him a remedy, is it a mandamus issuing from this Court? ...

It is ... the opinion of the Court,

1st. That by signing the commission of Mr. Marbury, the President of the United States appointed him a justice of peace for the county of Washington, in the District of Columbia; and that the seal of the United States, affixed thereto by the Secretary of State, is conclusive testimony of the verity of the signature, and of the completion of the appointment, and that the appointment conferred on him a legal right to the office for the space of five years.

2dly. That, having this legal title to the office, he has a consequent right to the commission; a refusal to deliver which is a plain violation of that right, for which the laws of his country afford him a remedy.

It remains to be inquired whether,

3dly. He is entitled to the remedy for which he applies. This depends on,

1st. The nature of the writ applied for; and,

2dly. The power of this Court.

[Answering the first question, it was held to be "a plain case for a mandamus, either to deliver the commission, or a copy of it from the record."] ... it only remains to be inquired, ... [w]hether it can issue from this Court.

The act to establish the judicial courts of the United States authorizes the Supreme Court "to issue writs of mandamus in cases warranted by the principles and usages of law, to any courts appointed, or persons holding office, under the authority of the United States."

The Secretary of State, being a person holding an office under the authority of the United States, is precisely within the letter of the description, and if this Court is not authorized to issue a writ of mandamus to such an officer, it must be because the law is unconstitutional, and therefore absolutely incapable of conferring the authority, and assigning the duties which its words purport to confer and assign.

The Constitution vests the whole judicial power of the United

States in one Supreme Court, and such inferior courts as Congress shall, from time to time, ordain and establish. This power is expressly extended to all cases arising under the laws of the United States; and, consequently, in some form, may be exercised over the present case; because the right claimed is given by a law of the United States.

In the distribution of this power it is declared that "the Supreme Court shall have original jurisdiction in all cases affecting ambassadors, other public ministers and consuls, and those in which a state shall be a party. In all other cases, the Supreme Court shall have appellate jurisdiction." [Art. 3, sec. 2, cl. 2, paraphrased.]

It has been insisted, at the bar, that as the original grant of jurisdiction, to the supreme and inferior courts, is general, and the clause, assigning original jurisdiction to the Supreme Court, contains no negative or restrictive words, the power remains to the legislature, to assign those specified in the article which has been recited; provided those cases belong to the judicial power of the United States.

If it had been intended to leave it in the discretion of the legislature to apportion the judicial power between the supreme and inferior courts according to the will of that body, it would certainly have been useless to have proceeded further than to have defined the judicial power, and the tribunals in which it should be vested. The subsequent part of the section is mere surplusage, is entirely without meaning, if such is to be the construction. If Congress remains at liberty to give this Court appellate jurisdiction, where the Constitution has declared their jurisdiction shall be original; and original jurisdiction where the Constitution has declared it shall be appellate; the distribution of jurisdiction, made in the Constitution, is form without substance.

Affirmative words are often, in their operation, negative of other objects than those affirmed; and in this case, a negative or exclusive sense must be given to them, or they have no operation at all.

It cannot be presumed that any clause in the Constitution is intended to be without effect; and, therefore, such a construction is inadmissible, unless the words require it.

The authority, therefore, given to the Supreme Court, by the act establishing the judicial courts of the United States, to issue writs of mandamus to public officers, appears not to be warranted by the Constitution; and it becomes necessary to inquire whether a jurisdiction so conferred can be exercised.

The question, whether an act, repugnant to the Constitution, can become the law of the land, is a question deeply interesting to the United States; but, happily, not of an intricacy proportioned to its interest. It seems only necessary to recognize certain principles supposed to have been long and well established, to decide it.

That the people have an original right to establish, for their future government such principles, as, in their opinion, shall most conduce to their own happiness is the basis on which the whole American fabric has been erected. The exercise of this original right is a very great exertion; nor can it, nor ought it, to be frequently repeated. The principles, therefore, so established, are deemed fundamental. And as the authority from which they proceed is supreme, and can seldom act, they are designed to be permanent.

This original and supreme will organizes the government, and assigns to different departments their respective powers. It may either stop here, or establish certain limits not to be transcended by those departments.

The government of the United States is of the latter description. The powers of the legislature are defined and limited; and that those limits may not be mistaken, or forgotten, the Constitution is written. To what purpose are powers limited, and to what purpose is that limitation committed to writing, if these limits may, at any time, be passed by those intended to be restrained? The distinction between a government with limited and unlimited powers is abolished, if those limits do not confine the persons on whom they are imposed, and if acts prohibited and acts allowed, are of equal obligation. It is a proposition too plain to be contested, that the Constitution controls any legislative act repugnant to it; or, that the legislature may alter the Constitution by an ordinary act.

Between these alternatives there is no middle ground. The Constitution is either a superior paramount law, unchangeable by ordinary means, or it is on a level with ordinary legislative acts, and, like other acts, is alterable when the legislature shall please to alter it.

If the former part of the alternative be true, then a legislative act contrary to the Constitution is not law; if the latter part be true, then written constitutions are absurd attempts, on the part of the people, to limit a power in its own nature illimitable.

Certainly all those who have framed written constitutions contemplate them as forming the fundamental and paramount law of the nation, and consequently, the theory of every such government must be, that an act of the legislature, repugnant to the constitution, is void.

This theory is essentially attached to a written constitution, and is, consequently, to be considered, by this Court, as one of the fundamental principles of our society. It is not therefore to be lost sight of in the further consideration of this subject.

If any act of the legislature, repugnant to the Constitution, is void, does it, notwithstanding its invalidity, bind the courts, and oblige them to give it effect? Or, in other words, though it be not law, does it constitute a rule as operative as if it was a law? This would be to overthrow in fact what was established in theory; and would seem, at first view, an absurdity too gross to be insisted on. It shall, however, receive a more attentive consideration.

It is emphatically the province and duty of the judicial department to say what the law is. Those who apply the rule to particular cases, must of necessity expound and interpret that rule. If two laws conflict with each other, the courts must decide on the operation of each.

So if a law be in opposition to the Constitution; if both the law and the Constitution apply to a particular case, so that the court must either decide that case conformably to the law, disregarding the Constitution; or conformably to the Constitution, disregarding the law; the court must determine which of these conflicting rules governs the case. This is of the very essence of judicial duty.

If, then, the courts are to regard the Constitution, and the Constitution is superior to any ordinary act of the legislature, the Constitution, and not such ordinary act, must govern the case to which they both apply.

Those, then, who controvert the principle that the Constitution is to be considered, in court, as a paramount law, are reduced to the necessity of maintaining that courts must close their eyes on the Constitution, and see only the law.

This doctrine would subvert the very foundation of all written constitutions. It would declare that an act which, according to the principles and theory of our government, is entirely void, is yet, in practice, completely obligatory. It would declare that if the legislature shall do what is expressly forbidden, such act, notwithstanding the express prohibition, is in reality effectual. It would be giving to the legislature a practical and real omnipotence, with the same breath which professes to restrict their powers within narrow limits. It is prescribing limits, and declaring that those limits may be passed at pleasure.

That it thus reduces to nothing what we have deemed the greatest improvement on political institutions, a written constitution, would of itself be sufficient, in America, where written constitutions have been viewed with so much reverence, for rejecting the construction. But the peculiar expressions of the Constitution of the United States furnish additional arguments in favor of its rejection.

The judicial power of the United States is extended to all cases arising under the Constitution.

Could it be the intention of those who gave this power, to say that in using it the Constitution should not be looked into? That a case arising under the Constitution should be decided without examining the instrument under which it rises?

This is too extravagant to be maintained.

In some cases, then, the Constitution must be looked into by the judges. And if they can open it at all, what part of it are they forbidden to read or to obey?

There are many other parts of the Constitution which serve to illustrate this subject.

It is declared that "no tax or duty shall be laid on articles exported from any state." Suppose a duty on the export of cotton, of tobacco, or of flour; and a suit instituted to recover it. Ought judgment to be rendered in such a case? Ought the judges to close their eyes on the Constitution, and only see the law?

The Constitution declares "that no bill of attainder or ex post facto law shall be passed."

If, however, such a bill should be passed, and a person should be prosecuted under it, must the court condemn to death those victims whom the Constitution endeavors to preserve?

"No person," says the Constitution, "shall be convicted of treason unless on the testimony of two witnesses to the same overt act, or on confession in open court."

Here the language of the Constitution is addressed especially to the courts. It prescribes, directly for them, a rule of evidence not to be departed from. If the legislature should change that rule, and declare one witness, or a confession out of court, sufficient for conviction, must the constitutional principle yield to the legislative act?

From these, and many other selections which might be made, it is apparent that the framers of the Constitution contemplated that instrument as a rule for the government of courts, as well as of the legislature.

Why otherwise does it direct the judges to take an oath to support it? This oath certainly applies in an especial manner to their conduct in their official character. How immoral to impose it on them, if they were to be used as the instruments, and the knowing instruments, for violating what they swear to support!

The oath of office, too, imposed by the legislature, is completely demonstrative of the legislative opinion on this subject. It is in these words: "I do solemnly swear that I will administer justice without respect to persons, and do equal right to the poor and to the rich; and that I will faithfully and impartially discharge all the duties incumbent on me as _____, according to the best of my abilities and understanding agreeably to the Constitution and laws of the United States."

Why does a judge swear to discharge his duties agreeably to the Constitution of the United States, if that Constitution forms no rule for his government? If it is closed upon him, and cannot be inspected by him?

If such be the real state of things, this is worse than solemn mockery. To prescribe, or to take this oath, becomes equally a crime.

It is also not entirely unworthy of observation, that in declaring what shall be the supreme law of the land, the Constitution itself is first mentioned; and not the laws of the United States generally, but those only which shall be made in pursuance of the Constitution, have that rank.

Thus, the particular phraseology of the Constitution of the United States confirms and strengthens the principle, supposed to be essential to all written constitutions, that a law repugnant to the Constitution is void; and that courts, as well as other departments, are bound by that instrument.

The rule must be discharged [i.e., Marbury's request for a writ of mandamus is denied].

2. CHRONOLOGY OF EVENTS RELATED TO MARBURY v. MADISON

November 4, 1800: John Adams, Federalist and second President of the United States, is defeated for re-election by the Republican Jefferson-Burr ticket. The Federalists also lose control of both houses of Congress.

January 20, 1801: President Adams names his Secretary of State, John Marshall, to be Chief Justice of the United States. (Marshall continues as acting Secretary of State until the naming of a successor by President Jefferson.)

February 13, 1801: The "lame-duck" Federalist Congress enacts the Judiciary Act of 1801, relieving the justices of the Supreme Court of "circuit-riding" duties, creating a number of new judgeships, and reducing the number of Supreme Court justices from six to five effective with the next vacancy.

February 27, 1801: Congress passes the Organic Act for the District of Columbia, providing for appointment of justices of the peace by the President.

March 2, 1801: President Adams appoints forty-two justices of the peace for the District of Columbia, including one William Marbury. Because of the pressure of other business some of the warrants of appointment are not delivered.

March 4, 1801: Thomas Jefferson is inaugurated as third President of the United States.

December 8, 1801: President Jefferson, in a message to Congress, by implication invites repeal of the Judiciary Act of 1801.

December 21, 1801: William Marbury asks the Supreme Court to compel Secretary of State Madison to deliver to him (Marbury) the warrant of his appointment as justice of the peace for the District of Columbia. Chief Justice Marshall issues a writ ordering Madison to show cause, at the next session of the Court (in June 1802), why he should not be compelled to make delivery of the warrant.

March 31, 1802: Congress repeals the Judiciary Act of 1801, thus re-imposing on the Supreme Court justices the duty of circuit-riding.

April 23, 1802: Congress changes the date of Supreme Court sessions from semiannual terms in June and December to one annual meeting in February. This move postpones the next convening of the Court until February, 1803.

January 1803: Possible impeachment of Supreme Court Justice Samuel Chase and District Judges Peters and Pickering is discussed in Congress and in the press.

February 3, 1803: President Jefferson asks the House of Representatives to impeach Judge Pickering on grounds of misconduct in office.

February 24, 1803: Chief Justice Marshall announces the Court's decision in *Marbury* v. *Madison*.

March 2, 1803: The Supreme Court acquiesces in the repeal of the Judiciary Act of 1801. *Stuart* v. *Laird,* 1 Cranch 299.

3. CRITICISMS OF THE DECISION

EAKIN v. RAUB

12 Sergeant & Rawle (Pa. Supr. Ct.) 330 (1825)

.   .   .   .   .

GIBSON, J., dissenting:

.   .   .   .   .

The Constitution and the right of the legislature to pass the act, may be in collision. But is that a legitimate subject for judicial determination? If it be, the judiciary must be a peculiar organ, to revise the proceedings of the legislature, and to correct its mistakes; and in what part of the Constitution are we to look for this proud preeminence? Viewing the matter in the opposite direction, what would be thought of an act of assembly in which it should be declared that the Supreme Court had, in a particular case, put a wrong construction on the Constitution of the United States, and that the judgment should therefore be reversed? It would doubtless be thought a usurpation of judicial power. But it is by no means clear, that to declare a law void which has been enacted according to the forms prescribed in the Constitution, is not a usurpation of legislative power. It is an act of sovereignty; and sovereignty and legislative power are said by Sir William Blackstone to be convertible terms. It is the business of the judiciary to interpret the laws, not scan the authority of the lawgiver; and without the latter, it cannot take cognizance of a collision between a law and the Constitution. So that to affirm that the judiciary has a right to judge of the existence of such collision, is to take for granted the very thing to be proved. And, that very cogent argument may be made in this way, I am not disposed to deny; for no conclusions are so strong as those that are drawn from the *petitio principii* [the Latin term for "begging the question," a logical fallacy in which that which is to be proved is, implicitly or otherwise, taken for granted].

.   .   .   .   .

But the judges are sworn to support the Constitution, and are they not bound by it as the law of the land? In some respects they are. In the very few cases in which the judiciary, and not the legislature, is the immediate organ to execute its provisions, they are bound by it in preference to any act of assembly to the contrary. In such cases, the Constitution is a rule to the courts. But what I have in view in this inquiry, is the supposed right of the judiciary to interfere, in cases where the Constitution is to be carried into effect through the instrumentality of the legislature, and where that organ must necessarily first decide on the constitutionality of its own act. The oath to support the Constitution is not peculiar to the judges, but is taken indiscriminately by every officer of the government, and is designed rather as a test of the political principles of the man, than to bind the officer in the discharge of his duty: otherwise it were difficult to determine what operation it is to have in the case of a recorder of deeds, for instance, who, in the execution of his office, has nothing to do with the Constitution. But granting it to relate to the official conduct of the judge, as well as every other officer, and not to his political principles, still it must be understood in reference to supporting the Constitution, only as far as that may be involved in his official duty; and, consequently, if his official duty does not comprehend an inquiry into the authority of the legislature, neither does his oath. It is worthy of remark here, that the foundation of every argument in favor of the right of the judiciary, is found at last to be an assumption of the whole ground in dispute. . . .

But do not the judges do a positive act in violation of the Constitution, when they give effect to an unconstitutional law? Not if the law has been passed according to the forms established in the Constitution. The fallacy of the question is, in supposing that the judiciary adopts the acts of the legislature as its own; whereas the enactment of a law and the interpretation of it are not concurrent acts, and as the judiciary is not required to concur in the enactment, neither is it in the breach of the Constitution which may be the consequence of the enactment. The fault is imputable to the legislature, and on it the responsibility exclusively rests. In this respect, the judges are in the predicament of jurors who are bound to serve in capital cases, although unable, under any circumstances, to reconcile it to their duty to deprive a human being of life. To one of these, who applied to be discharged from the panel, I once heard it remarked, by an eminent and humane judge: "You do not deprive a prisoner of life by finding him guilty of a capital crime; you but pronounce his case to be within the law, and it is therefore those who declare the law, and not you, who deprive him of life."

MARSHALL'S CHOICE
By Robert K. Carr[2]

Two further alternatives were open to Chief Justice Marshall in disposing of the case. In the first place a way was open whereby the relevant portion of the Judiciary Act of 1789 might have been interpreted to avoid any conflict between the statute and Article III of the Constitution. It has been pointed out that the wording of the act was sufficiently general that it might have been held to provide that the power given to the Court to grant writs of mandamus was to be exercised only in cases which the Constitution permitted it to hear by exercise of original jurisdiction. Had the Court so interpreted the law it would have had to refuse jurisdiction in the case as it actually did, but without the necessity of invalidating a law in order to reach such a result.[3]

Second, Chief Justice Marshall might have taken the point of view that Article III of the Constitution, involving as it does the organization and jurisdiction of the judiciary, belonged to the peculiar province of the courts to protect. Accordingly, any law which sought to impose upon the Court a task in connection with its judicial function which seemed to be forbidden by the Constitution might be resisted. The relevant portion of the Judiciary Act of 1789 could then have been invalidated on the basis of such reasoning, and a limited version of judicial review established. This power would have enabled the Court to invalidate, as it later did, certain laws dealing with the judicial process, such as those which the Court felt attempted to impose non-judicial duties upon it.[4] As a matter of fact, with the single exception of the invalidation of the Missouri Compromise in the *Dred Scott* case, all acts of Congress invalidated by the Supreme Court up to 1868 did concern matters of court organization

[2] Reprinted from *The Supreme Court and Judicial Review*, pp. 67–70, by permission of Rinehart & Company. Copyright 1942 by Robert K. Carr. Footnotes with this selection are those of the original, renumbered for the present purpose.

[3] Edward S. Corwin, "Marbury v. Madison and the Doctrine of Judicial Review," 12 *Michigan Law Review* (1914) 538; I *Selected Essays* 128, 132–133.

[4] See, for example, *Gordon* v. *United States*, 2 Wallace 561 (1865); *United States* v. *Evans*, 213 U.S. 297 (1909); *Muskrat* v. *United States*, 219 U.S. 346 (1911).

and jurisdiction.[5] But in *Marbury* v. *Madison*, Marshall chose to base his decision upon the much broader ground that the Court must refuse to enforce any act of Congress which it considers contrary to the Constitution, regardless of whether the act is one pertaining to the work of the judiciary or dealing with some other matter altogether.

Enough has now been said about the situation in which the Court found itself in deciding the case of *Marbury* v. *Madison* to indicate that it had several alternative paths available, almost any one of which might have been followed with logical and legal justification. Why did Chief Justice Marshall choose the path that he did? It may be conceded that the decision in the case was in part the result of the justices' conclusions on the high level of constitutional principles, but there were certainly other factors of a more realistic character which influenced a Federalist Court in its decision.

It may be noted that the Court did not render the most obvious "political" decision available. It refrained from exercising a power which Congress had granted to it and which in the case at hand it might have used in partisan fashion to accomplish an act of judicial interference with the conduct of administrative affairs of the government by the President of the United States and his first assistant, the Secretary of State. In other words, the Court might have tried to force Jefferson and Madison to give Marbury his commission, and Federalists the country over would have applauded. But instead, in an act of seeming self-abnegation, the Court said "No" and dismissed the case for want of jurisdiction. There are two possible reasons, apart from the compulsion of the Constitution, for this action.

In the first place, Marshall and his colleagues were undoubtedly deterred from a decision ordering Madison to deliver Marbury's commission because of a fear that Jefferson and his Secretary of State might flatly refuse to obey such a court order and, succeeding in such refusal, thereby weaken respect for the power of the judiciary. Or worse still, the Republican administration might even have attempted to take drastic steps of reprisal against the Court. As it was, even though the Court refrained from granting Marbury the writ he was seeking, Marshall's obiter dictum in his opinion—that Marbury seemed to have a very good case against Madison—stirred up a hornet's nest of criticism by Republicans against the Court. Indeed, as

[5] Charles G. Haines, *The American Doctrine of Judicial Supremacy* (2d ed., 1932), p. 401 n.

Professor Corwin has said, "The case in fact smells strongly of powder, for the battle between the chief justice and President Jefferson was already on."[6] The Federalist Court, then, went as far as it dared in its opposition to the Jefferson administration. Further it dared not go, for fear of goading Republicans beyond the endurance point. After all, the Federalists held only the judiciary and in the face of a determined onslaught against them by President and Congress, their position would surely have proved untenable.

But, it may be asked, if Marshall thought it wise for the Court to avoid deciding the case on its merits, why did he not seize upon the argument already discussed: that the Act of 1789 did not authorize the Court to issue a writ of mandamus in a case like the one at hand? In that way, as has been pointed out, the Court could have dismissed the case for want of jurisdiction without declaring a statute invalid.

It looks very much as though Marshall and his Court wanted to exercise the power of judicial review and declare congressional legislation void. Does it not seem, then, in the second place, that Marshall was playing for much higher stakes than a mere decision supporting the Federalist position in the petty squabble involving Marbury and his claim to the office of justice of the peace? In the pages of American history William Marbury was an insignificant figure at best, and what matter if he be sacrificed for a worthy cause? Having read his lecture condemning Jefferson and Madison for their highhanded action, the chief justice went on to accomplish his greater purpose of establishing once and for all in very positive fashion a strong precedent for the power of judicial review. Professor Haines has thus indicated the importance of the chief justice's action: ". . . Marshall, who was an ardent Federalist, was aware of a rising opposition to the theory of judicial control over legislation, and he no doubt concluded that the wavering opinions on federal judicial supremacy needed to be replaced by a positive and unmistakable assertion of authority."[7] Another eminent constitutional historian, Andrew C. McLaughlin, agrees that "the learned Justice really manufactured an opportunity to declare an act void."[8]

4. ANTECEDENTS

Although the question might appear to be largely academic today, there has been considerable scholarly and polemic controversy over

[6] E. S. Corwin, "Judicial Review," *Encyclopaedia of the Social Sciences,* VIII, 457, 601.
[7] Haines, *op. cit.,* p. 202.
[8] A. C. McLaughlin, "Marbury v. Madison Again," 14 *American Bar Association Journal* (1928) 155, 157.

the origins of judicial review. Historians and political scientists of eminent name have sought to determine whether or not the Framers —who made no mention of the practice in the Constitution—intended the Supreme Court to exercise the power of declaring acts of the Congress unconstitutional. See Charles A. Beard, *The Supreme Court and the Constitution* (1912), Louis B. Boudin, *Government by Judiciary* (1932), Edward S. Corwin, *The Doctrine of Judicial Review* (1914), H. A. Davis, *The Judicial Veto* (1914), A. C. McLaughlin, *The Courts, the Constitution, and Parties* (1912), Frank E. Melvin, "The Judicial Bulwark of the Constitution,"8 *American Political Science Review* 167 (1914). In its most extreme form the critics' argument accuses the Supreme Court, and Marshall in particular, of having "usurped" the power. From the other side considerable evidence is offered to show that the idea of judicial review antedated the Constitution, hence that the Framers should be presumed to have taken it for granted. To that it is countered that much of this supporting evidence may be challenged. Thus it has been stated that "constitutional historians have scrutinized the isolated assertions of judicial supremacy in the colonial and revolutionary periods, but have sharply divided on accepting them as legitimate precedents."[9]

It is worthy of note, however, that John Marshall's law teacher, George Wythe, is on record as enunciating the idea of judicial review most emphatically as early as 1782. In the Virginia case of *Commonwealth* v. *Caton*, 4 Call (8 Va.) 5, 8, he announced that "if the whole legislature, an event to be deprecated, should attempt to overleap the bounds prescribed for them by the people, I, in administering the public justice of the country, will meet the united powers at my seat in this tribunal; and pointing to the Constitution, will say to them, here is the limit of your authority, and hither you shall go, but no further." While this statement was not necessary to the decision of the particular case, it stands, of course, as the view of one of the outstanding jurists of the Revolutionary period and one who, but five years later, represented his state at the Philadelphia Convention.

It is perhaps useful to recall that in Wythe's and Marshall's generation the colonial legislatures had found themselves suddenly freed of the overruling authority of the English Privy Council. The analogy of the Supreme Court's power to declare laws unconstitutional and the Privy Council's control of colonial lawmaking is, of course, analytically imperfect. However, it might be surmised that colonial experi-

[9] Richard B. Morris, "Judicial Supremacy and the Inferior Courts in the American Colonies," 55 *Political Science Quarterly* 429 (1940).

ence might thus have prepared Americans to expect legislation to be reviewed and, occasionally, rejected.

It has also been urged that the idea of a higher law to which legislative action would have to conform had been known to English lawyers because of Sir Edward Coke's dictum in *Bonham's Case* in 1610.[10] In that famous litigation Dr. Thomas Bonham, a doctor of medicine of the University of Cambridge, had been confined to jail by order of the Royal College of Physicians for practicing medicine in the city of London without their certificate. An Act of Parliament had set up the College as the governing body for all physicians practicing in London, had given it power to license for such practice and to fine all who would practice in London without a license from the College. One-half of all the fines so collected was to go to the King and one-half to the College. It was under this statute that Dr. Bonham was fined and, on refusal to pay, committed to jail. In the course of his opinion Coke, then chief justice, averted to the College's interest in the fines which in effect made it a judge in its own cause. It was then that he said (and this was clearly dictum): "And it appears in our books that in many cases the common law will controul acts of parliament and sometimes adjudge them to be utterly void: for when an act of parliament is against common right or reason, or repugnant, or impossible to be performed, the common law will controul it and adjudge such act to be void." Citing this dictum, it has frequently been alleged that the principle of a higher law which acts of Parliament might not contravene was established in English law and hence accepted by the colonists. On the other hand, modern scholarship has argued that Coke had no reference to higher law notions—which, it is urged, were read into his statement by later commentators—but was stating a rule of statutory interpretation only. In any case, it is undisputed that English practice has established and maintained the principle of parliamentary supremacy, unlimited and illimitable by any legal power.[11]

A further factor which enters into considerations of the problem of the origins of judicial review is the jealousy of the judges of the period for their position and independence. It needs to be remem-

[10] 8 Coke Rep. 118a.

[11] On *Bonham's Case* see T. R. Plucknett, "Bonham's Case and Judicial Review," 40 *Harvard Law Review* 30 (1926), Thorne, "The Constitution and the Courts: a Reexamination of the Famous Case of Dr. Bonham," in Conyers Read, ed., *The Constitution Reconsidered*, New York: Columbia University Press, 1938, pp. 15–24, and works cited there.

bered that only since the Act of Settlement (1700) had English judges been assured of their tenure. Thus neither in 1789 nor in 1803 could judicial independence have been viewed as so long and so fully established as not to require continuous vigilance by the judges. It is to be noted that virtually all of the cases in the state courts in which the power to declare legislation unconstitutional was asserted prior to *Marbury* v. *Madison* involved attempts by the lawmakers to arrogate judicial functions to themselves or to establish their control over the judiciary by one means or another. As Professor Cushman points out (in the selection to be found in the next section), *Marbury* v. *Madison* itself partakes of this "defensive" characteristic of early judicial review.

This concern for the protection and preservation of judicial independence was apparently not dictated by partisan considerations. Spencer Roane, who is generally regarded as having been the man whom Jefferson would have named to the Chief Justiceship, did not consider himself bound by an act of the legislature which he interpreted as interfering with his judicial status. His views were stated in a letter to the governor of the state, but had the matter resolved itself into a justiciable controversy one may well assume from the tenor of the letter that he would not have hesitated to assert, as his antagonist Marshall had done, that such legislation was invalid.

Spencer Roane, Senior Judge of the Court of Appeals of Virginia, to Thomas Mann Randolph[12]

Richmond, April 16th, 1820

Sir,

I have duly considered your message, received some time since, requesting my attendance at the board of directors of the literary fund, under an act of the last session of Assembly, entitled "An Act concerning the directors of the literary fund, and the board of public works."

That act provides, that, whenever, from any cause, the president of the Court of Appeals shall be unable to attend the said board, "it shall be the duty of the senior judge of the said Court, capable of attending, to act as a director thereof, in lieu of the said president." —Under the present circumstances of the Court of Appeals, this provision applies to me; and it may apply, eventually, to every other member of the Court. —The Duty imposed by this act, is not a judicial duty, and much less is

[12] Original letter in the archives of the Virginia State Library, which has kindly given permission to reproduce the text.

it one which attaches on me, as a judge of The Court of Appeals. If it were, I ought to endeavor to discharge it, under any circumstances. That it is not a judicial duty is evinced, both by the nature of the duty, in itself, and by my being associated, for its discharge, with members of the Executive department of the Government.

This duty is not only not a judicial one, but it is incompatible with the due discharge of the arduous and important duties, confided to the Court of which I am a member.—The board of directors aforesaid, will have many important duties to perform, which will require great consideration, and consume much of its time. If, therefore, they are discharged by a member of the Court of Appeals, they would interfere with his actual duties as a judge. They would conflict with his duties as such, as well in term-time as in vacation; and it is well ascertained, that the whole of the time of the judges of that Court, is requisite to the due discharge of its duties. —These new duties would, therefore, disable a judge of that Court from discharging, efficiently, his previous and paramount duties, and they operate injuriously to the public interests.

. . . . .

In short, Sir, I conceive that few objects are more to be desired, in our administration, than that the judges in the last resort, should be permitted to devote their whole time, and their undivided attention, to the important controversies submitted to their decision; . . .

These are the reasons which have weighed with me, on the present occasion. I have submitted them to the better judgment of my brother judges; and it is, also, their unanimous opinion, that I ought to decline obeying your summons.

. . . . .

With high respect I have the honour to be, Sir, your Excellency's

most obt. servant,

SPENCER ROANE

5. EFFECTS OF THE DECISION IN MARBURY v. MADISON

THREE STAGES IN THE RISE OF JUDICIAL REVIEW
By Robert E. Cushman[13]

. . . . .

Now there are two facts about *Marbury* v. *Madison* which should be carefully noted. In the first place, the act of Congress held void was an act in which Congress had, in the Court's opinion, unconstitu-

[13] From his James Lecture, "The Role of the Supreme Court in a Democratic Nation," 1938. Reproduced by permission of Professor Cushman and of the University of Illinois Press.

tionally tampered with the Court's own jurisdiction. It had tried to give to the Court powers which could not validly be given and the Court had protected itself against this legislative assault on its own integrity. Jefferson himself could not logically quarrel with the basic theory of the Court's action. He believed that each of the three departments of the Government must interpret the Constitution in so far as it bears upon its own powers and status, and may properly follow its own interpretation. No department is bound by the constitutional interpretation of any other department. In *Marbury* v. *Madison* the Court is simply saying to the Congress, "You must keep your hands off from us. You cannot enlarge our jurisdiction beyond constitutional limits." While some of Marshall's language is more generous, the case of *Marbury* v. *Madison,* viewed on its facts, does not establish the power of the Court to reach over its own fence and pass upon the validity of Congressional or Presidential acts which in no way affect the prerogatives or jurisdiction of the Court itself. Marshall nowhere asserts the superiority of the Court over Congress or the Executive, nor does he lay claim on the Court's behalf to any general power of supervision over the other two departments. In the second place, no other act of Congress was invalidated until the Dred Scott case in 1857. If the Supreme Court, under the doctrine of *Marbury* v. *Madison,* was supposed to enjoy the broad power to supervise the constitutional correctness with which Congress and the President exercised their own powers, it is rather surprising that during the fifty years following no attempt was made to seek the Court's decision as to the constitutionality of the Bank of the United States, a protective tariff, the acquisition of Louisiana, the annexation of Texas, and numerous other legislative or executive acts which aroused bitter constitutional dispute.

The second stage in the development of the power of judicial review was reached in the Dred Scott case decided in 1857. We cannot go into the fascinating story of this great case. It is enough for our purposes to know that the Court held that a Negro slave could not become a citizen of the United States, and that the Missouri Compromise Act of 1820, which forbade slavery in the federal territories north of 36° 30′, was unconstitutional. In thus forbidding slavery in the territories Congress had exercised a power not granted to it in the Constitution, a power which could not validly be implied from the delegated power to govern the territories. This represents an important enlargement of the scope of judicial review over the doctrine of

Marbury v. *Madison.* Marshall's early decision had held that the Court could refuse to enforce laws purporting to change its own jurisdiction when the Court believed those laws to be invalid. In the Dred Scott case Taney and his colleagues go much further. They hold that the judgment of Congress as to the scope of one of its own legislative powers, this time a power in no way concerning the Court, is wrong and that the act so passed is unconstitutional. The Court, in other words, takes on the task of determining whether Congress has exercised powers which the Constitution has not delegated to it. Congress must stay in its own constitutional backyard and the Supreme Court, not Congress, is to determine whether it has done so.

The third stage in the growth of judicial guardianship over legislation came in the late eighties with the emergence of the Court's modern doctrine of due process of law. Here the Court added to its power of deciding whether Congress exercised undelegated power the much more far-reaching power of deciding whether Congress has exercised delegated power in an improper manner. Due process of law is a test, not of the existence of legislative power, but of the method of its exercise. . . .

TREND OF JUDICIAL REVIEW

Figure 2 attempts to portray in graphical form the rise of judicial review. It should be noted that, with two exceptions, every instance of a finding of unconstitutionality applied to an Act of Congress occurred within the eighty-year span of 1857 to 1937. It will be noted that the graph indicates increased use of the judicial acts whenever a strong personality in the White House appeared to dominate the national scene. It may be surmised that there is less occasion or less demand for judicial intervention in periods when the executive and the legislative branches of the government check each other's endeavors and plans; it is in times of executive leadership and Congressional harmony that the next echelon in the machinery of checks and balances is brought into play.

The Court has usually been a willing agent in this interplay of power. Of necessity, because its membership as a rule antedates the incumbent administration, it has been inclined to view critically legislative enactments which sought innovation at the expense of stability. This fact, and the entire trend of judicial review, would be brought into still sharper focus if judicial disapproval of state legislation were tabulated in a manner similar to that applied to Acts of

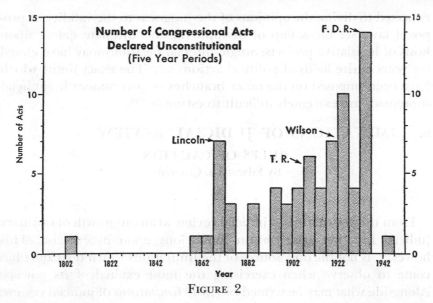

FIGURE 2

Congress in Figure 2. Such a graph is not feasible because of the technical difficulty of arriving at precise data, but the trend of any resultant curve would not be dissimilar. It would, however, not be entirely negative for the years since 1937 or before 1857. Following *Marbury* v. *Madison* and beginning with *Fletcher* v. *Peck*[14] in 1810 the Supreme Court exercised judicial review over state legislation so that by the middle of the nineteenth century its function as a council of revision had come to be taken for granted. The pro-Federalist, pro-Hamiltonian tone of the popular historical writers of the period lent authority to the commonly accepted belief that judicial review had been intended by the Framers and was essential to the operation of the constitutional system.

This acceptance of judicial review was not limited to the Supreme Court alone. Lower federal courts and state courts in all jurisdictions wielded the power of veto and met with few objections. Nor could one ignore the extra-judicial repercussions of the practice. As Charles Grove Haines has suggested, arithmetic totals of laws held invalid "by no means exhaust the limitations placed upon the doctrine [of judicial review]. On account of the fact that courts might hold acts invalid, the debates in legislative halls have more frequently centered on the subject of constitutionality than on the issue of policy or expediency. ... In the state legislatures the judiciary committees which were

14 6 Cranch 87, *infra* p. 271.

expected to divine the opinions of the judges as to the validity of proposed laws set the stamp of disapproval and ultimate defeat upon hosts of legislative projects. Single judicial decisions may have closed for years entire fields of political action. . . . The exact limits which have been imposed on the other branches of government by judicial supremacy are extremely difficult to estimate."[15]

6. LIMITATIONS OF JUDICIAL REVIEW

RULES OF CAUTION
By Edward S. Corwin[16]

.   .   .   .   .

From the very nature of judicial review as an outgrowth of ordinary judicial function arise certain limitations upon its exercise. This however, is not the only source of the limitations which the Court has come to observe when exercising the most exalted of its powers. Alongside what may be termed *intrinsic limitations* of judicial review, and often modifying them, are others which owe their existence to *cautionary considerations*—to the desire of the Court to avoid occasions of direct conflict with the political branches of the government, and especially with that branch which wields the physical forces of government, the President.

Neither of these factors of judicial review, it should be added, is an altogether constant one. The Court's theory of the nature of judicial power will itself be found to have undergone development, and to this development judicial review has responded. More changeable has been the other factor, varying in its force with the times and with the personalities of the judges—and perhaps also with personalities of Presidents. Marshall, for example, was a bold and enterprising magistrate, constantly ready to put the pretensions of the Court to the test; while his successor, on the contrary, was—save on one fatal occasion[17]—a notably cautious man. . . .

Among the rules which the Supreme Court has recognized as governing judicial review are the following:[18]

1. A decision disallowing a legislative act, either national or state,

---

[15] *op. cit. supra*, n. 5, pp. 426–427.

[16] Extracts from "Judicial Review in Action," 74 *University of Pennsylvania Law Review* 639 (1926). Copyright by University of Pennsylvania Law Review and reproduced by their permission.

[17] The allusion is to the Dred Scott case.

[18] A similar set of rules was listed by Mr. Justice Brandeis in his concurring opinion in *Ashwander* v. *Tennessee Valley Authority*, 297 U.S. 288, 346–348 (1936).

must be concurred in by a majority of the entire membership of the Bench. This is a cautionary rule—originally a concession to state pride —for other kinds of decisions are binding when concurred in by a majority of a quorum[19] of the Court.

2. The Court will pronounce on the constitutionality of legislative acts only in connection with "cases." . . . A *case* in this sense . . . must be a real case—not a simulated or "moot" case. That is, it must involve a real contest of antagonistic interests, requiring for its solution a judicial pronouncement on opposed views of law. . . . [The Court has not always observed this rule in practice.] . . . The Court at an early date refused to render an advisory opinion . . . and it has subsequently extended its scruple to the rendition of "declaratory judgments." . . .

. . . . .

3. Corollary of the rule against moot cases is the rule that nobody may attack the constitutionality of a legislative act in a case before the Court unless his rights are actually affected or clearly menaced by such legislative act; and also the rule, which is the converse of this, that the Court will pass on the constitutional question raised by such an attack only when it is necessary to do so in order to determine the rights of parties to a case before it. . . .

. . . . .

4. Another maxim stated with great positiveness by the writers is that no legislative act may be pronounced void by a court on the ground of its being in conflict with natural justice, the social compact, fundamental principles, etc.—in short, on any other than strictly constitutional grounds. . . . [But note that juristic usage of such constitutional concepts as "liberty" or "due process of law" frequently has the effect of reference to such broad principles or ideas outside the context of the Constitution.]

. . . . .

5. Probably no maxim of judicial review is encountered in the decisions more frequently than that which says that a statute may be declared unconstitutional only in "a clear case"; or as it is also phrased, that all legislative acts are "presumed to be constitutional" until shown to be otherwise, and that all "reasonable doubts" concerning their constitutionality will be resolved in their favor. . . . [To

[19] By Act of Congress any six members of the Court constitute a quorum.

this is related] the maxim that of two possible constructions of the statute one of which renders a statute constitutional and the other unconstitutional, the former is to be preferred as presumably representing the legislature's intention. . . . [But note that in recent years the Court has declared that state laws infringing upon the liberties guaranteed by the First Amendment are "prima facie void."]

6. Another limitation on judicial review, which is partially cautionary, partially logical, grows out of the doctrine of "political questions." [See below.] . . .

• • • • •

7. . . . It has become in recent years a rather common practice for legislatures, in enacting elaborate and complex measures, to declare the separate paragraphs thereof independent, and to direct that the holding of any paragraph or part of the statute invalid shall not affect the question of the validity of the rest. Such declarations are apparently regarded as binding by the Court. [But cf. *Carter* v. *Carter Coal Co.*, 298 U.S. 238, where the Court, in the face of an express separability clause, declared that invalidation of the contested portion of the act voided the whole.]

8. A further limitation on the exercise of the power of judicial review arises from the doctrine of precedent; but the real force of this limitation in the case of the Supreme Court of the United States is difficult to estimate. Logically the Court should, no doubt, regard its own past interpretations of the Constitution in the same light as it does its past interpretations of any law whatsoever. But in the first place, unlike the House of Lords, the Supreme Court has never said that it considered itself absolutely bound by its own previous decisions, while, in the second place, its construction of certain acts of Congress—the Sherman Act is an especially glaring example—has been characterized by anything but hidebound deference to the logic of decided cases.

That, therefore, the Court should claim equal freedom in relation to the Constitution—a law not amendable by ordinary legislative processes—is not strange. It has, to be sure, decided many cases by reference to the authority of past decisions, but this may have been because it still approved of the reasoning upon which these decisions rest. It has frequently shown itself astute to "distinguish" the case before it from analogous cases previously decided—a method of escape from the thraldom of stare decisis recognized by the doctrine itself.

Lastly it has on several occasions, with varying degrees of candor, overruled past decisions,[20] and sometimes it has silently suppressed them.

LUTHER v. BORDEN
17 How. 1 (1849)

[This suit grew out of the so-called "Dorr Rebellion" in Rhode Island, 1841–1842. That state had continued to be governed under the terms of the charter which the colony had received in 1663, with the result that suffrage was greatly limited and representation highly unequal. Dorr headed an insurgency which established a rival government, basing its authority derived on the will of the people and proclaiming universal manhood suffrage. The old (charter) government, however, suppressed the uprising and Dorr was tried for treason in the state supreme court and sentenced to life imprisonment. His purpose was accomplished nevertheless when the charter forces yielded to the popular pressure manifested by his movement and consented to revision of the state's basic law and the introduction of wider electoral rights. Dorr's cause had evoked widespread sympathy outside the state, particularly in Democratic circles. There was some hope that the Supreme Court of the United States, composed largely of members previously associated with that party, might rule that Dorr's government, because it represented the majority of the people, was the rightful one. In order to bring this case before the federal courts, Luther, a follower of Dorr who had been arrested in his home by government militia, moved to Massachusetts and from there, on the basis of diversity of citizenship, brought an action of trespass against the arresting officer, Borden.]

Mr. Chief Justice TANEY delivered the opinion of the Court:

The fourth section of the fourth article of the Constitution of the United States provides that the United States shall guarantee to every state in the Union a republican form of government, and shall protect each of them against invasion; and on the application of the legislature or of the executive (when the legislature cannot be convened) against domestic violence.

Under this article of the Constitution it rests with Congress to de-

[20] Charlotte C. Bernhardt offers a tabulation and appraisal of "Supreme Court Reversals on Constitutional Issues" in 34 *Cornell Law Quarterly* 55 (1948).

cide what government is the established one in a state. For as the United States guarantee to each state a republican government, Congress must necessarily decide what government is established in the state before it can determine whether it is republican or not. And when the senators and representatives of a state are admitted into the councils of the Union, the authority of the government under which they are appointed, as well as its republican character, is recognized by the proper constitutional authority. And its decision is binding on every other department of the government, and could not be questioned in a judicial tribunal. It is true that the contest in this case did not last long enough to bring the matter to this issue; and as no senators or representatives were elected under the authority of the government of which Mr. Dorr was the head, Congress was not called upon to decide the controversy. Yet the right to decide is placed there, and not in the courts.

So, too, as relates to the clause in the above-mentioned article of the Constitution, providing for cases of domestic violence. It rested with Congress, too, to determine upon the proper means to be adopted to fulfill this guarantee. They might, if they had deemed it most advisable to do so, have placed it in the power of a court to decide when the contingency had happened which required the federal government to interfere. But Congress thought otherwise, and no doubt wisely; and by the act of February 28, 1795, provided, that, "in case of an insurrection in any state against the government thereof, it shall be lawful for the President of the United States, on application of the legislature of such state or of the executive, when the legislature cannot be convened, to call forth such number of militia of any other state or states as may be applied for, as he may judge sufficient to suppress such insurrection."

By this act, the power of deciding whether the exigency had arisen upon which the government of the United States is bound to interfere, is given to the President. He is to act upon the application of the legislature, or of the executive, and consequently he must determine what body of men constitute the legislature, and who is the governor, before he can act. The fact that both parties claim the right to the government, cannot alter the case, for both cannot be entitled to it. If there is an armed conflict, like the one of which we are speaking, it is a case of domestic violence, and one of the parties must be in insurrection against the lawful government. And the President must, of necessity, decide which is the government, and which party is unlawfully arrayed against it, before he can perform the duty imposed upon him by the act of Congress.

After the President has acted and called out the militia, is a circuit court of the United States authorized to inquire whether his decision was right? Could the court, while the parties were actually contending in arms for the possession of the government, call witnesses before it and inquire which party represented a majority of the people? If it could then it would become the duty of the court (provided it came to the conclusion that the President had decided incorrectly) to discharge those who were arrested or detained by the troops in the service of the United States or the government which the President was endeavoring to maintain. If the judicial power extends so far, the guarantee contained in the Constitution of the United States is a guarantee of anarchy, and not of order. Yet if this right does not reside in the courts when the conflict is raging, if the judicial power is, at that time, bound to follow the decision of the political, it must be equally bound when the contest is over. It cannot, when peace is restored, punish as offenses and crimes the acts which it before recognized, and was bound to recognize, as lawful.

It is true that in this case the militia were not called out by the President. But upon the application of the governor under the charter government, the President recognized him as the executive power of the state, and took measures to call out the militia to support his authority, if it should be found necessary for the general government to interfere; and it is admitted in the argument, that it was the knowledge of this decision that put an end to the armed opposition to the charter government, and prevented any further efforts to establish by force the proposed constitution. The interference of the President, therefore, by announcing his determination, was as effectual as if the militia had been assembled under his orders. And it should be equally authoritative. For certainly no court of the United States, with a knowledge of this decision, would have been justified in recognizing the opposing party as the lawful government; or in treating as wrongdoers or insurgents the officers of the government which the President had recognized, and was prepared to support by an armed force. In the case of foreign nations, the government acknowledged by the President is always recognized in the courts of justice. And this principle has been applied by the act of Congress to the sovereign states of the Union.

It is said that this power in the President is dangerous to liberty, and may be abused. All power may be abused if placed in unworthy hands. But it would be difficult, we think, to point out any other hands in which this power would be more safe, and at the same time equally effectual. When citizens of the same state are in arms against each other, and the constituted authorities unable to execute the laws, the interposition of the United States must be prompt, or it is of little value. The ordinary course of proceedings in courts of justice would be utterly unfit for the crisis. And the elevated office of the President, chosen as he is by the people of the United States, and the high responsibility he could not fail to feel when acting in a case of so much moment, appear to furnish as strong safeguards against a wilful abuse of power as human prudence and foresight could well provide. At all events, it is conferred upon him by the Constitution and laws of the United States and must, therefore, be respected and enforced in its judicial tribunals.

.   .   .   .   .

Much of the argument on the part of the plaintiff turned upon political rights and political questions, upon which the Court has been urged to express an opinion. We decline doing so. The high power has been conferred on this Court of passing judgment upon the acts of the state sovereignties, and of the legislative and executive branches of the federal government, and of determining whether they are beyond the limits of power marked out for them respectively by the Constitution of the United States. This tribunal, therefore, should be the last to overstep the boundaries which limit its own jurisdiction. And while it should always be ready to meet any question confided to it by the Constitution, it is equally its duty not to pass beyond its appropriate sphere of action, and to take care not to involve itself in discussions which properly belong to other forums. No one, we believe, has ever doubted the proposition, that, according to the institutions of this country, the sovereignty in every state resides in the people of the state, and that they may alter and change their form of government at their own pleasure. But whether they have changed it or not, by abolishing an old government, and establishing a new one in its place, is a question to be settled by the political power. And when that power has decided, the courts are bound to take notice of its decision, and follow it.

The judgment of the Circuit Court must, therefore, be affirmed.

Mr. Justice WOODBURY, dissenting [on other grounds]. . . .[21]

[In *Pacific States Telephone and Telegraph Co.* v. *Oregon,* 223 U.S. 118 (1912), it was alleged that the insertion in the state constitution of Oregon of a provision for direct legislation through the popular initiative and referendum deprived the state of a republican form of government as guaranteed by the Federal Constitution. And hence it was argued that acts of the state government operating under this constitution, in this case a tax levied on plaintiff corporation, were invalid. "As the issues presented," said the Court, "in their very essence, are, and have long since by this Court been, definitely determined to be political and governmental, and embraced within the scope of the powers conferred upon Congress, and not therefore within the reach of judicial power, it follows that the case presented is not within our jurisdiction. . . ."]

COLEMAN v. MILLER
307 U.S. 433 (1939)

Mr. Chief Justice HUGHES delivered the opinion of the Court:

In June, 1924, the Congress proposed an amendment to the Constitution, known as the Child Labor Amendment. In January, 1925, the legislature of Kansas adopted a resolution rejecting the proposed amendment and a certified copy of the resolution was sent to the Secretary of State of the United States. In January, 1937, a resolution . . . was introduced in the senate of Kansas ratifying the proposed amendment. There were forty senators. When the resolution came up for consideration, twenty senators voted in favor of its adoption and twenty voted against it. The lieutenant governor, the presiding officer of the senate, then cast his vote in favor of the resolution. The resolution was later adopted by the house of representatives on the vote of a majority of its members.

This original proceeding in mandamus was then brought in the Supreme Court of Kansas by twenty-one members of the senate, including the twenty senators who had voted against the resolution, and three members of the house of representatives, to compel the secretary of the senate to erase an endorsement on the resolution to the effect that it had been adopted by the senate and to endorse thereon the words "was not passed," and to restrain the officers of the senate and

---

[21] The circumstances surrounding this case may be found interestingly discussed in Charles Warren, *The Supreme Court in United States History,* vol. II, pp. 186–195.

house of representatives from signing the resolution and the secretary of state of Kansas from authenticating it and delivering it to the governor. The petition challenged the right of the lieutenant governor to cast the deciding vote in the senate. The petition also set forth the prior rejection of the proposed amendment and alleged that in the period from June, 1924, to March, 1927, the amendment had been rejected by both houses of the legislatures of twenty-six states, and had been ratified in only five states, and that by reason of that rejection and the failure of ratification within a reasonable time the proposed amendment had lost its vitality.

[The Court here considered at length the question whether the petitioners had sufficient interest to invoke the jurisdiction of the Court, holding that they had. It next affirmed, by a tie vote of four-to-four, the decision of the state supreme court that the lieutenant governor could legally cast the deciding vote in the state senate.]

Third. The effect of the previous rejection of the amendment and of the lapse of time since its submission.

1. The state court adopted the view expressed by textwriters that a state legislature which rejected an amendment proposed by the Congress may later ratify. The argument in support of that view is that Article V says nothing of rejection but speaks only of ratification and provides that a proposed amendment shall be valid as part of the Constitution when ratified by three-fourths of the states; that the power to ratify is thus conferred upon the state by the Constitution and, as a ratifying power, persists despite a previous rejection. The opposing view proceeds on an assumption that if ratification by conventions were prescribed by the Congress, a convention could not reject and, having adjourned sine die, be reassembled and ratify. It is also premised, in accordance with views expressed by textwriters, that ratification if once given cannot afterwards be rescinded and the amendment rejected, and it is urged that the same effect in the exhaustion of the state's power to act should be ascribed to rejection; that a state can act "but once, either by convention or through its legislature."

Historic instances are cited. . . .

[These show that] . . . the political departments of the government dealt with the effect both of previous rejection and of attempted withdrawal and determined that both were ineffectual in the presence of an actual ratification. . . . This decision by the political department of the government as to the validity of the adoption of the Fourteenth Amendment has been accepted.

We think that in accordance with this historic precedent the question of the efficacy of ratification by state legislatures, in the light of previous rejection or attempted withdrawal, should be regarded as a political question pertaining to the political departments, with the ultimate authority in the Congress in the exercise of its control over the promulgation of the adoption of the amendment. . . .

2. The more serious question is whether the proposal by the Congress of the amendment had lost its vitality through lapse of time and hence it could not be ratified by the Kansas legislature in 1937. . . .

We have held that the Congress in proposing an amendment may fix a reasonable time for ratification. *Dillon* v. *Gloss*, 256 U.S. 368. . . . But petitioners contend that in the absence of a limitation by the Congress, the Court can and should decide what is a reasonable period within which ratification may be had. We are unable to agree with that contention.

Where are to be found the criteria for such a judicial determination? None are to be found in Constitution or statute. In their endeavor to answer this question petitioners' counsel have suggested that at least two years should be allowed; that six years would not be unreasonably long; that seven years had been used by the Congress as a reasonable period; that one year, six months and thirteen days was the average time used in passing upon amendments which had been ratified since the first ten amendments; that three years, six months and twenty-five days has been the longest time used in ratifying. To this list of variables, counsel add that "the nature and extent of publicity and the activity of the public and of the legislatures of the several states in relation to any particular proposal should be taken into consideration." That statement is pertinent, but there are additional matters to be examined and weighed. When a proposed amendment springs from a conception of economic needs, it would be necessary, in determining whether a reasonable time had elapsed since its submission to consider the economic conditions prevailing in the country, whether these had so far changed since the submission as to make the proposal no longer responsive to the conception which inspired it or whether conditions were such as to intensify the feeling of need and the appropriateness of the proposed remedial action. In short, the question of a reasonable time in many cases would involve, as in this case it does involve, an appraisal of a great variety of relevant conditions, political, social and economic, which can hardly be said to be within the appropriate range of evidence receivable in a court of justice and as to which it would be an extravagant extension of judicial authority to assert judicial notice as the basis of deciding a controversy with respect to the validity of an amendment actually ratified. On the other hand, these conditions are appropriate for the consideration of the political departments of the government. The questions they involve are essentially political and not justiciable. They can be decided by the Congress with the full knowledge and appreciation ascribed to the national legislature of the political, social and economic conditions which have prevailed during the period since the submission of the amendment.

. . . The decision by the Congress, in its control of the action of the Secretary of State [of promulgating the amendment], of the question whether the amendment had been adopted within a reasonable time would not be subject to review by the courts.

.   .   .   .   .

For the reasons we have stated . . . we think that the Congress in controlling the promulgation of the adoption of the amendment has the final determination of the question whether by lapse of time its proposal of the amendment had lost its vitality prior to the required ratifications. The state officials should not be restrained from certifying to the Secretary of State the adoption by the legislature of Kansas of the resolution of ratification.

As we find no reason for disturbing the decision of the Supreme Court of Kansas in denying the mandamus sought by petitioners, its judgment is affirmed but upon grounds stated in this opinion.

Mr. Justice BLACK (Mr. Justice ROBERTS, Mr. Justice FRANKFURTER, and Mr. Justice DOUGLAS joining with him), concurring in the result.

. . . Congress, possessing exclusive power over the amending process, cannot be bound by and is under no duty to accept the pronouncements upon that exclusive power by this Court or by the Kansas courts. Neither state nor federal courts can review that power. Therefore, any judicial expression amounting to more than mere acknowledgement of exclusive Congressional power over the political process of amendment is a mere admonition to the Congress in the nature of an advisory opinion, given wholly without constitutional authority. ...

Mr. Justice BUTLER (Mr. Justice McREYNOLDS joining with him), dissenting: [The Court should assume jurisdiction and find that more than a reasonable time has elapsed. Past pronouncements by the Court on matters involving the amending process have been accepted by the Congress, indicating that that body recognized the judicial authority in such matters.]

[*Note on The Amending Power*: Prior to *Coleman* v. *Miller* the Court had decided a number of cases touching on the procedure for amending the Constitution. The earliest of these was *Hollingsworth* v. *Virginia,* 3 Dallas 378 (1798), involving the Eleventh Amendment. It decided that the proposal of an amendment was a constituent, not a legislative act and that it was therefore not necessary to submit it to the President for signature or veto. Also bearing on the proposal stage is the ruling in the *National Prohibition Cases,* 253 U.S. 350 (1920), that the requirement of a two-thirds vote pertains to the quorum, not the total membership of each house.

[That Congress may impose a time limit within which a proposed amendment is to be ratified was approved in *Dillon* v. *Gloss,* 256 U.S. 368 (1921). On the other hand, an attempt by the state of Ohio to accomplish ratification by referendum was held to contravene the specific stipulations of the Constitution. *Hawke* v. *Smith,* 253 U.S. 221 (1920).

[Query: does the decision in *Coleman* v. *Miller* mean a complete surrender of the Court's jurisdiction in cases involving the amending power? Note the sweeping assertion of the concurring opinion on that question. Would the Court, for instance, consider whether or not a two-thirds vote of the quorum was mustered for a proposal? See *Christoffel* v. *United States,* 338 U.S. 84 (1949), where the Court decided that a Congressional committee was not "a competent tribunal" in the absence of quorum.

[The entire subject of amendments to the Federal Constitution is covered in an authoritative monograph *Amending the Federal Constitution* by Lester B. Orfield (Ann Arbor: The University of Michigan Press, 1942).]

COLEGROVE v. GREEN
328 U.S. 549 (1946)

[An effort by some qualified voters in Illinois to compel redistricting of the state for Congressional elections, a task which had been passed over since 1901, with the result that urban districts, which had registered great gains in the meantime, did not have a fair share of the state's representation in Congress. The state courts held themselves powerless to interfere with the inaction of the legislature.]

Mr. Justice FRANKFURTER announced the judgment of the Court and an opinion in which Mr. Justice REED and Mr. Justice BURTON concur.

We are of the opinion that the petitioners ask of this Court what is beyond its competence to grant. This is one of those demands on judicial power which cannot be met by verbal fencing about "jurisdiction." It must be resolved by considerations on the basis of which this Court, from time to time, has refused to intervene in controversies. It has refused to do so because due regard for the effective working of our government revealed this issue to be of a peculiarly political nature and therefore not meet for judicial determination.

This is not an action to recover for damage because of the discriminatory exclusion of a plaintiff from rights enjoyed by other citizens. The basis for the suit is not a private wrong, but a wrong suffered by Illinois as a polity. In effect this is an appeal to the federal courts to reconstruct the electoral process of Illinois in order that it may be adequately represented in the councils of the Nation. Because the Illinois legislature has failed to revise its Congressional Representative districts in order to reflect great changes, during more than a generation, in the distribution of its population, we are asked to do this, as it were, for Illinois.

Of course no court can affirmatively remap the Illinois districts so as to bring them more in conformity with the standards of fairness for a representative system. At best we could only declare the existing electoral system invalid. The result would be to leave Illinois undistricted and to bring into operation, if the Illinois legislature chose not to act, the choice of members for the House of Representatives on a state-wide ticket. The last stage may be worse than the first. The upshot of judicial action may defeat the vital political principle which led Congress, more than a hundred years ago, to require districting.

... Nothing is clearer than that this controversy concerns matters that bring courts into immediate and active relations with party contests. From the determination of such issues this Court has traditionally held aloof. It is hostile to a democratic system to involve the judiciary in the politics of the people. And it is not less pernicious if such judicial intervention in an essentially political contest be dressed up in the abstract phrases of the law.

To sustain this action would cut very deep into the very being of Congress. Courts ought not to enter this political thicket. The remedy for unfairness in districting is to secure state legislatures that will apportion properly or to invoke the ample powers of Congress. ...

Mr. Justice JACKSON took no part in the consideration of this case.

Mr. Justice RUTLEDGE. I concur in the result. ...

Mr. Justice BLACK (Mr. Justice DOUGLAS and Mr. Justice MURPHY concurring with him), dissenting.

It is difficult for me to see why the 1901 State Apportionment Act does not deny petitioners equal protection of the laws. The failure of the legislature to reapportion the congressional election districts for forty years, despite census figures indicating great changes in the distribution of the population, has resulted in election districts, the populations of which range from 112,000 to 900,000 people. One of the petitioners lives in a district of more than 900,000 people. His vote is consequently less effective than that of each of the citizens living in the district of 112,000. And such a gross inequality in the voting power of citizens irrefutably demonstrates a complete lack of effort to make an equitable apportionment. The 1901 State Apportionment Act if applied to the next election would thus result in a wholly indefensible discrimination against petitioners and all other voters in heavily populated districts. The equal protection clause of the Fourteenth Amendment forbids such discrimination. ...

In this case, no supervision over elections is asked for. ... What is involved here is the right to vote guaranteed by the Federal Constitution. It has always been the rule that where a federally protected right has been invaded the federal courts will provide the remedy to rectify the wrong done. Federal courts have not hesitated to exercise their equity power in cases involving deprivation of property and liberty. ... There is no reason why they should do so where the case involves the right to choose representatives that make laws affecting liberty and property.

Nor is there any more difficulty in enforcing a decree in this case than there was in the Smiley Case [*Smiley* v. *Holm,* 285 U.S. 355, upheld a state court order declaring a state apportionment bill invalid]. It is true that declaration of invalidity of the State Act and the enjoining of State officials would result in prohibiting the State from electing Congressmen under the system of old Congressional districts. But it would leave the State free to elect them from the State at large, which, as we held in the Smiley Case, is a manner authorized by the Constitution. It is said that it would be inconvenient for the State to conduct the election in this manner. But it has an element of virtue that the more convenient method does not have—namely, it does not discriminate against some groups to favor others, it gives all people an equally effective voice in electing their representatives as is essential under a free government, and it is Constitutional.

Mr. Justice DOUGLAS and Mr. Justice MURPHY join in this dissent.

Separation of Powers

1. THE STATEMENT

[From *The Spirit of the Laws,* by Charles Louis de Secondat, Baron de Montesquieu, Book IX, chapter 6 (Nugent-Prichard translation of 1878).]

In every government there are three sorts of power: the legislative, the executive. . ., and . . . [the judiciary]. . . . When the legislative and executive powers are united in the same person, or in the same body of magistrates, there can be no liberty; . . . Again, there is no liberty if the judiciary power be not separated from the legislative and executive. Were it joined with the legislative, the life and liberty of the subject would be exposed to arbitrary control; for the judge would then be legislator. Were it joined to the executive, the judge might behave with violence and oppression.

There would be an end of everything were the same men or the same body (whether of nobles or of the people) to exercise all three powers, that of enacting laws, that of executing the public resolutions, and of trying the causes of individuals.

[Massachusetts Constitution of 1780]

Article XXX: In the government of this commonwealth the legislative department shall never exercise the executive and judicial powers or either of them; the executive shall never exercise the legislative and judicial powers or either of them; the judicial shall never exercise the legislative and executive powers or either of them: to the end it may be a government of laws and not of men.

[Constitution of the United States, 1787]

Article I, Section 1: All legislative powers herein granted shall be vested in a Congress of the United States, ...

.   .   .

Article II, Section 1: The executive power shall be vested in a President of the United States of America. . . .

.   .   .

Article III, Section 1: The judicial power of the United States shall be vested in one Supreme Court, and in such inferior courts as the Congress may from time to time ordain and establish. . . .

.   .   .

[*The Federalist*, No. XLVII, by James Madison]

One of the principal objections inculcated by the more respectable adversaries to the constitution, is its supposed violation of the political maxim, that the legislative, executive, and judiciary departments, ought to be separate and distinct. In the structure of the federal government, no regard, it is said, seems to have been paid to this essential precaution in favour of liberty. The several departments of power are distributed and blended in such a manner, as at once to destroy all symmetry and beauty of form; and to expose some of the essential parts of the edifice to the danger of being crushed by the disproportionate weight of other parts.

No political truth is certainly of greater intrinsic value, or is stamped with the authority of more enlightened patrons of liberty, than that on which the objection is founded. The accumulation of all powers, legislative, executive, and judiciary, in the same hands, whether of one, a few, or many, and whether hereditary, self-appointed, or elective, may justly be pronounced the very definition of tyranny. . . .

The oracle who is always consulted and cited on this subject, is the celebrated Montesquieu. If he be not the author of this invaluable precept in the science of politics, he has the merit of at least displaying and recommending it most effectually to the attention of mankind. . . .

... In saying, "there can be no liberty, where the legislative and executive powers are united in the same person, or body of magistrates;" or "if the power of judging be not separated from the legislative and executive powers," he did not mean that these departments ought to have no *partial agency* in, or no *control* over, the acts of each other. His meaning, as his own words import, and still more conclusively as illustrated by the example in his eye [the British constitution], can amount to no more than this, that where the *whole* power of one department is exercised by the same hands which possess the *whole* power of another department, the fundamental principles of a free constitution are subverted. . . .

... The charge brought against the proposed constitution, of violating a sacred maxim of free government, is warranted neither by the real meaning annexed to that maxim by its author, nor by the sense in which it has hitherto been understood in America. . . .

2. THE PRACTICE

McGRAIN v. DAUGHERTY
273 U.S. 135 (1927)

[A Senate committee called Daugherty as a witness and, when he refused to appear, had him arrested to be brought before them. Daugherty asked a federal district court for a writ of *habeas corpus,* i.e., an order directing the person detaining him to show under what authority the arrest or detention was claimed. The district court held that the Senate committee had no power to order the arrest and that Daugherty should be released.]

Mr. Justice VAN DEVANTER delivered the opinion of the Court. . . .

Harry M. Daugherty became the Attorney General March 5, 1921, and held that office until March 28, 1924, when he resigned. Late in that period various charges of misfeasance and nonfeasance in the Department of Justice after he became its supervising head were brought to the attention of the Senate by individual senators and made the basis of an insistent demand that the department be investigated to the end that the practices and deficiencies which, according to the charges, were operating to prevent or impair its right administration might be definitely ascertained and that appropriate and effective measures might be taken to remedy or eliminate the evil. The Senate regarded the charges as grave and requiring legislative attention and action. Accordingly it . . . adopted a resolution authorizing and directing a select committee of five senators "to investigate circumstances and facts, to report same to the Senate, concerning the alleged failure of Harry M. Daugherty, Attorney General of the United States, to arrest and prosecute Albert B. Fall, Harry F. Sinclair, E. L. Doheny, C. R. Forbes, and their co-conspirators in defrauding the Government, as well as the alleged neglect and failure of the said Attorney General to arrest and prosecute many others for violation of Federal statutes, and his alleged failure to prosecute properly, efficiently, and promptly, and to defend all manner of civil and criminal actions wherein the Government of the United States is interested as a party plaintiff or defendant." . . .

[The first question is] . . . whether the Senate—or the House of Representatives, both being on the same plane in this regard—has power, through its own process, to compel a private individual [the brother of the ex-Attorney General, Ohio banker Mally S. Daugherty] to appear before it or one of its committees and give testimony needed to enable it efficiently to exercise a legislative function belonging to it under the Constitution. . . .

The Constitution provides for a Congress consisting of a Senate and House of Representatives and invests it with "all legislative Powers" granted to the United States, and with power "to make all laws which shall be necessary and proper" for carrying into execution these powers and "all other powers" vested by the Constitution in the United States or in any department or officer thereof. Article I, sections 1, 8 . . . But there is no provision expressly investing either house with power to make investigations and exact testimony to the end that it may exercise its legislative function advisedly and effectively. So the question arises whether this power is so far incidental to the legislative function as to be implied.

In actual legislative practice power to secure needed information by such means has long been treated as an attribute of the power to legislate. It was so regarded in the British Parliament and in the colonial legislatures before the American Revolution; and a like view has prevailed and been carried into effect in both houses of Congress and in most of the state legislatures. [Citing examples of its application by the House of Representatives in 1792 and 1859, and referring to state practices as well as to Congressional enactments facilitating investigations].

.   .   .   .   .

Four decisions of this Court are cited and more or less relied on, and we now turn to them.

The first decision was in *Anderson* v. *Dunn,* 6 Wheat. 204. . . . The question there was whether, under the Constitution, the House of Representatives has power to attach and punish a person other than a member for contempt of its authority—in fact, an attempt to bribe one of its members. The Court regarded the power as essential to the effective exertion of other powers expressly granted, and therefore implied. . . .

The next decision was in *Kilbourn* v. *Thompson,* 103 U.S. 168. The question there was whether the House of Representatives had exceeded its power in directing one of its committees to make a particular investigation. The decision was that it had. The principles announced and applied in the case are—that neither house of Congress possesses a "general power of making inquiry into the private affairs of the citizen;" that the power actually possessed is limited to inquiries relating to matters of which the particular house "has jurisdiction" and in respect of which it rightfully may take other action; that if the inquiry relates to "a matter wherein relief or redress could be had only by a judicial proceeding" it is not within the range of this power, but must be left to the courts, conformably to the constitutional separation of governmental powers; and that for the purpose of determining the essential character of the inquiry recourse may be had to the resolution or order under which it is made. The Court examined the resolution which was the basis of the particular inquiry, and ascertained therefrom that the inquiry related to a private real estate pool or partnership in the District of Columbia. Jay Cooke & Company had had an interest in the pool, but had become bankrupts, and their estate was in course of administration in a federal bankruptcy court in Pennsylvania. The United States was one of their creditors. The trustee in the bankruptcy proceeding had effected a settlement of the bankrupts' interest in the pool, and of course his action was subject to examination and approval or disapproval by the bankruptcy court. Some of the creditors, including the United States, were dissatisfied with the settlement. In these circumstances, disclosed in the preamble, the resolution directed the committee "to inquire into the matter and history of said real estate pool and the character of said settlement, with the amount of property involved in which Jay Cooke & Company were interested, and the amount paid or to be paid in said settlement, with power to send for persons and papers and report to the House." The Court pointed out that the resolution contained no suggestion of contemplated legislation; that the matter was one in respect to which no valid legislation could be had; that the bankrupts' estate and the trustee's settlement were still pending in the bankruptcy court; and that the United States and other creditors were free to press their claims in that proceeding. And on these grounds the Court held that in undertaking the investigation "the House of Representatives not only exceeded the limit of its own authority, but assumed power which could only be properly exercised by another branch of the government, because it was in its nature clearly judicial."

[Discussion of *In re Chapman*, 166 U.S. 661, and *Marshall* v. *Gordon*, 243 U.S. 521, omitted.]

While these cases are not decisive of the question we are considering, they definitely settle two propositions which we recognize as entirely sound and having a bearing on its solution: One, that the two houses of Congress, in their separate relations, possess not only such powers as are expressly granted to them by the Constitution, but such auxiliary powers as are necessary and appropriate to make the express powers effective; and, the other, that neither house is invested with "general" power to inquire into private affairs and compel disclosures, but only with such limited power of inquiry as is shown to exist when the rule of constitutional interpretation just stated is rightly applied. . . .

With this review of the legislative practice, congressional enactments and court decisions, we proceed to a statement of our conclusions on the question.

We are of the opinion that the power of inquiry—with process to enforce it—is an essential and appropriate auxiliary to the legislative function. It was so regarded and employed in American legislatures before the Constitution was framed and ratified. Both houses of Congress took this view of it early in their history—the House of Representatives with the approving votes of Mr. Madison and other members whose service in the convention which framed the Constitution gives special significance to their action—and both houses have employed the power accordingly up to the present time. The acts of 1798 and 1857, judged by their comprehensive terms, were intended to recognize the existence of this power in both houses and to enable them to employ it "more effectually" than before. So, when their practice in the matter is appraised according to the circumstances in which it was begun and to those in which it has been continued, it falls nothing short of a practical construction, long continued, of the constitutional provisions respecting their powers, and therefore should be taken as fixing the meaning of those provisions, if otherwise doubtful.

We are further of opinion that the provisions are not of doubtful meaning, but, as was held by the Court in the cases we have reviewed, are intended to be effectively exercised, and therefore to carry with them such auxiliary powers as are necessary and appropriate to that end. While the power to exact information in aid of the legislative function was not involved in those cases, the rule of interpretation applied there is applicable here. A legislative body cannot legislate wisely or effectively in the absence of information respecting the conditions which the legislation is intended to affect or change; and where the legislative body does not itself possess the requisite information—which not infrequently is true—recourse must be had to others who do possess it. Experience has taught that mere requests for such information often are unavailing, and also, that information which is volunteered is not always accurate or complete; so some means of compulsion are essential to obtain what is needed. . . .

The contention is earnestly made on behalf of the witness that this power of inquiry, if sustained, may be abusively and oppressively exerted. If this be so, it affords no ground for denying the power. . . .

We come now to the question whether it sufficiently appears that the purpose for which the witness's testimony was sought was to obtain information in aid of the legislative function. . . .

We are of the opinion that the [lower] court's ruling on this question was wrong, and that it sufficiently appears, when the proceedings are rightly interpreted that the object of the investigation and of the effort to secure the witness's testimony was to obtain information for legislative purposes.

It is quite true that the resolution directing the investigation does not in terms avow that it is intended to be in aid of legislation; but it does show that the subject to be investigated was the administration of the Department of Justice—whether its functions were being properly discharged or were being neglected or misdirected, and particularly whether the Attorney General and his assistants were performing or neglecting their duties in respect of the institution and prosecution of proceedings to punish crimes and enforce appropriate remedies against the wrongdoers—specific instances of alleged neglect being recited. Plainly the subject was one on which legislation could be had and would be materially aided by the information which the investigation was calculated to elicit. This becomes manifest when it is reflected that the functions of the Department of Justice, the powers and duties of the Attorney General and the duties of his assistants, are all subject to regulation by congressional legislation, and that the department is maintained . . . under [Congressional] appropriations. . . .

Reversed.

[Note that in the precedent cited for limitation of Congressional power of investigation *(Kilbourn* v. *Thompson)* the subject matter was in the hands of the courts; thus this was, like *Marbury* v. *Madison,* a defensive move of the judiciary. Consider the consequences if the Court had held the Daugherty investigation unconstitutional: this was the government's effort to clear itself of the bad odors left over by the Teapot Dome scandal—might Congress have chosen to ignore the Court?]

3. DELEGATION OF LEGISLATIVE POWER

PANAMA REFINING CO. v. RYAN (The "Hot Oil" Case)
293 U.S. 388 (1935)

Mr. Chief Justice HUGHES delivered the opinion of the Court.

On July 11, 1933, the President, by Executive Order, prohibited "the transportation in interstate and foreign commerce of petroleum and the products thereof produced or withdrawn from storage in excess of the amount permitted to be produced or withdrawn from storage by any state law or valid regulation or order prescribed thereunder, by any board, commission, officer, or other duly authorized agency of a state." This action was based on Section 9 (c) of Title I of the National Industrial Recovery Act of June 16, 1933. 48 Stat. 195–200, 15 U.S.C. Tit. I, sec. 709 (c). That section provides:

"Sec. 9 . . .

"(c) The President is authorized to prohibit the transportation in interstate and foreign commerce of petroleum and the products thereof produced or withdrawn from storage in excess of the amount permitted to be produced or withdrawn from storage by any state law or valid regulation or order prescribed thereunder, by any board, commission, officer, or other duly authorized agency of a state. Any violation of any order of the President issued under the provisions of this subsection shall be punishable by fine of not to exceed $1,000, or imprisonment for not to exceed six months, or both." . . .

On August 19, 1933, the President, by Executive Order, stating that his action was taken under Title I of the National Industrial Recovery Act, approved a "Code of Fair Competition for the Petroleum Industry." . . .

This "Petroleum Code" (in its original form and as officially printed) provided in Section 3 of Article III relating to "Production" for estimates of "required production of crude oil to balance consumer demand for petroleum products" to be made at intervals by the federal agency. This "required production" was to be "equitably allocated" among the several states. These estimates and allocations, when approved by the President, were to be deemed to be "the net reasonable market demand" and the allocations were to be recommended "as the operating schedules for the producing states and for the industry." By section 4 of Article III, the subdivision, with respect to producing properties, of the production allocated to each state, was to be made within the state. . . .

. . . The Panama Refining Company, as owner of an oil refining plant in Texas, and its co-plaintiff, a producer having oil and gas leases in Texas, sued to restrain the defendants, who were federal officials, from enforcing Regulations . . . prescribed by the Secretary of the Interior under Section 9 (c) of the National Industrial Recovery Act. Plaintiffs attacked the validity of Section 9(c) as an unconstitutional delegation to the President of legislative power and as transcending the authority of the Congress under the commerce clause. The regulations, and the attempts to enforce them by coming upon the properties of the plaintiffs, gauging their tanks, digging up pipe lines, and otherwise, were also assailed under the Fourth and Fifth Amendments of the Constitution. . . .

[A permanent injunction was granted by the District Court, but this order was reversed and the bills dismissed by the Circuit Court of Appeals. The Supreme Court took the case on certiorari.]

.   .   .   .   .

Fourth. Section 9 (c) is assailed upon the ground that it is an unconstitutional delegation of legislative power. The section purports to authorize the President to pass a prohibitory law. The subject to which this authority relates is defined. It is the transportation in interstate and foreign commerce of petroleum and petroleum products which are produced or withdrawn from storage in excess of the amount permitted by state authority. Assuming for the present purpose, without deciding, that the Congress has power to interdict the transportation of that excess in interstate and foreign commerce, the question whether that transportation shall be prohibited by law is obviously one of legislative policy. Accordingly, we look to the statute to see whether the Congress has declared a policy with respect to that subject; whether the Congress has set up a standard for the President's action; whether the Congress has required any finding by the President in the exercise of the authority to enact the prohibition.

Section 9(c) is brief and unambiguous. It does not attempt to control the production of petroleum and petroleum products within a state. It does not seek to lay down rules for the guidance of state legislatures or state officers. It leaves to the states and to their constituted authorities the determination of what production shall be permitted. It does not qualify the President's authority by reference to the basis, or extent, of the state's limitation of production. Section 9(c) does not state whether, or in what circumstances or under what conditions, the President is to prohibit the transportation of the amount of petroleum or petroleum products produced in excess of the state's permission. It establishes no criterion to govern the President's course. It does not require any finding by the President as a condition of his action. The Congress in Section 9(c) thus declares no policy as to the transportation of the excess production. So far as this section is concerned, it gives the President an unlimited authority to determine the policy and to lay down the prohibition, or not to lay it down, as he may see fit. And disobedience to his order is made a crime punishable by fine and imprisonment.

We turn to the other provisions of Title I of the Act. The first section is a "declaration of policy." It declares that a national emergency exists "which is productive of widespread unemployment and disorganization of industry, which burdens interstate and foreign commerce, affects public welfare, and undermines the standards of living of the American people." It is declared to be the policy of Congress "to remove obstructions to the free flow of interstate and foreign commerce which tend to diminish the amount thereof;" "to provide for the general welfare by promoting the organization of industry for the purpose of cooperative action among trade groups;" "to induce and maintain united action of labor and management under adequate governmental sanctions and supervision;" "to eliminate unfair competition practices, to promote the fullest possible utilization of the present productive capacity of industries, to avoid undue restriction of production (except as may be temporarily required), to increase the consumption of industrial and agricultural products by increasing purchasing power, to reduce and relieve unemployment, to improve standards of labor, and otherwise to rehabilitate industry and to conserve natural resources."

This general outline of policy contains nothing as to the circumstances or conditions in which transportation of petroleum or petroleum products should be prohibited,—nothing as to the policy of prohibiting, or not prohibiting, the transportation of production exceeding what the states allow. The general policy declared is "to remove obstructions to the free flow of interstate and foreign commerce." As to production, the section lays down no policy of limitation. It favors the fullest possible utilization of the present productive capacity of industries. It speaks, parenthetically, of a possible temporary restriction of production, but of what, or in what circumstances, it gives no suggestion. The section also speaks in general terms of the conservation of natural resources but it prescribes no policy for the achievement of that end. It is manifest that this broad outline is simply an introduction of the Act, leaving the legislative policy as to particular subjects to be declared and defined, if at all, by the subsequent sections.

It is no answer to insist that deleterious consequences follow the transportation of "hot oil"—oil exceeding state allowances. The Congress did not prohibit that transportation. The Congress did not undertake to say that the transportation of "hot oil" was injurious. The Congress did not say that transportation of that oil was "unfair competition." The Congress did not declare in what circumstances that transportation should be forbidden, or require the President to make any determination as to any facts or circumstances. Among the numerous and diverse objectives broadly stated, the President was not required to ascertain and proclaim the conditions prevailing in the industry which made the prohibition necessary. The Congress left the matter to the President without standard or rule, to be dealt with as he pleased. The effort by ingenious and diligent construction to supply a criterion still permits such a breadth of authorized action as essentially to commit to the President the functions of a legislature rather than those of an executive or administrative officer executing a declared legislative policy. We find nothing in Section 1 which limits or controls the authority conferred by Section 9(c).

We pass to the other sections of the Act. . . .

None of these provisions can be deemed to prescribe any limitation of the grant of authority in Section 9(c).

Fifth. The question whether such a delegation of legislative power is permitted by the Constitution is not answered by the argument that it should be assumed that the President has acted, and will act, for what he believes to be the public good. The point is not one of motives but of constitutional authority, for which the best of motives is not a substitute.

.   .   .   .   .

The Constitution provides that "All legislative powers herein granted shall be vested in a Congress of the United States, which shall consist of a Senate and House of Representatives." Art. I, Sec. 1. And the Congress is empowered "To make all laws which shall be necessary and proper for carrying into execution" its general powers. Art. I, Sec. 8, § 18. The Congress manifestly is not permitted to abdicate, or to transfer to others, the essential legislative functions with which it is thus vested. Undoubtedly legislation must often be adapted to complex conditions involving a host of details with which the national legislature cannot deal directly. The Constitution has never been regarded as denying to the Congress the necessary resources of flexibility and practicality, which will enable it to perform its function in laying down policies and establishing standards, while leaving to selected instrumentalities the making of subordinate rules within prescribed limits and the determination of facts to which the policy as declared by the legislature is to apply. Without capacity to give authorizations of that sort we should have the anomaly of a legislative power which in many circumstances calling for its exertion would be but a futility. But the constant recognition of the necessity and validity of such provisions, and the wide range of administrative authority which has been developed by means of them, cannot be allowed to obscure the limitations of the authority to delegate, if our constitutional system is to be maintained.

The Court has had frequent occasion to refer to these limitations and to review the course of congressional action. [Cases reviewed.]

.   .   .   .   .

. . . In every case in which the question has been raised, the Court has recognized that there are limits of delegation which there is no constitutional authority to transcend. We think that Section 9(c) goes beyond these limits. As to the transportation of oil production in excess of state permission, the Congress has declared no policy, has established no standard, has laid down no rule. There is no requirement, no definition of circumstances and conditions in which the transportation is to be allowed or prohibited.

If Section 9(c) were held valid, it would be idle to pretend that anything would be left of limitations upon the power of Congress to delegate its law-making function. The reasoning of the many decisions we have reviewed would be made vacuous and their distinctions nugatory. Instead of performing its law-making function the Congress could at will and as to such objects as it chooses transfer that function to the President or other officer or to an administrative body. The question is not of the intrinsic importance of the particular statute before us, but of the constitutional processes of legislation which are an essential part of our system of government. . . .

We see no escape from the conclusion that the Executive Orders of July 11, 1933, and July 14, 1933, and the Regulations issued by the Secretary thereunder, are without constitutional authority. . . .

Reversed.

Mr. Justice CARDOZO, dissenting. . . .

I am unable to assent to the conclusion that Section 9(c) of the National Industrial Recovery Act, a section delegating to the President a very different power from any that is involved in the regulation of production or in the promulgation of a code, is to be nullified upon the ground that his discretion is too broad or for any other reason. My point of difference with the Court is narrow. I concede that to uphold the delegation there is need to discover in the terms of the act a standard reasonably clear whereby discretion must be governed. I deny that such a standard is lacking in respect of the prohibitions permitted by this section when the act with all its reasonable implications is considered as a whole. What the standard is becomes the pivotal inquiry.

As to the nature of the *act* which the President is authorized to perform there is no need for implication. That at least is definite beyond the possibility of challenge. He may prohibit the transportation in interstate and foreign commerce of petroleum and the products thereof produced or withdrawn from storage in excess of the amount permitted by any state law or valid regulation or order prescribed thereunder. He is not left to roam at will among all the possible subjects of interstate transportation, picking and choosing as he pleases. I am far from asserting now that delegation would be valid if accompanied by all that latitude of choice. In the laying of his interdict he is to confine himself to a particular commodity, and to that commodity when produced or withdrawn from storage in contravention of the policy and statutes of the states. He has choice, though within limits, as to the occasion, but none whatever as to the means. The means have been prescribed by Congress. There has been no grant to the Executive of any roving commission to inquire into evils and then, upon discovering them, do anything he pleases. His act being thus defined, what else must he ascertain in order to regulate his discretion and bring the power into play? The answer is not given if we look to Section 9 (c) only, but it comes to us by implication from a view of other sections where the standards are defined. . . . If we look to the whole structure of the statute, the test is plainly this, that the President is to forbid the transportation of the oil when he believes, in the light of the conditions of the industry as disclosed from time to time, that the prohibition will tend to effectuate the declared policies of the act,—not merely his own conceptions of its policies, undirected by any intrinsic guide, but the policies announced by Section 1 in the forefront of the statute as an index to the meaning of everything that follows.

I am persuaded that a reference, express or implied, to the policy of Congress as declared in Section 1 is a sufficient definition of a standard to make the statute valid. Discretion is not unconfined and vagrant. It is canalized within banks that keep it from overflowing. . . . The separation of powers between the Executive and Congress is not a doctrinaire concept to be made use of with pedantic rigor. There must be sensible approximation, there must be elasticity of adjustment, in response to the practical necessities of government, which cannot foresee today the developments of tomorrow in their nearly infinite variety. . . . In the complex life of today, the business of government could not go on without the delegation, in greater or less degree, of the power to adapt the rule to the swiftly moving facts.

A. L. A. SCHECHTER POULTRY CORP. v. UNITED STATES
295 U.S. 495 (1935)

[In this case, a landmark in constitutional and political history, the Supreme Court struck down the key section of the National Industrial Recovery Act of 1933. The Court's attack on the statute used two principal approaches: that based upon the commerce clause will be found discussed in another context; the following extracts from the opinions offer the substance of the reasoning based on excessive delegation of legislative power.]

Mr. Chief Justice HUGHES delivered the opinion of the Court.

. . . .

Second. The question of delegation of legislative power. We recently had occasion to review the pertinent decisions and the general principles which govern the determination of this question. *Panama Refining Co.* v. *Ryan,* [*supra*] . . . . The Congress is not permitted to abdicate or to transfer to others the essential legislative functions with which it is . . . vested. We have repeatedly recognized the necessity of adapting legislation to complex conditions involving a host of details with which the national legislature cannot deal directly. We pointed out in the Panama Company case that the Constitution has never been regarded as denying Congress the necessary resources of flexibility and practicability, which will enable it to perform its function in laying down policies and establishing standards, while leaving to selected instrumentalities the making of subordinate rules within prescribed limits and the determination of facts to which the policy as declared by the legislature is to apply. But we said that the constant recognition of the necessity and validity of such provisions, and the wide range of administrative authority which has been developed by means of them, cannot be allowed to obscure the limitations of the authority to delegate, if our constitutional system is to be maintained.

Accordingly, we look to the statute to see whether Congress has overstepped these limitations,—whether Congress in authorizing "codes of fair competition" has itself established the standards of legal obligation, thus performing its essential legislative function, or, by failure to enact such standards, has attempted to transfer that function to others. . . .

What is meant by "fair competition" as the term is used in the Act? Does it refer to a category established in the law, and is the authority to make codes limited accordingly? Or is it used as a convenient designation for whatever set of laws the formulators of a code for a particular trade or industry may propose and the President may approve (subject to certain restrictions), or the President may himself prescribe, as being wise and beneficent, provisions for the government of the trade or industry in order to accomplish the broad purposes of rehabilitation, correction, and the expansion which are stated in the first section of Title I?

The Act does not define "fair competition." "Unfair competition," as known to the common law, is a limited concept. Primarily, and strictly, it relates to the palming off of one's goods as those of a rival trader. . . . In recent years, its scope has been extended. . . . But it is evident that in its widest range, "unfair competition," as it has been understood in the law, does not reach the objectives of the codes which are authorized by the National Industrial Recovery Act.

. . . . .

The Government urges that the codes will "consist of rules of competition deemed fair for each industry by representative members of that industry—by the persons most vitally concerned and most familiar with its problems." But would it be seriously contended that Congress could delegate its legislative authority to trade or industrial associations or groups so as to empower them to enact the laws they deem to be wise and beneficent for the rehabilitation and expansion of their trade or industries? Could trade or industrial associations or groups be constituted legislative bodies for that purpose because such associations or groups are familiar with the problems of their enterprises? And, could an effort of that sort be made valid by such a preface of generalities as to permissible aims as we find in section one of title I? The answer is obvious. Such a delegation of legislative power is unknown to our law and is utterly inconsistent with the constitutional prerogatives and duties of Congress.

The question, then, turns upon the authority which section 3 of the Recovery Act vests in the President to approve or prescribe. If the codes have standing as penal statutes, this must be due to the effect of the executive action. But Congress cannot delegate legislative power to the President to exercise an unfettered discretion to make whatever laws he thinks may be needed or advisable for the rehabilitation and expansion of trade or industry. . . .

. . . These restrictions [of Section 3 of the Act] leave virtually untouched the field of policy envisaged by Section 1, and, in that wide field of legislative possibilities, the proponents of a code, refraining from monopolistic designs, may roam at will and the President may approve or disapprove their proposals as he may see fit. That is the precise effect of the . . . finding that the President is to make—that the code "will tend to effectuate the policy of this title." While this is called a finding, it is really but a statement of an opinion as to the general effect upon the promotion of trade or industry of a scheme of laws.

. . . . .

Section 3 of the Recovery Act is without precedent. It supplies no standards for any trade, industry or activity. It does not undertake to prescribe rules of conduct to be applied to particular states of fact determined by appropriate administrative procedure. Instead of prescribing rules of conduct, it authorized the making of codes to prescribe them. For that legislative undertaking, Section 3 sets up no standards, aside from the statement of the general aims of rehabilitation, correction and expansion described in section one. In view of the few restrictions that are imposed, the discretion of the President in approving or prescribing codes, and thus enacting laws for the government of trade and industry throughout the country, is virtually unfettered. We think that the code-making authority thus conferred is an unconstitutional delegation of legislative power.

Mr. Justice CARDOZO, concurring.

The delegated power of legislation which has found expression in this code is not canalized within banks to keep it from overflowing. It is unconfined and vagrant, if I may borrow my own words in an earlier opinion. . . .

. . . Here . . . is an attempted delegation not confined to any single act nor to any class or group of acts identified or described by reference to a standard. Here in effect is a roving commission to inquire into evils and upon discovery correct them.

. . . . .

. . . This is delegation running riot. No such plenitude of power is susceptible of transfer. The statute, however, aims at nothing less, as one can learn both from its terms and from the administrative practice under it. Nothing less is aimed at by the code now submitted to our scrutiny. . . .

I am authorized to state that Mr. Justice STONE joins in this opinion.

OPP COTTON MILLS v. ADMINISTRATOR OF THE WAGE AND HOUR DIVISION OF THE DEPARTMENT OF LABOR
312 U.S. 126 (1941)

Mr. Justice STONE delivered the opinion of the Court.

Three types of questions are presented by the petition of certiorari in this case:

First, whether the Fair Labor Standards Act of (June 25) 1938 . . . is authorized by the Commerce Clause, violates the Tenth Amendment and the Due Process Clause of the Fifth Amendment and is an unconstitutional delegation of the legislative power of Congress to the Administrator of the Wage and Hour Division of the Department of Labor, appointed pursuant to Section 4 (a) of the Act. . . .

Constitutionality of the Act. The objections that the sections of the Act imposing a minimum wage and maximum hours are not within the commerce power and infringe the Tenth and Fifth Amendment were discussed and disposed of in our opinion in . . . *United States* v. *Darby,* 312 U.S. 100 [*infra,* p. 233]. Since petitioner concedes that he is engaged in the manufacture of cotton goods for interstate commerce it is unnecessary to consider these contentions further here.

There remains the question whether the Act is an unconstitutional delegation of the legislative power of Congress. Petitioner urges that the standards prescribed for fixing the authorized minimum wages between 30 and 40 cents per hour are too vague and indefinite to admit of any judicial determination whether they are within or without the standards prescribed by Congress.

It is not seriously urged that the policy and standards of the statute are subject to these criticisms independently of the provisions relating to classification. Section 8 defines, with precision, the policy of the Act to raise the minimum wage to the 40 cents per hour limit "as rapidly as economically feasible without substantially curtailing employment" in each industry, and the standards of the administrative action applicable to the Administrator are those made applicable to the committees [in each industry] which it is provided "shall recommend to the Administrator the highest minimum wage rates for the industry which it determines, having due regard to economic and competitive conditions, will not substantially curtail employment in the industry." But it is said that application of these standards in an industry is made contingent upon the determination whether the industry is to be classified and if so, whether it is to be subject to particular wage differentials, and that these determinations in turn depend upon factors so inadequately defined as to afford no standard of administrative action.

Committee and Administrator are required, as prerequisites for the classification, to determine that it will not give a competitive advantage to any group in the industry, and that the prescribed wage will not substantially curtail employment in each classification, and in making these determinations the committee and Administrator must consider "among other relevant factors," competitive conditions as affected by transportation, living and production costs, and the wage scale for comparable work established by collective bargaining labor agreements, and by employers who voluntarily maintain minimum wage standards.

It is urged that the statute does not prescribe the relative weight to be given to the specified factors or the other unnamed "relevant factors." It is said that this, with the further requirements that the prescribed wage is to be fixed with "due regard to economic and competitive conditions;" that the classification if made shall not "give a competitive advantage to any group in the industry," and the prescribed wage must be one fixed "without substantially curtailing employment," leave the function which the committee and Administrator are to perform so vague and indefinite as to be practically without any Congressional guide or control.

The mandate of the Constitution that all legislative powers granted "shall be vested" in Congress has never been thought to preclude Congress from resorting to the aid of administrative officers or boards as fact-finding agencies whose findings, made in conformity to previously adopted legislative standards or definitions of congressional policy, have been made prerequisite to the operation of its statutory command. The adoption of the declared policy by Congress and its definition of the circumstances in which its command is to be effective, constitute the performance, in the constitutional sense, of the legislative function.

True, the appraisal of facts in the light of the declared policy and in conformity to prescribed legislative standards, and the inferences to be drawn by the administrative agency from the facts, so appraised, involve the exercise of judgment within the prescribed limits. But where, as in the present case, the standards set up for guidance of the administrative agency, the procedure which it is directed to follow and the record of its action which is required by the statute to be kept or which is in fact preserved, are such that Congress, the courts and the public can ascertain whether the agency has conformed to the standards which Congress has prescribed, there is no failure of performance of the legislative function.

While fact finding may be and often is a step in the legislative process, the Constitution does not require that Congress should find for itself every fact upon which it bases legislation. "It is a constitution we are expounding" "intended to endure for ages to come, and consequently, to be adapted to the various crises of human affairs." *McCulloch* v. *Maryland,* 4 Wheat. (U.S.) 316, 407, 415. . . . In an increasingly complex society Congress obviously could not perform its functions if it were obliged to find all the facts subsidiary to the basic conclusions which support the defined legislative policy in fixing, for example, a tariff rate, a railroad rate, or the rate of wages to be applied in particular industries by a minimum wage law. The Constitution, viewed as a continuously operative charter of Government, is not to be interpreted as demanding the impossible or the impracticable. The essentials of the legislative function are the determination of the legislative policy and its formulation as a rule of conduct. Those essentials are preserved when Congress specifies the basic conclusions of fact upon ascertainment of which, from relevant data by a designated administrative agency, it ordains that its statutory command is to be effective.

The present statute satisfies those requirements. . . .

Affirmed.

LIMITS OF LEGISLATIVE DELEGATION
By James Hart[1]

This brief section will seek not so much to solve as to point up what is believed to be the central problem relating to the delegation by Congress of legislative power. This problem may be stated

[1] Reproduced with the permission of the author and the publisher from *The Annals of the American Academy of Political and Social Science,* May, 1942, pp. 87–100.

as a question: Does the "rule against delegation," as applied by the Supreme Court, threaten to defeat the efforts of our political democracy to use government as an instrumentality for the effective control of our national economy?

The importance of this question derives from the apparent conflict between the traditional constitutional doctrine that Congress may not delegate its legislative power, and the practical necessity that, when Congress undertakes to establish regulation of major aspects or segments of an economy so complex and changing as our own has now become, it must devolve the job in large measure upon the administrative agencies of the government.

．　．　．　．　．

As an able teacher used always to remind his classes, the rule or doctrine is nowhere expressed in the National Constitution. Nowhere does the constitutional text state that Congress may not delegate its legislative power. Such validity and meaning as the doctrine may have, therefore, must rest upon inference. . . .

[The author examines four inferential bases of the rule and finds them insufficient supports.] . . .

5. *The separation of powers*: The doctrine [forbidding delegation of legislative power] is usually called a corollary of the separation of powers. But the Constitution of the United States contains no "distributing clause"; and the separation of powers is a principle of that document only insofar as it is an incident of another principle which is itself an inference. For this other principle, see the sixth basis, stated below. The fact that the framers believed with Montesquieu that political liberty depended upon the separation of powers does indeed strengthen this other inference, but no further than to support the second alternative given below. If the first alternative were adopted, it would no more run counter to the separation of powers than to the broader principle of the distribution of powers as usually interpreted. Hence, the whole matter may be discussed in terms of the latter, rather than of the separation-of-powers doctrine of Montesquieu. . . .

6. A sixth basis for the rule is that when a written, rigid constitution has distributed the powers of government between different organs, these organs may not in their discretion redistribute such powers. This involves the classical tripartite separation of powers only because the organs set up—the Congress, the President, and

the constitutional courts—are invested, respectively, with "All legislative powers herein granted," "the executive Power," and "the judicial Power of the United States."

Re-examination of this sixth basis offers a choice of alternatives. The first alternative is to conclude that it is meaningless to say that Congress *may* not do that which it *cannot* do. For it is impossible for Congress to abdicate or transfer its legislative power. Congress, so long as it exists under the Constitution, cannot abdicate, because it may at any time take back what it has given, or simply make new enactments to supersede prior delegations or the regulations made thereunder. In this sense it cannot transfer full discretion in the premises even if it says, "Mr. President, you shall henceforth have power to enact any measure we may enact under the commerce clause"; for the very decision to do so is a primary exercise of legislative discretion which only Congress can make, and the "henceforth" lasts only until Congress sees fit to provide otherwise. Though it takes a two-thirds vote in both houses to provide otherwise in the face of a presidential veto, this may be a political but cannot be a constitutional objection, since the Constitution itself gives the President this check upon every legislative measure.

Acceptance of this first alternative eliminates the central problem by removing the last support from under the "rule against delegation."

There remains, however, the second alternative, according to which the first is a technical evasion rather than a substantial avoidance of the consequences of the principle that the creatures of the Constitution may not in their discretion alter its allotment of powers. Certainly it cannot honestly be denied that this principle is necessarily implicit in the constitutional allotment. To deny this would make that allotment meaningless. While not even the first alternative denies it, it does, in the view of the second alternative, go far toward achieving the same result by a bit of sophistry.

At the same time, to hold, even on the second alternative, that Congress violates the principle unless it specifies everything in detail, and if it delegates to those charged with the administration of its policies wide rule-making discretion, is to give an unnecessary meaning to "legislative power," to ignore the "necessary and proper" clause, to forget a good deal of legislative history, and to make modern government unworkable by treating a written constitution as if it were a code of civil practice.

The necessary conclusion is to draw a distinction between Congressional abdication or transference of its legislative power and Congressional delegation of rule-making discretion for the implementation of its policies. Such a distinction is but a way of saying that the so-called "rule against delegation" means that there is an outer limit beyond which delegation may not in honesty be allowed to go. The distinction does not, however, fix this outer limit with precision. As with all such broad distinctions, this must be done in particular instances by the exercise of judgment in weighing such factors as: the scope of the subject; the clarity of the main objective; the adequacy of standards; the limits which canalize the rule-making discretion; the procedural safeguards with which the exercise of the rule-making power is surrounded; and whether the character of the subject will enable the courts to determine when the resulting rules and regulations are unreasonable [citing illustrative cases with each item]. There is a variety of permutations and combinations of such relevant factors; and the matter is necessarily one of scope, of degree, and of circumstances.

This analysis assumes with Mr. Justice Holmes that it is impossible to "carry out the distinction between legislative and executive action with mathematical precision and divide the branches into watertight compartments." If a geometric or physical analogy hypostatizes the legislative power of Congress as a circle or a compartment, then every delegation, however minor, involves carving out a segment of the legislative and attaching it to the executive circle, or bailing water from the legislative to the executive compartment. So conceived, every delegation is literally an alteration of the allotment of powers made by the framers. Such an analogy, however, is fallacious. The terms "legislative" and "executive" are not constitutionally defined, and have no such sharply distinguished meanings as the analogy implies.

Aside from the constitutional executive powers of the President, executive power means, generally, the carrying out of the operations authorized by the statutes from time to time enacted. Executive power is thus necessarily relative to the statutes. Until statutes are enacted, it has no content, but only potentiality. After statutes are passed, its content is derived by grant or implication from their provisions. There is nothing in the nature of executive power which requires such content to be confined to clerical, ministerial functions. Neither is this required by the nature of the legislative power.

The idea that it is, was merely an assumption of the transitory philosophy of the laissez faire age. If in an era of interventionism the idea is utterly impracticable, then to hold that it is forever frozen into the Constitution is to deny Congress part of its legislative discretion. For it is a "necessary and proper" part of that discretion to determine that executive agents shall have choices in the implementation of its objectives. It is properly within the power of Congress to adopt the policy that minimum wages shall be what an administrator decides, within the framework of its expressed purposes and its prescribed limits and procedures, fully as much as it is to adopt the policy that minimum wages shall be 40 cents per hour. To hold otherwise is to substitute pedantry for constitutional statesmanship.

An examination of the cases suggests that the Supreme Court in effect accepts this meaning of the second alternative. From the *Brig Aurora* case in 1812 to the *Opp Cotton Mills* case in 1941, it has on the one hand assumed or asserted that Congress may not abdicate or transfer its legislative power, and on the other hand upheld more or less broad delegations of rule-making power in a long series of cases. In only three cases in its entire history has it invalidated attempted delegations on this score. These were the *Hot Oil* and *Schechter* cases [*supra*], decided in 1935, and the *Carter Coal Co.* case [*Carter* v. *Carter Coal Co.,* 298 U.S. 238], decided in 1936....

. . . . . .

4. THE SPECIAL PROBLEM OF FOREIGN RELATIONS

UNITED STATES v. CURTISS-WRIGHT EXPORT CORPORATION

299 U.S. 304 (1936)

[On May 28, 1934, the Congress adopted a Joint Resolution authorizing the President, if he found such a prohibition to be beneficial for the restoration of peace in the then raging Chaco War between Bolivia and Paraguay, to prohibit the sale of arms and munitions to the belligerents or to any parties acting on their behalf or in their interest. The same day, the President issued his proclamation in pursuance of this resolution. The Curtiss-Wright company subsequently was charged with having conspired to sell fifteen machine guns to Bolivia in violation of the presidential proclamation. On behalf of the company it was argued that the

Joint Resolution constituted an abdication of Congress's legislative function.]

Mr. Justice SUTHERLAND delivered the opinion of the Court:

Whether, if the Joint Resolution had related solely to internal
affairs it would be open to challenge that it constituted an unlawful
delegation of legislative power to the Executive, we find it unnecessary to determine. The whole aim of the resolution is to affect
a situation entirely external to the United States, and falling within
the category of foreign affairs. The determination which we are
called to make, therefore, is whether the Joint Resolution, as applied
to that situation, is vulnerable to attack under the rule that forbids
a delegation of the lawmaking power. In other words, assuming
(but not deciding) that the challenged delegation, if it were confined
to internal affairs, would be invalid, may it nevertheless be sustained
on the ground that its exclusive aim is to afford a remedy to a hurt-
ful condition within foreign territory?

It will contribute to the elucidation of the question if we first
consider the differences between the powers of the federal government in respect of foreign or external affairs and those in respect
of domestic or internal affairs. That there are differences between
them, and that these differences are fundamental, may not be
doubted.

The two classes of powers are different, both in respect of their
origin and their nature. The broad statement that the federal government can exercise no powers except those specifically enumerated
in the Constitution, and such implied powers as are necessary and
proper to carry into effect the enumerated powers, is categorically
true only in respect of our internal affairs. In that field, the primary
purpose of the Constitution was to carve from the general mass
of legislative powers *then possessed by the states* such portions as it
was thought desirable to vest in the federal government, leaving
those not included in the enumeration still in the states. That this
doctrine applies only to powers which the states had, is self-evident.
And since the states severally never possessed international powers,
such powers could not have been carved from the mass of state powers
but obviously were transmitted to the United States from some other
source. During the colonial period, those powers were possessed exclusively by and were entirely under the control of the Crown. By

the Declaration of Independence, "the Representatives of the United States of America" declared the United (not the several) Colonies to be free and independent states, and as such to have "full power to levy War, conclude Peace, contract Alliances, establish Commerce and to do all other Acts and Things which Independent states may of right do."

As a result of the separation from Great Britain by the colonies, acting as a unit, the powers of external sovereignty passed from the Crown not to the colonies severally, but to the colonies in their collective and corporate capacity as the United States of America. Even before the Declaration, the colonies were a unit in foreign affairs, acting through a common agency—namely the Continental Congress, composed of delegates from the thirteen colonies. That agency exercised the powers of war and peace, raised an army, created a navy, and finally adopted the Declaration of Independence. Rules come and go; governments end and forms of government change; but sovereignty survives. A political society cannot endure without a supreme will somewhere. Sovereignty is never held in suspense. When, therefore, the external sovereignty of Great Britain in respect of the colonies ceased, it immediately passed to the Union. See *Penhallow* v. *Doane,* 3 Dall. 54, 80–81. That fact was given practical application almost at once. The treaty of peace, made on September 23, 1783, was concluded between his Britannic Majesty and the "United States of America." 8 Stat.—European Treaties—80.

The Union existed before the Constitution, which was ordained and established among other things to form "a more perfect Union." Prior to that event, it is clear that the Union, declared by the Articles of Confederation to be "perpetual," was the sole possessor of external sovereignty, and in the Union it remained without change save insofar as the Constitution in express terms qualified its exercise. The Framers' Convention was called and exerted its powers upon the irrefutable postulate that though the states were several their people in respect of foreign affairs were one. . . .

.   .   .   .   .

It results that the investment of the federal government with the powers of external sovereignty did not depend upon the affirmative grants of the Constitution. The powers to declare and wage war, to conclude peace, to make treaties, to maintain diplomatic relations with other sovereignties, if they had never been mentioned in the

Constitution, would have vested in the federal government as necessary concomitants of nationality. . . .

Not only, as we have shown, is the federal power over external affairs in origin and essential character different from that over internal affairs, but participation in the exercise of the power is significantly limited. In this vast realm, with its important, complicated, delicate and manifold problems, the President alone has the power to speak or listen as a representative of this nation. He *makes* treaties with the advice and consent of the Senate; but he alone negotiates. Into the field of negotiations the Senate cannot intrude; and Congress itself is powerless to invade it. As Marshall said in his great argument of March 7, 1800, in the House of Representatives, "The President is the sole organ of the nation in its external relations, and its sole representative with foreign nations." Annals, 6th Cong., col. 613. [There follows an amplification of the same position in the words of the Senate Committee on Foreign Relations, in 1816.]

It is important to bear in mind that we are here dealing not alone with an authority vested in the President by an exertion of legislative power, but with such an authority plus the very delicate, plenary and exclusive power of the President as the sole organ of the federal government in the field of international relations—a power which does not require as a basis for its exercise an act of Congress, but which, of course, like every other governmental power, must be exercised in subordination to the applicable provisions of the Constitution. It is quite apparent that if, in the maintenance of our international relations, embarrassment—perhaps serious embarrassment—is to be avoided and success for our aims achieved, congressional legislation which is to be made effective through negotiation and inquiry within the international field must often accord the President a degree of discretion and freedom from statutory restriction which would not be admissible were domestic affairs alone involved.

In the light of the foregoing observations, it is evident that this Court should not be in haste to apply a general rule which will have the effect of condemning legislation like that under review as constituting an unlawful delegation of legislative power. The principles which justify such legislation find overwhelming support in the unbroken legislative practice which has prevailed almost from the inception of the national government to the present day.... [Citing examples.] ...

Practically every volume of the United States Statutes contains one or more acts or joint resolutions of Congress authorizing action by the President in respect of subjects affecting foreign relations, which either leave the exercise of the power to his unrestricted judgment, or provide a standard far more general than that which has always been considered requisite with regard to domestic affairs. ...

The uniform, long-continued and undisputed legislative practice just disclosed rests upon an admissible view of the Constitution which, even if the practice found far less support in principle than we think it does, we should not feel at liberty at this late date to disturb.

... We conclude there is sufficient warrant for the broad discretion vested in the President to determine whether the enforcement of the statute will have a beneficial effect upon the reestablishment of peace in the affected countries; whether he shall make proclamation to bring the resolution into operation; whether and when the resolution shall cease to operate and to make proclamation accordingly; and to prescribe limitations and exceptions to which the enforcement of the resolution shall be subject. ...

Justice McReynolds does not agree. He is of opinion that the court below reached the right conclusion and its judgment ought to be affirmed.

5. MAY CONGRESS LIMIT THE PRESIDENT'S REMOVAL POWER?

MYERS v. UNITED STATES
272 U.S. 52 (1926)

[This case and the following one, *Humphrey's Executor* v. *United States,* deal with the question of the President's power to remove federal officials from their posts. The Constitution is silent on the subject. The First Congress, in setting up the first of the major departments, side-stepped the issue, thus creating the inference that the President's removal power was an established fact. This is what

Chief Justice Taft refers to as "the decision of 1789."[2] Its ramifications were exploited to the fullest extent by Andrew Jackson, who freely dismissed officials in order to make room for patronage appointment. This so-called "spoils system" was followed by his successors without any particular objections from Congress. In the presidency of Andrew Johnson, however, the struggle between the President and the Republican leadership in Congress led to the passage of the Tenure of Office Act which sought to prevent the removal of any official for whose appointment the concurrence of the Senate was required, without in turn obtaining Senatorial approval for his dismissal. This formula was subsequently re-enacted in a statute of 1876 pertaining to postmasters of the first three classes; concurrence of the Senate was stipulated as necessary for removal as well as appointment. In 1920, Frank S. Myers, the postmaster of Portland, Oregon, was removed by President Wilson, without the consent of the Senate being obtained or even requested. Myers claimed that, under the terms of the 1876 statute, his removal was unlawful and sued for salary due him. The Court of Claims ruled against him and his widow (he had died in the meantime) appealed to the Supreme Court. The Court carefully reviewed the history of the removal power and summarized as follows:]

Mr. Chief Justice TAFT delivered the opinion of the Court:

We have, first, a construction of the Constitution made by a Congress which was to provide by legislation for the organization of the government in accord with the Constitution which had just then been adopted, and in which there were, as Representatives and Senators, a considerable number of those who had been members of the convention that framed the Constitution and presented it for ratification. It was the Congress that launched the government. . . . It was a Congress whose constitutional decisions have always been regarded, as they should be regarded, as of the greatest weight in the interpretation of that fundamental instrument. This construction was followed by the legislative department and the executive department continuously for 73 years, and this, although the matter, in the heat of political differences between the executive and the Senate in President Jackson's time, was the subject of bitter controversy. . . . This Court has repeatedly laid down the

[2] For an exhaustive and authoritative discussion, see James Hart, *The American Presidency in Action 1789*, New York: The Macmillan Co., 1948, pp. 155–214.

principle that a contemporaneous legislative exposition of the Constitution, when the founders of our government and framers of our Constitution were actively participating in public affairs, acquiesced in for a long term of years, fixes the construction to be given its provisions. . . .

[Earlier in the same opinion, the Court had placed the removal power in the context of administrative theory and practice:]

The power to prevent the removal of an officer who has served under the President is different from the authority to consent to or reject his appointment. When a nomination is made, it may be presumed that the Senate is, or may become, as well advised as to the fitness of the nominee as the President, but in the nature of things the defects in ability or intelligence or loyalty in the adminis- tration of the laws of one who has served as an officer under the President are facts as to which the President, or his trusted sub- ordinates, must be better informed than the Senate, and the power to remove him may therefore be regarded as confined for very sound and practical reasons, to the governmental authority which has administrative control. . . .

Made responsible under the Constitution for the effective enforce- ment of the law, the President needs as an indispensable aid to meet it the disciplinary influence upon those who act under him of a reserve power of removal.[3]

[It followed that the attempt by Congress to restrict the removal power by the statute of 1876 was unconstitutional. The opinion intimated that its ruling applied to all positions under the executive department. Acting in reliance on this rule, President Franklin D. Roosevelt in 1933 removed William E. Humphrey, a member of the Federal Trade Commission. The following case arose upon the removed commissioner's suit for his salary.]

HUMPHREY'S EXECUTOR v. UNITED STATES
295 U.S. 602 (1935)

Mr. Justice SUTHERLAND delivered the opinion of the Court.

The court below has certified to this Court two questions . . . in respect of the power of the President to make the removal.

---

[3] Professor Edward S. Corwin invites attention to the fact that the Chief Justice had himself once been President and was therefore strongly influenced by "practical consid- erations" in deciding this case. *The President: Office and Powers,* New York: New York University Press, 3rd ed., 1948, pp. 106–107.

"1. Do the provisions of Section 1 of the Federal Trade Commission Act, stating that 'any commissioner may be removed by the President for inefficiency, neglect of duty, or malfeasance in office,' restrict or limit the power of the President to remove a commissioner except upon one or more of the causes named?

"If the foregoing question is answered in the affirmative, then—

"2. If the power of the President to remove a commissioner is restricted or limited as shown by the foregoing interrogatory and the answer made thereto, is such a restriction or limitation valid under the Constitution of the United States?"

.   .   .   .   .

First. The question first to be considered is whether, by the provisions of Section 1 of the Federal Trade Commission Act already quoted, the President's power is limited to removal for the specific causes enumerated therein. . . .

.   .   .   .   .

. . . The statute fixes a term of office, in accordance with many precedents. The first commissioners appointed are to continue in office for terms of three, four, five, six, and seven years, respectively; and their successors are to be appointed for terms of seven years— any commissioner being subject to removal by the President for inefficiency, neglect of duty, or malfeasance in office. The words of the act are definite and unambiguous.

. . . The fixing of a definite term subject to removal for cause, unless there be some countervailing provision or circumstance indicating the contrary, which here we are unable to find, is enough to establish the legislative intent that the term is not to be curtailed in the absence of such cause. But if the intention of Congress that no removal should be made during the specified term except for one or more of the enumerated causes were not clear upon the face of the statute, as we think it is, it would be made clear by a consideration of the character of the commission, and the legislative history which accompanied and preceded the passage of the act.

The commission is to be non-partisan; and it must, from the very nature of its duties, act with entire impartiality. It is charged with the enforcement of no policy except the policy of the law. Its duties are neither political nor executive, but predominantly *quasi*-judicial and *quasi*-legislative. . . .

.   .   .   .   .

. . . The language of the act, the legislative reports, and the general purposes of the legislation as reflected by the debates, all combine to demonstrate the congressional intent to create a body of experts who shall gain experience by length of service; a body which shall be independent of executive authority, except in its selection, and free to exercise its judgment without the leave or hindrance of any other official or any department of the government. To the accomplishment of these purposes, it is clear that Congress was of the opinion that length and certainty of tenure would vitally contribute. And to hold that, nevertheless, the members of the commission continue in office at the mere will of the President, might be to thwart, in large measure, the very ends which Congress sought to realize by definitely fixing the term of office.

We conclude that the intent of the act is to limit the executive power of removal to the causes enumerated, the existence of none of which is claimed here; and we pass to the second question.

Second. To support its contention that the removal provision of Section 1, as we have just construed it, is an unconstitutional interference with the executive power of the President, the government's chief reliance is *Myers* v. *United States,* 272 U.S. 52. That case has been so recently decided, and the prevailing and dissenting opinions so fully review the general subject of the power of executive removal, that further discussion would add little value to the wealth of material there collected. These opinions examine at length the historical, legislative, and judicial data bearing upon the question, beginning with what is called "the decision of 1789" in the first Congress and coming down almost to the day when the opinions were delivered. They occupy 243 pages of the volume in which they are printed. Nevertheless, the narrow point actually decided was only that the President had power to remove a postmaster of the first class, without the advice and consent of the Senate as required by act of Congress. In the course of the opinion of the Court, expressions occur which tend to sustain the government's contention, but these are beyond the point involved and, therefore, do not come within the rule of *stare decisis.* Insofar as they are out of harmony with the views here set forth, these expressions are disapproved. . . .

The office of a postmaster is so essentially unlike the office now involved that the decision in the *Myers* case cannot be accepted as controlling our decision here. A postmaster is an executive officer restricted to the performance of executive functions. He is charged with no duty at all related to either the legislative or judicial power. The actual decision in the *Myers* case finds support in the theory that such an officer is merely one of the units in the executive department and, hence, inherently subject to the exclusive and illimitable power of removal by the Chief Executive, whose subordinate and aid he is. Putting aside dicta, which may be followed if sufficiently persuasive but which are not controlling, the necessary reach of the decision goes far enough to include all purely executive officers. It goes no farther; much less does it include an officer who occupies no place in the executive department and who exercises no part of the executive power vested by the Constitution in the President.

The Federal Trade Commission is an administrative body created by Congress to carry into effect legislative policies embodied in the statute in accordance with the legislative standard therein prescribed, and to perform other specified duties as a legislative or as a judicial aid. Such a body cannot in any proper sense be characterized as an arm or an eye of the executive. Its duties are performed without executive leave and, in the contemplation of the statute, must be free from executive control. In administering the provisions of the statute in respect of "unfair methods of competition," that is to say, in filling in and administering the details embodied by that general standard, the commission acts in part *quasi*-legislatively and in part *quasi*-judicially. In making investigations and reports thereon for the information of Congress under Section 6, in aid of the legislative power, it acts as a legislative agency. Under Section 7, which authorizes the commission to act as a master in chancery under rules prescribed by the court, it acts as an agency of the judiciary. To the extent that it exercises any executive function, as distinguished from executive power in the constitutional sense, it does so in the discharge and effectuation of its *quasi*-legislative or *quasi*-judicial powers, or as an agency of the legislative or judicial departments of the government.

If Congress is without authority to prescribe causes for removal of members of the trade commission and limit executive power of removal accordingly, that power at once becomes practically all-inclusive in respect to civil officers with the exception of the judiciary provided for by the Constitution. The Solicitor General, at the bar, apparently recognizing this to be true, with commendable candor, agreed that his view in respect of the removability of members of the Federal Trade Commission necessitated a like view in respect of the Interstate Commerce Commission and the Court of Claims. We are thus confronted with the serious question whether not only the members of these *quasi*-legislative and *quasi*-judicial bodies, but the judges of the legislative Court of Claims, exercising judicial power *(Williams* v. *United States,* 289 U.S. 553, 565–567), continue in office at the pleasure of the President.

We think it plain under the Constitution that illimitable power of removal is not possessed by the President in respect of officers of the character of those just named. The authority of Congress, in creating *quasi*-legislative or *quasi*-judicial agencies, to require them to act in discharge of their duties independently of executive control cannot well be doubted; and that authority includes, as an appropriate incident, power to fix the period during which they shall continue, and to forbid their removal except for cause in the meantime. For it is quite evident that one who holds his office only during the pleasure of another cannot be depended upon to maintain an attitude of independence against the latter's will.

The fundamental necessity of maintaining each of the three general departments of government entirely free from control or coercive influence, direct or indirect, of either of the others, has often been stressed and is hardly open to serious question. So much is implied in the very fact of the separation of the powers of these departments by the Constitution; and in the rule which recognizes their essential coequality. The sound application of a principle that makes one master in his own house precludes him from imposing his control in the house of another who is master there.

. . . . . .

The result of what we now have said is this: Whether the power of the President to remove an officer shall prevail over the authority of Congress to condition the power by fixing a definite term and precluding a removal except for cause will depend upon the character of the office; the *Myers* decision, affirming the power of the President alone to make the removal, is confined to purely executive officers; and as to officers of the kind here under consideration, we hold that no removal can be made during the prescribed term for

which the officer is appointed, except for one or more of the causes
named in the applicable statute.

To the extent that, between the decision in the *Myers* case,
which sustains the unrestrictable power of the President to remove
purely executive officers, and our present decision that such power
does not extend to an officer such as that here involved, there shall
remain a field of doubt, we leave such cases as may fall within it
for future consideration and determination as they may arise.

In accordance with the foregoing, the questions submitted are
answered:

    Question No. 1, Yes.

    Question No. 2, Yes.

*　———————　*
　　　　＊

E Pluribus Unum: The Federal System

1. THE NATIONALISM OF JOHN MARSHALL

McCULLOCH v. MARYLAND
4 Wheat. 316 (1819)

[The division of powers between the federal government and the states constitutes the core of the constitutional arrangement. The issue of the proper relationship of the two spheres of government recurs throughout the political history of the nation, to be fought on the hustings, in the legislatures, in the courts, and indeed on the field of battle. The ramifications of the question will be encountered in the consideration of most of the topics of constitutional law, most prominently in the discussions of the commerce clause. *McCulloch* v. *Maryland,* however, continues to be the classic statement of the doctrine of national supremacy. Chief Justice Marshall's opinion in this case has probably been more frequently cited than any other judicial expression.

[The controversy involved in this suit arose from the pronounced antagonism of many of the states to the Bank of the United States. This bank in 1817 established a branch in Baltimore. The following year the legislature of the state of Maryland enacted a tax on "all banks, or branches thereof, in the state of Maryland, not chartered by the legislature [of Maryland]." Obviously the tax was aimed exclusively at the Bank of the United States. McCulloch, the cashier of the Baltimore branch, was promptly sued for failure to pay the tax, and there was thus presented to the courts an opportunity to pass, first, on the power of Congress to incorporate a bank, and second, the power of a state to tax such a bank.

[Daniel Webster, in his argument for the Bank, employed all the reasons which Alexander Hamilton had advanced to argue for the constitutionality of a national bank in 1791.[1] Marshall's opinion, in turn, leaned heavily on Webster's presentation, to the extent of borrowing entire passages from his argument. Thus, for instance, the phrase "the power to tax is the power to destroy," to which Marshall gave fame and currency, originated with Webster.]

Mr. Chief Justice MARSHALL delivered the opinion of the Court.

In the case now to be determined, the defendant, a sovereign state, denies the obligation of a law enacted by the legislature of the Union; and the plaintiff, on his part, contests the validity of an act which has been passed by the legislature of that state. The Constitution of our country, in its most interesting and vital parts, is to be considered; the conflicting powers of the government of the Union and of its members, as marked in that Constitution, are to be discussed; and an opinion given, which may essentially influence the great operations of the government. . . .

The first question made in the cause is, has Congress power to incorporate a bank? . . .

Among the enumerated powers [of the federal government] we do not find that of establishing a bank or creating a corporation. But there is no phrase in the instrument [the Constitution] which, like the Articles of Confederation, excludes incidental or implied powers; and which requires that everything granted shall be expressly and minutely described. Even the 10th Amendment, which was framed for the purpose of quieting the extreme jealousies which had been excited, omits the word "expressly," and declares only that the powers "not delegated to the United States, nor prohibited to the states, are reserved to the states or to the people;" thus leaving the question, whether the particular power which may become the subject of contest, has been delegated to the one government, or prohibited to the other, to depend on a fair construction of the whole instrument. The men who drew and adopted this amendment had experienced the embarrassments resulting from the insertion of this word in the Articles of Confederation, and probably omitted it, to avoid those

[1] See *The Works of Alexander Hamilton*, ed. by J. C. Hamilton, vol. IV, pp. 104 ff.

embarrassments. A constitution, to contain an accurate detail of all the subdivisions of which its great powers will admit, and of all means by which they may be carried into execution, would partake of the prolixity of a legal code, and could scarcely be embraced by the human mind. It would, probably, never be understood by the public. Its nature, therefore, requires that only its great outlines should be marked, its important objects designated, and the minor ingredients which compose those objects be deduced from the nature of the objects themselves. That this idea was entertained by the framers of the American Constitution, is not only to be inferred from the nature of the instrument, but from the language. Why else were some of the limitations, found in the 9th section of the 1st article, introduced? It is also, in some degree, warranted, by their having omitted to use any restrictive term which might prevent its receiving a fair and just interpretation. In considering this question, then, we must never forget that it is a *constitution* we are expounding.

Although, among the enumerated powers of government, we do not find the word "bank," or "incorporation," we find the great powers, to lay and collect taxes; to borrow money; to regulate commerce; to declare and conduct war; and to raise and support armies and navies. The sword and the purse, all the external relations, and no inconsiderable portion of the industry of the nation, are intrusted to its government. It can never be pretended, that these vast powers draw after them others of inferior importance, merely because they are inferior. Such an idea can never be advanced. But it may with great reason be contended, that a government, intrusted with such ample powers, on the due execution of which the happiness and prosperity of the nation so vitally depends, must also be intrusted with ample means for their execution. It can never be their interest, and cannot be presumed to have been their intention, to clog and embarrass its execution, by withholding the most appropriate means. Throughout this vast republic, from the St. Croix to the Gulf of Mexico, from the Atlantic to the Pacific, revenue is to be collected and expended, armies are to be marched and supported. The exigencies of the nation may require, that the treasure raised in the north should be transported to the south, that raised in the east conveyed to the west, or that this order should be reversed. Is that construction of the Constitution to be preferred, which would render these operations difficult, hazardous, and expensive? Can we adopt that construction (unless the words imperiously require it) , which would impute to the framers of that instrument, when granting these powers for the public good, the intention of impeding their exercise by withholding a choice of means? If, indeed, such be the mandate of the Constitution, we have only to obey; but that instrument does not profess to enumerate the means by which the powers it confers may be executed; nor does it prohibit the creation of a corporation, if the existence of such a being be essential to the beneficial exercise of those powers. It is, then, the subject of fair inquiry, how far such means may be employed.

... The Constitution of the United States has not left the right of Congress to employ the necessary means, for the execution of the powers conferred upon the government, to general reasoning. To its enumeration of powers is added, that of making "all laws which shall be necessary and proper, for carrying into execution the foregoing powers, and all other powers vested by this Constitution, in the government of the United States, or in any department thereof." The counsel for the state of Maryland have urged various arguments, to prove that this clause, though in terms a grant of power, is not so in effect; but is really restrictive of the general right, which might otherwise be implied, of selecting means for executing the enumerated powers. In support of this proposition, they have found it necessary to contend, that this clause was inserted for the purpose of conferring on Congress the power of making laws. That, without it, doubts might be entertained whether Congress could exercise its powers in the form of legislation.

But could this be the object for which it was inserted? A government is created by the people, having legislative, executive, and judicial powers. Its legislative powers are vested in a Congress, which is to consist of a Senate and a House of Representatives. ... That a legislature, endowed with legislative powers, can legislate, is a proposition too self-evident to have been questioned.

But the argument on which most reliance is placed, is drawn from the peculiar language of this clause. Congress is not empowered by it to make all laws, which may have relation to the powers conferred on the government, but only such as may be "necessary and proper" for carrying them into execution. The word "necessary" is considered as controlling the whole sentence, and as limiting the right to pass laws for the execution of the granted powers, to such as are indispensable, and without which the power would be nugatory. That it excludes the choice of means, and leaves to Congress, in each case, that only which is most direct and simple.

... This clause, as construed by the state of Maryland, would abridge, and almost annihilate, the useful and necessary right of the legislature to select its means. That this could not be intended is, we should think, had it not already been controverted, too apparent for controversy.

We think so for the following reasons: 1st. The clause is placed among the powers of Congress, not among the limitations on those powers. 2d. Its terms purport to enlarge, not to diminish the powers vested in the government. It purports to be an additional power, not a restriction on those already granted. ... Had the intention been to make this clause restrictive, it would unquestionably have been so in form as well as in effect.

We admit, as all must admit, that the powers of the government are limited, and that its limits are not to be transcended. But we think the sound construction of the Constitution must allow to the national legislature that discretion, with respect to the means by which the powers it confers are to be carried into execution, which will enable that body to perform the high duties assigned to it, in the manner most beneficial to the people. Let the end be legitimate, let it be within the scope of the Constitution, and all means are appropriate, which are plainly adapted to that end, which are not prohibited, but consist with the letter and spirit of the Constitution, are constitutional.

... The choice of means implies a right to choose a national bank in preference to state banks, and Congress alone can make the election.

After the most deliberate consideration, it is the unanimous opinion of this Court, that the act to incorporate the Bank of the United States is a law made in pursuance of the Constitution, and is a part of the supreme law of the land.

It being the opinion of the Court, that the act incorporating the bank is constitutional; that the power of establishing a branch in the state of Maryland might be properly exercised by the bank itself, we proceed to inquire—

2. Whether the state of Maryland may, without violating the Constitution, tax that branch? . . . Whether this power can be exercised by the respective states, consistently with a fair construction of the Constitution? That the power to tax involved the power to destroy; that the power to destroy may defeat and render useless the power to create; that there is a plain repugnance in conferring on one government a power to control the constitutional measures of another, which other, with respect to those very measures, is declared to be supreme over that which exerts the control, are propositions not to be denied. . . .

If we apply the principle for which the state of Maryland contends, to the Constitution generally, we shall find it capable of changing totally the character of that instrument. We shall find it capable of arresting all the measures of government and of prostrating it at the foot of the states. The American people have declared their Constitution and the laws made in pursuance thereof, to be supreme; but this principle would transfer the supremacy, in fact, to the states. If the states may tax one instrument, employed by the government in the execution of its powers, they may tax any and every other instrument. They may tax the mail; they may tax the mint; they may tax patent rights; they may tax the papers of the customs-house; they may tax judicial process; they may tax all the means employed by the government, to an excess which would defeat all the ends of government. This was not intended by the American people. They did not design to make their government dependent on the states.

. . . The question is, in truth, a question of supremacy; and if the right of the states to tax the means employed by the general government be conceded, the declaration that the Constitution, and the laws made in pursuance thereof, shall be the supreme law of the land, is empty and unmeaning declamation. . . .

It is the opinion of this Court that the act of the legislature of Maryland is contrary to the Constitution of the United States, and void.

[Marshall's biographer, Albert J. Beveridge, acclaims the opinion in *McCulloch* v. *Maryland* as "among the very first of the greatest judicial utterances of all times." Certainly it has come to be looked upon as a vital foundation stone for the modern structure of national government in the United States. In contrast to *Marbury* v. *Madison,* the significance of which was hardly recognized at the time of the decision, the opinion in the Bank case drew immediate attention. Conservative circles, industrial interests, and New England in general applauded it. From the South and West, however, came loud and angry protests.

[In Virginia in particular, where feeling against the Court was already intense as a result of another recent decision, the opposition assumed formidable proportions. Judge Spencer Roane and John Taylor of Caroline rushed into print to denounce the Supreme Court's reading of the Constitution as an attack on the sovereignty of the states. Southern newspapers heaped censure and calumny on Marshall's head. State legislatures heard the Court attacked in the strongest terms; constitutional amendments were urged to halt the "pernicious design of the judges." Two ex-presidents, Jefferson and Madison, added their voices to the storm of criticism. Madison's acknowledgment of the receipt of some of Roane's polemics is one of the more temperate expressions of disapproval and offers a succinct summary of the principal legal arguments against the opinion.]

JAMES MADISON to SPENCER ROANE, September 2, 1819[2]

Dear Sir:

I have received your favor of the 22d ult. inclosing a copy of your observations on the judgment of the Supreme Court of the United States in the case of McCulloch against the State of Maryland; and I have found their latitudinary mode of expounding the Constitution, combated in them with the ability and the force which were to be expected.

It appears to me as it does to you that the occasion did not call for the general and abstract doctrine interwoven with the decision of a particular case. I have always supposed that the meaning of a law, and for a like reason, of a Constitution, so far as it depends on judicial interpretation, was to result from a course of particular decisions, and not these from a previous and abstract comment on the subject. The example in this instance tends to reverse the rule and to forego the illustration to be derived from a series of cases actually occurring for adjudication.

[2] James Madison, *Writings* (Hunt ed.) , vol. viii, pp. 447–453.

I could have wished also that the Judges had delivered their opinions *seriatim*. The case was of such magnitude, in the scope given to it, as to call, if any case could do so, for the views of the subject separately taken by them. This might either by the harmony of their reasoning have produced a greater conviction in the public mind; or by its discordance have impaired the force of the precedent now ostensibly supported by a unanimous and perfect concurrence in every argument and dictum in the judgment pronounced.

But what is of most importance is the high sanction given to a latitude in expounding the Constitution which seems to break down the landmarks intended by a specification of the powers of Congress, and to substitute for a definite connection between means and ends, a legislative discretion as to the former to which no practical limit can be assigned. In the great system of Political Economy having for its general object the national welfare, everything is related immediately or remotely to every other thing; and consequently a power over any one thing, if not limited by some obvious and precise affinity, may amount to a power over every other. Ends and means may shift their character at will and according to the ingenuity of the legislative body. What is an end in one case may be a means in another; nay in the same case, may be either an end or a means at the legislative option. The British Parliament in collecting a revenue from the commerce of America found no difficulty in calling it either a tax for the regulation of trade, or a regulation of trade with a view to the tax, as it suited the argument or the policy of the moment.

Is there a legislative power in fact, not expressly prohibited by the Constitution, which might not, according to the doctrine of the Court, be exercised as a means of carrying into effect some specified power?

Does not the Court also relinquish by their doctrine, all control on the legislative exercise of unconstitutional powers? According to that doctrine, the expediency and constitutionality of means for carrying into effect a specified power are convertible terms; and Congress are admitted to be judges of the expediency. The Court certainly cannot be so; a question, the moment it assumes the character of mere expediency or policy, being evidently beyond the reach of judicial cognizance.

It is true, the Court are disposed to retain a guardianship of the Constitution against legislative encroachments. "Should Congress," say they, "under the pretext of executing its powers, pass laws for the accomplishment of objects not entrusted to the government, it would become the painful duty of this Tribunal to say that such an act was not the law of the land." But suppose Congress should, as would doubtless happen, pass unconstitutional laws not to accomplish objects not specified in the Constitution, but the same laws as means expedient, convenient or conducive to the accomplishment of objects entrusted to the government; by what handle could the Court take hold of the case? We are told that it was the policy of the old government of France to grant monopolies, such as that of tobacco, in order to create funds in particular hands from which loans could be made to the public, adequate capitalists not being formed in that country in the ordinary course of commerce. Were Congress to grant a like monopoly merely to aggrandize those enjoying it, the Court might consistently say, that this not being an object entrusted to the government the grant was unconstitutional and void. Should Congress however grant the monopoly according to the French policy as a means judged by them to be necessary, expedient or conducive to the borrowing of money, which is an object entrusted to them by the Constitution, it seems clear that the Court, adhering to its doctrine, could not interfere without stepping on legislative ground, to do which they justly disclaim all pretension.

It could not but happen, and was foreseen at the birth of the Constitution, that difficulties and differences of opinion might occasionally arise in expounding terms and phrases necessarily used in such a charter; more especially those which divide legislation between the general and local governments; and that it might require a regular course of practice to liquidate and settle the meaning of some of them. But it was anticipated I believe by few if any of the friends of the Constitution, that a rule of construction would be introduced as broad and as pliant as what has occurred. And those who recollect, and still more those who shared in what passed in the State Conventions, through which the people ratified the Constitution, with respect to the extent of the powers vested in Congress, cannot easily be persuaded that the avowal of such a rule would not have prevented its ratification. It has been the misfortune, if not the reproach, of other nations, that their governments have not been freely and deliberately established by themselves. It is the boast of ours that such has been its source and that it can be altered by the same authority only which established it. It is a further boast that a regular mode of making proper alterations has been providently inserted in the Constitution itself. It is anxiously to be wished therefore, that no innovations may take place in other modes, one of which would be a constructive assumption of powers never meant to be granted. If the powers be deficient, the legitimate source of additional ones is always open, and ought to be resorted to.

Much of the error in expounding the Constitution has its origin in the use made of the species of sovereignty implied in the nature of government. The specified powers vested in Congress, it is said, are sovereign powers, and that as such they carry with them an unlimited discretion as to the means of executing them. It may surely be remarked that a limited government may be limited in its sovereignty as well with respect to the means as to the objects of his powers; and that to give an extent to the former, superseding the limits to the latter, is in effect to convert a limited into an unlimited government. There is certainly a reasonable medium between expounding the Constitution with the strictness of a penal law, or other ordinary statute, and expounding it with a laxity which may vary its essential character, and encroach on the local sovereignties with which it was meant to be reconcilable.

The very existence of these local sovereignties is a control on the pleas for a constructive amplification of the powers of the general government. Within a single State possessing the entire sovereignty, the powers given to the government by the people are understood to extend to all the acts whether as means or ends required for the welfare of the community, and falling within the range of just government. To withhold from such a government any particular power necessary or useful in itself, would be to deprive the people of the good dependent on its exercise; since the power must be there or not exist at all. In the government of the United States the case is obviously different. In establishing that government the people retained other governments capable of exercising such necessary and useful powers as were not to be exercised by the general government. No necessary presumption therefore arises from the importance of any particular power in itself, that it has been vested in that government because though not vested there, it may exist elsewhere, and the exercise of it elsewhere might be preferred by those who alone had a right to make the distribution. The presumption which ought to be indulged is that any improvement of the distribution sufficiently pointed out by experience would not be withheld. . . .

COHENS v. VIRGINIA
6 Wheat. 264 (1821)

[In order to effect improvements in the new city of Washington, Congress in 1802 authorized the District of Columbia to conduct lotteries. Acting under this authority the city passed an ordinance creating a lottery. The neighboring state of Virginia had a statute prohibiting the sale of lottery tickets in the state except for lotteries established under the laws of the state. The Cohens were arrested on a charge of violating this state statute by the sale, in Norfolk, Virginia, of tickets for the Washington lottery. The borough court found them guilty and imposed a fine of one hundred dollars. From this conviction they appealed directly to the Supreme Court of the United States, a procedure to which the state did not object as the political leaders were desiring to force the issue of the Supreme Court's authority over state acts. Counsel for the state were instructed by legislative resolution to confine their arguments before that court to the question of jurisdiction alone.

[Haines[3] summarized the arguments for the parties as follows: ". . . Senator Barbour, arguing for the state, said it seemed strange that a lottery authorized by the municipal corporation of the city of Washington for the local purpose of the city should be regarded as a law of the United States so as to give the federal courts jurisdiction for its enforcement beyond the confines of the District of Columbia. The absurdity of the local ordinances of the city being considered laws of the United States and having effect in the adjoining states was clearly pointed out. Because a state was a party in the case, it was contended that the Supreme Court could have neither original nor appellate jurisdiction. The Eleventh Amendment was declared to mean that 'a State can never be subjected, at the suit of any individual, to any judicial tribunal, without its own consent.' Defending the cause of the state, Mr. Smith insisted that 'there is not a word in the Constitution that goes to set up the federal Judiciary above the state Judiciary.' If the ordinance enacted in accordance with the acts of Congress relating to the District has no application to the state of Virginia, then the Supreme Court has no basis for its claim of jurisdiction.

["D. B. Ogden, supporting the claim of the Cohens, maintained that the District of Columbia, with all its subordinate agencies, was

---

[3] *The Role of the Supreme Court in American Government and Politics 1789–1835*, Berkeley: University of California Press, 1944, p. 431. Copyright, 1944, by the Regents of the University of California. Reprinted with the permission of the University of California Press.

a creature of the Constitution and that all regulations relating thereto were laws of the United States. The contention that Virginia, as a sovereign state, was exempt from suit was denied on the ground that 'since the establishment of the national Constitution, there is no such thing as a sovereign State, independent of the Union. The people of the United States are the sole sovereign authority of this country.' To William Pinkney, also counsel for the Cohens, the supremacy of the national Constitution was a fundamental principle of the federal system which would be rendered abortive by state action if Congress could not invest the courts of the union with either exclusive or appellate jurisdiction over such cases as the one before the Supreme Court. 'It is the case, then,' said he, 'and not the *forum* in which it arises, that is to determine whether the judicial authority of the Union shall be exercised over it.' "]

Chief Justice MARSHALL delivered the opinion of the Court.

The first question to be considered is, whether the jurisdiction of this Court is excluded by the character of the parties, one of them being a State, and the other a citizen of that State? . . .

We think, . . . that, as the Constitution originally stood, the appellate jurisdiction of this Court, in all cases arising under the Constitution, laws, or treaties of the United States, was not arrested by the circumstance that a State was a party.

This leads to a consideration of the 11th amendment.

It is in these words: "The Judicial power of the United States shall not be construed to extend to any suit in law or equity commenced or prosecuted against one of the United States, by citizens of another State, or by citizens or subjects of any foreign State."

It is a part of our history, that, at the adoption of the Constitution, all the States were greatly indebted; and the apprehension that these debts might be prosecuted in the federal courts, formed a very serious objection to that instrument. Suits were instituted; and the Court maintained its jurisdiction. The alarm was general; and, to quiet the apprehensions that were so extensively entertained, this amendment was proposed in Congress, and adopted by the State legislatures. That its motive was not to maintain the sovereignty of a State from the degradation supposed to attend a compulsory appearance before the tribunal of the nation, may be inferred from the terms of the amendment. It does not comprehend controversies between two or more States, or between a State and a foreign State. The jurisdiction of the Court still extends to these cases: and in these a State may still be sued. We must ascribe the amendment, then, to some other cause than the dignity of a State. There is no difficulty in finding this cause. Those who were inhibited from commencing a suit against a State, or from prosecuting one which might be commenced before the adoption of the amendment, were persons who might probably be its creditors. There was not much reason to fear that foreign or sister States would be creditors to any considerable amount, and there was reason to retain the jurisdiction of the Court in those cases, because it might be essential to the preservation of peace. The amendment, therefore, extended to suits commenced or prosecuted by individuals, but not to those brought by States. . . .

What is a suit? . . . In law language, it is the prosecution of some demand in a court of justice. . . .

To commence a suit, is to demand something by the institution of process in a court of justice; and to prosecute the suit, is, according to the common acceptation of language, to continue that demand. By a suit commenced by an individual against a State, we should understand process sued out by that individual against the State, for the purpose of establishing some claim against it by the judgment of a court; and the prosecution of that suit is its continuance. Whatever may be the stages of its progress, the actor is still the same. . . .If a suit, brought in one court, and carried by legal process to a supervising court, be a continuation of the same suit, then this suit is not commenced or prosecuted against a State. It is clearly in its commencement the suit of a State against an individual, which suit is transferred to this Court, not for the purpose of asserting any claim against the State, but for the purpose of asserting a constitutional defence against a claim made by a State.

A writ of error is defined to be, a commission by which the judges of one court are authorized to examine a record upon which a judgment was given in another court, and, on such examination, to affirm or reverse the same according to law. . . .

Under the Judiciary Act, the effect of a writ of error is simply to bring the record into court, and submit the judgment of the inferior tribunal to re-examination. It does not in any manner act upon the parties; it acts only on the record. It removes the record into the supervising tribunal. Where, then, a State obtains a judgment against an individual, and the court, rendering such judgment, overrules a defence set up under the Constitution or laws of the United States, the transfer of this record into the Supreme Court, for the sole purpose of inquiring whether the judgment violates the Constitution or laws of the United States, can, with no propriety, we think, be denominated a suit commenced or prosecuted against the State whose judgment is so far re-examined. Nothing is demanded from the State. No claim against it of any description is asserted or prosecuted. The party is not to be restored to the possession of anything. . . . Whether it be by writ of error or appeal, no claim is asserted, no demand is made by the original defendant; he only asserts the constitutional right to have his defence examined by that tribunal whose province it is to construe the Constitution and laws of the Union.

. . . . .

It is, then, the opinion of the Court, that the defendant who removes a judgment rendered against him by a State court into this Court, for the purpose of re-examining the question, whether that judgment be in violation of the Constitution or laws of the United States, does not commence or prosecute a suit against the State, whatever may be its opinion where the effect of the writ may be to restore the party to the possession of a thing which he demands. . . .

[The Court thus rejected the contention made by counsel for Virginia and asserted its predominance as interpreter of federal law. The opposite case would, of course, have resulted in a radical reduction of the number of cases which would have been reviewed by the Court. It is interesting to note that, as in *Marbury* v. *Madison* so in the *Cohens* case, Marshall struck a resounding blow for judicial power while at the same time adjudging the specific controversy in favor of the Court's opponents. For, having decided that his Court might properly entertain the Cohens' appeal he then proceeded to affirm the judgment of the Virginia court on its merits.]

IN PRAISE OF JOHN MARSHALL[4]

. . . The opinion of John Marshall in the Cohens case is one of the strongest and most enduring strands of that mighty cable woven by him to hold the American people together as a united and imperishable nation.

Fortunate, indeed, for the Republic that Marshall's fateful pronouncement came forth at such a critical hour, even if technicalities were waived in bringing before him a case in which he could deliver

[4] Albert J. Beveridge, *The Life of John Marshall*, vol. IV, pp. 343–344 and 353. Reproduced by permission of the publishers, Houghton Mifflin Company, Boston.

that opinion. For, in conjunction with his exposition in *McCulloch* v. *Maryland,* it was the most powerful answer that could be given, and from the source of greatest authority, to that defiance of the National Government and to the threats of disunion then growing ever bolder and more vociferous. Marshall's utterances did not still those hostile voices, it is true, but they gave strength and courage to Nationalists and furnished to the champions of the Union arguments of peculiar force as coming from the supreme tribunal of the Union.

. . . . . .

This is a direct reply to the Southern arguments in the Missouri debate which secessionists were now using wherever those who opposed National laws and authority raised their voices. John Marshall is blazing the way for Abraham Lincoln. . . .

The Chief Justice is exerting to the utmost his tremendous powers, not to protect two furtive peddlers of lottery tickets, but to check a powerful movement that, if not arrested, must destroy the Republic. Should that movement go forward thereafter, it must do so over every Constitutional obstacle which the Supreme Court of the Nation could throw in its way. In *Cohens* v. *Virginia,* John Marshall stamped upon the brow of Localism the brand of illegality. . . .

A NOTE ON THE LAW OF THE FEDERAL COURTS

The decision in *Cohens* v. *Virginia,* as has been seen, embedded in our constitutional system the proposition that the Supreme Court could hear appeals from the state courts and determine whether or not the "supreme law of the land" had been properly applied. The next question to be determined in the twilight zones of federal and state jurisdiction was what law should be applied in federal cases where the Constitution was not involved. The typical situation arises under the "diversity of citizenship" clause of the Judiciary Article of the Constitution. A and B are in an automobile collision; if both are citizens of Kansas it is plain that trial would be had in a Kansas court, according to Kansas law; but if A hails from Kansas and B is a resident of Missouri this is a case for a federal court. Is it to be tried in accordance with the law of Kansas, or of Missouri, or on some other legal basis?

When the First Congress implemented the Constitution by the passage of the Judiciary Act of 1789 it provided that "the laws of the several states . . . shall be regarded as rules of decision in trials at common law, in the courts of the United States, in cases where they apply." In 1842, in *Swift* v. *Tyson*,[5] Justice Story confined the meaning of "laws" to "enactments promulgated by the legislative authority of the state," with the result that federal courts were free to disregard decisions of state courts in common law cases. Two reasons have commonly been ascribed for Story's decision: first, that Story, the most eminent law teacher of his day, was convinced of the existence of an ultimate right answer, the search for which ought not to be frustrated by adherence to, possibly erroneous, state precedents; secondly, that it was hoped that the independent judgment of the federal courts would result in greater uniformity of the legal system.

The rule of *Swift* v. *Tyson* persisted for ninety-six years, though in the face of ever-increasing criticism. Justice Field was a vocal dissenter in his day,[6] but it was Holmes whose penetrating analysis laid the foundation for reversal. The following paragraph is illustrative of the dispelling clarity of the "Great Dissenter."

Books written about any branch of the common law treat it as a writ, cite cases from this Court, from the Circuit Courts of Appeals, from the state courts, from England and from the Colonies of England indiscriminately, and criticize them as right or wrong according to the writer's notion of a single theory. It is very hard to resist the impression that there is one august corpus, to understand which clearly is the only task of any court concerned. If there were such a transcendental body of law outside of any particular state but obligatory within it unless and until changed by statute, the courts of the United States might be right in using their independent judgment as to what it was. But there is no such body of law. The fallacy and illusion that I think exist consist in supposing that there is this outside thing to be found. Law is a word used with different meanings, but law in the sense in which courts speak of it today does not exist without some definite authority behind it. The common law so far as it is enforced in a state, whether called common law or not, is not the common law generally, but the law of that state existing by the authority of that state without regard to what it may have been in England or elsewhere.[7]

The case in which Holmes thus blasted the foundations of Story's doctrine was a signal demonstration of its malfunctioning. Brown &

[5] 16 Pet. 1.
[6] See, for instance, *Baltimore & Ohio R.R. Co.* v. *Baugh*, 149 U.S. 368, 403 (1893).
[7] *Black & White Taxicab and Transfer Co.* v. *Brown & Yellow Taxicab and Transfer Co.*, 276 U.S. 518, 532–533 (1928).

Yellow and Black & White were competing cab companies, both operating in Bowling Green, Kentucky. Both were incorporated in Kentucky as was the Louisville & Nashville Railroad, servicing that community. Brown & Yellow sought to secure the exclusive right to solicit customers at the railroad's depot but a contract to grant such a monopoly would have been invalid under the common law of Kentucky. In order to avoid this result, Brown & Yellow, without changing its membership or purposes, obtained reincorporation in Tennessee and in that state executed the desired agreement with the railroad concerning depot taxi service at Bowling Green, Kentucky. The Supreme Court held that the "general" common law of the federal courts did not forbid an arrangement which, but for the ruse of reincorporation, would have been voided by local policy. To the dissenters (Holmes, Brandeis, and Stone) the case represented a signal example of the "mischievous results" of *Swift* v. *Tyson*. Rather than enhancing uniformity of legal rules the doctrine had created increased uncertainty and subjected the outcome of legal conflict to the chance selection of the jurisdiction.

In 1938, six members of the Court agreed to jettison the old rule. "This Court and the lower courts," they announced through Justice Brandeis, "have invaded rights which in our opinion are reserved by the Constitution to the several states."[8]

The result has been to impose upon the federal courts the common law of the state in which the trial court sits and to disavow emphatically the existence of any "federal common law." With reference to crimes, this proposition had been well established since 1812.[9] *Erie Railroad Co.* v. *Tompkins* extends it to the other branches of law.

2. "THE POWER TO TAX IS THE POWER TO DESTROY"?

GRAVES v. NEW YORK ex rel. O'KEEFE
306 U.S. 466 (1939)

Mr. Justice STONE delivered the opinion of the Court.

We are asked to decide whether the imposition by the state of New York of an income tax on the salary of an employee of the Home Owners' Loan Corporation places an unconstitutional burden upon the federal government.

Respondent, a resident of New York, was employed during 1934

[8] *Erie Railroad Co.* v. *Tompkins*, 304 U.S. 64.
[9] *United States v. Hudson*, 7 Cranch 32.

as an examining attorney for the Home Owners' Loan Corporation at an annual salary of $2400. Petitioners, New York State Tax Commissioners, rejected respondent's claim for a refund of the [state income] tax based on the ground that his salary was constitutionally exempt from state taxation. . . .

For the purposes of this case we may assume that the creation of the Home Owners' Loan Corporation was a constitutional exercise of the powers of the federal government. . . . As that government derives its authority wholly from powers delegated to it by the Constitution, its every action within its constitutional power is governmental action, and since Congress is made the sole judge of what powers within the constitutional grant are to be exercised, all activities of government constitutionally authorized by Congress must stand on a parity with respect to their constitutional immunity from taxation. . . . And when the national government lawfully acts through a corporation which it owns and controls, those activities are governmental functions entitled to whatever tax immunity attaches to those functions when carried on by the government itself through its departments. . . .

The single question with which we are now concerned is whether the tax laid by the state upon the salary of respondent, employed by a corporate instrumentality of the federal government, imposes an unconstitutional burden upon that government. The theory of the tax immunity of either government, state or national, and its instrumentalities, from taxation by the other, has been rested upon an implied limitation of the taxing power of each, such as to forestall undue interference, through the exercise of that power, with the governmental activities of the other. That the two types of immunity may not, in all respects, stand on a parity has been recognized from the beginning, *McCulloch* v. *Maryland* (4 Wheat. 316, 435–436), and possible differences in application, deriving from differences in the source, nature and extent of the immunity of the governments and their agencies, were pointed out and discussed by this Court in detail during the last term. . . . [Citation of cases omitted.]

So far as now relevant, those differences have been thought to be traceable to the fact that the federal government is one of delegated powers in the exercise of which Congress is supreme; so that every agency which Congress can constitutionally create is a governmental agency. And since the power to create the agency includes the implied power to do whatever is needful or appropriate, if not expressly prohibited, to protect the agency, there has been attributed to Congress some scope, the limits of which it is not now necessary to define, for granting or withholding immunity of federal agencies from state taxation. . . . Whether its power to grant tax exemptions as an incident to the exercise of powers specifically granted by the Constitution can ever, in any circumstances, extend beyond the constitutional immunity of federal agencies which courts have implied, is a question which need not now be determined.

Congress has declared in section 4 of the Act [establishing that agency] that the Home Owners' Loan Corporation is an instrumentality of the United States and that its bonds are exempt, as to principal and interest, from federal and state taxation, except surtaxes, estate, inheritance and gift taxes. The corporation itself, "including its franchise, its capital, reserves and surplus, and its loans and income," is likewise exempted from taxation; its real property is subject to tax to the same extent as other real property. But Congress has given no intimation of any purpose either to grant or withhold immunity from state taxation of the salary of the corporation's employees, and the congressional intention is not to be gathered from the statute by implication. . . .

It is true that the silence of Congress, when it has authority to speak, may sometimes give rise to an implication as to the congressional purpose. The nature and extent of that implication depend upon the nature of the congressional power and the effect of its exercise. But there is little scope for the application of that doctrine to the tax immunity of governmental instrumentalities. The constitutional immunity of either government from taxation by the other, where Congress is silent, has its source in an implied restriction upon the powers of the taxing government. So far as the implication rests upon the purpose to avoid interference with the functions of the taxed government or the imposition upon it of the economic burden of the tax, it is plain that there is no basis for implying a purpose of Congress to exempt the federal government or its agencies from tax burdens which are unsubstantial or which courts are unable to discern. Silence of Congress implies immunity no more than does the silence of the Constitution. It follows that when exemption from state taxation is claimed on the ground that the federal government is burdened by the tax, and Congress has disclosed no intention with respect to the claimed immunity, it is in order to consider the nature and effect of the alleged burden, and if it appears that there is no ground for implying a constitutional immunity, there is equally a want of any ground for assuming any purpose on the part of Congress to create an immunity.

The present tax is a nondiscriminatory tax on income applied to salaries at a specified rate. It is not in form or substance a tax upon the Home Owners' Loan Corporation or its property or income, nor is it paid by the corporation or the government from their funds. It is measured by income which becomes the property of the taxpayer when received as compensation for his services; and the tax laid upon the privilege of receiving it is paid from his private funds and not from the funds of the government, either directly or indirectly. The theory, which once won a qualified approval, that a tax on income is legally or economically a tax on its source, is no longer tenable, . . . and the only possible basis for implying a constitutional immunity from state income tax of the salary of an employee of the national government or of a governmental agency is that the economic burden of the tax is in some way passed on so as to impose a burden on the national government tantamount to an interference by one government with the other in the performance of its functions.

.   .   .   .   .   .

The conclusion reached in the Gerhardt Case [*Helvering* v. *Gerhardt,* 304 U.S. 405] that in terms of constitutional tax immunity a federal income tax on the salary of an employee is not a prohibited burden on the employer makes it imperative that we should consider anew the immunity here claimed for the salary of an employee of a federal instrumentality. As already indicated, such differences as there may be between the implied tax immunity of a state and the corresponding immunity of the national government and its instrumentalities may be traced to the fact that the national government is one of delegated powers, in the exercise of which it is supreme. Whatever scope this may give to the national government to claim immunity from state taxation of all instrumentalities which it may constitutionally create, and whatever authority Congress may possess as incidental to the exercise of its delegated powers to grant or withhold immunity from state taxation, Congress has not sought in this case to exercise such power. Hence these distinctions between the two types of immunity cannot affect the question with which we are now concerned. The burden on government of a non-discriminatory income tax applied to the salary of the employee of a government is the same, whether a state or national government is concerned. The determination in the Gerhardt Case that the federal income tax imposed on the employees of the [New York] Port Authority was not a burden on the Port Authority made it unnecessary to consider whether the Authority itself was immune from federal taxation; the claimed immunity failed because even if the Port Authority were itself immune from federal income tax, the tax upon the income of its employees cast upon it no unconstitutional burden.

Assuming, as we do, that the Home Owners' Loan Corporation is clothed with the same immunity from state taxation as the government itself, we cannot say that the present tax upon the income of its employees lays any unconstitutional burden upon it. All the reasons for refusing to imply a constitutional prohibition of federal income taxation of salaries of state employees, stated at length in the Gerhardt Case, are of equal force when immunity is claimed from state income tax on salaries paid by the national government or its agencies. In this respect we perceive no basis for a difference in result whether the taxed income be salary or some other form of compensation, or whether the taxpayer be an employee or an officer of either a state or the national government, or of its instrumentalities. In no case is there basis for the assumption that any such tangible or certain economic burden is imposed on the government concerned as would justify a court's declaring that the taxpayer is clothed with the implied constitutional tax immunity of the government by which he is employed. That assumption, made in *Collector* v. *Day*, 11 Wall. 113 [1871], and *New York* ex rel. *Rogers* v. *Graves*, 299 U.S. 401 [1936], is contrary to the reasoning and to the conclusions reached in the Gerhardt Case and in *Metcalf & Eddy* v. *Mitchell*, 269 U.S. 514.... In their light the assumption can no longer be made. *Collector* v. *Day* and *New York* ex rel. *Rogers* v. *Graves* are overruled so far as they recognize an implied constitutional immunity from income taxation of the salaries of officers or employees of the national or a state government or their instrumentalities.

So much of the burden of a non-discriminatory general tax upon the incomes of employees of a government, state or national, as may be passed on economically to that government, through the effect of the tax on the price level of labor or materials, is but the normal

incident of the organization within the same territory of two governments, each possessing the taxing power. The burden, so far as it
can be said to exist or to affect the government in any indirect or
incidental way, is one which the Constitution presupposes, and
hence it cannot rightly be deemed to be within an implied restriction upon the taxing power of the national and state governments
which the Constitution has expressly granted to one and has confirmed to the other. The immunity is not one to be implied from
the Constitution, because if allowed it would impose to an inadmissible extent a restriction on the taxing power which the Constitution has reserved to the state governments.

Reversed.

Mr. Chief Justice Hughes concurs in the result.

Mr. Justice Frankfurter, concurring. . . .

The arguments upon which *McCulloch* v. *Maryland,* 4 Wheat.
316, rested had their roots in actuality. But they have been distorted
by sterile refinements unrelated to affairs. These refinements derived
authority from an unfortunate remark in the opinion in *McCulloch*
v. *Maryland.* Partly as a flourish of rhetoric and partly because the
intellectual fashion of the times indulged a free use of absolutes,
Chief Justice Marshall gave currency to the phrase that "the power
to tax involves the power to destroy." *Ibid.* at page 431 of 4 Wheat.
This dictum was treated as though it were a constitutional mandate.
But not without a protest. One of the most trenchant minds on the
Marshall court, Justice William Johnson, early analyzed the dangerous inroads upon the political freedom of the states and the Union
within their respective orbits resulting from a doctrinaire application of the generalities uttered in the course of the opinion in *Mc-
Culloch* v. *Maryland.* The seductive cliché that the power to tax
involves the power to destroy was fused with another assumption,
likewise not to be found in the Constitution itself, namely the doctrine that the immunities are correlative—because the existence of
the national government implied immunities from state taxation,
the existence of state governments implies equivalent immunities
from federal taxation. When this doctrine was first applied Mr.
Justice Bradley registered a powerful dissent, the force of which
gathered rather than lost strength with time, *Collector* v. *Day,* 11
Wall. 113, 128.

All these doctrines of intergovernmental immunity have until recently been moving in the realm of what Lincoln called "pernicious abstractions." The web of unreality spun from Marshall's famous dictum was brushed away by one stroke of Mr. Justice Holmes's pen: "The power to tax is not the power to destroy while this Court sits." *Panhandle Oil Co.* v. *Mississippi*, 277 U.S. 218, 223 (dissent). Failure to exempt public functionaries from the universal duties of citizenship to pay for the costs of government was hypothetically transmuted into hostile action of one government against the other. A succession of decisions thereby withdrew from the taxing power of the states and nation a very considerable range of wealth without regard to the actual workings of our federalism, and this, too, when the financial needs of all governments began steadily to mount. These decisions have encountered increasing dissent. In view of the powerful pull of our decisions upon the courts charged with maintaining the constitutional equilibrium of the two other great English federalisms, the Canadian and the Australian courts were at first inclined to follow the earlier doctrines of this Court regarding intergovernmental immunity. Both the Supreme Court of Canada and the High Court of Australia on fuller consideration—and for present purposes the British North America Act, 30 & 31 Vict., c.3, and the Commonwealth of Australia Constitution Act, 63 & 64 Vict., c.12, raise the same legal issues as does our Constitution—have completely rejected the doctrine of intergovernmental immunity. In this Court dissents have gradually become majority opinions, and even before the present decision the rationale of the doctrine had been undermined.

. . . Whether Congress may, by express legislation, relieve its functionaries from their civic obligations to pay for the benefits of the state governments under which they live is matter for another day.

Mr. Justice BUTLER (Mr. Justice McREYNOLDS concurring with him), dissented. . . .

NEW YORK v. UNITED STATES
326 U.S. 572 (1946)

Mr. Justice FRANKFURTER announced the judgment of the Court and delivered an opinion in which Mr. Justice RUTLEDGE joined.

Section 615 (a) (5) of the 1932 Revenue Act, 47 Stat. 169, 264, imposed a tax on mineral waters. The United States brought this suit to recover taxes assessed against the State of New York on the sale of mineral waters taken from Saratoga Springs, New York. The State claims immunity from this tax on the ground that "in the bottling and sale of the said waters the defendant State of New York was engaged in the exercise of a usual, traditional and essential governmental function." The claim was rejected by the District Court and judgment went for the United States. 48 F. Supp. 15. The judgment was affirmed by the Circuit Court of Appeals for the Second Circuit. 140 F. (2d) 608. The strong urging of New York for further clarification of the amenability of States to the taxing power of the United States led us to grant certiorari. . . .

On the basis of authority the case is quickly disposed of. When States sought to control the liquor traffic by going into the liquor business, they were denied immunity from federal taxes upon the liquor business. *South Carolina* v. *United States,* 199 U.S. 437; *Ohio* v. *Helvering,* 292 U.S. 360. And in rejecting a claim of immunity from federal taxation when Massachusetts took over the street railways of Boston, this Court a decade ago said: "We see no reason for putting the operation of a street railway [by a State] in a different category from the sale of liquors." *Helvering* v. *Powers,* 293 U.S. 214, 227. We certainly see no reason for putting soft drinks in a different constitutional category from hard drinks. . . .

One of the greatest sources of strength of our law is that it adjudicates concrete cases and does not pronounce principles in the abstract. But there comes a time when even the process of empiric adjudication calls for a more rational disposition than that the immediate case is not different from preceding cases. The argument pressed by New York and the forty-five other States who, as amici curiae,[10] have joined her deserves an answer.

Enactments levying taxes made in pursuance of the Constitution are, as other laws are, "the supreme Law of the Land." Art. 6, Constitution of the United States; . . . the first of the powers conferred upon Congress is the power "To lay and collect Taxes, Duties, Imposts and Excises. . . ." Art. I, § 8. By its terms the Constitution has placed only one limitation upon this power, other than limitations upon methods of laying taxes not here relevant: Congress can lay no tax "on articles exported from any State." Art. I, § 9. Barring only exports, the power of Congress to tax "reaches every subject." *License Tax Cases,* 5 Wall. (U.S.) 462, 471. But the fact that ours is a federal

---

[10] An *amicus curiae* (Latin for "friend of the court") is one not a party to the controversy who, because of some special interest in the case, is permitted to present briefs and arguments to the court.

constitutional system, as expressly recognized in the Tenth Amendment, carries with it implications regarding the taxing power as in other aspects of government. . . . Thus, for Congress to tax State activities while leaving untaxed the same activities pursued by private persons would do violence to the presuppositions derived from the fact that we are a Nation composed of States.

But the fear that one government may cripple or obstruct the operations of the other early led to the assumption that there was a reciprocal immunity of the instrumentalities of each from taxation by the other. It was assumed that there was an equivalence in the implications of taxation by a State of the governmental activities of the National Government and the taxation by the National Government of State instrumentalities. This assumed equivalence was nourished by the phrase of Chief Justice Marshall that "the power to tax involves the power to destroy." *McCulloch* v. *Maryland, 4* Wheat. (U.S.) 316, 431. To be sure, it was uttered in connection with a tax of Maryland which plainly discriminated against the use by the United States of the Bank of the United States as one of its instruments. What he said may not have been irrelevant in its setting. But Chief Justice Marshall spoke at a time when social complexities did not so clearly reveal as now the practical limitations of a rhetorical absolute. See Holmes, J., in *Long* v. *Rockwood,* 277 U.S. 142, 148, and in *Panhandle Oil Co.* v. *Mississippi,* 277 U.S. 218, 223.[11] The phrase was seized upon as the basis of a broad doctrine of intergovernmental immunity, while at the same time an expansive scope was given to what were deemed to be "instrumentalities of government" for purposes of tax immunity. As a result, immunity was until recently accorded to all officers of one government from taxation by the other, and it was further assumed that the economic burden of a tax on any interest derived from a government imposes a burden on that government so as to involve an interference by the taxing government with the functioning of the other government. . . .

To press a juristic principle designed for the practical affairs of government to abstract extremes is neither sound logic nor good sense. And this Court is under no duty to make law less than sound logic and good sense. When this Court for the first time relieved State officers from a non-discriminatory Congressional tax, not because of anything said in the Constitution but because of the supposed implications of our federal system, Mr. Justice Bradley pointed

---

[11] "The power to tax is not the power to destroy while this Court sits."

out the invalidity of the notion of reciprocal intergovernmental immunity. The considerations bearing upon taxation by the States of activities or agencies of the federal government are not correlative with the considerations bearing upon federal taxation of State agencies or activities. The federal government is the government of all the States, and all the States share in the legislative process by which a tax of general applicability is laid. "The taxation by the State governments of the instruments employed by the general government in the exercise of its powers," said Mr. Justice Bradley, "is a very different thing. Such taxation involves an interference with the powers of a government in which other States and their citizens are equally interested with the State which imposes the taxation." Since then we have moved away from the theoretical assumption that the National Government is burdened if its functionaries, like other citizens, pay for the upkeep of their State governments, and we have denied the implied constitutional immunity of federal officials from State taxes. *Graves* v. *New York,* 306 U.S. 466, *supra.* . . .

In the meantime, cases came here, as we have already noted, in which States claimed immunity from a federal tax imposed generally on enterprises in which the State itself was also engaged. This problem did not arise before the present century, partly because State trading did not actively emerge until relatively recently, and partly because of the narrow scope of federal taxation. In *South Carolina* v. *United States,* 199 U.S. 437, immunity from a federal tax on a dispensary system, whereby South Carolina monopolized the sale of intoxicating liquors, was denied by drawing a line between taxation of the historically recognized governmental functions of a State, and business engaged in by a State of a kind which theretofore had been pursued by private enterprise. The power of the federal government thus to tax a liquor business conducted by the State was derived from an appeal to the Constitution "in the light of conditions surrounding at the time of its adoption." . . . That there is a Constitutional line between the State as government and the State as trader, was still more recently made the basis of a decision sustaining a liquor tax against Ohio. *Ohio* v. *Helvering,* 292 U.S. 360. When the Ohio Case was decided it was too late in the day not to recognize the vast extension of the sphere of government, both State and national, compared with that with which the Fathers were familiar. It could hardly remain a satisfactory constitutional doctrine that only such State activities are immune from federal taxation as were engaged in by the States in 1787. Such a static concept of government denies its essential nature. . . .

When this Court came to sustain the federal taxing power upon a transportation system operated by a State, it did so in ways familiar in developing the law from precedent to precedent. It edged away from reliance on a sharp distinction between the "governmental" and the "trading" activities of a State, by denying immunity from federal taxation to a State when it "is undertaking a business enterprise of a sort that is normally within the reach of the federal taxing power and is distinct from the usual governmental functions that are immune from federal taxation in order to safeguard the necessary independence of the State." *Helvering* v. *Powers,* 293 U.S. 214, 227. But this likewise does not furnish a satisfactory guide for dealing with such a practical problem as the constitutional power of the United States over State activities. To rest the federal taxing power on what is "normally" conducted by private enterprise in contradiction to the "usual" governmental functions is too shifting a basis for determining constitutional power and too entangled in expediency to serve as a dependable legal criterion. The essential nature of the problem cannot be hidden by an attempt to separate manifestations of indivisible governmental powers. . . .

The present case illustrates the sterility of such an attempt. New York urges that in the use it is making of Saratoga Springs it is engaged in the disposition of its natural resources. And so it is. But in doing so it is engaged in an enterprise in which the State sells mineral waters in competition with private waters, the sale of which Congress has found necessary to tap as a source of revenue for carrying on the National Government. To say that the States cannot be taxed for enterprises generally pursued, like the sale of mineral water, because it is somewhat connected with a State's conservation policy, is to invoke an irrelevance to the federal taxing power. Liquor control by a State certainly concerns the most important of a State's natural resources—the health and well-being of its people. . . . If in its wisdom a State engages in the liquor business and may be taxed by Congress as others engaged in the liquor business are taxed, so also Congress may tax the States when they go into the business of bottling water as others in the mineral water business are taxed even though a State's sale of its mineral waters has relation to its conservation policy.

In the older cases, the emphasis was on immunity from taxation.

The whole tendency of recent cases reveals a shift in emphasis to that of limitation upon immunity. They also indicate an awareness of the limited role of courts in assessing the relative weight of the factors upon which immunity is based. Any implied limitation upon the supremacy of the federal power to levy a tax like that now before us, in the absence of discrimination against State activities, brings fiscal and political factors into play. The problem cannot escape issues that do not lend themselves to judgment by criteria and methods of reasoning that are within the professional training and special competence of judges. Indeed the claim of implied immunity by States from federal taxation raises questions not wholly unlike provisions of the Constitution, such as that of Art. 4, § 4, guaranteeing States a republican form of government, see *Pacific States Teleph. & Teleg. Co.* v. *Oregon,* 223 U.S. 118 [*supra,* p. 55], which this Court has deemed not within its duty to adjudicate.

... So long as Congress generally taps a source of revenue by whomsoever earned and not uniquely capable of being earned only by a State, the Constitution of the United States does not forbid it merely because its incidence falls also on a State. If Congress desires, it may of course leave untaxed enterprises pursued by States for the public good while it taxes like enterprises organized for private ends. ... If Congress makes no such differentiation and, as in this case, taxes all vendors of mineral water alike, whether State vendors or private vendors, it simply says, in effect, to a State: "You may carry out your own notions of social policy in engaging in what is called business, but you must pay your share in having a nation which enables you to pursue your policy." After all, the representatives of all the States, having, as the appearance of the Attorneys General of forty-six States at the bar of this Court shows, common interests, alone can pass such a taxing measure and they alone in their wisdom can grant or withhold immunity from federal taxation of such State activities.

... We decide enough when we reject limitations upon the taxing power of Congress derived from such untenable criteria as "proprietary" against "governmental" activities of the States, or historically sanctioned activities of Government, or activities conducted merely for profit, and find no restriction upon Congress to include the States in levying a tax exacted equally from private persons upon the same subject matter.

Judgment affirmed.

[Mr. Justice RUTLEDGE and Mr. Chief Justice STONE wrote concurring opinions.]

Mr. Justice DOUGLAS, with whom Mr. Justice BLACK concurs, dissenting.

If *South Carolina* v. *United States,* 199 U.S. 437, is to stand, the present judgment would have to be affirmed. For I agree that there is no essential difference between a federal tax on South Carolina's liquor business and a federal tax on New York's mineral water business. Whether *South Carolina* v. *United States* reaches the right result is another matter.

.   .   .   .   .

I do not believe *South Carolina* v. *United States* states the correct rule. A State's project is as much a legitimate governmental activity whether it is traditional, or akin to private enterprise, or conducted for profit. A State may deem it as essential to its economy that it own and operate a railroad, a mill, or an irrigation system as it does to own and operate bridges, street lights, or a sewage disposal plant. What might have been viewed in an earlier day as an improvident or even dangerous extension of state activities may today be deemed indispensable. But as Mr. Justice White said in his dissent in *South Carolina* v. *United States,* any activity in which a State engages within the limits of its police power is a legitimate governmental activity. Here a State is disposing of some of its natural resources. Tomorrow it may issue securities, sell power from its public power project, or manufacture fertilizer. Each is an exercise of its power of sovereignty. Must it pay the federal government for the privilege of exercising that inherent power? If the Constitution grants it immunity from a tax on the issuance of securities, on what grounds can it be forced to pay a tax when it sells power or disposes of other natural resources?

.   .   .   .   .

A tax is a powerful, regulatory instrument. Local government in this free land does not exist for itself. The fact that local government may enter the domain of private enterprise and operate a project for profit does not put it in the class of private business enterprise for tax purposes. Local government exists to provide for the welfare of its people, not for a limited group of stockholders. If the federal government can place the local governments on its tax collector's list, their capacity to serve the needs of their citizens is at once hampered or curtailed. The field of federal excise taxation alone is practically without limits. Many state activities are in marginal enterprises where private capital refuses to venture. Add to the cost of these projects a federal tax and the social program may be destroyed before it can be launched. In any case, the repercussions of such a fundamental change on the credit of the States and on their programs to take care of the needy and to build for the future would be considerable. To say the present tax will be sustained because it does not impair the State's functions of government is to conclude either that the sale by the State of its mineral water is not a function of government or that the present tax is so slight as to be no burden. The former obviously is not true. The latter overlooks the fact that the power to tax lightly is the power to tax severely. The power to tax is indeed one of the most effective forms of regulation. And no more powerful instrument for centralization of government could be devised. For with the federal government immune and the States subject to tax, the economic ability of the federal government to expand its activities at the expense of the States is at once apparent. That is the result whether the rule of *South Carolina* v. *United States* be perpetuated or a new rule of discrimination be adopted.

The notion that the sovereign position of the States must find its protection in the will of a transient majority of Congress is foreign to and a negation of our constitutional system. There will often be vital regional interests represented by no majority in Congress. The Constitution was designed to keep the balance between the States and the nation outside the field of legislative controversy.

The immunity of the States from federal taxation is no less clear because it is implied. The States on entering the Union surrendered some of their sovereignty. It was further curtailed as various Amendments were adopted. But the Tenth Amendment provides that "The powers not delegated to the United States by the Constitution, nor prohibited by it to the States, are reserved to the States respectively, or to the people." The Constitution is a compact between sovereigns. The power of one sovereign to tax another is an innovation so startling as to require explicit authority if it is to be allowed. If the power of the federal government to tax the States is conceded, the reserved power of the States guaranteed by the Tenth Amendment does not give them the independence which they have always been assumed to have. They are relegated to a more servile status. They become subject to interference and control both in the functions which they exercise and the methods which they employ. They must pay the federal government for the privilege of exercising the powers of sovereignty guaranteed them by the Constitution, whether, as here, they are disposing of their natural resources, or tomorrow they issue securities or perform any other acts within the scope of their police power.

. . . . . .

Those who agreed with *South Carolina* v. *United States* had the fear that an expanding program of state activity would dry up sources of federal revenues and thus cripple the national government. . . . That was in 1905. That fear is expressed again today when we have the federal income tax, from which employees of the States may not claim exemption on constitutional grounds. *Helvering* v. *Gerhardt,* 304 U.S. 405. The fear of depriving the national government of revenue if the tax immunity of the States is sustained has no more place in the present decision than the spectre of socialism, the fear of which, said Holmes, "was translated into doctrines that had no proper place in the Constitution or common law."

There is no showing whatsoever that an expanding field of state activity even faintly promises to cripple the federal government in its search for needed revenues. If the truth were known, I suspect it would show that the activity of the States in the fields of housing, public power and the like have increased the level of income of the people and have raised the standards of marginal or sub-marginal groups. Such conditions affect favorably, not adversely, the tax potential of the federal government.

3. FEDERAL ACTIVITIES AND STATE AUTHORITY

TARBLE'S CASE
13 Wall. 397 (1872)

[May a state court order the release of a person under the authority of the United States? Young Tarble enlisted in the army; his father, contending that his son was too young to be enlisted, sought to have him returned to parental custody. The state court granted a writ of habeas corpus ordering the army recruiting officer to release the youth. The government contested the validity of this order and carried the case to the Supreme Court of the United States.]

FIELD, J.: ... The important question is presented by this case, whether a state court commissioner has jurisdiction, upon *habeas corpus,* to inquire into the validity of the enlistment of soldiers into the military service of the United States, and to discharge them from such service when, in his judgment, their enlistment has not been made in conformity with the laws of the United States. The question presented may be more generally stated thus: Whether any judicial officer of a State has jurisdiction to issue a writ of *habeas corpus,* or to continue proceedings under the writ when issued, for the discharge of a person held under the authority, or claim and color of the authority, of the United States, by an officer of that government. For it is evident, if such jurisdiction may be exercised by the court commissioner within the county for which he is appointed; and if it may be exercised with reference to soldiers detained in the military service of the United States, whose enlistment is alleged to have been illegally made, it may be exercised with reference to persons employed in any other department of the public service when their illegal detention is asserted. It may be exercised in all cases where parties are held under the authority of the United States, whenever the invalidity of the exercise of that authority is affirmed. The jurisdiction, if it exists at all, can only be limited in its application by the legislative power of the State. It may even reach to parties imprisoned under sentence of the National courts, after regular indictment, trial, and conviction, for offenses against the laws of the United States. As we read the opinion of the Supreme Court of Wisconsin in this case, this is the claim of authority asserted by that tribunal for itself and for the judicial officers of that State. It does, indeed, disclaim any right of either to interfere with parties in custody, under judicial sentence, when the National court pronouncing sentence had jurisdiction to try and punish the offenders, but it asserts, at the same time, for itself and for each of those officers, the right to determine, upon *habeas corpus,* in all cases, whether that court ever had such jurisdiction.

It is in the consideration of this distinct and independent character of the government of the United States, from that of the government of the several States, that the solution of the question presented in this case, and in similar cases, must be found. There are within the territorial limits of each State two governments, restricted in their spheres of action, but independent of each other, and supreme within their respective spheres. Each has its separate departments; each has its distinct laws, and each has its own tribunals for their enforcement. Neither government can intrude within the jurisdiction, or authorize any interference therein by its judicial officers with the action of the other. The two governments in each State stand in their respective spheres of action in the same independent relation to each other, except in one particular, that they would if their authority embraced distinct territories. That particular consists in the supremacy of the authority of the United States when any conflict arises between the two governments. The Constitution and the laws passed in pursuance of it, are declared by the Constitution itself to be the supreme law of the land, and the judges of every State are bound thereby, "anything in the constitution or laws of any State to the contrary notwithstanding." Whenever, therefore, any conflict arises between the enactments of the two sovereignties, or in the enforcement of their asserted authorities, those of the National government must have supremacy until the validity of the different enactments and authorities can be finally determined by the tribunals of the United States. This temporary supremacy until judicial decision by the National tribunals, and the ultimate determination of the conflict by such decision, are essential to the preservation of order and peace, and the avoidance of forcible collision between the two governments. "The Constitution," as said by Mr. Chief Justice Taney,[12] "was not framed merely to guard the States against danger from abroad, but chiefly to secure union and harmony at home; and to accomplish this end it was deemed necessary, when the Constitution was framed, that many of the rights of sovereignty which the States then possessed should be ceded to the General government; and that in the sphere of action assigned to it, it should be supreme and strong enough to execute its own laws by its own tribunals, without interruption from a State, or from State authorities." . . .

Such being the distinct and independent character of the two governments, within their respective spheres of action, it follows that neither can intrude with its judicial processes into the domain of the other, except so far as such intrusion may be necessary on the part of the National government to preserve its rightful supremacy in cases of conflict of authority. In their laws, and mode of enforcement, neither is responsible to the other. How their respective laws

[12] In *Ableman* v. *Booth,* 21 How. 506 (1859).

shall be enacted; how they shall be carried into execution; and in what tribunals, or by what officers; and how much discretion, or whether any at all shall be vested in their officers, are matters subject to their own control, and in the regulation of which neither can interfere with the other.

Now, among the powers assigned to the National government, is the power "to raise and support armies," and the power "to provide for the government and regulation of the land and naval forces." The execution of these powers falls within the line of its duties; and its control over the subject is plenary and exclusive. It can determine, without question from any State authority, how the armies shall be raised, whether by voluntary enlistment or forced draft, the age at which the soldier shall be received, and the period for which he shall be taken, the compensation he shall be allowed, and the service to which he shall be assigned. And it can provide the rules for the government and regulation of the forces after they are raised, define what shall constitute military offenses, and prescribe their punishment. No interference with the execution of this power of the National government in the formation, organization, and government of its armies by any State officials could be permitted without greatly impairing the efficiency, if it did not utterly destroy, this branch of the public service. Probably in every county and city in the several States there are one or more officers authorized by law to issue writs of *habeas corpus* on behalf of persons alleged to be illegally restrained of their liberty; and if soldiers could be taken from the army of the United States, and the validity of their enlistment inquired into by any of these officers, such proceeding could be taken by all of them, and no movement could be made by the National troops without their commanders being subjected to constant annoyance and embarrassment from this source. . . . In many exigencies the measures of the National government might in this way be entirely bereft of their efficacy and value. An appeal in such cases to this Court, to correct the erroneous action of these officers, would afford no adequate remedy. Proceedings on *habeas corpus* are summary, and the delay incident to bringing the decision of a State officer, through the highest tribunal of the State, to this Court for review, would necessarily occupy years, and in the meantime, where the soldier was discharged, the mischief would be accomplished. It is manifest that the powers of the National government could not be exercised with energy and efficiency at all times, if its acts could be interfered with and controlled for any period by officers or tribunals of another sovereignty.

. . . . .

State judges and State courts, authorized by laws of their States to issue writs of *habeas corpus,* have undoubtedly a right to issue the writ in any case where a party is alleged to be illegally confined within their limits, unless it appear upon his application that he is confined under the authority, or claim and color of the authority, of the United States, by an officer of that government. If such fact appear upon the application the writ should be refused. If it do not appear, the judge or court issuing the writ has a right to inquire into the cause of imprisonment, and ascertain by what authority the person is held within the limits of the State; and it is the duty of the marshal, or other officer having the custody of the prisoner, to give, by a proper return, information in this respect. . . .

". . . But [again quoting Chief Justice Taney], after the return is made, and the State judge or court judicially apprised that the party is in custody under the authority of the United States, they can proceed no further. They then know that the prisoner is within the dominion and jurisdiction of another government, and that neither the writ of *habeas corpus* nor any other process issued under State authority can pass over the line of division between the two sovereignties. He is then within the dominion and exclusive jurisdiction of the United States. If he has committed an offense against their laws, their tribunals alone can punish him. If he is wrongfully imprisoned, their judicial tribunals can release him and afford him redress." . . .

This limitation upon the power of State tribunals and State officers furnishes no just ground to apprehend that the liberty of the citizen will thereby be endangered. The United States are as much interested in protecting the citizen from illegal restraint under their authority, as the several States are to protect him from like restraint under their authority, and are no more likely to tolerate any oppression. Their courts and judicial officers are clothed with the power to issue the writ of *habeas corpus* in all cases, where a party is illegally restrained of his liberty by an officer of the United States, whether such illegality consists in the character of the process, the authority of the officer, or the invalidity of the law under which he is held. And there is no just reason to believe that they will exhibit any hesitation to exert their power, when it is properly invoked. Certainly there can be no ground for supposing that their action will be less prompt and efficient in such cases than would be that of State tribunals and State officers....

It follows, from the views we have expressed, that the court commissioner of Dane County was without jurisdiction to issue the writ of *habeas corpus* for the discharge of the prisoner in this case; it appearing, upon the application presented to him for the writ, that the prisoner was held by an officer of the United States, under claim and color of the authority of the United States, as an enlisted soldier mustered into the military service of the National government; and the same information was imparted to the commissioner by the return of the officer. The commissioner was, both by the application for the writ and the return to it, apprised that the prisoner was within the dominion and the jurisdiction of another government, and that no writ of *habeas corpus* issued by him could pass over the line which divided the two sovereignties....

Judgment reversed.

CHASE, C. J., dissenting....

IN RE NEAGLE
135 U.S. 1 (1890)

[By direction of the Attorney General of the United States, Neagle, a deputy U.S. marshal, accompanied Supreme Court Justice Field while on circuit in California. There was reason to believe that one Terry and his wife, driven by motives of revenge, might physically attack the Justice. In fact, while eating at a station restaurant, Field was assaulted by Terry, whereupon Neagle shot and killed the latter. California authorities arrested Neagle on a charge of murder. His petition for a writ of habeas corpus reached the Supreme Court of the United States.]

Mr. Justice MILLER delivered the opinion of the Court.

. . . .

These are the material circumstances produced in evidence before the Circuit Court on the hearing of this *habeas corpus* case. It is but a short sketch of a history which is given in over five hundred pages in the record, but we think it is sufficient to enable us to apply the law of the case to the question before us. Without a more minute discussion of this testimony, it produces upon us the conviction of a settled purpose on the part of Terry and his wife, amounting to a conspiracy, to murder Justice Field. And we are quite sure that if Neagle had been merely a brother or a friend of Judge Field, travelling with him, and aware of all the previous relations of Terry to the Judge,—as he was,—of his bitter animosity, his declared purpose to have revenge even to the point of killing him, he would have been justified in what he did in defense of Mr. Justice Field's life, and possibly of his own.

But such a justification would be proper subject for consideration on a trial of the case for murder in the courts of the State of California, and there exists no authority in the courts of the United States to discharge the prisoner while held in custody by the State authorities for this offense, unless there be found in aid of the defense of the prisoner some element of power and authority asserted under the government of the United States.

This element is said to be found in the facts that Mr. Justice Field, when attacked, was in the immediate discharge of his duty as judge of the Circuit Court of the United States within California; that the assault upon him grew out of the animosity of Terry and his wife, arising out of the previous discharge of his duty as circuit justice in the case for which they were committed for contempt of court; and that the deputy marshal of the United States, who killed Terry in defense of Field's life, was charged with a duty under the law of the United States to protect Field from the violence which Terry was inflicting, and which was intended to lead to Field's death.

To the inquiry whether this proposition is sustained by law and the facts which we have recited, we now address ourselves. . . .

.   .   .   .   .

We have no doubt that Mr. Justice Field when attacked by Terry was engaged in the discharge of his duties as Circuit Justice of the Ninth Circuit, and was entitled to all the protection under those circumstances which the law could give him.

It is urged, however, that there exists no statute authorizing any such protection as that which Neagle was instructed to give Judge Field in the present case, and indeed no protection whatever against a vindictive or malicious assault growing out of the faithful discharge of his official duties, and that the language of section 753 of the Revised Statutes, that the party seeking the benefit of the writ of *habeas corpus* must in this connection show that he is "in custody for an act done or omitted in pursuance of a law of the United States," makes it necessary that upon this occasion it should be shown that the act for which Neagle is imprisoned was done by virtue of an act of Congress. It is not supposed that any special act of Congress exists which authorizes the marshals or deputy marshals of the United States in express terms to accompany the judges of the Supreme Court through their circuits, and act as a body-guard to them, to defend them against malicious assaults against their persons. But we are of opinion that this view of the statute is an unwarranted restriction of the meaning of a law designed to extend in a liberal manner the benefit of the writ of *habeas corpus* to persons imprisoned for the performance of their duty. And we are satisfied that if it was the duty of Neagle, under the circumstances, a duty which could only arise under the laws of the United States, to defend Mr. Justice Field from a murderous attack upon him, he brings himself within the meaning of the section we have recited. This view of the subject is confirmed by the alternative provision, that he must be in custody "for an act done or omitted in pursuance of a law of the United States or of an order, process, or decree of a court or judge thereof, or is in custody in violation of the Constitution or of a law or treaty of the United States."

In the view we take of the Constitution of the United States, any obligation fairly and properly inferable from that instrument, or any duty of the marshal to be derived from the general scope of his duties under the laws of the United States, is "a law" within the meaning of this phrase. It would be a great reproach to the system of government of the United States, declared to be within its sphere sovereign and supreme, if there is to be found within the domain of its powers no means of protecting the judges, in the conscientious and faithful discharge of their duties, from the malice and hatred of those upon whom their judgment may operate unfavorably.

.   .   .   .   .

Where, then, are we to look for the protection which we have shown Judge Field was entitled to when engaged in the discharge of his official duties? ...

.   .   .   .   .

... The Constitution, Article 2, section 3, declares that the

President "shall take Care that the Laws be faithfully executed," and he is provided with the means of fulfilling this obligation by this authority to commission all the officers of the United States, and, by and with the advice and consent of the Senate, to appoint the most important of them and to fill vacancies. He is declared to be commander in chief of the army and navy of the United States. The duties which are thus imposed upon him he is further enabled to perform by the recognition in the Constitution, and the creation by acts of Congress, of executive departments, which have varied in number from four or five to seven or eight, the heads of which are familiarly called cabinet ministers. These aid him in the performance of the great duties of his office, and represent him in a thousand acts to which it can hardly be supposed his personal attention is called, and thus he is enabled to fulfill the duty of his great department, expressed in the phrase that "he shall take Care that the Laws be faithfully executed."

Is this duty limited to the enforcement of acts of Congress or of treaties of the United States according to their *express terms,* or does it include the rights, duties and obligations growing out of the Constitution itself, our international relations, and all the protection implied by the nature of the government under the Constitution? ...

We cannot doubt the power of the President to take measures for the protection of a judge of one of the courts of the United States, who, while in the discharge of the duties of his office, is threatened with a personal attack which may probably result in his death, and we think it clear that where this protection is to be afforded through the civil power, the Department of Justice is the proper one to set in motion the necessary means of protection. The correspondence already cited in this opinion between the marshal of the Northern District of California, and the Attorney General, is sufficient, we think, to warrant the marshal in taking the steps which he did take, in making the provision which he did make, for the protection and defense of Mr. Justice Field.

But there is positive law investing the marshals and their deputies with powers which not only justify what Marshal Neagle did in this matter, but which imposed it upon him as a duty. In chapter 14 of the Revised Statutes of the United States, which is devoted to the appointment and duties of the district attorneys, marshals, and clerks of the courts of the United States, section 788 declares:

"The marshals and their deputies shall have, in each state, the same powers, in executing the laws of the United States, as the sheriffs and their deputies in such state may have, by law, in executing the laws thereof."

If, therefore, a sheriff of the state of California was authorized to do in regard to the laws of California what Neagle did, that is, if he is authorized to keep the peace, to protect a judge from assault and murder, then Neagle was authorized to do the same thing in reference to the laws of the United States.

That there is a peace of the United States; that a man assaulting a judge of the United States while in the discharge of his duties violates that peace; that in such case the marshal of the United States stands in the same relation to the peace of the United States which the sheriff of the county does to the peace of the state of California are questions too clear to need argument to prove them. That it would be the duty of a sheriff, if one had been present at this assault by Terry upon Judge Field, or of himself, to kill Terry, in a case where, like this, it was evidently a question of the choice of who should be killed, the assailant and violator of the law and disturber of the peace, or the unoffending man who was in his power, there can be no question of the authority of the sheriff to have killed Terry. So the marshal of the United States, charged with the duty of protecting and guarding the judge of the United States court against this special assault upon his person and his life, being present at the critical moment, when prompt action was necessary, found it to be his duty, a duty which he had no liberty to refuse to perform, to take the steps which resulted in Terry's death. This duty was imposed on him by the section of the Revised Statutes which we have cited, in connection with the powers conferred by the state of California upon its peace officers, which become, by this statute, in proper cases, transferred as duties to the marshals of the United States. . . .

The result at which we have arrived upon this examination is, that in the protection of the person and the life of Mr. Justice Field while in the discharge of his official duties, Neagle was authorized to resist the attack of Terry upon him; that Neagle was correct in the belief that without prompt action on his part the assault of Terry upon the judge would have ended in the death of the latter; that such being his well-founded belief, he was justified in taking the life of Terry, as the only means of preventing the death of the man who was intended to be his victim; that in taking the life of Terry, under the circumstances, he was acting under the authority of the law of the United States, and was justified in so doing; and that he is not liable to answer in the courts of California on account of his part in that transaction.

We therefore affirm the judgment of the Circuit Court authorizing his discharge from the custody of the sheriff of San Joaquin County.

Mr. Justice LAMAR, with whom concurred Mr. Chief Justice FULLER, dissenting [opinion omitted].

JOHNSON v. MARYLAND
254 U.S. 51 (1920)

Mr. Justice HOLMES delivered the opinion of the Court.

The plaintiff in error was an employee of the Post Office Department of the United States, and while driving a government motor truck in the transportation of mail over a post road from Mt. Airy, Maryland, to Washington, was arrested in Maryland, and was tried, convicted, and fined for so driving without having obtained a license from the state. . . . The naked question is whether the state has power to require such an employee to obtain a license by submitting to an examination concerning his competence and paying $3, before performing his official duty in obedience to superior command.

. . . [More broadly expressed,] the question is whether the state can interrupt the acts of the general government itself. With regard to taxation, . . . the state's inability to interfere has been regarded as established since *McCulloch* v. *Maryland,* 4 Wheat. 316. The decision in that case was not put upon any consideration of degree, but upon the entire absence of power on the part of the states to touch, in that way, at least, the instrumentalities of the United States; . . . and that is the law today. . . . In more recent days the principle was applied when the governor of a soldiers' home was convicted for disregard of a state law concerning the use of oleomargarine, while furnishing it to the inmates of the home as part of their rations. It was said that the federal officer was not "subject to the jurisdiction of the state in regard to those very matters of administration which are thus approved by federal authority." *Ohio* v. *Thomas,* 173 U.S. 276, 283. It seems to us that the foregoing decisions establish the law governing this case.

Of course, an employee of the United States does not secure a general immunity from state law while acting in the course of his employment. . . . It very well may be that, when the United States has not spoken, the subjection to local law would extend to general rules that might affect incidentally the mode of carrying out the employment, —as, for instance, a statute or ordinance regulating the mode of turning at the corners of streets. . . . But even the most unquestionable and most universally applicable of state laws, such as those concerning murder, will not be allowed to control the conduct of a marshal of the United States, acting under and in pursuance of the laws of the United States. *In re Neagle,* 135 U.S. 1 [*supra*].

It seems to us that the immunity of the instruments of the United States from state control in the performance of their duties extends to a requirement that they desist from performance until they satisfy a state officer upon examination that they are competent for a necessary part of them and pay a fee for permission to go on. Such a requirement does not merely touch the government servants remotely by a general rule of conduct; it lays hold of them in their specific attempt to obey orders, and requires qualifications in addition to those that the government has pronounced sufficient. It is the duty of the Department to employ persons competent for their work, and that duty it must be presumed to have performed. . . .

Judgment reversed.

Mr. Justice PITNEY and Mr. Justice McREYNOLDS dissent.

PENN DAIRIES, INC. v. MILK CONTROL COMMISSION
318 U.S. 261 (1943)

Mr. Chief Justice STONE delivered the opinion of the Court.

Decision of this case turns on the question whether the minimum price regulations of the Pennsylvania Milk Control Law of 1937, . . . may constitutionally be applied to the sale of milk by a dealer to the United States, the sale being consummated within the territorial limits of the state in a place subject to its jurisdiction.

The Pennsylvania Milk Control Law establishes a milk control commission, with authority to fix prices for milk sold within the state wherever produced, including minimum wholesale and retail prices for milk sold by milk dealers to consumers, and to issue rules, regulations and orders to effectuate this authority.

In the fall of 1940 the United States established, under a permit from the Commonwealth of Pennsylvania, a military encampment [at Indiantown Gap] on lands belonging to the Commonwealth. As is conceded, the permit involved no surrender of state jurisdiction or authority over the area occupied by the camp. On February 1, 1941, the purchasing and contracting officer at the encampment, an officer of the Quartermaster's Corps of the United States Army, invited bids for a supply of milk for the period from March 1 to June 30, 1941, for consumption by troops stationed at the camp. On February 4, the Milk Control Commission sent a notice to interested parties, including appellant, Penn Dairies, Inc., a Pennsylvania corporation, addressed to "all milk dealers interested in submitting bids to furnish milk to the United States Government" at the encampment. The notice was accompanied by the Commission's Official General Order No. A-14, section 4-B of which prescribed the "minimum wholesale prices to be charged by or paid to milk dealers." The notice announced that the unit prices should be considered in the preparation of bids and that sales of milk at prices below the prescribed minima would be construed as violations of the milk control law. The dairy submitted a bid offering to sell milk in wholesale quantities at prices substantially below those prescribed by the Commission. Its bid was accepted by a War Department Purchase Order of March 1, 1941, the contract was awarded to it as the lowest bidder, and it performed the contract by deliveries of the milk at the contract price—all within the state.

On March 5, 1941, the Commission, pursuant to sections 404 and 405 of the Milk Control Act, issued a citation to the dairy to show cause why its application for a milk dealer's license for the year beginning May 1, 1941, should not be denied because of its sale and delivery of the milk at prices below the minima fixed by the Commission's order. Section 404 makes the grant of a license mandatory save in circumstances not now material, but provides that the Commission may deny or cancel a license where the applicant or licensee "has violated any of the provisions of this act, or any of the rules, regulations or orders of the commission. . . ."

. . . . .

Appellants urge that the Pennsylvania Milk Control Act, as applied to a dealer selling to the United States, violates a constitutional immunity of the United States, and also conflicts with federal legislation regulating purchases by the United States and therefore cannot constitutionally apply to such purchases.

Appellants' first proposition proceeds on the assumption that local price regulations normally controlling milk dealers who carry on their business within the state, when applied to sales made to the government, so burden it or so conflict with the Constitution as to render the regulations unlawful. We may assume that Congress, in aid of its granted power to raise and support armies, Article I, section 8, § 12, and with the support of the supremacy clause, Article VI, § 2 could declare state regulations like the present inapplicable to sales to the government. . . . But there is no clause of the Constitution which purports, unaided by Congressional enactment, to prohibit such regulations, and the question with which we are now concerned is whether such a prohibition is to be implied from the relationship of the two governments established by the Constitution.

We may assume also that, in the absence of congressional consent, there is an implied constitutional immunity of the national government from state taxation and from state regulation of the performance, by federal officers and agencies, of governmental functions. . . . But those who contract to furnish supplies or render services to the government are not such agencies and do not perform governmental functions, . . . and the mere fact that non-discriminatory taxation or regulation of the contractor imposes an increased economic burden on the government is no longer regarded as bringing the contractor within any implied immunity of the government from state taxation or regulation. *Alabama* v. *King & Boozer*, 314 U.S. 1, 9, and cases cited. . . .

Here the state regulation imposes no prohibition on the national government or its officers. They may purchase milk from whom and at what price they will, without incurring any penalty. . . . As in the case of state taxation of the seller, the government is affected only as the state's regulation may increase the price which the government must pay for milk. By the exercise of control over the seller, the regulation imposes or may impose an increased economic burden on the government, for it may be assumed that the regulation if enforceable and enforced will increase the price of the milk purchased for the consumption in Pennsylvania, unless the government is able to procure a supply from without the state. . . . But in this burden, if Congress has not acted to forbid it, we can find no different or greater impairment of federal authority than in the tax on sales to a government contractor sustained in *Alabama* v. *King & Boozer, supra;* or the state regulation of the operations of a trucking company in performing its contract with the government to transport workers employed on a Public Works Administration project, upheld in *Baltimore & A. R. Co.* v. *Lichtenberg* [308 U.S. 525], or the local building restrictions applied to a contractor engaged in constructing a postoffice building for the government, sustained in *James Stewart & Co.* v. *Sadrakula,* 309 U.S. 94.

The trend of our decisions is not to extend governmental immunity from state taxation and regulation beyond the national government itself and governmental functions performed by its officers and agents. We have recognized that the Constitution presupposes the continued existence of the states functioning in coordination with the national government, with authority in the states to lay taxes and to regulate their internal affairs and policy, and that state regulation like state taxation inevitably imposes some burdens on the national government of the same kind as those imposed on citizens of the United States within the state's borders. And we have held that those burdens, save as Congress may act to remove them, are to be regarded as the normal incidents of the operation within the same territory of a dual system of government, and that no immunity of the national government from such burdens is to be implied from the Constitution which established the system, see *Graves* v. *New York* ex rel. *O'Keefe,* 306 U.S. 466, 483, 487 [*supra*].

Since the Constitution has left Congress free to set aside local taxation and regulation of government contractors which burden the national government, we see no basis for implying from the Constitution alone a restriction upon such regulations which Congress has seen fit to impose, unless the regulations are shown to be inconsistent with Congressional policy. Even in the case of agencies created or appointed to do the government's work we have been slow to infer an immunity which Congress has not granted and which Congressional policy does not require. . . . Our inquiry here, therefore, must be whether the state's regulation of this contractor in a matter of local concern conflicts with Congressional legislation or with any discernible Congressional policy.

.   .   .   .   .

We are unable to find in Congressional legislation, either as read in the light of its history or as construed by the executive officers charged with the exercise of the contracting power, any disclosure of a purpose to immunize government contractors from local price-fixing regulations which would otherwise be applicable. Nor, in the circumstances of this case, can we find that the Constitution, unaided by Congressional enactment, confers such an immunity. It follows that the Pennsylvania courts rightly held that the Constitution and laws of the United States did not preclude the application of the Pennsylvania Milk Control Law to appellant Penn Dairies, Inc., by denial of its license application.

Affirmed.

Mr. Justice MURPHY, concurring.

. . . . . .

We are not concerned here with just an ordinary state regulatory statute of non-discriminatory character which affects the federal government in some degree, but with a general measure designed to safeguard the health and well-being of the public by insuring an adequate supply of wholesome milk at stable prices. . . . In my opinion it is of greater importance to the nation at war and to its military establishment that high standards of health be maintained than that the military procurement authorities have the benefit of unrestricted competitive bidding and lower prices in the purchase of milk supplies. . . .

In the conduct of the war as well as in other relations, the larger interests of the federal government and the nation as a whole will not suffer, nor will constitutional arrangements be prejudiced, if procurement officers are obliged to conduct their activities within the general framework of state laws enacted within reasonable limits to safeguard the public health and safety. . . .

[Justices DOUGLAS, BLACK and JACKSON contended that Congressional authorization of War Department procurement regulations constituted an assertion of federal power in this field which excluded exercise of conflicting state powers. Justice DOUGLAS wrote the dissent.]

4. STATE VERSUS STATE: JUDICIAL DILEMMAS

"SOVEREIGN" EQUALITY OF THE STATES

Constitutional historians have reserved the name of the "Great Compromise" for the formula proposed by Connecticut's delegation to the Philadelphia Convention by which the deadlock between large and small states was finally broken and agreement accomplished on the basis of representation in the national legislature. It may well be equally feasible to denominate the entire proceedings as a "great compromise," a model lesson in the art of the possible. Throughout the records of the assembly the assertions and suspicions, fears and prides, of the new states are eloquently expressed; but overshadowing them is the desire to attain a better association of these states and the—eminently practical—realization that the forms of such a proposed association would have to allay all those elements of local pride and local fear if the labors of the delegates were not to be for naught.

The pattern that emerged left the states free in every respect not especially singled out for prohibition by the Constitution. The members of the union relinquished parts only of their powers and reserved to themselves and even a minority of themselves the right and power to withhold assent to any future change of the arrangement. As among themselves, the states remained as independent of one another and as equal to each other as fully sovereign political units might be. Their equality is asserted whenever a new state is admitted by the inclusion in the act of admission of a recital to that effect. Yet this Congressional assurance is indeed superfluous, for statehood implies equality of status with all states. Congress is powerless to attach conditions to admission to statehood that would bind the state or limit its freedom of action beyond constitutional bounds. Thus when Congress admitted Oklahoma on condition that the state capital should not be moved from Guthrie for a specified number of years the Supreme Court gave its approval to an earlier removal of the seat of government to Oklahoma City. "The constitutional equality of the states," it was said, "is essential to the harmonious operation of the scheme upon which the Republic was organized."[13]

The theme of equality may also be recognized in the numerous instances in which the national judiciary resolved controversies between the states. The authority for the adjuciation by the Supreme Court of such issues arising between states of the union stems from the judiciary article of the Constitution and derives from a similar provision under the Articles of Confederation which directed Congress to set up special tribunals as needed in such cases.

The number of cases in this category decided by the Supreme Court is rather surprisingly high. James Brown Scott collected all

---

[13] *Coyle* v. *Smith,* 221 U.S. 559 (1911). However, a condition in an act of admission that the state should not, for a period of ten years after admission, levy taxes on land owned by private individuals but purchased from the United States Government was interpreted as a compact between the state and the union and taxes imposed in contravention of the agreement were held void. *Stearns* v. *Minnesota,* 179 U.S. 223 (1900). Note, however, that this construction of the agreement made it in effect separate from the act of admission and hence did not contradict the basic assumption of state equality.

prior decisions of this nature in two bulky volumes in 1918.[14] Charles Warren, writing in 1924, listed over eighty instances.[15] A sizeable portion of these conflicts have involved boundary disputes. See *Virginia v. Tennessee,* below. In a number of other instances the Court entertained suits brought by a state on behalf of its citizens against another state. Thus when inhabitants of Missouri who depended on the Mississippi River for their water supply sought to prevent Illinois from polluting the stream, the state of Missouri acted on their behalf; the Eleventh Amendment barring suits of citizens against states, the device of substituting the state for its citizens affords one avenue of judicial relief. The Supreme Court has acquiesced to this practice.[16] But it has drawn the line where the state accommodated its citizens by acting as collecting agency on the defaulted bonds of a sister state. This was the case in *New Hampshire* v. *Louisiana,* 108 U.S. 76 (1883), where individual owners of Louisiana bonds had assigned them to the state of New Hampshire but, under the laws of that state, were to receive any proceeds materialized from the suit on the bonds. The Court found the individuals to be the real parties in interest and dismissed the suit on the authority of the Eleventh Amendment.[17]

The exercise of judicial authority by the national Supreme Court over individual states of the union contains, of course, within itself numerous potential problems of enforcement. What would the Court do if a state refused to abide by its decree? The controversy between Virginia and West Virginia over the payment of the pre-Civil War debt of the former state bade fair to bring that issue into the open. West Virginia had obligated herself, at the time of her separation from Virginia in 1863, to assume a proportionate share of the debt of the parent state. After a protracted series of suits, extending from 1906 to 1915, the Supreme Court set the sum to be paid at twelve million dollars. Virginia then asked for a writ of execution, analogous to a court order for a sheriff's sale. West Virginia countered by asserting that all her property was used for public purposes and hence was not subject to execution. The Supreme Court side-stepped the issue

[14] *Judicial Settlement of Controversies Between States of the American Union,* Washington: Carnegie Institution, 1918.

[15] *The Supreme Court and Sovereign States,* Princeton: Princeton University Press, 1924.

[16] *Missouri* v. *Illinois,* 180 U.S. 208 (1901); 200 U.S. 496 (1906). In *Kansas* v. *Colorado,* 185 U.S. 125 (1902); 206 U.S. 46 (1907), the Court similarly allowed a suit by Kansas to prevent depletion of the waters of the Arkansas River by Colorado; each state was held entitled to an equitable share of the water of the river.

[17] But where the transfer of bonds was without reservation the Court took jurisdiction and ordered the defaulting state to honor the bonds. *South Dakota* v. *North Carolina,* 192 U.S. 286 (1904).

by pointing out that the debtor state's legislature had not met since the award of the judgment and that it should be afforded an opportunity to determine means for the payment of the debt. Virginia then asked the Supreme Court to issue a writ of mandamus to the West Virginia legislature directing them to levy a tax in order to meet the judicially approved obligation. Speculation was rife as to the possible compulsions which could be applied if the writ were not complied with. The Court postponed decision and set a date for further hearing to determine what remedies might be appropriate. Fortunately for the justices, West Virginia provided for the payment of the debt before the hearing date came around.[18]

The Court's regard for the sensitivities of the states and the difficulties of enforcement in respect to them had previously been demonstrated in cases involving other interstate problems. The constitutional provisions for the extradition of fugitives from justice was given an interpretation which converted it from a mandatory to a permissive clause. See *Kentucky* v. *Dennison,* below. The state's police power was given ample latitude in dealing with corporations domiciled in other states. "Full Faith and Credit," stipulated by the Constitution for the public records of sister states, has not prevented the confusing welter of (to name but one subject) divorce jurisdictions. Congress has shown no inclination to assume the responsibility of implementing the constitutional language and the Court has done little to advance the cause of legal simplification.[19] On the contrary one could cite several instances, not necessarily consistent with one another, where the only plausible rationale for the Court's decision must be found in the desire to avoid possible defiance of its holding by the state. In the realm of federalism as in that of interdepartmental relations judicial strategy is often dictated by the tactics of caution.

VIRGINIA v. TENNESSEE
148 U.S. 503 (1893)

Mr. Justice FIELD delivered the opinion of the Court.

This is a suit to establish by judicial decree the true boundary line between the states of Virginia and Tennessee. It embraces a contro-

---

[18] *Virginia* v. *West Virginia,* 264 U.S. 565 (1918).

[19] See Robert H. Jackson, "Full Faith and Credit: The Lawyers' Clause of the Constitution," 45 *Columbia Law Review* 1 (1945), extracts from which may be found *infra,* p. 150; and William H. Page, "Full Faith and Credit: The Discarded Constitutional Provision," *Wisconsin Law Review* (1948), 265–329.

versy of which this Court has original jurisdiction, and in this respect the judicial department of our government is distinguished from the judicial department of any other country, drawing to itself by the ordinary modes of peaceful procedure the settlement of questions as between the states, possessed, for purposes of internal government of the powers of independent communities, which otherwise might be fruitful cause of prolonged and harassing conflicts. . . .

The Constitution provides that "no state shall, without the consent of Congress, lay any duty of tonnage, keep troops or ships of war in time of peace, enter into any agreement or compact with another state, or with a foreign power, or engage in war, unless actually invaded, or in such immediate danger as will not admit of delay.". . .

[By resolutions of January, 1800, and November, 1801, respectively, Virginia and Tennessee agreed to appoint commissioners to survey and find part of the boundary line between them that had been in dispute since the formation of the latter state. This preliminary agreement the Court held was not one requiring the consent of Congress. "There are many matters," said the Court, "upon which different states may agree that can in no respect concern the United States." The final ratification of the boundary fixed by the commissioners took place in 1803, and these acts, being mutually done by each state in consideration of the act of the other, constituted an agreement of the character requiring the consent of Congress. This consent, however, might be expressed or implied; and in the case before the Court it was to be implied from the "subsequent legislation and proceedings" of Congress, in the assignment of the area in question to one state or the other in the making of congressional and judicial district lines.]

Independently of any effect due to the compact as such, a boundary line between states or provinces, as between private persons, which has been run out, located, and marked upon the earth, and afterwards recognized and acquiesced in by the parties for a long course of years, is conclusive, even if it be ascertained that it varies somewhat from the courses given in the original grant; and the line so established takes effect, not as an alienation of territory, but as a definition of the true and ancient boundary. . . . In the case of *Rhode Island* v. *Massachusetts,* 4 How. (45 U.S.) 591, this Court, speaking of the long possession of Massachusetts, and the delays in alleging any mistake in the action of the commissioners of the colonies, said: "Surely this, connected with the lapse of time, must remove all doubts as to the right of the respondent under the agreements of 1711 and 1718. No human transactions are unaffected by time. Its influence is seen on all things subject to change. And this is peculiarly the case in regard to matters which rest in memory, and which consequently fade with the lapse of time and fall with the lives of individuals. For the security of rights, whether of states or individuals, long possession under a claim of title is protected. And there is no controversy in which this great principle may be invoked with greater justice and propriety than in a case of disputed boundary.". . .

The compact in this case having received the consent of Congress, though not in express terms, yet impliedly, and subsequently, which is equally effective, became obligatory and binding upon all the citizens of both Virginia and Tennessee. Nor is it any objection that there may have been errors in the demarcation of the line which the states thus by their compact sanctioned. After such compacts have been adhered to for years, neither party can be absolved from them upon showing errors, mistakes, or misapprehension of their terms, or in the line established; and this is a complete and perfect answer to the complainant's position in this case. . . .

Our judgment, therefore, is that the boundary line established by the states of Virginia and Tennessee by the compact of 1803 is the true boundary between them, and that on a proper application, based upon a showing that any marks for the identification of that line have been obliterated or have become indistinct, an order may be made at any time during the present term for the restoration of such marks without any change of the line. . . .

It is so ordered.

KENTUCKY v. DENNISON
24 How. 66 (1861)

On petition of mandamus, or for a rule on William Dennison, the governor of Ohio, to show cause why a mandamus should not be issued by this Court, commanding him to cause Willis Lago, a fugitive from justice, to be delivered up to be removed to the state of Kentucky, having jurisdiction of the crime with which he is charged. . . .[20]

Mr. Chief Justice TANEY delivered the opinion of the Court.

The Court is sensible of the importance of this case, and of the

[20] This was a test case on the extradition of runaway slaves. It was argued and decided in the months immediately preceding the secession of the Southern states.

great interest and gravity of the questions involved in it, and which have been raised and fully argued at the bar.

. . . The clause which has given rise to this controversy . . . is in the following words:

"A person charged in any state with treason, felony or other crime who shall flee from justice, and be found in another state, shall, on demand of the executive authority of the state from which he fled, be delivered up, to be removed to the state having jurisdiction of the crime."

.   .   .   .   .   .

Looking, therefore, to the words of the Constitution—to the obvious policy and necessity of this provision to preserve harmony between the states, and order and law within their respective borders, and to its early adoption by the colonies, and then by the confederated states, whose mutual interest it was to give each other aid and support whenever it was needed—the conclusion was irresistible, that this compact engrafted in the Constitution included, and was intended to include, every offense made punishable by the law of the state in which it was committed, and that it gives the right to the executive authority of the state to demand the fugitive from the executive authority of the state in which he is found; that the right given to "demand" implies that it is an absolute right; and that it follows that there must be a correlative obligation to deliver, without any reference to the character of the crime charged, or to the policy or laws of the state to which the fugitive has fled. . . .

This duty, of providing by law the regulations necessary to carry this compact into execution, from the nature of the duty and the object in view was manifestly devolved upon Congress; . . . as early as 1791, in a demand by the Governor of Pennsylvania upon the Governor of Virginia, . . . both of them admitted the propriety of bringing the subject before the President, who immediately submitted the matter to the consideration of Congress. And this led to the act of 1793. . . .

The demand being . . . made, the act of Congress declares that "it shall be the duty of the executive authority of the state" to cause the fugitive to be arrested and secured, and delivered to the agent of the demanding state. The words, "it shall be the duty," in ordinary legislation, imply the assertion of the power to command and to coerce obedience. But looking to the subject matter of this law, and the relations which the United States and the several states bear to each other, the Court is of opinion, the words "it shall be the duty," were not used as mandatory and compulsory, but as declaratory of the moral duty which this compact—the Constitution—created, when Congress had provided the mode of carrying it into execution. The act does not provide any means to compel the execution of this duty, nor inflict any punishment for neglect or refusal on the part of the executive of the state; nor is there any clause or provision in the Constitution which arms the government of the United States with this power. Indeed, such a power would place every state under the control and dominion of the general government, even in the administration of its internal concerns and reserved rights.

It is true that Congress may authorize a particular state officer to perform a particular duty; but if he declines to do so, it does not follow that he may be coerced, or punished for his refusal. And we are very far from supposing, that in using this word "duty," the statesmen who framed and passed the law, or the President who approved and signed it, intended to exercise a coercive power over state officers not warranted by the Constitution.

. . .

If the governor of Ohio refuses to discharge this [moral] duty, there is no power delegated to the general government, either through the judicial department or any other department, to use any coercive means to compel him.

And upon this ground the motion for the mandamus must be overruled.

FULL FAITH AND CREDIT: THE LAWYER'S CLAUSE OF THE CONSTITUTION[21]

. . .

To a foreign observer the United States may well appear to be "a nation concealed under the form of a federation." However true this may be as to political power and economic controls, it is far wide of the truth as to administration of internal justice among our forty-eight state legal systems. Indeed, today in respect of our legal administrations we have not achieved a much "more perfect union" than that of the colonies under the Articles of Confederation. We have so far

[21] By Justice Robert H. Jackson. Reprinted from 45 *Columbia Law Review* 1 (1945), with permission of the editors.

as I can ascertain the most localized and conflicting system of any country which presents the external appearance of nationhood. But we are so accustomed to the delays, expense, and frustrations of our system that it seldom occurs to us to inquire whether these are wise or constitutionally necessary.

If we look about us, we see that peoples who, no less than we, love local independence and home rule have in the nineteenth and twentieth centuries got away from the sharp territorial delimitations on court process which prevailed in the eighteenth. Both process to initiate and process to terminate actions are regulated, not by the accidents of geography, but by the appropriateness of a particular venue[22] in which to commence an action and by universal respect for the judgment which settles it. We alone in a century and a half have made no effort better to integrate our judicial systems. These confining concepts, which do so much to make our judgments ineffective or to delay and increase the costs of their execution and do so much to complicate our choice of law problems[23] presents a challenge to our times and most of all to our [the legal] profession.

The fact is that today, except in the few cases of which the United States Supreme Court has original jurisdiction, the litigant can go into no court of the land whose judgment will have any effect outside a very limited area except as a record on which to sue for another judgment. If such parochial limitations serve any good purpose in modern society, I do not know what they are.

Congress, instead of using its powers to integrate the legal systems of the states, has impressed the state limitations upon the federal courts.

Thus, when one must seek a remedy, whether he turns to state courts or to federal courts, he finds them subject to territorial limitations which often force one injured in person or property to go far from the only place he ever had lived or traded, to some distant forum.

. . . . .

Always to be kept in mind in dealing with these problems is that the policy ultimately to be served in application of the clause is the federal policy of "a more perfect union" of our legal systems. No local interest and no balance of local interests can rise above this consideration. It is hard to see how the faith and credit clause would

22 Place where the trial is held.
23 I.e., the problem of which law to apply, that of State A or State B.

have any practical meaning as to statutes if the Court should adhere to the statement that "a state is not required to enforce a law obnoxious to its public policy."

The distinction between federal interest and local interest may be elusive, but always it is present in these conflicts. Fundamental to every such conflict of law is that separate states consider that their own interests require inconsistent social or economic policies. The legal controversy as to whether Dred Scott's sojourn in a free state invested him with rights which must be respected when he returned to a slave state had its roots in the two incompatible social systems. Conflicts which we face day after day are less deep and less bitter, but nonetheless, they grow out of disagreement between states as to the policies that will promote their social welfare. One state thinks it needs to encourage industrial capital to come and exploit its latent resources and therefore is niggardly about putting the burden of industrial accidents upon industry. Another, more fully industrialized, perhaps, adopts a policy of more generous workmen's compensation. Or religious convictions prevailing in one state may lead to a highly restrictive policy of divorce, while another grants it on easy terms. . . .

. . . Only a singularly balanced mind could weigh relative state interests in such subject matters except by resort to what are likely to be strong preferences in sociology, economics, governmental theory, and politics. There are no judicial standards of valuation of such imponderables. . . . But, even if we could appraise or compare relative local interests, we must lift these questions above the control of local interests and must govern conflict in these cases by the wider considerations arising out of the federal order. . . .

.   .   .   .   .

It is doubtful if a century and a half of constitutional interpretation has advanced us much beyond where we would be if there had never been a [full faith and credit] clause. Local policies and balance of local interest still dominate the application of the federal requirement. . . .

It seems easier for the Court to put aside parochialism and to think in terms of a national economy or of a national social welfare than to think in terms of a truly national legal system. . . .

But the full faith and credit clause is the foundation of any hope we may have for a truly national system of justice, based on the preservation but better integration of the local jurisdictions we have.

The Power of the Purse: Money and Taxation

1. THE COIN OF THE REALM

The Constitution confers upon the federal government the power "to coin money" and "regulate the value thereof" (Art. I, sec. 8, cl. 5). Read in conjunction with the constitutional prohibition on the coinage of money by the states (Art. I, sec. 10, cl. 1), this grant makes the issuance of metallic currency an exclusively national prerogative. Paper certificates in lieu of metallic tokens had not yet acquired respectability in the Framers' day. On the contrary, they enjoined the states not to "make anything but gold and silver coin a tender in payment of debts."[1] But the language of the Constitution neither authorizes nor prohibits the issuance by the federal government of paper money to be used in lieu of specie.

Then, in the dark days of the Civil War, Congress passed the Legal Tender Act of 1862, authorizing "greenbacks" in the amount of $150,000,000 to be printed and making them legal tender in payment of all private and public debts (with minor exceptions). Subsequently this amount was increased to $450,000,000. Salmon P. Chase, as Secretary of the Treasury, reluctantly urged that these acts be passed, believing them to be necessary to the successful prosecution of the war. In 1870, as Chief Justice, Chase wrote the opinion for the majority in *Hepburn* v. *Griswold*, 8 Wall. 603, declaring the Legal Tender Act unconstitutional. In effect, he announced that the stipulation set up

[1] *Constitution*, Art. I, sec. 10, cl. 1.

by the Constitution for the states should apply with equal force against the national government and nothing but gold and silver be prescribed as legal tender.

There followed a dramatic, politics-laden interlude. *Hepburn* v. *Griswold* had been decided by a seven-man Court dividing four-to-three. The Court, at the time of this decision, was short two members, one as the result of legislation increasing the number of judges, the other by virtue of the resignation of Justice Grier. President Grant at once appointed two new justices, Bradley and Strong, both considered friendly toward "greenback" policies. It is unlikely that Grant obtained any formal commitments from the two appointees. But he undoubtedly availed himself of the prerogative of any appointing authority to select his candidates from among his sympathizers rather than his opponents.

Within fifteen months, the reconstituted Court discarded *Hepburn* v. *Griswold* and, by a vote of five-to-four, upheld the legal tender legislation, but as an outgrowth of the war powers of the Congress *(Knox* v. *Lee,* 12 Wall. 457 [1871]). It should also be noted that in 1869 Congress had resolved to redeem "at the earliest practicable period" the notes issued during the war (16 Stat. 1).

There came, however, the panic of 1873, ushering in one of the worst depressions of the American economy (prior to 1929). The demand for more money in circulation, for "cheap money," increased sharply and became a major political issue. In the end Congress instructed the Secretary of the Treasury to reissue any notes presented for redemption or otherwise received by the Treasury. Debtors were interested in the maintenance of this money supply; creditors urged that, because the earlier Court validation of legal tender notes had been based on the war power, such notes could not constitutionally be reissued in time of peace. This led to the case of *Juilliard* v. *Greenman.*

JUILLIARD v. GREENMAN
110 U.S. 421 (1884)

[In payment of an obligation totaling $5122.90, the defendant tendered gold coins to the total of $22.50; 40 cents in silver coin; and $5100 in United States notes. The plaintiff refused to accept the notes; the defendant insisted that, under the Act of Congress, the notes had to be accepted as legal tender and declined to make payment in any other form or specie. The plaintiff sued for the amount due, plus interest, but the defendant was awarded judgment in the lower court.]

Mr. Justice GRAY delivered the opinion of the Court. . . .

The notes of the United States, tendered in payment of the defendant's debt to the plaintiff, were originally issued under the acts of Congress . . . passed during the war of the rebellion, and enacting that these notes should "be lawful money and a legal tender in payment of all debts, public and private, within the United States," except for duties on imports and interest on the public debt. 12 Stat. 345, 709. . . .

The act of January 14th, 1875, ch. 15, "to provide for the resumption of specie payments," enacted that on and after January 1st, 1879, "the Secretary of the Treasury shall redeem in coin the United States legal tender notes then outstanding. . . ."

The act of May 31st, 1878, ch. 146, under which the notes in question were reissued, is entitled "An act to forbid the further retirement of United States legal tender notes. . . ."

The manifest intention of this act is that the notes which it directs, after having been redeemed, to be reissued and kept in circulation, shall retain their original quality of being a legal tender.

The single question . . . to be considered . . . is whether notes of the United States, issued in time of war . . . and afterwards in time of peace redeemed . . . and then reissued . . . can, under the Constitution of the United States, be a legal tender in payment of . . . debts.

Upon full consideration of the case, the Court is unanimously of opinion that it cannot be distinguished in principle from the cases heretofore determined, reported under the names of the *Legal Tender Cases,*[2] 12 Wall. 457, . . . and all the judges, except Mr. Justice Field, who adheres to the views expressed in his dissenting opinions in those cases, are of opinion that they were rightly decided.

No question of the scope and extent of the implied powers of Congress under the Constitution can be satisfactorily discussed without repeating much of the reasoning of Chief Justice Marshall in the great judgment in *McCulloch* v. *Maryland,* 4 Wheat. 316. . . .

A constitution, establishing a frame of government, declaring fundamental principles, and creating a national sovereignty, and intended to endure for ages and to be adapted to the various crises

[2] *Knox* v. *Lee* and companion cases.

of human affairs, is not to be interpreted with the strictness of a private contract. . . .

That clause of the Constitution which declares that "the Congress shall have the power to lay and collect taxes, duties, imposts and excises, to pay the debts and provide for the common defence and general welfare of the United States," either embodies a grant of power to pay the debts of the United States, or presupposes and assumes that power as inherent in the United States as a sovereign government. But, in whichever aspect it be considered, neither this nor any other clause of the Constitution makes any mention of priority or preference of the United States as a creditor over other creditors of an individual debtor. Yet this Court, in the early case of *United States* v. *Fisher,* 2 Cranch, 358, held that, under the power to pay the debts of the United States, Congress had the power to enact that debts due to the United States should have that priority of payment out of the estate of an insolvent debtor, which the law of England [then] gave to debts due the Crown.

In delivering judgment in that case, Chief Justice Marshall expounded the clause giving Congress power to make all necessary and proper laws, as follows: "In construing this clause, it would be incorrect, and would produce endless difficulties, if the opinion should be maintained that no law was authorized which was not indispensably necessary to give effect to a specified power. Where various systems might be adopted for that purpose, it might be said with respect to each, that it was not necessary, because the end might be obtained by other means. Congress must possess the choice of means, and must be empowered to use any means which are in fact conducive to the exercise of a power granted by the Constitution. The government is to pay the debt of the Union, and must be authorized to use the means which appear to itself the most eligible to effect that object." 2 Cranch, 396.

In *McCulloch* v. *Maryland,* he more fully developed the same view, concluding thus: ". . . Let the end be legitimate, let it be within the scope of the Constitution, and all means which are appropriate, which are plainly adapted to that end, which are not prohibited, but consistent with the letter and spirit of the Constitution, are constitutional." 4 Wheat. 421.

The rule of interpretation thus laid down has been constantly adhered to and acted on by this Court, and was accepted as expressing the true test by all the judges who took part in the former discussions of the power of Congress to make the treasury notes of the United States a legal tender in payment of private debts . . . [i.e., the *Legal Tender Cases*].

The words "to borrow money," as used in the Constitution, to designate a power vested in the national government, for the safety and welfare of the whole people, are not to receive that limited and restricted interpretation and meaning which they would have in a penal statute, or in an authority conferred, by law or by contract, upon trustees or agents for private purposes.

The power "to borrow money on the credit of the United States" is the power to raise money for the public use on a pledge of the public credit, and may be exercised to meet either present or anticipated expenses and liabilities of the government. It includes the power to issue, in return for the money borrowed, the obligations of the United States in any appropriate form, of stock, bonds, bills or notes. . . . Congress has authority to issue these obligations in a form adapted to circulation from hand to hand in the ordinary transactions of commerce and business. In order to promote and facilitate such circulation, to adapt them to use as currency, and to make them more current in the market, it may provide for their redemption in coin or bonds, and may make them receivable in payment of debts to the government. So much is settled beyond doubt, and was asserted or distinctly admitted by the judges who dissented from the decision in the *Legal Tender Cases,* as well as by those who concurred in that decision. . . .

. . . Congress has the power to issue the obligations of the United States in such form, and to impress upon them such qualities as currency for the purchase of merchandise and the payment of debts, as accord with the usage of sovereign governments. The power . . . was a power universally understood to belong to sovereignty, in Europe and America, at the time of the framing and adoption of the Constitution of the United States. . . . The exercise of this power not being prohibited to Congress by the Constitution, it is included in the power expressly granted to borrow money on the credit of the United States. . . .

The power of making the notes of the United States a legal tender in payment of private debts, being included in the power to borrow money and to provide a national currency, is not defeated or restricted by the fact that its exercise may affect the value of private contracts. . . .

. . . As observed by Mr. Justice Strong, in delivering the opinion of the Court in the *Legal Tender Cases*, "Every contract for the payment of money, simply, is necessarily subject to the constitutional power of the government over the currency, whatever that power may be, and the obligation of the parties is, therefore, assumed with reference to that power." 12 Wall. 549.

Congress, as the legislature of a sovereign nation, being expressly empowered by the Constitution "to lay and collect taxes, to pay the debts and provide for the common defence and general welfare of the United States," and "to borrow money on the credit of the United States," and "to coin money and regulate the value thereof and of foreign coin;" and being clearly authorized, as incidental to the exercise of those great powers, to emit bills of credit, to charter national banks, and to provide a national currency for the whole people, in the form of coin, treasury notes, and national bank bills; and the power to make the notes of the government a legal tender in payment of private debts being one of the powers belonging to sovreignty in other civilized nations, and not expressly withheld from Congress by the Constitution; we are irresistibly impelled to the conclusion that the impressing upon the treasury notes of the United States the quality of being legal tender in payment of private debts is an appropriate means, conducive and plainly adapted to the execution of the undoubted powers of Congress, consistent with the letter and spirit of the Constitution, and therefore, within the meaning of that instrument, "necessary and proper for carrying into execution the powers vested by this Constitution in the government of the United States."

Such being our conclusion in matter of law, the question whether at any particular time, in war or in peace, the exigency is such, by reason of unusual or pressing demands on the resources of the government, or of the inadequacy of the supply of gold and silver coin to furnish the currency needed for the uses of the government and of the people, that it is, as matter of fact, wise and expedient to resort to this means, is a political question, to be determined by Congress when the question of exigency arises, and not a judicial question, to be afterwards passed upon by the courts. . . .

It follows that the act of May 31st, 1878, ch. 146, is constitutional and valid; . . . that the tender in treasury notes, reissued and kept in circulation under that act, was a tender of lawful money in payment of the defendant's debt to the plaintiff.

Judgment affirmed.

Mr. Justice FIELD, dissenting.

From the judgment of the Court in this case, and from all the positions advanced in its support, I dissent. . . .

. . . Beyond and above all the objections which I have stated to the decision recognizing a power in Congress to impart the legal tender quality to the notes of the government, is my objection to the rule of construction adopted by the Court to reach its conclusions, a rule which fully carried out would change the whole nature of our Constitution and break down the barriers which separate a government of limited from one of unlimited powers. When the Constitution came before the conventions of the several States for adoption, apprehension existed that other powers than those designated might be claimed; and it led to the first ten amendments. . . . The Tenth Amendment . . . declares that "the powers not delegated to the United States by the Constitution, nor prohibited by it to the States, are reserved to the States respectively, or to the people." . . . Of what purpose is it then to refer to the exercise of the power by the absolute or the limited governments of Europe, or by the States previous to our Constitution? Congress can exercise no power by virtue of any supposed inherent sovereignty in the general government. . . . It is a government of delegated powers, supreme within its prescribed sphere, but powerless outside of it. In this country sovereignty resides in the people, and Congress can exercise no power which they have not, by their Constitution, entrusted to it; all else is withheld. It seems, however, to be supposed that, as the power was taken from the States, it could not have been intended that it should disappear entirely, and therefore it must in some way adhere to the general government, notwithstanding the Tenth Amendment and the nature of the Constitution. The doctrine, that a power not expressly forbidden may be exercised, would, as I have observed, change the character of our government. If I have read the Constitution aright, if there is any weight to be given to the uniform teachings of our great jurists and of commentators previous to the late civil war, the true doctrine is the very opposite of this. If the power is not in terms granted, and is not necessary and proper for the exercise of a power which is thus granted, it does not exist. . . .

From the decision of the Court I see only evil likely to follow.

There have been times within the memory of all of us when the legal tender notes of the United States were not exchangeable for more than one half of their nominal value. The possibility of such depreciation will always attend paper money. This inborn infirmity no mere legislative declaration can cure. If Congress has the power to make the notes a legal tender and to pass as money or its equivalent, why should not a sufficient amount be issued to pay the bonds of the United States as they mature? Why pay interest on the millions of dollars of bonds now due, when Congress can in one day make the money to pay the principal? And why should there be any restraint upon unlimited appropriations by the government for all imaginary schemes of public government, if the printing press can furnish the money that is needed for them?

NOTE ON THE GOLD CLAUSE CASES[3]

In the case of *Norman* v. *Baltimore & Ohio R. R. Co.*,[4] decided in February 1935, the Court was called upon to decide the validity of the Joint Resolution of Congress, of June 5, 1933, which nullified the "gold clauses" in existing contractual obligations. The resolution provided that "every provision contained in . . . any obligation which purports to give the obligee a right to require payment in gold" is "against public policy," and that every such obligation, "whether or not any such provision is contained therein . . . shall be discharged upon payment, dollar for dollar, in any coin or currency which at the time of payment is legal tender for public and private debts." By this simple resolution Congress at one stroke reduced the value of existing contracts by many billions of dollars; and by upholding its validity, the Court, in effect, eliminated the Fifth Amendment as a limitation upon legislative interference with vested rights. In deciding the case favorably to the government, the Court clearly established the proposition that Congress, in the exercise of its delegated powers, may impair or even destroy private obligations without compensation whenever the enforcement of such private obligations would tend to interfere with the exercise by Congress of its constitutional powers.

Nor is this conclusion applicable to the revenue powers only. The comprehensive argument made by Chief Justice Hughes, who wrote

[3] From Dean Alfange, *The Supreme Court and the National Will,* New York: Doubleday, Doran & Co., 1937, pp. 198–202. Copyright by the author and reproduced here with his permission.

[4] 294 U.S. 240.

the prevailing opinion, covered the exercise of every congressional power and touched contracts of every description save those made by the United States. After citing the *Legal Tender Cases* as illustrations of the power of Congress to impair private obligations in the exercise of its money powers, the chief justice said:

The instant cases involve contracts between private parties, but the question necessarily relates as well to the contracts or obligations of States and municipalities, or of their political subdivisions, that is, to such engagements as are within the reach of the applicable national power. . . . Contracts, however express, cannot fetter the constitutional authority of the Congress. Contracts may create rights of property, but when contracts deal with a subject matter which lies within the control of the Congress, they have a congenital infirmity. Parties cannot remove their transactions from the reach of dominant constitutional power by making contracts about them. This principle has familiar illustration in the exercise of the power to regulate commerce. If shippers and carriers stipulate for specified rates, although the rates may be lawful when the contracts are made, if Congress through the Interstate Commerce Commission exercises its authority and prescribes different rates, the latter control and override inconsistent stipulations in contracts previously made. This is so, even if the contract be a charter granted by a State and limiting rates, or a contract between municipalities and carriers. . . . The reason is manifest. To subordinate the exercise of the Federal authority to the continuing operation of previous contracts would be to place to this extent the regulation of inter-State commerce in the hands of private individuals and to withdraw from the control of the Congress so much of the field as they might choose by "prophetic discernment" to bring within the range of their agreements. The Constitution recognizes no such limitation. The same reasoning applies to the constitutional authority of the Congress to regulate the currency and to establish the monetary system of the country. If the gold clauses now before us interfere with the policy of the Congress in the exercise of that authority, they cannot stand.

In the case of *Perry* v. *United States*,[5] decided on the same day, the Court said that the same reasoning does not apply to United States government obligations. This is so, said the Court, because the sovereign cannot use a power—i.e. the power to "coin money"—in a way to destroy what it had already done under another power i.e. the power to borrow money "on the credit of the United States." But because the export or possession of gold was unlawful, continued the

[5] 294 U.S. 330.

Court, "the question of value, in relation to transactions legally available to the plaintiff, would require a consideration of the purchasing power of the dollars which the plaintiff could have received." Thus, while theoretically denying to the government the right to abrogate the gold clause in its obligations, it prevented the claimant from recovering the difference between the depreciated and the former standard gold dollars by changing the legal meaning of the term "value." The term previously meant gold of a certain weight and fineness; but the Court, in order to avoid an impossible situation, now declared that value meant purchasing power and that plaintiff could not recover damages because he could not prove that he sustained a loss of purchasing power.

The Gold Clause decisions then are another striking example of the Court's willingness and ability to adjust constitutional law to dominant political and economic realities. The President, supported by Congress, and acting to meet the exigencies of a grave domestic and international situation, abandoned the gold standard and depreciated the currency. The repercussions of these acts affected drastically not only our own national economy but world markets and the fiscal policies of other nations. The Court was, therefore, confronted with a *fait accompli* which it knew it could not upset. Moreover, it knew that no decision it could make or dare to make could restore the *status quo* which existed before the executive and legislative branches had caused abandonment of the gold standard; and it probably realized that any attempt to do so might result in the impairment of its own power and prestige. The majority of the Court wisely subordinated the constitutional issues involved to these paramount considerations; and, following the precedent established during the Civil War, it upheld the measures initiated by the President and Congress with overwhelming popular support in order to meet a comparable national emergency.

The *Perry Case,* which involved government obligations, illustrates the Court's ability to bow to expediency and to impart new meanings to legal terms in order to meet an unalterable *de facto* situation. The *Norman Case,* on the other hand, which involved private contracts, hit at the very heart of the Fifth Amendment. As Mr. Justice Mc-Reynolds said in his dissenting opinion, "the Fifth Amendment limits all governmental powers." It qualifies all the substantive powers of Congress and the powers implied from them. If Congress by direct action—the joint resolution abrogating the gold clauses—

can destroy contract rights, of what efficacy is "due process"? "Contracts, however express," said the chief justice, "cannot fetter the constitutional authority of the Congress." It would seem to follow then that Congress may exert its lawful powers notwithstanding the effect upon vested rights.

2. THE GOVERNMENT AND THE PEOPLE'S MONEY[6]

THE POWER TO TAX

Resistance to taxation, as every schoolboy knows, has been a powerful factor in English and American history. In conjunction with the religious question, it precipitated in seventeenth-century England the long revolution which ultimately established the sovereignty of Parliament; and it was the vital issue in the conflict between the landowning and commercial oligarchy of England and the thirteen colonies which led to their armed secession and the eventual independence of the United States of America. Yet despite this strong tradition, and a Constitution so framed and interpreted as to afford the maximum protection to private property, in no other field is the authority of the federal government less encumbered by constitutional limitations than in taxing, spending, coining money and regulating its value. It is true that the power to tax and its derivative, the power to spend, as well as the power "to coin money" and "regulate the value thereof," are deemed subject to the Fifth Amendment, which decrees, among other things, that the federal government shall not deprive any person of his liberty or property without due process of law. But the efficacy of the "due process" clause as a curb on these particular powers and a safeguard of fiscal security has been inferior to its restrictive effect on the other substantive powers of Congress. The following discussion will attempt to substantiate this thesis and to appraise briefly its far-reaching implications.

The taxing power, the first in the list of powers expressly delegated to Congress, is couched in the following language:

The Congress shall have power to lay and collect taxes, duties, imposts and excises to pay the debts and provide for the common defense and general welfare of the United States; but all duties, imposts and excises shall be uniform throughout the United States.

[6] The first selection and the paragraphs preceding the report of *United States* v. *Butler* are from the chapter by the above title in Dean Alfange's *The Supreme Court and the National Will*, pp. 171–188, and are reproduced by permission of the author.

It has been argued by staunch nationalists that this provision gave to Congress two separate and distinct substantive powers: (1) the power to lay and collect taxes, and (2) the power to provide for the common defense and general welfare of the United States. The opponents of this view, however, have pointed to the syntax and punctuation of the provision, and to the intent of its framers as disclosed by the proceedings of the Constitutional Convention. They have contended, moreover, that the reading of an independent grant of power into the "general welfare" clause would be inconsistent with the fundamental purpose of the Constitution, for it would tend to create a national government vested with general and unlimited powers. "Congress," said Jefferson, "are not to lay taxes *ad libitum,* for any purpose they please; but only to pay the debts or provide for the welfare of the Union. In like manner they are not to do any thing they please, to provide for the general welfare; but only to lay taxes for that purpose. To consider the latter phrase, not as describing the purpose of the first, but as giving a distinct and independent power to do any act they please, which might be for the good of the Union, would render all the preceding and subsequent enumerations of power completely useless. It would reduce the whole instrument to a single phrase, that of instituting a congress with power to do whatever would be for the good of the United States; and, as they would be the sole judges of the good or evil, it would also be a power to do whatever evil they pleased."

Hence, the words "and provide for the common defense and general welfare," read in sequential conjunction with "to pay the debts," have come to be construed as specifying the second and third of the purposes of federal taxation, and, therefore, as a limitation on the taxing power. According to Justice Story's illuminating paraphrase, the subsection in question should be understood to say that "the Congress shall have power to lay and collect taxes . . . *in order* to pay the debts, and to provide for the common defense and general welfare of the United States." This reading leaves no doubt as to the dependence of the "general welfare" clause on the part of the subsection immediately preceding it. In the words of the same authoritative commentator: "A power to lay taxes for any purposes whatever is a general power; a power to lay taxes for certain specified purposes is a limited power. A power to lay taxes for the common defense and general welfare . . . is not in common sense a general power. It is limited to those objects."

With this much conceded, it is obvious that the extent to which Congress may tax and spend in order to provide for the *general welfare* depends on the meaning of these two words. As was to be expected, the strict-constructionists have advocated such an interpretation as would confine taxing and spending under the "general welfare" clause to those activities which the Constitution specifically delegates to the national legislature. "Whenever . . . money has been raised by the general authority," said Madison, "and is to be applied to a particular measure, a question arises whether the particular measure be within the enumerated authorities vested in Congress. If it be, the money requisite for it may be applied to it. If it be not, no such application can be made." This narrow interpretation, however, would have precluded any expenditure from the national treasury for roads, canals, and other internal improvements; and it was therefore practically abandoned by Madison's successor. When Justice Story wrote his Commentaries, he was describing the actual "practice of the government" when he said: "Appropriations have never been limited by Congress to cases falling within the specific powers enumerated in the Constitution, whether those powers be construed in their broad or in their narrow sense. And in an especial manner appropriations have been made to aid internal improvements of various sorts, in our roads, our navigation, our streams, and other objects of a national character and importance."

With the Supreme Court following presidential and congressional leadership to a greater extent in the domain of taxing and spending than in any other department of constitutional law, the taxing power has come to be qualified only in the sense that it must be exercised for the purpose of providing for the general welfare. This means, in theory at least, that Congress cannot collect taxes from all or part of the people and apply them for the private benefit of individuals or groups. But if taxes are collected for a *public* purpose, there is no limit to the taxing power, regardless of whether it is exercised for the purpose of revenue, regulation or even destruction of the thing taxed. This is true despite Chief Justice Marshall's dictum that "the power to tax is the power to destroy," which can be construed as a limitation on the taxing power only when torn from its context. "But this reasoning," said the Court in *Knowlton* v. *Moore*,[7] referring to Marshall's celebrated aphorism, "has no application to a lawful tax, for if it had there would be an end to all taxation; that is to say, if a lawful tax

[7] 178 U.S. 41 (1900).

can be defeated because the power which is manifested by its imposition may when further exercised be destructive, it would follow that every lawful tax would become unlawful, and therefore no taxation whatever could be levied." This was an elaboration of the principle that the destructive potentialities of a given tax do not constitute any limitation of the taxing power. In the concise language of Justice Swayne, "the right of taxation where it exists, is necessarily unlimited in its nature. It carries with it inherently the power to embarrass and destroy."

The constitutional muniments of private property have been of relatively little avail against this all-embracing scope of the taxing power, and there is no clearer evidence of this fact than the decisions of the Court itself. The opinion rendered in *Veazie Bank* v. *Fenno*[8] was one of the earlier indications of the vast purview of this power. In that case the Supreme Court was called upon to review an act of Congress imposing a 10 per cent tax on the notes of state banks with a view to restraining their circulation and thus establishing a uniform national currency. The Veazie Bank contended that the imposition of this tax impaired its franchise, granted by the state; but the Court, while admitting the possible validity of this contention, refused to enjoin Congress by invoking the "contract" or "due process" clause. Chief Justice Chase proclaimed the supremacy of the congressional taxing prerogative in the following words:

It is insisted, however, that the tax in the case before us is excessive, and so excessive as to indicate a purpose on the part of Congress to destroy the franchise of the bank, and is, therefore, beyond the constitutional power of Congress. The first answer to this is that the judicial cannot prescribe to the legislative departments of the government limitations upon the exercise of its acknowledged powers. The power to tax may be exercised oppressively upon persons, but the responsibility of the legislature is not to the courts, but to the people by whom its members are elected. So if a particular tax bears heavily upon a corporation, or a class of corporations, it cannot, for that reason only, be pronounced contrary to the Constitution.

The only constitutional barriers to the taxing power were defined by the same chief justice in the *License Tax Cases*[9] as follows: "It is true that the power of Congress to tax is a very extensive power. It is

[8] See *infra*, p. 167.
[9] 5 Wall. 462 (1866).

given in the Constitution, with only one exception and only two qualifications. Congress cannot tax exports, and it must impose direct taxes by the rule of apportionment, and indirect taxes by the rule of uniformity. Thus limited, and thus only, it reaches every subject and may be exercised at discretion."

This means that the taxing power may be exercised not only despite the consequent impairment of contractual obligations but with scant regard to "due process.". . . With respect to the taxing power . . ."due process" has been shorn of its efficacy. The extent of its emasculation is made clear in the following exerpt from Justice White's opinion in *McCray* v. *United States*[10]:

Whilst undoubtedly both the Fifth and Tenth Amendments qualify, insofar as they are applicable, all the provisions of the Constitution, nothing in those amendments operates to take away the grant of power to tax conferred by the Constitution upon Congress. . . . The right of Congress to tax within its delegated power being unrestricted, except as limited by the Constitution, it was within the authority conferred on Congress to select the objects upon which an excise should be laid. It therefore follows that, in exerting its power, no want of due process of law could possibly result. . . . The judicial power may not usurp the functions of the legislative in order to control that branch of the government in the performance of its lawful duties. . . . The judiciary is without authority to avoid an act of Congress exerting the taxing power, even in a case where to the judicial mind it seems that Congress had in putting such power in motion abused its lawful authority by levying a tax which was unwise or oppressive, or the result of the enforcement of which might be to indirectly affect subjects not within the powers delegated to Congress.

VEAZIE BANK v. FENNO
8 Wall. 533 (1869)

[Following the issuance of legal tender notes by the United States, Congress placed a tax of 10 percent on all notes issued by state and national banks. The Veazie Bank, under a charter granted by the state of Maine, had issued notes and placed them in circulation. Compelled to pay the new federal tax thereon, it had done so under protest and then sued Fenno, the Collector of Internal Revenue, to recover its payment on the ground that the Act of Congress violated the Constitution.]

Mr. Chief Justice CHASE delivered the opinion of the Court. . . .

[10] *Infra*, p. 170.

The general question now before us is, whether or not the tax of ten per cent., imposed on State banks or National banks paying out the notes of individuals or State banks used for circulation, is repugnant to the Constitution of the United States.

In support of the position that the act of Congress, so far as it provides for the levy and collection of this tax, is repugnant to the Constitution, two propositions have been argued with much force and earnestness.

The first is that the tax in question is a direct tax, and has not been apportioned among the States agreeably to the Constitution.

The second is that the act imposing the tax impairs a franchise granted by the State, and that Congress has no power to pass any law with that intent or effect.

The first of these propositions will be first examined. . . .

Much diversity of opinion has always prevailed upon the question, what are direct taxes? Attempts to answer it by reference to the definitions of political economists have been frequently made, but without satisfactory results. The enumeration of the different kinds of taxes which Congress was authorized to impose was probably made with little reference to their speculations. . . .

We are obliged therefore to resort to historical evidence, and to seek the meaning of the words in the use and in the opinion of those whose relations to the government, and means of knowledge, warranted them in speaking with authority.

And considered in this light, the meaning and application of the rule, as to direct taxes, appears to us quite clear.

It is, as we think, distinctly shown in every act of Congress on the subject. . . .

. . . This review [of Congressional statutes] shows that personal property, contracts, occupations, and the like have never been regarded by Congress as proper subjects of direct tax. . . .

. . . And it may further be taken as established . . . that the words direct taxes, as used in the Constitution, comprehended only capitation taxes, and taxes on land, and perhaps taxes on personal property by general valuation and assessment of the various descriptions possessed within the several States.

It follows necessarily that the power to tax without apportionment extends to all other objects. Taxes on other objects are included under the heads of taxes not direct, duties, imposts, and excises, and must be laid and collected by the rule of uniformity. The tax under consideration is a tax on bank circulation, and may very well be classed under the head of duties. Certainly it is not, in the sense of the Constitution, a direct tax. It may be said to come within the same category of taxation as the tax on incomes of insurance companies, which this Court, at the last term, in the case of *Pacific Insurance Company* v. *Soule,* 7 Wallace, 433, held not to be a direct tax.

.   .   .   .   .

It is insisted, however, that the tax in the case before us is excessive, and so excessive as to indicate a purpose on the part of Congress to destroy the franchise of the bank, and is, therefore, beyond the constitutional power of Congress.

The first answer to this is that the judicial cannot prescribe to the legislative department of the government limitations upon the exercise of its acknowledged powers. The power to tax may be exercised oppressively upon persons, but the responsibility of the legislature is not to the courts, but to the people by whom its members are elected. So if a particular tax bears heavily upon a corporation, or a class of corporations, it cannot, for that reason only, be pronounced contrary to the Constitution.

But there is another answer which vindicates equally the wisdom and the power of Congress.

It cannot be doubted that under the Constitution the power to provide a circulation of coin is given to Congress. And it is settled by the uniform practice of the government and by repeated decisions, that Congress may constitutionally authorize the emission of bills of credit. It is not important here, to decide whether the quality of legal tender in payment of debts, can be constitutionally imparted to those bills; it is enough to say, that there can be no question of the power of the government to emit them; to make them receivable in payment of debts to itself; to fit them for use by those who see fit to use them in all the transactions of commerce; to provide for their redemption; to make them a currency, uniform in value and description, and convenient and useful for circulation. These powers, until recently, were only partially and occasionally exercised. Lately, however, they have been called into full activity, and Congress has undertaken to supply a currency for the entire country.

.   .   .   .

Having thus, in the exercise of undisputed constitutional powers, undertaken to provide a currency for the whole country, it cannot be questioned that Congress may, constitutionally, secure the benefit of it to the people by appropriate legislation. To this end, Congress has denied the quality of legal tender to foreign coins, and has provided by law against the imposition of counterfeit and base coin on the community. To the same end, Congress may restrain, by suitable enactment, the circulation as money of any notes not issued under its own authority. Without this power, indeed, its attempts to secure a sound and uniform currency for the country must be futile.

Viewed in this light, as well as in the other light of a duty on contracts or property, we cannot doubt the constitutionality of the tax under consideration. . . .

Mr. Justice NELSON, with whom concurred Mr. Justice DAVIS, dissenting. . . .

McCRAY v. UNITED STATES
195 U.S. 27 (1904)

The United States sued McCray for a statutory penalty of $50, alleging that, being a licensed retail dealer in oleomargarine, he had, in violation of the acts of Congress (1886, 24 Stat. 200 and its amendment, 1902, 32 Stat. 93), knowingly purchased for resale a fifty-pound package of oleomargarine, artificially colored to look like butter, to which there were affixed internal revenue stamps at the rate of onefourth of a cent a pound, upon which the law required stamps at the rate of ten cents per pound. The answer of McCray . . . set up two defenses.

First . . . It was asserted that whilst it was true that the oleomargarine . . . was of a yellow color, that this result was not caused by artificial coloration, but was solely occasioned by the fact that the butter which was bought in the open market and used in making the oleomargarine had a deep yellow color imparted to it (the butter) by a substance known as Wells-Richardson's improved butter color. . . .

Second. If the act of Congress imposing the tax, when rightfully construed, required stamps at the rate of ten cents per pound upon oleomargarine, colored as described in the first defense, the act levying such tax was charged to be repugnant to the Constitution of the United States. . . .

Mr. Justice WHITE, after making the foregoing statement, delivered the opinion of the Court. . . .

Whilst, as a result of our written constitution, it is axiomatic that the judicial department of the government is charged with the solemn duty of enforcing the Constitution, and therefore in cases properly presented, of determining whether a given manifestation of authority has exceeded the power conferred by that instrument, no instance is afforded from the foundation of the government where an act, which was within a power conferred, was declared to be repugnant to the Constitution, because it appeared to the judicial mind that the particular exertion of constitutional power was either unwise or unjust. . . . So to hold . . . would be a mere act of judicial usurpation.

It is, however, argued if a lawful power may be exerted for an unlawful purpose, and thus by abusing the power it may be made to accomplish a result not intended by the Constitution, all limitations of power must disappear, and the grave function lodged in the judiciary, to confine all the departments within the authority conferred by the Constitution, will be of no avail. . . . But this reduces itself to the contention that, under our constitutional system, the abuse by one department of the government of its lawful powers is to be corrected by the abuse of its powers by another department. . . .

It is, of course, true, as suggested, that if there be no authority in the judiciary to restrain a lawful exercise of power by another department of the government, where a wrong motive or purpose has impelled to the exertion of the power, that abuses of a power conferred may be temporarily effectual. The remedy for this, however, lies, not in the abuse by the judicial authority of its functions, but in the people, upon whom, after all, under our institutions, reliance must be placed for the correction of abuses committed in the exercise of a lawful power.

. . . . .

It being thus demonstrated that the motive or purpose of Congress in adopting the acts in question may not be inquired into, we are brought to consider the contentions relied upon to show that the acts assailed were beyond the power of Congress, putting entirely out of view all considerations based upon purpose or motive.

1. Undoubtedly, in determining whether a particular act is within a granted power, its scope and effect are to be considered. Applying this rule to the acts assailed, it is self-evident that on their face they levy an excise tax. That being their necessary scope and operation, it

follows that the acts are within the grant of power. The argument to the contrary rests on the proposition that, although the tax be within the power, as enforcing it will destroy or restrict the manufacture of artificially colored margarine, therefore the power to levy the tax did not obtain. This, however, is but to say that the question of power depends, not upon the authority conferred by the Constitution, but upon what may be the consequence arising from the exercise of the lawful authority.

Since . . . the taxing power conferred by the Constitution knows no limits except those expressly stated in that instrument, it must follow, if a tax be within the lawful power, the exertion of that power may not be judicially restrained because of the results to arise from its exercise. . . .

2. The proposition that where a tax is imposed which is within the grant of powers, and which does not conflict with any express constitutional limitation, the courts may hold the tax to be void because it is deemed that the tax is too high, is absolutely disposed of by the opinions in the cases. . . .

3. Whilst undoubtedly both the Fifth and Tenth Amendments qualify, in so far as they are applicable, all the provisions of the Constitution, nothing in those amendments operates to take away the grant of power to tax conferred by the Constitution upon Congress. . . .

The right of Congress to tax within its delegated power being unrestrained, except as limited by the Constitution, it was within the authority conferred on Congress to select the objects upon which an excise should be laid. It therefore follows that, in exerting its power, no want of due process of law could possibly result, because that body chose to impose an excise on artificially colored oleomargarine and not upon natural butter artificially colored. . . .

.   .   .   .   .

4. Lastly we come to consider the argument that, even though as a general rule a tax of the nature of the one in question would be within the power of Congress, in this case the tax should be held not to be within such power, because of its effect. This is based on the contention that, as the tax is so large as to destroy the business of manufacturing oleomargarine artificially colored to look like butter it thus deprives the manufacturers of that article of their freedom to engage in a lawful pursuit, and hence, irrespective of the distribution of powers made by the Constitution, the taxing laws are void, because

they violate those fundamental rights which it is the duty of every free government to safeguard, and which, therefore, should be held to be embraced by implied though none the less potential guaranties, or in any event to be within the protection of the due process clause of the Fifth Amendment.

Let us concede, for the sake of argument only, the premise of fact upon which the proposition is based. . . .

Such concession, however, is not controlling in this case. This follows when the nature of oleomargarine, artificially colored to look like butter, is recalled. As we have said, it has been conclusively settled by this Court that the tendency of that article to deceive the public into buying it for butter is such that the States may, in the exertion of their police powers, without violating the due process clause of the Fourteenth Amendment, absolutely prohibit the manufacture of the article. It hence results, that even although it be true that the effect of the tax in question is to repress the manufacture of artificially colored oleomargarine, it cannot be said that such repression destroys rights which no free government could destroy, and, therefore, no ground exists to sustain the proposition that the judiciary may invoke an implied prohibition, upon the theory that to do so is essential to save such rights from destruction. And the same considerations dispose of the contention based upon the due process clause of the Fifth Amendment. . . .

Let us concede that if a case was presented where the abuse of the taxing power was so extreme as to be beyond the principles which we have previously stated, and where it was plain to the judicial mind that the power had been called into play not for revenue but solely for the purpose of destroying rights which could not be rightfully destroyed consistently with the principles of freedom and justice upon which the Constitution rests, that it would be the duty of the courts to say that such an arbitrary act was not merely an abuse of a delegated power, but was the exercise of an authority not conferred. This concession, however, like the one previously made, must be without influence upon the decision of this cause for the reasons previously stated; that is, that the manufacture of artificially colored oleomargarine may be prohibited by a free government without a violation of fundamental rights.[11]

- - - - - -

[11] The oleomargarine tax was repealed in 1950. Public Law 459, 81st Cong., 2d Session, approved March 16, 1950.

The Chief Justice [FULLER], Mr. Justice BROWN and Mr. Justice PECKHAM dissent.

SONZINSKY v. UNITED STATES
300 U.S. 506 (1937)

Mr. Justice STONE delivered the opinion of the Court.

The question for decision is whether Section 2 of the National Firearms Act of June 26, 1934, . . . which imposes a $200 annual license tax on dealers in firearms, is a constitutional exercise of the legislative power of Congress. . . .

Section 2 of the National Firearms Act requires every dealer in firearms to register with the Collector of Internal Revenue in the district where he carries on business, and to pay a special excise tax of $200 a year. Importers or manufacturers are taxed $500 a year. Section 3 imposes a tax of $200 on each transfer of a firearm, payable by the transferor, and Section 4 prescribes regulations for the identification of purchasers. The term "firearm" is defined by Section 1 as meaning a shotgun or a rifle having a barrel less than eighteen inches in length, or any other weapon, except a pistol or revolver, from which a shot is discharged by an explosive, if capable of being concealed on the person, or a machine gun, and includes a muffler or silencer for any firearm. . . . Section 16 declares that the provisions of the Act are separable. Each tax is on a different activity and is collectible independently of the other. . . .

In the exercise of its constitutional power to lay taxes, Congress may select the subjects of taxation, choosing some and omitting others. . . . Its power extends to the imposition of excise taxes upon the doing of business. . . . Petitioner does not deny that Congress may tax his business as a dealer in firearms. He insists that the present levy is not a true tax, but a penalty imposed for the purpose of suppressing traffic in a certain noxious type of firearms, the local regulation of which is reserved to the states because not granted to the national government. To establish its penal and prohibitive character, he relies on the amounts of the tax imposed by Section 2 on dealers, manufacturers and importers, and of the tax imposed by Section 3 on each transfer of a "firearm," payable by the transferor. The cumulative effect on the distribution of a limited class of firearms, of relatively small value, by the successive imposition of different taxes, one on the business of the importer or manufacturer, another on that of the dealer, and a third on the transfer to a buyer, is said to be prohibitive in effect and to disclose unmistakably the legislative purpose to regulate rather than to tax.

The case is not one where the statute contains regulatory provisions related to a purported tax in such a way as has enabled this Court to say in other cases that the latter is a penalty resorted to as a means of enforcing the regulations. See *Child Labor Tax Case*, 259 U.S. 20, 35; *Hill* v. *Wallace*, 259 U.S. 44; *Carter* v. *Carter Coal Co.*, 298 U.S. 238. Nor is the subject of the tax described or treated as criminal by the taxing statute. . . . Here Section 2 contains no regulation other than the mere registration provisions, which are obviously supportable as in aid of a revenue purpose. On its face it is only a taxing measure, and we are asked to say that the tax, by virtue of its deterrent effect on the activities taxed, operates as a regulation which is beyond the congressional power.

Every tax is in some measure regulatory. To some extent it interposes an economic impediment to the activity taxed as compared with others not taxed. But a tax is not any the less a tax because it has a regulatory effect . . . and it has long been established that an Act of Congress which on its face purports to be an exercise of the taxing power is not any the less so because the tax is burdensome or tends to restrict or suppress the thing taxed. . . . *McCray* v. *United States*, 195 U.S. 27, 60–61. . . .

Here the annual tax of $200 is productive of some revenue. We are not free to speculate as to the motives which moved Congress to impose it, or as to the extent to which it may operate to restrict the activities taxed. As it is not attended by an offensive regulation, and since it operates as a tax, it is within the national taxing power. . . .

[The conviction of Sonzinsky, on a charge of dealing in firearms without payment of the tax, was affirmed.]

THE POWER TO SPEND[12]

The spending power, though not expressly granted, is, paradoxically, even broader than the taxing power from which it is impliedly derived. Once the money collected by taxation goes into the treasury, there is no way to question by court action the validity of the method by which it is spent. And though the spending of public money may vitally affect contracts and property rights, there is no way by which

[12] From Dean Alfange, *The Supreme Court and the National Will*.

the person affected may invoke the protection of "due process" or the "contract clause." It is true that attempts in this direction have been made, but the Court has repeatedly refused jurisdiction in such cases. Moreover, congressional spending without judicial restraint has been the practice for so long that it has become one of the firmly established conventions of the American system, and it is extremely doubtful that the Court at this late stage will attempt to disturb it. The principle of judicial noninterference with federal spending was stated most categorically in the case of *Massachusetts* v. *Mellon*[13] which involved the so-called Maternity Act passed by Congress in 1921. The act was challenged and an attempt was made to restrain the appropriations provided therein on the ground that they were intended for local, and not for national, purposes and hence constituted an invasion of the powers reserved to the states under the Tenth Amendment. The Court, however, speaking through Mr. Justice Sutherland, dismissed the cases and refused to consider the constitutional issues involved with the following conclusive argument:

The right of a taxpayer to enjoin the execution of a Federal appropriation act, on the ground that it is invalid and will result in taxation for illegal purposes, has never been passed upon by this Court. In cases where it was presented, the question has either been allowed to pass sub silentio, or the determination of it expressly withheld. . . . If one taxpayer may champion and litigate such a cause, then every other taxpayer may do the same, not only in respect to the statute here under review, but also in respect of every other appropriation act and statute whose administration requires the outlay of public money, and whose validity may be questioned. The bare suggestion of such a result, with its attendant inconveniences, goes far to sustain the conclusion which we have reached, that a suit of this character cannot be maintained. It is of much significance that no precedent sustaining the right to maintain suits like this has been called to our attention although since the formation of the government, as an examination of the acts of Congress will disclose, a large number of statutes appropriating or involving the expenditure of moneys for non-Federal purposes have been enacted and carried into effect.

The Court's readiness to seize almost any pretext in order to avoid the issue is a gauge of the unfettered power of Congress to spend for any purpose and the futility of attempting to frustrate this established and popular prerogative by judicial action. The Court has appar-

13 262 U.S. 447 (1922).

ently made up its mind not to attempt to exercise any restraint beyond the constitutional limitation of Article I, Section 9, Subsection 7, which provides that "no money shall be drawn from the treasury, but in consequence of appropriations made by law." Once the appropriation has been duly made, Congress may draw upon the treasury for any purpose that the legislators may judge to be within the ambit of the general welfare. This was precisely the conception of the "general welfare" clause expounded by Hamilton. "The terms 'general welfare'," he said, "were doubtless intended to signify more than was expressed or imported in those which preceded; otherwise numerous exigencies incident to the force of a nation would have been left without provision. The phrase is as comprehensive as any that could have been used, because it is not fit that the constitutional authority of the Union to appropriate its revenues should have been restricted within narrower limits than the 'general welfare,' and because this necessarily embraces a vast variety of particulars which are susceptible neither of specification nor of definition. It is therefore of necessity left to the discretion of the National Legislature to pronounce upon the subjects which concern the general welfare, and for which, under that description, an appropriation of money is requisite and proper."[14]

Though feints at challenge have been made, the Hamiltonian conception of the power to spend for the general welfare has never been upset by the Supreme Court, not even in the much misunderstood *Hoosac Mills Case (United States* v. *Butler)* which invalidated the AAA. For while the Court outlawed the processing taxes, it was powerless to stop the spending contemplated by the Agricultural Adjustment Act, and the government continued its benefit payments to farmers, notwithstanding the nullification of the whole plan.

· · · · ·

UNITED STATES v. BUTLER
297 U.S. 1 (1935)

Mr. Justice ROBERTS delivered the opinion of the Court.

In this case we must determine whether certain provisions of the Agricultural Adjustment Act, 1933, conflict with the Federal Constitution.

Title I of the statute is captioned "Agricultural Adjustment." Section 1 recites that an economic emergency has arisen, due to disparity between the prices of agricultural and other commodities,

[14] From the *Report on Manufactures*.

with consequent destruction of farmers' purchasing power and break-down in orderly exchange, which, in turn, have affected transactions in agricultural commodities with a national public interest and burdened and obstructed the normal currents of commerce, calling for the enactment of legislation.

Section 2 declares it to be the policy of Congress:

"To establish and maintain such balance between the production and consumption of agricultural commodities, and such marketing conditions therefor, as will reestablish prices to farmers at a level that will give agricultural commodities a purchasing power with respect to articles that farmers buy, equivalent to the purchasing power of agricultural commodities in the base period." . . .

Section 8 provides, amongst other things, that "in order to effectuate the declared policy," the Secretary of Agriculture shall have power

" (1) To provide for reduction in acreage or reduction in the production for market, or both, of any basic agricultural commodity, through agreements with producers or by other voluntary methods, and to provide for rental or benefit payments in connection therewith . . . to be payable out of any moneys available for such payments. . . .

"(2) To enter into marketing agreements with processors, associations of producers, and others engaged in the handling, in the current of interstate or foreign commerce of any agricultural commodity or product thereof. . . .

"(3) To issue licenses permitting processors, associations of producers, and others to engage in the handling, in the current of interstate or foreign commerce, of any agricultural commodity or product thereof, ..."

It will be observed that the Secretary is not required, but is permitted, if, in his uncontrolled judgment, the policy of the act will so be promoted, to make agreements with individual farmers for a reduction of acreage or production upon such terms as he may think fair and reasonable.

Section 9 (a) enacts:

"To obtain revenue for extraordinary expenses incurred by reason of the national economic emergency, there shall be levied processing taxes as hereinafter provided. When the Secretary of Agriculture determines that rental or benefit payments are to be made with respect to any basic agricultural commodity, he shall proclaim such determination, and a processing tax shall be in effect with respect to such commodity from the beginning of the marketing year therefor next following the date of such proclamation. The processing tax shall be levied, assessed, and collected upon the first domestic production of the commodity, . . . and shall be paid by the processor. . . ."

. . . . .

. . . Section 12 (b) appropriates the proceeds from all taxes imposed under the act "to be available to the Secretary of Agriculture for expansion of markets and removal of surplus agricultural products, . . . administrative expenses, rental and benefit payments, and refunds on taxes."

. . . . .

On July 14, 1933, the Secretary of Agriculture, with the approval of the President, proclaimed that he had determined rental and benefit payments should be made with respect to cotton; that the marketing year for that commodity was to begin August 1, 1933; and calculated and fixed the rates of processing and floor taxes on cotton in accordance with the terms of the act.

The United States presented a claim to the respondents as receivers of the Hoosac Mills Corporation for processing and floor taxes on cotton. . . . The receivers recommended that the claim be disallowed. The District Court found the taxes valid and ordered them paid. Upon appeal the Circuit Court of Appeals reversed the order. . . .

First. At the outset the United States contends that the respondents have no standing to question the validity of the tax. The position is that the act is merely a revenue measure levying an excise upon the activity of processing cotton,—a proper subject for the imposition of such a tax,—the proceeds of which go into the federal treasury and thus become available for appropriation for any purpose. . . .

The tax can only be sustained by ignoring the avowed purpose and operation of the act, and holding it a measure merely laying an excise upon processors to raise revenue for the support of government. Beyond cavil the sole object of the legislation is to restore the purchasing power of agricultural products to a parity with that prevailing in an earlier day; to take money from the processor for the accomplishment of the proposed end, and, meanwhile, to aid these farmers during the period required to bring the prices of their crops to the desired level.

The tax plays an indispensable part in the plan of regulation. . . .

A tax automatically goes into effect for a commodity when the Secretary of Agriculture determines that rental or benefit payments are to be made for reduction of production of that commodity. The tax is to cease when rental or benefit payments cease. . . .

The statute not only avows an aim foreign to the procurement of revenue for the support of government, but by its operation shows the exaction laid upon processors to be the necessary means for the intended control of agricultural production. . . .

It is inaccurate and misleading to speak of the exaction from processors prescribed by the challenged act as a tax, or to say that as a tax it is subject to no infirmity. A tax, in the general understanding of the term, and as used in the Constitution, signifies an exaction for the support of the Government. The word has never been thought to connote the expropriation of money from one group for the benefit of another. We may concede that the latter sort of imposition is constitutional when imposed to effectuate regulation of a matter in which both groups are interested and in respect of which there is a power of legislation. But manifestly no justification for it can be found unless as an integral part of such regulation. The exaction cannot be wrested out of its setting, denominated an excise for raising revenue and legalized by ignoring its purpose as a mere instrumentality for bringing about a desired end. To do this would be to shut our eyes to what all others than we can see and understand. *Child Labor Tax Case,* 259 U.S. 20, 37.

We conclude that the act is one regulating agricultural production; that the tax is a mere incident of such regulation and that the respondents have standing to challenge the legality of the exaction.

It does not follow that as the act is not an exertion of the taxing power and the exaction not a true tax, the statute is void or the exaction uncollectible. For, to paraphrase what was said in the *Head Money Cases*[15] if this is an expedient regulation by Congress, of a subject within one of its granted powers, "and the end to be attained is one falling within that power, the act is not void, because, within a loose and more extended sense than was used in the Constitution," the exaction is called a tax.

Second. The Government asserts that even if the respondents may question the propriety of the appropriation embodied in the statute their attack must fail because Article I, Section 8 of the Constitution authorizes the contemplated expenditure of the funds raised by the

[15] 112 U.S. 580 (1884).

tax. This contention presents the great and the controlling question in the case. We approach its decision with a sense of our grave responsibility to render judgment in accordance with the principles established for the governance of all three branches of the Government.

There should be no misunderstanding as to the function of this Court in such a case. It is sometimes said that the Court assumes a power to overrule or control the action of the people's representatives. This is a misconception. The Constitution is the supreme law of the land ordained and established by the people. All legislation must conform to the principles it lays down. When an act of Congress is appropriately challenged in the courts as not conforming to the constitutional mandate the judicial branch of the Government has only one duty,—to lay the article of the Constitution which is invoked beside the statute which is challenged and to decide whether the latter squares with the former. All the Court does, or can do, is to announce its considered judgment upon the question. The only power it has, if such it may be called, is the power of judgment. This Court neither approves nor condemns any legislative policy. Its delicate and difficult office is to ascertain and declare whether the legislation is in accordance with, or in contravention of, the provisions of the Constitution; and, having done that, its duty ends.

The question is not what power the Federal Government ought to have but what powers in fact have been given by the people. It hardly seems necessary to reiterate that ours is a dual form of government; that in every state there are two governments,—the state and the United States. Each State has all governmental powers save such as the people, by their Constitution, have conferred upon the United States, denied to the States, or reserved to themselves. The federal union is a government of delegated powers. It has only such as are expressly conferred upon it and such as are reasonably to be implied from those granted. In this respect we differ radically from nations where all legislative power, without restriction or limitation, is vested in a parliament or other legislative body subject to no restrictions except the discretion of its members.

Article I, Section 8, of the Constitution vests sundry powers in the Congress. But two of its clauses have any bearing upon the validity of the statute under review.

The third clause endows the Congress with power "to regulate Commerce . . . among the several States." Despite a reference in its first section to a burden upon, and an obstruction of the normal currents of commerce, the act under review does not purport to regulate transactions in interstate or foreign commerce. Its stated purpose is the control of agricultural production, a purely local activity, in an effort to raise the prices paid the farmer. Indeed, the Government does not attempt to uphold the validity of the act on the basis of the commerce clause, which, for the purpose of the present case, may be put aside as irrelevant.

The clause thought to authorize the legislation—the first,—confers upon the Congress power "to lay and collect Taxes, Duties, Imposts and Excises, to pay the Debts and provide for the common Defence and general Welfare of the United States. . . ." It is not contended that this provision grants power to regulate agricultural production upon the theory that such legislation would promote the general welfare. The Government concedes that the phrase "to provide for the general welfare" qualifies the power "to lay and collect taxes." The view that the clause grants power to provide for the general welfare, independently of the taxing power, has never been authoritatively accepted. . . . The true construction undoubtedly is that the only thing granted is the power to tax for the purpose of making funds for payment of the nation's debts and making provisions for the general welfare.

Nevertheless the Government asserts that warrant is found in this clause for the adoption of the Agricultural Adjustment Act. The argument is that Congress may appropriate and authorize the spending of moneys for the "general welfare"; that the phrase should be liberally construed to cover anything conducive to national welfare; that decision as to what will promote such welfare rests with Congress alone, and the courts may not review its determination; and finally that the appropriation under attack was in fact for the general welfare of the United States. The Congress is expressly empowered to lay taxes to provide for the general welfare. . . .

Since the foundation of the Nation sharp differences of opinion have persisted as to the true interpretation of the phrase. Madison asserted it amounted to no more than a reference to the other powers enumerated in the subsequent clauses of the same section; that, as the United States is a government of limited and enumerated powers, the grant of power to tax and spend for the general national welfare must be confined to the enumerated legislative fields committed to the Congress. In this view the phrase is mere tautology, for taxation and appropriation are or may be necessary incidents to the exercise of any of the enumerated legislative powers. Hamilton, on the other hand, maintained the clause confers a power separate and distinct from those later enumerated, is not restricted in meaning by the grant of them, and Congress consequently has a substantive power to tax and to appropriate, limited only by the requirement that it shall be exercised to provide for the general welfare of the United States. Each contention has had the support of those whose views are entitled to great weight. This Court has noticed the question, but has never found it necessary to decide which is the true construction. Mr. Justice Story, in his Commentaries espouses the Hamiltonian position. We shall not review the writings of public men and commentators or discuss the legislative practice. Study of all these leads us to conclude that the reading advocated by Mr. Justice Story is the correct one. While, therefore, the power to tax is not unlimited, its confines are set in the clause which confers it, and not in those of Section 8 which bestow and define the legislative powers of the Congress. It results that the power of Congress to authorize expenditure of public moneys for public purposes is not limited by the direct grants of legislative power found in the Constitution.

.   .   .   .   .

We are not now required to ascertain the scope of the phrase "general welfare of the United States" or to determine whether an appropriation in aid of agriculture falls within it. Wholly apart from that question, another principle enbedded in our Constitution prohibits the enforcement of the Agricultural Adjustment Act. The act invades the reserved rights of the states. It is a statutory plan to regulate and control agricultural production, a matter beyond the powers delegated to the federal government. The tax, the appropriation of the funds raised, and the direction for their disbursement, are but parts of the plan. They are but means to an unconstitutional end.

From the accepted doctrine that the United States is a government of delegated powers, it follows that those not expressly granted, or reasonably to be implied from such as are conferred, are reserved to the states or to the people. To forestall any suggestion to the contrary, the Tenth Amendment was adopted. The same proposition, otherwise stated, is that powers not granted are prohibited. None to regulate agricultural production is given, and therefore legislation by Congress for that purpose is forbidden.

It is an established principle that the attainment of a prohibited end may not be accomplished under the pretext of the exertion of powers which are granted. . . .

The power of taxation, which is expressly granted, may, of course, be adopted as a means to carry into operation another power also expressly granted. But resort to the taxing power to effectuate an end which is not legitimate, not within the scope of the Constitution, is obviously inadmissible. . . .

Third. If the taxing power may not be used as the instrument to enforce a regulation of matters of state concern with respect to which the Congress has no authority to interfere, may it, as in the present case, be employed to raise the money necessary to purchase a compliance which the Congress is powerless to command? The Government asserts that whatever might be said against the validity of the plan if compulsory, it is constitutionally sound because the end is accomplished by voluntary cooperation. There are two sufficient answers to the contention. The regulation is not in fact voluntary. The farmer, of course, may refuse to comply, but the price of such refusal is the loss of benefits. The amount offered is intended to be sufficient to exert pressure on him to agree to the proposed regulation. The power to confer or withhold unlimited benefits is the power to coerce or destroy. If the cotton grower elects not to accept the benefits, he will receive less for his crops; those who receive payments will be able to undersell him. The result may well be financial ruin. The coercive purpose and intent of the statute is not obscured by the fact that it has not been perfectly successful. It is pointed out that, because there still remained a minority whom the rental and benefit payments were insufficient to induce to surrender their independence of action, the Congress has gone further and, in the Bankhead Cotton Act, used the taxing power in a more directly minatory fashion to compel submission. This progression only serves more fully to expose the coercive purpose of the so-called tax imposed by the present act. It is clear that the Department of Agriculture has properly described the plan as one to keep a non-cooperating minority in line. This is coercion by economic pressure. The asserted power of choice is illusory. . . .

But if the plan were one for purely voluntary cooperation it would stand no better so far as federal power is concerned. At best it is a scheme for purchasing with federal funds submission to federal regulation of a subject reserved to the states.

It is said that Congress has the undoubted right to appropriate money to executive officers for expenditure under contracts between the government and individuals; that much of the total expenditure is so made. But appropriations and expenditures under contracts for proper governmental purposes cannot justify contracts which are not within federal power. And contracts for the reduction of acreage and the control of production are outside the range of that power. An appropriation to be expended by the United States under contracts calling for violation of a state law clearly would offend the Constitution. Is a statute less objectionable which authorizes expenditure of federal moneys to induce action in a field in which the United States has no power to intermeddle? The Congress cannot invade state jurisdiction to compel individual action; no more can it purchase such action.

. . . . .

If the act before us is a proper exercise of the federal taxing power, evidently the regulation of all industry throughout the United States may be accomplished by similar exercises of the same power. It would be possible to exact money from one branch of an industry and pay it to another branch in every field of activity which lies within the province of the states. The mere threat of such a procedure might well induce the surrender of rights and the compliance with federal regulation as the price of continuance in business. . . .

. . . . .

Hamilton himself, the leading advocate of broad interpretation of the power to tax and to appropriate for the general welfare, never suggested that any power granted by the Constitution could be used for the destruction of local self-government in the states. Story countenances no such doctrine. It seems never to have occurred to them, that the general welfare of the United States, (which has aptly been termed "an indestructible Union, composed of indestructible States,") might be served by obliterating the constituent members of the Union. But to this fatal conclusion the doctrine contended for would inevitably lead. . . .

Mr. Justice STONE, dissenting. . . .

1. The power of courts to declare a statute unconstitutional is

subject to two guiding principles of decision which ought never to be absent from judicial consciousness. One is that courts are concerned only with the power to enact statutes, not with their wisdom. The other is that while unconstitutional exercise of power by the executive and legislative branches of the government is subject to judicial restraint, the only check upon our own exercise of power is our own sense of self-restraint. For the removal of unwise laws from the statute books appeal lies not to the courts but to the ballot and to the processes of democratic government.

2. The constitutional power of Congress to levy an excise tax upon the processing of agricultural products is not questioned. The present levy is held invalid, not for any want of power in Congress to lay such a tax to defray public expenditures, including those for the general welfare, but because the use to which its proceeds are put is disapproved.

3. As the present depressed state of agriculture is nation-wide in its extent and effects, there is no basis for saying that the expenditure of public money in aid of farmers is not within the specifically granted power of Congress to levy taxes to "provide for the . . . general welfare." The opinion of the Court does not declare otherwise.

.   .   .   .   .

It is with these preliminary and hardly controverted matters in mind that we should direct our attention to the pivot on which the decision of the Court is made to turn. It is that a levy unquestionably within the taxing power of Congress may be treated as invalid because it is a step in a plan to regulate agricultural production and is thus a forbidden infringement of the state power. . . .

.   .   .   .   .

The Constitution requires that public funds shall be spent for a defined purpose, the promotion of the general welfare. Their expenditure usually involves payment on terms which will insure use by the selected recipients within the limits of the constitutional purpose. Expenditures would fail of their purpose and thus lose their constitutional sanction if the terms of payment were not such that by their influence on the action of the recipients the permitted end would be attained. The power of Congress to spend is inseparable from persuasion to action over which Congress has no legislative control. Congress may not command that the science of agriculture be taught in state universities. But if it would aid the teaching of that science by grants to state institutions, it is appropriate, if not necessary, that the grant be on the condition . . . that it be used for the intended purpose. . . . It makes no difference that there is a promise to do an act which the condition is calculated to induce. Condition and promise are alike valid since both are in furtherance of the national purpose for which money is appropriated.

.   .   .   .   .

Congress through the Interstate Commerce Commission has set aside interstate railroad rates. It has made and destroyed intrastate industries by raising or lowering tariffs. These results are said to be permissible because they are incidents of the commerce power and the power to levy duties on imports. . . . The only conclusion to be drawn is that results become lawful when they are incidents of those powers but unlawful when incident to the similarly granted power to tax and spend.

Such a limitation is contradictory and destructive of the power to appropriate for the public welfare, and is incapable of practical application. The spending power of Congress is in addition to the legislative power and not subordinate to it. . . . It is a contradiction in terms to say that there is power to spend for the national welfare, while rejecting any power to impose conditions reasonably adapted to the attainment of the end which alone would justify the expenditure.

.   .   .   .

That the governmental power of the purse is a great one is not now for the first time announced. Every student of the history of government and economics is aware of its magnitude and of its existence in every civilized government. Both were well understood by the framers of the Constitution when they sanctioned the grant of the spending power to the federal government, and both were recognized by Hamilton and Story, whose views of the spending power as standing on a parity with the other powers specifically granted, have hitherto been generally accepted.

The suggestion that it must now be curtailed by judicial fiat because it may be abused by unwise use hardly rises to the dignity of the argument. So may judicial power be abused. . . .

. . . Courts are not the only agency of government that must be assumed to have capacity to govern. . . . But interpretation of our great charter of government which proceeds on any assumption that the responsibility for the preservation of our institutions is the exclusive concern of any one of the three branches of government, or that it alone can save them from destruction is far more likely, in the long run, "to obliterate the constituent members" of "an indestructible union of indestructible states" than the frank recognition that language, even of a constitution, may mean what it says: that the power to tax and spend includes the power to relieve a nation-wide economic maladjustment by conditional gifts of money.

Mr. Justice BRANDEIS and Mr. Justice CARDOZO join in this opinion.

HELVERING v. DAVIS
301 U.S. 619 (1937)

Mr. Justice CARDOZO delivered the opinion of the Court.

The Social Security Act . . . is challenged once again.

In *Steward Machine Co.* v. *Davis,* 301 U.S. 548, decided this day, we have upheld the validity of Title IX of the act, imposing an excise upon employers of eight or more. In this case Titles VIII and II are the subject of attack. Title VIII lays another excise upon employers in addition to the one imposed by Title IX (though with different exemptions). It lays a special income tax upon employees to be deducted from their wages and paid by the employers. Title II provides for the payment of Old Age Benefits, and supplies the motive and occasion, in the view of the assailants of the statute, for the levy of the taxes imposed by Title VIII. The plan of the two titles will now be summarized more fully.

Title VIII, as we have said, lays two different types of tax, an "income tax on employees," and "an excise tax on employers." The income tax on employees is measured by wages paid during the calendar year. . . . The excise tax on the employer is to be paid "with respect to having individuals in his employ," and, like the tax on employees, is measured by wages. . . . The two taxes are at the same rate. . . . In the computation of wages all remuneration is to be included except so much as is in excess of $3000 during the calendar year affected. . . . The proceeds of both taxes are to be paid into the Treasury like internal-revenue taxes generally, and not earmarked in any way. . . .

Title II has the caption "Federal Old-Age Benefits." The benefits are of two types, first, monthly pensions, and second, lump sum payments, the payments of the second class being relatively few and unimportant.

The first section of this title creates an account in the United States Treasury to be known as the "Old-Age Reserve Account." No present appropriation, however, is made to that account. . . .

Section 202 and later sections prescribe the form of benefits. The principal type is a monthly pension payable to a person after he has attained the age of 65. . . . In no event are they to exceed $85 a month. . . .

This suit is brought by [Davis] a shareholder of the Edison Electric Illuminating Company of Boston, a Massachusetts corporation, to restrain the corporation from making the payments and deductions called for by the act, which is stated to be void under the Constitution of the United States. . . .

First. [Whether Davis could properly challenge the payment of these taxes by the company; a majority held that he could.]

. . . . .

Second. The scheme of benefits created by the provisions of Title II is not in contravention of the limitations of the Tenth Amendment.

Congress may spend money in aid of the "general welfare." . . . There have been great statesmen in our history who have stood for other views. We will not resurrect the contest. It is now settled by decision. *United States* v. *Butler, [supra].* The conception of the spending power advocated by Hamilton and strongly reinforced by Story has prevailed over that of Madison, which has not been lacking in adherents. Yet difficulties are left when the power is conceded. The line must still be drawn between one welfare and another, between particular and general. Where this shall be placed cannot be known through a formula in advance of the event. There is a middle ground or certainly a penumbra in which discretion is at large. The discretion, however, is not confided to the courts. The discretion belongs to Congress, unless the choice is clearly wrong, a display of arbitrary power, not an exercise of judgment. This is now familiar law. "When such a contention comes here we naturally require a showing that by no reasonable possibility can the challenged legislation fall within the wide range of discretion permitted to the Congress." *United States* v. *Butler, [supra].* . . . Nor is the concept of the general welfare static. Needs that were narrow or parochial a century ago may be interwoven in our day with the well-being of the Nation. What is critical or urgent changes with the times.

The purge of nation-wide calamity that began in 1929 has taught us many lessons. Not the least is the solidarity of interests that may once have seemed to be divided. Unemployment spreads from State to State, the hinterland now settled that in pioneer days gave an avenue of escape. . . . Spreading from State to State, unemployment is an ill not particular but general, which may be checked, if Congress so determines, by the resources of the Nation. . . . But the ill is all one, or at least not greatly different, whether men are thrown out of work because there is no longer work to do or because the disabilities of age make them incapable of doing it. Rescue becomes necessary irrespective of the cause. The hope behind this statute is to save men and women from the rigors of the poor house as well as from the haunting fear that such a lot awaits them when journey's end is near.

Congress did not improvise a judgment when it found that the award of old age benefits would be conducive to the general welfare. . . . A great mass of evidence was brought together supporting the policy which finds expression in the act. Among the relevant facts are these: The number of persons in the United States 65 years of age or over is increasing proportionately as well as absolutely. What is even more important the number of such persons unable to take care of themselves is growing at a threatening pace. More and more our population is becoming urban and industrial instead of rural and agricultural. The evidence is impressive that among industrial workers the younger men and women are preferred over the older. In times of retrenchment the older are commonly the first to go, and even if retained, their wages are likely to be lowered. The plight of men and women at so low an age as 40 is hard, almost hopeless, when they are driven to seek for reemployment. Statistics are in the brief. . . .

The problem is plainly national in area and dimensions. Moreover, laws of the separate states cannot deal with it effectively. Congress, at least, had a basis for that belief. States and local governments are often lacking in the resources that are necessary to finance an adequate program of security for the aged. . . . Apart from the failure of resources, states and local governments are at times reluctant to increase so heavily the burden of taxation to be borne by their residents for fear of placing themselves in a position of economic disadvantage as compared with neighbors or competitors. . . . A system of old age pensions has special dangers of its own, if put in force in one state and rejected in another. The existence of such a system is a bait to the needy and dependent elsewhere, encouraging them to migrate and seek a haven of repose. Only a power that is national can serve the interests of all.

Whether wisdom or unwisdom resides in the scheme of benefits in Title II, it is not for us to say. . . . Counsel for respondent has recalled to us the virtues of self-reliance and frugality. . . . But the answer is not doubtful. . . . The issue is a closed one. It was fought out long ago. When money is spent to promote the general welfare, the concept of welfare or the opposite is shaped by Congress, not the states. So the concept be not arbitrary, the locality must yield. Constitution, Art. VI, § 2.

[Discussion of other points omitted.]

Mr. Justice McReynolds and Mr. Justice Butler are of opinion that the provisions of the Act here challenged are repugnant to the Tenth Amendment. . . .

CHAPTER VI

The Power to Govern[1]:
Interstate Commerce

1. A NATIONAL ECONOMY[2]

When victory relieved the Colonies from the pressure for solidarity that war had exerted, a drift toward anarchy and commercial warfare between states began. ". . . each State would legislate according to its estimate of its own interests, the importance of its own products, and the local advantages or disadvantages of its position in a political or commercial view." This came "to threaten at once the peace and safety of the Union." Story, *The Constitution*, §§ 259, 260. See Fiske, *The Critical Period of American History* 144; Warren, *The Making of the Constitution* 567. The sole purpose for which Virginia initiated the movement which ultimately produced the Constitution was "to take into consideration the trade of the United States; to examine the relative situations and trade of the said states; to consider how far a uniform system in their commercial regulation may be necessary to their common interest and their permanent harmony" and for that purpose the General Assembly of Virginia in January of 1786 named commissioners and proposed their meeting with those from other states. . . .

The desire of the Forefathers to federalize regulation of foreign and interstate commerce stands in sharp contrast to their jealous

[1] Walton H. Hamilton and Douglass Adair gave this title to their illuminating study of the commerce clause (New York: W. W. Norton & Co., 1937).

[2] From Mr. Justice Jackson's majority opinion in *Hood* v. *Du Mond*, 336 U.S. 525, 533–535, 538–539 (1949).

preservation of power over their internal affairs. No other federal power was so universally assumed to be necessary, no other state power was so readily relinquished. There was no desire to authorize federal interference with social conditions or legal institutions of the states. Even the Bill of Rights amendments were framed only as a limitation upon the powers of Congress. The states were quite content with their several and diverse controls over most matters but, as Madison has indicated, "want of a general power over Commerce led to an exercise of this power separately, by the States, which not only proved abortive, but engendered rival, conflicting and angry regulations." 3 Farrand, *Records of the Federal Convention* 547.

The necessity of centralized regulation of commerce among the states was so obvious and so fully recognized that the few words of the Commerce Clause were little illuminated by debate. But the significance of the clause was not lost and its effect was immediate and salutary. We are told by so responsible an authority as Mr. Jefferson's first appointee to this Court [Mr. Justice Johnson] that "there was not a State in the Union, in which there did not, at that time, exist a variety of commercial regulations; concerning which it is too much to suppose, that the whole ground covered by those regulations was immediately assumed by actual legislation, under the authority of the Union. But where was the existing statute on this subject, that a State attempted to execute? or by what State was it ever thought necessary to repeal those statutes? By common consent, these laws dropped lifeless from their statute books, for want of the sustaining power, that had been relinquished to Congress." *Gibbons* v. *Ogden,* 9 Wheat. (U.S.) 1, concurring opinion at 226.

The Commerce Clause is one of the most prolific sources of national power and an equally prolific source of conflict with legislation of the state. While the Constitution vests in Congress the power to regulate commerce among the states, it does not say what the states may or may not do in the absence of congressional action, nor how to draw the line between what is and what is not commerce among the states. Perhaps even more than by interpretation of its written word, this [the Supreme] Court has advanced the solidarity and prosperity of this Nation by the meaning it has given to these great silences of the Constitution.

The material success that has come to inhabitants of the states which make up this federal free trade unit has been the most impressive in the history of commerce, but the established interdependence of the states only emphasizes the necessity of protecting interstate movement of goods against local burdens and repressions. We need only consider the consequences if each of the few states that produce copper, lead, high-grade iron ore, timber, cotton, oil or gas should decree that industries located in that state shall have priority. What fantastic rivalries and dislocations and reprisals would ensue if such practices were begun! Or suppose that the field of discrimination and retaliation be industry. May Michigan provide that automobiles cannot be taken out of that State until local dealers' demands are fully met? . . . Could Ohio then pounce upon the rubber-tire industry, on which she has a substantial grip, to retaliate for Michigan's auto monopoly?

Our system, fostered by the Commerce Clause, is that every farmer and every craftsman shall be encouraged to produce by the certainty that he will have free access to every market in the Nation, that no home embargoes will withhold his export, and no foreign state will by customs duties or regulations exclude them. Likewise, every consumer may look to the free competition from every producing area in the Nation to protect him from exploitation by any. Such was the vision of the Founders; such has been the doctrine of this Court which has given it reality.

GIBBONS v. OGDEN
9 Wheat. 1 (1824)

[The subject of the controversy in this case, the first to elaborate upon the commerce clause, was the steamboat monopoly granted to Robert Livingston by the New York state legislature. It was the trend of the time to encourage inventors and entrepreneurs by the grant of exclusive privileges. Livingston, in partnership with the inventor Robert Fulton, had secured an exclusive franchise for steam navigation in New York waters even before the "Clairmont's" first successful trip. Subsequently he obtained similar rights in Louisiana, thus combining control of the steamboat traffic in the nation's two most important port cities, New York and New Orleans. Other individuals obtained monopolies for steam navigation from the state legislatures of Georgia, Massachusetts, New Hampshire, and Vermont. "These," says Albert J. Beveridge in his *Life of John Marshall*, "are some examples of the general tendency of States and the promoters of steam navigation to make commerce pay tribute to monopoly by the exercise of the sovereignty of States over waters within their jurisdiction. Retaliation of State upon State again appeared—and in the same fashion that wrecked the States under the Confederation."[3]

[Ogden enjoyed a monopoly on steam navigation between New York City and Elizabethtown, New Jersey, by virtue of an assignment of this part of their franchise from Livingston and Fulton (through a middleman). Gibbons had obtained a federal license for coastwise shipping (under an Act of Congress of 1793) and under it operated two steamboats between the same two points. Ogden claimed that this violated his exclusive right to navigate in New York waters and sought an injunction to restrain Gibbons. The New York courts granted his request and ordered Gibbons to discontinue the use of any steam vessels in the territorial waters of New York. Gibbons appealed to the Supreme Court.]

MARSHALL, C. J., delivered the opinion of the Court.

. . . . . .

The appellant contends that this decree is erroneous, because the laws which purport to give the exclusive privilege it sustains, are repugnant to the Constitution and laws of the United States.

They are said to be repugnant—

1. To that clause in the Constitution which authorizes Congress to regulate commerce.

2. To that which authorizes Congress to promote the progress of science and the useful arts:

. . . . . .

This instrument [the Constitution] contains an enumeration of powers expressly granted by the people to their government. It has been said that these powers ought to be construed strictly. But why ought they be so construed? Is there one sentence in the Constitution which gives countenance to this rule? In the last of the enumerated powers, that which grants, expressly, the means of carrying all others into execution, Congress is authorized "to make all laws which shall be necessary and proper" for the purpose. But this limitation on the means which may be used, is not extended to the powers which are conferred; nor is there one sentence in the Constitution . . . that prescribes this rule. We do not, therefore, think ourselves justified in

[3] Vol. IV, p. 415.

adopting it. . . . We know of no rule for construing the extent of such powers, other than is given by the language of the instrument which confers them, taken in connection with the purposes for which they are conferred.

The words are: "Congress shall have power to regulate commerce with foreign nations, and among the several States, and with the Indian tribes."

The subject to be regulated is commerce; and our Constitution being, as was aptly said at the bar, one of enumeration, and not of definition, to ascertain the extent of the power, it becomes necessary to settle the meaning of the word. The counsel for the appellee would limit it to traffic, to buying and selling, or the interchange of commodities, and do not admit that it comprehends navigation. . . . Commerce, undoubtedly, is traffic, but it is something more: it is intercourse. It describes the commercial intercourse between nations, and parts of nations, in all its branches, and is regulated by prescribing rules for carrying on that intercourse. The mind can scarcely conceive a system for regulating commerce between nations which shall exclude all laws concerning navigation. . . .

If commerce does not include navigation, the government of the United States has no direct power over that subject. . . . Yet this power has been exercised from the commencement of the government, has been execised with the consent of all, and has been understood by all to be a commercial regulation. All America understands, and has uniformly understood, the word, "commerce," to comprehend navigation. It was so understood, and must have been so understood, when the Constitution was framed. The power over commerce, including navigation, was one of the primary objects for which the people of America adopted their government, and must have been contemplated in forming it. The convention must have used the word in that sense, because all have understood it in that sense; and the attempt to restrict it comes too late.

The word used in the Constitution, then, comprehends, and has been always understood to comprehend, navigation within its meaning; and a power to regulate navigation, is as expressly granted, as if that term had been added to the word "commerce."

To what commerce does this power extend? The Constitution informs us, to commerce "with foreign nations, and among the several States, and with the Indian tribes."

It has, we believe, been universally admitted that these words comprehend every species of commercial intercourse between the United States and foreign nations. No sort of trade can be carried on between this country and any other, to which this power does not extend. It has been truly said that commerce, as the word is used in the Constitution, is a unit, every part of which is indicated by the term.

If this be the admitted meaning of the word, in its application to foreign nations, it must carry the same meaning throughout the sentence, and remain a unit, unless there be some plain intelligible cause which alters it.

The subject to which the power is next applied, is to commerce "among the several States." . . .

It is not intended to say that these words comprehend that commerce which is completely internal . . . and which does not extend to or affect other States. . . . The genius and character of the whole government seem to be, that its action is to be applied to all the external concerns of the nation, and to those internal concerns which affect the States generally; but not to those which are completely within a particular State, which do not affect other States, and with which it is not necessary to interfere, for the purpose of executing some of the general powers of the government. . . .

But, in regulating commerce with foreign nations, the power of Congress does not stop at the jurisdictional lines of the several States. . . . If Congress has the power to regulate it, that power must be exercised whenever the subject exists. If it exists within the States, if a foreign voyage may commence or terminate at a port within a State, then the power of Congress may be exercised within a State.

The principle is, if possible, still more clear when applied to commerce "among the several States." . . . What is commerce "among" them; and how is it to be conducted? Can a trading expedition between two adjoining States, commence and terminate outside of each? And if the trading intercourse be between two States remote from each other, must it not commence in one, terminate in the other, and probably pass through a third? Commerce among the States must, of necessity, be commerce with the States. . . . The power of Congress, then, whatever it may be, must be exercised within the territorial jurisdiction of the several States. . . .

We are now arrived at the inquiry—what is this power?

It is the power to regulate; that is, to prescribe the rule by which commerce is to be governed. This power, like all others vested in Congress, is complete in itself, may be exercised to its utmost extent, and acknowledges no limitations other than are prescribed in the Constitution.

But it has been urged, with great earnestness, that although the power of Congress to regulate commerce ... be coextensive with the subject itself, ... yet the States may severally exercise the same power, within their respective jurisdictions. ...

.   .   .   .   .

The grant of the power to lay and collect taxes is, like the power to regulate commerce, made in general terms, and has never been understood to interfere with the exercise of the same power by the States. ... But the two grants are not, it is conceived, similar in their terms or their nature. ... Taxation is the simple operation of taking small portions from a perpetually accumulating mass, susceptible of almost infinite division; and a power in one to take what is necessary for certain purposes, is not, in its nature, incompatible with a power in another to take what is necessary for other purposes. ... In imposing taxes for State purposes, they are not doing what Congress is empowered to do. Congress is not empowered to tax for these purposes which are within the exclusive province of the States. When, then, each government exercises the power of taxation, neither is exercising the power of the other. But, when a State proceeds to regulate commerce with foreign nations, or among the several States, it is exercising the very power that is granted to Congress, and is doing the very thing which Congress is authorized to do. ...

.   .   .   .   .

But the inspection laws are said to be regulations of commerce, and are certainly recognized in the Constitution as being passed in the exercise of a power remaining with the States.

That inspection laws may have a remote and considerable influence on commerce will not be denied; but that a power to regulate commerce is the source from which the right to pass them is derived, cannot be admitted. ... They act upon the subject before it becomes an article of foreign commerce, or of commerce among the States, and prepare it for that purpose. They form a portion of that immense mass of legislation, which embraces everything within the territory of a State, not surrendered to a general government. . . . Inspection laws, quarantine laws, health laws of every description, as well as laws for regulating the internal commerce of a State, and those which respect turnpike roads, ferries, etc., are component parts of this mass.

No direct general power over these objects is granted to Congress and, consequently, they remain subject to state legislation. If the legislative power of the Union can reach them, it must be for national purposes; it must be where the power is expressly given for a special purpose, or is clearly incidental to some power which is expressly given. It is obvious that the government of the Union, in the exercise of its express powers, that, for example, of regulating commerce with foreign nations and among the States, may use means that may also be employed by a State, in the exercise of its acknowledged powers; that, for example, of regulating commerce within the State. . . . So if a State, in passing laws on subjects acknowledged to be within its control, and with a view to those subjects, shall adopt a measure of the same character with one which Congress may adopt, it does not derive its authority from the particular power which has been granted, but from some other which remains with the State, and may be executed by the same means. All experience shows that the same measures, or measures scarcely distinguishable from each other, may flow from distinct powers; but this does not prove that the powers themselves are identical. . . .

. . . . . .

It has been contended, by the counsel for the appellant [Daniel Webster], that, as the word to "regulate" implies in its nature full power over the thing to be regulated, it excludes, necessarily, the action of all others that would perform the same operation on the same thing. That regulation is designed for the entire result. . . . It produces a uniform whole, which is as much disturbed and deranged by changing what the regulating power designs to leave untouched, as that on which it has operated.

There is great force in this argument, and the Court is not satisfied that it has been refuted.

Since, however, in exercising the power of regulating their own purely internal affairs, whether of trading or police, the States may sometimes enact laws, the validity of which depends on their interfering with, and being contrary to, an act of Congress passed in pursuance of the Constitution, the Court will enter upon the inquiry, whether the laws of New York, as expounded by the highest tribunal of that State, have, in their application to this case, come into collision with an act of Congress, and deprived a citizen of a right to which that act entitled him. Should this collision exist, it will be immaterial whether those laws were passed in virtue of a concurrent power "to regulate commerce with foreign nations and among the several States," or in virtue of a power to regulate their domestic trade and police. In one case and the other, the acts of New York must yield to the law of Congress; and the law sustaining the privilege they confer, against a right given by a law of the union, must be erroneous.

This opinion has been frequently expressed in this Court, and is founded as well on the nature of the government as on the words of the Constitution. In argument, however, it has been contended that, if a law passed by a State, in the exercise of its acknowledged sovereignty, comes into conflict with a law passed by Congress in pursuance of the Constitution, they affect the subject, and each other, like equal opposing powers.

But the framers of our Constitution foresaw this state of things, and provided for it by declaring the supremacy not only of itself, but of the laws made in pursuance of it. The nullity of any act, inconsistent with the Constitution, is produced by the declaration that the Constitution is the supreme law. The appropriate application of that part of the clause which confers the same supremacy on laws and treaties, is to such acts of the state legislatures as do not transcend their powers, but, though enacted in the execution of acknowledged state powers, interfere with, or are contrary to the laws of Congress, made in pursuance of the Constitution, or some treaty made under the authority of the United States. In every such case, the act of Congress, or the treaty, is supreme; and the law of the State, though enacted in the exercise of powers not controverted, must yield to it. . . .

The questions . . . whether the conveyance of passengers be a part of the coasting trade, and whether a vessel can be protected in that occupation by a coasting license, are not, and cannot be, raised in this case. The real and sole question seems to be, whether a steam machine, in actual use, deprives a vessel of the privilege conferred by a license. . . .

But all inquiry into this subject seems to the Court to be put completely at rest, by the act already mentioned, entitled, "An act for the enrolling and licensing of steamboats." . . .

This act demonstrates the opinion of Congress, that steamboats may be enrolled and licensed, in common with vessels using sails. They are, of course, entitled to the same privileges, and can no more be restrained from navigating waters, and entering ports which are free to such vessels, than if they were wafted on their voyage by the winds, instead of being propelled by the agency of fire. The one element may be as legitimately used as the other, for every commercial purpose authorized by the laws of the Union: and the act of a State inhibiting the use of either to any vessel having a license under the act of Congress, comes, we think, in direct collision with that act.

As this decides the cause, it is unnecessary to enter in an examination of that part of the Constitution which empowers Congress to promote the progress of science and the useful arts. . . .

Reversed and annulled.

[Mr. Justice JOHNSON, in a concurring opinion, maintained that the power of Congress over interstate commerce was intended to be wholly exclusive.]

COOLEY v. BOARD OF WARDENS OF THE PORT OF PHILADELPHIA
12 How. 299 (1851)

Mr. Justice CURTIS delivered the opinion of the Court.

These cases are . . . actions to recover half-pilotage fees under the 29th section of the act of the Legislature of Pennsylvania, passed on the second day of March, 1803. The plaintiff in error alleges that the highest court of the State has decided against a right claimed by him under the Constitution of the United States. That right is, to be exempted from the payment of sums of money, demanded pursuant to the state law above referred to, because that law contravenes several provisions of the Constitution of the United States.

The particular section of the state law drawn in question is as follows: "That every ship or vessel arriving from or bound to any foreign port or place, and every ship or vessel of the burden of seventy-five tons or more, sailing from or bound to any port not within the river Delaware, shall be obliged to receive a pilot. . . . And it shall be the duty of the wardens to enter every such vessel in a book to be kept by them for that purpose, without fee or reward.

And if the master of any ship or vessel shall neglect to make such report, he shall forfeit and pay the sum of sixty dollars. And if the master of any such ship or vessel shall refuse or neglect to take a pilot, the master, owner or consignee of such vessel shall forfeit and pay to the warden aforesaid a sum equal to the half-pilotage of such ship or vessel. . . ."

We think this particular regulation concerning half-pilotage fees, is an appropriate part of a general system of regulations of this subject. Testing it by the practice of commercial states and countries legislating on this subject, we find it has usually been deemed necessary to make similar provisions. Numerous laws of this kind are cited in the learned argument of the counsel for the defendant in error; and their fitness, as part of a system of pilotage, in many places, may be inferred from their existence in so many different states and countries. . . .

It remains to consider the objection that it is repugnant to the third clause of the eighth section of the first article. "The Congress shall have power to regulate commerce with foreign nations and among the several States, and with the Indian tribes."

That the power to regulate commerce includes the regulation of navigation, we consider settled. And when we look to the nature of the service performed by pilots, to the relations which that service and its compensations bear to navigation between the several States, and between the ports of the United States and foreign countries, we are brought to the conclusion, that the regulation of the qualifications of pilots, of the modes and times of offering and rendering their services, of the responsibilities which shall rest upon them, of the powers they shall possess, of the compensation they may demand, and of the penalties by which their rights and duties may be enforced, do constitute regulations of navigation, and consequently of commerce, within the just meaning of this clause of the Constitution. . . .

It becomes necessary, therefore, to consider whether this law of Pennsylvania, being a regulation of commerce, is valid.

The act of Congress of the 7th of August, 1789, sect. 4, is as follows:

"That all pilots . . . shall continue to be regulated in conformity with the existing laws of the States, respectively, wherein such pilots may be, or with such laws as the States may respectively hereafter enact for the purpose, until further legislative provision shall be made by Congress."

.   .   .   .   .

If the States were divested of the power to legislate on this subject by the grant of the commercial power to Congress, it is plain this act could not confer upon them power thus to legislate. If the Constitution excluded the States from making any law regulating commerce, certainly Congress cannot regrant, or in any manner reconvey that power. . . . Entertaining these views, we are brought directly and unavoidably to the consideration of the question, whether the grant of the commercial power to Congress, did *per se* deprive the States of all power to regulate pilots. This question has never been decided by this Court, nor, in our judgment, has any case depending upon all the considerations which must govern this one, come before this Court. The grant of commercial power to Congress does not contain any terms which expressly exclude the States from exercising an authority over its subject-matter. If they are excluded, it must be because the nature of the power, thus granted to Congress, requires that a similar authority should not exist in the States. If it were conceded on the one side, that the nature of this power . . . is absolutely and totally repugnant to the existence of a similar power in the States, probably no one would deny that the grant of the power to Congress, as effectually and perfectly excludes the States from all future legislation on the subject, as if express words had been used to exclude them. And on the other hand, if it were admitted that the existence of this power in Congress, like the power of taxation, is compatible with the existence of a similar power in the States, then it would be in conformity with the contemporary exposition of the Constitution *(Federalist,* No. 32), and with the judicial construction, given from time to time by this Court, after the most deliberate consideration, to hold that the mere grant of such a power to Congress, did not imply a prohibition on the States to exercise the same power; that it is not the mere existence of such a power, but its exercise by Congress, which may be incompatible with the exercise of the same power by the States, and that the States may legislate in the absence of Congressional regulations. . . .

The diversities of opinion, therefore, which have existed on this subject, have arisen from the different views taken of the nature of this power. But when the nature of a power like this is spoken of, when it is said that the nature of the power requires that it should be exercised exclusively by Congress, it must be intended to refer to the subjects of that power, and to say they are of such a nature as to require exclusive legislation by Congress. Now the power to regulate commerce, embraces a vast field, containing not only many, but exceedingly various subjects, quite unlike in their nature; some imperatively demanding a single uniform rule, operating equally on the commerce of the United States in every port; and some, like the subject now in question, as imperatively demanding that diversity which alone can meet the local necessities of navigation.

Either absolutely to affirm, or deny that the nature of this power requires exclusive legislation by Congress, is to lose sight of the nature of the subjects of this power, and to assert concerning all of them, what is really applicable but to a part. Whatever subjects of this power are in their nature national, or admit only of one uniform system, or plan of regulation, may justly be said to be of such a nature as to require exclusive legislation by Congress. That this cannot be affirmed of laws for the regulation of pilots and pilotage is plain. . . .

Viewed in this light, so much of this act of 1789 as declares that pilots shall continue to be regulated "by such laws as the States may respectively hereafter enact for that purpose," instead of being held to be inoperative, as an attempt to confer on the States a power to legislate, of which the Constitution had deprived them, is allowed an appropriate and important signification. It manifests the understanding of Congress, at the outset of the government, that the nature of this subject is not such as to require exclusive legislation. The practice of the States, and of the national government, has been in conformity with this declaration, from the origin of the national government to this time; and the nature of the subject when examined is such as to leave no doubt of the superior fitness and propriety, not to say the absolute necessity, of different systems of regulation, drawn from local knowledge and experience, and conformed to local wants. How, then, can we say, that by the mere grant of power to regulate commerce, the States are deprived of all the power to legislate on this subject, because from the nature of the power the legislation of Congress must be exclusive. This would be to affirm that the nature of the power is, in any case, something different from the nature of the subject to which, in such case, the power extends, and that the nature of the power necessarily demands, in all cases, exclusive legislation by Congress, while the nature of one of the subjects of that power, not only does not require such exclusive legislation but may be best provided for by many different systems enacted by the States, in conformity with the circumstances of the ports within their limits. In construing an instrument designed for the formation of a government, and in determining the extent of one of its important grants of power to legislate, we can make no such distinction between the nature of the power and the nature of the subject on which that power was intended practically to operate, nor consider the grant more extensive by affirming of the power, what is not true of its subject now in question.

It is the opinion of a majority of the Court that the mere grant to Congress of the power to regulate commerce did not deprive the States of power to regulate pilots, and that although Congress has legislated on this subject, its legislation manifests an intention, with a single exception, not to regulate this subject, but to leave its regulation to the several States. To these precise questions, which are all we are called on to decide, this opinion must be understood to be confined. It does not extend to the question what other subjects, under the commercial power, are within the exclusive control of Congress, or may be regulated by the States in the absence of all Congressional legislation; nor to the general question, how far any regulation of a subject by Congress, may be deemed to operate as an exclusion of all legislation by the States upon the same subject. We decide the precise questions before us, upon what we deem sound principles, applicable to this particular subject in the state in which the legislation of Congress has left it. We go no further. . . .

[Affirmed.]

[Mr. Justice McLEAN and Mr. Justice WAYNE dissented; Mr. Justice DANIEL wrote a concurring opinion arguing that the control of pilotage was inherently a right of the States, "not one merely to be tolerated, or held subject to the sanction of the federal government."]

REGULATION UNDER THE COMMERCE CLAUSE[4]

The restrictive effects of the commerce clause, even as ameliorated by the principles of *Cooley* v. *Board of Port Wardens* and the recognition of the states' police powers, interfered frequently with the effective execution of important state policies. A situation finally arose that led to Congressional intervention to relieve the states of some of the then existing restraints of their powers. During the seventies and eighties of the last century several midwestern states had prohibited the manufacture and sale of intoxicating beverages. The

[4] From: *The Constitution and Socio-Economic Change,* the first Thomas M. Cooley Lecture delivered at the University of Michigan by Henry Rottschaefer; Ann Arbor: University of Michigan Law School, 1948, pp. 28–32. Copyright by University of Michigan Law School. Reproduced by permission of the author and publishers.

enforcement of this policy against interstate sales, and local original package sales of intoxicants brought in from other states, was held to conflict with the commerce clause. Their [the dry states'] appeals to Congress led to the enactment of the Wilson Act in 1890, which subjected intoxicants to the laws of those states upon their arrival therein. The validity of that Act was a fairly debatable matter when the issue came before the Supreme Court. In *Gibbons* v. *Ogden*, Chief Justice Marshall, in meeting the contention that the Pilot Act of August 7, 1789, impliedly acknowledged a concurrent power in the states to regulate interstate commerce, had stated that "Congress cannot enable a State to legislate" but might adopt the provisions of state laws on any subject. In *Cooley* v. *Board of Port Wardens,* Justice Curtis drew from the enactment of that Act the very conclusion that Chief Justice Marshall had denied. In his opinion, he had used the following language:

"If the States were divested of the power to legislate on this subject [of pilotage] by the grant of the commercial power to Congress, it is plain this act could not confer upon them power thus to legislate. If the Constitution excluded the States from making any law regulating commerce, certainly Congress cannot regrant it, or in any manner reconvey to the States that power."

When *In re Rahrer*[5] was decided the commerce power was being quite uniformly treated as an exclusive power, and the regulation of original package sales as within its scope. It was not unreasonable to view the Wilson Act as conferring that power upon the states in the case of intoxicants; that is, granting them a right to exercise part of an exclusively federal power. The Court met this difficulty by a rather ingenious argument substantially as follows. Since the matter is one within the federal commerce power, the silence of Congress would operate to exclude states from its regulation. Action by Congress is no less potent than its silence. Its action in removing "an impediment to the enforcement of the state laws in respect to imported packages in their original condition, created by the absence of a specific utterance on its part" does not delegate any federal powers to the states. The Wilson Act was viewed as merely divesting intoxicants of their character as subjects of interstate commerce "at an earlier period of time than would otherwise be the case." The same

[5] 140 U.S. 545 (1891).

technique was later used to protect the economic interests of a state, as it conceived those interests, against injury from competition by prison-made goods.[6] Whatever the theory invoked to sustain it, it was a device for expanding the operative effect of state laws governing transactions within them. The limits of its availability have never been precisely defined. . . .

The principles formulated by Chief Justice Marshall in *McCulloch* v. *Maryland* furnished a favorable basis for a broad expansion of federal powers in general. His opinion in *Gibbons* v. *Ogden* performed the same function for the commerce power. Its scope is defined by reference to the "Genius and character of the whole government" which seems "to be, that its action is to be applied to all the external concerns of the nation, and to those internal concerns which affect the States generally; but not to those which are completely within a particular State, which do not affect other States, and with which it is not necessary to interfere, for the purpose of executing some of the general powers of the government." This language, though applied to federal powers generally, states his theory of the scope of the commerce power as well. Equally comprehensive was his view as to the scope of the power to regulate. It is defined as the power "to prescribe the rule by which commerce is to be governed," and, "like all others vested in Congress, is complete in itself, may be exercised to its utmost extent, and acknowledges no limitations, other than are prescribed in the Constitution . . . the power over commerce with foreign nations, and among the several States, is vested in Congress as absolutely as it would be in a single government, having in its constitution the same restrictions in the exercise of the power as are found in the Constitution of the United States."

It remained for his successors on the Court to develop the implications of these premises. The conditions in the nation in his time

[6] *Kentucky Whip & Collar Company* v. *Illinois Central R. Co.*, 299 U.S. 334 (1937). The same formula for "divesting" items in interstate commerce of their protected status was employed in 1940 when Congress made prize-fight films shipped into a state subject to the laws of that state in spite of the interstate character of the shipment. 54 Stat. 686. In the *Whip & Collar* case Chief Justice Hughes summarized the cases which sanctioned use of the commerce power for police power objectives and concluded that Congress may properly formulate these objectives "in the light of the fact that the transportation in interstate commerce, if permitted, would aid in the frustration of valid state laws. . . ." *United States* v. *Darby, post,* apparently sets at rest any speculation over possible limits to the power of Congress to prohibit the movement of goods in interstate commerce and, correspondingly, to divest goods of their interstate character. See also Holmes' famous dissent in *Hammer* v. *Dagenhart,* 247 U.S. 251 (1918), (overruled by the *Darby* case) : "Congress . . . may carry out its views of public policy whatever indirect effect they may have upon the activities of the states. . . ."

did not call for any extensive exercise of the commerce power by Congress. It did enact legislation regulating navigation, providing for the construction of interstate highways, and imposing protective tariffs against foreign imports. During the Civil War, and for some time thereafter, it chartered corporations for the construction of railroads. The beginning of its active interposition to regulate the nation's economic life dates from the eighties of the last century. This was in no small measure due to evils that had arisen with which the individual states were unable to cope. Their inability was due in part to the restraints imposed on them by the commerce clause as construed by the Supreme Court. The most important laws inacted in these early stages of what proved to be a permanent movement were the Interstate Commerce Act of 1887 and the Sherman Anti-Trust Act of 1890. The former dealt directly with interstate transportation; the latter sought to protect the then existing national market against the evils of monopoly by prohibiting contracts in restraint of, or aiming to monopolize, interstate trade. That Congress possessed the power to regulate interstate transportation in some respects had never been denied since *Gibbons* v. *Ogden.* The Act of 1887 marked the beginning of a federal program for the regulation of interstate carriers that was far advanced by 1933. No difficulty was found in sustaining laws regulating the operating conditions of railroads, their relations to patrons, the rates that might be charged, and the relations between carriers in connection with through routes and joint rates. The basic justification for such measures was that they protected interstate traffic against unreasonable burdens. That the commerce power could be used to promote the growth of interstate commerce and control it with an eye to the welfare not only of those immediately concerned but also of the general public was expressly affirmed in the *Recapture Clause Case* [which follows]. . . .

DAYTON-GOOSE CREEK RY. CO. v. UNITED STATES
263 U.S. 456 (1924)

Mr. Chief Justice TAFT delivered the opinion of the Court.

The main question in this case is whether the so-called "recapture" paragraphs of the Transportation Act of 1920, c. 91, Section 422 (15a) , paragraphs 5–17, 41 Stat. 456, 489–491, are constitutional.

The Dayton-Goose Creek Railway Company is a corporation of Texas, engaged in intrastate, interstate and foreign commerce. Its volume of intrastate traffic exceeds that of its interstate and foreign traffic. In response to orders of the Interstate Commerce Commission, the carrier made returns for ten months of 1920, and for the full year of 1921, reporting the value of its railroad property employed in commerce and its net revenue therefrom. It earned $21,666.24 more than six per cent. on the value of its property in the ten months of 1920, and $33,766.99 excess in the twelve months of 1921. The Commission requested it to report what provision it had made for setting up a fund to preserve one-half of these excesses, and to remit the other half to the Commission. The carrier then filed the present bill, setting forth the constitutional invalidity of the recapture provisions. . . .

This Court has recently had occasion to construe the Transportation Act. In *Wisconsin R. R. Commission* v. *C. R. & Q. R. R. Co.,* 257 U.S. 563, it was held that the act in seeking to render the interstate commerce railway system adequate to the country's needs had . . . conferred on the Commission valid power and duty to raise the level of intrastate rates when it found that they were so low as to discriminate against interstate commerce and unduly to burden it. In the *New England Divisions Case,* 261 U.S. 184, it was held that . . . the Commission in making division of joint rates between groups of carriers might in the public interest consult the needs of a weaker group in order to maintain it in effective operation as part of an adequate transportation system, and give it a greater share of such rates if the share of the other group was adequate to avoid a confiscatory result.

In both cases it was pointed out that the Transportation Act adds a new and important object to previous interstate commerce legislation, which was designed primarily to prevent unreasonable or discriminatory rates against persons and localities. The new act seeks affirmatively to build up a system of railways prepared to handle promptly all the interstate traffic of the country. It aims to give the owners of the railways an opportunity to earn enough to maintain their properties and equipment in such a state of efficiency that they can carry well this burden. To achieve this great purpose, it puts the railroad systems of the country more completely than ever under the fostering guardianship and control of the Commission, which is to supervise their issue of securities, their car supply and distribution, their joint use of terminals, their construction of new lines, their abandonment of old lines, and by a proper division of joint rates, and by fixing adequate rates for interstate commerce, to secure a fair return upon the properties of the carriers engaged.

It was insisted in the two cases referred to, and it is insisted here, that the power to regulate interstate commerce is limited to the fixing of reasonable rates and the prevention of those which are discriminatory, and that when these objects are attained, the power of regulation is exhausted. This is too narrow a view of the commerce clause. To regulate in the sense intended is to foster, protect and control the commerce with appropriate regard to the welfare of those who are immediately concerned, as well as the public at large, and to promote its growth and insure its safety. . . .

. . . . . .

Title IV of the Transportation Act, embracing §§ 418 and 422, is carefully framed to achieve its expressly declared objects. Uniform rates enjoined for all shippers will tend to divide the business in proper proportions so that, when the burden is great, the railroad of each carrier will be used to its capacity. If the weaker roads were permitted to charge higher rates than their competitors, the business would seek the stronger roads with the lower rates, and congestion would follow. The directions given to the Commission in fixing uniform rates will tend to put them on a scale enabling a railroad of average efficiency among all the carriers of the section to earn the prescribed maximum return. Those who earn more must hold one-half of the excess primarily to preserve their sound economic condition and avoid wasteful expenditures and unwise dividends. Those who earn less are to be given help by credit secured through a fund made up of the other half of the excess. By the recapture clauses Congress is enabled to maintain uniform rates for all shippers and yet keep the net returns of railways, whether strong or weak, to the varying percentages which are fair respectively to them. The recapture provisions are thus the key provision of the whole plan.

Having regard to the property rights of the carriers and the interest of the shipping public, the validity of the plan depends on two propositions.

First. Rates which as a body enable all the railroads necessary to do the business of a rate territory or section, to enjoy not more than a fair net operating income on the aggregate value of their properties therein economically and efficiently operated, are reasonable from the standpoint of the individual shipper in that section. He with every other shipper similarly situated in the same section is vitally interested in having a system which can do all the business offered. If there is congestion, he suffers with the rest. He may, therefore, properly be required in the rates he pays to share with all other shippers of the same section the burden of maintaining an adequate railway capacity to do their business.

It should be noted that, in reaching a conclusion, upon the first proposition, we are only considering the general level of rates and their direct bearing upon the net return of the entire group. . . .

Second. The carrier owning and operating a railroad, however strong financially, however economical in its facilities, or favorably situated as to traffic, is not entitled as of constitutional right to more than a fair net operating income upon the value of its properties which are being devoted to transportation. . . . If it receives a fair return on its property, why should it make any difference that other and competing railroads in the same section are permitted to receive higher rates for a service which it costs them more to render and from which they receive no better net return? . . .

The reduction of the net operating return provided by the recapture clause is, as near as may be, the same thing as if rates had all been reduced proportionately before collection. It is clearly unsound to say that the net operating profit accruing from a whole rate structure is not relevant evidence in determining whether the sum of the rates is fair. The investment is made on the faith of a profit, the profit accrues from the balance left after deducting expenses from the product of the rates, and the assumption is that the operation is economical and the expenditures are reasonably necessary. If the profit is fair, the sum of the rates is so. If the profit is excessive, the sum of the rates is so. One obvious way to make the sum of the rates reasonable so far as the carrier is concerned is to reduce its profit to what is fair.

.   .   .   .   .   .

The third question for our consideration is whether the recapture clause, by reducing the net income from intrastate rates, invades the reserved power of the States and is in conflict with the Tenth Amendment. In solving the problem of maintaining the efficiency of an interstate commerce railway system which serves both the States and the Nation, Congress is dealing with a unit in which state and interstate operations are often inextricably commingled. When the adequate maintenance of interstate commerce involves and makes necessary on this account the incidental and partial control of intrastate commerce, the power of Congress to exercise such control has been clearly established.

... *The Shreveport Case*, 234 U.S. 342, 352 [below]; ... The combination of uniform rates with the recapture clauses is necessary to the better development of the country's interstate transportation system as Congress has planned it. The control of the excess profit due to the level of the whole body of rates is the heart of the plan. To divide that excess and attempt to distribute one part to interstate traffic and the other to intrastate traffic would be impracticable and defeat the plan. This renders indispensable the incidental control by Congress of that part of the excess possibly due to intrastate rates which if present is indistinguishable. ...

HOUSTON, E. & W. T. RY. CO. v. UNITED STATES
("The Shreveport Case")
234 U.S. 342 (1914)

Mr. Justice HUGHES delivered the opinion of the Court.

These suits were brought in the Commerce Court[7] by the Houston, East & West Texas Railway Company and the Houston & Shreveport Railroad Company, and by the Texas & Pacific Railway Company, respectively, to set aside an order of the Interstate Commerce Commission, dated March 11, 1912, upon the ground that it exceeded the Commission's authority. Other railroad companies intervened in support of the petitions, and the Interstate Commerce Commission and the Railroad Commission of Louisiana intervened in opposition. The petitions were dismissed. ...

The order of the Interstate Commerce Commission was made in a proceeding initiated in March, 1911, by the Railroad Commission of Louisiana. The complaint was that the appellants, and other interstate carriers, maintained unreasonable rates from Shreveport, Louisiana, to various points in Texas, and further, that these carriers, in the adjustment of rates over their respective lines, unjustly discriminated in favor of traffic within the state of Texas, and against similar traffic between Louisiana and Texas. The carriers filed answers; numerous pleas of intervention by shippers and commercial bodies were allowed; testimony was taken and arguments were heard.

The gravamen of the complaint, said the Interstate Commerce

---

[7] A special court set up in 1910 to review and to enforce findings of the Interstate Commerce Commission. It was abolished in 1913.

Commission, was that the carriers made rates out of Dallas and other Texas points into eastern Texas which were much lower than those which they extended into Texas from Shreveport. The situation may be briefly described: Shreveport, Louisiana, is about 40 miles from the Texas state line, and 231 miles from Houston, Texas, on the line of the Houston, East & West Texas and Houston & Shreveport Companies (which are affiliated in interest); it is 189 miles from Dallas, Texas, on the line of the Texas and Pacific. Shreveport competes with both cities for the trade of the intervening territory. The rates on these lines from Dallas and Houston, respectively, eastward to intermediate points in Texas, were much less, according to distance, than from Shreveport westward to the same points. It is undisputed that the difference was substantial, and injuriously affected the commerce of Shreveport. It appeared, for example, that a rate of 60 cents carried first-class traffic a distance of 160 miles to the eastward from Dallas, while the same rate would carry the same class of traffic only 55 miles into Texas from Shreveport. . . .

The Interstate Commerce Commission found that the interstate class rates out of Shreveport to named Texas points were unreasonable, and it established maximum class rates for this traffic. These rates, we understand, were substantially the same as the class rates fixed by the Railroad Commission of Texas, and charged by the carriers, for transportation for similar distances in that state. The Interstate Commerce Commission also found that the carriers maintained "higher rates from Shreveport to points in Texas" than were in force "from cities in Texas to such points under substantially similar conditions and circumstances," and that thereby "an unlawful and undue preference and advantage" was given to the Texas cities, and a "discrimination" that was "undue and unlawful" was effected against Shreveport. In order to correct this discrimination, the carriers were directed to desist from charging higher rates for the transportation of any commodity from Shreveport to Dallas and Houston, respectively, and intermediate points, than were contemporaneously charged for the carriage of such commodity from Dallas and Houston toward Shreveport for equal distances, as the Commission found that relation of rates to be reasonable. . . . The report states that under this order it will be the duty of the companies "to duly and justly equalize the terms and conditions" upon which they will extend "transportation to traffic of a similar character, moving into Texas from Shreveport, with that moving wholly within Texas," but that, in effecting such equalization, the class scale rates as prescribed shall not be exceeded.

The point of the objection to the order is that, as the discrimination found by the Commission to be unjust arises out of the relation of intrastate rates, maintained under state authority, to interstate rates that have been upheld as reasonable, its correction was beyond the Commission's power. Manifestly the order might be complied with, and the discrimination avoided, either by reducing the interstate rate from Shreveport to the level of the competing intrastate rates, or by raising these intrastate rates to the level of the interstate rate, or by such reduction in the one case and increase in the other as would result in equality. But it is urged that, so far as the interstate rates were sustained by the Commission as reasonable, the Commission was without authority to compel their reduction in order to equalize them with the lower intrastate rates. The holding of the commerce court was that the order relieved the appellants from further obligation to observe the intrastate rates, and that they were at liberty to comply with the Commission's requirements by increasing these rates sufficiently to remove the forbidden discrimination. The invalidity of the order in this aspect is challenged upon two grounds:

(1) That Congress is impotent to control the intrastate charges of an interstate carrier even to the extent necessary to prevent injurious discrimination against interstate traffic; and

(2) That, if it be assumed that Congress has this power, still it has not been exercised, and hence the action of the Commission exceeded the limits of the authority which has been conferred upon it.

First. It is unnecessary to repeat what has frequently been said by this Court with respect to the complete and paramount character of the power confided to Congress to regulate commerce among the several states. It is of the essence of this power that, where it exists, it dominates. Interstate trade was not left to be destroyed or impeded by the rivalries of local government. The purpose was to make impossible the recurrence of the evils which had overwhelmed the Confederation, and to provide the necessary basis of national unity by insuring "uniformity of regulation against conflicting and discriminating state legislation." By virtue of the comprehensive terms of the grant, the authority of Congress is at all times adequate to meet the varying exigencies that arise, and to protect the national interest by securing the freedom of interstate commercial intercourse from local control. . . .

Congress is empowered to regulate,—that is, to provide the law for the government of interstate commerce; to enact "all appropriate legislation" for its "protection and advancement" (*The Daniel Ball,* 10 Wall. 557, 564); to adopt measures "to promote its growth and insure its safety" (*Mobile County* v. *Kimball,* 102 U.S. 691, 696, 697) ; "to foster, protect, control, and restrain" (*Second Employers' Liability Cases,* 223 U.S. 1, 47, 53, 54). Its authority, extending to these interstate carriers as instruments of interstate commerce, necessarily embraces the right to control their operations in all matters having such a close and substantial relation to interstate traffic that the control is essential or appropriate to the security of that traffic, to the efficiency of the interstate service, and to the maintenance of conditions under which interstate commerce may be conducted upon fair terms and without molestation or hindrance. As it is competent for Congress to legislate to these ends, unquestionably it may seek their attainment by requiring that the agencies of interstate commerce shall not be used in such manner as to cripple, retard, or destroy it. The fact that carriers are instruments of intrastate commerce, as well as of interstate commerce, does not derogate from the complete and paramount authority of Congress over the latter, or preclude the Federal power from being exerted to prevent the intrastate operations of such carriers from being made a means of injury to that which has been confided to Federal care. Wherever the interstate and intrastate transactions of carriers are so related that the government of the one involves the control of the other, it is Congress, and not the State, that is entitled to prescribe the final and dominant rule, for otherwise Congress would be denied the exercise of its constitutional authority, and the State, and not the Nation, would be supreme within the national field. . . .

. . . . . .

While . . . [prior] decisions sustaining the Federal power relate to measures adopted in the interest of the safety of persons and property, they illustrate the principle that Congress, in the exercise of its paramount power, may prevent the common instrumentalities of interstate and intrastate commercial intercourse from being used in their intrastate operations to the injury of interstate commerce. This is not to say that Congress possesses the authority to regulate the internal commerce of a State, as such, but that it does possess the power to foster and protect interstate commerce, and to take all measures necessary or appropriate to that end, although intrastate transactions of interstate carriers may thereby be controlled.

This principle is applicable here. We find no reason to doubt that Congress is entitled to keep the highways of interstate communication open to interstate traffic upon fair and equal terms. That an unjust discrimination in the rates of a common carrier, by which one person or locality is unduly favored as against another under substantially similar conditions of traffic, constitutes an evil, is undeniable; and where this evil consists in the action of an interstate carrier in unreasonably discriminating against interstate traffic over its line, the authority of Congress to prevent it is equally clear. It is immaterial, so far as the protecting power of Congress is concerned, that the discrimination arises from intrastate rates as compared with interstate rates. The use of the instrument of interstate commerce in a discriminatory manner so as to inflict injury upon that commerce, or some part thereof, furnishes abundant ground for Federal intervention. Nor can the attempted exercise of state authority alter the matter, where Congress has acted, for a State may not authorize the carrier to do that which Congress is entitled to forbid and has forbidden.

It is to be noted—as the government has well said in its argument in support of the Commission's order—that the power to deal with the relation between the two kinds of rates, as a relation, lies exclusively with Congress. It is manifest that the state cannot fix the relation of the carrier's interstate and intrastate charges without directly interfering with the former, unless it simply follows the standard set by Federal authority. . . . It is for Congress to supply the needed correction where the relation between intrastate and interstate rates presents the evil to be corrected, and this it may do completely, by reason of its control over the interstate carrier in all matters having such a close and substantial relation to interstate commerce that it is necessary and appropriate to exercise the control for the effective government of that commerce.

It is also clear that, removing the injurious discriminations against interstate traffic arising from the relation of intrastate to interstate rates, Congress is not bound to reduce the latter below what it may deem to be a proper standard, fair to the carrier and to the public. Otherwise, it could prevent the injury to interstate commerce only by the sacrifice of its judgment as to interstate rates. Congress is entitled to maintain its own standard as to these rates, and to forbid any discriminatory action by interstate carriers which will obstruct the freedom of movement of interstate traffic over their lines in accordance with the terms it establishes.

Having this power, Congress could provide for its execution through the aid of a subordinate body; and we conclude that the order of the Commission now in question cannot be held invalid upon the ground that it exceeded the authority which Congress could lawfully confer.

Second. The remaining question is with regard to the scope of the power which Congress has granted to the Commission. [Discussion omitted].

.   .   .   .   .   .

Affirmed.

Mr. Justice LURTON and Mr. Justice PITNEY dissent.

2. THE POWER EXPANDING

A. L. A. SCHECHTER POULTRY CORP. v. UNITED STATES
295 U.S. 495 (1935)

Mr. Chief Justice HUGHES delivered the opinion of the Court.

Petitioners . . . were convicted in the District Court of the United States for the Eastern District of New York on eighteen counts of an indictment charging violations of what is known as the "Live Poultry Code," and on an additional count for conspiracy to commit such violations. . . . The defendants contended (1) that the Code had been adopted pursuant to an unconstitutional delegation by Congress of legislative power; (2) that it attempted to regulate intrastate transactions which lay outside the authority of Congress; and (3) that in certain provisions it was repugnant to the due process clause of the Fifth Amendment.

.   .   .   .   .   .

New York City is the largest live-poultry market in the United States. Ninety-six per cent of the live poultry there marketed comes from other States. Three-fourths of this amount arrives by rail and is consigned to commission men or receivers. . . . The commission men transact by far the greater part of the business on a commission basis, representing the shippers as agents, and remitting to them the proceeds of sale, less commissions, freight and handling charges.

Otherwise, they buy for their own account. They sell to slaughter-house operators who are also called marketmen.

The defendants [Schechter Poultry Corporation et al.] are slaugh-terhouse operators of the latter class. . . . Defendants ordinarily pur-chase their live poultry from commission men at the West Washing-ton Market in New York City or at the railroad terminals serving the City, but occasionally they purchase from commission men in Phila-delphia. They buy the poultry for slaughter and resale. After the poultry is trucked to their slaughterhouse markets in Brooklyn, it is there sold, usually within twenty-four hours, to retail poultry dealers and butchers who sell directly to consumers. The poultry purchased from defendants is immediately slaughtered, prior to deliv-ery, by schochtim[8] in defendants' employ. Defendants do not sell poultry in interstate commerce.

The "Live Poultry Code" was promulgated under section 3 of the National Industrial Recovery Act. That section . . . authorizes the President to approve "codes of fair competition." Such a code may be approved for a trade or industry, upon application by one or more trade or industrial associations or groups if the President finds that such associations or groups "impose no inequitable restrictions on admission to membership therein and are truly representative," and (2) that such codes are not designed "to promote monopolies or to eliminate or oppress small enterprises and will not operate to discriminate against them, and will tend to effectuate the policy" of Title I of the act. Such codes "shall not permit monopolies or mo-nopolistic practices.". . . Where such a code has not been approved, the President may prescribe one, either on his own motion or on complaint. Violation of any provision of a code (so approved or prescribed) "in any transaction in or affecting interstate or foreign commerce" is made a misdemeanor punishable by a fine of not more than $500 for each offense, and each day the violation continues is to be deemed a separate offense.

The "Live Poultry Code" was approved by the President on April 13, 1934. . . .

The declared purpose is "To effect the policies of title I of the National Industrial Recovery Act." The code is established as "a code for fair competition for the live poultry industry of the metro-politan area in and about the City of New York."

---

[8] Persons authorized by rabbinical authority to slaughter animals for use as food in accordance with orthodox Jewish laws.

The Code fixes the number of hours for work-days. It provides that no employee, with certain exceptions, shall be permitted to work in excess of forty (40) hours in any one week, and that no employee, save as stated, "shall be paid in any pay period less than at the rate of fifty (50) cents per hour." The article containing "general labor provisions" prohibits the employment of any person under sixteen years of age, and declares that employees shall have the right of "collective bargaining," and freedom of choice with respect to labor organizations, in the terms of section 7 (a) of the Act. The minimum number of employees, who shall be employed by slaughterhouse operators, is fixed, the number being graduated according to the average volume of weekly sales. . . .

The seventh article, containing "trade practice provisions," prohibits various practices which are said to constitute "unfair methods of competition." . . .

The President approved the Code by an executive order. . . .

Of the eighteen counts of the indictment upon which the defendants were convicted, aside from the count for conspiracy, two counts charged violation of the minimum wage and maximum hour provisions of the Code, and ten counts were for violation of the requirement (found in the "trade practice provisions") of "straight killing." This requirement was really one of "straight" selling. The term "straight killing" was defined in the Code as "the practice of requiring persons purchasing poultry for resale to accept the run of any half coop, coop, or coops, as purchased by slaughterhouse operators, except for culls." The charges in the ten counts, respectively, were that the defendants in selling to retail dealers and butchers had permitted "selections of individual chickens taken from particular coops and half coops."

Of the other six counts, one charged the sale to a butcher of an unfit chicken; two counts charged the making of sales without having the poultry inspected or approved in accordance with regulations or ordinances of the City of New York; two counts charged the making of false reports or the failure to make reports relating to the range of daily prices and volume of sales for certain periods; and the remaining count was for sales to slaughterers or dealers who were without licenses required by the ordinances and regulations of the City of New York.

First. Two preliminary points are stressed by the Government with respect to the appropriate approach to the important questions presented. We are told that the provision of the statute authorizing the adoption of codes must be viewed in the light of the grave national crisis with which Congress was confronted. Undoubtedly, the conditions to which power is addressed are always to be considered when the exercise of power is challenged. Extraordinary conditions may call for extraordinary remedies. But the argument necessarily stops short of an attempt to justify action which lies outside the sphere of constitutional authority. Extraordinary conditions do not create or enlarge constitutional power. The Constitution established a national government with powers deemed to be adequate, as they have proved to be both in war and peace, but these powers of the national government are limited by the constitutional grants. Those who act under these grants are not at liberty to transcend the imposed limits because they believe that more or different power is necessary. Such assertions of extraconstitutional authority were anticipated and precluded by the explicit terms of the Tenth Amendment,—"The powers not delegated to the United States by the Constitution, nor prohibited by it to the States, are reserved to the States, respectively, or to the people."

The further point is urged that the national crisis demanded a broad and intensive cooperative effort by those engaged in trade and industry, and that this necessary cooperation was sought to be fostered by permitting them to initiate the adoption of codes. But the statutory plan is not simply one for voluntary effort. It does not seek merely to endow voluntary trade or industrial associations or groups with privileges or immunities. It involves the coercive exercise of the law-making power. The codes of fair competition, which the statute attempts to authorize, are codes of laws. If valid, they place all persons within their reach under the obligation of positive law, binding equally those who assent and those who do not assent. Violations of the provisions of the codes are punishable as crimes. . . .

[The second part of the opinion, dealing with the delegation of legislative power, is reproduced in Chapter III, at p. 77.]

Third. The question of the application of the provisions of the Live Poultry Code to intrastate transactions. Although the validity of the codes (apart from the question of delegation) rests upon the commerce clause of the Constitution, section 3 (a) is not in terms limited to interstate and foreign commerce. From the generality of its terms, and from the argument of the Government at the bar, it would appear that section 3(a) was designed to authorize codes without that limitation. But under section 3(f) penalties are confined to violations of a code provision "in any transaction in or affecting interstate or foreign commerce." This aspect of the case presents the question whether the particular provisions of the Live Poultry Code, which the defendants were convicted for violating and for having conspired to violate, were within the regulating power of Congress.

These provisions relate to the hours and wages of those employed by defendants in their slaughterhouses in Brooklyn and to the sales there made to retail dealers and butchers.

(1) Were these transactions *"in"* interstate commerce? Much is made of the fact that almost all the poultry coming to New York is sent there from other States. But the code provisions, as here applied, do not concern the transportation of the poultry from other States to New York, or the transaction of the commission men or others to whom it is consigned, or the sales made by such consignees to defendants. When defendants had made their purchases, whether at the West Washington Market in New York City or at the railroad terminals serving the City, or elsewhere, the poultry was trucked to their slaughterhouses in Brooklyn for local disposition. The interstate transactions in relation to that poultry then ended. Defendants held the poultry at their slaughterhouse markets for slaughter and local sale to retail dealers and butchers who in turn sold directly to consumers. Neither the slaughtering nor the sales by defendants were transactions in interstate commerce. . . .

The undisputed facts thus afford no warrant for the argument that the poultry handled by defendants at their slaughterhouse markets was in a *"current"* or *"flow"* of interstate commerce and was thus subject to congressional regulation. The mere fact that there may be a constant flow of commodities into a State does not mean that the flow continues after the property has arrived and has become commingled with the mass of property within the State and is there held solely for local disposition and use. So far as the poultry here in question is concerned, the flow in interstate commerce had ceased. The poultry had come to a permanent rest within the State. It was not held, used, or sold by defendants in relation to any further transactions in interstate commerce and was not destined for transportation to other States. Hence, decisions which deal with a stream of interstate commerce—where goods come to rest within a State temporarily and are later to go forward in interstate commerce—and with the regulations of transactions involved in that practical continuity of movement, are not applicable here. . . .

(2) Did the defendants' transactions directly *"affect"* interstate commerce so as to be subject to federal regulation? The power of Congress extends not only to the regulation of transactions which are part of interstate commerce, but to the protection of that commerce from injury. . . .

In determining how far the federal government may go in controlling intrastate transactions upon the ground that they "affect" interstate commerce, there is a necessary and well-established distinction between direct and indirect effects. The precise line can be drawn only as individual cases arise, but the distinction is clear in principle. Direct effects are illustrated by . . . e.g., the effects of failure to use prescribed safety appliances on railroads which are the highways of both interstate and intrastate commerce, injury to an employee engaged in interstate transportation by the negligence of an employee engaged in an intrastate movement, the fixing of rates for intrastate transportation which unjustly discriminate against interstate commerce. But where the effect of intrastate transaction upon interstate commerce is merely indirect, such transactions remain within the domain of state power. If the commerce clause were construed to reach all enterprises and transactions which could be said to have an indirect effect upon interstate commerce, the federal authority would embrace practically all the activities of the people and the authority of the State over its domestic concerns would exist only by sufferance of the federal government. Indeed, on such a theory, even the development of the State's commercial facilities would be subject to federal control. . . .

It is not the province of the Court to consider the economic advantages or disadvantages of such a centralized system. It is sufficient to say that the Federal Constitution does not provide for it. Our growth and development have called for wide use of the commerce power of the federal government in its control over the expanded activities of interstate commerce, and in protecting that commerce from burdens, interferences, and conspiracies to restrain and monopolize it. But the authority of the federal government may not be pushed to such an extreme as to destroy the distinction, which the commerce clause itself establishes, between commerce "among the several States" and the internal concerns of a State. The same answer must be made to the contention that is based upon the serious economic situation which led to the passage of the Recovery Act,—the fall in prices, the decline in wages and employment, and the curtailment of the market for commodities. Stress is laid upon the great importance of maintaining wage distributions which would provide the necessary stimulus in starting "the cumulative forces making for expanding commercial activity." Without in any way disparaging this motive, it is enough to say that the recuperative efforts of the federal government must be made in a manner consistent with the authority granted by the Constitution.

We are of the opinion that the attempt through the provisions of the Code to fix the hours and wages of employees of defendants in their intrastate business was not a valid exercise of federal power. . . .

. . . . .

Mr. Justice CARDOZO, concurring. . . .

. . . . .

I find no authority in that grant [the commerce clause] for the regulation of wages and hours of labor in the intrastate transactions that make up the defendants' business. As to this feature of the case little can be added to the opinion of the Court. There is a view of causation that would obliterate the distinction between what is national and what is local in the activities of commerce. Motion at the outer rim is communicated perceptibly, though minutely to recording instruments at the center. A society such as ours "is an elastic medium which transmits all tremors through its territory; the only question is of their size." Per Learned Hand, J., in the court below. The law is not indifferent to considerations of degree. Activities local in their immediacy do not become interstate and national because of distant repercussions. What is near and what is distant may at times be uncertain. . . . There is no penumbra of uncertainty obscuring judgment here. To find immediacy or directness here is to find it almost everywhere. If centripetal forces are to be isolated to the exclusion of the forces that oppose and counteract them, there will be an end to our federal system.

. . . . . .

I am authorized to state that Mr. Justice STONE joins in this opinion.

NATIONAL LABOR RELATIONS BOARD v. JONES & LAUGHLIN STEEL CORP.
301 U.S. 1 (1937)

Mr. Chief Justice HUGHES delivered the opinion of the Court.

In a proceeding under the National Labor Relations Act of 1935, (49 Stat. 449), the National Labor Relations Board found that the respondent, Jones & Laughlin Steel Corporation, had violated the Act by engaging in unfair labor practices affecting commerce. The proceeding was instituted by the Beaver Valley Lodge No. 200, affiliated with the Amalgamated Association of Iron, Steel and Tin Workers of America, a labor organization. The unfair labor practices charged were that the corporation was discriminating against members of the union with regard to hire and tenure of employment, and was coercing and intimidating its employees in order to interfere with their self-organization. The discriminatory and coercive action alleged was the discharge of certain employees.

The National Labor Relations Board, sustaining the charge, ordered the corporation to cease and desist from such discrimination and coercion, to offer reinstatement to ten of the employees named, to make good their losses in pay, and to post for thirty days notices that the corporation would not discharge or discriminate against members, or those desiring to become members, of the labor union. As the corporation failed to comply, the Board petitioned the Circuit Court of Appeals to enforce the order. The court denied the petition, holding that the order lay beyond the range of federal power. . . . We granted certiorari.

The scheme of the National Labor Relations Act—which is too long to be quoted in full—may be briefly stated. The first section sets forth findings with respect to the injury to commerce resulting from the denial by employers of the right of employees to organize and from the refusal of employers to accept the procedure of collective bargaining. There follows a declaration that it is the policy of the United States to eliminate these causes of obstruction to the free flow of commerce. The Act then defines the terms it uses, including the terms "commerce" and "affecting commerce." Section 2. It creates the National Labor Relations Board and prescribes its organization. . . . Section 7. It defines "unfair labor practices." Section 8. It lays down rules as to the representation of employees for the purpose of collective bargaining. Section 9. . . . The findings of the Board as to the facts, if supported by evidence, are to be conclusive. . . . Any person aggrieved by a final order of the Board may obtain a review in the designated courts. . . . Section 10. The Board has broad powers of investigation. . . .

Contesting the ruling of the Board, the respondent argues (1) that the Act is in reality a regulation of labor relations and not of interstate commerce; (2) that the Act can have no application to the respondent's relations with its production employees because they are not subject to regulation by the federal government; and (3) that the provisions of the Act violate Section 2 of Article III and the Fifth and Seventh Amendments of the Constitution of the United States.

The facts as to the nature and scope of the business of the Jones & Laughlin Steel Corporation have been found by the Labor Board and, so far as they are essential to the determination of this controversy, they are not in dispute. The Labor Board has found: The corporation . . . [is] the fourth largest producer of steel in the United States. With its subsidiaries—nineteen in number—it is a completely integrated enterprise, owning and operating ore, coal and limestone properties, lake and river transportation facilities and terminal railroads located at its manufacturing plants. . . . Much of its product is shipped to its warehouses in Chicago, Detroit, Cincinnati and Memphis,—to the last two places by means of its own barges and transportation equipment. In Long Island City, New York, and in New Orleans it operates structural steel fabricating shops in connection with the warehousing of semi-finished materials sent from its works. Through one of its wholly-owned subsidiaries it owns, leases and operates stores, warehouses and yards for the distribution of equipment and supplies for drilling and operating oil and gas wells and for pipe lines, refineries and pumping stations. It has sales offices in twenty cities in the United States and a wholly-owned subsidiary which is devoted exclusively to distributing its product in Canada. Approximately 75 per cent of its product is shipped out of Pennsylvania.

Summarizing these operations, the Labor Board concluded that the works in Pittsburgh and Aliquippa "might be likened to the heart of a self-contained, highly integrated body. They draw in the raw materials from Michigan, Minnesota, West Virginia, Pennsylvania in part through arteries and by means controlled by the respondent;

they transform the materials and then pump them out to all parts of the nation through the vast mechanism which the respondent has elaborated." . . .

Practically all the factual evidence in the case, except that which dealt with the nature of the respondent's business, concerned its relations with the employees in the Aliquippa plant whose discharge was the subject of the complaint. These employees were active leaders in the labor union. Several were officers and others were leaders of particular groups. Two of the employees were motor inspectors; one was a tractor driver; three were crane operators; one was a washer in a coke plant; and three were laborers.

While respondent criticizes the evidence and the attitude of the Board, which is described as being hostile toward employers and particularly toward those who insisted upon their constitutional rights, respondent did not take advantage of its opportunity to present evidence to refute that which was offered to show discrimination and coercion. In this situation, the record presents no ground for setting aside the order of the Board so far as the facts pertaining to the circumstances and purpose of the discharge of the employees are concerned. Upon that point it is sufficient to say that the evidence supports the findings of the Board that respondent discharged these men "because of their union activity and for the purpose of discouraging membership in the union." We turn to the questions of law which the respondent urges in contesting the validity and application of the Act.

First. The scope of the Act.—The Act is challenged in its entirety as an attempt to regulate all industry, thus invading the reserved powers of the States over their local concerns. It is asserted that the references in the Act to interstate and foreign commerce are colorable at best. . . . And it is further insisted that its legislative history shows an essential universal purpose in the light of which its scope cannot be limited by either construction or by the application of the separability clause.

If this conception of terms, intent and consequent inseparability were sound, the Act would necessarily fall by reason of the limitation upon the federal power which inheres in the constitutional grant, as well as because of the explicit reservation of the Tenth Amendment. *Schechter Corporation* v. *United States,* [*supra*]. The authority of the federal government may not be pushed to such an extreme as to destroy the distinction, which the commerce clause itself establishes, between "commerce among the several States" and the internal concerns of a State. That distinction between what is national and what is local in the activities of commerce is vital to the maintenance of our federal system.

But we are not at liberty to deny effect to specific provisions, which Congress has constitutional power to enact, by superimposing upon them inferences from general legislative declarations of an ambiguous character, even if found in the same statute. The cardinal principle of statutory construction is to save and not to destroy. We have repeatedly held that as between two possible interpretations of a statute, by one of which it would be unconstitutional and by the other valid, our plain duty is to adopt that which will save the act. Even to avoid a serious doubt the rule is the same. . . .

We think it clear that the National Labor Relations Act may be construed so as to operate within the sphere of constitutional authority. . . .

There can be no question that the commerce . . . contemplated by the Act . . . is interstate and foreign commerce in the constitutional sense. . . .

. . . The grant of authority to the Board does not purport to extend to the relationship between all industrial employees and employers. Its terms do not impose collective bargaining upon all industry regardless of effects upon interstate or foreign commerce. . . . It is a familiar principle that acts which directly burden or obstruct interstate or foreign commerce, or its free flow, are within the reach of the congressional power. Acts having that effect are not rendered immune because they grow out of labor disputes. It is the effect upon commerce, not the source of the injury, which is the criterion. Whether or not particular action does affect commerce in such a close and intimate fashion as to be subject to federal control, and hence to lie within the authority conferred upon the Board, is left by the statute to be determined as individual cases arise. We are thus to inquire whether in the instant case the constitutional boundary has been passed.

Second. The unfair labor practices in question. . . . [The Court upholds the principle of collective bargaining.]

.   .   .   .   .   .

Third. The application of the Act to employees engaged in pro-

duction. Respondent says that whatever may be said relations and activities in the manufacturing department of respondent's enterprise are not subject to federal regulation. The argument rests upon the proposition that manufacturing in itself is not commerce. . . .

The Government . . . [describes] . . . the various parts of respondent's enterprise . . . as interdependent and as thus involving "a great movement of iron ore, coal and limestone along well-defined paths to the steel mills, then through them, and thence in the form of steel products into the consuming centers of the country—a definite and well-understood course of business." It is urged that these activities constitute a "stream" or "flow" of commerce, of which the Aliquippa manufacturing plant is the focal point, and that industrial strife at that point would cripple the entire movement. . . .

. . . The congressional authority to protect interstate commerce from burdens and obstructions is not limited to transactions which can be deemed to be an essential part of a "flow" of interstate or foreign commerce. Burdens and obstructions may be due to injurious action springing from other sources. The fundamental principle is that the power to regulate commerce is the power to enact "all appropriate legislation" for "its protection and advancement"; to adopt measures "to promote its growth and insure its safety"; "to foster, protect, control and restrain." . . . Although activities may be intrastate in character when separately considered, if they have such a close and substantial relation to interstate commerce that their control is essential or appropriate to protect that commerce from burdens and obstructions, Congress cannot be denied the power to exercise that control.

The close and intimate effect which brings the subject within the reach of federal power may be due to activities in relation to productive industry although the industry when separately viewed is local. This has been abundantly illustrated in the application of the federal Anti-Trust Act. . . .

Upon the same principle, the Anti-Trust Act has been applied to the conduct of employees engaged in production. . . .

It is thus apparent that the fact that the employees here concerned were engaged in production is not determinative. The question remains as to the effect upon interstate commerce of the labor practice involved. . . .

Fourth. Effects of the unfair labor practice in respondent's enterprise.—Giving full weight to respondent's contention with respect to a break in the complete continuity in the "stream of commerce" by reason of respondent's manufacturing operations, the fact remains that the stoppage of those operations by industrial strife would have a most serious effect upon interstate commerce. In view of respondent's far-flung activities, it is idle to say that the effect would be indirect or remote. It is obvious that it would be immediate and might be catastrophic. We are asked to shut our eyes to the plainest facts of our national life and to deal with the question of direct and indirect effects in an intellectual vacuum. . . . When industries organize themselves on a national scale, making their relation to interstate commerce the dominant factor in their activities, how can it be maintained that their industrial labor relations constitute a forbidden field into which Congress may not enter when it is necessary to protect interstate commerce from the paralyzing consequences of industrial war? We have often said that interstate commerce itself is a practical conception. It is equally true that interferences with that commerce must be appraised by a judgment that does not ignore actual experience.

Experience has abundantly demonstrated that the recognition of the right of employees to self-organization and to have representatives of their own choosing for the purpose of collective bargaining is often an essential condition of industrial peace. . . . This is such an outstanding fact in the history of labor disturbances that it is a proper subject of judicial notice and requires no citation of instances. . . . And of what avail is it to protect the facility of transportation, if interstate commerce is throttled with respect to the commodities to be transported! . . .

Our conclusion is that the order of the Board was within its competency and that the Act is valid as here applied. . . .

Mr. Justice McREYNOLDS.

Mr. Justice VAN DEVANTER, Mr. Justice SUTHERLAND, Mr. Justice BUTLER and I are unable to agree with the decisions just announced. . . .

MULFORD v. SMITH
307 U.S. 38 (1939)

Mr. Justice ROBERTS delivered the opinion of the Court.

The appellants [Mulford et al.], producers of flue-cured tobacco, assert that the Agricultural Adjustment Act of 1938, is unconstitutional as it affects their 1938 crop.

The portions of the statute involved are those included in Title III, providing marketing quotas for flue-cured tobacco. The Act directs that when the supply is found to exceed the level defined in the Act as the "reserve supply level" a national marketing quota shall become effective which will permit enough flue-cured tobacco to be marketed during the ensuing marketing year to maintain the supply at the reserve supply level. The quota is to be apportioned to the farms on which tobacco is grown. Penalties are to be paid by tobacco auction warehousemen for marketing tobacco from a farm in excess of its quota.

Section 311 is a finding by the Congress that the marketing of tobacco is a basic industry which directly affects interstate and foreign commerce; that stable conditions in such marketing are necessary to the general welfare; that tobacco is sold on a national market and it and its products move almost wholly in interstate and foreign commerce; that without federal assistance the farmers are unable to bring about orderly marketing, with the consequence that abnormally excessive supplies are produced and dumped indiscriminately on the national market; that this disorderly marketing of excess supply burdens and obstructs interstate and foreign commerce, causes reduction in prices and consequent injury to commerce, creates disparity between the prices of tobacco in interstate and foreign commerce and the prices of industrial products in such commerce, and diminishes the volume of interstate commerce in industrial products; and that the establishment of quotas as provided by the Act is necessary and appropriate to promote, foster and obtain an orderly flow of tobacco in interstate and foreign commerce.

. . . The Act provided, with respect to the marketing year beginning July 1, 1938, for which the quotas involved in this case were in effect, that the determination and proclamation of the national marketing quota should be made within fifteen days after the statute's approval.

Within thirty days after proclamation, the Secretary is to conduct a referendum of the producers of the crop of the preceding year to ascertain whether they favor or oppose the imposition of a quota. If more than one-third oppose, the Secretary is to proclaim the result before January 1st and the quota is not to be effective.

By Section 313(a) it is directed that the quota is to be first apportioned among the states based on the total quantity of tobacco produced in each state during the five years immediately preceding the year in question, plus the normal production of any acreage diverted under any agricultural adjustment and conservation program in any of the years. . . . A limit is set below which the quota of any state may not be reduced.

The Act provides for the apportionment of the state allotment amongst the farms which produced tobacco in the current year or have produced previously in one or more of the four preceding years. Apportionment to these farms is to be made on the basis of past marketing, after due allowance for . . . [various factors]. A limit is fixed below which the adjustment may not reduce the production of a given farm. Allotment to new tobacco farms is to be made on a slightly different basis.

Apportionment of the quota amongst individual farms is to be by local committees of farmers according to standards prescribed in the Act, amplified by regulations and instructions issued by the Secretary. Each farmer is to be notified of his marketing quota and the quotas of individual farms are to be kept available for public inspection in the county or district where the farm is located. If the farmer is dissatisfied with his allotment he may have his quota reviewed by a local review committee, and, if dissatisfied with the determination of that committee, he may obtain judicial review.

Section 314 provides that if tobacco in excess of the quota for the farm on which the tobacco is produced is marketed through a warehouseman, the latter must pay to the Secretary a penalty equal to fifty per cent. of the market price of the excess, and may deduct an amount equivalent to the penalty from the price paid the producer. . . .

A few days before the 1938 auction sales were to take place, the appellants, who produce flue-cured tobacco in southern Georgia and northern Florida, filed a . . . [complaint] . . . in a Georgia state court against local warehousemen [Smith et al.] to restrain them from deducting penalties under the Act from the sales price of tobacco to be sold at their auction warehouses on behalf of appellants. The . . . [complaint] alleged that the Act is unconstitutional. . . . The cause was set down before a [District] court consisting of three judges, which heard it on a stipulation of facts and entered a decree dismissing the bill. . . .

The appellants [Mulford et al.] plant themselves upon three propositions: (1) that the Act is a statutory plan to control agricultural production and, therefore, beyond the powers delegated to Congress;

(2) that the standard for calculating farm quotas is uncertain, vague, and indefinite, resulting in an unconstitutional delegation of legislative power to the Secretary; (3) that, as applied to appellants' 1938 crop, the Act takes their property without due process of law.

First. The statute does not purport to control production. It sets no limit upon the acreage which may be planted or produced and imposes no penalty for the planting and producing of tobacco in excess of the marketing quota. It purports to be solely a regulation of interstate commerce, which it reaches and affects at the throat where tobacco enters the stream of commerce,—the marketing warehouse. The record discloses that at least two-thirds of all flue-cured tobacco sold at auction warehouses is sold for immediate shipment to an interstate or foreign destination. In Georgia nearly one hundred per cent. of the tobacco so sold is purchased by extrastate purchasers. In markets where tobacco is sold to both interstate and intrastate purchasers it is not known, when the grower places his tobacco on the warehouse floor for sale, whether it is destined for interstate or intrastate commerce. Regulation to be effective, must, and therefore may constitutionally, apply to all sales. . . . Any rule, such as that embodied in the Act, which is intended to foster, protect and conserve that commerce, or to prevent the flow of commerce from working harm to the people of the nation, is within the competence of Congress. Within these limits the exercise of the power, the grant being unlimited in its terms, may lawfully extend to the absolute prohibition of such commerce, and *a fortiori* to limitation of the amount of a given commodity which may be transported in such commerce. The motive of Congress in exerting the power is irrelevant to the validity of the legislation.

The provisions of the Act under review constitute a regulation of interstate and foreign commerce within the competency of Congress under the power delegated to it by the Constitution.

Second. . . .

Third. . . .

The decree is affirmed.

Mr. Justice BUTLER, dissenting. . . .

The penalty is laid on the farmer to prevent production in excess of his quota. It is therefore invalid.

If the penalty is imposed for marketing in interstate commerce, it is a regulation not authorized in the commerce clause.

To impose penalties for marketing in excess of quotas not disclosed before planting and cultivation is to deprive plantiffs of their liberty and property without due process of law.

The judgment of the district court should be reversed.

Mr. Justice McReynolds concurs in this opinion.

UNITED STATES v. DARBY
312 U.S. 100 (1941)

Mr. Justice Stone delivered the opinion of the Court.

The two principal questions raised by the record in this case are, first, whether Congress has constitutional power to prohibit the shipment in interstate commerce of lumber manufactured by employees whose wages are less than a prescribed minimum or whose weekly hours of labor at that wage are greater than a prescribed maximum, and second, whether it has power to prohibit the employment of workmen in the production of goods "for interstate commerce" at other than prescribed wages and hours. A subsidiary question is whether in connection with such prohibitions Congress can require the employer subject to them to keep records showing the hours worked each day and week by each of his employees including those engaged "in the production and manufacture of goods to wit, lumber, for 'interstate commerce'."

. . . . . .

The Fair Labor Standards Act set up a comprehensive legislative scheme for preventing the shipment in interstate commerce of certain products and commodities produced in the United States under labor conditions as respects wages and hours which fail to conform to standards set up by the Act. Its purpose, as we judicially know from the declaration of policy in § 2(a) of the Act, and the reports of Congressional committees proposing the legislation, . . . is to exclude from interstate commerce goods produced for the commerce and to prevent their production for interstate commerce, under conditions detrimental to the maintenance of the minimum standards of living necessary for health and general well-being; and to prevent the use of interstate commerce as the means of competition in the distribution of goods so produced, and as the means of spreading and perpetuating such substandard labor conditions among the workers of the several states. The Act also sets up an administrative procedure whereby those standards may from time to time be modified generally as to industries subject to the Act or within an industry in accordance with specified standards, by an administrator acting in collaboration with "Industry Committees" appointed by him.

... Section 15(a)(1) makes unlawful the shipment in interstate commerce of any goods "in the production of which any employee was employed in violation of section 6 or section 7," which provide, among other things, that during the first year of operation of the Act a minimum wage of 25 cents per hour shall be paid to employees "engaged in [interstate] commerce or in the production of goods for [interstate] commerce," § 6, and the maximum hours of employment for employees "engaged in commerce or in the production of goods for commerce" without increased compensation for overtime, shall be forty-four hours a week. § 7.

Section 15(a)(2) makes it unlawful to violate the provisions of §§ 6 and 7 including the minimum wage and maximum hour requirements just mentioned for employees engaged in production of goods for commerce. Section 15 (a)(5) makes it unlawful for an employer subject to the Act to violate § 11(c) which requires him to keep such records of the persons employed by him and of their wages and hours of employment as the administrator shall prescribe by regulation or order.

The indictment charges that appellee is engaged, in the state of Georgia, in the business of acquiring raw materials, which he manufactures into finished lumber with the intent, when manufactured, to ship it in interstate commerce to customers outside the state, and that he does in fact so ship a large part of the lumber so produced. There are numerous counts charging appellee with the shipment in interstate commerce from Georgia to points outside the state of lumber in the production of which, for interstate commerce, appellee has employed workmen at less than the prescribed minimum wage or more than the prescribed maximum hours without payment to them of any wage for overtime. . . .

... The district court quashed the indictment in its entirety upon the broad grounds that the Act, which it interpreted as a regulation of manufacture within the states, is unconstitutional. It declared that manufacture is not interstate commerce and that the regulation by the Fair Labor Standards Act of wages and hours of employment of those engaged in the manufacture of goods which it is intended at the time of production "may or will be" after production "sold in interstate commerce in part or in whole" is not within the congressional power to regulate interstate commerce.

The effect of the court's decision and judgment are thus to deny the power of Congress to prohibit shipment in interstate commerce of lumber produced for interstate commerce under the proscribed substandard labor conditions of wages and hours, its power to penalize the employer for his failure to conform to the wage and hour provisions in the case of employees engaged in the production of lumber which he intends thereafter to ship in interstate commerce in part or in whole according to the normal course of his business and its power to compel him to keep records of hours of employment as required by the statute and the regulations of the administrator.

. . . [We] confine our decision to the validity and construction of the statute.

The prohibition of shipment of the proscribed goods in interstate commerce. Section 15 (a)(1) prohibits, and the indictment charges, the shipment in interstate commerce, of goods produced for interstate commerce by employees whose wages and hours of employment do not conform to the requirements of the Act. Since this section is not violated unless the commodity shipped has been produced under labor conditions prohibited by § 6 and § 7, the only question arising under the commerce clause with respect to such shipments is whether Congress has the constitutional power to prohibit them.

While manufacture is not of itself interstate commerce the shipment of manufactured goods interstate is such commerce and the prohibition of such shipment by Congress is indubitably a regulation of the commerce. The power to regulate commerce is the power "to prescribe the rule by which commerce is to be governed." *Gibbons* v. *Ogden,* 9 Wheat. 1, 196. It extends not only to those regulations which aid, foster and protect the commerce, but embraces those which prohibit it. . . . It is conceded that the power of Congress to prohibit transportation in interstate commerce includes noxious articles, *Lottery Case,* 188 U.S. 321; *Hipolite Egg Co.* v. *United States,* 220 U.S. 45; cf. *Hoke* v. *United States,* 227 U.S. 308; stolen articles, *Brooks* v. *United States,* 267 U.S. 432; kidnapped persons, *Gooch* v. *United States,* 297 U.S. 124, and articles such as intoxicating liquor or convict made goods, traffic in which is forbidden or restricted by the laws of the state of destination. *Kentucky Whip & Collar Co.* v. *Illinois Central R. Co.,* 299 U.S. 334.[9]

But it is said that the present prohibition falls within the scope of none of these categories; that while the prohibition is nominally a

[9] See *supra,* note 6, p. 207.

regulation of the commerce its motive or purpose is regulation of wages and hours of persons engaged in manufacture, the control of which has been reserved to the states and upon which Georgia and some of the states of destination have placed no restriction; that the effect of the present statute is not to exclude the prescribed articles from interstate commerce in aid of state regulation as in *Kentucky Whip & Collar Co.* v. *Illinois Central R. Co., supra,* but instead under the guise of a regulation of interstate commerce, it undertakes to regulate wages and hours within the state contrary to the policy of the state which has elected to leave them unregulated.

The power of Congress over interstate commerce "is complete in itself, may be exercised to its utmost extent, and acknowledges no limitations, other than are prescribed by the Constitution." *Gibbons* v. *Ogden, supra,* 9 Wheat. 196. That power can neither be enlarged nor diminished by the exercise or non-exercise of state power. . . . Congress, following its own conception of public policy concerning the restrictions which may appropriately be imposed on interstate commerce, is free to exclude from the commerce articles whose use in the states for which they are destined it may conceive to be injurious to the public health, morals or welfare, even though the state has not sought to regulate their use. . . .

Such regulation is not a forbidden invasion of state power merely because either its motive or its consequence is to restrict the use of articles of commerce within the states of destination and is not prohibited unless by other Constitutional provisions. It is no objection to the assertion of the power to regulate interstate commerce that its exercise is attended by the same incidents which attend the exercise of the police power of the states. . . .

The motive and purpose of the present regulation is plainly to make effective the Congressional conception of public policy that interstate commerce should not be made the instrument of competition in the distribution of goods produced under substandard labor conditions, which competition is injurious to the commerce and to the states from and to which the commerce flows. The motive and purpose of a regulation of interstate commerce are matters for the legislative judgment upon the exercise of which the Constitution places no restriction and over which the courts are given no control. . . . Whatever their motive and purpose, regulations of commerce which do not infringe some constitutional prohibition are within the plenary power conferred on Congress by the Commerce Clause. . . .

In the more than a century which has elapsed since the decision of *Gibbons* v. *Ogden,* these principles of constitutional interpretation have been so long and repeatedly recognized by this Court as applicable to the Commerce Clause, that there would be little occasion for repeating them now were it not for the decision of this Court twenty-two years ago in *Hammer* v. *Dagenhart,* 247 U.S. 251. In that case it was held by a bare majority of the Court over the powerful and now classic dissent of Mr. Justice Holmes setting forth the fundamental issues involved, that Congress was without power to exclude the products of child labor from interstate commerce. The reasoning and conclusion of the Court's opinion there cannot be reconciled with the conclusion which we have reached. . . .

. . . *Hammer* v. *Dagenhart* was a departure from the principles which have prevailed in the interpretation of the commerce clause both before and since the decision and . . . such vitality, as a precedent, as it then had has long since been exhausted. It should be and now is overruled.

Validity of the wage and hour requirements. Section 15 (a) (2) and §§ 6 and 7 require employers to conform to the wage and hour provisions with respect to all employees engaged in the production of goods for interstate commerce. As appellee's employees are not alleged to be "engaged in interstate commerce" the validity of the prohibition turns on the question whether the employment, under other than the prescribed labor standards, of employees engaged in the production of goods for interstate commerce is so related to the commerce and so affects it as to be within the reach of the power of Congress to regulate it.

To answer this question we must at the outset determine whether the particular acts charged in the counts which are laid under § 15(a)(2) . . . constitute "production for commerce" within the meaning of the statute. . . .

Without attempting to define the precise limits of the phrase, we think the acts alleged in the indictment are within the sweep of the statute. The obvious purpose of the Act was not only to prevent the interstate transportation of the proscribed product, but to stop the initial step toward transportation, production with the purpose of so transporting it. Congress was not unaware that most manufacturing businesses shipping their product in interstate commerce make it in their shops without reference to its ultimate destination and then after manufacture select some of it for shipment interstate and some intrastate according to the daily demands of their business, and that it would be practically impossible, without disrupting manufacturing businesses, to restrict the prohibited kind of production to the particular pieces of lumber, cloth, furniture or the like which later move in interstate rather than intrastate commerce.

The recognized need of drafting a workable statute and the well known circumstances in which it was to be applied are persuasive of the conclusion, which the legislative history supports, . . . that the "production for commerce" intended includes at least production of goods, which, at the time of production, the employer, according to the normal course of his business, intends or expects to move in interstate commerce although, through the exigencies of the business, all of the goods may not thereafter actually enter interstate commerce.

There remains the question whether such restriction on the production of goods for commerce is a permissible exercise of the commerce power. The power of Congress over interstate commerce is not confined to the regulation of commerce among the states. It extends to those activities intrastate which so affect interstate commerce or the exercise of the power of Congress over it as to make regulation of them appropriate means to the attainment of a legitimate end, the exercise of the granted power of Congress to regulate interstate commerce.

. . . This Court has many times held that the power of Congress to regulate interstate commerce extends to the regulation through legislative action of activities intrastate which have a substantial effect on the commerce or the exercise of the Congressional power over it.

In such legislation Congress has sometimes left it to the courts to determine whether the intrastate activities have the prohibited effect on the commerce, as in the Sherman Act. It has sometimes left it to an administrative board or agency to determine whether the activities sought to be regulated or prohibited have such effect, as in the case of the Interstate Commerce Act and National Labor Relations Act. . . . And sometimes Congress itself has said that a particular activity affects the commerce as it did in the present act, the Safety Appliance Act and the Railway Labor Act. In passing on the validity of legislation of the class last mentioned the only function of courts is to determine whether the particular activity regulated or prohibited is within the reach of the federal power.

Congress, having by the present Act adopted the policy of excluding from interstate commerce all goods produced for the commerce which do not conform to the specified labor standards, it may choose the means reasonably adapted to the attainment of the permitted end, even though they involve control of intrastate activities. Such legislation has often been sustained with respect to powers, other than the commerce power granted to the national government, when the means chosen, although not themselves within the granted power, were nevertheless deemed appropriate aids to the accomplishment of some purpose within an admitted power of the national government.

. . . . .

A familiar like exercise of power is the regulation of intrastate transactions which are so commingled with or related to interstate commerce that all must be regulated if the interstate commerce is to be effectively controlled. *Shreveport Case,* 234 U.S. 342.[10]

. . . . .

The means adopted by § 15 (a) (2) for the protection of interstate commerce by the suppression of the production of the condemned goods for interstate commerce is so related to the commerce and so affects it as to be within the reach of the commerce power. Congress, to attain its objective in the suppression of nationwide competition in interstate commerce by goods produced under substandard labor conditions, has made no distinction as to the volume or amount of shipments in the commerce or of production for commerce by any particular shipper or producer. It recognized that in present day industry, competition by a small part may affect the whole and that the total effect of the competition of many small producers may be great. . . .

. . . . .

Our conclusion is unaffected by the Tenth Amendment which provides: "The powers not delegated to the United States by the Constitution, nor prohibited by it to the States are reserved to the States respectively, or to the people." The amendment states but a

[10] *Supra,* p. 212.

truism that all is retained which has not been surrendered. There is nothing in the history of its adoption to suggest that it was more than declaratory of the relationship between the national and state government as it had been established by the Constitution before the amendment or that its purpose was other than to allay fears that the new national government might seek to exercise powers not granted, and that the states might not be able to exercise fully their reserved powers. . . .

From the beginning and for many years the amendment has been construed as not depriving the national government of authority to resort to all means for the exercise of a granted power which are appropriate and plainly adapted to the permitted end. . . . Whatever doubts may have arisen of the soundness of that conclusion they have been put at rest by the decisions under the Sherman Act and National Labor Relations Act. . . .

We have considered, but find it unnecessary to discuss other contentions.

Reversed.

WICKARD v. FILBURN
317 U.S. 111 (1942)

Mr. Justice JACKSON delivered the opinion of the Court.

The appellee filed his complaint against the Secretary of Agriculture of the United States, three members of the County Agricultural Conservation Committee for Montgomery County, Ohio, and a member of the State Agricultural Conservation Committee for Ohio. He sought to enjoin enforcement against himself of the marketing penalty imposed by the amendment of May 26, 1941, to the Agricultural Adjustment Act of 1938, upon that part of his 1941 wheat crop which was available for marketing in excess of the marketing quota established for his farm. He also sought a declaratory judgment that the wheat marketing quota provisions of the Act as amended and applicable to him were unconstitutional because not sustainable under the Commerce Clause or consistent with the Due Process Clause of the Fifth Amendment.

. . . . . .

The appellee for many years past has owned and operated a small farm in Montgomery County, Ohio, maintaining a herd of dairy cattle, selling milk, raising poultry, and selling poultry and eggs. It has been his practice to raise a small acreage of winter wheat, sown in the fall and harvested in the following July; to sell a portion of the crop; to feed part to poultry and livestock on the farm, some of which is sold; to use some in making flour for home consumption; and to keep the rest for the following seeding. The intended disposition of the crop here involved has not been expressly stated.

In July of 1940, pursuant to the Agricultural Adjustment Act of 1938, as then amended, there was established for the appellee's 1941 crop a wheat acreage allotment of 11.1 acres and a normal yield of 20.1 bushels of wheat an acre. He was given notice of such allotment in July of 1940 before the fall planting of his 1941 crop of wheat, and again in July of 1941, before it was harvested. He sowed, however, 23 acres, and harvested from his 11.9 acres of excess acreage 239 bushels, which under the terms of the Act as amended on May 26, 1941, constituted farm marketing excess, subject to a penalty of 49 cents a bushel, or $117.11 in all. The appellee has not paid the penalty and he has not postponed or avoided it by storing the excess under regulations of the Secretary of Agriculture, or by delivering it up to the Secretary. . . .

The general scheme of the Agricultural Adjustment Act of 1938 as related to wheat is to control the volume moving in interstate and foreign commerce in order to avoid surpluses and shortages and the consequent abnormally low or high wheat prices and obstructions to commerce. Within prescribed limits and by prescribed standards the Secretary of Agriculture is directed to ascertain and proclaim each year a national acreage allotment for the next crop of wheat, which is then apportioned to the states and their counties, and is eventually broken up into allotments for individual farms. Loans and payments to wheat farmers are authorized in stated circcumstances.

The Act provides further that whenever it appears that the total supply of wheat as of the beginning of any marketing year, beginning July 1, will exceed a normal year's domestic consumption and export by more than 35 per cent, the Secretary shall so proclaim not later than May 15 prior to the beginning of such marketing year; and that during the marketing year a compulsory national marketing quota shall be in effect with respect to the marketing of wheat. Between the issuance of the proclamation and June 10, the Secretary must, however, conduct a referendum of farmers who will be subject to the quota to determine whether they favor or oppose it; and if more than one-third of the farmers voting in the referendum do oppose, the

Secretary must prior to the effective date of the quota by proclamation suspend its operation.

It is urged that under the Commerce Clause of the Constitution, Article I, § 8, clause 3, Congress does not possess the power it has in this instance sought to exercise. The question would merit little consideration since our decision in *United States* v. *Darby*, 312 U.S. 100[11] sustaining the federal power to regulate production of goods for commerce except for the fact that this Act extends federal regulation to production not intended in any part for commerce but wholly for consumption on the farm. The Act includes a definition of "market" and its derivatives so that as related to wheat in addition to its conventional meaning it also means to dispose of "by feeding (in any form) to poultry or livestock which, or the products of which, are sold, bartered, or exchanged or to be so disposed of." Hence, marketing quotas not only embrace all that may be sold without penalty but also what may be consumed on the premises. Wheat produced on excess acreage is designated as "available for marketing" as so defined and the penalty is imposed thereon. Penalties do not depend upon whether any part of the wheat either within or without the quota is sold or intended to be sold. The sum of this is that the Federal Government fixes a quota including all that the farmer may harvest for sale or for his own farm needs, and declares that wheat produced on excess acreage may neither be disposed of nor used except upon payment of the penalty or except it is stored as required by the Act or delivered to the Secretary of Agriculture.

Appellee says that this is a regulation of production and consumption of wheat. Such activities are, he urges, beyond the reach of Congressional power under the Commerce Clause, since they are local in character, and their effects upon interstate commerce are at most "indirect." In answer the Government argues that the statute regulates neither production nor consumption, but only marketing; and, in the alternative, that if the Act does go beyond the regulation of marketing it is sustainable as a "necessary and proper" implementation of the power of Congress over interstate commerce.

The Government's concern lest the Act be held to be a regulation of production or consumption rather than of marketing is attributable to a few dicta and decisions of this Court which might be

[11] *Supra,* p. 233.

understood to lay it down that activities such as "production," "manufacturing," and "mining" are strictly "local" and, except in special circumstances which are not present here, cannot be regulated under the commerce power because their effects upon interstate commerce are, as matter of law, only "indirect." Even today, when this power has been held to have great latitude, there is no decision of this Court that such activities may be regulated where no part of the product is intended for interstate commerce or intermingled with the subjects thereof. We believe that a review of the course of decision under the Commerce Clause will make plain, however, that questions of the power of Congress are not to be decided by reference to any formula which would give controlling force to nomenclature such as "production" and "indirect" and foreclose consideration of the actual effects of the activity in question upon interstate commerce.

At the beginning Chief Justice Marshall described the federal commerce power with a breadth never yet exceeded. *Gibbons* v. *Ogden*, 9 Wheat. 1, 194, 195. He made emphatic the embracing and penetrating nature of this power by warning that effective restraints on its exercise must proceed from political rather than from judicial processes. *Id.* at 197.

Once an economic measure of the reach of the power granted to Congress in the Commerce Clause is accepted, questions of federal power cannot be decided simply by finding the activity in question to be "production" nor can consideration of its economic effects be foreclosed by calling them "indirect." The present Chief Justice[12] has said in summary of the present state of the law: "The commerce power is not confined in its exercise to the regulation of commerce among the states. It extends to those activities intrastate which so affect interstate commerce, or the exertion of the power of Congress over it, as to make regulation of them appropriate means to the attainment of a legitimate end, the effective execution of the granted power to regulate interstate commerce is plenary and complete in itself, may be exercised to its utmost extent, and acknowledges no limitations other than are prescribed in the Constitution. . . . It follows that no form of state activity can constitutionally thwart the regulatory power granted by the commerce clause to Congress. Hence the reach of that power extends to those intrastate activities which in

---

[12] Harlan F. Stone (died 1946) .

a substantial way interfere with or obstruct the exercise of the granted power." *United States* v. *Wrightwood Dairy Co.,* 315 U.S. 110, 119.

Whether the subject of the regulation in question was "production," "consumption," or "marketing" is, therefore, not material for purposes of deciding the question of federal power before us. That an activity is of local character may help in a doubtful case to determine whether Congress intended to reach it. The same consideration might help in determining whether in the absence of Congressional action it would be permissible for the state to exert its power on the subject matter, even though in so doing it to some degree affected interstate commerce. But even if appellant's activity be local and though it may not be regarded as commerce, it may still, whatever its nature, be reached by Congress if it exerts a substantial economic effect on interstate commerce and this irrespective of whether such effect is what might at some earlier time have been defined as "direct" or "indirect."

.   .   .   .   .

The maintenance by government regulation of a price for wheat undoubtedly can be accomplished as effectively by sustaining or increasing the demand as by limiting the supply. The effect of the statute before us is to restrict the amount which may be produced for market and the extent as well to which one may forestall resort to the market by producing to meet his own needs. That appellee's own contribution to the demand for wheat may be trivial by itself is not enough to remove him from the scope of federal regulation where, as here, his contribution, taken together with that of many others similarly situated, is far from trivial. *National Labor Relations Board* v. *Fainblatt,* 306 U.S. 601, 606, *et seq.; United States* v. *Darby, supra* at 123.

It is well established by decisions of this Court that the power to regulate commerce includes the power to regulate the prices at which commodities in that commerce are dealt in and practices affecting such prices. One of the primary purposes of the Act in question was to increase the market price of wheat and to that end to limit the volume thereof that could affect the market. It can hardly be denied that a factor of such volume and variability as home-consumed wheat would have a substantial influence on price and market conditions. This may arise because being in marketable condition such homegrown wheat overhangs the market and if induced by rising prices tends to flow into the market and check price increases. But if we assume that it is never marketed, it supplies a need of the man who grew it which would otherwise be reflected by purchases in the open market. Homegrown wheat in this sense competes with wheat in commerce. The stimulation of commerce is a use of the regulatory function quite as definitely as prohibitions or restrictions thereon. This record leaves us in no doubt that Congress may properly have considered that wheat consumed on the farm where grown if wholly outside the scheme of regulation would have a substantial effect in defeating and obstructing its purpose to stimulate trade therein at increased prices.

It is said, however, that this Act, forcing some farmers into the market to buy what they could provide for themselves, is an unfair promotion of the markets and prices of specializing wheat growers. It is of the essence of regulation that it lays a restraining hand on the self-interest of the regulated and that advantages from the regulation commonly fall to others. The conflicts of economic interest between the regulated and those who advantage by it are wisely left under our system to resolution by the Congress under its more flexible and responsible legislative process. Such conflicts rarely lend themselves to judicial determination. And with the wisdom, workability, or fairness, of the plan of regulation we have nothing to do.

The statute is also challenged as a deprivation of property without due process of law contrary to the Fifth Amendment, both because of its regulatory effect on the appellee and because of its alleged retroactive effect. [The due process contentions were rejected; the discussion is omitted.]

Reversed.

3. COMMERCE CLAUSE AND STATE ACTION

THE PROBLEM STATED[13]

It has already been shown that the commerce clause has been the most important instrument in the expansion of federal powers, and that this has subjected to federal control many local matters because of their relation to interstate commerce. Some of them were being

[13] By Henry Rottschaefer in *The Constitution and Socio-Economic Change;* Ann Arbor: University of Michigan Law School, 1948, pp. 97–103. Reprinted by permission of the author and the publishers.

regulated by the states when Congress intervened, and state control of some came subsequent thereto. In either case, the question arose how far state regulations could still be enforced in the face of federal assumption of some control of the same field. It was a variant of the problem that dated back as far as *Cooley* v. *Board of Port Wardens*. It differed from the earlier one in that the local matter regulated was not itself a part of interstate commerce. That case had divided the subject matter of the commerce power into matters requiring uniformity of treatment on a national basis and those permitting diversity of treatment. It had affirmed the inability of the states to regulate the former, and their competence to regulate the latter in the absence of federal action undertaking to do so. That the only federal legislation concerning pilots had accepted the rules established by the states was held to show a Congressional intent to leave their regulation to the states. The principal opinion in the case expressly excluded from what was being decided the "question how far any regulation of a subject by Congress, may be deemed to operate as an exclusion of all legislation by the States upon the same subject." It was recognized that any state rules that conflicted with a valid federal regulation would be invalid or, as would be said today, unenforceable. That the state pilotage laws did not interfere with any system of regulation established by Congress was among the reasons for sustaining them. The problem of how far the enactment of any legislation by Congress operated to exclude state action, even when not in conflict with federal regulations, was thus posed at a relatively early date with respect to state regulation of interstate transactions. The same question as to the effect of such federal legislation upon state regulation of matters not constituting a part of interstate commerce arose later. The importance of this latter question has transcended that of the former as Congress has used its commerce power more and more to control local matters substantially affecting interstate commerce.

There is no way of preventing federal intervention to regulate local matters under the commerce clause from limiting the potential sphere of state action. The most that the states can hope for is that the Court will so construe federal legislation as to preserve as much of their power as possible. The Court is impotent to help where the state regulations are clearly in conflict with those enacted by Congress. If the conflict is not so clear, it has considerable freedom in choosing between protecting the states' powers and expanding the area of effective federal control. Its discretion becomes the decisive factor when there is no direct conflict. However, the mere absence thereof does not mean that the states' regulations may be enforced. Their enforcement may be incompatible with the execution of the policy of the federal legislation. The decision on such an issue depends largely on how the Court exercises the discretion necessarily vested in it. This is especially true when the question is to what extent federal regulation of some parts of the field indicated a Congressional intent to leave all other parts thereof free from regulation by the states as well as by itself. It is apparent from this analysis that the actual extent to which federal regulation of local matters related to interstate commerce reduces the field for potential state action depends on how the Court uses the discretion belonging to it in deciding issues of the kind just described. The question is, how has it exercised this discretion while the recent broad expansion of federal powers was occurring? In several cases a conflict was discovered by reasoning somewhat forced. In others the finding was clearly justified. The data are insufficient to warrant a conclusion that the Court is tending more and more to use its discretion in favor of restricting state powers whenever possible. But certainly the decisions do not reveal any trend in the opposite direction. The states would not be justified in relying upon the Court to preserve for them the control of local matters by limiting the effect thereon of federal assumption of some control in that field. . . .

The most that could be achieved by use of the technique just described would be to decrease the rate at which federal intervention ousted state control of local matters. It could operate only in that negative manner. The situation is different when the only obstacle to state regulation is the commerce clause itself. A great deal of state legislation has been held invalid because it directly burdened interstate commerce. Much of it that affected such commerce has been sustained because the burden imposed by it was merely indirect. The formulation of the tests in terms of direct and indirect burdens continued in use after 1933 and is used occasionally even today. But there now is a distinct trend in favor of substituting for them the substantial or insubstantial character of the burden. This has been noticeable especially in the decisions of the last decade. In *Parker* v. *Brown*[14] the Court sustained a state act applying to the marketing of locally produced fruits a system of control along the lines of the fed-

[14] 317 U.S. 341 (1943).

eral statutes regulating the marketing of agricultural products. The bulk of the fruit was destined for the national market after being processed locally. The first argument to sustain it was based on the factor that the transactions regulated were not part of interstate commerce. The opinion next denies that courts are "confined to so mechanical a test." It cites many cases in which broader considerations were relied upon, and expressly states that the local regulations involved were sustained "not because they are 'indirect' rather than 'direct'" but because they were appropriate means for protecting local interests which might never be adequately dealt with by Congress. The "direct-indirect" test has seldom been resorted to by the Court since that decision.

The substitution of one method of formulating a problem for another generally does not change its character. The new method will sometimes be better adapted than the old to directing attention to the fundamental factors that should influence, and in some instances, determine the solution. One aim of the commerce clause was the protection of interstate trade against state interference. As a limit on state powers, it is a free trade charter for national commerce. The motives that lead to protective tariffs at the international level are present in each state and have induced a variety of measures to protect the local market from out-of-state competitors. But free trade implies freedom of exportation as well as freedom of importation. The extent to which a state regulation in fact hampers the flow of goods in interstate commerce does not depend upon the nearness of its point of incidence to the transactions that constitute interstate commerce. It depends on the actual results of the regulation. The "direct-indirect" test has fallen into disfavor because it tended to focus attention upon the point of incidence of the regulation upon interstate commerce. The "substantial-insubstantial" test is better devised to suggest an inquiry into the actual results of the regulation upon such commerce. The courts, including the Supreme Court, cannot decide a case involving the validity of a state regulation without answering it, either explicitly or implicitly. That arriving at an answer is not always easy and simple is apparent from *Southern Pacific Company* v. *Arizona* in which there was a marked difference of opinion on that matter between the Court's majority and minority. Furthermore, judicial excursions into this field of fact-finding in practice may result in courts substituting their view of the facts for those of the legislature, and in lessening whatever vague influence the presumption of constitutionality may heretofore have had in this field. The minority in the case just referred to made much of these points. But apart from these considerations, determining the existence or nonexistence of the factual burden is but the first step in the judicial process of deciding the validity *vel non* of such state regulations. A burden may exist, and also be a heavy one, and yet the regulation be held valid. The Court must answer the further question "whether the relative weights of the state and national interests involved are such as to make inapplicable the rule, generally observed, that the free flow of interstate commerce and its freedom from local restraints in matters requiring uniformity of regulation are interests safeguarded by the commerce clause from state interference." This involves a balancing of the two interests mentioned in the quotation. The question is posed how far the policy of freedom of trade among the states may be sacrificed to promote a state policy. This is no mere question of fact, but a most difficult problem in value theory. It is fundamentally the same as that which ultimately emerged when the main issue was phrased in terms of the "direct-indirect" test. It is with respect to this element that the problem has remained the same despite the change in the terms of its formulation. But this is precisely its most decisive element.

SOUTHERN PACIFIC CO. v. ARIZONA
325 U.S. 761 (1945)

Mr. Chief Justice STONE delivered the opinion of the Court.

The Arizona Train Limit Law of May 16, 1912, Arizona Code Ann., § 69–119, makes it unlawful for any person or corporation to operate within the state a railroad train of more than fourteen passenger or seventy freight cars, and authorizes the state to recover a money penalty for each violation of the Act. The questions for decision are whether Congress has, by legislative enactment, restricted the power of the states to regulate the length of interstate trains as a safety measure and, if not, whether the statute contravenes the commerce clause of the Federal Constitution.

In 1940 the State of Arizona brought suit in the Arizona Superior Court against appellant, the Southern Pacific Company, to recover the statutory penalties for operating within the state two interstate trains, one a passenger train of more than fourteen cars. Appellant answered, admitting the train operations, but defended on the ground that the statute offends against the commerce clause and the due process clause of the Fourteenth Amendment and conflicts with federal legislation. After an extended trial, without a jury, the court ... gave judgment for the railroad company. The Supreme Court of Arizona reversed and directed judgment for the state. . . . The case comes here on appeal. . . .

The Supreme Court [of Arizona] ... held that the power of the state to regulate the length of interstate trains had not been restricted by Congressional action. It sustained the Act as a safety measure to reduce the number of accidents attributed to the operation of trains of more than the statutory maximum length, enacted by the state legislature in the exercise of the "police power." This power the court held extended to the regulation of the operations of interstate commerce in the interests of local health, safety and well-being. It thought that a state statute, enacted in the exercise of the police power, and bearing some reasonable relation to the health, safety and well-being of the people of the state, of which the state legislature is the judge, was not to be judicially overturned, notwithstanding its admittedly adverse effect on the operation of interstate trains.

... Paragraph 15 of § 1 of the Interstate Commerce Act empowers the [Interstate Commerce] Commission, when it is "of opinion that shortage of equipment, congestion of traffic, or other emergency requiring immediate action exists in any section of the country," to make or suspend rules and practices "with respect to car service," which includes by paragraph 10 of § 1 "the use, control, supply, movement, distribution, exchange, interchange, and return" of locomotives and cars, and the "supply of trains." . . .

... We are of opinion that, in the absence of administrative implementation by the Commission, § 1 does not of itself curtail state power to regulate train lengths. . . . We can hardly suppose that Congress, merely by conferring authority on the Commission to regulate car service in an "emergency," intended to restrict the exercise, otherwise lawful, of state power to regulate train lengths before the Commission finds an "emergency" to exist.

Congress, in enacting legislation within its constitutional authority over interstate commerce, will not be deemed to have intended to strike down a state statute designed to protect the health and safety of the public unless its purpose to do so is clearly manifested, . . . or unless the state law, in terms or in its practical administration, conflicts with the Act of Congress, or plainly and palpably infringes its policy. . . .

The contention, faintly urged, that the provisions of the Safety Appliance Act, 45 U.S.C. §§ 1 and 9, providing for brakes on trains, and of § 25 of Part I of the Interstate Commerce Act, 49 U.S.C. § 26(b), permitting the Commission to order the installation of train stop and control devices, operate of their own force to exclude state regulation of train lengths, has even less support. Congress, although asked to do so, has declined to pass legislation specifically limiting trains to seventy cars. We are therefore brought to appellant's principal contention, that the state statute contravenes the commerce clause of the Federal Constitution.

Although the commerce clause conferred on the national government power to regulate commerce, its possession of the power does not exclude all state power of regulation. Ever since ... *Cooley* v. *Board of Wardens,* 12 How. 299, it has been recognized that, in the absence of conflicting legislation by Congress, there is a residuum of power in the state to make laws governing matters of local concern which nevertheless in some measure affect interstate commerce or even, to some extent, regulate it. . . . Thus the states may regulate matters which, because of their number and diversity, may never be adequately dealt with by Congress. *Cooley* v. *Board of Wardens, supra,* 319; *South Carolina Highway Dept.* v. *Barnwell Bros.,* 303 U.S. 177, 185. . . . When the regulation of matters of local concern is local in character and effect, and its impact on the national commerce does not seriously interfere with its operation, and the consequent incentive to deal with them nationally is slight, such regulation has been generally held to be within state authority. *South Carolina Highway Dept.* v. *Barnwell Bros., supra,* 188 and cases cited; . . . .

But ever since *Gibbons* v. *Ogden,* 9 Wheat. 1, the states have not been deemed to have authority to impede substantially the free flow of commerce from state to state, or to regulate those phases of the national commerce which, because of the need of national uniformity, demand that their regulation, if any, be prescribed by a single authority. Whether or not this long-recognized distribution of power between the national and the state governments is predicated upon the implications of the commerce clause itself, . . . or upon the presumed intention of Congress, where Congress has not spoken, . . . the result is the same.

In the application of these principles some enactments may be found to be plainly within and others plainly without state power. But between these extremes lies the infinite variety of cases, in which regulation of local matters may also operate as a regulation of commerce, in which reconciliation of the conflicting claims of state and national power is to be attained only by some appraisal and accommodation of the competing demands of the state and national interests involved. . . .

For a hundred years it has been accepted constitutional doctrine that the commerce clause, without aid of Congressional legislation, thus affords some protection from state legislation inimical to the national commerce, and that in such cases, where Congress has not acted, this Court, and not the state legislature, is under the commerce clause the final arbiter of the competing demands of state and national interests. *Cooley* v. *Board of Wardens, supra; Kansas City Southern R. Co.* v. *Kaw Valley District,* 233 U.S. 75, 79; *South Covington R. Co.* v. *Covington,* 235 U.S. 537, 546; *Missouri, K. & T. R. Co.* v. *Public Service Comm'n,* 254 U.S. 535, 537; *Foster-Fountain Packing Co.* v. *Haydel,* 278 U.S. 1, 10; *Gwin, White & Price* v. *Henneford,* 305 U.S. 434, 441; *McCarroll* v. *Dixie Lines,* 309 U.S. 176.

Congress has undoubted power to redefine the distribution of power over interstate commerce. It may either permit the states to regulate the commerce in a manner which would otherwise not be permissible, . . . or exclude state regulation even of matters of peculiarly local concern which nevertheless affect interstate commerce.

But in general Congress has left it to the courts to formulate the rules thus interpreting the commerce clause in its application, doubtless because it has appreciated the destructive consequences to the commerce of the nation if their protection were withdrawn, . . . and has been aware that in their application state laws will not be invalidated without the support of relevant factual material which will "afford a sure basis" for an informed judgment. . . . Meanwhile, Congress has accommodated its legislation, as have the states, to these rules as an established feature of our constitutional system. There has thus been left to the states wide scope for the regulation of matters of local state concern, even though it in some measure affects the commerce, provided it does not materially restrict the free flow of commerce across state lines, or interfere with it in matters with respect to which uniformity of regulation is of predominant national concern.

Hence the matters for ultimate determination here are the nature and extent of the burden which the state regulation of interstate trains, adopted as a safety measure, imposes on interstate commerce, and whether the relative weights of the state and national interests involved are such as to make inapplicable the rule, generally observed, that the free flow of interstate commerce and its freedom from local restraints in matters requiring uniformity of regulation are interests safeguarded by the commerce clause from state interference.

. . . . .

The findings [of the trial court] show that the operation of long trains, that is trains of more than fourteen passenger and more than seventy freight cars, is standard practice over the main lines of the railroads of the United States, and that, if the length of trains is to be regulated at all, national uniformity in the regulation adopted, such as only Congress can prescribe, is practically indispensable to the operation of an efficient and economical national railway system. . . .

In Arizona, approximately 93% of the freight traffic and 95% of the passenger traffic is interstate. Because of the Train Limit Law appellant is required to haul over 30% more trains in Arizona than would otherwise have been necessary. The record shows a definite relationship between operating costs and the length of trains, the increase in length resulting in a reduction of operating costs per car. The additional cost of operation of trains complying with the Train Limit Law in Arizona amounts for the two railroads traversing that state to about $1,000,000 a year. The reduction in train lengths also impedes efficient operation. More locomotives and more manpower are required; the necessary conversion and reconversion of train lengths at terminals and the delay caused by breaking up and remaking long trains upon entering and leaving the state in order to comply with the law, delays the traffic and diminishes its volume moved in a given time, especially when traffic is heavy.

. . . . .

The unchallenged findings leave no doubt that the Arizona Train Limit Law imposes a serious burden on the interstate commerce conducted by appellant. It materially impedes the movement of appellant's interstate trains through that state and interposes a substantial obstruction to the national policy proclaimed by Congress, to promote adequate, economical and efficient railway transportation service. Interstate Commerce Act, preceding § 1, 54 Stat. 899. Enforcement of the law in Arizona, while train lengths remain unregulated or are regulated by varying standards in other states, must inevitably result in an impairment of uniformity of efficient railroad operation because the railroads are subjected to regulation which is not uniform in its application. Compliance with a state statute limiting train lengths requires interstate trains of a length lawful in other states to be broken up and reconstituted as they enter each state according as it may impose varying limitations upon train lengths. The alternative is for the carrier to conform to the lowest train limit restriction of any of the states through which its trains pass, whose laws thus control the carriers' operations both within and without the regulating state.

Although the seventy car maximum for freight trains is the limitation which has been most commonly proposed, various bills introduced in the state legislatures provided for maximum freight train lengths of from fifty to one hundred and twenty-five cars, and maximum passenger train lengths of from ten to eighteen cars. With such laws in force in states which are interspersed with those having no limit on train lengths, the confusion and difficulty with which interstate operations would be burdened under the varied system of state regulations and the unsatisfied need for uniformity in such regulation, if any, are evident.

.   .   .   .   .

The trial court found that the Arizona law had no reasonable relation to safety, and made train operation more dangerous. Examination of the evidence and the detailed findings makes it clear that this conclusion was rested on facts found which indicate that such increased danger of accident and personal injury as may result from the greater length of trains is more than offset by the increase in the number of accidents resulting from the larger number of trains when train lengths are reduced. In considering the effect of the statute as a safety measure, therefore, the factor of controlling significance for present purposes is not whether there is basis for the conclusion of the Arizona Supreme Court that the increase in length of trains beyond the statutory maximum has an adverse effect upon safety of operation. The decisive question is whether in the circumstances the total effect of the law as a safety measure in reducing accidents and casualties is so slight or problematical as not to outweigh the national interest in keeping interstate commerce free from

interferences which seriously impede it and subject it to local regulation which does not have a uniform effect on the interstate train
journey which it interrupts.

.   .   .   .   .

We think, as the trial court found, that the Arizona Train Limit
Law, viewed as a safety measure, affords at most slight and dubious
advantage, if any, over unregulated train lengths, because it results in
an increase in the number of trains and train operations and the
consequent increase in train accidents of a character generally more
severe than those due to slack action. Its undoubted effect on the
commerce is the regulation, without securing uniformity, of the
length of trains operated in interstate commerce, which lack is itself
a primary cause of preventing the free flow of commerce by delaying
it and by substantially increasing its cost and impairing its efficiency.
In these respects the case differs from those where a state, by regulatory measures affecting the commerce, has removed or reduced safety
hazards without substantial interference with the interstate movement of trains. Such are measures abolishing the car stove, *New York,
N. H. & H. R. Co.* v. *New York,* 165 U.S. 628; requiring locomotives
to be supplied with electric headlights, *Atlantic Coast Line R. Co.* v.
Georgia, 234 U.S. 280; providing for full train crews, *Chicago, R. I.
& P. R. Co.* v. *Arkansas,* 219 U.S. 453; *St. Louis & I. M. R. Co.* v.
Arkansas, 240 U.S. 518; *Missouri Pacific R. Co.* v. *Norwood,* 283 U.S.
249; and for the equipment of freight trains with cabooses, *Terminal
Railroad Assn.* v. *Brotherhood,* 318 U.S. 1.

.   .   .   .   .

... Recently in *Kelly* v. *Washington,* 302 U.S. 1, 15, we have
pointed out that when a state goes beyond safety measures which are
permissible because only local in their effect upon interstate commerce, and "attempts to impose particular standards as to structure,
design, equipment and operation [of vessels plying interstate] which
in the judgment of its authorities may be desirable but pass beyond
what is plainly essential to safety and seaworthiness, the State will
encounter the principle that such requirements, if imposed at all,
must be through the action of Congress which can establish a uniform rule. Whether the State in a particular matter goes too far must
be left to be determined when the precise question arises."
Here we conclude that the state does go too far. Its regulation of

train lengths, admittedly obstructive to interstate train operation, and having a seriously adverse effect on transportation efficiency and economy, passes beyond what is plainly essential for safety since it does not appear that it will lessen rather than increase the danger of accident. Its attempted regulation of the operation of interstate trains cannot establish nation-wide control such as is essential to the maintenance of an efficient transportation system, which Congress alone can prescribe. The state interest cannot be preserved at the expense of the national interest by an enactment which regulates interstate train lengths without securing such control, which is a matter of national concern. To this the interest of the state here asserted is subordinate.

Appellees especially rely . . . on *South Carolina Highway Dept.* v. *Barnwell Bros., supra,* as supporting the state's authority to regulate the length of interstate trains. . . .

[That case] . . . was concerned with the power of the state to regulate the weight and width of motor cars passing interstate over its highways, a legislative field over which the state has a far more extensive control than over interstate railroads. In that case, . . . we were at pains to point out that there are few subjects of state regulation affecting interstate commerce which are so peculiarly of local concern as is the use of the state's highways. Unlike the railroads local highways are built, owned and maintained by the state or its municipal subdivisions. The state is responsible for their safe and economical administration. Regulations affecting the safety of their use must be applied alike to intrastate and interstate traffic. The fact that they affect alike shippers in interstate and intrastate commerce in great numbers, within as well as without the state, is a safeguard against regulatory abuses. Their regulation is akin to quarantine measures, game laws, and like local regulations of rivers, harbors, piers, and docks, with respect to which the state has exceptional scope for the exercise of its regulatory power, and which, Congress not acting, have been sustained even though they materially interfere with interstate commerce (303 U.S. at 187–188 and cases cited).

The contrast between the present regulation and . . . the highway safety regulations, in point of the nature of the subject of regulation and the state's interest in it, illustrate and emphasize the considerations which enter into a determination of the relative weights of state and national interests where state regulation affecting interstate commerce is attempted. Here examination of all the relevant factors makes it plain that the state interest is out-weighed by the interest

of the nation in an adequate, economical and efficient railway transportation service, which must prevail.

Reversed.

Mr. Justice RUTLEDGE concurs in the result.

Mr. Justice BLACK, dissenting.

In *Hennington* v. *Georgia*, 163 U.S. 299, 304, a case which involved
the power of a state to regulate interstate traffic, this Court said,
"The whole theory of our government, federal and state, is hostile to
the idea that questions of legislative authority may depend . . . upon
opinions of judges as to the wisdom or want of wisdom in the enactment of laws under powers clearly conferred upon the legislature."
What the Court decides today is that it is unwise governmental
policy to regulate the length of trains. I am therefore constrained to
note my dissent.

For more than a quarter of a century, railroads and their employees
have engaged in controversies over the relative virtues and dangers
of long trains. Railroads have argued that they could carry goods and
passengers cheaper in long trains than in short trains. They have also
argued that while the danger of personal injury to their employees
might in some respects be greater on account of the operation of long
trains, this danger was more than offset by an increased number of
accidents from other causes brought about by the operation of a much
larger number of short trains. These arguments have been, and are
now, vigorously denied. While there are others, the chief causes assigned for the belief that long trains unnecessarily jeopardize the
lives and limbs of railroad employees relate to "slack action." Cars
coupled together retain a certain free play of movement, ranging between 1½ inches and 1 foot, and this is called "slack action." Train
brakes do not ordinarily apply or release simultaneously on all cars.
This frequently results in a severe shock or jar to cars, particularly
those in the rear of a train. It has always been the position of the employees that the dangers from "slack action" correspond to and are
proportionate with the length of the train. The argument that "slack
movements" are more dangerous in long trains than in short trains
seems never to have been denied. The railroads have answered it by
what is in effect a plea of confession and avoidance. They say that the
added cost of running short trains places an unconstitutional burden
on interstate commerce. Their second answer is that the operation of
short trains requires the use of more separate train units; that a
certain number of accidents resulting in injury are inherent in the

operation of each unit, injuries which may be inflicted either on employees or on the public; consequently, they have asserted that it is not in the public interest to prohibit the operation of long trains.

. . . I . . . think that the "findings" of the state court do not authorize today's decision. That court did not find that there is no unusual danger from slack movements in long trains. It did decide on disputed evidence that the long train "slack movement" dangers were more than offset by prospective dangers as a result of running a larger number of short trains, since many people might be hurt at grade crossings. There was undoubtedly some evidence before the state court from which it could have reached such a conclusion. There was undoubtedly as much evidence before it which would have justified a different conclusion.

Under those circumstances, the determination of whether it is in the interest of society for the length of trains to be governmentally regulated is a matter of public policy. Someone must fix that policy—either the Congress, or the state, or the courts. A century and a half of constitutional history and government admonishes this Court to leave that choice to the elected legislative representatives of the people themselves, where it properly belongs both on democratic principles and the requirements of efficient government.

I think that legislatures, to the exclusion of courts, have the constitutional power to enact laws limiting train lengths, for the purpose of reducing injuries brought about by "slack movements." Their power is not less because a requirement of short trains might increase grade crossing accidents. This latter fact raises an entirely different element of danger which is itself subject to legislative regulation. For legislatures may, if necessary, require railroads to take appropriate steps to reduce the likelihood of injuries at grade crossings. *Denver & R. G. R. Co.* v. *Denver,* 250 U.S. 241. And the fact that grade-crossing improvements may be expensive is no sufficient reason to say that an unconstitutional "burden" is put upon a railroad even though it be an interstate road. *Erie R. Co.* v. *Public Utility Commissioners,* 254 U.S. 394, 408–411.

But, it is said today, . . . [that] . . . if one state applies a regulation of its own to interstate trains, "uniformity" in regulation or rather non-regulation, is destroyed. Justice Hughes speaking for the Court in the *Atlantic Coast Line* case[15] made short shrift of that same argument. He there referred to the contention that "if state requirements conflict, it will be necessary to carry additional apparatus and to make various adjustments at state lines which would delay and inconvenience interstate traffic." In answer to this argument he reiterated a former declaration of this Court in *New York, N. H. & H. R. Co.* v. *New York,* 165 U.S. 628, on this subject, and added that "If there is a conflict in such local regulations, by which interstate commerce may be inconvenienced—if there appears to be need of standardization of safety appliances and of providing rules of operation which will govern the entire interstate road irrespective of state boundaries —there is a simple remedy; and it cannot be assumed that it will not be readily applied if there be real occasion for it. That remedy does not rest in a denial to the state, in the absence of conflicting federal action, of its power to protect life and property within its borders, but it does lie in the exercise of the paramount authority of Congress in its control of interstate commerce to establish such regulations as in its judgment may be deemed appropriate and sufficient. Congress, when it pleases, may give the rule and make the standard to be observed on the interstate highway." P. 292.

That same statement has in substance been made in many other decisions of this Court, a number of which are cited in the *Atlantic Coast Line* case, and all of them are today swept into the discard. In no one of all these previous cases was it more appropriate than here to call attention to the fact that Congress could when it pleased establish a uniform rule as to the length of trains. Congress knew about the Arizona law. It is a common knowledge that the Interstate Commerce Committees of the House and the Senate keep in close and intimate touch with the affairs of railroads and other national means of transportation. Every year brings forth new legislation which goes through those Committees, much of it relating to safety. The attention of the members of Congress and of the Senate have been focused on the particular problem of the length of railroad trains. We cannot assume that they were ignorant of the commonly known fact that a long train might be more dangerous in some territories and on some particular types of railroad. The history of congressional consideration of this problem leaves little if any room to doubt that the choice of Congress to leave the state free in this field was a deliberate choice, which was taken with a full knowledge of the complexities of the

---

[15] *Atlantic Coast Line R. Co.* v. *Georgia,* 234 U.S. 280.

problems and the probable need for diverse regulations in different localities. I am therefore compelled to reach the conclusion that today's decision is the result of the belief of a majority of this Court that both the legislature of Arizona and the Congress made wrong policy decisions in permitting a law to stand which limits the length of railroad trains. I should at least give the Arizona statute the benefit of the same rule which this Court said should be applied in connection with state legislation under attack for violating the Fourteenth Amendment, that is, that legislative bodies have "a wide range of legislative discretion, . . . and their conclusions respecting the wisdom of their legislative acts are not reviewable by the courts." *Arizona Employer's Liability Cases*, 250 U.S. 400, 419.

When we finally get down to the gist of what the Court today actually decides, it is this: Even though more railroad employees will be injured by "slack action" movements on long trains than on short trains, there must be no regulation of this danger in the absence of "uniform regulations." That means that no one can legislate against this danger except the Congress; and even though the Congress is perfectly content to leave the matter to the different state legislatures, this Court, on the ground of "lack of uniformity," will require it to make an express avowal of that fact before it will permit a state to guard against that admitted danger.

We are not left in doubt as to why, as against the potential peril of injuries to employees, the Court tips the scales on the side of "uniformity." For the evil it finds in a lack of uniformity is that it (1) delays interstate commerce, (2) increases its cost and (3) impairs its efficiency. All three of these boil down to the same thing, and that is that running shorter trains would increase the cost of railroad operations. The "burden" on commerce reduces itself to mere cost because there was no finding, and no evidence to support a finding, that by the expenditure of sufficient sums of money, the railroads could not enable themselves to carry goods and passengers just as quickly and efficiently with short trains as with long trains. Thus the conclusion that a requirement for long trains will "burden interstate commerce" is a mere euphemism for the statement that a requirement for long trains will increase the cost of railroad operations.

. . . .

. . . I would affirm the judgment of the Supreme Court of Arizona. [Mr. Justice DOUGLAS also wrote a dissenting opinion].

EDWARDS v. CALIFORNIA
314 U.S. 160 (1941)

Mr. Justice BYRNES delivered the opinion of the Court.

The facts of this case are simple and are not disputed. Appellant [Edwards] is a citizen of the United States and a resident of California. In December, 1939, he left his home in Marysville, California, for Spur, Texas, with the intention of bringing back to Marysville his wife's brother, Frank Duncan, a citizen of the United States and a resident of Texas. When he arrived in Texas, appellant learned that Duncan had last been employed by the Works Progress Administration. Appellant thus became aware of the fact that Duncan was an indigent person and he continued to be aware of it throughout the period involved in this case. The two men agreed that appellant should transport Duncan from Texas to Marysville in appellant's automobile. Accordingly, they left Spur on January 1, 1940, entered California by way of Arizona on January 3, and reached Marysville on January 5. When he left Texas, Duncan had about $20. It had all been spent by the time he reached Marysville. He lived with appellant for about ten days until he obtained financial assistance from the Farm Security Administration. During the ten days interval, he had no employment.

In Justice Court a complaint was filed against appellant under Section 2615 of the Welfare and Institutions Code of California, which provides: "Every person, firm or corporation or officer or agent thereof that brings or assists in bringing into the State any indigent person who is not a resident of the State, knowing him to be an indigent person, is guilty of a misdemeanor."... The appellant was convicted and sentenced to six months imprisonment in the county jail, and sentence was suspended....

Article I, Section 8 of the Constitution delegates to the Congress the authority to regulate interstate commerce. And it is settled beyond question that the transportation of persons is "commerce," within the meaning of that provision. It is nevertheless true that the States are not wholly precluded from exercising their police power in matters of local concern even though they may thereby affect interstate commerce. The issue presented in this case, therefore, is whether the prohibition embodied in Section 2615 against the "bringing" or transportation of indigent persons into California is within the police power of that State. We think that it is not, and hold that it is an unconstitutional barrier to interstate commerce.

The grave and perplexing social and economic dislocation which this statute reflects is a matter of common knowledge and concern. We are not unmindful of it. We appreciate that the spectacle of large segments of our population constantly on the move has given rise to urgent demands upon the ingenuity of government. . . . The State asserts that the huge influx of migrants into California in recent years has resulted in problems of health, morals, and especially finance, the proportions of which are staggering. It is not for us to say that this is not true. We have repeatedly and recently affirmed, and we now reaffirm, that we do not conceive it our function to pass upon "the wisdom, need, or appropriateness" of the legislative efforts of the States to solve such difficulties.

But this does not mean that there are no boundaries to the permissible area of State legislative activity. There are. And none is more certain than the prohibition against attempts on the part of any single State to isolate itself from difficulties common to all of them by restraining the transportation of persons and property across its borders. It is frequently the case that a State might gain a momentary respite from the pressure of events by the simple expedient of shutting its gates to the outside world. But, in the words of Mr. Justice Cardozo: "The Constitution was framed under the dominion of a political philosophy less parochial in range. It was framed upon the theory that the peoples of the several States must sink or swim together, and that in the long run prosperity and salvation are in union and not division." *Baldwin* v. *Seelig*, 294 U.S. 511.

It is difficult to conceive of a statute more squarely in conflict with this theory than the section challenged here. Its express purpose and inevitable effect is to prohibit the transportation of indigent persons across the California border. The burden upon interstate commerce is intended and immediate; it is the plain and sole function of the statute. . . . We think this statute must fail under any known test of the validity of State interference with interstate commerce.

It is urged, however, that the concept which underlies Section 2615 enjoys a firm basis in English and American history. This is the notion that each community should care for its own indigent, that relief is solely the responsibility of local government. Of this it must first be said that we are not now called upon to determine anything other than the propriety of an attempt by a State to prohibit the transportation of indigent non-residents into its territory. The nature and extent of its obligation suggest that the theory of the Elizabethan poor laws no longer fits the facts. Recent years, and particularly the past decade, have been marked by a growing recognition that in an industrial society the task of providing assistance to the needy has ceased to be local in character. The duty to share the burden, if not wholly to assume it, has been recognized not only by State governments, but by the Federal government as well. The changed attitude is reflected in the Social Security laws under which the Federal and State governments cooperate for the care of the programs under which work is furnished the unemployed, with the State supplying approximately 25% and the Federal government approximately 75% of the cost. It is further reflected in the Farm Security laws, under which the entire cost of the relief provisions is borne by the Federal government.

Indeed, the record in this case illustrates the inadequate basis in fact for the theory that relief is presently a local matter. Before leaving Texas, Duncan had received assistance from the Works Progress Administration. After arriving in California he was aided by the Farm Security Administration, which, as we have said, is wholly financed by the Federal government. This is not to say that our judgment would be different if Duncan had received relief from local agencies in Texas and California. Nor is it to suggest that the financial burden of assistance to indigent persons does not continue to fall heavily upon local and State governments. It is only to illustrate that in not inconsiderable measure the relief of the needy has become the common responsibility and concern of the whole nation.

What has been said with respect to financing relief is not without its bearing upon the regulation of the transportation of indigent persons. For the social phenomenon of large-scale interstate migration is as certainly a matter of national concern as the provision of assistance to those who have found a permanent or temporary abode. Moreover, and unlike the relief problem, this phenomenon does not admit of diverse treatment by the several States. The prohibition against transporting indigent non-residents into one State is an open invitation to retaliatory measures, and the burdens upon the transportation of such persons become cumulative. Moreover, it would be a virtual impossibility for migrants and those who transport them to acquaint themselves with the peculiar rules of admission of many States. "This Court has repeatedly declared that the grant [the commerce clause] established the immunity of interstate commerce from the control of the States respecting all those subjects embraced within the grant which are of such a nature as to demand that, if regulated at all, their regulation must be prescribed by a single authority." *Milk Control Board* v. *Eisenberg Farm Products,* 306 U.S. 346. We are of the opinion that the transportation of indigent persons from State to State clearly falls within this class of subjects. The scope of congressional power to deal with this problem we are not now called upon to decide.

There remains to be noticed only the contention that the limitation upon State power to interfere with the interstate transportation of persons is subject to an exception in the case of "paupers." It is true that support for this contention may be found in early decisions of this Court. In *New York* v. *Miln,* 11 Pet. 102, it was said that it is "as competent and as necessary for a State to provide precautionary measures against the moral pestilence of paupers, vagabonds, and possibly convicts, as it is to guard against the physical pestilence which may arise from unsound and infectious articles imported. . . ." This language has been casually repeated in numerous later cases up to the turn of the century. In none of these cases, however, was the power of a State to exclude "paupers" actually involved.

Whether an able-bodied but unemployed person like Duncan is a "pauper" within the historical meaning of the term is open to considerable doubt. But assuming that the term is applicable to him and to persons similarly situated, we do not consider ourselves bound by the language referred to. *City of New York* v. *Miln* was decided in 1837. Whatever may have been the notion then prevailing, we do not think that it will now be seriously contended that because a person is without employment and without funds he constitutes a "moral pestilence." Poverty and immorality are not synonymous.

We are of the opinion that Section 2615 is not a valid exercise of the police power of California, that it imposes an unconstitutional burden upon interstate commerce, and that the conviction under it cannot be sustained. In the view we have taken it is unnecessary to decide whether the section is repugnant to other provisions of the Constitution.

Reversed.

[Mr. Justice DOUGLAS wrote a concurring opinion, in which Justices BLACK and MURPHY joined; Mr. Justice JACKSON concurred separately. Both concurring opinions would declare the right to move freely from state to state to be an incident of *national* citizenship protected by the privileges and immunities clause of the Fourteenth Amendment against state interference. See *post,* p. 327, for extracts.]

AERO MAYFLOWER TRANSIT COMPANY v. BOARD OF R. R. COMM'RS OF MONTANA
332 U.S. 495 (1947)

Mr. Justice RUTLEDGE delivered the opinion of the Court.

Again we are asked to decide whether state taxes as applied to an interstate motor carrier run afoul of the commerce clause, Art. 1, § 8, of the Federal Constitution.

Two distinct Montana levies are questioned. Both are imposed by that state's Motor Carriers Act, Mont. Rev. Codes (1935) §§ 3847.1-3847.28. One is a flat tax of $10 for each vehicle operated by a motor carrier over the state's highways, payable on issuance of a certificate or permit, which must be secured before operations begin, and annually thereafter. § 3847.16(a). The other is a quarterly fee of one-half of one per cent of the motor carrier's "gross operating revenue," but with a minimum annual fee of $15 per vehicle for class C carriers, in which group appellant falls. § 3847.27. Each tax is declared expressly to be laid "in consideration of the use of the highways of this state" and to be "in addition to all other licenses, fees and taxes imposed upon motor vehicles in this state."

Prior to July 1, 1941, the fees collected pursuant to §§ 3847.16 (a) and 3847.27 were paid into the state treasury and credited to "the motor carrier fund." After that date, by virtue of Mont. Laws 1941, c. 14, § 2, they were allocated to the state's general fund.

Appellant is a Kentucky corporation, with its principal offices in Indianapolis, Indiana. Its business is exclusively interstate. It consists in transporting household goods and office furniture from points in one state to destinations in another. Appellant does no intrastate business in Montana. The volume of its interstate business there is continuous and substantial, not merely casual or occasional. It holds a certificate of convenience and necessity issued by the Interstate Commerce Commission, pursuant to which its business in Montana and elsewhere is conducted.

In 1935 appellant received a class C permit to operate over Montana highways, as required by state law. Until 1937, apparently, it complied with Montana requirements, including the payment of registration and license plate fees for its vehicles operating in Montana and of the 5c per gallon tax on gasoline purchased there. However, in 1937 and thereafter appellant refused to pay the flat $10 fee imposed by § 3847.16 (a) and the $15 minimum "gross revenue" tax laid by § 3847.27. In consequence, after hearing on order to show cause, the appellee board in 1939 revoked the 1935 permit and brought this suit in a state court to enjoin appellant from further operations in Montana. [On appeal, the state Supreme Court held both exactions valid.]

... We have, in effect, two flat taxes, one for $10, the other for $15, payable annually upon each vehicle operated on Montana highways in the course of appellant's business, with each tax expressly declared to be in addition to all others and to be imposed "in consideration of the use of the highways of this state."

Neither exaction discriminates against interstate commerce. Each applies alike to local and interstate operations. Neither undertakes to tax traffic or movements taking place outside Montana or the gross returns from such movements or to use such returns as a measure of the amount of the tax. Both levies apply exclusively to operations wholly within the state or the proceeds of such operations, although those operations are interstate in character.

Moreover, it is not material to the validity of either tax that the state also imposes and collects the vehicle registration and license fee and the gallonage tax on gasoline purchased in Montana. The validity of those taxes neither is questioned nor well could be.... Nor does their exaction have any significant relationship to the imposition of the taxes now in question.... They are imposed for distinct purposes and the proceeds, as appellant concedes, are devoted to different uses, namely, the policing of motor traffic and the maintenance of the state's highways.

Concededly the proceeds of the two taxes presently involved are not allocated to those objects. Rather they now go into the state's general fund, subject to appropriation for general state purposes. Indeed this fact, in appellant's view, is the vice of the statute. But in that view appellant misconceives the nature and legal effect of the exactions. It is far too late to question that a state, consistently with the commerce clause, may lay upon motor vehicles engaged exclusively in interstate commerce, or upon those who own and so operate them, a fair and reasonable, nondiscriminatory tax as compensation for the use of its highways.... Moreover "common carriers for hire, who make the highways their place of business, may properly be charged an extra tax for such use." *Clark* v. *Poor,* 274 U.S. 554, 557.

The present taxes on their face are exacted "in consideration of the use of the highways of this state," that is, they are laid for the privilege of using those highways. . . . The state builds the highways and owns them. Motor carriers for hire, and particularly truckers of heavy goods, like appellant, make especially arduous use of roadways, entailing wear and tear much beyond that resulting from general indiscriminate public use. . . . Although the state may not discriminate against or exclude such interstate traffic generally in the use of its highways, this does not mean that the state is required to furnish those facilities to it free of charge or indeed on equal terms with other traffic not inflicting similar destructive effects. . . . Interstate traffic equally with intrastate may be required to pay a fair share of the cost and maintenance reasonably related to the use made of the highways.

This does not mean, as appellant seems to assume, that the proceeds of all taxes levied for the privilege of using the highways must be allocated directly and exclusively to maintaining them. . . . That is true, although this Court has held invalid, as forbidden by the commerce clause, certain state taxes on interstate motor carriers because laid "not as compensation for the use of the highways but for the privilege of doing the interstate bus business." *Interstate Transit v. Lindsey,* 283 U.S. 183, 186; cf. *McCarroll v. Dixie Greyhound Lines,* 309 U.S. 176, 179. Those cases did not hold that all state exactions for the privilege of using the state's highways are valid only if their proceeds are required to go directly and exclusively for highway maintenance, policing and administration. Both before and after the Interstate Transit decision this Court has sustained state taxes expressly laid on the privilege of using the highways, as applied to interstate motor carriers, declaring in each instance that it is immaterial whether the proceeds are allocated to highway uses or others.

Appellant therefore confuses a tax "assessed for a proper purpose and . . . not objectionable in amount," *Clark v. Poor, supra* (274 U.S. at 557), that is, a tax affirmatively laid for the privilege of using the state's highways, such as the privilege of doing the interstate business. Though necessarily related, in view of the nature of interstate motor traffic, the two privileges are not identical, and it is useless to confuse them or to confound a tax for the privilege of using the highways with one the proceeds of which are necessarily devoted to maintaining them. Whether the proceeds of a tax are used or required to be used for highway maintenance "may be of significance," as the Court has said, "when the point is otherwise in doubt, to show that the fee is in fact laid for that purpose and is thus a charge for the privilege of using the highways. *Interstate Transit* v. *Lindsey,* 283 U.S. 183. But where the manner of the levy, like that prescribed by the present statute, definitely identifies it as a fee charged for the grant of the privilege, it is immaterial whether the state places the fees collected in the pocket out of which it pays highway maintenance charges or in some other." *Morf* v. *Bingaman,* 298 U.S. 407, 412.

It is of no consequence that the state has seen fit to lay two exactions, substantially identical, rather than combine them into one, or that appellant pays other taxes which in fact are devoted to highway maintenance. For the state does not exceed its constitutional powers by imposing more than one form of tax. . . .

Neither is there merit in its other arguments, which we have considered, including those urging due process and equal protection grounds for invalidating the levies.

The judgment of the Supreme Court of Montana is affirmed.

THE COURT'S CHOICE[16]

It is apparent that the weighing of the interest which the state regulation aims to protect against those which the commerce clause was adopted to secure necessarily forces courts to make decisions on important matters of policy. This cannot be avoided as long as they are charged with the task of reconciling or choosing between competing interests. The existence, character, and extent of the effects of a regulation are undoubtedly questions of fact. And in many instances evidence thereof must be, and is before the Court. But they furnish but one element in the judgment that must be made in deciding cases in this field. Unless it be assumed that the mere existence of any effects tending to reduce the flow of interstate trade suffices to render the regulation invalid, the problem becomes one of degree. Courts have never adopted this extreme position. The normal result of a regulation that increases either the cost of producing goods for the interstate market, or the cost of their transportation in

[16] From Henry Rottschaefer, *The Constitution and Socio-Economic Change,* Ann Arbor: University of Michigan Law School, 1948, pp. 22–24. Reprinted by permission of the author and the publishers.

interstate commerce, would be a reduction in the volume of such commerce. Yet the Supreme Court has stated more than once that a state tax having that effect does not violate the commerce clause on that account. Judicial recognition that the protection of some state interests justifies a larger interference with interstate trade than does the protection of others further complicates the matter. No court has yet devised any scale for measuring the relative values of freedom of interstate trade and the numerous local interests which a state may wish to protect at the former's expense. This is not necessarily a disadvantage. It has facilitated adapting the commerce clause to changing social and economic needs and philosophies. This is not a new phenomenon peculiar to our own times. The shift of judicial opinion on the issue of the exclusive or concurrent nature of the commerce clause was not uninfluenced by factors present in the political and economic environment of the period. No one would doubt that this process would have occurred had the power of construing the commerce clause been vested in Congress alone. History has proved that the Supreme Court has responded to the impact of the same necessity and forces. No one would question that, on the assumption just made, the interpretations of Congress inevitably would have involved value judgments. The need for them cannot be eliminated by conferring the power of final construction of the commerce clause, and, for that matter, most other provisions of the Constitution, upon the judiciary....

CHAPTER VII

The Obligation of Contracts

1. THE PROTECTION OF VESTED INTERESTS

THE FRAMERS' PURPOSES

The inclusion in the Constitution of a specific guarantee of contractual obligations against state action is commonly attributed to the desire of creditor classes to forestall a repetition of the debtors' relief legislation enacted by many states during the 1780's. The dislocations of the Revolutionary War had resulted in widespread economic distress, with farmers in particular being sorely afflicted. As a result of their agitation, several state legislatures passed remedial acts offering stay of execution on existing obligations and providing for cheaper money with which the debts could be discharged.

How desperately the debtor classes strove for these forms of relief was dramatically and almost tragically demonstrated in 1786 when the state legislature of Massachusetts refused to pass a cheap money bill. An armed insurrection led by Captain Daniel Shays threatened to compel by force what the legislature would not grant of its own. Boston merchants raised the necessary funds to assemble the military force necessary to suppress this so-called Shays' Rebellion.

As Charles A. Beard has authoritatively shown, every member of the Philadelphia Convention (with one possible exception) shared the interests and attitudes of the creditor classes (see his *Economic Interpretation of the Constitution*). To these men the type of legislation sought by Shays and actually passed in some of the states was, of course, anathema. The restoration of commerce and credit seemed to them to demand that the sanctity of contractual obligations be protected by the supreme law of the land. The contract clause of the Constitution was thus to insure that any future attempt to emulate Shays would be met not only by the regular force of the state government but by the accumulated power of the Union.

Throughout the period of Federalist domination of the Supreme Court the clause was applied in keeping with these sentiments of the Framers. State control was permitted no inroads where contractual agreement had created interests and vested them in individuals or corporations. Indeed, the Court's interpretation even expanded the protective coverage of the contract clause by ruling that grants and charters issued by a State were contracts within the meaning of the Constitution.

FLETCHER v. PECK
6 Cr. 87 (1810)

[In the year 1795 the legislature of Georgia passed an act for the sale of twenty million acres of the State's western lands to four land companies for the sum of $500,000. Virtually every member of the legislature was bribed to secure this grant for the land companies, control of which was primarily in the hands of Northern speculators. Popular resentment ran high and, following an election, the entire deal was rescinded by the lawmakers in 1796. Meanwhile title to land parcels in the grant area had been sold to numerous individuals not parties to nor aware of the fraud in obtaining the original grant. These new owners, of course, claimed that the State could not withdraw from them the interests which the original transfer had given. Georgia, on the other hand, maintained that, because of the fraud involved, no valid title could derive from the original grant. In 1802, Georgia ceded its claims to the United States and the scene of the debate over these so-called Yazoo Frauds was transferred to the Congress. There, however, the efforts to obtain compensation for the claimants under the 1795 grant ran into heavy and continuous opposition. At last it was arranged to bring the question to a court test. Peck, who held his land under a title derived from the allegedly invalid grant, conveyed a parcel to Fletcher, with the customary warranty of title, i.e., an undertaking that the title conveyed was clear and good. Fletcher then sued Peck, alleging that, because the title was not good, the transfer price should be refunded. The Circuit Court found for the defendant, Peck; that is, it held that the title was good. Fletcher then carried the case to the Supreme Court.]

MARSHALL, C. J., delivered the opinion of the Court. . . .

The lands in controversy vested absolutely in . . . the original grantees, by the conveyance of the governor, made in pursuance of an act of assembly, to which the legislature was fully competent. Being thus in full possession of the legal estate, they, for a valuable consideration, conveyed portions of the land to those who were willing to purchase. If the original transaction was infected with fraud, these purchasers did not participate in it, and had no notice of it. They were innocent. Yet the legislature of Georgia has involved them in the fate of the first parties to the transaction, and, if the act be valid, has annihilated their rights also. . . .

In this case, the legislature may have had ample proof that the original grant was obtained by practices which can never be too much reprobated, and which would have justified its abrogation, so far as respected those to whom crime was imputable. But the grant, when issued, conveyed . . . [a right in the land] . . . to the grantee, clothed with all the solemnities which law can bestow. This . . . [right] . . . was transferable; and those who purchased parts of it were not stained by that guilt which infected the original transaction. Their case is not distinguishable from the ordinary case of purchasers of a legal estate, without knowledge of any secret fraud which might have led to the emanation of the original grant. According to the well-known course of equity, their rights could not be affected by such fraud. Their situation was the same, their title was the same, with that of every other member of the community who holds land by regular conveyances from the original patentee.

Is the power of the legislature competent to the annihilation of such title, and to a resumption of the property thus held? The principle asserted is, that one legislature is competent to repeal any act which a former legislature was competent to pass; and that one legislature cannot abridge the powers of a succeeding legislature. The correctness of this principle, so far as respects general legislation, can never be controverted. But, if an act be done under a law, a succeeding legislature cannot undo it. The past cannot be recalled by the most absolute power. Conveyances have been made, those conveyances have vested legal estates, and, if those estates may be seized by the sovereign authority, still, that they originally vested is a fact, and cannot cease to be a fact. When, then, a law is in its nature a contract, when absolute rights have vested under that contract, a repeal of the law cannot divest those rights; and the act of annulling them, if legitimate, is rendered so by a power applicable to the case of every individual in the community.

It may well be doubted, whether the nature of society and of government does not prescribe some limits to the legislative power; and if any be prescribed, where are they to be found, if the property of an individual, fairly and honestly acquired, may be seized without compensation? To the legislature, all legislative power is granted; but the question, whether the act of transferring the property of an individual to the public, be in the nature of the legislative power, is well worthy of serious reflection. It is the peculiar province of the legislature, to prescribe general rules for the government of society; the application of those rules to individuals in society would seem to be the duty of other departments. How far the power of giving the law may involve every other power, in cases where the constitution is silent, never has been, and perhaps never can be, definitely stated.

The validity of this rescinding act, then, might well be doubted, were Georgia a single sovereign power. But Georgia cannot be viewed as a single, unconnected, sovereign power, on whose legislature no other restrictions are imposed than may be found in its own constitution. She is a part of a large empire; she is a member of the American union; and that union has a Constitution, the supremacy of which all acknowledge, and which imposes limits to the legislatures of the several states, which none claim a right to pass. The Constitution of the United States declares that no state shall pass any bill of attainder, *ex post facto* law, or law impairing the obligation of contracts.

Does the case now under consideration come within this prohibitory section of the Constitution? In considering this very interesting question, we immediately ask ourselves what is a contract? Is a grant a contract? A contract is a compact between two or more parties, and is either executory or executed. An executory contract is one in which a party binds himself to do, or not do, a particular thing; such was the law under which the conveyance was made by the governor. A contract executed is one in which the object of contract is performed; and this, says Blackstone, differs in nothing from a grant. The contract between Georgia and the purchasers was executed by the agent. A contract executed, as well as one which is executory, contains obligations binding on the parties. A grant, in its own nature, amounts to an extinguishment of the right of the grantor, and implies a contract not to reassert that right. A party is, therefore, always estopped by his own grant. Since, then, in fact, a grant is a contract executed, the obligation of which still continues, and since the Constitution uses the general term contract, without distinguishing between those which are executory and those which are executed, it must be construed to comprehend the latter as well as the former. A law annulling conveyances between individuals, and declaring that the grantors should stand seized of their former estates, notwithstanding those grants, would be as repugnant to the Constitution, as a law discharging the vendors of property from the obligation of executing their contracts by conveyances. It would be strange, if a contract to convey was secured by the Constitution, while an absolute conveyance remained unprotected.

If, under a fair construction of the Constitution, grants are comprehended under the term contracts, is a grant from the state excluded from the operation of the provision? Is the clause to be considered as inhibiting the state from impairing the obligation of contracts between two individuals, but as excluding from that inhibition contracts made with itself? The words themselves contain no such distinction. They are general, and are applicable to contracts of every description. If contracts made with the state are to be exempted from their operation, the exception must arise from the character of the contracting party, not from the words which are employed. . . .

It is, then, the unanimous opinion of the Court, that, in this case, the estate having passed into the hands of a purchaser for a valuable consideration, without notice, the state of Georgia was restrained, either by general principles which are common to our free institutions, or by the particular provisions of the Constitution of the United States, from passing a law whereby the estate of the plaintiff in the premises so purchased could be constitutionally and legally impaired and rendered null and void. . . .

Judgment affirmed, with costs.

[Mr. Justice JOHNSON concurred in a separate opinion.]

DARTMOUTH COLLEGE v. WOODWARD
4 Wheat. 518 (1819)

[Dartmouth College was established in 1769, by the grant of a charter from the royal governor of the Province of New Hampshire to one Eleazar Wheelock. By this charter the Trustees of Dartmouth

College were constituted as a corporate body and given full power to control the affairs of the new college.

[In 1793, one Nathaniel Niles became a trustee of the college and soon thereafter gained control of the board. Meanwhile Wheelock's son had succeeded his father in the presidency of the college. Relations between him and the Niles-controlled board rapidly deteriorated. Finally, in 1815, the trustees removed Wheelock from his position.

[Meanwhile the intramural conflict in the college had aroused state-wide attention and the two political parties had aligned themselves with the warring factions. The Federalists sided with the trustees while the Republicans gave their support to Wheelock. In 1816, the Republicans elected the state governor and secured a majority in the legislature. Among the reform measures instituted by the new administration was an act changing the name of the college to "Dartmouth University," increasing the number while curtailing the power of the trustees, and generally subjecting the institution to the control of the state.

[The old trustees refused to accept the new law and continued to run the college. New trustees and overseers were appointed by the governor and ejected the old group from the college premises. Dartmouth University assumed operation, with Wheelock as President. Meanwhile the old college carried on in a nearby building, with most of the students following their faculty.

[With Wheelock at the new university was William H. Woodward, for many years secretary and treasurer of the college trustees. He held the records, the books, and the seal of the college, all of which he carried with him when he followed Wheelock to the new institution. The college trustees brought suit against him to compel the surrender of the seal and papers. This raised the question of the effect of the legislative action of 1816: could a state law thus change the college charter? If the answer was in the affirmative, the trustees of the college had no claim to records and seal; if the power was denied, "Dartmouth University" had no legal existence and Woodward had illegally removed the items in issue.

[The state supreme court, consisting of three Republicans, found against the college. The case was taken to the Supreme Court of the United States, where Daniel Webster offered the principal argument on behalf of the college from which he had graduated. After some delay, the Court's decision was announced on February 2, 1819.]

The opinion of the Court was delivered by MARSHALL, C. J.

This is an action ... brought by the Trustees of Dartmouth College against William H. Woodward ... for the book of records, corporate seal, and other corporate property, to which the plaintiffs allege themselves to be entitled.... The single question now to be considered is, do the acts ... [of the state legislature] ... violate the Constitution of the United States?

This Court can be insensible neither to the magnitude nor to the delicacy of this question. The validity of a legislative act is to be examined; and the opinion of the highest law tribunal of a State is to be revised—an opinion which carries with it intrinsic evidence of the diligence, of the ability, and the integrity, with which it was formed. On more than one occasion, this Court has expressed the cautious circumspection with which it approaches the consideration of such questions; and has declared that, in no doubtful case, would it pronounce a legislative act to be contrary to the Constitution. But the American people have said, in the Constitution of the United States, that "no state shall pass any bill of attainder, *ex post facto* law, or law impairing the obligation of contracts." In the same instrument, they have also said, "that the judicial power shall extend to all cases in law and equity arising under the Constitution." On the judges of this Court, then, is imposed the high and solemn duty of protecting, from even legislative violation, those contracts which the Constitution of our country has placed beyond legislative control; and, however irksome the task may be, this is a duty from which we dare not shrink.

The title of the plaintiffs originates in a charter dated the 13th day of December, in the year 1769, incorporating twelve persons therein mentioned, by the name of "The Trustees of Dartmouth College," granting to them and their successors the usual corporate privileges and powers, and authorizing the trustees, who are to govern the college, to fill up all vacancies which may be created in their own body.

The defendant claims under three acts of the legislature of New Hampshire, the most material of which was passed on the 27th of June, 1816, and is entitled, "An act to amend the charter, and enlarge and improve the corporation of Dartmouth College." Among other alterations in the charter, this act increases the number of trustees to twenty-one, gives the appointment of the additional members to the executive of the state, and creates a board of overseers, with power to inspect and control the most important acts of the trustees. This board consists of twenty-five persons. The president of the senate, the speaker of the house of representatives of New Hampshire, and the governor and the lieutenant-governor of Vermont, for the time being, are to be members *ex officio*. The board is to be completed by the governor and council of New Hampshire, who are also empowered to fill all vacancies which may occur. The acts of the 18th and 26th of December are supplemental to that of the 27th of June, and are principally intended to carry that act into effect. The majority of the trustees of the college have refused to accept this amended charter, and have brought this suit for the corporate property, which is in possession of a person [Woodward] holding by virtue of the acts which have been stated.

It can require no argument to prove that the circumstances of this case constitute a contract. An application is made to the crown for a charter to incorporate a religious and literary institution. In the application, it is stated, that large contributions have been made for the object, which will be conferred on the corporation, as soon as it shall be created. The charter is granted, and on its faith the property is conveyed. Surely, in this transaction every ingredient of a complete and legitimate contract is to be found. The points for consideration are, 1. Is this contract protected by the Constitution of the United States? 2. Is it impaired by the acts under which the defendant holds?

1. On the first point, it has been argued that the word "contract," in its broadest sense, would comprehend the political relations between the government and its citizens, would extend to offices held within a state, for state purposes, and to many of those laws concerning civil institutions, which must change with circumstances, and be modified by ordinary legislation; which deeply concern the public, and which, to preserve good government, the public judgment must control. That even marriage is a contract, and its obligations are affected by the laws respecting divorces. That the clause in the Constitution, if construed in its greatest latitude, would prohibit these laws. Taken in its broad, unlimited sense, the clause would be an unprofitable and vexatious interference with the internal concerns of a state, would unnecessarily and unwisely embarrass its legislation, and render immutable those civil institutions, which are established for purpose of internal government, and which, to subserve those purposes, ought to vary with varying circumstances. That

as the framers of the Constitution could never have intended to in-
sert in that instrument, a provision so unnecessary, so mischievous,
and so repugnant to its general spirit, the term "contract" must be
understood in a more limited sense. That it must be understood as
intended to guard against a power, of at least doubtful utility, the
abuse of which had been extensively felt; and to restrain the legislature in future from violating the right to property. That, anterior
to the formation of the Constitution, a course of legislation had prevailed in many, if not in all, of the states, which weakened the confidence of man in man, and embarrassed all transactions between
individuals, by dispensing with a faithful performance of engagements. To correct this mischief, by restraining the power which produced it, the state legislatures were forbidden "to pass any law impairing the obligation of contracts," that is, of contracts respecting
property, under which some individual could claim a right to something beneficial to himself; and that, since the clause in the Constitution must in construction receive some limitation, it may be confined, and ought to be confined, to cases of this description; to cases
within the mischief it was intended to remedy.

The general correctness of these observations cannot be controverted. . . .

The parties in this case differ less on general principles, less on
the true construction of the Constitution in the abstract, than on
the application of those principles to this case, and on the true construction of the charter of 1769. This is the point on which the cause
essentially depends. If the act of incorporation be a grant of political
power, if it creates a civil institution, to be employed in the administration of the government, or if the funds of the college be public
property, or if the state of New Hampshire, as a government, be
alone interested in its transactions, the subject is one in which the
legislature of the state may act according to its judgment, unrestrained by any limitation of its power imposed by the Constitution
of the United States.

But if this be a private eleemosynary institution, endowed with
a capacity to take property, for objects unconnected with government, whose funds are bestowed by individuals, on the faith of the
charter; if the donors have stipulated for the future disposition and
management of those funds, in the manner prescribed by themselves; there may be more difficulty in the case, although neither

the persons who have made these stipulations, nor those for whose benefit they were made, should be parties to the cause. . . .

. . . It appears, that Dartmouth College is an eleemosynary institution, incorporated for the purpose of perpetuating the application of the bounty of the donors, to the specified objects of that bounty; that its trustees or governors were originally named by the founder, and invested with the power of perpetuating themselves; that they are not public officers, nor is it a civil institution, participating in the administration of government; but a charity school, or a seminary of education, incorporated for the preservation of its property, and the perpetual application of that property to the objects of its creation.

This is plainly a contract to which the donors, the trustees, and the crown (to whose rights and obligations New Hampshire succeeds) were the original parties. It is a contract made on a valuable consideration. It is a contract for the security and disposition of property. It is a contract, on the faith of which, real and personal estate has been conveyed to the corporation. It is, then, a contract within the letter of the Constitution. . . .

The opinion of the Court, after mature deliberation, is, that this is a contract, the obligation of which cannot be impaired, without violating the Constitution of the United States. This opinion appears to us to be equally supported by reason, and by the former decisions of this Court.

2. We next proceed to the inquiry, whether its obligation has been impaired by those acts of the legislature of New Hampshire. . . .

On the effect of this law, two opinions cannot be entertained. Between acting directly, and acting through the agency of trustees and overseers, no essential difference is perceived. The whole power of governing the college is transferred from trustees, appointed according to the will of the founder, expressed in the charter, to the executive of New Hampshire. The management and application of the funds of this eleemosynary institution, which are placed by the donors in the hands of trustees named in the charter, and empowered to perpetuate themselves, are placed by this act under the control of the government of the state. The will of the state is substituted for the will of the donors, in every essential operation of the college. This is not an immaterial change. The founders of the college contracted, not merely for the perpetual application of the funds which they gave, to the objects for which those funds were given; they contracted also, to secure that application by the constitution of the corporation. They contracted for a system, which should, as far as human foresight can provide, retain forever the government of the literary institution they had formed, in the hands of persons approved by themselves. This system is totally changed. The charter of 1769 exists no longer. It is reorganized; and reorganized in such a manner, as to convert a literary institution, moulded according to the will of its founders, and placed under the control of private literary men, into a machine entirely subservient to the will of government. This may be for the advantage of the college in particular, and may be for the advantage of literature in general; but it is not according to the will of the donors, and is subversive of that contract, on the faith of which their property was given. . . .

It results from this opinion, that the acts of the legislature of New Hampshire, which are stated in the special verdict found in this cause, are repugnant to the Constitution of the United States; and that the judgment on this special verdict ought to have been for the plaintiffs. The judgment of the state court must, therefore, be reversed. . . .

[Mr. Justice WASHINGTON and Mr. Justice STORY delivered concurring opinions. Mr. Justice DUVALL dissented.]

CONSEQUENCES OF THE "DARTMOUTH" DECISION[1]

Important, indeed, were the consequences of the Dartmouth decision. Everywhere corporations were springing up in response to the necessity for large and more constant business units and because of the convenience and profit of such organizations. Marshall's opinion was a tremendous stimulant to this natural economic tendency. It reassured investors in corporate securities and gave confidence and steadiness to the business world. It is undeniable and undenied that America could not have been developed so rapidly and solidly with-

[1] From Albert J. Beveridge, *The Life of John Marshall*, vol. IV, pp. 276–278. Reprinted by permission of the publishers, Houghton Mifflin Co., Boston.

out the power which the law as announced by Marshall gave to industrial organization.

One result of his opinion was, for the period, of even higher value than the encouragement it gave to private enterprise and the steadiness it brought to business generally; it aligned on the side of nationalism all powerful economic forces operating through corporate organization. A generation passed before railway development began in America; but Marshall lived to see the first stage of the evolution of that mighty element in American commercial, industrial, and social life; and all of that force, except the part of it which was directly connected with and under the immediate influence of the slave power, was aggressively and most effectively nationalist.

That this came to be the fact was due to Marshall's Dartmouth opinion more than to any other single cause. The same was true of other industrial corporate organizations. John Fiske does not greatly exaggerate in his assertion that the law as to corporate franchises declared by Marshall, in subjecting to the national Constitution every charter granted by a State "went farther, perhaps, than any other in our history toward limiting State sovereignty and extending the Federal jurisdiction."

Sir Henry Sumner Maine has some ground for his rather dogmatic statement that the principle of Marshall's opinion "is the basis of credit of many of the great American Railway Incorporations," and "has . . . secured full play to the economical forces by which the achievement of cultivating the soil of the North American Continent has been performed." Marshall's statesmanship is, asserts Maine, "the bulwark of American individualism against democratic impatience and Socialistic fantasy." Such views of the Dartmouth decision are remarkably similar to those which Story himself expressed soon after it was rendered. Writing to Chancellor Kent Story says: "Unless I am very much mistaken the principles on which that decision rests will be found to apply with an extensive reach to all the great concerns of the people, and will check any undue encroachments upon civil rights, which the passions or the popular doctrines of the day may stimulate our State Legislatures to adopt."

The Court's decision, however, made corporate franchises infinitely more valuable and strengthened the motives for procuring them, even by corruption In this wise tremendous frauds have been perpetrated upon negligent, careless, and indifferent publics; and "enormous and threatening powers," selfish and non-public in their purposes and methods, have been created. But Marshall's opinion put the public on its guard. Almost immediately the States enacted laws reserving to the legislature the right to alter or repeal corporate charters; and the constitutions of several States now include this limitation on corporate franchises. Yet these reservations did not, as a practical matter, nullify or overthrow Marshall's philosophy of the sacredness of contracts.

2. BUSINESS WITHOUT PRIVILEGE

CHARLES RIVER BRIDGE v. WARREN BRIDGE
11 Pet. 420 (1837)

["While the state legislatures were writing Jacksonian ideals into the law of corporations, a Jacksonian Supreme Court under Chief Justice Taney was reading them into the clauses of the Constitution. Taney, appointed by Jackson in 1836, sat on the Court until his death in 1864, and during his long tenure the Court propagated the Jacksonian view of business without privilege. . . . Taney's most startling case, as symbolic of the fight against privilege in the juridical sphere as the bank was in politics, was the Charles River Bridge case. The majority decision, prepared by Taney, which represented a long forward step in detaching from the corporation the stigma of monopoly, stands as a classic of the Jacksonian faith." Richard Hofstadter, *The American Political Tradition and the Men Who Made It*.[2]]

[In 1650 the Legislature of Massachusetts granted to the president of Harvard College "the liberty and power" to dispose of the ferry over the Charles River from Charlestown to Boston, and under this grant Harvard College received the profits of this ferry until 1785, when the legislature incorporated "The Proprietors of the Charles River Bridge," and authorized the company to construct a bridge at the place where the ferry then was. Provision was made for compensating Harvard College for the impairment of the value of its ferry franchise. In 1828 the legislature incorporated another company by the name of "The Proprietors of the Warren Bridge," and authorized it to construct another bridge in the immediate proximity of the Charles River Bridge, the new bridge to be free of toll charges after an initial period.

[The Charles River Bridge Company asked for an injunction to stop the construction of the new bridge on the ground that the act authorizing the building of Warren Bridge was an impairment by

---

[2] New York: Alfred A. Knopf, Inc., 1948. Reprinted by permission.

the state legislature of the obligation of the contract between the state and the Charles River Bridge Company. The Massachusetts supreme court declined to issue the injunction.]

Mr. Chief Justice TANEY delivered the opinion of the Court. . . .

The plaintiffs in error insist, mainly, upon two grounds: 1st. That by virtue of the grant of 1650, Harvard College was entitled, in perpetuity, to the right of keeping a ferry between Charlestown and Boston; that this right was exclusive; and that the legislature had not the power to establish another ferry on the same line of travel, because it would infringe the rights of the college; and that these rights, upon the erection of the bridge in the place of the ferry, under the charter of 1785, were transferred to, and became vested in "the proprietors of the Charles River Bridge"; and that under, and by virtue of this transfer of the ferry-right, the rights of the bridge company were as exclusive in that line of travel, as the rights of the ferry. 2d. That independently of the ferry-right, the acts of the legislature of Massachusetts, of 1785 and 1792, by their true construction, necessarily implied, that the legislature would not authorize another bridge, and especially a free one, by the side of this, and placed in the same line of travel, whereby the franchise granted to the "Proprietors of the Charles River Bridge" should be rendered of no value, and the plaintiffs in error contend, that the grant of the ferry to the college, and of the charter to the proprietors of the bridge, are both contracts on the part of the state; and that the law authorizing the erection of the Warren Bridge in 1828, impairs the obligation of one or both of these contracts. . . .

This brings us to the act of the legislature of Massachusetts of 1785, by which the plaintiffs were incorporated by the name of "The Proprietors of the Charles River Bridge"; and it is here, and in the law of 1792, prolonging their charter, that we must look for the extent and nature of the franchise conferred upon the plaintiffs. Much has been said in the argument of the principles of construction by which this law is to be expounded, and what undertakings, on the part of the state, may be implied. The Court think there can be no serious difficulty on that head. It is the grant of certain franchises, by the public, to a private corporation, and in a matter where the public interest is concerned. The rule of construction in such cases is well settled, both in England, and by the decision of our tribunals. ". . . The rule of construction in all such cases is now fully established to be this—that any ambiguity in the terms of the contract, must operate against the adventurers, and in favor of the public, and the plaintiffs can claim nothing that is not clearly given them by the act.". . .

Borrowing, as we have done, our system of jurisprudence from the English law; and having adopted, in every other case, civil and criminal, its rules for the construction of statutes; is there anything in our local situation, or in the nature of our political institutions, which should lead us to depart from the principle, where corporations are concerned? Are we to apply to acts of incorporation a rule of construction differing from that of the English law and, by implication, make the terms of a charter in one of the states more unfavorable to the public than upon an act of parliament, framed in the same words, would be sanctioned in an English court? Can any good reason be assigned, for excepting this particular class of cases from the operation of the general principle; and for introducing a new and adverse rule of construction in favor of corporations, while we adopt and adhere to the rules of construction known to the English common law, in every other case, without exception? We think not; and it would present a singular spectacle, if, while the courts in England are restraining, within the strictest limits, the spirit of monopoly, and exclusive privileges in nature of monopolies, and confining corporations to the privileges plainly given to them in their charter; the courts of this country should be found enlarging these privileges by implication; and construing a statute more unfavorably to the public, and to the rights of the community, than would be done in a like case in an English court of justice.

Adopting the rule of construction above stated as the settled one, we proceed to apply it to the charter of 1785 to the proprietors of the Charles River Bridge. This act of incorporation is in the usual form, and the privileges such as are commonly given to corporations of that kind. It confers on them the ordinary faculties of a corporation, for the purpose of building the bridge; and establishes certain rates of toll, which the company are authorized to take: this is the whole grant. There is no exclusive privilege given to them over the waters of Charles River, above or below their bridge; no right to erect another bridge themselves, nor to prevent other persons from erecting one, no engagement from the state, that another shall not be erected; and no undertaking not to sanction competition, nor to make improvements that may diminish the amount of its income. Upon all these subjects, the charter is silent; and nothing is said in it about a line of travel, so much insisted on in the argument, in which they are to have exclusive privileges. No words are used from which an intention to grant any of these rights can be inferred; if the plaintiff is entitled to them, it must be implied, simply, from the nature of the grant; and cannot be inferred, from the words by which the grant is made.

The relative position of the Warren Bridge has already been described. It does not interrupt the passage over the Charles River Bridge, nor make the way to it, or from it, less convenient. None of the faculties or franchises granted to the corporation, have been revoked by the legislature; and its right to take the tolls granted by the charter remains unaltered. In short, all the franchises and rights of property, enumerated in the charter, and there mentioned to have been granted to it, remain unimpaired. But its income is destroyed by the Warren Bridge; which, being free, draws off the passengers and property which would have gone over it, and renders their franchise of no value. This is the gist of the complaint. For it is not pretended, that the erection of the Warren Bridge would have done them any injury, or in any degree affected their right of property, if it had not diminished the amount of their tolls. In order, then, to entitle themselves to relief, it is necessary to show, that the legislature contracted not to do the act of which they complain; and that they impaired, or in other words, violated, that contract by the erection of the Warren Bridge.

The inquiry, then, is, does the charter contain such a contract on the part of the state? Is there any such stipulation to be found in that instrument? It must be admitted on all hands, that there is none; no words that even relate to another bridge, or to the diminution of their tolls, or to the line of travel. If a contract on that subject can be gathered from the charter, it must be by implication; and cannot be found in the words used. Can such an agreement be implied? The rule of construction before stated is an answer to the question; in charters of this description, no rights are taken from the public, or given to the corporation, beyond those which the words of the charter, by their natural and proper construction, purport to convey. . . . The whole community . . . have a right to require that the power of promoting their comfort and convenience, and of advancing the public prosperity, by providing safe, convenient and cheap ways for the transportation of produce and the purposes of travel shall not be construed to have been surrendered or diminished by the state, unless it shall appear by plain words, that it was intended to be done....

The judgment of the supreme judicial court of the commonwealth of Massachusetts, dismissing the plaintiff's bill, must therefore, be affirmed, with costs.

Mr. Justice STORY, dissenting....

... It is conceded that the legislature cannot revoke or resume this grant. Why not, I pray to know? There is no negative covenant in the charter; there is no express prohibition to be found there. The reason is plain. The prohibition arises by natural, if not by necessary implication. It would be against the first principles of justice to presume that the legislature reserved a right to destroy its own grant. That was the doctrine in *Fletcher* v. *Peck,* 6 Cranch 87, in this Court and in other cases turning upon the same great principle of political and constitutional duty and right. Can the legislature have power to do that indirectly which it cannot do directly? If it cannot take away, or resume, the franchise itself, can it take away its whole substance and value?...

No principle is better established than the principle that, when a thing is given or granted, the law giveth, impliedly, whatever is necessary for the taking and enjoying the same....

What objection can there be to implications if they arise from the very nature and objects of the grant? If it be indispensable to the full enjoyment of the right to take toll that it should be exclusive within certain limits, is it not just and reasonable that it should be so construed?

I maintain that, upon the principles of common reason and legal interpretation, the present grant carries with it a necessary implication that the legislature shall do no act to destroy or essentially to impair the franchise; that (as one of the learned judges of the state court expressed it) there is an implied agreement that the state will not grant another bridge between Boston and Charlestown, so near as to draw away the custom from the old one; and (as another learned judge expressed it) that there is an implied agreement of the state to grant the undisturbed use of the bridge and its tolls, so far as respects any acts of its own, or of any persons acting under its authority.

HOME BUILDING & LOAN ASSOCIATION v. BLAISDELL
290 U.S. 398 (1934)

Mr. Chief Justice HUGHES delivered the opinion of the Court.

Appellant [Home Building & Loan Association] contests the validity of chapter 339 of the Laws of Minnesota of 1933, . . . called the Minnesota Mortgage Moratorium Law, as being repugnant to the contract clause (article 1, § 10) and the due process and equal protection clauses of the Fourteenth Amendment of the Federal Constitution. The statute was sustained by the Supreme Court of Minnesota, and the case comes here on appeal.

The act provides that, during the emergency declared to exist, relief may be had through authorized judicial proceedings with respect to foreclosures of mortgages, and execution sales, of real estate; that sales may be postponed and periods of redemption may be extended. The act does not apply to mortgages subsequently made nor to those made previously which shall be extended for a period ending more than a year after the passage of the act (part 1, § 8). . . . The act is to remain in effect "only during the continuance of the emergency and in no event beyond May 1, 1935." . . .

The act declares that the various provisions for relief are severable; that each is to stand on its own footing with respect to validity. Part 1, § 9. We are here concerned with the provisions of part 1, § 4, authorizing the district court of the county to extend the period of redemption from foreclosure sales "for such additional time as the court may deem just and equitable," subject to the above-described limitation. The extension is to be made upon application to the court, on notice, for an order determining the reasonable value of the income on the property involved in the sale, or, if it has no income, then the reasonable rental value of the property, and directing the mortgagor "to pay all or a reasonable part of such income or rental value, in or toward the payment of taxes, insurance, interest, mortgage . . . indebtedness at such times and in such manner" as shall be determined by the court. . . .

Invoking the relevant provision of the statute, appellees [J. H. Blaisdell and wife] applied to the district court of Hennepin county for an order extending the period of redemption from a foreclosure sale. Their petition stated that they owned a lot in Minneapolis which they had mortgaged to appellant; that the mortgage contained a valid power of sale by advertisement, and that by reason of their default the mortgage had been foreclosed and sold to appellant on

May 2, 1932, for $3,700.98; that appellant was the holder of the sheriff's certificate of sale; that, because of the economic depression, appellees had been unable to obtain a new loan or to redeem, and that, unless the period of redemption were extended, the property would be irretrievably lost; and that the reasonable value of the property greatly exceeded the amount due on the mortgage, including all liens, costs, and expenses. . . .

. . . The court found that the time to redeem would expire on May 2, 1933, under the laws of the state as they were in effect when the mortgage was made and when it was foreclosed; that the reasonable value of the income on the property, and the reasonable rental value, was $40 a month; that the bid made by appellant on the foreclosure sale, and the purchase price, were the full amount of the mortgage indebtedness, and that there was no deficiency after the sale; that the reasonable market value of the premises was $6,000; and that the total amount of the purchase price, with taxes and insurance premiums subsequently paid by appellant, but exclusive of interest from the date of sale, was $4,056.39. The court also found that the property was situated in the closely built-up portions of Minneapolis; that it had been improved by a two-car garage, together with a building two stories in height which was divided into fourteen rooms; that the appellees, husband and wife, occupied the premises as their homestead, occupying three rooms and offering the remaining rooms for rental to others.

The court entered its judgment extending the period of redemption to May 1, 1935, subject to the condition that the appellees should pay to the appellant $40 a month through the extended period from May 2, 1933; that is, that in each of the months of August, September, and October, 1933, the payments should be $80, in two installments, and thereafter $40 a month, all these amounts to go to the payment of taxes, insurance, interest, and mortgage indebtedness. It is this judgment, sustained by the Supreme Court of the state on the authority of its former opinion, which is here under review.

The state court upheld the statute as an emergency measure. Although conceding that the obligations of the mortgage contract were impaired, the court decided that what it thus described as an impairment was, notwithstanding the contract clause of the Federal Constitution, within the police power of the state as that power was called into exercise by the public economic emergency which the Legislature had found to exist. Attention is thus directed to the preamble and first section of the statute which described the existing emergency in terms that were deemed to justify the temporary relief which the statute affords. The state court, declaring that it could not say that this legislative finding was without basis, supplemented that finding by its own statement of conditions of which it took judicial notice. The court said:

" . . . It is common knowledge that in the last few years land values have shrunk enormously. Loans made a few years ago upon the basis of the then going values cannot possibly be replaced on the basis of present values. We all know that when this law was enacted the large financial companies, which had made it their business to invest in mortgages, had ceased to do so. No bank would directly or indirectly loan on real estate mortgages. Life insurance companies, large investors on such mortgages, had even declared a moratorium as to the loan provisions of their policy contracts. The President had closed banks temporarily. The Congress, in addition to many extraordinary measures looking to the relief of the economic emergency, had passed an act to supply funds whereby mortgagors may be able within a reasonable time to refinance their mortgages or redeem from sales where the redemption has not expired. With this knowledge the court cannot well hold that the Legislature had no basis in fact for the conclusion that an economic emergency existed which called for the exercise of the police power to grant relief." . . .

We approach the question thus presented upon the assumption made below, as required by the law of the state, that the mortgage contained a valid power of sale to be exercised in case of default; that this power was validly exercised; that under the law then applicable the period of redemption from the sale was one year, and that it has been extended by the judgment of the court over the opposition of the mortgagee-purchaser; and that, during the period thus extended, and unless the order for extension is modified, the mortgagee-purchaser will be unable to obtain possession, or to obtain or convey title in fee, as he would have been able to do had the statute not been enacted. The statute does not impair the integrity of the mortgage indebtedness. The obligation for interest remains. The statute does not affect the validity of the sale or the right of a mortgagee-purchaser to title in fee, or his right to obtain a deficiency judgment, if the mortgagor fails to redeem within the prescribed period. Aside from the extension of time, the other conditions of redemption are unaltered. While the mortgagor remains in possession, he must pay the rental value as that value has been determined, upon notice and hearing, by the court. The rental value so paid is devoted to the carrying of the property by the application of the required payments to taxes, insurance, and interest on the mortgage indebtedness. While the mortgagee-purchaser is debarred from actual possession, he has, so far as rental value is concerned, the equivalent of possession during the extended period.

In determining whether the provision for this temporary and conditional relief exceeds the power of the state by reason of the clause of the Federal Constitution prohibiting impairment of the obligations of contracts, we must consider the relation of emergency to constitutional power, the historical setting of the contract clause, the development of the jurisprudence of this Court in the construction of that clause, and the principles of construction which we may consider to be established.

Emergency does not create power. Emergency does not increase granted power or remove or diminish the restrictions imposed upon power granted or reserved. The Constitution was adopted in a period of grave emergency. Its grants of power to the federal government and its limitations of the power of the States were determined in the light of emergency. What power was thus granted and what limitations were thus imposed are questions which have always been, and always will be, the subject of close examination under our constitutional system.

While emergency does not create power, emergency may furnish the occasion for the exercise of power. . . . The constitutional question presented in the light of an emergency is whether the power possessed embraces the particular exercise of it in response to particular conditions. Thus, the war power of the federal government is not created by the emergency of war, but it is a power given to meet that emergency. It is a power to wage war successfully, and thus it permits the harnessing of the entire energies of the people in a supreme co-operative effort to preserve the nation. But even the war power does not remove constitutional limitations safeguarding essential liberties. When the provisions of the Constitution, in grant or restriction, are specific, so particularized as not to admit of construction, no question is presented. Thus, emergency would not permit a state to have more than two Senators in the Congress, or permit the election of President by a general popular vote without regard to the number of electors to which the States are respectively entitled, or permit the States to "coin money" or to "make anything but gold and silver coin a tender in payment of debts." But, where constitutional grants and limitations of power are set forth in general clauses, which afford a broad outline, the process of construction is essential to fill in the details. That is true of the contract clause. . . .

In the construction of the contract clause, the debates in the Constitutional Convention are of little aid. But the reasons which led to the adoption of that clause, and of the other prohibitions of section 10 of article 1, are not left in doubt, and have frequently been described with eloquent emphasis. The widespread distress following the revolutionary period and the plight of debtors had called forth in the States an ignoble array of legislative schemes for the defeat of creditors and the invasion of contractual obligations. Legislative interferences had been so numerous and extreme that the confidence essential to prosperous trade had been undermined and the utter destruction of credit was threatened. . . .

But full recognition of the occasion and general purpose of the clause does not suffice to fix its precise scope. Nor does an examination of the details of prior legislation in the States yield criteria which can be considered controlling. To ascertain the scope of the constitutional prohibition, we examine the course of judicial decisions in its application. These put it beyond question that the prohibition is not an absolute one and is not to be read with literal exactness like a mathematical formula. . . .

The inescapable problems of construction have been: What is a contract? What are the obligations of contract? What constitutes impairment of these obligations? What residuum of power is there still in the States, in relation to the operation of contracts, to protect the vital interests of the community? Questions of this character, "of no small nicety and intricacy, have vexed the legislative halls, as well as the judicial tribunals, with an uncounted variety and frequency of litigation and speculation." Story on the Constitution, § 1375.

The obligation of a contract is the law which binds the parties to perform their agreement. . . . This Court has said that "the laws which subsist at the time and place of the making of a contract, and where it is to be performed, enter into and form a part of it, as if they were expressly referred to or incorporated in its terms. This principle embraces alike those which affect its validity, construction, discharge, and enforcement. . . . Nothing can be more material to the obligation than the means of enforcement. . . . The ideas of validity and remedy are inseparable, and both are parts of the obligation, which is guaranteed by the Constitution against invasion." *Von Hoffman* v. *City of Quincy,* 4 Wall. 535, 550, 552. But this broad language cannot be taken without qualification. Chief Justice Marshall pointed out the distinction between obligation and remedy. *Sturges* v. *Crowninshield,* 4 Wheat. 122, 200. Said he: "The distinction between the obligation of a contract, and the remedy given by the legislature to enforce that obligation, has been taken at the bar, and exists in the nature of things. Without impairing the obligation of the contract, the remedy may certainly be modified as the wisdom of the nation shall direct." And in *Von Hoffman* v. *City of Quincy, supra,* 4 Wall. 553, 554, the general statement above quoted was limited by the further observation that "it is competent for the States to change the form of the remedy, or to modify it otherwise, as they may see fit, provided no substantial right secured by the contract is thereby impaired. No attempt has been made to fix definitely the line between alterations of the remedy, which are to be deemed legitimate, and those which, under the form of modifying the remedy, impair substantial rights. Every case must be determined upon its own circumstances." . . .

[Discussion of other cases omitted.]

.   .   .   .   .

None of these cases, and we have cited those upon which appellant chiefly relies, is directly applicable to the question now before us in view of the conditions with which the Minnesota statute seeks to safeguard the interests of the mortgagee-purchaser during the extended period. . . .

Not only is the constitutional provision qualified by the measure of control which the state retains over remedial processes, but the state also continues to possess authority to safeguard the vital interests of its people. It does not matter that legislation appropriate to that end "has the result of modifying or abrogating contracts already in effect." *Stephenson* v. *Binford,* 287 U.S. 251, 276. Not only are existing laws read into contracts in order to fix obligations as between the parties, but the reservation of essential attributes of sovereign power is also read into contracts as a postulate of the legal order. The policy of protecting contracts against impairment pre-supposes the maintenance of a government by virtue of which con-tractual relations are worth while,—a government which retains adequate authority to secure the peace and good order of society. This principle of harmonizing the constitutional prohibition with the necessary residuum of state power has had progressive recogni-tion in the decisions of this Court.

. . . . .

The legislature cannot "bargain away the public health or the public morals." Thus the constitutional provision against the im-pairment of contracts was held not to be violated by an amendment of the state constitution which put an end to a lottery theretofore authorized by the legislature. *Stone* v. *Mississippi,* 101 U.S. 814, 819. . . . A similar rule has been applied to the control by the state of the sale of intoxicating liquors. *Boston Beer Company* v. *Massachusetts,* 97 U.S. 25, 32, 33. . . . The states retain adequate power to protect the public health against the maintenance of nuisances despite in-sistence upon existing contracts. . . .

. . . . .

The argument is pressed that in the cases we have cited the obli-gation of contracts was affected only incidentally. This argument proceeds upon a misconception. The question is not whether the legislative action affects contracts incidentally, or directly or indi-rectly, but whether the legislation is addressed to a legitimate end and the measures taken are reasonable and appropriate to that end. Another argument, which comes more closely to the point, is that the state power may be addressed directly to the prevention of the enforcement of contracts only when these are of a sort which the legislature in its discretion may denounce as being in themselves hostile to public morals, or public health, safety, or welfare, or where the prohibition is merely of injurious practices; that inter-ference with the enforcement of other and valid contracts according to appropriate legal procedure, although the interference is tem-porary and for a public purpose, is not permissible. This is but to contend that in the latter case the end is not legitimate in the view that it cannot be reconciled with a fair interpretation of the consti-tutional provision.

Undoubtedly, whatever is reserved of state power must be consistent with the fair intent of the constitutional limitation of that power. The reserved power cannot be construed so as to destroy the limitation, nor is the limitation to be construed to destroy the reserved power in its essential aspects. They must be construed in harmony with each other. This principle precludes a construction which would permit the state to adopt as its policy the repudiation of debts or the destruction of contracts or the denial of means to enforce them. But it does not follow that conditions may not arise in which a temporary restraint of enforcement may not be consistent with the spirit and purpose of the constitutional provision and thus be found to be within the range of the reserved power of the state to protect the vital interests of the community. It cannot be maintained that the constitutional prohibition should be so construed as to prevent limited and temporary interpositions with respect to the enforcement of contracts if made necessary by a great public calamity such as fire, flood, or earthquake. . . . The reservation of state power appropriate to such extraordinary conditions may be deemed to be as much a part of all contracts as is the reservation of state power to protect the public interest in the other situations to which we have referred. And, if state power exists to give temporary relief from the enforcement of contracts in the presence of disasters due to physical causes such as fire, flood, or earthquake, that power cannot be said to be nonexistent when the urgent public need demanding such relief is produced by other and economic causes.

It is manifest from . . . [the] . . . review of our decisions that there has been a growing appreciation of public needs and of the necessity of finding ground for a rational compromise between individual rights and public welfare. The settlement and consequent contraction of the public domain, the pressure of a constantly increasing density of population, the inter-relation of the activities of our people and the complexity of our economic interests, have inevitably led to an increased use of the organization of society in order to protect the very bases of individual opportunity. Where, in earlier days, it was thought that only the concerns of individuals or of classes were involved, and that those of the state itself were touched only remotely, it has later been found that the fundamental interests of the state are directly affected; and that the question is no longer merely that of one party to a contract as against another, but of the use of reasonable means to safeguard the economic structure upon which the good of all depends.

It is no answer to say that this public need was not apprehended a century ago, or to insist that what the provision of the Constitution meant to the vision of that day it must mean to the vision of our time. If by the statement that what the Constitution meant at the time of its adoption it means to-day, it is intended to say that the great clauses of the Constitution must be confined to the interpretation which the framers, with the conditions and outlook of their time, would have placed upon them, the statement carries its own refutation. It was to guard against such a narrow conception that Chief Justice Marshall uttered the memorable warning: "We must never forget, that it is a *constitution* we are expounding" (*McCulloch* v. *Maryland,* 4 Wheat. 316, 407); "a constitution intended to endure for ages to come, and consequently, to be adapted to the various crises of human affairs." *Id.* page 415 of 4 Wheat. When we are dealing with the words of the Constitution, said this Court in *Missouri* v. *Holland,* 252 U.S. 416, 433, "we must realize that they have called into life a being the development of which could not have been foreseen completely by the most gifted of its begetters. . . . The case before us must be considered in the light of our whole experience and not merely in that of what was said a hundred years ago."

Nor is it helpful to attempt to draw a fine distinction between the intended meaning of the words of the Constitution and their intended application. When we consider the contract clause and the decisions which have expounded it in harmony with the essential reserved power of the states to protect the security of their peoples, we find no warrant for the conclusion that the clause has been warped by these decisions from its proper significance or that the founders of our government would have interpreted the clause differently had they had occasion to assume that responsibility in the conditions of the later day. The vast body of law which has been developed was unknown to the fathers, but it is believed to have preserved the essential content and the spirit of the Constitution. With a growing recognition of public needs and the relation of individual right to public security, the Court has sought to prevent the perversion of the clause through its use as an instrument to throttle the capacity of the states to protect their fundamental interests. This development is a growth from the seeds which the fathers planted. . . . And the germs of the later decisions are found in the *Charles River Bridge* [case] . . . *supra,* which upheld the public right against strong insistence upon the contract clause. The principle of this development is, as we have seen, that the reservation of the reasonable exercise of the protective power of the state is read into all contracts. . . .

We are of the opinion that the Minnesota statute as here applied does not violate the contract clause of the Federal Constitution. Whether the legislation is wise or unwise as a matter of policy is a question with which we are not concerned.

The judgment of the Supreme Court of Minnesota is affirmed.

Mr. Justice SUTHERLAND, dissenting.

Few questions of greater moment than that just decided have been submitted for judicial inquiry during this generation. He simply closes his eyes to the necessary implications of the decision who fails to see in it the potentiality of future gradual but ever-advancing encroachments upon the sanctity of private and public contracts. The effect of the Minnesota legislation, though serious enough in itself, is of trivial significance compared with the far more serious and dangerous inroads upon the limitations of the Constitution which are almost certain to ensue as a consequence naturally following any step beyond the boundaries fixed by that instrument. And those of us who are thus apprehensive of the effect of this decision would, in a matter so important, be neglectful of our duty should we fail to spread upon the permanent records of the Court the reasons which move us to the opposite view.

A provision of the Constitution, it is hardly necessary to say, does not admit of two distinctly opposite interpretations. It does not mean one thing at one time and an entirely different thing at another time. If the contract impairment clause, when framed and adopted, meant that the terms of a contract for the payment of money could not be altered . . . by a state statute enacted for the relief of hardly pressed debtors to the end and with the effect of postponing payment or enforcement during and because of an economic or financial emergency, it is but to state the obvious to say that it means the same now. . . .

The Minnesota statute either impairs the obligation of contracts or it does not. If it does not, the occasion to which it relates becomes immaterial, since then the passage of the statute is the exercise of a normal, unrestricted, state power and requires no special occasion to render it effective. If it does, the emergency no more furnishes a proper occasion for its exercise than if the emergency were non-existent. And so, while, in form, the suggested distinction seems to put us forward in a straight line, in reality it simply carries us back in a circle, like bewildered travelers lost in a wood, to the point where we parted company with the view of the state court.

A statute which materially delays enforcement of the mortgagee's contractual right of ownership and possession does not modify the remedy merely; it destroys, for the period of delay, *all* remedy so far as the enforcement of that right is concerned. The phrase, "obligation of a contract," in the constitutional sense imports a legal duty to perform the specified obligation of *that* contract, not to substitute and perform, against the will of one of the parties, a different, albeit equally valuable, obligation. And a state, under the contract impairment clause, has no more power to accomplish such a substitution than has one of the parties to the contract against the will of the other. It cannot do so either by acting directly upon the contract, or by bringing about the result under the guise of a statute in form acting only upon the remedy. If it could, the efficacy of the constitutional restriction would, in large measure, be made to disappear.

I am authorized to say that Mr. Justice VAN DEVANTER, Mr. Justice MCREYNOLDS and Mr. Justice BUTLER concur in this opinion.

[A statute not dissimilar to the Minnesota law involved in the *Blaisdell* case was enacted by the New York legislature in 1933. In subsequent years, the statute was renewed annually or biennially; mortgages contracted before the cut-off date in 1932 thus continued to enjoy protection against foreclosure. The extention of this provision in 1943 was made the subject of attack before the Supreme Court. Justice Frankfurter, speaking for a unanimous Court (Mr. Justice Rutledge concurring without opinion), declined to set aside or question the legislative finding that "the sudden termination of the legislation . . . might well result in an emergency more acute than that which the original legislation was intended to alleviate." Thus contractual remedies may not only be postponed in order to offer relief in depression situations, but apparently also as a measure to bar the recurrence of such economic dangers. *East New York Savings Bank* v. *Hahn,* 326 U.S. 230 (1945).]

CHAPTER VIII

The Fourteenth Amendment:
Due Process v. Wise Policy

1. THE PATH OF DUE PROCESS OF LAW[1]

By WALTER H. HAMILTON

[This essay by a distinguished member (now emeritus) of the Yale law faculty was originally presented to the American Historical Association as a part of that organization's observance of the sesquicentennial of the Constitutional Convention of 1787. Professor Hamilton's narrative traces the broad outlines of doctrinal development against a background of history and economy. The cases discussed in this essay are collected in the later sections of this chapter.]

I

In the law the judgment of yesterday is the precedent of today. The words are set down in the reports and there they abide for all time, to be drawn upon now and then as "the opinion of the court" demands. The meaning is rooted in the case and the occasion—the exchange of views in executive session, the idiom of the day, the temper of the times, the preferences of the judges. Its specific reference and concrete meaning are inseparable from the record which called it into being; and, along with these, it gradually recedes into the mists of legal history. As in a continuous process judgment follows judgment into precedent, a doctrine is fashioned. Its raw material is a

[1] Reprinted from Conyers Read, editor, *The Constitution Reconsidered*. Copyright 1938 by Columbia University Press.

298

common sense which comes from without the law; its lines take on content from the prevailing opinion to which it is exposed; it is hammered into shape through a conflict of interests within a formidable procedure of litigation by unlike-minded jurists. As a product of a protracted intellectual process, it is a part of all that it has met. It is rare that a legal rule which rides high is the rule "originally laid down" in "the leading case"; and a doctrine on the make, like its human kin, usually exhibits scant respect for its humble beginnings.

In an era of constitutional law that flickers to a close [this was written in 1937], no doctrine has enjoyed greater prestige than "due process." It has come to be the symbol habitually invoked by private right, the barrier that guards the frontiers of business against the interference of the state, a sanction by which the judiciary reviews the work of the legislature. It has woven itself into the folkways of an industrial culture and called into being an august corpus of the law. Yet into an eminence that already shows signs of decay it has emerged out of an estate of little repute. The account of its coming up in the world is among the most dramatic of stories. It bristles with color and conflict, with surprise and paradox. A novelist who made ideas his characters would not—for fear of provoking disbelief—have dared to allow his imagination to contrive such a series of events. Yet beneath the curious rhetoric of case and coincidence, of confused citation and vagrant judgment, the logic of events was always in command of a doctrine headed for parts unknown.

It all began quietly enough. The phrase "due process of law" is of ancient lineage. For a long time it had been an authoritative term for the established ways of justice. An injunction that "no person" shall "be deprived of life, liberty, or property without due process of law" had for decades reposed quietly within the Fifth Amendment. It served a necessary purpose in preventing arbitrary imprisonments, in forbidding seizures of possessions, in compelling resort to ordinary procedures, and in restraining public officials from acting without legal warrant. But in all the years that stretched away from the early days of the Constitution to the close of the Civil War, it was not an invitation to those who found Acts of Congress distasteful to appeal to the judiciary for relief. Save for an obiter dictum here and there—as by Mr. Chief Justice Taney in the Dred Scott Case—the records of the United States Supreme Court are singularly unconcerned over what later became so mighty a matter. A like provision adorned with procedural concern the constitution of many a state. As the Civil War approached, a New York court declared that due process had to do with the substance of legislation; and in litigious cause or congressional speech state acts which denied to freedmen of color the full privileges of citizenship were challenged as against due process of law. But such a demand for a substantive reading was casual and lacked authority. If there was a higher law in whose name legislation might be struck down by a court, it was elsewhere in the Constitution or in the great unchartered domain of natural rights. In reputable opinion due process of law was firmly fixed within the ancient domain of procedure.

It was the Civil War which disturbed the verbal calm. The course of events made the emancipation of the slaves a military and political necessity. The ways of thought again became receptive to the philosophy of Mr. Jefferson, and to the self-evident truths of the Declaration of Independence. The rights "to life, liberty, and the pursuit of happiness"—already inalienable within an order of nature—were written into the constitutions of the conquered Southern States. An injunction in perpetuity against slavery and involuntary servitude was made a part of the supreme law of the land, and a correlative amendment undertook to safeguard the rights of the newly enfranchised blacks. It began with the novel declaration that "all persons born or naturalized in the United States, and subject to the jurisdiction thereof, are citizens of the United States and of the state wherein they reside." Then, in words whose revolutionary character could be appreciated only by men of the age who had been steeped in an older political philosophy, it was provided that "no State shall make or enforce any law which shall abridge the privileges or immunities of citizens of the United States; nor shall any State deprive any person of life, liberty, or property without due process of law; nor deny to any person within its jurisdiction the equal protection of the laws." A number of other provisions, all relating to matters growing out of the late rebellion, were followed by a final section which granted, not to the courts, but "to the Congress," "power to enforce, by appropriate legislation, the provisions of this article." A little later the Constitution was made further to stipulate that "the right of citizens of the United States to vote shall not be denied or abridged by the United States or by any state on account of race, color, or previous condition of servitude." In occasion, ideology, and intent the Fourteenth Amendment seems clearly of a piece with the Thirteenth and the Fifteenth.

Yet high authority would dismiss context as irrelevance and would have construction accept "the plain and obvious meaning of the words." The bother is that the language is general and abstract. The clauses are filled with verbal symbols quite receptive to a content strong enough to possess them; not one single concretion is to be found to suggest interpretation or to point direction. The language is exposed to the greatest of all historical fallacies, which is to confuse event with intent and to read the exposition of a later age back into the pristine statement. The men who framed and ratified the amendment had only the dimmest knowledge of events to come; they had to explore its constitutional possibilities without benefit of the labors of jurists recently seated or not yet upon the bench; they had to set down general words in terms of the problems then current. For them the clauses lived with the breath of their own age. It is only by historical reconstruction that the contemporary meaning of the Fourteenth Amendment is to be rediscovered. An understanding requires an appreciation of the crisis, the intellectual heritage and the expediencies out of which it emerged. It demands even more an oblivion to the gloss of a later day which lies thick upon the text. It is easy enough from the vantage point of what came of it all to look back over our shoulders and to give order and purpose to the course of judicial events. But in 1868—and decreasingly in the years to come—the immediate past was more insistent than the distant future. The folk of the time had to meet events head-on.

II

If words are in want of definition, the proper appeal is to the law. And it was hardly half a decade after the amendment had been adopted before the meaning of its high-sounding phrases became the concern of the United States Supreme Court. Due process made its judicial entry with the fanfare of trumpets and in the livery of a strange master. The men who had taken part in the late rebellion had been disenfranchised; the reconstruction program of the Black Republican Congress was in full swing; and in the states which had made up the Confederacy, the legislatures had fallen into the hands of freedmen of color and carpetbaggers. A flood of reckless legislation ensued; some marked by social vision, some savoring strongly of privilege and corruption, all anathema to the white aristocracy which before the war had been in the saddle. The old South had lost in war and at the polls. But someone within its defeated ranks had the vague idea that an appeal to the courts might yet save the situation. Whose idea it was is lost to history. But an adage was current—"Leave it to God and Mr. Campbell"—and presently the Hon. John Archibald Campbell was putting his ex-judicial mind to a difficult problem.[2]

Who chose the particular statute which in single combat was to stand for hundreds of its kind has escaped the record. But whether choice fell to an unknown, to Mr. Campbell, or to a group, a more strategic selection could not have been made. An act of the legislature of Louisiana had granted to a corporation of seventeen persons for a period of twenty-five years an exclusive franchise in respect to the slaughtering of animals for meat in the parish of New Orleans and the two next adjacent. In giving effect to the act a citizen has been enjoined from the sale of his land for a rival slaughterhouse; a like interdict had been laid upon a boatload of cattle headed for market by an unorthodox route; butchers who for years had done their deadly work were no longer free to follow their trade; and the local public was forced to have commerce with a monopoly or turn vegetarian. Here were, ready at hand, causes as perfect as if they had been fashioned for the oncoming judicial ordeal. They offered all the raw materials which a popular legal crusade demanded; they gave opportunity to all the symbols by which the emotions are stirred and the judge-within-the-man is moved. American institutions were being flaunted; a monopoly, odious at law and to the people, had been given a legislative blessing; the laborer had been denied his Biblical doom and God-given right to work. The enemy was an octopus of a corporation; the cause was the cause of the workingman; the rights at stake were the rights of man. The requisite stuff of persuasion was there; there was need only to chisel it into a compelling legal argument.[3]

The situation clearly invited a challenge of the statute in the name of the higher law. But to Mr. Campbell no readymade formula was at hand. He had daringly to blaze a new trail; and a number of briefs which are rather successive drafts of the same argument than complementary lines of reasoning attest the arduous progress of his labor. It is impossible for the lawyer of today, with a head full of the things that came later, to appraise the quality of his perform-

---

[2] Campbell had sat on the bench of the Supreme Court from 1853 to 1861 when he resigned to "follow the fortunes" of his fellow-citizens of Alabama. He was probably one of the most outstanding lawyers of his generation.

[3] *The Slaughter House Cases, infra.*

ance, and even the historian with his art of re-creation can form no certain judgment. In his briefs there is nothing of clean-cut concept, of rule of law chiseled with neatness and precision, of sweep of syllogism to its inevitable therefore. They are clothed in a rhetoric alien to the legal persuasion of today. But history is here—its pages are filled with the conditions of the working classes in America, in England and Scotland, in France and Prussia. Learning is here— there is hardly a page not adorned with its apt quotation from some writer on government, jurisprudence, economics, or philosophy. Authority is here—citations of cases are alternated with statements from Turgot and Guizot; Buckle and de Tocqueville; Hallam, Macaulay, and G. C. Lewis; Mr. Jefferson and Adam Smith; John C. Calhoun, Mr. Justice Curtis, and Cooley on *Constitutional Limitations*. A sentence from the *Wealth of Nations* which makes of a man's right to his trade both a liberty and a property was copied from the brief into a dissenting opinion and to this day goes resounding down the law reports. Even the arts have their dialectical due in an occasional line of poetry or a rhymed couplet of a Negro minstrel.

The books were at hand—and a skill in their use—to serve the cause of the butchers. The task was to mold a medley of materials into a legal entity. Mr. Campbell had only foresight—not the hindsight of a later generation. His endeavor is marked, not with the delicate articulation of the codifier, but by the daring of the adventurer and the fumbling of the pioneer. His strategy had the audacity of an ex-member pleading before his own court, of an ex-rebel confronting his victorious enemies. He abandoned the older parts of the Constitution, whose well-litigated clauses did not point his way, and took his stand upon an article which as yet had drawn forth no judicial utterance. He decided to add another to the many paradoxes with which the history of legal doctrine is strewn. The Fourteenth Amendment was intended to secure the rights of the recently emancipated blacks against their former masters. The ink upon the fresh constitutional entry was hardly dry; yet he proposed to use the self-same article to guard the rights of the Southern whites against the political power of the newly liberated Negroes.

In spite of a wandering style that jumps from Illinois to Norway and takes the distance from Scotch thralldom to Southern slavery in a stride, the substance of his contention is clear and its focus never lost. His oral argument before the Supreme Court was an exposition of the unity of the Thirteenth and Fourteenth Amendments; and the great objective of which they are instruments is the theme of all the briefs. All over the Western world, and almost within a century, a revolution had taken place in the status of the workingman. In France thralls had been eased of their ancient dues; in Prussia serfs had become their own masters; everywhere the feudal ties which had bound vassal to lord had been loosed. Even in the United States of before the war there had been slaves, freedmen, and free-born citizens and "the state might and did make large differences in the positions of men in the social and political system." The Thirteenth Amendment ended not only slavery but involuntary servitude in every degree and form; it made forever unlawful throughout the whole land a servitude for a year, for an hour, or even for an occasion. A master could no longer command a servant to dance, to frolic, or to make merry before him.

But the impulse of a mighty revolution was not spent in a single enactment. In the Fourteenth Amendment all ranks were leveled, all marks and perquisites of social status were obliterated. All classes, whatever had been their previous conditions, were made a single people. "The law of citizenship became as broad as the law of freedom"; and every person became the equal of every other person before the legislature and at law. In respect to "conscience, speech, publication, security, occupation, freedom, and whatever else is essential to liberty or is proper as an attribute of citizenship," every man became equal to every other man. The amendment—a political as well as a social revolution—"brought the federal government into immediate contact with every person and gave to every citizen a claim upon its protecting power." The natural rights of men, "life, liberty, property, protection, privilege, and immunity"—their reiterated beat falls upon page after page—are "the sacred inheritance of the people." The Fourteenth Amendment "was designed to afford a permanent and powerful guarantee to them." They are to be recognized as "the assured estate of the population"; the mandate to the states is, not "to abridge or destroy," but "to maintain and preserve them." In respect to these rights, inalienable and indefeasible, the federal government becomes every man's guardian.

With such a philosophic start it was easy to get down to constitutional concretions. Although the reasons are not neatly tooled, the substance of the argument is repeated again and again with cumulative effect. The Fourteenth Amendment created a national citizen-

ship, fitted it out with "privileges and immunities," and placed this
heritage from times of old beyond the power of the state government.
These privileges and immunities are nothing other than the natural
rights of man. Among these rights—quoting Mr. Jefferson and the
new constitution of Louisiana—are "life, liberty, and the pursuit
of happiness." It is—in an argument helped along by Turgot, Adam
Smith, and Mr. Campbell's own common sense—impossible for a
man to sustain life, to enjoy liberty and to pursue happiness if denied
the chance to work. Man "has a right to labor for himself and not
at the will or under the constraint of another." Moreover, a man's
right in his own labor is not only a liberty but a property as well. As
"a natural right of person" it is a liberty; in "its results or the expec-
tation of results" it is a property—the only property of substance the
working man possesses. It follows that he has a natural right to dispose of his service—note the quiet appearance of a term which later
made a mighty sound—by "freedom of contract." An argument so
surely upon its way was not to be halted here; and, with strokes so
deft that the transition is unobtrusive, Mr. Campbell converts an
abstract right to work into the worker's vested interest in his occupation. Every trade must—in an order of nature to which the Constitution has come into accord—be open to all who choose to take its
chances; and "no kind of occupation, employment or trade can be
imposed upon" the workingman "or prohibited to him so as to avoid
election on his part." Here, then, in tangible and specific terms is
a constitutional right, a privilege and an immunity of citizenship,
a liberty and a property, a claim to the equal protection of the laws,
which the national government must under solemn mandate maintain against a state legislature gone astray.

And, having given concretion to his absolutes, with telling strokes
the attorney drove the argument home. He had no quarrel with the
state in its exercise of the police power; its right to promote by legislation "salubrity, security, and order" is not challenged; but the
statute on trial is not a health measure. Instead "the recitals of concern for the general welfare," the "delusive and deceitful promises
of public good," the "expression of an unusual benevolence for the
domestic comfort or the sanitary care of a neglected community"
are sheer pretense. The statute emerges from "no proper legislative
procedure"; it serves no motive—note the usage of the time—"of the
public utility." On the contrary its one characteristic, its sole import,
is to create a private corporation and to grant to a favored group of

seventeen the exclusive privilege of an ordinary occupation. The ordinance was a return to the age of feudalism; it had created a banality in favor of a single firm; Louisiana had, in defiance of the federal Constitution, become "enthralled ground." There is at issue not one jot or tittle of regulation by the state which those who are pressing the suits wish to avoid. Instead a monopoly—under the ban of the common law, intolerable in a democracy, forbidden by the Fourteenth Amendment—had been created at the expense of men who have made "an ancient trade the business of their lives." The Louisiana statute abridges the privileges and immunities of citizens of the United States; it denies to persons life, liberty, and property without due process of law; it takes from them the equal protection of the laws. Liberty and property were before there was law. The rights of man, which belong to the order of nature, are above "the chartered rights" of a corporation. The cause is that of the workingman, of the community, and of the Constitution.

It was a powerful—even if not quite successful—appeal. In the decision all the justices who spoke for the Court or in dissent addressed themselves to Mr. Campbell's argument. At its judicial debut four out of nine were converted to a novel constitutional doctrine and the majority of five found it hard going to contrive a dialectical answer. Chance got in its deft stroke and shaped the course of constitutional events by a single vote. As Mr. ex-Justice Campbell, the Southerner, argued for national sovereignty, Mr. Justice Miller, the Northerner, denied it. As the native of Georgia argued that all citizens were one people in an indivisible union, the unionist from Iowa refused to curb the authority of the states. As the ex-Confederate asserted that whites and blacks were equal before the Constitution, the abolitionist on the bench refused to erase the color line. There was, according to the Court, a citizenship of the United States, but Mr. Justice Miller neglected to remove it from the realm of the abstract, to define its terms or to endow it with substantive rights. The Fourteenth was an addendum to the Thirteenth Amendment; it had been designed to make secure the rights of the blacks. But white men, though industrious artisans, were without benefit of its coverage. The legislature had passed the statute as a health measure, and with the act of a sovereign state the Court would not interfere.

It was, however, only as a judgment to go at that. Mr. Justice Field boldly spread upon the record a powerful dissent. The Court, like lost sheep, had gone astray; he with three of his colleagues—

especially he—was sound in a just-discovered faith. There was a citizenship of the United States, whose privileges and immunities had by the Constitution been put beyond the reach of the state, and that citizenship knew neither race nor color. The rhetoric was the rhetoric of Field, but the ideas were visible imports from the Campbell briefs. A milder echo of the same argument reappeared as the opinion of Mr. Justice Bradley. In the midst of a paragraph toward the end—as if it were a passing thought—he set it down that a possible mandate with which to curb the power of the legislature might be found in "due process of law." So the cause was lost. The "privileges and immunities of citizenship" disappeared from constitutional law—and we hear little more of it until its ghost returns after sixty-five years to serve a cause of tax avoidance of the vintage of 1935.[4]

But the loss of a cause is not the loss of a doctrine. . . .

. . . . . .

[Notwithstanding its initial defeat,] . . . the Fourteenth Amendment came quietly into constitutional law. The pomp and circumstance which had attended the previous causes was absent. A municipal ordinance in California had made a pretty verbal display to the effect that laundries carried on in brick buildings were within the law; but if they were housed in wooden structures, the authorities must be satisfied that the chance of fire was not a hazard to public safety. In obvious intent and in administration it said that the trade was open to the whites but that Orientals were to be subjected to the closest scrutiny before admission to so exclusive a club. Yick Wo, denied the right to work at his chosen trade, essayed judicial combat, had syllogisms broken in his behalf, and came away with the signal victory of the highest court in the land.[5] His right to his trade was as good as that of any other man. The victory was scored, not by a recently emancipated black, not by a Southern white whose pride in race did not forbid the use of the Negro's legal protection, but by a yellow man from China. Against the arbitrary act of the state, "equal protection of the laws" came into constitutional law where "privileges and immunities" and "due process" had been denied admission. And the new doctrine had been accepted by the Court without a single vote in dissent.

4 *Colgate* v. *Harvey*, see note on p. 326.
5 *Yick Wo* v. *Hopkins*, *infra*, p. 410.

The breath of life had been breathed into the Fourteenth Amendment. The right to work at one's chosen occupation had at last become a part of the supreme law of the land. The substance to which "equal protection" gave a verbal home could pass on by contagion into a liberty and a property fortified by "due process." Eighteen years had passed since the amendment was adopted and fourteen since Mr. Campbell had blazed the path for a novel doctrine. But at last, in 1886, even against the action of the state, the rights of man had been accorded the protection of the Constitution.

III

Yet long before this decision another course of events was under way. The Campbell arguments were much too useful to be left to butchers, bakers, and laundry workers. At the bar, and at least before the bench, we find them presently clad in the livery of an alien master. In his briefs—with all their concern for the liberties of the workingman—ex-Justice Campbell could not leave the word "property" alone. He made the right to work a property; and somewhat abstractly, on his own and within quotation marks, he declared the idea that property derives from the state to be the most revolutionary of notions; for, "if the state creates, the state can destroy." As with the individual, so with the nation-on-the-make, no clean-cut line was to be drawn; liberty was the liberty to acquire property. To Mr. Justice Field, rounding out his decades on the high judicial bench, liberty and property came to be a single word with a constant shift of accent to the right. . . . And, long before Yick Wo won his legal tilt against Hopkins and California, attorneys for corporations as plaintiffs in error were presenting in brief and oration a round of exquisite variations on a theme of Campbell.

Although lawyers were admonished for pleading reasons that had been rejected, the recitation went on. In the challenge to the regulation of grain elevators, to the railway legislation of Granger days, to legislative attempts to abate or to subdue the trade in alcoholic beverages, the theme was omnipresent. It was always put forward as a defense of the frontiers of business enterprise against legislative attack. If invariably it fell before the police powers of the state, it acquired momentum and an enhancing repute in the opinions in dissent. As the decade of the eighties moved along, general admissions that legislation must meet the standards of due process were wrung from the Court, while it was still loath to apply the doctrine in the instant case. It was, however, not until the nineties that the personnel of the bench became radical enough to give effect to novel doctrine. . . .

The first decisive commitments came—if not off stage—at least in the realm of dicta. In arguing a case of tax avoidance for a railway company[6] Mr. Roscoe Conkling attempted to use a humble confession to advance the cause of his client. He hinted that the Fourteenth Amendment was the result of a conspiracy between politicians and industrialists; and admitted that, in Congressional committee, the word "person" had been chosen instead of "citizen" to extend the protection of the due process clause to the corporation. His prestige at the bar was at its height; he had refused the high office then held by Mr. Chief Justice Waite and the hardly less honored seat then occupied by Mr. Justice Blatchford. He quoted at some length from the minutes of the Congressional committee; and although the record had not been published and he did not produce it, his remarks made quite an impression. They left no decisive imprint in the reports; for although the Court found it easy to listen to elaborate constitutional argument, it found it difficult to resolve the issue. As the months passed without result, a motion to dismiss was allowed on the ground that the question had become moot, and the issue was left in abeyance. It was long afterward that the minutes of the committee were made available and it was discovered that Conkling had taken excerpts from their context, tempered entries to his cause and reshaped quotations to serve his argumentative purpose.[7]

But decades before historical research was to reveal a deliberate indulgence in historical error, his confidential knowledge had had its effect. Four years later, in 1886, an attorney for the same railroad, in another case of tax avoidance, proposed to argue the same issue.[8] He was stopped by Mr. Chief Justice Waite, who announced that the Court was prepared to admit, without argument, that a corporation was a person within the intendment of the equal protection clause. Again a case, elaborately argued on constitutional grounds, was disposed of without recourse to constitutional doctrine; and the elevation of the corporation to the protective eminence of a person remained a dictum. But the dictum was set down in the re-

---

[6] San Mateo County v. Southern Pacific R. Co., 116 U. S. 138; argued in 1882.

[7] Cf. Howard Jay Graham, "The Conspiracy Theory of the Fourteenth Amendment," 47 Yale Law Journal 371 (1938).

[8] Santa Clara County v. Southern Pacific R. Co., 118 U.S. 394.

ports; and, oblivious to its lack of authority, it began presently to assert its claim as a holding.[9]

The eighties gave way to the more receptive attitude of the nineties. Courts must await their causes; and from the play of minds upon issues which are potential the law takes its course. . . .

. . . . .

But not until 1897—and then only through a reaching out toward issues that need not have been raised—did an opportunity come for a better fitting of due process to the current temper of the Court.[10] A Louisiana statute had prescribed a regulation of insurance companies within the state; the officials had attempted to bring under its penal provisions a firm which had contracted for marine insurance upon shipments of cotton with a New York company. It seems to have been admitted by all concerned that the contracts had been made in New York and that in the instant case the only matter of local concern was the notices sent of shipments upon which the insurance was to take effect. It was easy enough for the Court to waive so incidental a part of the transaction out from under the Act. That done, the decision of the case demanded no more than the simple comment that an act of Louisiana had no application to a matter beyond the jurisdiction of the state. It might even have been declared null and void as an interference with commerce among the several states. But so obvious a disposition was not for the new blood within the Court. Mr. Justice Peckham, a fresh recruit, had the zeal of the reformer and a faith in the enlightened opinion of his own day untroubled by doubt. The holding depends upon the way the question is put; and he chose—with the consent of his brethren—to view the Act as a "real" interference with "the liberty of the defendants to place insurance on property of their own" where they pleased. Thus the issue became larger, more general, and more significant than the unresolved query in the litigation. As thus stated no question of the right of the Court to review the matter was raised by any of the nine justices. That hurdle had been got over by a succession of rhetorical yieldings in a number of important cases. . . . As formulated by the spokesman for the Court, business privilege was square-

[9] Only recently have individual Justices begun to register dissent from this rule; thus Mr. Justice Black in *Connecticut General Life Ins. Co.* v. *Johnson*, 303 U.S. 77 (1938), and Mr. Justice Douglas in *Wheeling Steel Corp.* v. *Glander*, 337 U.S. 562 (1949).

[10] *Allgeyer* v. *Louisiana, infra,* p. 333.

ly opposed to state regulation with "due process of law" as the arbiter.

It is idle to argue that he went out of his way to do it; for, to the individualistic mind of Mr. Justice Peckham, his was the only way. It was a superb opportunity to bring the orthodoxy of classical economics into the higher law and he was not going to allow it to pass. In a rhetoric which is strangely familiar the dissent of yesterday becomes the opinion of the Court. . . . The familiar arguments, even the illustrations of the Campbell brief, are repeated. The "inalienable rights" of the Declaration of Independence; the pursuit of happiness; the right of the butcher, the baker, and the candlestick-maker are all there. As Peckham quotes Bradley, who paraphrases Campbell—thus piling a superfluous Ossa upon a Pelion of dicta—"I hold that the liberty of pursuit—the right to follow any of the ordinary callings of life—is one of the privileges of a citizen of the United States." Although the path of his argument is beset with questions, his faith in the efficacy of free contract to take care of all the affairs of business rises above all bother over relevance. The privileges and immunities of citizenship may be outmoded, but there is a constitutional successor. A nimble sentence may be made to travel a long doctrinal way; its hurried words may overcome formidable obstacles where the argument at a leisurely pace would break down. Thus, "it is true that these remarks are made in regard to questions of monopoly, but they well describe the rights which are covered by the word 'liberty,' as contained in the Fourteenth Amendment." The "privilege" quoted is that of "pursuing an ordinary calling or trade"; but—without setting down a period or evoking a therefore—smoothly he glides along through "the acquiring, holding, and selling" of "property" to "the right to make all proper contracts in relation thereto." Thus, in the name of due process of law, freedom of contract is thrown up as a fence about the domain of business enterprise against the incursions of the state. And no one on the high bench said to the contrary.

In the Allgeyer case "the police power" remained in the background. The cause had little concern with human rights; a trio of judicial bows acknowledged an abstract authority to regulate; and judicial silence prevented a conflict between an upstart due process and the more venerable doctrine. . . . It was only in 1905 that due process first won in a clean-cut combat with the police power. A statute of New York had limited the hours of employees in bake-shops to ten in any one day or sixty in any one week; and, because of his lack of workaday respect for the Act, the People of New York were at odds with a certain Mr. Lochner.[11] The judgment of the Supreme Court—one of the habitual five to four variety—was again delivered by the learned jurist and sound economist, Mr. Justice Peckham. He had only to elaborate his former argument, now fortified by the official citation of *Allgeyer* v. *Louisiana*. Freedom of contract, in respect to trade or employment, was an aspect of the liberty and property which a state might not abridge without due process of law. The challenge of the police power was met by a formidable parade of personal and common-sense opinion that the hours of bakers had little or no relation to the public health.

Again the distinguished jurist made the question before the Court far broader than the issue which the case presented. If such an act were allowed to stand, "a printer, a tinsmith, a locksmith, a carpenter, a cabinetmaker, a dry-goods clerk, a bank's, a lawyer's, or a physi-cian's clerk"—in inelegant verbal parade—would "all come under the power of the legislature." In fact "no trade, no occupation, no mode of earning one's living, could escape this all-pervading power." Since "there is no contention that bakers as a class are not equal in intelligence and capacity to men in other trades" or are "not able to assert their rights and care for themselves," the real question is the general use of "the protecting arm of the state" to interfere with "the independence of judgment and of action" among men of every occupation. "Statutes of the nature of that under review, limiting the hours in which grown and intelligent men may labor to earn their living, are meddlesome interference with the rights of the in-dividual." And, since such "interference on the part of the legisla-tures of the several states with the ordinary trades and occupations of the people" seemed "to be on the increase," it was time to call a halt. The opinion of the Court was intended to be an apostolic let-ter to the many legislatures in the land, appointing limits to their police power and laying a ban upon social legislation.

So it might have become but for the dissent. Mr. Justice Harlan objected that the question of the relation of hours to health was one of fact; that as reasonable men, members of the legislature were en-titled to their opinion; and that "there are few, if any, questions in political economy about which entire certainty may be predicated."

[11] *Lochner* v. *New York, infra*, p. 336.

With him White and Day, JJ., concurred. A youngster of sixty-four, newly come to the Court, seized his chance and scribbled the most famous dissent in all legal history. Mr. Justice Holmes insisted that "general propositions do not decide concrete cases." He accused the Court of interpolating economic doctrine, insisted that "a constitution is not intended to embody a particular economic theory, whether of paternalism and the organic relation of the citizen to the state or of laissez faire"; and protested against freezing the law into "Mr. Herbert Spencer's *Social Statics.*" It is common for latter-day liberals to set this down as the first blast of the trumpet in behalf of a social oversight of human rights; but the historian is more likely to view it as a lance worthily broken in behalf of an ancient cause now in retreat. But the four dissenters saw as clearly as the five—who, by virtue of being one more, were the Court—that the challenged act might be "the first installment of a general regulation of the hours of work"; and they wished to keep the way open. It was probably too late for Harlan, J., or even for Holmes, J., to argue that in such matters the legislature was the sole and exclusive judge and that the Court had no rightful power of review; at least such an argument was not attempted. The all-but-equal vote led to an even balance of doctrines. Neither the police power nor due process was to be preferred; in an even-handed formula, liberty and property are to be set against public policy; as case follows case, these concepts are to be filled with the values of life, a balance is to be struck, and a judgment rendered. An engaging number of rules for the game of review have come and gone; the decisions of the Court have with the circumstances, its personnel, and the temper of the times swung now toward one side, now toward the other. But the balance of values recorded in *Lochner* v. *the People of New York* has endured as the judicial formula for the ultimate judgment upon legislation designed to promote the public interest.

Thus a collusion of occasions and persons, causes and ideas, shaped the course of doctrinal events. It was quite untouched by conspiracy, unless it be of the gods or of that Providence which is said to preside over American institutions. A constitutional doctrine contrived to protect the natural rights of men against corporate monopoly was little by little commuted into a formula for safeguarding the domain of business against the regulatory power of the state. The chartered privileges of the corporation became rights which could be pleaded in equity and at law against the government which created them.

In a litigious procedure in which private right was balanced against the general good, the ultimate word was given to the judiciary. . . .

IV

All of this has to do with the rhetoric of the coming of due process. The account has as its narrow concern a sequence of judicial events; it is drawn from the official records of a single court; in all its detail it can be supported by the sanctions of exact documentation. But the larger story of the making of the doctrine lies elsewhere; in the development of industrialism, in the changing state of opinion, in the assembly of ideas from far and near into a principle of law, in urges within an economic order that could not be judicially denied. A part of that history has been written; distinguished scholars have garnered from legal literature the germs of the doctrine and have shown how the catholic concept of due process offered a home to notions of natural rights. But if the raw material has been exhibited and the verbal history of the doctrine written, the impulses within the social order—in particular, economic interest and legal persuasion—have not been accorded their part in the drama. Here off stage are the forces which give life to abstractions. The records of the Court reflect only in a series of passing shadows their tumultuous vitality. And the history of due process is far more than the judicial record it has left.

A shift from rhetoric to logic, from recorded doctrine to compelling impulse, is an engaging hazard. It is an inquiry into a series of "if's," many of which escaped actuality by the narrowest of margins. If in the Slaughter House Cases, the Campbell argument had commanded just one vote more, what difference would it have made? We would doubtless by now possess an august corpus on the privileges and immunities of citizenship, and the entries under due process would be correspondingly thin. But would the hypothetical domain be a great and humane code concerned with the rights of man? Or would the corporation, which became a person, just as easily have passed into the protected position of a citizen of the United States? And, in such an event, would the only change be that all that is now written down as liberty and property would be entered as the privileges of citizenship?

Or was the logic of the commitment inevitable—and the specific legal doctrine by which business enterprise sought immunity from regulation a mere rhetorical device? Due process was fashioned from the most respectable ideological stuff of the later nineteenth century. The ideas out of which it was shaped were in full accord with the dominant thought of the age. They were an aspect of common sense, a standard of economic orthodoxy, a test of straight thinking and sound opinion. In the domain of thought their general attitude was omnipresent. In philosophy it was individualism, in government laissez faire, in economics the natural law of supply and demand, in law the freedom of contract. The system of thought had possessed every other discipline; it had in many a domain reshaped the law to its teachings. . . . An impact that had been irresistible elsewhere should surely have won its way into constitutional law. Its coming seemed inevitable; the constitutional concept which it made its domicile was a mere matter of doctrinal accident. Words on parchment could not be adamant before so powerful a thrust; privileges and immunities, due process, equal protection, were all available; and, had there been no Fourteenth Amendment, "the obligations" might have been made to encompass "the freedom" of contract; or as a last resort, a vague "natural rights" as a higher law might have been found to permeate the whole Constitution.

The wonder is, not that laissez faire made its entrance, but that it found so insecure a lodgment within the Constitution. Ex-Justice Campbell had a superb case, his strategy was adroit, he suited his arguments to a state of mind which it took a civil war to produce— yet he could not quite command a majority of the Court. It was nearly twenty years before even as a dictum the protection of the Fourteenth Amendment was accorded to a corporation and it was nearly twenty more before the first installment in a program of social legislation was struck down by the Court. Even when it was at last accorded constitutional standing, its victories were often obtained by the narrow margin of five to four. Its triumph did not come until half a decade after the turn of the century, when it had ceased to be common sense, when legislators were forsaking its precepts, and when in philosophy, economics, and government it was on the way out. Even then its victory was inconclusive; it could never claim the faith of the full bench, and it had to share its sovereignty with the antithetical doctrine of the police power.

. . . It seems strange that so many jurists stood steadfast against the seductions of laissez faire; history, political science, and economics can boast no such record. Or it may be due to the older and established doctrine that the state might intervene with regulation to promote public safety, public health, public morals, and public welfare—against which the cause of the independence of the business system could achieve only a partial success. Or does the whole story, in irony, paradox, and compromise, derive from the innate conservatism of the law—a rock of ages which even the untamed strength of laissez faire could move but could not blast?

2. THE FAILURE OF "PRIVILEGES AND IMMUNITIES"

LEGISLATIVE HISTORY OF THE FOURTEENTH AMENDMENT[12]

Attempts to extend the protection of individuals in the enjoyment of their liberties so as to shield them against state action as well as against the potential arbitrariness of the federal government date from the earliest beginnings of government under the Constitution. Indeed, one of the propositions offered by Madison as part of the prospective Bill of Rights would have provided that "No State shall infringe the equal rights of conscience, nor the freedom of speech or of the press, nor the right of trial by jury in criminal cases." While this proposal gained the approval of the House of Representatives, it failed to pass the Senate, much to the regret of Madison, who said that it had been "much the most valuable of the whole list."

In the 39th Congress, when the proposal of a new amendment to the Constitution was under discussion, the extension of the guarantees of the Bill of Rights to the states received ample and vocal consideration. From an examination of the debates in the Congress some eminent scholars and jurists have concluded that, in the words of Robert E. Cushman,[13] "there seems no doubt that as a matter of historical fact the framers of the Amendment meant by 'privileges and immunities of citizens of the United States' the whole body of ordinary civil rights and especially those enumerated in the Bill of Rights of the Federal Constitution," and that at least some of the key movers for the new (14th) amendment intended it to operate as an extension of the protection afforded by the federal Bill of

---

[12] Adapted from Carl B. Swisher, *American Constitutional Development*, pp. 331–334, and "Appendix" to dissenting opinion of Mr. Justice Black in *Adamson* v. *California*, 332 U.S. 46, 92.

[13] *Leading Constitutional Decisions*, 8th edition, p. 41; in the new, 9th edition of this standard collection, Professor Cushman allows some doubt, in the light of recent research, and begins the quoted sentence with "it has been claimed . . . ."

Rights. However, constitutional historians of no less eminence have been able to reach the opposite conclusion; see, e.g., Andrew C. Mc-Laughlin, *A Constitutional History of the United States,* pp. 730–731.

Leading among the proponents of the new amendment was Congressman John A. Bingham of Ohio. He was a member of the Joint Committee on Reconstruction, of its subcommittee which deliberated on necessary constitutional changes, and of the select committee of three which prepared specific proposals. It was he who, on February 13, 1866, introduced in the House of Representatives a proposed constitutional amendment which, eventually, became the Fourteenth Amendment. As offered by him, this proposal provided that "The Congress shall have power to make all laws which shall be necessary and proper to secure to the citizens of each State all privileges and immunities of citizens in the several States; and to all persons in the several States equal protection in the rights of life, liberty, and property."[14]

On February 26, 1866, the proposed amendment came up for debate. In support of the proposal Mr. Bingham said:

... The amendment proposed stands in the very words of the Constitution of the United States as it came to us from the hands of its illustrious framers. Every word of the proposed amendment is to-day in the Constitution of our country, save the words conferring the express grant of power upon the Congress of the United States. ...

Sir, it has been the want of the Republic that there was not an express grant of power in the Constitution to enable the whole people of every State, by congressional enactment, to enforce obedience to these requirements of the Constitution. Nothing can be plainer to thoughtful men than that if the grant of power had been originally conferred upon the Congress of the nation, and legislation had been upon your statute books to enforce these requirements of the Constitution in every State, that rebellion, which has scarred and blasted the land, would have been an impossibility. ...

And later:

The question is, simply, whether you will give by this amendment to the people of the United States the power, by legislative enactment, to punish officials of the States for violation of oaths enjoined upon them by

[14] 36 Congressional Globe 1034.

the Constitution? . . . Is the Bill of Rights to stand in our Constitution hereafter, as in the past five years within eleven States, a mere dead letter? It is absolutely essential to the safety of the people that it should be enforced.

. . . . .

But, sir, there never was even colorable excuse, much less apology, for any man North or South claiming that any State Legislature or State court, or State Executive, has any right to deny protection to any free citizens of the United States within their limits in the rights of life, liberty, and property. Gentlemen who oppose this amendment oppose the grant of power to enforce the bill of rights. Gentlemen who oppose this amendment simply declare to these rebel States, "Go on with your confiscation statutes, your statutes of banishment, your statutes of unjust imprisonment, your statutes of murder and death against men because of their loyalty to the Constitution and Government of the United States."

. . . Where is the power in Congress, unless this or some similar amendment be adopted, to prevent the reenactment of those infernal statutes . . . ? Let some man answer. Why, sir, the gentleman from New York [Mr. Hale] . . . yesterday gave up the argument on this point. He said that the citizens must rely upon the State for their protection. I admit that such is the rule under the Constitution as it now stands.[15]

But the sentiment of the House was apparently not yet sufficiently crystallized. On a motion to lay on the table the proposal was, with Bingham's concurrence, postponed until April, 1866. In the intervening period, however, a number of events, notably the sharpening of the conflict between Congress and President Johnson, served to effect a swing in public and legislative opinion. The Committee on Reconstruction utilized the time by rephrasing the amendment in the form it presently holds. Reintroduced in this modified version it was accepted by both Houses of Congress.

The change from an affirmative grant of power to Congress to a negative prohibition of state action was apparently considered negligible by Bingham. A few years later he argued eloquently that the version adopted differed from the February proposals only in that it had been made more comprehensive. Addressing himself specifically to the meaning of "privileges and immunities," he offered the following explanation:

Mr. Speaker, that the scope and meaning of the limitations imposed by the first section, fourteenth amendment of the Constitution may be more

[15] *Ibid.*, 1033–1034, 1089–1091, 1093.

fully understood, permit me to say that the privileges and immunities of citizens of the United States, as contradistinguished from citizens of a State, are chiefly defined in the first eight amendments to the Constitution of the United States. . . . [He then proceeded to recite the Bill of Rights in full.]

These eight articles . . . never were limitations upon the power of the States, until made so by the fourteenth amendment. The words of that amendment, "no State shall make or enforce any law which shall abridge the privileges or immunities of citizens of the United States," are an express prohibition upon every State of the Union, which may be enforced under existing laws of Congress, and such other laws for their better enforcement as Congress may make.[16]

But the wording of the amendment permitted different interpretation. Nor should it be overlooked that, regardless of Bingham's statements, there is a plain and undeniable difference between the phraseology of the February proposal ("Congress shall have the power . . .") and the adopted language ("No state shall . . ."). Congress declined, although not on formal vote, to accept the affirmative grant of power. This may well give rise to at least a substance of doubt as to the general acceptance of Bingham's assumption that no material change was made in the wording. Of Bingham's own intentions the quoted passages leave little doubt.

THE SLAUGHTER HOUSE CASES
16 Wall. 36 (1873)

[The state of Louisiana, in the exercise of its police power, enacted a law conferring upon the Crescent City Live-Stock Landing and Slaughter House Company the exclusive right of slaughtering animals for food within the city of New Orleans. The state supreme court held this monopoly valid. The company, as well as the legislature of the state, were then dominated by so-called "carpetbagger" elements. The effect of the legislation would have been to deprive some one thousand butchers in the city of New Orleans of their means of livelihood. In attacking the law, John A. Campbell urged that the right to engage in business was one of the privileges and immunities of national citizenship.]

Mr. Justice MILLER delivered the opinion of the Court. . .

The plaintiffs . . . allege that the statute is a violation of the Constitution of the United States in these several particulars:

[16] *Ibid.*, App., 42d Cong., 1st Sess., pp. 83–84.

That it creates an involuntary servitude forbidden by the thirteenth article of amendment;

That it abridges the privileges and immunities of citizens of the United States;

That it denies to the plaintiffs the equal protection of the laws; and,

That it deprives them of their property without due process of law; contrary to the provisions of the first section of the fourteenth article of amendment.

This Court is thus called upon for the first time to give construction to these articles. . . .

[The Court begins its examination of the fourteenth amendment by an inquiry into the provisions on citizenship, arriving at the conclusion "that there is a citizenship of the United States, and a citizenship of a State, which are distinct from each other, and which depend upon different characteristics or circumstances in the individual."]

We think this distinction and its explicit recognition in this amendment of great weight in this argument, because the next paragraph of this same section, which is the main one relied on by the plaintiffs . . ., speaks only of privileges and immunities of citizens of the United States, and does not speak of those of citizens of the several states. The argument, however, in favor of plaintiffs rests wholly on the assumption that the citizenship is the same, and the privileges and immunities granted by the clause are the same.

The language is, "No State shall make or enforce any law which shall abridge the privileges or immunities of citizens of *the United States.*" It is a little remarkable, if this clause was intended as a protection to the citizen of a state against the legislative power of his own state, that the word citizen of the state should be left out when it is so carefully used, and used in contradistinction to citizens of the United States, in the very sentence which precedes it. It is too clear for argument that the change in phraseology was adopted understandingly and with a purpose.

Of the privileges and immunities of the citizen of the United States, and of the privileges and immunities of the citizen of the state, and what they respectively are, we will presently consider; but we wish to state here that it is only the former which are placed by this clause under the protection of the Federal Constitution, and that the latter, whatever they might be, are not intended to have any additional protection by this paragraph of the amendment.

If, then, there is a difference between the privileges and immunities belonging to a citizen of the United States as such, and those belonging to the citizen of the state as such, the latter must rest for their security and protection where they have heretofore rested; for they are not embraced by this paragraph of the amendment.

The first occurrence of the words "privileges and immunities" in our constitutional history, is to be found in the fourth of the articles of the old Confederation.

It declares "that the better to secure and perpetuate mutual friendship and intercourse among the people of the different States in this Union, the free inhabitants of each of these States, paupers, vagabonds, and fugitives from justice excepted, shall be entitled to all the privileges and immunities of free citizens in the several States; and the people of each State shall have free ingress and regress to and from any other State, and shall enjoy therein all the privileges of trade and commerce, subject to the same duties, impositions, and restrictions as the inhabitants thereof respectively."

In the Constitution of the United States, which superseded the Articles of Confederation, the corresponding provision is found in section two of the fourth article, in the following words: "The citizens of each State shall be entitled to all the privileges and immunities of citizens of the several States."

The constitutional provision . . . did not create those rights, which it called privileges and immunities of citizens of the states. It threw around them in that clause no security for the citizen of the state in which they were claimed or exercised. Nor did it profess to control the power of the state governments over the rights of its own citizens.

Its sole purpose was to declare to the several states, that whatever those rights, as you grant or establish them to your own citizens, or as you limit or qualify, or impose restrictions on their exercise, the same, neither more nor less, shall be the measure of the rights of citizens of other states within your jurisdiction.

It would be the vainest show of learning to attempt to prove by citation of authority, that up to the adoption of the recent amendments, no claim or pretense was set up that those rights depended on the Federal government for their existence or protection, beyond the very few express limitations which the Federal Constitution imposed upon the states—such, for instance, as the prohibition against *ex post facto* laws, bills of attainder, and laws impairing the obligation of contracts. But with the exception of these and a few other restrictions, the entire domain of the privileges and immunities of citizens of the states, . . . lay within the constitutional and legislative power of the states, and without that of the Federal government. Was it the purpose of the Fourteenth Amendment, by the simple declaration that no state should make or enforce any law which shall abridge the privileges and immunities of citizens of the United States, to transfer the security and protection of all the civil rights . . ., from the states to the Federal government? And where it is declared that Congress shall have the power to enforce that article, was it intended to bring within the power of Congress the entire domain of civil rights heretofore belonging exclusively to the states?

All this and more must follow, if the proposition of the plaintiffs . . . be sound. For not only are these rights subject to the control of Congress whenever in its discretion any of them are supposed to be abridged by state legislation, but that body may also pass laws in advance, limiting and restricting the exercise of legislative power by the states, in their most ordinary and usual function, as in its judgment it may think proper on all such subjects. And still further, such a construction followed by the reversal of the Supreme Court of Louisiana in these cases, would constitute this Court a perpetual censor upon all legislation of the states, on the civil rights of their own citizens, with authority to nullify such as it did not approve as consistent with those rights, as they existed at the time of the adoption of this amendment. The argument, we admit, is not always the most conclusive which is drawn from the consequences urged against the adoption of a particular construction of an instrument. But when, as in the case before us, these consequences are so serious, so far-reaching and pervading, so great a departure from the structure and spirit of our institutions, when the effect is to fetter and degrade the state governments by subjecting them to the control of Congress, in the exercise of powers heretofore universally conceded to them of the most ordinary and fundamental character;

when in fact it radically changes the whole theory of the relations of the state and Federal governments to each other and of both these governments to the people; the argument has a force that is irresistible, in the absence of language which expresses such a purpose too clearly to admit of doubt.

We are convinced that no such results were intended by the Congress which proposed these amendments, nor by the legislatures of the states which ratified them.

Having shown that the privileges and immunities relied on in the argument are those which belong to citizens of the states as such, and that they are left to the state governments for security and protection, and not by this article placed under the special care of the Federal government, we may hold ourselves excused from defining the privileges and immunities of citizens of the United States which no state can abridge, until some case involving those privileges may make it necessary to do so.

But lest it should be said that no such privileges and immunities are to be found if those we have been considering are excluded, we venture to suggest some which owe their existence to the Federal government, its national character, its Constitution, or its laws.

One of these is well described in the case of *Crandall* v. *Nevada*, 6 Wall. 35. It is said to be the right of the citizens of this great country, protected by implied guarantees of the Constitution, "to come to the seat of government to assert any claim he may have upon that government, to transact any business he may have with it, to seek its protection, to share its offices, to engage in administering its functions. He has the right of free access to its seaports, through which all operations of foreign commerce are conducted, to the sub-treasuries, and offices, and courts of justice in the several states." And quoting from the language of Chief Justice Taney in another case, it is said "that for all the great purposes for which the Federal government was established, we are one people, with one common country, we are all citizens of the United States;" and it is, as such citizens, that their rights are supported in this Court in *Crandall* v. *Nevada*.

. . . . .

In the early history of the organization of the government, its statesmen seem to have divided on the line which should separate the power of the national government from those of the state governments, and though this line has never been very well defined in public opinion, such a division has continued from that day to this.

The adoption of the first eleven amendments to the Constitution so soon after the original instrument was accepted, shows a prevailing sense of danger at that time from the Federal power. And it cannot be denied that such jealousy continued to exist with many patriotic men until the breaking out of the Civil War. It was then discovered that the true danger of the perpetuity of the Union was in the capacity of the state organizations to combine and concentrate all the powers of the state, and of contiguous states, for a determined resistance to the general government.

Unquestionably, this has given great force to the argument, and added largely to the number, of those who believe in the necessity of a strong national government.

But, however pervading this sentiment, and however it may have contributed to the adoption of the amendments we have been considering, we do not see in those amendments any purpose to destroy the main features of the general system. Under the pressure of all the excited feeling growing out of the war, our statesmen have still believed that the existence of the states with powers for domestic and local government, including the regulation of civil rights—the rights of person and property—was essential to the perfect working of our complex form of government, though they may have thought proper to impose additional limitations on the states, and to confer additional power on that of the nation.

The judgments of the Supreme Court of Louisiana in these cases are affirmed.

Mr. Justice FIELD (Mr. Chief Justice CHASE and Justices BRADLEY and SWAYNE joining with him), dissenting.

No one will deny the abstract justice which lies in the position of the plaintiffs . . .; and I shall endeavor to show that the position has some support in the fundamental law of the country.

It is contended in justification for the act in question that it was adopted in the interest of the city, to promote its cleanliness and protect its health, and was the legitimate exercise of what is termed the police power of the state. That power undoubtedly extends to all regulations affecting the health, good order, morals, peace, and safety of society, and is exercised on a great variety of subjects, and in almost numberless ways. All sorts of restrictions and burdens are imposed under it, and when these are not in conflict with any constitutional prohibitions, or fundamental principles, they cannot be successfully assailed in a judicial tribunal. With this power of the state and its legitimate exercise I shall not differ from the majority of the Court. But under the pretense of prescribing a police regulation the state cannot be permitted to encroach upon any of the just rights of the citizens which the Constitution intended to secure against abridgement.

What, ... are the privileges and immunities which are secured against abridgement by state legislation? ...

... The immortal document which proclaimed the independence of the country declared as self-evident truths that the Creator had endowed all men "with certain inalienable rights, [and] that among these are life, liberty, and the pursuit of happiness,—[and] that to secure these rights, governments are instituted among men."

... That [the Fourteenth] Amendment was intended to give practical effect to the declaration of 1776 of inalienable rights, rights which are the gift of the Creator; which the law does not confer, but only recognizes. ...

In all these cases [referring to several state and lower federal court decisions] there is a recognition of the equality of right among citizens in the pursuit of the ordinary avocations of life, and a declaration that all grants of exclusive privileges, in contravention of this equality, are against common right, and void.

This equality of right, with exemption from all disparaging and partial enactments, in the lawful pursuits of life, throughout the whole country, is the distinguishing privilege of citizens of the United States. To them, everywhere, all pursuits, all professions, all avocations are open without other restrictions than such as are imposed equally upon all others of the same age, sex and conditions. The state may prescribe such regulations for every pursuit and calling of life as will promote the public health, secure the good order and advance the general prosperity of society, but when once prescribed, the pursuit or calling must be free to be followed by every citizen who is within the conditions designated, and will conform to the regulations. This is the fundamental idea upon which our institutions rest, and unless adhered to in the legislation of the country our government will be a republic only in name. . . . That only is a free government, in the American sense of the term, under which the inalienable right of every citizen to pursue his happiness is unrestrained, except by just, equal, and impartial laws.

[Dissenting opinions were also written by Justices BRADLEY and SWAYNE.]

[With the Supreme Court's restrictive interpretation of the privileges and immunities clause established, the opponents of state legislation in the economic realm then turned to the due process clause and found it a useful instrument which the high Court appeared willing to apply. It was not until 1935 that privileges and immunities underwent a brief revival. In *Colgate* v. *Harvey,* 296 U.S. 404, the right to make loans across state lines was declared to be a privilege of United States citizenship and a Vermont tax on such out-of-state loans was struck down as a violation of the privileges and immunities clause of the Fourteenth Amendment. Justices Brandeis, Cardozo and Stone were in dissent, with Stone filing their opinion.

[Said Justice Stone: "The novel application thus given to the clause, and the arguments to support it, leave one in doubt whether it is thought to preclude all differences of taxation . . . of income, or only to forbid such inequality as is in some sense arbitrary and unreasonable. If the former, the clause becomes an inexhaustible source of immunities, incalculable in their benefit to taxpayers and in their harm to local government, by imposing on the states the heavy burden of an exact equality of taxation whenever transactions across state lines may be involved. If the latter, it would seem to add nothing to the guarantee of the equal protection clause, which extends to all 'persons,' including citizens of the United States."

[In *Hague* v. *C. I. O.,* 307 U.S. 496 (1939), two of the Justices, Roberts and Black, urged that the right to discuss national legislation should be declared a privilege derived from national citizenship. Again Stone disagreed, stressing that freedom of speech was not to be confined by subject matter or citizenship. The following year, *Colgate* v. *Harvey* was expressly overruled in *Madden* v.

Kentucky, 309 U.S. 83 (1940). Only Roberts, now joined by Mc-Reynolds, continued to argue for a rebirth of privileges and immunities.

[In the case of the California Anti-Okie law, however, a minority of four Justices, while concurring in the result reached by the majority on interstate commerce grounds, contended that the law ran afoul of the privileges and immunities clause and should have been voided for that reason. Two separate concurring opinions presented this argument, one by Justice Douglas, joined in by Murphy and Black, and the other by Justice Jackson. The facts of the case and parts of the majority opinion have been presented in connection with the discussion of the commerce clause, *supra,* p. 261. Extracts from the concurring opinions follow.]

EDWARDS v. CALIFORNIA
314 U.S. 160 (1941)

Mr. Justice Douglas, concurring.

I express no view on whether or not the statute here in question runs afoul of Art. I, Sec. 8 of the Constitution granting to Congress the power "to regulate Commerce with foreign Nations, and among the several States." But I am of the opinion that the right of persons to move freely from state to state occupies a more protected position in our constitutional system than does the movement of cattle, fruit, steel and coal across state lines. While the opinion of the Court expresses no view on that subject, I deem it appropriate to indicate the reach of the constitutional question which is present.

The right to move freely from state to state is an incident of *national* citizenship, protected by the privileges and immunities clause of the Fourteenth Amendment against state interference.... Now it is apparent that this right is not specifically granted by the Constitution. Yet before the Fourteenth Amendment it was recognized as a right fundamental to the national character of our Federal government. It was so decided in 1867 in *Crandall* v. *Nevada,* 6 Wall. 35. In that case this Court struck down a Nevada tax "upon every person leaving the state" by common carrier. Mr. Justice Miller writing for the Court held that the right to move freely throughout the nation was a right of *national* citizenship. That the right was implied did not make it any the less "guaranteed" by the Constitution.... To be sure, he emphasized that the Nevada statute would obstruct the right of a citizen to travel to the seat of his national government or its offices throughout the country. . . . But there is not a shred of evidence in the record of the *Crandall* case that the persons there involved were en route on any such mission any more than it appears in the present case that Duncan entered California to interview some federal agency. The point which Mr. Justice Miller made was merely in illustration of the damage and havoc which would ensue if the states had the power to prevent the free movement of citizens from one state to another. . . .

So, when the Fourteenth Amendment was adopted in 1868 it had been squarely and authoritatively settled that the right to move freely from state to state was a right of *national* citizenship. As such it was protected by the privileges and immunities clause of the Fourteenth Amendment against state interference. *Slaughter House Cases,* 16 Wall. 36.

Mr. Justice JACKSON, concurring.

I concur in the result reached by the Court, and I agree that the grounds of its decision are permissible ones under applicable authorities. But the migrations of a human being, of whom it is charged that he possesses nothing that can be sold and has no wherewithal to buy, do not fit easily into my notions as to what is commerce. To hold that the measure of his rights is the commerce clause is likely to result eventually either in distorting the commercial law or in denaturing human rights. I turn, therefore, away from principles by which commerce is regulated to that clause of the Constitution by virtue of which Duncan is a citizen of the United States and which forbids any state to abridge his privileges and immunities as such.

This Court should, . . . hold squarely that it is a privilege of citizenship of the United States, protected from state abridgement, to enter any state of the Union, either for temporary sojourn or for the establishment of permanent residence therein and for gaining the resultant citizenship thereof. If national citizenship means less than this, it means nothing.

The right of the citizen to migrate from state to state which, I agree with Mr. Justice Douglas, is shown by our precedents to be one of national citizenship, is not, however, an unlimited one. In addition to being subject to all constitutional limitations imposed by the federal government, such citizen is subject to some control by state governments. He may not, if a fugitive from justice, claim freedom to migrate unmolested, nor may he endanger others by carrying contagion about. These causes, and perhaps others that do not occur to me now, warrant any public authority in stopping a man where it finds him and arresting his progress across a state line quite as much as from place to place within the state.

It is here that we meet the real crux of this case. Does "indigence" as defined by the application of the California statute constitute a basis for restricting the freedom of a citizen, as crime or contagion warrant its restriction? We should say now, and in no uncertain terms, that a man's mere property status, without more, cannot be used by a state to test, qualify, or limit his rights as a citizen of the United States. "Indigence" in itself is neither a source of rights nor a basis for denying them. The mere state of being without funds is a neutral fact—constitutionally an irrelevance, like race, creed, or color. . . .

Any measure which would divide our citizenry on the basis of property into one class free to move from state to state and another class that is poverty-bound to the place where it has suffered misfortune is not only at war with the habit and custom by which our country has expanded, but is also a short-sighted blow at the security of property itself. Property can have no more dangerous, even if unwitting, enemy than one who would make its possession a pretext for unequal or exclusive civil rights. Where those rights are derived from national citizenship no state may impose such a test, and whether the Congress could do so we are not called upon to inquire.

. . . . . .

3. THE RISE AND DECLINE OF SUBSTANTIVE DUE PROCESS

DAVIDSON v. NEW ORLEANS
96 U.S. 97 (1878)

[A Louisiana statute authorized the city of New Orleans to make assessments against real estate in the city, for draining swamp lands within certain areas. Various parcels belonging to the estate of John

Davidson were assessed for approximately $50,000. Upon failure to receive payment the city sought a court order which was refused. The state supreme court, however, reversed. Then Mrs. Davidson, the widow and executrix of the estate, carried the case to the Supreme Court of the United States, urging that the assessment and court order enforcing it constituted a denial of due process of law under the Fourteenth Amendment.

[The case illustrates and contrasts the procedural and substantive approaches, respectively, to the concept of due process of law.]

Mr. Justice MILLER delivered the opinion of the Court. . . .

It is easy to see that when the great barons of England wrung from King John, at the point of the sword, the concession that neither their lives nor their property should be disposed of by the crown, except as provided by the law of the land, they meant by "law of the land" the ancient and customary laws of the English people, or laws enacted by the Parliament of which those barons were a controlling element. It was not in their minds, therefore, to protect themselves against the enactment of laws by the Parliament of England. But when, in the year of grace 1866, there is placed in the Constitution of the United States a declaration that "no State shall deprive any person of life, liberty, or property without due process of law," can a State make anything due process of law which, by its own legislation, it chooses to declare such? To affirm this is to hold that the prohibition to the States is of no avail, or has no application where the invasion of private rights is effected under the forms of State legislation. . . .

A most exhaustive judicial inquiry into the meaning of the words "due process of law," as found in the Fifth Amendment, resulted in the unanimous decision of this Court, that they do not necessarily imply a regular proceeding in a court of justice, or after the manner of such courts. *Murray's Lessee* v. *Hoboken Land & Improvement Co.,* 12 How. 272. . . .

It is not a little remarkable, that while this provision has been in the Constitution of the United States, as a restraint upon the authority of the Federal government, for nearly a century, and while, during all that time, the manner in which the powers of that government have been exercised has been watched with jealousy, and subjected to the most rigid criticism in all its branches, this special limitation upon its powers has rarely been invoked in the judicial forum or the more enlarged theatre of public discussion. But while it has been a part of the Constitution, as a restraint upon the power of the States, only a very few years, the docket of this Court is crowded with cases in which we are asked to hold that state courts and state legislatures have deprived their own citizens of life, liberty, or property without due process of law. There is here abundant evidence that there exists some strange misconception of the scope of this provision as found in the Fourteenth Amendment. In fact, it would seem, from the character of many of the cases before us, and the arguments made in them, that the clause under consideration is looked upon as a means of bringing to the test of the decision of this Court the abstract opinions of every unsuccessful litigant in a state court of the justice of the decision against him, and of the merits of the legislation on which such a decision may be founded. If, therefore, it were possible to define what it is for a State to deprive a person of life, liberty, or property without due process of law, in terms which would cover every exercise of power thus forbidden to the State, and exclude those which are not, no more useful construction could be furnished by this or any other court to any part of the fundamental law.

But, apart from the risk of a failure to give any definition which would be at once perspicuous, comprehensive, and satisfactory, there is a wisdom, we think, in the ascertaining of the intent and application of such an important phrase in the Federal Constitution, by the gradual process of judicial inclusion and exclusion, as the cases presented for decision shall require, with the reasoning on which such decisions may be founded. This Court is, after an experience of nearly a century, still engaged in defining the obligation of contracts, the regulation of commerce, and other powers conferred on the Federal government, or limitations imposed upon the States.

As contributing, to some extent, to this mode of determining what class of cases do not fall within its provision, we lay down the following proposition, as applicable to the case before it:—

That whenever by the laws of a State, or by state authority, a tax, assessment, servitude, or other burden is imposed upon property for the public use, whether it be for the whole State or of some more limited portion of the community, and those laws provide for a mode of confirming or contesting the charge thus imposed, in the ordinary courts of justice, with such notice to the person, or such proceeding in regard to the property as is appropriate to the nature of the case, the judgment in such proceedings cannot be said to deprive the owner of his property without due process of law, however obnoxious it may be to other objections.

It may violate some provision of the state constitution against unequal taxation; but the Federal Constitution imposes no restraint on the States in that regard. . . . It may possibly violate some of those principles of general constitutional law, of which we could take jurisdiction if we were sitting in review of a Circuit Court of the United States. . . . But however this may be, or under whatever other clause of the Federal Constitution we may review the case, it is not possible to hold that a party has, without due process of law, been deprived of his property, when, as regards the issues affecting it, he has, by the laws of the State, a fair trial in a court of justice, according to the modes of proceeding applicable to such a case. . . .

This proposition covers the present case. Before the assessment could be collected, or become effectual, the statute required that the tableau of assessments should be filed in the proper District Court of the State; the personal service of notice, with reasonable time to object, should be served on all owners who were known and within reach of process, and due advertisement made as to those who were unknown, or could not be found. This was complied with; and the party complaining here appeared, and had a full and fair hearing in the court of the first instance, and afterwards in the Supreme Court [of the state]. If this be not due process of law, then the words can have no definite meaning as used in the Constitution.

Affirmed.

Mr. Justice BRADLEY. In the conclusion and general tenor of the opinion just read, I concur. But I think it narrows the scope of inquiry as to what is due process of law more than it should do.

It seems to me that private property may be taken by a State without due process of law in other ways than by mere direct enactment, or the want of a judicial proceeding. . . . The exceptions noted imply that the nature and cause of the taking are proper to be considered. . . . I think, therefore, we are entitled, under the Fourteenth Amendment, not only to see that there is some process of law, but "due process of law," provided by the state law when a citizen is deprived of his property; and that, in judging what is "due process of law," respect must be had to the cause and object of the taking, whether under the taxing power, the power of eminent domain, or the power of assessment for local improvements, or none of these; and if found to be suitable or admissible in this special case, it will be adjudged to be "due process of law;" but if found to be arbitrary, oppressive, and unjust, it may be declared to be not "due process of law." Such an examination may be made without interfering with that large discretion which every legislative power has of making wide modifications in the forms of procedure in each case, according as the laws, habits, customs, and preferences of the people of the particular State may require.

ALLGEYER v. LOUISIANA
165 U.S. 578 (1897)

[A Louisiana statute prescribed a fine of $1000 for any person who "does any act in this State to effect, for himself or for another, insurance on property, then in this State, in any marine insurance company which has not complied in all respects with the laws of this State." Defendant, Allgeyer, insured some marine cargo, to be shipped from New Orleans, with a New York firm which had not qualified under Louisiana law. When the defendant mailed a notice under the policy to the New York insurance company he was fined in accordance with the statute.]

Mr. Justice PECKHAM delivered the opinion of the Court....

In this case the only act which it is claimed was a violation of the statute in question consisted in sending the letter through the mail notifying the company of the property to be covered by the policy already delivered. We have, then, a contract which it is conceded was made outside and beyond the limits of the jurisdiction of the State of Louisiana, being made and to be performed within the State of New York, where the premiums were to be paid, and losses, if any, adjusted. The letter of notification did not constitute a contract made or entered into within the State of Louisiana. It was but the performance of an act rendered necessary by the provisions of the contract already made between the parties outside of the State. It was a mere notification that the contract already in existence would attach to that particular property. In any event, the contract was made in New York, outside the jurisdiction of Louisiana, even though the policy was not to attach to the particular property until the notification was sent.

It is natural that the state court should have remarked that there is in this "statute an apparent interference with the liberty of defendants in restricting their rights to place insurance on property of their own whenever and in what company they desired." Such interference is not only apparent, but it is real, and we do not think that it is justified for the purpose of upholding what the State says is its policy with regard to foreign insurance companies which had not complied with the laws of the State for doing business within its limits. In this case the company did no business within the State, and the contracts were not therein made.

The supreme court of Louisiana says that the act of writing within that State the letter of notification was an act therein done to effect an insurance on property then in the State, in a marine insurance company which had not complied with its laws, and such act was therefore prohibited by the statute. As so construed, we think the statute is a violation of the fourteenth amendment of the federal Constitution, in that it deprives the defendants of their liberty without due process of law. The statute which forbids such act does not become due process of law, because it is inconsistent with the provisions of the Constitution of the Union. The "liberty" mentioned in that amendment means, not only the right of the citizen to be free from the mere physical restraint of his person, as by incarceration, but the term is deemed to embrace the right of the citizen to be free in the enjoyment of all his faculties; to be free to use them in all lawful ways; to live and work where he will; to earn his livelihood by any lawful calling; to pursue any livelihood or avocation; and for that purpose to enter into all contracts which may be proper, necessary, and essential to his carrying out to a successful conclusion the purposes above mentioned.

It was said by Mr. Justice Bradley, in *Butchers' Union Slaughter-House Co.* v. *Crescent City Live-Stock Landing Co.*, 111 U.S. 746, at page 762, . . . in the course of his concurring opinion in that case, that "the right to follow any of the common occupations of life is an inalienable right. It was formulated as such under the phrase 'pursuit of happiness' in the Declaration of Independence, which commenced with the fundamental proposition that 'all men are created equal; that they are endowed by their Creator with certain inalienable rights; that among these are life, liberty, and the pursuit of happiness.' This right is a large ingredient in the civil liberty of the citizen." Again, on page 764 of 111 U.S., . . . the learned justice said: "I hold that the liberty of pursuit—the right to follow any of the ordinary callings of life—is one of the privileges of a citizen of the United States." And again, on page 765 of 111 U.S., . . . : "But if it does not abridge the privileges and immunities of a citizen of the United States to prohibit him from pursuing his chosen calling, and giving to others the exclusive right of pursuing it, it certainly does deprive him (to a certain extent) of his liberty; for it takes from him the freedom of adopting and following the pursuit which he prefers, which, as already intimated, is a material part of the liberty of the citizen." It is true that these remarks were made in regard to questions of monopoly, but they well describe the rights which are covered by the word "liberty," as contained in the fourteenth amendment.

Again in *Powell* v. *Pennsylvania*, 127 U.S. 678, . . . Mr. Justice Harlan, in stating the opinion of the Court, said: "The main proposition advanced by the defendant is that his enjoyment upon terms of equality with all others in similar circumstances of the privilege of pursuing an ordinary calling or trade, and of acquiring, holding, and selling property, is an essential part of his rights of liberty and property, as guaranteed by the fourteenth amendment. The Court assents to this general proposition as embodying a sound principle of constitutional law." It was there held, however, that the legislation under consideration in that case did not violate any of the constitutional rights of the plaintiff in error.

The foregoing extracts have been made for the purpose of showing what general definitions have been given in regard to the meaning of the word "liberty" as used in the amendment, but we do not intend to hold that in no such case can the State exercise its police power. When and how far such power may be legitimately exercised with regard to these subjects must be left for determination to each case as it arises. . . .

In the privilege of pursuing an ordinary calling or trade, and of acquiring, holding, and selling property, must be embraced the right to make all proper contracts in relation thereto; and although it may be conceded that this right to contract in relation to persons or property or to do business within the jurisdiction of the State may be regulated, and sometimes prohibited, when the contracts or business conflict with the policy of the State as contained in its statutes, yet the power does not and cannot extend to prohibiting a citizen from making contracts of the nature involved in this case outside of the limits and jurisdiction of the State, and which are also to be performed outside of such jurisdiction; nor can the State legally prohibit its citizens from doing such an act as writing this letter of notification, even though the property which is the subject of the insurance may at the time when such insurance attaches be within the limits of the State. The mere fact that a citizen may be within the limits of a particular State does not prevent his making a contract outside its limits while he himself remains within it. . . . The giving of the notice is a mere collateral matter. It is not the contract itself, but is an act performed pursuant to a valid contract. . . .

LOCHNER v. NEW YORK
198 U.S. 45 (1905)

[A New York state statute limited employment in bakeries to ten-hour days or sixty-hour weeks. The state court upheld the act.]

Mr. Justice PECKHAM . . . delivered the opinion of the Court. . . .

The statute necessarily interferes with the right of contract between the employer and employes, concerning the number of hours in which the latter may labor in the bakery of the employer. The general right to make a contract in relation to his business is part of the liberty of the individual protected by the Fourteenth Amendment of the Federal Constitution. *Allgeyer* v. *Louisiana*, 165 U.S. 578.

The State . . . has power to prevent the individual from making certain kinds of contracts, and in regard to them the Federal Constitution offers no protection. If the contract be one which the State, in the legitimate exercise of its police power, has the right to prohibit, it is not prevented from prohibiting it by the Fourteenth Amendment. Contracts in violation of a statute, either of the Federal or State government, or a contract to let one's property for immoral purposes, or to do any other unlawful act, could obtain no protection from the Federal Constitution, as coming under the liberty of person or of free contract. Therefore, when the State, by its legislature, in the assumed exercise of its police powers, has passed an act which seriously limits the right to labor or the right of contract in regard to their means of livelihood between persons who are *sui juris* (both employer and employe), it becomes of great importance to determine which shall prevail—the right of the individual to labor for such time as he may choose, or the right of the State to prevent the individual from laboring or from entering into contract to labor, beyond a certain time prescribed by the State.

This Court has recognized the existence and upheld the exercise of the police powers of the States in many cases which might fairly be considered as border ones, and it has, in the course of its determination of questions regarding the asserted invalidity of such statutes, on the ground of their violation of the rights secured by the Federal Constitution, been guided by rules of a very liberal nature, the application of which has resulted, in numerous instances, in upholding the validity of state statutes thus assailed. . . .

It must, of course, be conceded that there is a limit to the valid exercise of the police power by the State. There is no dispute concerning this general proposition. Otherwise the Fourteenth Amendment would have no efficacy and the legislatures of the States would have unbounded power, and it would be enough to say that any piece of legislation was enacted to conserve the morals, the health or the safety of the people; such legislation would be valid, no matter how absolutely without foundation the claim might be. The claim of the police power would be a mere pretext—become another and elusive name for the supreme sovereignty of the State to be exercised free from constitutional restraint. This is not contended for. In every case that comes before this Court, therefore, where legislation of this character is concerned and where the protection of the Federal Constitution is sought, the question necessarily arises: Is this a fair, reasonable and appropriate exercise of the police power of the State, or is it an unreasonable and arbitrary interference with the right of the individual to his personal liberty or to enter into those contracts in relation to labor which may seem to him appropriate or necessary for the support of himself and his family. Of course the liberty of contract relating to labor includes both parties to it. The one has as much right to purchase as the other to sell labor.

This is not a question of substituting the judgment of the Court for that of the legislature. If the act be within the power of the State it is valid, although the judgment of the Court might be totally opposed to the enactment of such a law. But the question would still remain: Is it within the police power of the State? and that question must be answered by the Court.

The question whether this act is valid as a labor law, pure and simple, may be dismissed in a few words. There is no reasonable ground for interfering with the liberty of person or the right of free contract, by determining the hours of labor, in the occupation of a baker. . . . The law must be upheld, if at all, as a law pertaining to the health of the individual engaged in the occupation of a baker. Clean and wholesome bread does not depend upon whether the baker works but ten hours per day or only sixty hours a week. The limitation of the hours of labor does not come within the police power on that ground.

. . . . .

We think the limit of the police power has been reached and passed in this case. There is, in our judgment, no reasonable foundation for holding this to be necessary or appropriate as a health law to safeguard the public health or the health of the individuals who are following the trade of a baker. If this statute be valid, and if, therefore, a proper case is made out in which to deny the right of an individual, *sui juris,* as employer or employe to make contracts for the labor of the latter under the protection of the provisions of the Federal Constitution, there would seem to be no length to which legislation of this nature might not go. . . .

We think that there can be no fair doubt that the trade of a baker, in and of itself, is not an unhealthy one to that degree which would authorize the legislature to interfere with the right to labor, and with the right of free contract on the part of the individual, either as employer or employe. In looking through statistics regarding all trades and occupations, it may be true that the trade of a baker does not appear to be as healthy as some other trades, and is also vastly more healthy than still others. To the common understanding the trade of a baker has never been regarded as an unhealthy one. Very likely physicians would not recommend the exercise of that or of any other trade as a remedy for ill health. . . . It might be safely affirmed that almost all occupations more or less affect the health. . . . But are we all, on that account, at the mercy of legislative majorities? . . .

Statutes of the nature of that under review, limiting the hours in which grown and intelligent men may labor to earn their living, are mere meddlesome interferences with the rights of the individual, and they are not saved from condemnation by the claim that they are passed in the exercise of the police power and upon the subject of the health of the individual whose rights are interfered with, unless there be some fair ground, reasonable in and of itself, to say that there is material danger to the public health or to the health of the employes, if the hours of labor are not curtailed. If this be not clearly the case the individuals, whose rights are thus made the subject of legislative interference, are under the protection of the Federal Constitution regarding their liberty of contract as well as of person; and the legislature of the State has no power to limit their right as proposed in this statute. . . .

It is impossible for us to shut our eyes to the fact that many of the laws of this character, while passed under what is claimed to be the police power for the purpose of protecting the public health or welfare, are, in reality, passed from other motives. We are justified in saying so when, from the character of the law and the subject upon which it legislates, it is apparent that the public health or welfare bears but the most remote relation to the law. The purpose of a statute must be determined from the natural and legal effect of the language employed; and whether it is or is not repugnant to the Constitution of the United States must be determined from the natural effect of such statutes when put into operation, and not from their proclaimed purpose. . . .

Judgment reversed.

Mr. Justice HARLAN, with whom Mr. Justice WHITE and Mr. Justice DAY concurred, dissenting. . . .

I find it impossible, in view of common experience, to say that there is here no real or substantial relation between the means employed by the State and the end sought to be accomplished by its legislation. . . .

We judicially know that the question of the number of hours during which a workman should continuously labor has been, for a long period, and is yet, a subject of serious consideration among civilized peoples, and by those having special knowledge of the laws of health. . . . What is the true ground for the State to take between legitimate protection, by legislation, of the public health and liberty of contract is not a question easily solved, nor one in respect of which there is or can be absolute certainty. There are very few, if any, questions in political economy about which entire certainty may be predicated. . . .

I do not stop to consider whether any particular view of this economic question presents the sounder theory. What the precise facts are it may be difficult to say. It is enough for the determination of this case, and it is enough for this Court to know, that the question is one about which there is room for debate and for an honest difference of opinion. There are many reasons of a weighty, substantial character, based upon the experience of mankind, in support of the theory that, all things considered, more than ten hours steady work each day, from week to week, in a bakery or confectionary establishment, may endanger the health and shorten the lives of the workmen, thereby diminishing their physical and mental capacity to serve the State and to provide for those dependent upon them.

If such reasons exist that ought to be the end of this case, for the State is not amenable to the judiciary, in respect of its legislative enactments, unless such enactments are plainly, palpably, beyond all question, inconsistent with the Constitution of the United States. . . .

Mr. Justice HOLMES, dissenting. . . .

This case is decided upon an economic theory which a large part of the country does not entertain. If it were a question whether I agreed with that theory, I should desire to study it further and long before making up my mind. But I do not conceive that to be my duty, because I strongly believe that my agreement or disagreement has nothing to do with the right of a majority to embody their opinions in law. It is settled by various decisions of this Court that state constitutions and state laws may regulate life in many ways which we as legislators might think as injudicious or if you will as tyrannical as this, and which equally with this interfere with the liberty to contract. Sundays laws and usury laws are ancient examples. A more modern one is the prohibition of lotteries. The liberty of the citizen to do as he likes so long as he does not interfere with the liberty of others to do the same, which has been a shibboleth for some well-known writers, is interfered with by school laws, by the Post Office, by every state or municipal institution which takes his money for purposes thought desirable, whether he likes it or not.

The Fourteenth Amendment does not enact Mr. Herbert Spencer's *Social Statics*. . . . United States and state statutes and decisions cutting down the liberty to contract by way of combination are familiar to this Court. . . . Two years ago we upheld the prohibition of sales of stock on margins or for future delivery in the constitution of California. . . . The decision sustaining an eight-hour law for minors is still recent. . . . Some of these laws embody convictions or prejudices which judges are likely to share. Some may not. But a constitution is not intended to embody a particular economic theory, whether of paternalism and the organic relation of the citizen to the State or of laissez faire. It is made for people of fundamentally differing views, and the accident of our finding certain opinions natural and familiar or novel and even shocking ought not to conclude our judgment upon the question whether statutes embodying them conflict with the Constitution of the United States.

General propositions do not decide concrete cases. The decision will depend on a judgment or intuition more subtle than any articulate major premise. But I think that the proposition just stated, if it is accepted, will carry us far toward the end. Every opinion tends to become a law. I think that the word "liberty" in the Fourteenth Amendment is perverted when it is held to prevent the natural outcome of a dominant opinion, unless it can be said that a rational and fair man necessarily would admit that the statute proposed would infringe fundamental principles as they have been understood by the traditions of our people and our law. It does not need research to show that no such sweeping condemnation can be passed upon the statute before us. A reasonable man might think it a proper measure on the score of health. Men whom I certainly could not pronounce unreasonable would uphold it as a first instalment of a general regulation of the hours of work. Whether in the latter aspect it would be open to the charge of inequality I think it unnecessary to discuss.

MEYER v. NEBRASKA
262 U.S. 390 (1923)

[Meyer was convicted of a violation of a Nebraska statute of 1919, which prohibited the teaching of any language other than English in the first eight grades of the secondary schools.]

Mr. Justice McReynolds delivered the opinion of the Court. . . .

The problem for our determination is whether the statute as construed and applied unreasonably infringes the liberty guaranteed to the plaintiff in error by the Fourteenth Amendment. . . .

While this Court has not attempted to define with exactness the liberty thus guaranteed, the term has received much consideration and some of the included things have been definitely stated. Without doubt, it denotes not merely freedom from bodily restraint but also the right of the individual to contract, to engage in any of the common occupations of life, to acquire useful knowledge, to marry, establish a home and bring up children, to worship God according to the dictates of his own conscience, and generally to enjoy those privileges long recognized at common law as essential to the orderly pursuit of happiness by free men. . . . The established doctrine is that this liberty may not be interfered with, under the guise of protecting the public interest, by legislative action which is arbitrary or without reasonable relation to some purpose within the competency of the State to effect. Determination by the legislature of what constitutes proper exercise of police power is not final or conclusive but is subject to supervision by the courts. *Lawton* v. *Steele,* 152 U.S. 133, 137.

The American people have always regarded education and acquisition of knowledge as matters of supreme importance which should be diligently promoted. The [Northwest] Ordinance of 1787 declares, "Religion, morality, and knowledge being necessary to good government and the happiness of mankind, schools and the means of education shall forever be encouraged." Corresponding to the right of control, it is the natural duty of the parent to give his children education suitable to their station in life; and nearly all the States, including Nebraska, enforce this obligation by compulsory laws.

Practically, education of the young is only possible in schools conducted by especially qualified persons who devote themselves thereto. The calling always has been regarded as useful and honorable, essential, indeed, to the public welfare. Mere knowledge of the German language cannot reasonably be regarded as harmful. Heretofore it has been commonly looked upon as helpful and desirable. Plaintiff in error taught this language in school as part of his occupation. His right thus to teach and the right of parents to engage him so to instruct their children, we think, are within the liberty of the Amendment.

The challenged statute forbids the teaching in school of any subject except in English; also the teaching of any other language until the pupil has attained and successfully passed the eighth grade, which is not usually accomplished before the age of twelve. The Supreme Court of the State has held that "the so-called ancient or dead languages" are not "within the spirit or the purpose of the act." . . . Latin, Greek, Hebrew are not proscribed; but German, French, Spanish, Italian and every other alien speech are within the ban. Evidently the legislature has attempted materially to interfere with the calling of modern language teachers, with the opportunities of pupils to acquire knowledge, and with the power of parents to control the education of their own.

It is said the purpose of the legislation was to promote civic development by inhibiting training and education of the immature in foreign tongues and ideals before they could learn English and acquire American ideals; and "that the English language should be and become the mother tongue of all children reared in this State." It is also affirmed that the foreign born population is very large, that certain communities commonly use foreign words, follow foreign leaders, move in a foreign atmosphere, and that the children are thereby hindered from becoming citizens of the most useful type and the public safety is imperiled.

That the State may do much, go very far, indeed, in order to improve the equality of its citizens, physically, mentally and morally, is clear; but the individual has certain fundamental rights which must be respected. The protection of the Constitution extends to all, to those who speak other languages as well as those born with English on the tongue. Perhaps it would be highly advantageous if all had ready understanding of our ordinary speech, but this cannot be coerced by methods which conflict with the Constitution—a desirable end cannot be promoted by prohibited means. . . .

The desire of the legislature to foster a homogeneous people with American ideals prepared readily to understand current discussions of civic matters is easy to appreciate. Unfortunate experiences during the late war and aversion toward every characteristic of truculent adversaries were certainly enough to quicken that aspiration. But the means adopted, we think, exceed the limitations upon the power of the State and conflict with rights assured to plaintiff in error. The interference is plain enough and no adequate reason therefor in time of peace and domestic tranquility has been shown. . . .

The judgment of the court below must be reversed and the cause remanded for further proceedings not inconsistent with this opinion.

Reversed.

Mr. Justice HOLMES, dissenting:

We all agree, I take it, that it is desirable that all citizens of the United States should speak a common tongue, and therefore that the end aimed at by the statute is a lawful and proper one. The only question is whether the means adopted deprive teachers of the liberty secured to them by the Fourteenth Amendment. It is with hesitation and unwillingness that I differ from my brethren with regard to a law like this but I cannot bring my mind to believe that in some circumstances, and circumstances it is said existing in Nebraska, the statute might not be regarded as a reasonable or even necessary method of reaching the desired result. . . . I think I appreciate the objection to the law but it appears to me to present a question upon which men reasonably might differ and therefore I am unable to say that the Constitution of the United States prevents the experiment being tried. . . .

Mr. Justice SUTHERLAND concurs in this opinion.

WEST COAST HOTEL CO. v. PARRISH
300 U.S. 379 (1937)

Mr. Chief Justice HUGHES delivered the opinion of the Court.

This case presents the question of the constitutional validity of the minimum wage law of the State of Washington.

The Act, entitled "Minimum Wages for Women," authorizes the fixing of minimum wages for women and minors. . . . It provides:

"Section 1. The welfare of the State of Washington demands that women and minors be protected from conditions of labor which have a pernicious effect on their health and morals. The State of Washington, therefore, exercising herein its police and sovereign power declares that inadequate wages and unsanitary conditions of labor exert such pernicious effect.

"Sec. 2. It shall be unlawful to employ women or minors in any industry or occupation within the State of Washington under conditions of labor detrimental to their health or morals; and it shall be unlawful to employ women workers in any industry within the State of Washington at wages which are not adequate for their maintenance.

"Sec. 3. There is hereby created, a commission to be known as the 'Industrial Welfare Commission' for the State of Washington, to establish such standards of wages and conditions of labor for women and minors employed within the State of Washington, as shall be held hereunder to be reasonable and not detrimental to health and morals, and which shall be sufficient for the decent maintenance of women."

Further provisions required the Commission to ascertain the wages and conditions of labor of women and minors within the State. Public hearings were to be held. If after investigation the Commission found that in any occupation, trade or industry the wages paid to women were "inadequate to supply them necessary cost of living and to maintain the workers in health," the Commission was empowered to call a conference of representatives of employers and employees together with disinterested persons representing the public. The conference was to recommend to the Commission, on its request, an estimate of a minimum wage adequate for the purpose above stated, and on the approval of such a recommendation it became the duty of the Commission to issue an obligatory order fixing minimum wages. Any such order might be reopened and the question reconsidered with the aid of the former conference or a new one. Special licenses were authorized for the employment of women who were "physically defective or crippled by age or otherwise," and also for apprentices, at less than the prescribed minimum wage.

. . . . . .

The appellant [West Coast Hotel Co.] conducts a hotel. The appellee Elsie Parrish was employed as a chambermaid and (with her husband) brought this suit to recover the difference between the wages paid her and the minimum wage fixed pursuant to the state law. The minimum wage was $14.50 per week of 48 hours. The appellant challenged the act as repugnant to the due process clause of the Fourteenth Amendment of the Constitution of the United States. The Supreme Court of the State, reversing the trial court, sustained the statute and directed judgment for the plaintiffs. . . . The case is here on appeal.

The appellant relies upon the decision of this Court in *Adkins* v. *Children's Hospital,* 261 U.S. 525, which held invalid the District of Columbia Minimum Wage Act which was attacked under the due process clause of the Fifth Amendment. . . .

The recent case of *Morehead* v. *New York ex rel. Tipaldo,* 298 U.S. 587 [1936], came here on certiorari to the New York court which had held the New York minimum wage act for women to be invalid. . . .

We think that the question [of the continued validity of the *Adkins* ruling] which was not deemed to be open in the *Morehead* case is open and is necessarily presented here. The Supreme Court of Washington has upheld the minimum wage statute of that State. It has decided that the statute is a reasonable exercise of the police power of the State. In reaching that conclusion the state court has invoked principles long established by this Court in the application of the Fourteenth Amendment. The state court has refused to regard the decision in the *Adkins* case as determinative and has pointed to our decisions both before and since that case as justifying its position. We are of the opinion that this ruling of the state court demands on our part a reexamination of the *Adkins* case. The importance of the question, in which many States having similar laws are concerned, the close division by which the decision in the *Adkins* case was reached, and the economic conditions which have supervened, and in the light of which the reasonableness of the exercise of the protective power of the State must be considered, make it not only appropriate, but we think imperative, that in deciding the present case the subject should receive fresh consideration.

[The Court here summarizes the decisions on the subject.]

The principle which must control our decision is not in doubt. The constitutional provision invoked is the due process clause of the Fourteenth Amendment governing the States, as the due process clause invoked in the *Adkins* case governed Congress. In each case the violation alleged by those attacking minimum wage regulation for women is deprivation of freedom of contract. What is this freedom? The Constitution does not speak of freedom of contract. It speaks of liberty and prohibits the deprivation of liberty without due process of law. In prohibiting that deprivation the Constitution does not recognize an absolute and uncontrollable liberty. Liberty in each of its phases has its history and connotation. But the liberty safeguarded is liberty in a social organization which requires the protection of law against the evils which menace the health, safety, morals and welfare of the people. Liberty under the Constitution is thus necessarily subject to the restraints of due process, and regulation which is reasonable in relation to its subject and is adopted in the interests of the community is due process.

This essential limitation of liberty in general governs freedom of contract in particular. . . .

This power under the Constitution to restrict freedom of contract has had many illustrations. That it may be exercised in the public interest with respect to contracts between employer and employee is undeniable. . . .

The point that has been strongly stressed that adult employees should be deemed competent to make their own contracts was decisively met nearly forty years ago in *Holden* v. *Hardy* [169 U.S. 366, involving a Utah statute limiting employment in underground mines and smelters to eight hours a day], where we pointed out the inequality in the footing of the parties. We said (*Id.*, 397):

"The legislature has also recognized the fact, which the experience of legislators in many States has corroborated, that the proprietors of these establishments and their operatives do not stand upon an equality, and that their interests are, to a certain extent, conflicting. The former naturally desire to obtain as much labor as possible from their employes, while the latter are often induced by the fear of discharge to conform to regulations which their judgment, fairly exercised, would pronounce to be detrimental to their health or strength. In other words, the proprietors lay down the rules and the laborers are practically constrained to obey them. In such cases self-interest is often an unsafe guide, and the legislature may properly interpose its authority." . . .

It is manifest that this established principle is peculiarly applicable in relation to the employment of women in whose protection the State has a special interest. That phase of the subject received elaborate consideration in *Muller* v. *Oregon* (1908), 208 U.S. 412, where the constitutional authority of the State to limit the working hours of women was sustained. . . .

This array of precedents and the principles they applied were thought by the dissenting justices in the *Adkins* case to demand that the minimum wage statute be sustained. The validity of the distinction made by the Court between a minimum wage and a maximum of hours in limiting liberty of contract was especially challenged. 261 U.S., p. 564. That challenge persists and is without any satisfactory answer. . . .

One of the points which was pressed by the Court in supporting its ruling in the *Adkins* case was that the standard set up by the District of Columbia Act did not take appropriate account of the value of the services rendered. In the *Morehead* case, the minority thought that the New York Statute had met that point in its definition of a "fair wage" and that it accordingly presented a distinguishable feature which the Court could recognize within the limits which the Morehead petition for certiorari was deemed to present. The Court, however, did not take that view and the New York Act was held to be essentially the same as that for the District of Columbia. The statute now before us is like the latter, but we are unable to conclude that in its minimum wage requirement the State has passed beyond the boundary of its broad protective power.

[The Court cites from the dissenting opinions of Justice Holmes and of Chief Justice Taft in the *Adkins* case.]

We think that the views thus expressed are sound and that the decision in the *Adkins* case was a departure from the true application of the principles governing the regulation by the State of the relation of employer and employed. Those principles have been reenforced by our subsequent decisions. . . .

With full recognition of the earnestness and vigor which characterize the prevailing opinion in the *Adkins* case, we find it impossible to reconcile that ruling with these well-considered declarations. What can be closer to the public interest than the health of women and their protection from unscrupulous and overreaching employers? And if the protection of women is a legitimate end of the exercise of state power, how can it be said that the requirement of the payment of a minimum wage fairly fixed in order to meet the very necessities of existence is not an admissible means to that end? The legislature of the State was clearly entitled to consider the situation of women in employment, the fact that they are in the class receiving the least pay, that their bargaining power is relatively weak, and that they are the ready victims of those who would take advantage of their necessitous circumstances. The legislature was entitled to adopt measures to reduce the evils of the "sweating system," the exploiting of workers at wages so low as to be insufficient to meet the bare cost of living thus making their very helplessness the occasion of a most injurious competition. The legislature had the right to consider that its minimum wage requirements would be an important aid in carrying out its policy of protection. The adoption of similar requirements by many States evidences a deepseated conviction both as to the presence of the evil and as to the means adapted to check it. Legislative response to that conviction cannot be regarded as arbitrary or capricious and that is all we have to decide. Even if the wisdom of the policy be regarded as debatable and its effects uncertain, still the legislature is entitled to its judgment.

There is an additional and compelling consideration which recent economic experience has brought into a strong light. The exploitation of a class of workers who are in an unequal position with respect to bargaining power and are thus relatively defenceless against the denial of a living wage is not only detrimental to their health and well being but casts a direct burden for their support upon the community. What these workers lose in wages the taxpayers are called upon to pay. The bare cost of living must be met. We may take judicial notice of the unparalleled demands for relief which arose during the recent period of depression and still continue to an alarming extent despite the degree of economic recovery which has been achieved. It is unnecessary to cite official statistics to establish what is of common knowledge through the length and breadth of the land. While in the instant case no factual brief has been presented, there is no reason to doubt that the State of Washington has encountered the same social problem that is present elsewhere. The community is not bound to provide what is in effect a subsidy for unconscionable employers. The community may direct its law-making power to correct the abuse which springs from their selfish disregard of the public interest. The argument that the legislation in question constitutes an arbitrary discrimination, because it does not extend to men, is unavailing. This Court has frequently held that the legislative authority, acting within its proper field, is not bound to extend its regulation to all cases which it might possibly reach. The legislature "is free to recognize degrees of harm and it may confine its restrictions to those classes of cases where the need is deemed to be clearest." If "the law presumably hits the evil where it is most felt, it is not to be overthrown because there are other instances to which it might have been applied." There is no "doctrinaire requirement" that the legislation should be couched in all embracing terms. . . . This familiar principle has repeatedly been applied to legislation which singles out women, and particular classes of women, in the exercise of the State's protective power. . . . Their relative need in the presence of the evil, no less than the existence of the evil itself, is a matter for the legislative judgment.

Our conclusion is that the case of *Adkins* v. *Children's Hospital, supra,* should be, and it is, overruled. The judgment of the Supreme Court of the State of Washington is affirmed.

Mr. Justice SUTHERLAND [dissenting].

Mr. Justice VAN DEVANTER, Mr. Justice MCREYNOLDS, Mr. Justice BUTLER and I think the judgment of the court below should be reversed.

The principles and authorities relied upon to sustain the judgment, were considered in *Adkins* v. *Children's Hospital,* 261 U.S. 525, and *Morehead* v. *New York ex rel. Tipaldo,* 298 U.S. 587; and their lack of application to cases like the one in hand was pointed out. A sufficient answer to all that is now said will be found in the opinions of the Court in those cases. Nevertheless, in the circumstances, it seems well to restate our reasons and conclusions.

Under our form of government, where the written Constitution, by its own terms, is the supreme law, some agency, of necessity, must have the power to say the final word as to the validity of a statute assailed as unconstitutional. The Constitution makes it clear that the power has been intrusted to this Court when the question arises in a controversy within its jurisdiction; and so long as the power remains there, its exercise cannot be avoided without betrayal of the trust.

It has been pointed out many times, as in the *Adkins* case, that this judicial duty is one of gravity and delicacy; and that rational doubts must be resolved in favor of the constitutionality of the statute. But whose doubts, and by whom resolved? Undoubtedly it is the duty of a member of the Court, in the process of reaching a right conclusion, to give due weight to the opposing views of his associates; but in the end, the question which he must answer is not whether such views seem sound to those who entertain them, but whether they convince him that the statute is constitutional or engender in his mind a rational doubt upon that issue. The oath which he takes as a judge is not a composite oath, but an individual one. And in passing upon the validity of a statute, he discharges a duty imposed upon him, which cannot be consummated justly by an automatic acceptance of the views of others which have neither convinced, nor created a reasonable doubt in, his mind. If upon a question so important he thus surrender his deliberate judgment, he stands forsworn. He cannot subordinate his convictions to that extent and keep faith with his oath or retain his judicial and moral independence.

The suggestion that the only check upon the exercise of the judicial power, when properly invoked, to declare a constitutional right superior to an unconstitutional statute is the judge's own faculty of self-restraint, is both ill considered and mischievous. Self-restraint belongs in the domain of will and not of judgment. The check upon the judge is that imposed by his oath of office, by the Constitution and by his own conscientious and informed convictions; and since he has the duty to make up his own mind and adjudge accordingly, it is hard to see how there could be any other restraint. This Court acts as a unit. It cannot act in any other way; and the majority (whether a bare majority or a majority of all but one of its members), therefore, establishes the controlling rule as the decision of the Court, binding, so long as it remains unchanged, equally upon those who disagree and upon those who subscribe to it. Otherwise, orderly administration of justice would cease. But it is the right of those in the minority to disagree, and sometimes, in matters of grave importance, their imperative duty to voice their disagreement at such length as the occasion demands—always, of course, in terms which, however forceful, do not offend the proprieties or impugn the good faith of those who think otherwise.

It is urged that the question involved should now receive fresh consideration, among other reasons, because of "the economic conditions which have supervened;" but the meaning of the Constitution does not change with the ebb and flow of economic events. We frequently are told in more general words that the Constitution must be construed in the light of the present. If by that it is meant that the Constitution is made up of living words that apply to every new condition which they include, the statement is quite true. But to say, if that be intended, that the words of the Constitution mean today what they did not mean when written—that is, that they do not apply to a situation now to which they would have applied then— is to rob that instrument of the essential element which continues it in force as the people have made it until they, and not their official agents, have made it otherwise. . . .

The judicial function is that of interpretation; it does not include the power of amendment under the guise of interpretation. To miss the point of difference between the two is to miss all that the phrase "supreme law of the land" stands for and to convert what was intended as inescapable and enduring mandates into mere moral reflections.

If the Constitution, intelligently and reasonably construed in the light of these principles, stands in the way of desirable legislation, the blame must rest upon that instrument, and not upon the Court for enforcing it according to its terms. The remedy in that situation— and the only true remedy—is to amend the Constitution. . . .

The *Adkins* case dealt with an act of Congress which had passed the scrutiny both of the legislative and executive branches of the government. We recognized that thereby these departments had affirmed the validity of the statute, and properly declared that their determination must be given great weight, but we then concluded, after thorough consideration, that their view could not be sustained. We think it not inappropriate now to add a word on that subject before coming to the question immediately under review.

The people by their Constitution created three separate, distinct, independent and coequal departments of government. The governmental structure rests, and was intended to rest, not upon any one or upon any two, but upon all three of these fundamental pillars. It seems unnecessary to repeat, what so often has been said, that the powers of these departments are different and are to be exercised independently. The differences clearly and definitely appear in the Constitution. Each of the departments is an agent of its creator; and one department is not and cannot be the agent of another. Each is answerable to its creator for what it does, and not to another agent. The view, therefore, of the Executive and of Congress that an act is constitutional is persuasive in a high degree; but it is not controlling.

Coming, then, to a consideration of the Washington statute, it first is to be observed that it is in every substantial respect identical with the statute involved in the *Adkins* case. Such vices as existed in the latter are present in the former. And if the *Adkins* case was properly decided, as we who join in this opinion think it was, it necessarily follows that the Washington statute is invalid.

An appeal to the principle that the legislature is free to recognize degrees of harm and confine its restrictions accordingly, is but to beg the question, which is—since the contractual rights of men and women are the same, does the legislation here involved, by restricting only the rights of women to make contracts as to wages, create an arbitrary discrimination? We think it does. Difference of sex affords no reasonable ground for making a restriction applicable to the wage contracts of all working women from which like contracts of all working men are left free. Certainly a suggestion that the bargaining ability of the average woman is not equal to that of the average man would lack substance. The ability to make a fair bargain, as everyone knows, does not depend upon sex.

4. DUE PROCESS AND PRICES

BUSINESS AFFECTED WITH A PUBLIC INTEREST[17]

Prices perform important functions under any economic system. It is difficult to conceive of the successful operation of a predominantly private enterprise system unless the entrepreneur is permitted to determine his own price policies. There is a sound basis for pro-

---

[17] From Henry Rottschaefer, *The Constitution and Socio-Economic Change*, Ann Arbor: University of Michigan Law School, 1948, pp. 156–159. Reproduced by permission of the author and the publishers.

tecting his power to do so if the purpose is to maintain that system. He was exercising it over a much larger area of economic activities than today when the validity of governmental price control came before the Court for the first time. The demand for it originated with the consumers who objected to what were charged to be exorbitant prices. The major problem from *Munn v. Illinois* in 1877 to *Nebbia v. New York* in 1934[18] concerned the fixing of maximum prices. The former of these decided that due process was not violated by a state statute regulating the price of grain elevation at commercial centers. The majority of the Court based its decision in part upon analogies found in the common law under which those who devoted their property to the public use subjected it thereby to public regulation requiring them to "take but reasonable toll." Such property was said to be affected with a public interest. As the policy was extended to additional businesses, the test was reformulated so as to subject to this form of control businesses affected with such an interest. This removed any implications that it was limited to cases in which the regulated subject was the use of property. A long series of decisions left it uncertain just how a business affected with a public interest was to be distinguished from one not so affected. The grant of a legal monopoly or other special privileges, the possession of a monopoly in fact, the existence of excessive competition among consumers and that the commodity or service belonged to the class of necessities, were all invoked to support the conclusion that a particular business had become affected with a public interest.[19] These reduced somewhat the vagueness of that expression, but still left sufficient room for differences of judicial opinion to render doubtful the validity of any extension of the field of government price control. There were situations in which it was sustained solely for the purpose of protecting a limited group from oppression and extortion by unscrupulous persons. No attempt was made to subsume these cases under the "affectation with a public interest" category. The usual form of price control has been that in which a government agency has fixed the price. Some legislation has merely required sellers or buyers to maintain in every locality in which they sell or buy a commodity the price maintained therefor in another locality except for differences due to variations in transportation costs to or from such localities. These

18 Both *infra*, pp. 355, 365.
19 See the *Wolff Packing Company* case, *infra*.

had been sustained only when justifiable as a means for combatting monopoly. Prior to 1933 there were quite a number of economic activities subject to governmental price control of one form or another. The due process clauses had prevented their application to others. The fixing of maximum, or maximum and minimum, prices was still considered to be valid in exceptional cases only. The principles developed to define those exceptions were looked upon as quite different from those applicable to other forms of regulation.

This was the situation when the *Nebbia Case* was decided in 1934. It involved the validity under the due process clause of the Fourteenth Amendment of a New York statute so far as it permitted fixing a minimum retail price for milk. The basic assumption underlying the attack was that governmental price-fixing could not validly be applied to a business not affected with a public interest as that concept had been defined by prior decisions. The Court's majority admitted that the dairy industry was not a public utility in the accepted sense of that term, and that the factors usually relied upon to put a business into the class of these affected with a public interest were absent. That which the majority admitted was the basis of the minority's condemnation of the statute. The majority in effect rejected price control by the due process clauses which had been gradually developed during a period of more than fifty years. Its general ideas are redefined. "The statement that one has dedicated his property to a public use" is stated to be "merely another way of saying that if one embarks in a business which public interest demands shall be regulated, he must know regulation will ensue." The definition of the phrase "affected with a public interest" is revised out of existence. It is stated that it "can, in the nature of things, mean no more than that an industry, for adequate reasons, is subject to control for the public good." The validity of price control was made to depend wholly upon the reasonableness of the legislative judgment that it was an appropriate means for remedying what it was free to regard as an evil or obstacle to the public welfare. This would permit it whenever the "economic maladjustment is one of price." Such was the situation of the dairy industry in New York when this legislation was enacted. The provision sustained was but one part of a general policy of protecting the dairy industry by raising the prices of its products. Though the majority attempted to relate it to the welfare of the consumers, the statute's principal purpose was to maintain the prices paid the producers. . . .

MUNN v. ILLINOIS
94 U.S. 113 (1877)

Mr. Chief Justice WAITE delivered the opinion of the Court.

The question to be determined in this case is whether the general assembly of Illinois can, under the limitations upon the legislative powers of the States imposed by the Constitution of the United States, fix by law the maximum of charges for the storage of grain in warehouses at Chicago and other places in the State ... "in which grain is stored in bulk, and in which the grain of different owners is mixed together, or in which grain is stored in such a manner that the identity of different lots or parcels cannot be accurately preserved."

It is claimed that such a law is repugnant—

1. To that part of sect. 8, art. I, of the Constitution of the United States which confers upon Congress the power "to regulate commerce with foreign nations and among the several States;"

2. To that part of sect. 9 of the same article, which provides that "no preference shall be given by any regulation of commerce or revenue to the ports of one State over those of another;" and

3. To that part of amendment 14 which ordains that no State shall "deprive any person of life, liberty, or property, without due process of law, nor deny to any person within its jurisdiction the equal protection of the laws."

We will consider the last of these objections first. . . .

The Constitution contains no definition of the word "deprive," as used in the Fourteenth Amendment. To determine its signification, therefore, it is necessary to ascertain the effect which usage has given it, when employed in the same or a like connection.

While this provision of the amendment is new in the Constitution of the United States, as a limitation upon the powers of the States, it is old as a principle of civilized government. It is found in Magna Charta, and, in substance if not in form, in nearly or quite all the constitutions that have been from time to time adopted by the several States of the Union. By the Fifth Amendment, it was introduced into the Constitution of the United States as a limitation upon the powers of the national government, and by the Fourteenth, as a guaranty against any encroachments upon an acknowledged right of citizenship by the legislatures of the States.

When the people of the United Colonies separated from Great Britain, they changed the form, but not the substance, of their government. They retained for the purposes of government all the powers of the British Parliament, and through their State constitutions, or other forms of social compact, undertook to give practical effect to such as they deemed necessary for the common good and the security of life and property. All the powers which they retained they committed to their respective States, unless in express terms or by implications reserved to themselves. Subsequently, when it was found necessary to establish a national government for national purposes, a part of the powers of the States and of the people of the States was granted to the United States and the people of the United States. This grant operated as a further limitation upon the powers of the States, so that now the governments of the States possess all the powers of the Parliament of England, except such as have been delegated to the United States or reserved by the people. The reservations by the people are shown in the prohibitions of the constitutions.

When one becomes a member of society, he necessarily parts with some rights or privileges which, as an individual not affected by his relations to others, he might retain. "A body politic," as aptly defined in the preamble of the Constitution of Massachusetts, "is a social compact by which the whole people covenants with each citizen, and each citizen with the whole people, that all shall be governed by certain laws for the common good." This does not confer power upon the whole people to control rights which are purely and exclusively private, . . . but it does authorize the establishment of laws requiring each citizen to so conduct himself, and so use his own property, as not unnecessarily to injure another. This is the very essence of government. . . . From this source come the police powers, which, as was said by Mr. Chief Justice Taney in the *License Cases,* 5 How. 583, "are nothing more or less than the powers of government inherent in every sovereignty, . . . that is to say, . . . the power to govern men and things." Under these powers the government regulates the conduct of its citizens one towards another, and the manner in which each shall use his own property, when such regulation becomes necessary for the public good. In their exercise it has been customary in England from time immemorial, and in this country from its first colonization, to regulate ferries, common carriers, hackmen, bakers, millers, wharfingers, innkeepers, &c., and in so doing to fix a maximum of charge to be made for services rendered, accommodations furnished, and articles sold. To this day, statutes are to be found in many of the States upon some or all these subjects; and we think it has never yet been successfully contended that such legislation came within any of the constitutional pro-hibitions against interference with private property. With the Fifth Amendment in force, Congress in 1820, conferred power upon the city of Washington "to regulate . . . the rates of wharfage at private wharves, . . . the sweeping of chimneys, and to fix the rates of fees therefor, . . . and the weight and quality of bread," 3 Stat. 587, sect. 7; and, in 1838, "to make all necessary regulations respecting hackney carriages and the rates of fare of the same, and the rates of hauling by cartmen, wagoners, carmen, and draymen, and the rates of commission of auctioneers," 9 *id.* 224, sect. 2.

From this it is apparent that, down to the time of the adoption of the Fourteenth Amendment, it was not supposed that statutes regulating the use, or even the price of the use, of private property necessarily deprived an owner of his property without due process of law. Under some circumstances they may, but not under all. The amendment does not change the law in this particular: it simply prevents the States from doing that which will operate as such a deprivation.

This brings us to inquire as to the principles upon which this power of regulation rests, in order that we may determine what is within and what is without its operative effect. Looking, then, to the common law, from whence came the right which the Constitu-tion protects, we find that when private property is "affected with a public interest, it ceases to be *juris privati* only." This was said by Lord Chief Justice Hale more than two hundred years ago, in his treatise *De Portibus Maris,* 1 Harg. Law Tracts, 78, and has been accepted without objection as an essential element in the law of property ever since. Property does become clothed with a public interest when used in a manner to make it of public consequence, and affect the community at large. When, therefore, one devotes his property to a use in which the public has an interest, he, in effect, grants to the public an interest in that use, and must submit to be controlled by the public for the common good, to the extent of the interest he has thus created. He may withdraw his grant by discon-tinuing the use; but, so long as he maintains the use, he must submit to the control. . . .

From the same source comes the power to regulate the charges of common carriers, which was done in England as long ago as the third year of the reign of William and Mary, and continued until within a comparatively recent period. And in the first statute we find the following suggestive preamble, to wit:—

"And whereas divers wagoners and other carriers, by combination amongst themselves, have raised the prices of carriage of goods in many places to excessive rates, to the great injury of the trade: Be it, therefore, enacted," &c. 3 W. & M. c. 12, § 24; 3 Stat. at Large (Great Britain), 481.

Common carriers exercise a sort of public office, and have duties to perform in which the public is interested. Their business is, therefore, "affected with a public interest," within the meaning of the doctrine which Lord Hale has so forcibly stated.

But we need not go further. Enough has already been said to show that, when private property is devoted to a public use, it is subject to public regulation. It remains only to ascertain whether the warehouses of these plaintiffs in error, and the business which is carried on there, come within the operation of this principle.

For this purpose we accept as true the statements of fact contained in the elaborate brief of one of the counsel of the plaintiffs in error. From these it appears that "the great producing region of the West and Northwest sends its grain by water and rail to Chicago, where the greater part of it is shipped by vessel for transportation to the seaboard by the Great Lakes, and some of it is forwarded by railway to the Eastern ports. . . . Vessels, to some extent, are loaded in the Chicago harbor, and sailed through the St. Lawrence directly to Europe. . . . The quantity [of grain] received in Chicago has made it the greatest grain market in the world. This business has created a demand for means by which the immense quantity of grain can be handled or stored, and these have been found in grain warehouses, which are commonly called elevators, because the grain is elevated from the boat or car, by machinery operated by steam, into the bins prepared for its reception, and elevated from the bins, by a like process, into the vessel or car which is to carry it on. . . . In this way the trade in grain is carried on by the inhabitants of seven or eight of the great States of the West with four or five of the States lying on the sea-shore, and forms the largest part of interstate commerce in these States. The grain warehouses or elevators in Chicago are immense structures, holding from 300,000 to 1,000,000 bushels at one time, according to size. They are divided into bins of large capacity and great strength. . . . They are located with the river harbor on one side and the railway tracks on the other; and the grain is run through them from car to vessel, or boat to car, as may be demanded in the course of business. It has been found impossible to preserve each owner's grain separate, and this has given rise to a system of inspection and grading, by which the grain of different owners is mixed, and receipts issued for the number of bushels which are negotiable, and redeemable in like kind, upon demand. This mode of conducting the business was inaugurated more than twenty years ago, and has grown to immense proportions. The railways have found it impracticable to own such elevators, and public policy forbids the transaction of such business by the carrier; the ownership has, therefore, been by private individuals, who have embarked their capital and devoted their industry to such business as a private pursuit."

In this connection it must also be borne in mind that, although in 1874 there were in Chicago fourteen warehouses adapted to this particular business, and owned by about thirty persons, nine business firms controlled them, and that the prices charged and received for storage were such "as have been from year to year agreed upon and established by the different elevators or warehouses in the city of Chicago, and which rates have been annually published in one or more newspapers printed in said city, in the month of January in each year, as the established rates for the year then next ensuing such publication." Thus it is apparent that all the elevating facilities through which these vast productions "of seven or eight great States of the West" must pass on the way "to four or five of the States on the sea-shore" may be a "virtual" monopoly.

Under such circumstances it is difficult to see why, if the common carrier, or the miller, or the ferryman, or the innkeeper, or the wharfinger, or the baker, or the cartman, or the hackney-coachman, pursues a public employment and exercises "a sort of public office," these plaintiffs in error do not. They stand, to use again the language of their counsel, in the very "gateway of commerce," and take toll from all who pass. Their business most certainly "tends to a common charge, and is become a thing of public interest and use." Every bushel of grain for its passage "pays a toll, which is a common charge," and, therefore, according to Lord Hale, every such ware houseman "ought to be under public regulation, viz., that he . . . take but reasonable toll." Certainly, if any business can be clothed "with a public interest and cease to be *juris privati* only," this has been. It may not be made so by the operation of the Constitution of Illinois or this statute, but it is by the facts. . . .

Neither is it a matter of any moment that no precedent can be found for a statute precisely like this. It is conceded that the business is one of recent origin, that its growth has been rapid, and it is already of great importance. And it must also be conceded that it is a business in which the whole public has a direct and positive interest. It presents, therefore, a case for the application of a long-known and well-established principle in social science, and this statute simply extends the law so as to meet this new development of commercial progress. There is no attempt to compel these owners to grant the public an interest in their property, but to declare their obligations, if they use it in this particular manner.

It matters not in this case that these plaintiffs in error had built their warehouses and established their business before the regulations complained of were adopted. What they did was from the beginning subject to the power of the body politic to require them to conform to such regulations as might be established by the proper authorities for the common good. They entered upon their business and provided themselves with the means to carry it on subject to this condition. If they did not wish to submit themselves to such interference, they should not have clothed the public with an interest in their concerns. The same principle applies to them that does to the proprietor of a hackney-carriage, and as to him it has never been supposed that he was exempt from regulating statutes or ordinances because he had purchased his horses and carriage and established his business before the statute or the ordinance was adopted. . . .

Judgment affirmed.

Mr. Justice FIELD. I am compelled to dissent. . . . The principle upon which the opinion of the majority proceeds is, in my judgment, subversive of the rights of private property . . . and is in conflict with the authorities cited in its support.

   . . . . .

The question presented . . . is one of the greatest importance,— whether it is within the competency of a State to fix the compensation which an individual may receive for the use of his own property in his private business, and for his services in connection with it.

   . . . . .

. . . It would seem from its opinion that the Court holds that property loses something of its private character when employed in such a way as to be generally useful. The doctrine declared is that property "becomes clothed with a public interest when used in a manner to make it of public consequence, and affect the community at large;" and from such clothing the right of the legislature is deduced to control the use of the property, and to determine the compensation which the owner may receive for it. When Sir Matthew Hale, and the sages of the law in his day, spoke of property as affected by a public interest, and ceasing from that cause to be *juris privati* solely, that is, ceasing to be held merely in private right, they referred to property dedicated by the owner to public uses, or to property the use of which was granted by the government, or in connection with which special privileges were conferred. Unless the property was thus dedicated, or some right bestowed by the government was held with the property . . . the property was not affected by any public interest so as to be taken out of the category of property held in private right. But it is not in any such sense that the terms "clothing property with a public interest" are used in this case. From the nature of the business under consideration—the storage of grain— which, in any sense in which the words can be used, is a private business . . . it is clear that the Court intended to declare that, whenever one devotes his property to a business which is useful to the public,—"affects the community at large,"—the legislature can regulate the compensation which the owner may receive for its use, and for his own services in connection with it. . . . The building used by the defendants was for the storage of grain: in such storage, says the Court, the public has an interest; therefore the defendants, by devoting the building to that storage, have granted the public an interest in that use, and must submit to have their compensation regulated by the legislature.

If this be sound law, . . . all property and all business in the State are held at the mercy of a majority of its legislature. . . . The public is interested in the manufacture of cotton, woolen, and silken fabrics, in the construction of machinery, in the printing and publication of books and periodicals, and in the making of utensils of every variety, useful and ornamental; indeed there is hardly an enterprise or business engaging the attention and labor of any considerable portion of the community, in which the public has not an interest in the sense in which that term is used by the Court in this opinion;

and the doctrine which allows the legislature to interfere with and regulate the charges which the owners of property thus employed shall make for its use, that is, the rates at which all these different kinds of business shall be carried on, has never before been asserted, so far as I am aware, by any judicial tribunal in the United States.

It is true that the legislation which secures to all protection in their rights, and the equal use and enjoyment of their property, embraces an almost infinite variety of subjects. Whatever affects the peace, good order, morals, and health of the community, comes within its scope; and every one must use and enjoy his property subject to the restrictions which such legislation imposes. What is termed the police power of the State, which, from the language often used respecting it, one would suppose to be an undefined and irresponsible element in government, can only interfere with the conduct of individuals in their intercourse with each other, and in the use of their property, so far as may be required to secure these objects. The compensation which the owners of property, not having any special rights or privileges from the government in connection with it, may demand for its use, or for their own services in union with it, forms no element of consideration in prescribing regulations for that purpose. . . .

There is nothing in the character of the business of the defendants as warehousemen which called for the interference complained of in this case. Their buildings are not nuisances; their occupation of receiving and storing grain infringes upon no rights of others, disturbs no neighborhood, infects not the air, and in no respect prevents others from using and enjoying their property as to them may seem best. The legislation in question is nothing less than a bold assertion of absolute power by the State to control at its discretion the property and business of the citizen, and fix the compensation he shall receive. . . . The decision of the Court in this case gives unrestrained license to legislative will. . . .

[Mr. Justice STRONG concurred in this dissent.]

WOLFF PACKING CO. v. COURT OF INDUSTRIAL RELATIONS
262 U.S. 522 (1923)

[The Industrial Court Act of Kansas (1920) declared a number of industrial enterprises to be affected with a public interest and authorized a three-man court to fix wages and other terms for the conduct of these industries.]

Mr. Chief Justice TAFT delivered the opinion of the Court. . . .

Businesses said to be clothed with a public interest justifying some public regulation may be divided into three classes:

(1) Those which are carried on under the authority of a public grant of privileges which either expressly or impliedly imposes the affirmative duty of rendering a public service demanded by any member of the public. Such are the railroads, other common carriers and public utilities.

(2) Certain occupations, regarded as exceptional, the public interest attaching to which, recognized from earliest times, has survived the period of arbitrary laws by Parliament or Colonial legislatures for regulating all trades and callings. Such are those of the keepers of inns, cabs and grist mills. . . .

(3) Businesses which though not public at their inception may be fairly said to have arisen to be such and have become subject in consequence to some government regulation. They have come to hold such a peculiar relation to the public that this is superimposed upon them. In the language of the cases, the owner by devoting his business to the public use, in effect grants the public an interest in that use and subjects himself to public regulation to the extent of that interest although the property continues to belong to its private owner and to be entitled to protection accordingly. . . .

It is manifest from an examination of the cases cited under the third head that the mere declaration by a legislature that a business is affected with a public interest is not conclusive of the question whether its attempted regulation on that ground is justified. The circumstances of its alleged change from the status of a private business and its freedom from regulation into one in which the public have come to have an interest are always a subject of judicial inquiry. . . .

It has never been supposed, since the adoption of the Constitution, that the business of the butcher, or the baker, the tailor, the wood chopper, the mining operator or the miner was clothed with such a public interest that the price of his product or his wages could be fixed by State regulation. It is true that in the days of the early common law an omnipotent Parliament did regulate prices and wages as it chose, and occasionally a Colonial legislature sought to exercise the same power; but nowadays one does not devote one's property or business to the public use or clothe it with a public interest merely because one makes commodities for, and sells to, the public in the common callings of which those above mentioned are instances. . . .

In nearly all the businesses included under the third head above, the thing which gave the public interest was the indispensable nature of the service and the exorbitant charges and arbitrary control to which the public might be subjected without regulation. . . .

It is very difficult under the cases to lay down a working rule by which readily to determine when a business has become "clothed with a public interest." All business is subject to some kinds of public regulation; but when the public becomes so peculiarly dependent upon a particular business that one engaging therein subjects himself to a more intimate public regulation is only to be determined by the process of exclusion and inclusion and to gradual establishment of a line of distinction. We are relieved from considering and deciding definitely whether preparation of food should be put in the third class of quasi-public businesses, noted above, because even so, the valid regulation to which it might be subjected as such, could not include what this act attempts.

To say that a business is clothed with a public interest, is not to determine what regulation may be permissible in view of the private rights of the owner. The extent to which an inn or a cab system may be regulated may differ widely from that allowable as to a railroad or other common carrier. It is not a matter of legislative discretion solely. It depends on the nature of the business, on the feature which touches the public, and on the abuses reasonably to be feared. To say that a business is clothed with a public interest is not to import that the public may take over its entire management and run it at the expense of the owner. The extent to which regulation may reasonably go varies with different kinds of business. The regulation of rates to avoid monopoly is one thing. The regulation of wages is another. A business may be of such character that only the first is permissible, while another may involve such a possible danger of monopoly on the one hand, and such disaster from stoppage on the other, that both come within the public concern and power of regulation.

If, as, in effect, contended by counsel for the State, the common callings are clothed with a public interest by a mere legislative declaration, which necessarily authorizes full and comprehensive regulation within legislative discretion, there must be a revolution in the relation of government to general business. . . . It will be impossible to reconcile such result with the freedom of contract and of labor secured by the Fourteenth Amendment. . . .

. . . . .

We think the Industrial Court Act, in so far as it permits the fixing of wages in plaintiff in error's packing house, is in conflict with the Fourteenth Amendment and deprives it of its property and liberty of contract without due process of law.

NEBBIA v. NEW YORK
291 U.S. 502 (1934)

Mr. Justice ROBERTS delivered the opinion of the Court.

The Legislature of New York established by chapter 158 of the Laws of 1933, a Milk Control Board with power, among other things, to "fix . . . minimum and maximum . . . retail prices to be charged by . . . stores to consumers for consumption off the premises where sold." Agriculture and Markets Law N. Y. (Consol. Laws, c. 69) § 312. The board fixed nine cents as the price to be charged by a store for a quart of milk. Nebbia, the proprietor of a grocery store in Rochester, sold two quarts and a 5-cent loaf of bread for 18 cents; and was convicted for violating the board's order. At his trial he asserted the statute and order contravene the equal protection clause and the due process clause of the Fourteenth Amendment, and renewed the contention in successive appeals to the county court and the Court of Appeals. Both overruled his claim and affirmed the conviction.

The question for decision is whether the Federal Constitution prohibits a state from so fixing the selling price of milk. We first inquire as to the occasion for the legislation and its history.

During 1932 the prices received by farmers for milk were much below the cost of production. The decline in prices during 1931 and 1932 was much greater than that of prices generally. The situation of the families of dairy producers had become desperate and called for state aid similar to that afforded the unemployed, if conditions should not improve.

On March 10, 1932, the senate and assembly resolved, "That a joint Legislative committee is hereby created . . . to investigate the causes of the decline of the price of milk to producers and the resultant effect of the low prices upon the dairy industry and the future supply of milk to the cities of the State; to investigate the cost of distribution of milk and its relation to prices paid to milk producers, to the end that the consumer may be assured of an adequate supply of milk at a reasonable price, both to producer and consumer." . . .

In part those conclusions [of the Committee] are:

. . . . . .

The fluid milk industry is affected by factors of instability peculiar to itself which call for special methods of control. Under the best practicable adjustment of supply to demand the industry must carry a surplus of about 20 per cent, because milk, an essential food, must be available as demanded by consumers every day in the year, and demand and supply vary from day to day and according to the season; but milk is perishable and cannot be stored. Close adjustment of supply to demand is hindered by several factors difficult to control. Thus surplus milk presents a serious problem, as the prices which can be realized for it are much less than those obtainable for milk sold for consumption in fluid form or as cream. A satisfactory stabilization of prices for fluid milk requires that the burden of surplus milk be shared equally by all producers and all distributors in the milk-shed. So long as the surplus burden is unequally distributed the pressure to market surplus milk in fluid form will be a serious disturbing factor. The fact that the larger distributors find it necessary to carry large quantities of surplus milk, while the smaller distributors do not, leads to price-cutting and other forms of destructive competition. Smaller distributors, who take no responsibility for the surplus, by purchasing their milk at the blended prices (i.e., an average between the price paid the producer for milk for sale as fluid milk, and the lower surplus milk price paid by the larger organizations) can undersell the larger distributors. Indulgence in this price-cutting often compels the larger dealer to cut the price to his own and the producer's detriment. . . .

The Legislature adopted chapter 158 as a method of correcting the evils, which the report of the committee showed could not be expected to right themselves through the ordinary play of the forces of supply and demand, owing to the peculiar and uncontrollable factors affecting the industry. . . .

Section 312 (3) on which the prosecution in the present case is founded, provides: "After the board shall have fixed prices to be charged or paid for milk in any form ... it shall be unlawful for a milk dealer to sell or buy or offer to sell or buy milk at any price less or more than such price, ... and no method or device shall be lawful whereby milk is bought or sold ... at a price less or more than such price ... whether by any discount, or rebate, or free service, or advertising allowance, or a combined price for such milk together with another commodity or commodities, or service or services, which is less or more than the aggregate of the prices for the milk and the price or prices for such other commodity or commodities, or service or services, when sold or offered for sale separately or otherwise. . . ."

Second. The more serious question is whether in the light of the conditions disclosed, the enforcement of section 312 (3) denied the appellant the due process secured to him by the Fourteenth Amendment.

The milk industry in New York has been the subject of long-standing and drastic regulation in the public interest. The legislative investigation of 1932 was persuasive of the fact that for this and other reasons unrestricted competition aggravated existing evils and the normal law of supply and demand was insufficient to correct maladjustments detrimental to the community. The inquiry disclosed destructive and demoralizing competitive conditions and unfair trade practices which resulted in retail price cutting and reduced the income of the farmer below the cost of production. ... In the light of the facts the order [of the Milk Control Board] appears not to be unreasonable or arbitrary, or without relation to the purpose to prevent ruthless competition from destroying the wholesale price structure on which the farmer depends for his livelihood, and the community for an assured supply of milk.

But we are told that because the law essays to control prices it denies due process. Notwithstanding the admitted power to correct existing economic ills by appropriate regulation of business, even though an indirect result may be a restriction of the freedom of contract or a modification of charges for services or the price of commodities, the appellant urges that direct fixation of prices is a type of regulation absolutely forbidden. His position is that the Fourteenth Amendment requires us to hold the challenged statute void for this reason alone. The argument runs that the public control of rates or prices is *per se* unreasonable and unconstitutional, save as applied to businesses affected with a public interest; that a business so affected is one in which property is devoted to an enterprise of a sort which the public itself might appropriately undertake, or one whose owner relies on a public grant or franchise for the right to conduct the business, or in which he is bound to serve all who apply; in short, such as is commonly called a public utility; or a business in its nature a monopoly. The milk industry, it is said, possesses none of these characteristics, and, therefore, not being affected with a public interest, its charges may not be controlled by the state. Upon the soundness of this contention the appellant's case against the statute depends.

We may as well say at once that the dairy industry is not, in the accepted sense of the phrase, a public utility. We think the appellant is also right in asserting that there is in this case no suggestion of any monopoly or monopolistic practice. It goes without saying that those engaged in the business are in no way dependent upon public grants or franchises for the privilege of conducting their activities. But if, as must be conceded, the industry is subject to regulation in the public interest, what constitutional principle bars the state from correcting existing maladjustments by legislation touching prices? We think there is no such principle. The due process clause makes no mention of sales or of prices any more than it speaks of business or contracts or buildings or other incidents of property. The thought seems nevertheless to have persisted that there is something peculiarly sacrosanct about the price one may charge for what he makes or sells, and that, however able to regulate other elements of manufacture or trade, with incidental effect upon price, the state is incapable of directly controlling the price itself. This view was negatived many years ago. *Munn* v. *Illinois,* 94 U.S. 113.

.   .   .   .   .

The touchstone of public interest in any business, its practices and charges, clearly is not the enjoyment of any franchise from the state, *Munn* v. *Illinois, supra.* . . .

Many other decisions show that the private character of a business does not necessarily remove it from the realm of regulation of charges or prices. . . .

It is clear that there is no closed class or category of businesses affected with a public interest, and the function of courts in the application of the Fifth and Fourteenth Amendments is to determine in each case whether circumstances vindicate the challenged regulation as a reasonable exertion of governmental authority or condemn it as arbitrary or discriminatory. *Wolff Packing Co.* v. *Court of Industrial Relations,* 262 U.S. 522, 535. The phrase "affected with a public interest" can, in the nature of things, mean no more than that an industry, for adequate reason, is subject to control for the public good. In several of the decisions of this Court wherein the expressions "affected with a public interest," and "clothed with a public use," have been brought forward as the criteria of the validity of price control, it has been admitted that they are not susceptible of definition and form an unsatisfactory test of the constitutionality of legislation directed at business practices or prices. These decisions must rest, finally, upon the basis that the requirements of due process were not met because the laws were found arbitrary in their operation and effect. But there can be no doubt that upon proper occasion and by appropriate measures the state may regulate a business in any of its aspects, including the prices to be charged for the products or commodities it sells.

So far as the requirement of due process is concerned, and in the absence of other constitutional restriction, a state is free to adopt whatever economic policy may reasonably be deemed to promote public welfare, and to enforce that policy by legislation adapted to its purpose. The courts are without authority either to declare such policy, or, when it is declared by the legislative arm, to override it. . . . Times without number we have said that the legislature is primarily the judge of the necessity of such an enactment, that every possible presumption is in favor of its validity, and that though the Court may hold views inconsistent with the wisdom of the law, it may not be annulled unless palpably in excess of legislative power.

The lawmaking bodies have in the past endeavored to promote free competition by laws aimed at trusts and monopolies. The consequent interference with private property and freedom of contract has not availed with the courts to set these enactments aside as denying due process. Where the public interest was deemed to require the fixing of minimum prices, that expedient has been sustained. If the lawmaking body within its sphere of government concludes that the conditions or practices in an industry make unrestricted competition an inadequate safeguard of the consumer's interest, produce waste harmful to the public, threaten ultimately to cut off the supply of a commodity needed by the public, or portend the destruction of the industry itself, appropriate statutes passed in an honest effort to correct the threatened consequences may not be set aside because the regulation adopted fixes prices reasonably deemed by the Legislature to be fair to those engaged in the industry and to the consuming public. And this is especially so where, as here, the economic maladjustment is one of price, which threatens harm to the producer at one end of the series and the consumer at the other. The Constitution does not secure to any one liberty to conduct his business in such fashion as to inflict injury upon the public at large, or upon any substantial group of the people. Price control, like any other form of regulation, is unconstitutional only if arbitrary, discriminatory, or demonstrably irrelevant to the policy the legislature is free to adopt, and hence an unnecessary and unwarranted interference with individual liberty.

Tested by these considerations we find no basis in the due process clause of the Fourteenth Amendment for condemning the provision of the Agriculture and Markets Law here drawn into question.

The judgment is affirmed.

Separate opinion of Mr. Justice MCREYNOLDS.

The statement by the court below that, "Doubtless the statute before us would be condemned by an earlier generation as a temerarious interference with the rights of property and contract . . . with the natural law of supply and demand," is obviously correct. But another, that "statutes aiming to . . . stimulate the production of a vital food product by fixing living standards of prices for the producer, are to be interpreted with that degree of liberality which is essential to the attainment of the end in view," conflicts with views of constitutional rights accepted since the beginning. An end although apparently desirable cannot justify inhibited means. . . .

The somewhat misty suggestion below that condemnation of the challenged legislation would amount to holding "that the due process clause has left milk producers unprotected from oppression,"

I assume, was not intended as a material contribution to the discussion upon the merits of the cause. Grave concern for embarrassed farmers is everywhere; but this should neither obscure the rights of others nor obstruct judicial appraisement of measures proposed for relief. The ultimate welfare of the producer, like that of every other class, requires dominance of the Constitution. And zealously to uphold this in all its parts is the highest duty intrusted to the courts.

The judgment of the court below should be reversed.

Mr. Justice VAN DEVANTER, Mr. Justice SUTHERLAND, and Mr. Justice BUTLER authorize me to say that they concur in this opinion.

————————⌣————————
*

The Fourteenth Amendment:
Due Process in Procedure

1. DUE PROCESS IN LAW ENFORCEMENT

TUMEY v. OHIO
273 U.S. 510 (1927)

Mr. Chief Justice TAFT delivered the opinion of the Court.

The question in this case is whether certain statutes of Ohio, in providing for the trial by the mayor of a village of one accused of violating the Prohibition Act of the state deprive the accused of due process of law and violate the Fourteenth Amendment to the Federal Constitution, because of the pecuniary and other interest which those statutes give the mayor in the result of the trial.

Tumey, the plaintiff in error hereafter to be called the defendant, was arrested and brought before Mayor Pugh, of the village of North College Hill, charged with unlawfully possessing intoxicating liquor. He moved for his dismissal because of the disqualification of the mayor to try him under the Fourteenth Amendment. The mayor denied the motion, proceeded to trial, convicted the defendant of unlawfully possessing intoxicating liquor within Hamilton County as charged, fined him $100, and ordered that he be imprisoned until the fine and costs were paid. He [Tumey] . . . carried the case to the court of common pleas of Hamilton County. That court heard the case and reversed the judgment, on the ground that the mayor was disqualified as claimed. . . . [The next higher state court then reversed the county court and affirmed the mayor's judgment. The state supreme court upheld that decision.]

. . . . .

The fees which the mayor and marshal received in this case came to them by virtue of the general statutes of the state applying to all state cases, liquor and otherwise. General Code Ohio, § 4270; ... Moreover, the North College Hill village council sought to remove all doubt on this point by providing ... that he [the mayor] should receive or retain the amount of his costs in each case in addition to his regular salary, as compensation for hearing such cases. But no fees or costs in such cases are paid him, except by the defendant, if convicted. There is, therefore, no way by which the mayor may be paid for his service as a judge, if he does not convict those who are brought before him; nor is there any fund from which marshals, inspectors and detectives can be paid for their services in arresting and bringing to trial and furnishing the evidence to convict in such cases, except it be from the initial $500 which the village may vote from its treasury to set the court going or from a fund created by the fines thereafter collected from convicted defendants. . . .

. . . . .

Between May 11, 1923, and December 31, 1923, the total amount of fines for violation of the prohibition law collected by this village court was upwards of $20,000, from which the state received $8,992.50, North College Hill received $4,471.25 for its general uses, $2,697.25 was placed to the credit of the village safety fund, and the balance was put in the secret service fund. Out of this, the person acting as prosecutor in the liquor court received in that period $1,796.50; the deputy marshals, inspectors and other employees, including the detectives, received $2,697.75; and $438.50 was paid for costs in transporting prisoners, serving writs and other services in connection with the trial of these cases. Mayor Pugh received $696.35 from these liquor cases during that period as his fees and costs, in addition to his regular salary.

That officers acting in a judicial or quasi-judicial capacity are disqualified by their interest in the controversy to be decided is of course the general rule. . . .

All questions of judicial qualification may not involve constitutional validity. Thus matters of kinship, personal bias, state policy, remoteness of interest would seem generally to be matters of mere legislative discretion.[1]... But it certainly violates the Fourteenth Amendment and deprives a defendant in a criminal case of due process of law to subject his liberty or property to the judgment of a court, the judge of which has a direct, personal, substantial pecuniary interest in reaching a conclusion against him in his case.

The mayor of the village of North College Hill, Ohio, had a direct personal pecuniary interest in convicting the defendant who came before him for trial, in the $12 costs imposed in his behalf, which he would not have received if the defendant had been acquitted. . . . Counsel contend that in Ohio and in other states, in the economy which it is found necessary to maintain in the administration of justice in the inferior courts by justices of the peace and by judicial officers of like jurisdiction, the only compensation which the state and the county and township can afford is the fees and costs earned by them, and that such compensation is so small that it is not to be regarded as likely to influence improperly a judicial officer in the discharge of his duty, or as prejudicing the defendant in securing justice, even though the magistrate will receive nothing if the defendant is not convicted.

We have been referred to no cases at common law in England, prior to the separation of the colonies from the mother country, showing a practice that inferior judicial officers were dependent upon their conviction of the defendant for receiving their compensation. Indeed, in analogous cases it is very clear that the slightest pecuniary interest of any officer, judicial or quasi-judicial, in the resolving of the subject-matter which he was to decide, rendered the decision voidable. . . .

[1] The law and practice of judicial disqualification are exhaustively surveyed in an article by John P. Frank in 56 *Yale Law Journal* 605 (1947). There are no statutes controlling disqualification of Supreme Court justices though they have increasingly inclined to withdraw from any case where their participation might be subject to criticism. Thus, while Justices Field and Curtis heard argument by their own brothers, Chief Justice Stone would remain in a case argued by his son (who had been assigned as one of counsel to defend the German saboteurs in *Ex parte Quirin,* 317 U.S. 1) only at the insistence of the parties. The tendency among the justices of the Supreme Court appears to be in the direction of more rather than less reluctance to participate in dubious instances. Note that justices do not, as a rule, assign reasons for their withdrawal from a case and that their decision to take part or to retire from a case is entirely within their discretion.

[The Court reviewed at length English and American state cases on the subject.]

.   .   .   .   .

From this review we conclude that a system by which an inferior judge is paid for his service only when he convicts the defendant has not become so embedded by custom in the general practice, either at common law or in this country, that it can be regarded as due process of law, unless the costs are so small that they may be properly ignored as within the maxim *de minimis non curat lex.*[2]

.   .   .   .   .

These are not cases in which the penalties and the costs are negligible. . . . There are doubtless mayors who would not allow such a consideration as $12 costs in each case to affect their judgment in it, but the requirement of due process of law in judicial procedure is not satisfied by the argument that men of highest honor and the greatest self-sacrifice could carry it on without danger of injustice. Every procedure which would offer a possible temptation to the average man as a judge to forget the burden of proof required to convict the defendant, or which might lead him not to hold the balance nice, clear, and true between the state and the accused denies the latter due process of law.

[The Court notes that the pecuniary interest of the entire village in these prosecutions places the mayor, as an elective official responsible to the villagers, in a position where a defendant might be doubly fearful that a fair trial could not be had.]

.   .   .   .   .

It is finally argued that the evidence shows clearly that the defendant was guilty and that he was only fined $100 which was the minimum amount, and therefore that he cannot complain of a lack of due process, either in his conviction or in the amount of the judgment. The plea was not guilty and he was convicted. No matter what the evidence was against him, he had the right to have an impartial judge. He seasonably raised the objection, and was entitled to halt the trial because of the disqualification of the judge, which existed both because of his direct pecuniary interest in the out-

[2] Freely translatable as "the law doesn't bother with trifles."

come, and because of his official motive to convict and to graduate the fine to help the financial needs of the village. There were thus presented at the outset both features of the disqualification.

The judgment of the Supreme Court of Ohio must be reversed, and the cause remanded for further proceedings not inconsistent with this opinion.

Judgment reversed.

POWELL v. ALABAMA[3]
287 U.S. 45 (1932)

Mr. Justice SUTHERLAND delivered the opinion of the Court.

These cases [including *Patterson* v. *Alabama* and *Weems* v. *Alabama*] were argued together and submitted for decision as one case.

The petitioners, hereinafter referred to as defendants, are negroes charged with the crime of rape, committed upon the persons of two white girls. The crime is said to have been committed on March 25, 1931. The indictment was returned in a state court of first instance on March 31, and the record recites that on the same day the defendants were arraigned and entered pleas of not guilty. There is a further recital to the effect that upon the arraignment they were represented by counsel. But no counsel had been employed, and aside from a statement made by the trial judge several days later during a colloquy immediately preceding the trial, the record does not disclose when, or under what circumstances, an appointment of counsel was made, or who was appointed. During the colloquy referred to, the trial judge, in response to a question, said that he had appointed all the members of the bar for the purpose of arraigning the defendants and then of course anticipated that the members of the bar would continue to help the defendants if no counsel appeared. Upon the argument here both sides accepted that as a correct statement of the facts concerning the matter.

There was a severance upon the request of the state, and the defendants were tried in three several groups, as indicated above. As each of the three cases was called for trial, each defendant was arraigned, and, having the indictment read to him, entered a plea of not guilty. Whether the original arraignment and pleas were

[3] This is known as the "First Scottsboro Case," one of a series of notorious cases which did much to focus national attention on the status of the racial minorities. The pathetic story of one of the "boys" in this trial has recently been published (Patterson, *Scottsboro Boy*).

regarded as ineffective is not shown. Each of the three trials was completed within a single day. Under the Alabama statute the punishment for rape is to be fixed by the jury, and in its discretion may be from ten years imprisonment to death. The juries found defendants guilty and imposed the death penalty upon all. The trial court overruled motions for new trials and sentenced the defendants in accordance with the verdicts. The judgments were affirmed by the state supreme court. Chief Justice Anderson thought the defendants had not been accorded a fair trial and strongly dissented. . . .

In this Court the judgments are assailed upon the grounds that the defendants, and each of them, were denied due process of law and the equal protection of the laws, in contravention of the Fourteenth Amendment, specifically as follows: (1) They were not given a fair, impartial, and deliberate trial; (2) they were denied the right of counsel, with the accustomed incidents of consultation and opportunity of preparation for trial; and (3) they were tried before juries from which qualified members of their own race were systematically excluded. These questions were properly raised and saved in the courts below.

The only one of the asignments which we shall consider is the second, in respect of the denial of counsel; and it becomes unnecessary to discuss the facts of the case or the circumstances surrounding the prosecution except in so far as they reflect light upon that question.

The record shows that on the day when the offense is said to have been committed these defendants, together with a number of other negroes, were upon a freight train on its way through Alabama. On the same train were seven white boys and the two white girls. A fight took place between the negroes and the white boys, in the course of which the white boys, with the exception of one named Gilley, were thrown off the train. A message was sent ahead, reporting the fight and asking that every negro be gotten off the train. The participants of the fight, and the two girls were in an open gondola car. The two girls testified that each of them was assaulted by six different negroes in turn, and they identified the seven defendants as having been among the number. None of the white boys was called to testify, with the exception of Gilley, who was called in rebuttal.

Before the train reached Scottsboro, Alabama, a sheriff's posse seized the defendants and two other negroes. Both girls and the negroes then were taken to Scottsboro, the county seat. Word of their coming and of the alleged assault had preceded them, and they were met at Scottsboro by a large crowd. It does not sufficiently appear that the defendants were seriously threatened with, or that they were actually in danger of, mob violence; but it does appear that the attitude of the community was one of great hostility. The sheriff thought it necessary to call for the militia to assist in safe-guarding the prisoners. Chief Justice Anderson pointed out in his opinion that every step taken from the arrest and arraignment to the sentence was accompanied by the military. Soldiers took the defendants to Gadsden for safekeeping, brought them back to Scottsboro for arraignment, returned them to Gadsden for safe-keeping while awaiting trial, escorted them to Scottsboro for trial a few days later, and guarded the courthouse and grounds at every stage of the proceedings. It is perfectly apparent that the proceed-ings, from the beginning to end, took place in an atmosphere of tense, hostile, and excited public sentiment. During the entire time, the defendants were closely confined or were under military guard. The record does not disclose their ages, except that one of them was nineteen; but the record clearly indicates that most, if not all, of them were youthful, and they are constantly referred to as "the boys." They were ignorant and illiterate. All of them were residents of other states, where alone members of their families or friends resided.

However guilty defendants, upon due inquiry, might prove to have been, they were, until convicted, presumed to be innocent. It was the duty of the court having their cases in charge to see that they were denied no necessary incident of a fair trial. . . .

First. The record shows that immediately upon the return of the indictment defendants were arraigned and pleaded not guilty. Ap-parently they were not asked whether they had, or were able to employ, counsel, or wished to have counsel appointed; or whether they had friends or relatives who might assist in that regard if com-municated with. That it would not have been an idle ceremony to have given the defendants reasonable opportunity to communicate with their families and endeavor to obtain counsel is demonstrated by the fact that very soon after conviction, able counsel appeared in their behalf. . . .

It is hardly necessary to say that the right to counsel being conceded, a defendant should be afforded a fair opportunity to secure counsel of his own choice. Not only was that not done here, but such designation of counsel as was attempted was either so indefinite or so close upon the trial as to amount to a denial of effective and substantial aid in that regard. . . .

Second. The Constitution of Alabama (Const. 1901, § 6) provides that in all criminal prosecutions the accused shall enjoy the right to have the assistance of counsel; and a state statute (Code 1923, § 5567) requires the court in a capital case, where the defendant is unable to employ counsel, to appoint counsel for him. The state Supreme Court held that these provisions had not been infringed, and with that holding we are powerless to interfere. The question, however, which it is our duty, and within our power, to decide, is whether the denial of the assistance of counsel contravenes the due process clause of the Fourteenth Amendment to the Federal Constitution.

[The Court here surveys the extent to which a defendant charged with a felony had a right to the aid of counsel at common law in England and in the colonies at the time of the adoption of their constitutions.]

.   .   .   .   .

It never has been doubted by this Court, or any other so far as we know, that notice and hearing are preliminary steps essential to the passing of an enforceable judgment, and that they, together with a legally competent tribunal having jurisdiction of the case, constitute basic elements of the constitutional requirement of due process of law. . . .

What, then, does a hearing include? Historically and in practice, in our own country at least, it has always included the right to the aid of counsel when desired and provided by the party asserting the right. The right to be heard would be, in many cases, of little avail if it did not comprehend the right to be heard by counsel. Even the intelligent and educated layman has small and sometimes no skill in the science of law. If charged with crime, he is incapable, generally, of determining for himself whether the indictment is good or bad. He is unfamiliar with the rules of evidence. Left without the aid of counsel he may be put on trial without a proper charge, and convicted upon incompetent evidence, or evidence irrelevant to the issue or otherwise inadmissible. He lacks both the skill and knowledge adequately to prepare his defense, even though he have a perfect one. He requires the guiding hand of counsel at every step in the proceedings against him. Without it, though he be not guilty, he faces the danger of conviction because he does not know how to establish his innocence. If that be true of men of intelligence, how much more true is it of the ignorant and illiterate, or those of feeble intellect. If in any case, civil or criminal, a state or federal court were arbitrarily to refuse to hear a party by counsel, employed by and appearing for him, it reasonably may not be doubted that such a refusal would be a denial of a hearing, and, therefore, of due process in the constitutional sense. . . .

In the light of the facts outlined in the forepart of this opinion— the ignorance and illiteracy of the defendants, their youth, the circumstances of public hostility, the imprisonment and the close surveillance of the defendants by the military forces, the fact that their friends and families were all in other states and communication with them necessarily difficult, and above all that they stood in deadly peril of their lives—we think the failure of the trial court to give them reasonable time and opportunity to secure counsel was a clear denial of due process.

But passing that, and assuming their inability, even if opportunity had been given, to employ counsel, as the trial court evidently did assume, we are of opinion that, under the circumstances just stated, the necessity of counsel was so vital and imperative that the failure of the trial court to make an effective appointment of counsel was likewise a denial of due process within the meaning of the Fourteenth Amendment. Whether this would be so in other criminal prosecutions, or under other circumstances, we need not determine. All that it is necessary now to decide, as we do decide, is that in a capital case, where the defendant is unable to employ counsel, and is incapable adequately of making his own defense because of ignorance, feeble-mindedness, illiteracy, or the like, it is the duty of the court, whether requested or not, to assign counsel for him as a necessary requisite of due process of law; and that duty is not discharged by an assignment at such a time or under such circumstances as to preclude the giving of effective aid in the preparation and trial of the case. To hold otherwise would be to ignore the fundamental postulate, already adverted to, "that there are certain immutable principles of justice which inhere in the very idea of free government which no member of the Union may disregard." *Holden* v. *Hardy*

[169 U.S. 366]. In a case such as this, whatever may be the rule in other cases, the right to have counsel appointed, when necessary, is a logical corollary from the constitutional right to be heard by counsel. . . .

The judgments must be reversed and the causes remanded for further proceedings not inconsistent with this opinion.

Judgments reversed.

Mr. Justice BUTLER, dissenting.

The Court, putting aside—they are utterly without merit—all other claims that the constitutional rights of petitioners were infringed, grounds its opinion and judgment upon a single assertion of fact. It is that petitioners "were denied the right of counsel, with the accustomed incidents of consultation and opportunity of preparation for trial." If that is true, they were denied due process of law and are entitled to have the judgments against them reversed.

But no such denial is shown by the record. . . .

The record wholly fails to reveal that petitioners have been deprived of any right guaranteed by the Federal Constitution, and I am of opinion that the judgment should be affirmed.

Mr. Justice McREYNOLDS concurs in this opinion.

BUTE v. ILLINOIS
333 U.S. 640 (1948)

Mr. Justice BURTON delivered the opinion of the Court.

In the Circuit Court of La Salle County, Illinois, the petitioner, Roy Bute, pleaded guilty to the crime of "taking indecent liberties with children" as charged in each of two indictments and, on each plea, was sentenced to confinement in the Illinois State Penitentiary for not less than one nor more than 20 years, the sentences to run consecutively. Each . . . record is silent on the subject of counsel for the petitioner's defense. The issue here is whether or not each state sentence shall be held to have been imposed in violation of the due process clause of the Fourteenth Amendment to the Constitution of the United States because each . . . record shows that the petitioner appeared "in his proper person" and does not show that the court inquired as to the petitioner's desire to be represented by counsel, or his ability to procure counsel, or his desire to have counsel assigned to him to assist him in his defense, or that such counsel was offered or assigned to him. We hold that such a silence in the respective records does not suffice to invalidate the sentences. We hold further that, in the absence of any showing beyond that in these records, the due process clause of the Fourteenth Amendment did not require the Illinois court to make the inquiries or the offer or assignment of counsel now claimed to have been the right of the petitioner.

. . . . .

The cases turn upon the meaning of "due process of law" under the Fourteenth Amendment in relation to the assistance of counsel for the defense of the accused in state criminal trials such as these. In *Powell* v. *Alabama,* 287 U.S. 45 (1932), this Court granted relief in a group of capital cases which demonstrated the essential need for applying the full force of the Fourteenth Amendment to the invalidation of purportedly valid judgments rendered in a state court under the circumstances there shown. These and other less extreme cases have well illustrated the kind of service to the cause of justice which can be rendered by the Court in thus giving effect to the Fourteenth Amendment.

. . . . .

The present case, on the other hand, illustrates equally well the kind of judgments by a state court that should not be invalidated as lacking in the due process of law required by the Fourteenth Amendment. This is so, although the procedure followed, in 1938, by the state court in the instant cases, as to counsel for the accused might not have satisfied the practice then required of a federal court in the case of comparable federal crimes. The Fourteenth Amendment, however, does not say that no state shall deprive any person of liberty without following the *federal* process of law as prescribed for the federal courts in comparable federal cases. It says merely "nor shall any state deprive any person of life, liberty, or property, without due process of law; . . ." This *due* process is not an equivalent for the process of the federal courts or for the process of any particular state. It has reference rather to a standard of process that may cover many varieties of processes that are expressive of differing combinations of historical or modern, local or other juridical standards, provided they do not conflict with the "fundamental principles of liberty and justice which lie at the base of all our civil and political institutions. . . ." *Hebert* v. *Louisiana,* 272 U.S. 312, 316. This clause in the Fourteenth Amendment leaves room for much of the freedom which, under the Constitution of the United States and in accordance with its purposes, was originally reserved to the states for their exercise of their own police powers and for their control over the procedure to be followed in criminal trials in their respective courts. It recognizes that differences arise naturally between the procedures in the state courts and those in the federal courts.

.   .   .   .   .

Until the taking effect of the Fourteenth Amendment in 1868, there was no question but that the states were free to establish their own court procedures. This freedom included state practice as to the assistance of counsel to be permitted or assigned to the accused for his defense in state criminal cases. Because the Constitution of the United States, during nearly 80 formative years, thus permitted each state to establish, maintain and accustom its people to that state's own forms of "due process of law," a substantial presumption arises in favor of, rather than against, the lawfulness of those procedures and in favor of their right to continued recognition by the federal government as "due process of law." While such a presumption does not arise in favor of any practice against which the Fourteenth Amendment was particularly directed, there is no reason to feel that, in 1868, such Amendment was particularly directed against the practice now before us.

.   .   .   .   .

After exhaustive consideration of the subject, this Court has decided that the Fourteenth Amendment does not, through its due process clause or otherwise, have the effect of requiring the several states to conform the procedure of their state criminal trials to the precise procedure of the federal courts, even to the extent that the procedure of the federal courts is prescribed by the federal Constitution or Bill of Rights. There is nothing in the Fourteenth Amendment specifically stating that the long recognized and then existing power of the states over the procedure of their own courts in criminal cases was to be prohibited or even limited. . . .

. . . We recognize that the Fourteenth Amendment, as part of the supreme law of the land under Article 6 of the original Constitution, supersedes "any Thing in the Constitution or Laws of any State to the Contrary notwithstanding." The important question remains, however: what shall be considered to be contrary? It is the established policy of both the state and federal governments to treat possible conflicts between their powers in such a manner as to produce as little conflict and friction as possible. So here the procedure followed by Illinois should not be held to violate the standard of permissible process of law broadly recognized by the Fourteenth Amendment unless the Illinois procedure violates "the very essence of a scheme of ordered liberty" and that to continue it would "violate 'a principle of justice so rooted in the tradition and conscience of our people as to be ranked as fundamental.' " Cardozo, J., in *Palko* v. *Connecticut*, 302 U.S. 319, 325, with quotation from his opinion in *Snyder* v. *Massachusetts*, 291 U.S. 97, 105. . . .

It is natural for state procedures to differ from each other in many ways. It is permissible for the states to establish ways of safeguarding the respective interests of the prosecution and of the accused in their courts. These may differ from comparable practices developed in the courts of other states or of the United States. . . .

. . . The states are free to determine their own practice as to the assistance of counsel, subject to the general limitation that such practice shall not deprive the accused of life, liberty, or property without due process of law. Accordingly, the lack of conformity of Illinois practice to the standards illustrated by the present Federal Rules of Criminal Procedure is by no means determinative of the issue before us.

As throwing light on the general practice in the several states, the National Commission on Law Observance and Enforcement, under the chairmanship of George W. Wickersham, in its Report on Prosecution, in 1931, said:

"In America counsel was allowed from an early date and state and federal Constitutions guarantee to accused in all prosecutions 'the assistance of counsel for his defense,' in this or some equivalent language. It will be seen from this bit of history that, as indeed the courts have held, the right guaranteed is one of employing counsel, not one of having counsel provided by the government. But in the spirit of the guaranty most of the states have by legislation authorized or even required the courts to assign counsel for the defense of indigent and unrepresented prisoners. As to capital cases, all the states so provide. Thirty-four states so provide for felonies and 28 for misdemeanors." Vol. I, p. 30.

The foregoing suggests the existence of a gradual voluntary trend

among the states toward the authorization by them of the appointment of counsel to assist the accused in his defense in all criminal
prosecutions, with special consideration to the seriousness of the
charge faced and to the actual needs of the accused under the circumstances of each case. Much of this trend has taken place since 1868.
It is neither universal nor uniform. The above summary shows that
20 states, in 1931, had no statute authorizing such appointments of
counsel in misdemeanor cases and 14 had none, even in felony cases,
unless the charges were for capital offenses. Furthermore, some of
the authorizations, as in Illinois, were subject to special limitations
requiring an affirmative showing to be made by the accused of his
inability to procure counsel for himself.

. . . .

It is not our province to prescribe which procedure we consider
preferable among many permissible procedures which lawfully could
be followed by an Illinois or any other state court in connection with
counsel for the defense of a party accused of a state crime. It is our
province to decide whether the practice of the Illinois court in these
cases, although admittedly in conformity with the law of Illinois, was
so clearly at variance with procedure constituting "due process of
law" under the Fourteenth Amendment that these sentences must
be completely invalidated. This brings us to an analysis of the precise facts presented by the records. Each crime was punishable by a
mandatory sentence of from one to 20 years in the penitentiary. The
charges were stated in simple terms, not ordinarily capable of being
misunderstood by a 57-year-old man,[4] however elementary or primitive his understanding. There is no claim that this petitioner failed
to understand the charges. Before he pleaded guilty, the court "admonished and explained to the said defendant the consequences and
penalties, . . ." which would result from his plea of guilty if made.
The records then recite, largely in the language of the statute, that
"the said defendant still persisted in his desire to enter his plea of
guilty to the crime of taking indecent liberties with children, in
manner and form as charged in the first count of the indictment
herein, the court grants such leave." We do not accept the argument
that these records are to be considered unreliable because they are
almost exactly in the language of the statute. The important point is

[4] Age and other circumstances of the appellant had been previously stated in a passage
of the opinion not here reproduced.

not so much that a certain phraseology is used, as it is that the court actually represented the state at the trial and that the court did what the statute required of it. It cannot be argued, without factual support, that the court failed to do its full duty with an intelligent, competent and understanding appreciation of all its state and federal obligations. In the light of all the circumstances which must have been obvious to the judge presiding in the courtroom, but are incapable of reproduction here, the court granted leave to the petitioner to enter his plea of guilty in each case. Before sentence was passed, the record shows that the state's attorney and the petitioner, in his own proper person, came before the court and the petitioner "not saying anything further why the judgment of the court should not now be pronounced . . ." the court pronounced, in each case, the mandatory sentence for the crime to which the petitioner had pleaded guilty. On the facts thus before us in these records, which must be our sole guides in these cases, there is no good reason to doubt either the due process or the propriety of the procedure followed by the trial court. There is nothing in the records on which to base a claim that the petitioner's conduct did not fit the charges made against him. There is nothing in them on which to base a claim of abnormality, intoxication, prejudice or emotional influence affecting the conduct or thought of anyone connected with these trials. The presence of the judge, the state's attorney, and the petitioner, together with a natural wish on the part of the petitioner not to expand upon the shame of these crimes, provide no ground for a conclusion that there has been any failure, much less any constitutional failure, of fair judicial process. Doubts should be resolved in favor of the integrity, competence and proper performance of their official duties by the judge and the state's attorney. They were state officials lawfully chosen to discharge serious responsibilities under their oaths of office. Especially in a self-governing state and nation, governmental stability depends upon the giving of full faith and credit in form, substance and spirit to public acts, records and judicial proceedings not only among the states but among individuals and between their state and federal governments.

Although the records disclose no affirmative bases for invalidating the sentences, it is suggested that an error of omission appears in the failure of the records to show either the presence of counsel for the accused, or an inquiry by the court as to counsel for the accused, or the appointment of counsel by the court to assist the accused. Here also if any presumption is to be indulged it should be one of regularity rather than irregularity. Eight years after the trial, in the complete absence of any showing to the contrary, such a presumption of regularity indicates that the court constitutionally discharged, rather than unconstitutionally disregarded, its state and federal duties to the petitioner, including those relating to his right, if any, to the assistance of counsel. . . . It is not necessary, however, for us to depend upon such a presumption.

. . . The state statute and practice . . . did not require that the accused must be so represented or that the trial court must initiate inquiry into the petitioner's desires. The statute did require that the court must assign counsel to conduct the defense for the accused if the accused stated under oath that he was unable to procure counsel. There is nothing in these records, however, either under oath or otherwise, to show that the petitioner, at the time of trial, either desired counsel or was unable to procure counsel.

The final question is therefore, whether, even in the absence of any state requirement to that effect, the provision requiring due process of law under the Fourteenth Amendment, in and of itself, required the court in these cases to initiate an inquiry into the desire of the accused to be represented by counsel, to inquire into the ability of the accused to procure counsel or, in the event of the inability of the accused to procure counsel, to assign competent counsel to the accused to conduct his defense. We recognize that, if these charges had been capital charges, the court would have been required, both by state statute and the decisions of this Court interpreting the Fourteenth Amendment, to take some such steps.

These, however, were not capital charges. They were charges of the commission of two elementary offenses, carrying mandatory sentences of from one to 20 years each. We have considered the special circumstances as shown by these records. We do not find in them adequate ground for concluding that the state court, by failing to take the affirmative procedure suggested, violated due process of law under the Fourteenth Amendment. . . .

. . . This Court repeatedly has held that failure to appoint counsel to assist a defendant or to give a fair opportunity to the defendant's counsel to assist him in his defense *where charged with a capital crime*[5] is a violation of due process of law under the Fourteenth Amendment. *Carter* v. *Illinois,* 329 U.S. 173 . . .; *Powell* v. *Alabama,* 287 U.S. 45. . . .

In a noncapital state felony case, this Court has recognized the constitutional right of the accused to the assistance of counsel for his defense *when there are special circumstances showing*[6] that, otherwise, the defendant would not enjoy that fair notice and adequate hearing which constitute the foundation of due process of law in the trial of any criminal charge. *Rice* v. *Olson,* 324 U.S. 786. . . .

For the foregoing reasons, and under the principles previously announced by the Court, the judgment of the Supreme Court of Illinois is affirmed.

Mr. Justice DOUGLAS, with whom Mr. Justice BLACK, Mr. Justice MURPHY and Mr. Justice RUTLEDGE concur, dissenting.

In considering cases like this and the ill-starred decision in *Betts* v. *Brady,* 316 U.S. 455 (1942), we should ask ourselves this question: Of what value is the constitutional guaranty of a fair trial if an accused does not have counsel to advise and defend him?

The Framers deemed the right of counsel indispensable, for they wrote into the Sixth Amendment that in all criminal prosecutions the accused "shall enjoy the right . . . to have the Assistance of Counsel for his defence." Hence, if this case had been tried in the federal court, appointment of counsel would have been mandatory, even though Bute did not request it. See *Johnson* v. *Zerbst,* 304 U.S. 458. I do not think the constitutional standards of fairness depend on what court an accused is in. I think that the Bill of Rights is applicable to all courts at all times. Mr. Justice Black demonstrated in his dissent in *Adamson* v. *California,* 332 U.S. 46, 68, 71, that a chief purpose of the Fourteenth Amendment was to protect the safeguards of the Bill of Rights against invasion by the states. If due process as defined in the Bill of Rights required appointment of counsel to represent defendants in federal prosecutions, due process demands that the same be done in state prosecutions. The basic requirements for fair trial are those which the Framers deemed so important to procedural due process that they wrote them into the Bill of Rights and thus made it impossible for either legislatures or courts to tinker with them. I fail to see why it is due process to deny an accused the benefit of counsel in a state court when by constitutional standards

[5] Italics added.
[6] Italics added.

that benefit could not be withheld from him in a federal court.

But if we take the view more hostile to the rights of the individual and assume that procedural due process guaranteed by the Fourteenth Amendment provides lesser safeguards than those of the Bill of Rights, the result should be the same. Then the question is whether the appointment of counsel for Bute was required "by natural, inherent, and fundamental principles of fairness." *Betts* v. *Brady, supra.*

Illinois allows counsel to everyone charged with crime. To obtain counsel, however, the accused has to ask for one and also state under oath that he is unable to procure counsel.... But, as held by the Illinois Supreme Court in the present case, the court need not advise him of his right to counsel. The Illinois rule apparently proceeds from the premise that the average person knows of his right to counsel and resorts to an attorney in case he gets caught in the toils of the law. That view, if logically applied, would not require appointment of counsel in any case—capital or otherwise. For a man charged with murder usually knows whether or not it was his blow or shot that killed the deceased and therefore whether he is unjustly accused. And he certainly knows he is in serious trouble when he is faced with such a charge. The logic of the Illinois view would lead to the conclusion that the average man in those circumstances would know enough to demand a lawyer to defend him and that the court need not offer one to him.

Fortunately for the liberal tradition the law has followed a different course. At least where the offense is a capital one, due process requires appointment of counsel in state as well as in federal prosecutions. *Powell* v. *Alabama*, 287 U.S. 45; .... The reason is that the guilty as well as the innocent are entitled to a fair trial, that a layman without the experience and skill of counsel to guide him may get lost in the intricacies of the law and lose advantages which it extends to every accused, that without expert appraisal of the circumstances surrounding his arrest, detention, arraignment, and conviction the penalties he suffers may be aggravated by his own ignorance or by overreaching of the prosecution or police. Hence the need for counsel exists in capital cases whether the accused contests the charge against him or pleads guilty. *Foster* v. *Illinois*, 332 U.S. 134, 137.

Those considerations are equally germane though liberty rather than life hangs in the balance. Certainly due process shows no less solicitude for liberty than for life. A man facing a prison term may, indeed, have as much at stake as life itself.

Bute was charged with a most repulsive crime. It may seem easy to say that it is a simple and uncomplicated one, and therefore that he should know whether he committed it and whether he stood in need of counsel. But it has long been recognized that the charge of taking indecent liberties with children is, like rape, "an accusation easily to be made and hard to be proved, and harder to be defended by the party accused, tho never so innocent." 1 Hale's Pleas of the Crown 634.... The weight of the prosecution's case, the character of the defense which is available are all questions which only a skilled lawyer can consider intelligently. A layman might rush to confession where counsel would see advantages in a trial before judge or jury. Counsel might see weakness in the prosecution's case which could be utilized either in standing trial or in pleading guilty to a lesser offense. These are the circumstances of the present case which Bute uses to appeal to our conscience. They without more convince me that we could be sure Bute had a fair trial only if counsel had stood at his side and guided him across the treacherous ground he had to traverse.

. . . . . .

HALEY v. OHIO
332 U.S. 596 (1948)

Mr. Justice Douglas announced the judgment of the Court and an opinion in which Mr. Justice Black, Mr. Justice Murphy, and Mr. Justice Rutledge join.

Petitioner was convicted in an Ohio court of murder in the first degree and sentenced to life imprisonment. The Court of Appeals of Ohio sustained the judgment over the objection that the admission of petitioner's confession at the trial violated the Fourteenth Amendment of the Constitution .... The Ohio Supreme Court ... dismissed the appeal. ...

A confectionery store was robbed near midnight on October 14, 1945, and William Karam, its owner, was shot. It was the prosecutor's theory, supported by some evidence which it is unnecessary for us to relate, that petitioner, a Negro boy aged 15, and two others, Willie Lowder, aged 16, and Al Parks, aged 17, committed the crime, petitioner acting as a lookout. Five days later—around midnight October 19, 1945—petitioner was arrested at his home and taken to police headquarters.

There is some contrariety in the testimony as to what then transpired. There is evidence that he was beaten. He took the stand and so testified. His mother testified that the clothes he wore when arrested, which were exchanged two days later for clean ones she brought to the jail, were torn and bloodstained. She also testified that when she first saw him five days after his arrest he was bruised and skinned. The police testified to the contrary on this entire line of testimony. So we put on one side the controverted evidence. Taking only the undisputed testimony we have the following sequence of events. Beginning shortly after midnight this 15-year-old lad was questioned by the police for about five hours. Five or six of the police questioned him in relays of one or two each. During this time no friend or counsel of the boy was present. Around 5 a.m.—after being shown alleged confessions of Lowder and Parks—the boy confessed. A confession was typed in question and answer form by the police. At no time was this boy advised of his right to counsel; but the written confession started off with the following statement:

We want to inform you of your constitutional rights, the law gives you the right to make this statement or not as you see fit. It is made with the understanding that it may be used at a trial in court either for or against you or anyone else involved in this crime with you, of your own free will and accord, you are under no force or duress or compulsion and no promises are being made to you at this time whatsoever.

Do you still desire to make this statement and tell the truth after having had the above clause read to you?

A. Yes.

He was put in jail about 6 or 6:30 a.m. on Saturday, the 20th, shortly after the confession was signed. Between then and Tuesday, the 23d, he was held incommunicado. A lawyer retained by his mother tried to see him twice but was refused admission by the police. His mother was not allowed to see him until Thursday, the 25th. But a newspaper photographer was allowed to see him and take his picture in the early morning hours of the 20th, right after he had confessed. He was not taken before a magistrate and formally charged with a crime until the 23d—three days after the confession was signed.

The trial court, after a preliminary hearing on the voluntary character of the confession, allowed it to be admitted in evidence over petitioner's objection that it violated his rights under the Fourteenth Amendment. The court instructed the jury to disregard the confession if it found that he did not make the confession voluntarily and of his free will.

But the ruling of the trial court and the finding of the jury on the voluntary character of the confession do not foreclose the independent examination which it is our duty to make here. *Ashcraft* v. *Tennessee*, 322 U.S. 143, 147, 148. If the undisputed evidence suggests that force or coercion was used to exact the confession, we will not permit the judgment of conviction to stand even though without the confession there might have been sufficient evidence for submission to the jury. *Malinsky* v. *New York*, 324 U.S. 401, and cases cited.

We do not think the methods used in obtaining this confession can be squared with that due process of law which the Fourteenth Amendment commands.

The age of the petitioner, the hours when he was grilled, the fact that he had no friend or counsel to advise him, the callous attitude of the police toward his rights combine to convince us that this was a confession wrung from a child by means which the law should not sanction. Neither man nor child can be allowed to stand condemned by methods which flout constitutional requirements of due process of law.

But we are told that this boy was advised of his constitutional rights before he signed the confession and that, knowing them, he nevertheless confessed. That assumes, however, that a boy of fifteen, without aid of counsel, would have a full appreciation of that advice and that on the facts of this record he had a freedom of choice. We cannot indulge those assumptions. Moreover, we cannot give any weight to recitals which merely formalize constitutional requirements. Formulas of respect for constitutional safeguards cannot prevail over the facts of life which contradict them. They may not become cloak for inquisitorial practices and make an empty form of the due process of law for which free men fought and died to obtain.

The course we followed in *Chambers* v. *Florida*, 309 U.S. 227, . . . [and subsequent cases] . . . must be followed here. The Fourteenth Amendment prohibits the police from using the private, secret custody of either man or child as a device for wringing confessions from them.

Reversed.

Mr. Justice FRANKFURTER, joining in reversal of judgment.

Whether a confession of a lad of fifteen is "voluntary" and as such admissible, or "coerced" and thus wanting in due process, is not a matter of mathematical determination. Essentially it invites psychological judgment—a psychological judgment that reflects deep, even if inarticulate feelings of our society. . . .

. . . Unfortunately, we cannot draw upon any formulated expression of the existence of such feeling. Nor are there available experts on such matters to guide the judicial judgment. Our Constitutional system makes it the Court's duty to interpret those feelings of society to which the Due Process Clause gives legal protection. Because of their inherent vagueness the tests by which we are to be guided are most unsatisfactory, but such as they are we must apply them.

Unhappily we have neither physical nor intellectual weights and measures by which judicial judgment can determine when pressures in securing a confession reach the coercive intensity that calls for the exclusion of a statement so secured. Of course, the police meant to exercise pressures upon Haley to make him talk. That was the very purpose of their procedure. In concluding that a statement is not voluntary which results from pressures such as were exerted in this case to make a lad of fifteen talk when the Constitution gave him the right to keep silent and when the situation was so contrived that appreciation of his rights and thereby the means of asserting them were effectively withheld from him by the police, I do not believe I express a merely personal bias against such a procedure. Such a finding, I believe, reflects those fundamental notions of fairness and justice in the determination of guilt or innocence which lie embedded in the feelings of the American people and are enshrined in the Due Process Clause of the Fourteenth Amendment. To remove the inducement to resort to such methods this Court has repeatedly denied use of the fruits of illicit methods.

Accordingly, I think Haley's confession should have been excluded and the conviction based upon it should not stand.

Mr. Justice BURTON, with whom the CHIEF JUSTICE, Mr. Justice REED, and Mr. Justice JACKSON concur, dissenting.

As admitted by the petitioner in this Court, the entire issue here resolves itself into a consideration of the methods used in obtaining the confession. This in turn resolves itself primarily into a question of the credibility of witnesses as a means of determining the contested question as to what methods in fact were used. A voluntary confession not only is valid but it is the usual, best and generally fairest kind of evidence. Often it is the only direct evidence obtainable as to the state of mind of the accused. The giving of such a confession promptly is to be encouraged in the interest of all concerned. The police are justified and under obligation to seek such confessions. At the same time, it is a primary part of their obligation to see to it that coercion, including intimidation, is not used to secure a confession. It should be evident to them not only that involuntary confessions are worthless as evidence, but that coercion applied in securing them itself constitutes a serious violation of duty.

The question in this case is the simple one—was the confession in fact voluntary? As in many other cases it is difficult, because of conflicting testimony, to determine this controlling fact. Self-serving perjury, however, must not be the pass-key to a mandatory exclusion of the confession from use as evidence. It is for the trial judge and the jury, under the safeguards of constitutional due process of criminal law, to apply even-handed justice to the determination of the factual issues. . . .

. . . . .

We are not in a position, on the basis of mere suspicion, to hold the trial court in error and to conclude "that this was a confession wrung from a child by means which the law should not sanction." While coercion and intimidation in securing a confession should be unequivocally condemned and punished and their product invalidated, nevertheless such coercion should not be presumed to exist because of a mere suggestion or suspicion, in the face of contrary findings by the triers of fact. On the basis of the undisputed testimony relied upon by the Court, it is not justified in making such a determination of "the callous attitude of the police" of Canton as thereby to override not only the sworn testimony of the State's public officials but also the conclusions of the triers of fact. The trial judge, with his first-hand knowledge, both of the credibility indicated by the testimony in open court and of the habitual "attitude of the police" of

Canton, if there be any such attitude, found to the contrary. That judge and the law enforcement officers of Canton have been entrusted by the State of Ohio with the enforcement of the constitutional obligations of the public to each individual and also of each individual to the public. In the absence of substantial proof to upset the findings of the trial court, these public officers should not be charged with callousness toward, or with violation of, their constitutional obligations.

. . . . .

In testing due process this Court must first make sure of its facts. Until a better way is found for testing credibility than by the examination of witnesses in open court, we must give trial courts and juries that wide discretion in this field to which a living record, as distinguished from a printed record, logically entitles them. In this living record there are many guideposts to the truth which are not in the printed record. Without seeing them ourselves, we will do well to give heed to those who have seen them.[7]

2. LEGISLATIVE AND ADMINISTRATIVE PROCEDURE[8]

BI-METALLIC INVESTMENT COMPANY v. COLORADO
239 U.S. 441 (1915)

Mr. Justice HOLMES delivered the opinion of the Court.

This is a suit to enjoin the State Board of Equalization and the Colorado Tax Commission from putting in force and the defendant Pitcher, as assessor of Denver, from obeying, an order of the board, increasing the valuation of all taxable property in Denver 40 per cent. The order was sustained and the suit directed to be dismissed by the supreme court of the state. . . . The plaintiff is the owner of real estate in Denver, and brings the case here on the ground that it was given no opportunity to be heard, and that therefore its property will be taken without due process of law, contrary to the Fourteenth Amendment of the Constitution of the United States. That is the only question with which we have to deal. . . .

For the purposes of decision we assume that the constitutional

[7] Some instructors may prefer to pass now to the subject of the extension of the Bill of Rights to include state action. The pertinent material will be found *infra*, Ch. XIII, pp. 580–610.

[8] *Davidson* v. *New Orleans, supra*, p. 329, should be reread in this context.

question is presented in the baldest way,—that neither the plaintiff nor the assessor of Denver, who presents a brief on plaintiff's side, nor any representative of the city and county, was given an opportunity to be heard, other than such as they may have had by reason of the fact that the time of the meeting of the board is fixed by law. On this assumption it is obvious that injustice may be suffered if some property in the county already has been valued at its full worth. But if certain property has been valued at a rate different from that generally prevailing in the county, the owner has had his opportunity to protest and appeal as usual in our system of taxation (*Hager* v. *Reclamation District,* 111 U.S. 701, 709, 710), so that it must be assumed that the property owners in the county all stand alike. The question, then, is whether all individuals have a constitutional right to be heard before a matter can be decided in which all are equally concerned,—here, for instance, before a superior board decided that the local taxing officers have adopted a system of undervaluation throughout a county, as notoriously often has been the case. . . .

Where a rule of conduct applies to more than a few people, it is impracticable that everyone should have a direct voice in its adoption. The Constitution does not require all public acts to be done in town meeting or an assembly of the whole. General statutes within the state power are passed that affect the person or property of individuals, sometimes to the point of ruin, without giving them a chance to be heard. Their rights are protected in the only way that they can be in a complex society, by their power, immediate or remote, over those who make the rule. If the result in this case had been reached, as it might have been, by the state's doubling the rate of taxation, no one would suggest that the Fourteenth Amendment was violated unless every person affected had been allowed an opportunity to raise his voice against it before the body intrusted by the state constitution with the power. In considering this case in this Court we must assume that the proper state machinery has been used, and the question is whether, if the state constitution had declared that Denver had been undervalued as compared with the rest of the state, and had decreed that for the current year the valuation should be 40 per cent higher, the objection now urged could prevail. It appears to us that to put the question is to answer it. There must be a limit to individual argument in such matters if government is to go on. . . .

Judgment affirmed.

LAWTON v. STEELE
152 U.S. 133 (1894)

[A New York statute provided that any fish nets used in violation of state laws for the protection of fish and game were to be considered public nuisances and should be summarily destroyed. Game constables and similar officials were charged with the duty of seizing any such nets and destroying them; they were not liable in damages or subject to suit for such summary destruction of property.

[Steele, an officer of the state, came upon fifteen nets belonging to Lawton which were either in use or had the signs of recent use in violation of state law. In accordance with the statute Steele seized the nets and destroyed them. Lawton then sued Steele for the value of the nets, $216; on appeal, the state supreme court held for the defendant.]

Mr. Justice BROWN delivered the opinion of the Court.

This case involves the unconstitutionality of an act of the legislature of the state of New York. . . .

The main and only real difficulty connected with the act in question is in its declaration that any net, etc., maintained in violation of any law for the protection of fisheries, is to be treated as a public nuisance, "and may be abated and summarily destroyed by any person, and it shall be the duty of each and every protector aforesaid and every game constable to seize, remove, and forthwith destroy the same." The legislature, however, undoubtedly possessed the power not only to protect fishing by nets in these waters, but to make it a criminal offense, and to take such measures as were reasonable and necessary to prevent such offenses in the future. It certainly could not do this more effectually than by destroying the means of the offense. If the nets were being used in a manner detrimental to the interests of the public, we think it was within the power of the legislature to declare them to be nuisances, and to authorize the officers of the state to abate them. . . .

An act of the legislature which has for its object the preservation of the public interests against the illegal depredations of private individuals ought to be sustained, unless it is plainly violative of the Constitution, or subversive of private rights. In this case there can be no doubt of the right of the legislature to authorize judicial proceedings to be taken for the condemnation of the nets in question, and their sale or destruction by process of law. Congress has assumed this power in a large number of cases, by authorizing the condemnation of property which has been made use of for the purpose of defrauding the revenue. . . . In all these cases, however, the forfeiture was decreed by judicial proceeding. But where the property is of little value, and its use for the illegal purpose is clear, the legislature may declare it to be a nuisance, and subject to summary abatement. Instances are the power to kill diseased cattle; to pull down houses in the path of conflagrations; the destruction of decayed fruit or fish or unwholesome meats, or infected clothing, obscene books or pictures, or instruments which can only be used for illegal purposes. While the legislature has no right arbitrarily to declare that to be a nuisance which is clearly not so, a good deal must be left to its discretion in that regard, and if the object to be accomplished is conducive to the public interests, it may exercise a large liberty of choice in the means employed. . . .

It is not easy to draw the line between cases where property illegally used may be destroyed summarily and where judicial proceedings are necessary for its condemnation. If the property were of great value, as, for instance, if it were a vessel employed for smuggling or other illegal purposes, it would be putting a dangerous power in the hands of a custom officer to permit him to sell or destroy it as a public nuisance, and the owner would have good reason to complain of such act as depriving him of his property without due process of law. But where the property is of trifling value, and its destruction is necessary to effect the object of a certain statute, we think it is within the power of the legislature to order its summary abatement. For instance, if the legislature should prohibit the killing of fish by explosive shells, and should order the cartridges so used to be destroyed, it would seem like belittling the dignity of the judiciary to require such destruction to be preceded by a solemn condemnation in a court of justice. The same remark might be made of the cards, chips, and dice of a gambling-room.

The value of the nets in question was but $15 apiece. The cost of condemning one (and the use of one is as illegal as the use of a dozen), by judicial proceedings, would largely exceed the value of the net, and doubtless the state would, in many cases, be deterred from executing the law by the expense. . . . It is evident that the efficacy of this statute would be very seriously impaired by requiring every net illegally used to be carefully taken from the water, carried before a court or magistrate, notice of the seizure to be given by publication, and regular judicial proceedings to be instituted for its condemnation.

. . . . .

Judgment affirmed.

The CHIEF JUSTICE [FULLER], with whom Mr. Justice FIELD and Mr. Justice BREWER concur, dissenting. [Opinion omitted.]

SOUTHERN RAILWAY CO. v. VIRGINIA ex rel. SHIRLEY
290 U.S. 190 (1933)

Mr. Justice McREYNOLDS delivered the opinion of the Court.

This appeal questions the validity of chap. 62, Acts General Assembly of Virginia, 1930; Michie's Code, § 3974a. ... The claim is that enforcement of the Act as construed by the state supreme court, would deprive appellant of property without due process of law and thus violate the Fourteenth Amendment.

Purporting to proceed under the challenged chapter, the Highway Commissioner, without prior notice, advised appellant that in his opinion public safety and convenience required elimination of the grade crossing near Antlers; also, he directed construction there of an overhead passage according to accompanying plans and specifications. Replying, the Company questioned the Commissioner's conclusion upon the facts, denied the validity of the Act, and refused to undertake the work. Thereupon, by petition he asked the State Corporation Commission for an order requiring it to proceed. A demurrer to this questioned the constitutionality of the statute. It especially pointed out that the Commissioner undertook to ordain, without prior notice, and that there was no provision for any review except in respect of the proposed plans for the structure. The commission overruled the demurrer and directed the railway to construct the overhead. The supreme court construed the statute and approved this action.

As authoritatively interpreted the challenged act permits the Highway Commissioner—an executive officer—without notice or hearing to command a railway company to abolish any designated grade crossing and construct an overhead when, in his opinion, necessary for public safety and convenience. His opinion is final upon the fundamental question whether public convenience and necessity require the elimination, unless what the supreme court denominates "arbitrary" exercise of the granted power can be shown. Upon petition, filed within sixty days, the Corporation Commission may consider the proposed plans and approve or modify them, but nothing more. The statute makes no provision for review by any court. But the supreme court has declared that a court of equity may give relief under an original bill where "arbitrary" action can be established.

As construed and applied, we think the statute conflicts with the Fourteenth Amendment.

Certainly, to require abolition of an established grade crossing and the outlay of money necessary to construct an overhead would take the railway's property in a very real sense. This seems plain enough both upon reason and authority. . . .

If we assume that by proper legislation a state may impose upon railways the duty of eliminating grade crossings, when deemed necessary for public safety and convenience, the question here is whether the challenged statute meets the requirements of due process of law. Undoubtedly, it attempts to give an administrative officer power to make final determination in respect of facts—the character of a crossing and what is necessary for the public safety and convenience—without notice, without hearing, without evidence; and upon this *ex parte* finding not subject to general review, to ordain that expenditures shall be made for erecting a new structure. The thing so authorized is no mere police regulation.

The claim that the questioned statute was enacted under the police power of the state and, therefore, is not subject to the standards applicable to legislation under other powers, conflicts with the firmly established rule that every state is limited by the inhibitions of the Fourteenth Amendment. . . .

Lawton v. *Steele,* 152 U.S. 133, points out that the right to destroy private property—nuisance, etc.—for protection against imminent danger, has long been recognized. Such action does no violence to the Fourteenth Amendment. The principles which control have no present application. Here, the statute itself contemplates material delay; no impending danger demands immediate action. During sixty days the railway may seek modification of the plans proposed.

Counsel submit that the legislature, without giving notice or opportunity to be heard, by direct order might have required elimination of the crossing. Consequently, they conclude the same may be accomplished in any manner which it deems advisable without violating the federal Constitution. But if we assume that a state legislature may determine what public welfare demands and by direct command require a railway to act accordingly, it by no means follows that an administrative officer may be empowered, without notice or hearing, to act with finality upon his own opinion and obtain the taking of private property. There is an obvious difference between legislative determination and the finding of an administrative official not supported by evidence. In theory, at least, the legislature acts upon adequate knowledge after full consideration and through members who represent the entire public.

Chapter 62 undertakes to empower the Highway Commissioner to take railway property if and when he deems it necessary for public safety and convenience. It makes no provision for a hearing, and grants no opportunity for a review in any court. This, we think, amounts to the delegation of purely arbitrary and unconstitutional power unless the indefinite right of resort to a court of equity referred to by the court below affords adequate protection.

Considering the decisions here, it is clear that no such authority as that claimed for the Commissioner could be entrusted to an administrative officer or body under the power to tax, to impose assessments for benefits, to regulate common carriers, to establish drainage districts or to regulate business.... Appellee makes no claim to the contrary. He affirms, however, that under the police power the legislature could rightly grant the challenged authority. But, as pointed out above, this is subject to the inhibitions of the Fourteenth Amendment, and we think the suggested distinction between it and other powers of the state is unsound.

This Court has often recognized the power of a state acting through an executive officer or body to order the removal of grade crossings, but in all cases there was a right to a hearing and review by some court....

After affirming appellant's obligation to comply with the Commissioner's order, the court below said: "The railroad is not without remedy. Should the power vested in the Highway Commissioner be arbitrarily exercised, equity's long arm will stay his hand." But by sanctioning the order directing the railway to proceed, it, in effect, approved action without hearing, without evidence, without opportunity to know the basis therefor. This was to rule that such action was not necessarily "arbitrary." There is nothing to indicate what that court would deem arbitrary action or how this could be established in the absence of evidence or hearing. In circumstances like those here disclosed no contestant could have fair opportunity for relief in a court of equity. There would be nothing to show the grounds upon which the Commissioner based his conclusion. He alone would be cognizant of the mental processes which begot his urgent opinion.

The infirmities of the enactment are not relieved by an indefinite right of review in respect of some action spoken of as arbitrary. Before it properly can be taken under the edict of an administrative officer the appellant is entitled to a fair hearing upon the fundamental facts. This has not been accorded. The judgment below must be reversed. The cause will be remanded for further proceedings not inconsistent with this opinion.

Reversed.

The CHIEF JUSTICE [HUGHES], Mr. Justice STONE and Mr. Justice CARDOZO dissent upon the ground that there has been a lawful delegation to the State Highway Commissioner of the power to declare the need for the abatement of a nuisance through the elimination of grade crossings dangerous to life and limb; that this power may be exercised without notice or hearing *(Chicago, B. & Q. R. Co.* v. *Nebraska,* 170 U.S. 57, 77), provided adequate opportunity is afforded for review in the event that the power is perverted or abused; and that such opportunity has been given by the statutes of Virginia as construed by its highest court.

BOURJOIS v. CHAPMAN
301 U.S. 183 (1937)

Mr. Justice BRANDEIS delivered the opinion of the Court.

Bourjois, Inc., a New York corporation, brought, in the federal court for Maine, this suit seeking to enjoin, both temporarily and permanently, the enforcement of Chapter 109 of the Public Laws of Maine, 1935, entitled "An Act for the Regulation of Cosmetics." . . .

Section 1 of the Act provides:

"Registration of cosmetics. On and after January 1, 1936, no person, firm, corporation or copartnership shall hold for sale, sell, offer for sale, in intrastate commerce, give away, deal in, within this state, supply or apply in the conduct of a beauty shop, barber shop, hairdressing establishment or similar establishment, any cosmetic preparation unless the said preparation has been registered with and a certificate of registration secured from the department of health and welfare."

Section 2 declares that the purpose of the Act is to safeguard the public health; and provides for the issue of certificates of registration by the department of health and welfare "to the manufacturer, proprietor, or producer of any cosmetic preparation." Other sections of the Act contain elaborate provisions for the seizure and forfeiture of "cosmetic preparations kept or deposited within the state for unlawful sale or use": and for imposition of fines upon violators of the statute.

. . . . . .

The plaintiff has not applied for a certificate of registration of any of its preparations; and it announces that it will refuse to do so, because the statute is void under the federal and state Constitutions. Sixteen distinct grounds of invalidity are argued with great earnestness. None is well founded. Only a few need to be discussed.

. . . . .

Third. The plaintiff contends that in other respects the statute violates rights protected by the Fourteenth Amendment and the Constitution of the United States. It objects that the power conferred upon the board to grant or deny a certificate is unlimited; that the board has issued no regulations; and that neither the statute nor the board has provided for hearing an applicant.... Section 2 defines the department's control of registration:

"The said department is authorized to regulate or to refuse the issuance of certificates or to prohibit the sale of cosmetic preparations which in its judgment contain injurious substances in such amounts as to be poisonous, injurious or detrimental to the person."

Delegation of the power to exercise that judgment is not obnoxious to the constitution of Maine.... And obviously, it contravenes no provision of the federal Constitution.... Neither constitution requires that exercise of such a power be preceded by the adoption of regulations. And neither constitution requires that there must be a hearing of the applicant before the board may exercise a judgment under the circumstances and of the character here involved. The requirement of due process of law is amply safeguarded by § 2 of the statute, which provides:

"From the refusal of said department to issue a certificate of registration for any cosmetic preparation appeal shall lie to the superior court in the county of Kennebec or any other county in the state from which the same was offered for registration."

Affirmed.

MODEL STATE ADMINISTRATIVE PROCEDURE ACT

[The National Conference of Commissioners on Uniform State Laws at its 1946 session produced a draft bill on administrative procedure from which the following extracts are taken. This draft is the second one, an earlier one having been formulated in 1943. That first draft has been adopted in Wisconsin; general legislation on administrative procedure has also been enacted in Ohio, California, North Carolina, and several other states. The 1946 Model Act shows marked influences from the Federal Administrative Procedure Act, 60 Stat. 237, adopted the same year. The federal law as well as this draft manifest, in the words of Professor Walter Gellhorn, "the drive among lawyers to standardize by statute the practices and principles of administrative agencies which adjudicate or make rules." To put it in other words, these enactments would seek to spell out criteria of due process of law in administrative procedure.]

Section 8. (Contested Cases; Notice, Hearings, Records.)

In any contested case all parties shall be afforded an opportunity for hearing after reasonable notice. The notice shall state the time, place, and issues involved, but if, by reason of the nature of the proceeding, the issues cannot be fully stated in advance of the hearing, or if subsequent amendment of the issues is necessary, they shall be fully stated as soon as practicable, and opportunity shall be afforded all parties to present evidence and argument with respect thereto. The agency shall prepare an official record, which shall include testimony and exhibits, in each contested case, but it shall not be necessary to transcribe shorthand notes requested for purposes of rehearing or court review. Informal disposition may also be made of any contested case by stipulation, consent order, or default. Each agency shall adopt appropriate rules of procedure for notice and hearing in contested cases.

Section 12. (Judicial Review of Contested Cases.)

(1) Any person aggrieved by a final decision in contested case, whether such decision is affirmative or negative in form, is entitled to judicial review thereof under this act (but nothing in this section shall be deemed to prevent resort to other means of review, redress, relief or trial de novo, provided by law).

. . . . .

UNITED STATES ex rel. KNAUFF v. SHAUGHNESSY[9]
338 U.S. 537 (1950)

Mr. Justice MINTON delivered the opinion of the Court.

May the United States exclude without hearing, solely upon a finding of the Attorney General that her admission would be prejudicial to the interests of the United States, the alien wife of a citizen who had served honorably in the armed forces of the United States during World War II? The District Court for the Southern District of New York held that it could, and the Court of Appeals for the Second Circuit affirmed. . . . We granted certiorari to examine the question especially in the light of the War Brides Act of December 28, 1945. . . .

Petitioner was born in Germany in 1915. She left Germany and went to Czechoslovakia during the Hitler regime. There she was married and divorced. She went to England in 1939 as a refugee. Thereafter she served with the Royal Air Force efficiently and honorably from January 1, 1943, until May 30, 1946. She then secured civilian employment with the War Department of the United States in Germany. Her work was rated "very good" and "excellent." On February 28, 1948, with the permission of the Commanding General at Frankfurt, Germany, she married Kurt W. Knauff, a naturalized citizen of the United States. He is an honorably discharged United States Army veteran of World War II. He is, as he was at the time of his marriage, a civilian employee of the United States Army at Frankfurt, Germany.

On August 14, 1948, petitioner sought to enter the United States to be naturalized. On that day she was temporarily excluded from the United States and detained at Ellis Island. On October 6, 1948, the Assistant Commissioner of Immigration and Naturalization recom-

---

[9] While this case involves federal rather than state action and is thus not a Fourteenth Amendment problem it raises a sharp and urgent issue of due process of law in the contemporary scene and is therefore included at this point.

mended that she be permanently excluded without a hearing on the ground that her admission would be prejudicial to the interests of the United States. On the same day the Attorney General adopted this recommendation and entered a final order of exclusion. . . .

The authority of the Attorney General to order the exclusion of aliens without a hearing flows from the Act of June 21, 1941, amending § 1 of the Act of May 22, 1918. By the 1941 amendment it was provided that the President might, upon finding that the interests of the United States required it, impose additional restrictions and prohibitions on the entry into and departure of persons from the United States during the national emergency proclaimed May 27, 1941. Pursuant to this Act of Congress the President on November 14, 1941, issued Proclamation 2523. . . .

Pursuant to the authority of this proclamation the Secretary of State and the Attorney General issued regulations governing the entry into and departure of persons from the United States during the national emergency. Subparagraphs (a) to (k) of § 175.53 of these regulations specified the classes of aliens whose entry into the United States was deemed prejudicial to the public interest. Subparagraph (b) of § 175.57 provided that the Attorney General might deny an alien a hearing before a board of inquiry in special cases where he determined that the alien was excludable under the regulations on the basis of information of a confidential nature, the disclosure of which would be prejudicial to the public interest.

It was under this regulation 175.57 (b) that petitioner was excluded by the Attorney General and denied a hearing. We are asked to pass upon the validity of this action.

At the outset we wish to point out that an alien who seeks admission to this country may not do so under any claim of right. Admission of aliens to the United States is a privilege granted by the sovereign United States Government. Such privilege is granted to an alien only upon such terms as the United States shall prescribe. It must be exercised in accordance with the procedure which the United States provided. . . .

.   .   .   .   .

Whatever the procedure authorized by Congress is, it is due process as far as an alien denied entry is concerned. . . .

.   .   .   .   .

... The contention of petitioner is that she is entitled to the statutory hearing [normally prescribed by Congress in time of peace, 8 U.S. Code §§ 152, 153] because ... the War Brides Act, within which she comes, ... discloses a congressional intent that special restrictions on the entry of aliens should cease to apply to war brides upon the cessation of hostilities.

The War Brides Act provides that World War II is the period from December 7, 1941, until the proclaimed termination of hostilities. This has nothing to do with the period for which the regulations here acted under were authorized. The beginning and end of the war are defined by the War Brides Act, we assume, for the purpose of ascertaining the period within which citizens must have served in the armed forces in order for their spouses and children to be entitled to the benefits of the Act. The special procedure followed in this case was authorized not only during the period of actual hostilities but during the entire war and the national emergency proclaimed May 27, 1941. The national emergency has never been terminated. Indeed, a state of war still exists. See *Woods* v. *Cloyd W. Miller Co.,* 333 U.S. 138.[10] Thus the authority upon which the Attorney General acted remains in force. . . .

The War Brides Act does not relieve petitioner of her alien status. Indeed, she sought admission in order to be naturalized and thus to overcome her alien status. The Act relieved her of certain physical, mental, and documentary requirements and of the quota provisions of the immigration laws. But she must, as the Act requires, still be "otherwise admissible under the immigration laws." In other words, aside from the enumerated relaxations of the immigration laws she must be treated as any other alien seeking admission. Under the immigration laws and regulations applicable to all aliens seeking entry into the United States during the national emergency, she was excluded by the Attorney General without a hearing. In such a case we have no authority to retry the determination of the Attorney General. . . .

. . . We find no legal defect in the manner of petitioner's exclusion, and the judgment is

Affirmed.

Mr. Justice DOUGLAS [who was convalescing from an accident] and Mr. Justice CLARK [who as Attorney General had issued the

[10] *Infra,* p. 625.

order excluding Mrs. Knauff] took no part in the consideration or decision of this case.

Mr. Justice FRANKFURTER, dissenting.

. . . . .

Mr. Justice JACKSON, whom Mr. Justice BLACK and Mr. Justice FRANKFURTER join, dissenting.

I do not question the constitutional power of Congress to authorize immigration authorities to turn back from our gates any alien or class of aliens. But I do not find that Congress has authorized an abrupt and brutal exclusion of the wife of an American citizen without a hearing.

Congress held out a promise of liberalized admission to alien brides, taken unto themselves by men serving in or honorably discharged from our armed services abroad, as the Act, set forth in the Court's opinion, indicated. The petitioning husband is honorably discharged and remained in Germany as a civilian employee. Our military authorities abroad require their permission before marriage. The Army in Germany is not without a vigilant and security-conscious intelligence service. This woman was employed by our European Command and her record is not only without blemish, but is highly praised by her superiors. The marriage of this alien woman to this veteran was approved by the Commanding General at Frankfurt-on-Main.

Now this American citizen is told he cannot bring his wife to the United States, but he will not be told why. He must abandon his bride to live in his own country or forsake his country to live with his bride.

So he went to court and sought a writ of habeas corpus, which we never tire of citing to Europe as the unanswerable evidence that our free country permits no arbitrary official detention. And the Government tells the Court that not even a court can find out why the girl is excluded. But it says we must find that Congress authorized this treatment of war brides and even if we cannot get any reasons for it, we must say it is legal; security requires it.

Security is like liberty in that many are the crimes committed in its name. The menace to the security of this country, be it great as it may, from this girl's admission is as nothing compared to the menace to free institutions in procedures of this pattern. In the name of security the police state justifies its arbitrary oppressions on evidence that is secret, because security might be prejudiced if it were brought to light in hearings. The plea that evidence of guilt must be secret is abhorrent to free men, because it provides a cloak for the malevolent, the misinformed, the meddlesome, and the corrupt to play the role of informer undetected and uncorrected. . . .

I am sure the officials here have acted from a sense of duty, with full belief in their lawful power, and no doubt upon information which, if it stood the test of trial, would justify the order of exclusion. But not even they know whether it would stand this test. And anyway, . . . personal confidence in the officials involved does not excuse a judge for sanctioning a procedure that is dangerously wrong in principle. . . .

Congress will have to use more explicit language than any yet cited before I will agree that it has authorized an administrative officer to break up the family of an American citizen or force him to keep his wife by becoming an exile. Likewise, it will have to be much more explicit before I can agree that it authorized a finding of serious misconduct against the wife of an American citizen without notice of charges, evidence of guilt and a chance to meet it.

I should direct the Attorney General either to produce his evidence justifying exclusion or to admit Mrs. Knauff to the country.

C H A P T E R *X*

The Fourteenth Amendment: Equal Protection of the Laws

1. CLASSIFICATION OR DISCRIMINATION?

YICK WO v. HOPKINS
118 U.S. 356 (1886)

[This case involved an ordinance of the City and County of San Francisco which made it unlawful "to carry on a laundry ... without having first obtained the consent of the board of supervisors, except the same be located in a building constructed either of brick or stone." Yick Wo and his associates were convicted of violation of this ordinance and sentenced to prison terms. They sought release through writs of habeas corpus which the state supreme court denied.]

Mr. Justice MATTHEWS delivered the opinion of the Court.

. . . . .

The determination of the question whether the proceedings under these ordinances and in enforcement of them are in conflict with the Constitution and laws of the United States necessarily involves the meaning of the ordinances, which, for that purpose, we are required to ascertain and adjudge.

We are consequently constrained, at the outset, to differ from the Supreme Court of California upon the real meaning of the ordinances in question. The court considered these ordinances as vesting in the board of supervisors a not unusual discretion in granting or withholding their assent to the use of wooden buildings as laundries, to be exercised in reference to the circumstances of each case, with a view to the protection of the public against the dangers of fire. We are not able to concur in that interpretation of the power conferred upon the supervisors. There is nothing in the ordinances which points to such a regulation of the business of keeping and conducting laundries. They seem intended to confer, and actually do confer, not a discretion to be exercised upon a consideration of the circumstances of each case, but a naked and arbitrary power to give or withhold consent, not only as to places, but as to persons. So that, if an applicant for such consent, being in every way a competent and qualified person, and having complied with every reasonable condition demanded by any public interest, should, failing to obtain the requisite consent of the supervisors to the prosecution of his business, apply for redress by the judicial process of mandamus, to require the supervisors to consider and act upon his case, it would be a sufficient answer for them to say that the law had conferred upon them authority to withhold their assent without reason and without responsibility. The power given to them is not confided to their discretion in the legal sense of that term, but is granted to their mere will. It is purely arbitrary, and acknowledges neither guidance nor restraint. . . .

The ordinance drawn in question in the present case . . . does not prescribe a rule and conditions for the regulation of the use of property for laundry purposes, to which all similarly situated may conform. It allows without restriction the use for such purposes of buildings of brick or stone; but, as to wooden buildings, constituting nearly all those in previous use, it divides the owners or occupiers into two classes, not having respect to their personal character and qualifications for the business, nor the situation and nature and adaptation of the buildings themselves, but merely by an arbitrary line, on one side of which are those who are permitted to pursue their industry by the mere will and consent of the supervisors, and on the other those from whom that consent is withheld, at their mere will and pleasure. And both classes are alike only in this, that they are tenants at will, under the supervisors, of their means of living. The ordinance, therefore, also differs from the not unusual case, where discretion is lodged by law in public officers or bodies to grant or withhold licenses to keep taverns, or places for the sale of spirituous liquors, and the like, when one of the conditions is that the applicant shall be a fit person for the exercise of the privilege, because in such cases the fact of fitness is submitted to the judgment of the officer, and calls for the exercise of a judicial nature.

The rights of the petitioners, as affected by the proceedings of which they complain, are not less, because they are aliens and subjects of the Emperor of China.

The Fourteenth Amendment to the Constitution is not confined to the protection of citizens. It says: "Nor shall any State deprive any person of life, liberty, or property without due process of law; nor deny to any person within its jurisdiction the equal protection of the laws." These provisions are universal in their application, to all persons within the territorial jurisdiction, without regard to any difference of race, or color, or of nationality, and the equal protection of the laws is a pledge of the protection of equal laws. . . .

It is contended on the part of the petitioners, that the ordinances for violations of which they are severally sentenced to imprisonment, are void on their face, as being within the prohibitions of the Fourteenth Amendment; and, in the alternative, if not so, that they are void by reason of their administration, operating unequally, so as to punish in the present petitioners what is permitted to others as lawful, without any distinction of circumstances—an unjust and illegal discrimination, it is claimed, which, though not made expressly by the ordinances, is made possible by them.

.   .   .   .   .

In the present cases we are not obliged to reason from the probable to the actual, and pass upon the validity of the ordinances complained of, as tried merely by the opportunities which their terms afford, of unequal and unjust discrimination in their administration. For the cases present the ordinances in actual operation, and the facts shown established an administration directed so exclusively against a particular class of persons as to warrant and require the conclusion that, whatever may have been the intent of the ordinances as adopted, they are applied by the public authorities charged with their administration, and thus representing the State itself, with a mind so unequal and oppressive as to amount to a practical denial by the State of that equal protection of the laws which is secured to the petitioners, as to all other persons, by the broad and benign provisions of the Fourteenth Amendment to the Constitution of the United States. Though the law itself be fair on its face and impartial in appearance, yet, if it is applied and administered by public authority with an evil eye and an unequal hand, so as practically to make unjust and illegal discriminations between persons in similar circumstances, material to their rights, the denial of equal justice is still within the prohibition of the Constitution.

The present cases, as shown by the facts disclosed in the record, are within this class. It appears that both petitioners have complied with every requisite, deemed by the law or by the public officers charged with its administration, necessary for the protection of neighboring property from fire, or as a precaution against injury to the public health. No reason whatever, except the will of the supervisors, is assigned why they should not be permitted to carry on, in the accustomed manner, their harmless and useful occupation, on which they depend for a livelihood. And while this consent of the supervisors is withheld from them and from two hundred others who have also petitioned, all of whom happen to be Chinese subjects, eighty others, not Chinese subjects, are permitted to carry on the same business under similar conditions. The fact of this discrimin-ation is admitted. No reason for it is shown, and the conclusion can-not be resisted, that no reason for it exists except hostility to the race and nationality to which the petitioners belong, and which in the eye of the law is not justified. The discrimination is, therefore, illegal, and the public administration which enforces it is a denial of the equal protection of the laws, and a violation of the Fourteenth Amendment of the Constitution. The imprisonment of the petition-ers is, therefore, illegal, and they must be discharged. . . .

Reversed.

TRUAX v. RAICH
239 U.S. 33 (1915)

Mr. Justice HUGHES delivered the opinion of the Court.

Under the initiative provision of the constitution of Arizona (Art. IV, sec. 1), there was adopted the following measure which was pro-claimed by the Governor as a law of the State on December 14, 1914:

An Act to protect the citizens of the United States in their employment against non-citizens of the United States, in Arizona, and to provide penal-ties and punishment for the violation thereof,

Be it enacted by the People of the State of Arizona:

Section 1. Any company, corporation, partnership, association or indi-vidual who is, or may hereafter become an employer of more than five (5) workers at any one time, in the State of Arizona, regardless of kind or class of work, or sex of workers, shall employ not less than eighty (80) per cent qualified electors or native-born citizens of the United States or some sub-division thereof. [Penalty provisions omitted.]

Mike Raich (the appellee), a native of Austria, and an inhabitant of the State of Arizona but not a qualified elector, was employed as a cook by the appellant William Truax, Sr., in his restaurant in the city of Bisbee, Cochise County. Truax had nine employees, of whom seven were neither "native-born citizens" of the United States nor qualified electors. After the election at which the act was passed Raich was informed by his employer that when the law was proclaimed, and solely by reason of its requirements and because of the fear of the penalties that would be incurred in case of its violation, he would be discharged. Thereupon, on December 15, 1914, Raich filed this bill in the District Court of the United States for the District of Arizona, asserting among other things that the act denied to him the equal protection of the laws and hence was contrary to the Fourteenth Amendment of the Constitution of the United States. Wiley E. Jones, the attorney general of the state, and W. G. Gilmore, the county attorney of Cochise County, were made defendants in addition to the employer Truax, upon the allegation that these officers would prosecute the employer unless he complied with its terms and that in order to avoid such a prosecution the employer was about to discharge the complainant. . . .

. . . . . .

The question then is whether the act assailed is repugnant to the Fourteenth Amendment. Upon the allegations of the bill, it must be assumed that the complainant, a native of Austria, has been admitted to the United States under the federal law. He was thus admitted with the privilege of entering and abiding in the United States, and hence of entering and abiding in any state of the union. . . . Being lawfully an inhabitant of Arizona, the complainant is entitled under the Fourteenth Amendment to the equal protection of its laws. The description—"any person within its jurisdiction"—as it has frequently been held, includes aliens. . . .

The act, it will be observed, provides that every employer (whether corporation, partnership, or individual) who employs more than five workers at any one time regardless of kind or class of work, or sex of workers shall employ "not less than eighty per cent qualified electors or native-born citizens of the United States or some sub-division thereof." It thus covers the entire field of industry with the exception of enterprises that are relatively very small. Its application in the present case is to employment in a restaurant the business of which requires nine employees. The purpose of an act must be found in its natural operation and effect, and the purpose of this act is not only plainly shown by its provisions, but it is frankly revealed in its title. It is there described as "An act to protect the citizens of the United States in their employment against non-citizens of the United States, in Arizona." As the appellants rightly say, there has been no subterfuge. It is an act aimed at the employment of aliens, as such, in the businesses described. Literally, its terms might be taken to include with aliens those naturalized citizens who by reason of change of residence might not be at the time qualified electors in any subdivision of the United States, but we are dealing with the main purpose of the statute, definitely stated, in the execution of which the complainant is to be forced out of his employment as a cook in a restaurant, simply because he is an alien.

It is sought to justify this act as an exercise of the power of the state to make reasonable classifications in legislating to promote the health, safety, morals and welfare of those within its jurisdiction. But this admitted authority, with the broad range of legislative discretion that it implies, does not go so far as to make it possible for the state to deny to lawful inhabitants, because of their race or nationality, the ordinary means of earning a livelihood. It requires no argument to show that the right to work for a living in the common occupations of the community is of the very essence of the personal freedom and opportunity that it was the purpose of the Amendment to secure. . . . If this could be refused solely upon the ground of race or nationality, the prohibition of the denial to any person of the equal protection of the laws would be a barren form of words. It is no answer to say, as it is argued, that the act proceeds upon the assumption that "the employment of aliens unless restrained was a peril to the public welfare." The discrimination against aliens in the wide range of employments to which the act relates is made an end in itself and thus the authority to deny to aliens, upon the mere fact of their alienage, the right to obtain support in the ordinary fields of labor is necessarily involved. It must also be said that reasonable classification implies action consistent with the legitimate interests of the state, and it will not be disputed that these cannot be so broadly conceived as to bring them into hostility to exclusive federal power. The authority to control immigration—to admit or exclude aliens— is vested solely in the Federal Government. *Fong Yue Ting* v. *United States*, 149 U.S. 698, 713. The assertion of an authority to deny to aliens the opportunity of earning a livelihood when lawfully admitted to the state would be tantamount to the assertion of the right to deny them entrance and abode, for in ordinary cases they cannot live where they cannot work. And, if such a policy were permissible, the practical result would be that those lawfully admitted to the country under the authority of acts of Congress, instead of enjoying in a substantial sense and in their full scope the privileges conferred by the admission, would be segregated in such of the states as chose to offer hospitality.

It is insisted that the act should be supported because it is not "a total deprivation of the right of the alien to labor"; that is, the restriction is limited to those businesses in which more than five workers are employed, and to the ratio fixed. It is emphasized that the employer in any line of business who employs more than five workers may employ aliens to the extent of twenty per cent of his employees. But the fallacy of this argument at once appears. If the state is at liberty to treat the employment of aliens as in itself a peril requiring restraint regardless of kind or class of work, it cannot be denied that the authority exists to make its measures to that end effective. . . . If the restriction to twenty per cent now imposed is maintainable the state undoubtedly has the power if it sees fit to make the percentage less. We have nothing before us to justify the limitation to 20 per cent save the judgment expressed in the enactment, and if that is sufficient, it is difficult to see why the apprehension and conviction thus evidenced would not be sufficient were the restriction extended so as to permit only ten per cent of the employees to be aliens or even a less percentage, or were it made applicable to all businesses in which more than three workers were employed instead of applying to those employing more than five. We have frequently said that the legislature may recognize degrees of evil and adapt its legislation accordingly . . . [citing cases]; but underlying the classification is the authority to deal with that at which the classification is aimed. The restriction now sought to be sustained is such as to suggest no limit to the state's power of excluding aliens from employment if the principle underlying the prohibition of the act is conceded. No special public interest with respect to any particular

business is shown that could possibly be deemed to support the enactment, for as we have said it relates to every sort. The discrimination
is against aliens as such in competition with citizens in the described
range of enterprises and in our opinion it clearly falls under the
condemnation of the fundamental law.

The question of rights under treaties was not expressly presented
by the bill, and, although mentioned in the argument, does not
require attention in view of the invalidity of the act under the Fourteenth Amendment.

[Mr. Justice McREYNOLDS dissented on the ground that this was a
suit against a state and as such prohibited by the Eleventh Amendment.]

DOMINION HOTEL, INC. v. ARIZONA
249 U.S. 265 (1919)

Mr. Justice HOLMES delivered the opinion of the Court.

This is an information alleging that the defendant, the plaintiff
in error, was engaged in the hotel business and permitted a woman
to work in the hotel for eight hours and that the "said eight hours
of work was not then and there performed within a period of twelve
hours," with a denial that the defendant was within the exceptions
made by the statute governing the case. The statute provides as follows: "Provided further, that the said eight hour period of work shall
be performed within a period of twelve hours, the period of twelve
hours during which such labor must be performed not to be applicable to railroad restaurants or eating houses located upon railroad
rights of way and operated by or under contract with any railroad
company." [Because of the exemption accorded to station restaurants, defendant claims denial of equal protection of the laws.] . . .
There was a trial and judgment against the defendant which was
sustained by the Supreme Court of the State, Arizona.

The Fourteenth Amendment is not a pedagogical requirement of
the impracticable. The equal protection of the laws does not mean
that all occupations that are called by the same name must be treated
in the same way. The power of the State "may be determined by degrees of evil or exercised in cases where detriment is especially experienced." *Armour & Co. v. North Dakota,* 240 U.S. 510, 517. . . . It
may do what it can to prevent what is deemed an evil and stop
short of those cases in which the harm to the few concerned
is thought less important than the harm to the public that would

ensue if the rule laid down were made mathematically exact. The only question is whether we can say on our judicial knowledge that the legislature of Arizona could not have had any reasonable ground for believing that there were such public considerations for the distinction made by the present law. The deference due to the judgment of the legislature on the matter has been emphasized again and again. . . . Of course, this is especially true when local conditions may affect the answer, conditions that the legislature does but that we cannot know. . . .

Presumably, or at least possibly, the main custom of restaurants upon railroad rights of way comes from the passengers upon trains that stop to allow them to eat. The work must be adjusted to the hours of the trains. This fact makes a practical and, it may be, an important distinction between such restaurants and others. If in its theory the distinction is justifiable, as for all that we know it is, the fact that some cases, including the plaintiff's, are very near to the line makes it none the worse. That is the inevitable result of drawing a line where the distinctions are distinctions of degree; and the constant business of the law is to draw such lines. "Upholding the act as embodying a principle generally fair and doing as nearly equal justice as can be expected seems to import that if a particular case of hardship arises under it in its natural and ordinary application, that hardship must be borne as one of the imperfections of human things." *Louisville & Nashville R. Co.* v. *Barber Asphalt Co.*, 197 U.S. 430, 434. . . . We cannot pronounce the statute void.

KOTCH v. BOARD OF RIVER PORT PILOT COMMISSIONERS FOR THE PORT OF NEW ORLEANS
330 U.S. 552 (1947)

Mr. Justice BLACK delivered the opinion of the Court.

Louisiana statutes provide in general that all seagoing vessels moving between New Orleans and foreign ports must be navigated through the Mississippi River approaches to the port of New Orleans and within it, exclusively by pilots who are state officers. New state pilots are appointed by the governor only upon certification of a State Board of River Pilot Commissioners, themselves pilots. Only those who have served a six month apprenticeship under incumbent pilots and who possess other specific qualifications may be certified to the governor by the board. Appellants here have had at least fifteen years experience in the river, the port, and elsewhere, as pilots of vessels whose pilotage was not governed by the state law in question. Although they possess all the statutory qualifications except that they have not served the requisite six months apprenticeship under Louisiana officer pilots, they have been denied appointment as state pilots. Seeking relief in a Louisiana state court, they alleged that the incumbent pilots, having unfettered discretion under the law in the selection of apprentices, had selected, with occasional exception, only the relatives and friends of incumbents; that the selections were made by electing prospective apprentices into the pilots' association, which the pilots have formed by authority of state law; that since "membership . . . is closed to all except those having the favor of the pilots" the result is that only their relatives and friends have and can become state pilots. The Supreme Court of Louisiana has held that the pilotage law so administered does not violate the equal protection clause of the Fourteenth Amendment. . . .

The constitutional command for a state to afford "equal protection of the laws" sets a goal not attainable by the invention and application of a precise formula. This Court has never attempted that impossible task. A law which affects the activities of some groups differently from the way in which it affects the activities of other groups is not necessarily banned by the Fourteenth Amendment. . . . Otherwise, effective regulation in the public interest could not be provided, however essential that regulation might be. For it is axiomatic that the consequence of regulating by setting apart a classified group is that those in it will be subject to some restrictions or receive certain advantages that do not apply to other groups or to all the public. . . . This selective application of a regulation is discrimination in the broad sense, but it may or may not deny equal protection of the laws. Clearly, it might offend that constitutional safeguard if it rested on grounds wholly irrelevant to achievement of the regulation's objectives. An example would be a law applied to deny a person a right to earn a living or hold any job because of hostility to his particular race, religion, beliefs, or because of any other reason having no rational relation to the regulated activities. . . .

. . . So here, we must consider the relationship of the method of appointing pilots to the broad objectives of the entire Louisiana pilotage law. . . . In so doing we must view the appointment system in the context of the historical evolution of the laws and institution of pilotage in Louisiana and elsewhere. . . . And an important factor in our consideration is that this case tests the right and power of a state to select its own agents and officers.

. . . . .

The history and practice of pilotage demonstrate that, although inextricably geared to a complex commercial economy, it is also a highly personalized calling. A pilot does not require a formalized technical education so much as a detailed and extremely intimate, almost intuitive, knowledge of the weather, waterways and conformation of the harbor or river which he serves. This seems to be particularly true of the approaches to New Orleans through the treacherous and shifting channel of the Mississippi River. Moreover, harbor entrances where pilots can most conveniently make their homes and still be close to places where they board incoming and leave outgoing ships are usually some distance from the port cities they serve. These "pilot towns" have begun, and generally exist today, as small communities of pilots perhaps near, but usually distinct from the port cities. In these communities young men have an opportunity to acquire special knowledge of the weather and water hazards of the locality and seem to grow up with ambitions to become pilots in the traditions of their fathers, relatives, and neighbors. We are asked, in effect, to say that Louisiana is without constitutional authority to conclude that apprenticeship under persons specially interested in a pilot's future is the best way to fit him for duty as a pilot officer in the service of the State.

The States have had full power to regulate pilotage of certain kinds of vessels since 1789 when the first Congress decided that then existing state pilot laws were satisfactory and made federal regulation unnecessary. 1 Stat. 53, 54 (1789), 46 U.S.C. § 211. Louisiana legislation has controlled the activities and appointment of pilots since 1805—even before the Territory was admitted as a State. The State pilotage system, as it has evolved since 1805, is typical of that which grew up in most seaboard states and in foreign countries. . . . Thus in Louisiana, as elsewhere, it seems to have been accepted at an early date that in pilotage, unlike other occupations, competition for appointment, for the opportunity to serve particular ships and for fees, adversely affects the public interest in pilotage.

It is within the framework of this longstanding pilotage regulation system that the practice has apparently existed of permitting pilots, if they choose, to select their relatives and friends as the only ones ultimately eligible for appointment as pilots by the governor. Many other states have established pilotage systems which make the selection of pilots on this basis possible. Thus it was noted thirty years ago in a Department of Commerce study of pilotage that membership of pilot associations "is limited to persons agreeable to those already members, generally relatives and friends of the pilots. Probably in pilotage more than in any other occupation of the United States the male members of a family follow the same work generation to generation."

The practice of nepotism in appointing public servants has been a subject of controversy in this country throughout our history. Some states have adopted constitutional amendments or statutes, to prohibit it. These have reflected state policies to wipe out the practice. But Louisiana and most other states have adopted no such general policy. We can only assume that the Louisiana legislature weighed the obvious possibility of evil against whatever useful function a closely knit pilotage system may serve. Thus the advantages of early experience under friendly supervision in the locality of the pilot's training, the benefits to morale and esprit de corps which family and neighborly tradition might contribute, the close association in which pilots must work and live in their pilot communities and on the water, and the discipline and regulation which is imposed to assure the State competent pilot service after appointment, might have prompted the legislature to permit Louisiana pilot officers to select those with whom they would serve.

The number of people, as a practical matter, who can be pilots is very limited. No matter what system of selection is adopted, all but the few occasionally selected must of necessity be excluded. . . . We are aware of no decision of this Court holding that the Constitution requires a state governor, or subordinates responsible to him and removable by him for cause, to select state public servants by competitive tests or by any other particular method of selection. The object of the entire pilotage law, as we have pointed out, is to secure for the State and others interested the safest and most efficiently operated pilotage system practicable. We cannot say that the method adopted in Louisiana for the selection of pilots is unrelated to this objective . . . Considering the entirely unique institution of pilotage in the light of its history in Louisiana, we cannot say that the practice appellants attack is the kind of discrimination which violates the equal protection clause of the Fourteenth Amendment.

Affirmed.

Mr. Justice RUTLEDGE, dissenting.

The unique history and conditions surrounding the activities of river port pilots, shortly recounted in the Court's opinion, justify a high degree of public regulation. But I do not think they can sustain a system of entailment for the occupation. If Louisiana were to provide by statute in haec verba that only members of John Smith's family would be eligible for the public calling of pilot, I have no doubt that the statute on its face would infringe the Fourteenth Amendment. And this would be true, even though John Smith and the members of his family had been pilots for generations. It would be true also if the right were expanded to include a number of designated families.

In final analysis this is, I think, the situation presented on this record. While the statutes applicable do not purport on their face to restrict the right to become a licensed pilot to members of the families of licensed pilots, the charge is that they have been so administered. And this charge not only is borne out by the record but is accepted by the Court as having been sustained.

The result of the decision therefore is to approve as constitutional state regulation which makes admission to the ranks of pilots turn finally on consanguinity. Blood is, in effect, made the crux of selection. That, in my opinion, is forbidden by the Fourteenth Amendment's guaranty against denial of the equal protection of the laws. The door is thereby closed to all not having blood relationship to presently licensed pilots. Whether the occupation is considered as having the status of "public officer" or of highly regulated private employment, it is beyond legislative power to make entrance to it turn upon such a criterion. The Amendment makes no exception from its prohibitions against state action on account of the fact that public rather than private employment is affected by the forbidden discriminations. That fact simply makes violation all the more clear where those discriminations are shown to exist.

It is not enough to avoid the Amendment's force that a familial system may have a tendency or, as the Court puts it, a direct relationship to the end of securing an efficient pilotage system. Classification based on the purpose to be accomplished may be said abstractly to be sound. But when the test adopted and applied in fact is race or consanguinity, it cannot be used constitutionally to bar all except a group chosen by such a relationship from public employment. That is not a test; it is a whole arbitrary exercise of power.

Conceivably the familial system would be the most effective possible scheme for training many kinds of artisans or public servants, sheerly from the viewpoint of securing the highest degree of skill and competence. Indeed, something very worth while largely disappeared from our national life when the once prevalent familial system of conducting manufacturing and mercantile enterprises went out and was replaced by the highly impersonal corporate system for doing business.

But that loss is not one to be repaired under our scheme by legislation framed or administered to perpetuate family monopolies of either private occupations or branches of the public service. It is precisely because the Amendment forbids enclosing those areas by legislative lines drawn on the basis of race, color, creed and the like, that, in cases like this, the possibly most efficient method of securing the highest development of skills cannot be established by law. Absent any such bar, the presence of such a tendency or direct relationship would be effective for sustaining the legislation. It cannot be effective to overcome the bar itself. The discrimination here is not shown to be consciously racial in character. But I am unable to differentiate in effects one founded on blood relationship.

The case therefore falls squarely within the ruling in *Yick Wo* v. *Hopkins,* 118 U.S. 356, not only with relation to the line of discrimination employed, but also in the fact that unconstitutional administration of a statute otherwise valid on its face incurs the same condemnation as if the statute had incorporated the discrimination in terms. Appellants here are entitled, in my judgment, to the same relief as was afforded in the *Yick Wo* case.

Mr. Justice REED, Mr. Justice DOUGLAS and Mr. Justice MURPHY join in this dissent.

2. EQUALITY OF THE RACES

STRAUDER v. WEST VIRGINIA
100 U.S. 303 (1880)

Mr. Justice STRONG delivered the opinion of the Court.

In this Court, several errors have been assigned, and the controlling questions underlying them all are, first, whether, by the Constitution and laws of the United States, every citizen of the United

States has a right to a trial of an indictment against him by a jury selected and impaneled without discrimination against his race or color, because of race or color; and, second, if he has such a right, and is denied its enjoyment by the State in which he is indicted, may he cause the case to be removed into the Circuit Court of the United States?

It is to be observed that the first of these questions is not whether a colored man, when an indictment has been preferred against him, has a right to a grand or a petit jury composed in whole or in part of persons of his own race or color, but it is whether, in the composition or selection of jurors by whom he is to be indicted or tried, all persons of his race or color may be excluded by law, solely because of their race or color, so that by no possibility can any colored man sit upon the jury. . . .

This [the Fourteenth Amendment] is one of a series of constitutional provisions having a common purpose; namely, securing to a race recently emancipated, a race that through many generations had been held in slavery, all the civil rights that the superior race enjoy. The true spirit and meaning of the amendments, as we said in the *Slaughter-House Case* (16 Wall. 36), cannot be understood without keeping in view the history of the times when they were adopted, and the general objects they plainly sought to accomplish. At the time when they were incorporated into the Constitution, it required little knowledge of human nature to anticipate that those who had long been regarded as an inferior and subject race would, when suddenly raised to the rank of citizenship, be looked upon with jealousy and positive dislike, and that State laws might be enacted or enforced to perpetuate the distinctions that had before existed. Discriminations against them had been habitual. It was well known that in some States laws making such discriminations then existed, and others might well be expected. The colored race, as a race, was abject and ignorant, and in that condition was unfitted to command the respect of those who had superior intelligence. Their training had left them mere children, and as such they needed the protection which a wise government extends to those who are unable to protect themselves. They especially needed protection against unfriendly action in the States where they were resident. It was in view of these considerations the Fourteenth Amendment was framed and adopted. It was designed to assure to the colored race the enjoyment of all the civil rights that under the law are enjoyed by white persons, and to give to that race the protection of the general government, in that enjoyment, whenever it should be denied by the States. It not only gave citizenship and the privileges of citizenship to persons of color, but it denied to any State the power to withhold from them the equal protection of the laws, and authorized Congress to enforce its provisions by appropriate legislation. . . .

If this is the spirit and meaning of the amendment, whether it means more or not, it is to be construed liberally, to carry out the purposes of its framers. It ordains that no State shall make or enforce any laws which shall abridge the privileges or immunities of citizens of the United States (evidently referring to the newly made citizens, who, being citizens of the United States, are declared to be also citizens of the State in which they reside). It ordains that no State shall deprive any persons of life, liberty, or property, without due process of law, or deny to any person within its jurisdiction the equal protection of the laws. What is this but declaring that the law in the States shall be the same for the black as for the white; that all persons, whether colored or white, shall stand equal before the laws of the States, and, in regard to the colored race, for whose protection the amendment was primarily designed, that no discrimination shall be made against them by law because of their color? The words of the amendment, it is true, are prohibitory, but they contain a necessary implication of a positive immunity, or right, most valuable to the colored race,—the right to exemption from unfriendly legislation against them distinctly as colored,—exemption from legal discriminations, implying inferiority in civil society, lessening the security of their enjoyment of the rights which others enjoy, and discriminations which are steps towards reducing them to the condition of a subject race.

That the West Virginia statute respecting juries—the statute that controlled the selection of the grand and petit jury in the case of the plaintiff in error—is such a discrimination ought not to be doubted. Nor would it be if the persons excluded by it were white men. If in those States where the colored people constitute a majority of the entire population a law should be enacted excluding all white men from jury service, thus denying to them the privilege of participating equally with the blacks in the administration of justice, we apprehend no one would be heard to claim that it would not be a denial to white men of the equal protection of the laws. Nor if a law should be passed excluding all naturalized Celtic Irishmen, would there be any doubt of its inconsistency with the spirit of the amendment. The very fact that colored people are singled out and expressly denied by a statute all right to participate in the administration of the law, as jurors, because of their color, though they are citizens, and may be in other respects fully qualified, is practically a brand upon them, affixed by the law, an assertion of their inferiority, and a stimulant to that race prejudice which is an impediment to securing to individuals of the race that equal justice which the law aims to secure to all others.

The right to a trial by jury is guaranteed to every citizen of West Virginia by the Constitution of that State, and the constitution of juries is a very essential part of the protection such a mode of trial is intended to secure. The very idea of a jury is a body of men composed of the peers or equals of the person whose rights it is selected or summoned to determine; that is, of his neighbors, fellows, associates, persons having the same legal status in society as that which he holds. . . . It is well known that prejudices often exist against particular classes in the community, which sway the judgment of jurors, and which, therefore, operate in some cases to deny to persons of those classes the full enjoyment of that protection which others enjoy. Prejudice in a local community is held to be a reason for a change of venue. The framers of the constitutional amendment must have known full well the existence of such prejudice and its likelihood to continue against the manumitted slaves and their race, and that knowledge was doubtless a motive that led to the amendment. By their manumission and citizenship the colored race became entitled to the equal protection of the laws of the States in which they resided; and the apprehension that through prejudice they might be denied that equal protection, that is, that there might be discrimination against them, was the inducement to bestow upon the national government the power to enforce the provisions that no State shall deny to them the equal protection of the laws. Without the apprehended existence of prejudice that portion of the amendment would have been unnecessary, and it might have been left to the States to extend equality of protection.

In view of these considerations, it is hard to see why the statute of West Virginia should not be regarded as discriminating against a colored man when he is put upon trial for an alleged criminal offense against the State. It is not easy to comprehend how it can be said that while every white man is entitled to a trial by a jury selected from persons of his own race or color, or rather, selected without discrimination against his color, and a negro is not, the latter is equally protected by the law with the former. Is not protection of life, and liberty against race or color prejudice a right, a legal right, under the constitutional amendment? And how can it be maintained that compelling a colored man to submit to a trial for his life by a jury drawn from a panel from which the State has expressly excluded every man of his race, because of color alone, however well qualified in other respects, is not a denial to him of equal legal protection?

. . . . . .

The judgment of the Supreme Court of West Virginia will be reversed, and the case remitted with instructions to reverse the judgment of the Circuit Court of Ohio County: and it is so ordered.

[Mr. Justice FIELD and Mr. Justice CLIFFORD dissented.]

NORRIS v. ALABAMA
294 U.S. 587 (1935)

Mr. Chief Justice HUGHES delivered the opinion of the Court.

Petitioner, Clarence Norris, is one of nine Negro boys who were indicted in March 1931 in Jackson county, Ala., for the crime of rape. On being brought to trial in that county eight were convicted. This Court reversed the judgments of conviction upon the ground that the defendants had been denied due process of law in that the trial court had failed in the light of the circumstances disclosed, and of the inability of the defendants at that time to obtain counsel, to make an effective appointment of counsel to aid them in preparing and presenting their defense. *Powell* v. *Alabama,* 287 U.S. 45.[1]

After the remand, a motion for change of venue [place of trial] was granted and the cases were transferred to Morgan county. Norris was brought to trial in November 1933. At the outset, a motion was made on his behalf to quash the indictment upon the ground of the exclusion of Negroes from juries in Jackson county where the indictment was found. A motion was also made to quash the trial venire [summons for jury duty] in Morgan county upon the ground of the exclusion of Negroes from juries in that county. In relation to each county, the charge was of long-continued, systematic and arbitrary exclusion of qualified Negro citizens from service on juries, solely because of their race and color, in violation of the Constitution of the United States. . . . The trial . . . proceeded and resulted in the

[1] *Supra,* p. 376.

conviction of Norris who was sentenced to death. On appeal, the Supreme Court of the state considered and decided the federal question which Norris had raised and affirmed the judgment. We granted a writ of certiorari.

First. There is no controversy as to the constitutional principle involved. . . . Summing up precisely the effect of earlier decisions, this Court thus stated the principle in *Carter* v. *Texas,* 177 U.S. 442, 447, in relation to exclusion from service on grand juries: "Whenever by any action of a state, whether through its legislature, through its courts, or through its executive or administrative officers, all persons of the African race are excluded, solely because of their race or color, from serving as grand jurors in the criminal prosecution of a person of the African race, the equal protection of the laws is denied to him, contrary to the Fourteenth Amendment." . . . The principle is equally applicable to a similar exclusion of Negroes from service on petit juries. And although the state statute defining the qualifications of jurors may be fair on its face, the constitutional provision affords protection against action of the state through its administrative officers in effecting the prohibited discrimination.

The question is of the application of this established principle to the facts disclosed by the record. That the question is one of fact does not relieve us of the duty to determine whether in truth a federal right has been denied. When a federal right has been specially set up and claimed in a state court, it is our province to inquire not merely whether it was denied in express terms but also whether it was denied in substance and effect. If this requires an examination of evidence, that examination must be made. Otherwise, review by this Court would fail of its purpose in safeguarding constitutional rights.

Second. The evidence on the motion to quash the indictment. In 1930, the total population of Jackson county, where the indictment was found, was 36,881, of whom 2688 were Negroes. The male population over 21 years of age numbered 8801, and of these 666 were Negroes.

The qualifications of jurors were thus prescribed by the state statute: "The jury commission shall place on the jury roll and in the jury box the names of all male citizens of the county who are generally reputed to be honest and intelligent men, and are esteemed in the community for their integrity, good character and sound judgment, but no person must be selected who is under 21 or over 65 years of age, or who is an habitual drunkard, or who, being afflicted with a permanent disease or physical weakness, is unfit to discharge the duties of a juror, or who cannot read English, or who has ever been convicted of any offense involving moral turpitude. If a person cannot read English and has all the other qualifications prescribed herein and is a freeholder or householder, his name may be placed on the jury roll and in the jury box."

Defendant adduced evidence to support the charge of unconstitutional discrimination in the actual administration of the statute in Jackson county. The testimony, as the state court said, tended to show that "in a long number of years no Negro had been called for jury service in that county." It appeared that no Negro had served on any grand or petit jury in that county within the memory of witnesses who had lived there all their lives. Testimony to that effect was given by men whose ages ran from 50 to 76 years. Their testimony was uncontradicted. It was supported by the testimony of officials. The clerk of the jury commission and the clerk of the circuit court had never known of a Negro serving on a grand jury in Jackson county. The court reporter, who had not missed a session in that county in 24 years, and two jury commissioners testified to the same effect. One of the latter, who was a member of the commission which made up the jury roll for the grand jury which found the indictment, testified that he had "never known of a single instance where any Negro sat on any grand or petit jury in the entire history of that county."

That testimony in itself made out a prima facie case of the denial of the equal protection which the Constitution guarantees. . . . The case thus made was supplemented by direct testimony that specified Negroes, 30 or more in number, were qualified for jury service. Among these were Negroes who were members of school boards, or trustees, of colored schools, and property owners and householders. It also appeared that Negroes from that county had been called for jury service in the federal court. Several of those who were thus described as qualified were witnesses. While there was testimony which cast doubt upon the qualifications of some of the Negroes who had been named, and there was also general testimony by the editor of a local newspaper who gave his opinion as to the lack of "sound judgment" of the "good Negroes" in Jackson county, we think that the definite testimony as to the actual qualifications of individual Negroes, which was not met by any testimony equally direct, showed that there were Negroes in Jackson county qualified for jury service. . . .

The state court rested its decision upon the ground that even if it were assumed that there was no name of a Negro on the jury roll, it was not established that race or color caused the omission. The court pointed out that the statute fixed a high standard of qualifications for jurors and that the jury commission was vested with a wide discretion. The court adverted to the fact that more white citizens possessing age qualifications had been omitted from the jury roll than the entire Negro population of the county, and regarded the testimony as being to the effect that "the matter of race, color, politics, religion or fraternal affiliations" had not been discussed by the commission and had not entered into their consideration, and that no one had been excluded because of race or color. . . .

We are of the opinion that the evidence required a different result from that reached in the state court. We think that the evidence that for a generation or longer no Negro had been called for service on any jury in Jackson county, that there were Negroes qualified for jury service, that according to the practice of the jury commission their names would normally appear on the preliminary list of male citizens of the requisite age but that no names of Negroes were placed on the jury roll, and the testimony with respect to the lack of appropriate consideration of the qualifications of Negroes, established the discrimination which the Constitution forbids. The motion to quash the indictment upon that ground should have been granted.

Third. The evidence on the motion to quash the trial venire. The population of Morgan county, where the trial was had, was larger than that of Jackson county, and the proportion of Negroes was much greater. The total population of Morgan county in 1930 was 46,176, and of this number 8311 were Negroes.

Within the memory of witnesses, long resident there, no Negro had ever served on a jury in that county or had been called for such service. Some of these witnesses were over 50 years of age and had always lived in Morgan county. Their testimony was not contradicted. A clerk of the circuit court, who had resided in the county for 30 years, and who had been in office for over four years, testified that during his official term approximately 2500 persons had been called for jury service and that not one of them was a Negro; that he did not recall "ever seeing any single person of the colored race serve on any jury in Morgan county."

There was abundant evidence that there were a large number of Negroes in the county who were qualified for jury service. Men of intelligence, some of whom were college graduates, testified to long lists (said to contain nearly 200 names) of such qualified Negroes, including many businessmen, owners of real property, and householders. When defendant's counsel proposed to call many additional witnesses in order to adduce further proof of qualifications of Negroes for jury service, the trial judge limited the testimony, holding that the evidence was cumulative.

We find no warrant for a conclusion that the names of any of the Negroes as to whom this testimony was given, or of any other Negroes, were placed on the jury rolls. No such names were identified. The evidence that for many years no Negro had been called for jury service itself tended to show the absence of the names of Negroes from the jury rolls, and the state made no effort to prove their presence.

For this long-continued, unvarying, and wholesale exclusion of Negroes from jury service we find no justification consistent with the constitutional mandate. We have carefully examined the testimony of the jury commissioners upon which the state court based its decision. . . .

We think that this evidence failed to rebut the strong prima facie case which defendant had made. That showing as to the long-continued exclusion of Negroes from jury service, and as to the many Negroes qualified for that service, could not be met by mere generalities. If, in the presence of such testimony as defendant adduced, the mere general assertions by officials of their performance of duty were to be accepted as an adequate justification for the complete exclusion of Negroes from jury service, the constitutional provision—adopted with special reference to their protection—would be but a vain and illusory requirement. . . .

We are concerned only with the federal question which we have discussed, and in view of the denial of the federal right suitably asserted, the judgment must be reversed and the cause remanded for further proceedings not inconsistent with this opinion.

Mr. Justice McREYNOLDS did not hear the argument and took no part in the consideration and decision of this case.

SHELLEY v. KRAEMER
334 U.S. 1 (1948)

Mr. Chief Justice VINSON delivered the opinion of the Court.

These cases present for our consideration questions relating to the validity of court enforcement of private agreements, generally described as restrictive covenants, which have as their purpose the exclusion of persons of designated race or color from the ownership or occupancy of real property. Basic constitutional issues of obvious importance have been raised.

. . . . .

It is well, at the outset, to scrutinize the terms of the restrictive agreements involved in these cases. In the Missouri case, the covenant declares that no part of the affected property shall be "occupied by any person not of the Caucasian race, it being intended hereby to restrict the use of said property . . . against the occupancy as owners or tenants of any portion of said property for resident or other purposes by people of the Negro or Mongolian Race." Not only does the restriction seek to proscribe use and occupancy of the affected property by members of the excluded class, but as construed by the Missouri courts, the agreement requires that title of any person who uses his property in violation of the restriction shall be divested. The restriction of the covenant in the Michigan case seeks to bar occupancy by persons of the excluded class. It provides that "This property shall not be used or occupied by any person or persons except those of the Caucasian race."

It should be observed that these covenants do not seek to proscribe any particular use of the affected properties. Use of the properties for residential occupancy, as such, is not forbidden. The restrictions of these agreements, rather, are directed toward a designated class of persons and seek to determine who may and who may not own or make use of the properties for residential purposes. The excluded class is defined wholly in terms of race or color; "simply that and nothing more."

It cannot be doubted that among the civil rights intended to be protected from discriminatory state action by the Fourteenth Amendment are the rights to acquire, enjoy, own and dispose of property. Equality in the enjoyment of property rights was regarded by the framers of that Amendment as an essential pre-condition to the realization of other basic civil rights and liberties which the Amendment was intended to guarantee. . . .

.   .   .   .   .

It is likewise clear that restrictions on the right of occupancy of the sort sought to be created by the private agreements in these cases could not be squared with the requirements of the Fourteenth Amendment if imposed by state statute or local ordinance. We do not understand respondents to urge the contrary. . . .

.   .   .   .   .

But the present cases . . . do not involve action by state legislatures or city councils. Here the particular patterns of discrimination and the areas in which the restrictions are to operate, are determined, in the first instance, by the terms of agreements among private individuals. Participation of the state consists in the enforcement of the restrictions so defined. The crucial issue with which we are here confronted is whether this distinction removes these cases from the operation of the prohibitory provisions of the Fourteenth Amendment.

Since the decision of this Court in the *Civil Rights Cases,* 109 U.S. 3 (1883), the principle has become firmly embedded in our constitutional law that the action inhibited by the first section of the Fourteenth Amendment is only such action as may fairly be said to be that of the states. That Amendment erects no shield against merely private conduct, however discriminatory or wrongful.

We conclude, therefore, that the restrictive agreements standing alone cannot be regarded as a violation of any rights guaranteed to petitioners by the Fourteenth Amendment. So long as the purposes of those agreements are effectuated by voluntary adherence to their terms, it would appear clear that there has been no action by the state and the provisions of the Amendment have not been violated. . . .

But here there was more. These are cases in which the purposes of the agreements were secured only by judicial enforcement by state courts of the restrictive terms of the agreements. The respondents urge that judicial enforcement of private agreement does not

amount to state action; or, in any event, the participation of the
States is so attenuated as not to amount to state action within the
Fourteenth Amendment. . . .

We have no doubt that there has been state action in these cases in
the full and complete sense of the phrase. . . .

These are not cases . . . in which the States have merely abstained
from action, leaving private individuals free to impose such discriminations as they see fit. Rather, these are cases in which the
States have made available to such individuals the full coercive power
of government to deny to petitioners, on the grounds of race or color,
the enjoyment of property rights in premises which petitioners are
willing and financially able to acquire and which the grantors are
willing to sell. The difference between judicial enforcement and
non-enforcement of the restrictive covenants is the difference to petitioners between being denied rights of property available to other
members of the community and being accorded full enjoyment of
those rights on an equal footing.

We hold that in granting judicial enforcement of the restrictive
agreements in these cases, the states have denied petitioners the equal
protection of the laws and that, therefore, the action of the state
courts cannot stand. We have noted that freedom from discrimination by the states in the enjoyment of property rights was among the
basic objectives sought to be effectuated by the framers of the Fourteenth Amendment. That such discrimination has occurred in these
cases is clear. . . .

Respondents urge, however, that since the state courts stand ready
to enforce restrictive covenants excluding white persons from the
ownership or occupancy of property covered by such agreements,
enforcement of covenants excluding colored persons may not be
deemed a denial of equal protection of the laws to the colored
persons who are thereby affected. This contention does not bear
scrutiny. The parties have directed our attention to no case in which
a court, state or federal, has been called upon to enforce a covenant
excluding members of the white majority from ownership or occupancy of real property on grounds of race or color. But there are
more fundamental considerations. The rights created by the first
section of the Fourteenth Amendment are, by its terms, guaranteed

to the individual. The rights established are personal rights. It is, therefore, no answer to these petitioners to say that the courts may also be induced to deny white persons rights of ownership and occupancy on grounds of race or color. Equal protection of the laws is not achieved through indiscriminate imposition of inequalities.

Nor do we find merit in the suggestion that property owners who are parties to these agreements are denied equal protection of the laws if denied access to the courts to enforce the terms of the restrictive covenants and to assert property rights which the state courts have held to be created by such agreements. The Constitution confers upon no individual the right to demand action by the state which results in the denial of equal protection of the laws to other individuals. And it would appear beyond question that the power of the state to create and enforce property interests must be exercised within the boundaries defined by the Fourteenth Amendment. . . .

The problem of defining the scope of the restrictions which the Federal Constitution imposes upon exertions of power by the states has given rise to many of the most persistent and fundamental issues which this Court has been called upon to consider. That problem was foremost in the minds of the framers of the Constitution, and since that early day, has arisen in a multitude of forms. The task of determining whether the action of a state offends constitutional provisions is one which may not be undertaken lightly. Where, however, it is clear that the action of the state violates the terms of the fundamental charter, it is the obligation of this Court so to declare.

The historical context in which the Fourteenth Amendment became a part of the Constitution should not be forgotten. Whatever else the framers sought to achieve, it is clear that the matter of primary concern was the establishment of equality in the enjoyment of basic civil and political rights and the preservation of those rights from discriminatory action on the part of the states based on considerations of race or color. Seventy-five years ago this Court announced that the provisions of the Amendment are to be construed with this fundamental purpose in mind. Upon full consideration, we have concluded that in these cases the states have acted to deny petitioners the equal protection of the laws guaranteed by the Fourteenth Amendment. Having so decided, we find it unnecessary to consider whether petitioners have also been deprived of property without due process of law or denied privileges and immunities of citizens of the United States.

For the reasons stated, the judgment of the Supreme Court of Missouri and the judgment of the Supreme Court of Michigan must be reversed.

Mr. Justice REED, Mr. Justice JACKSON, and Mr. Justice RUT-LEDGE took no part in the consideration or decision of these cases.[2]

TAKAHASHI v. FISH AND GAME COMMISSION
334 U.S. 410 (1948)

Mr. Justice BLACK delivered the opinion of the Court.

The respondent, Torao Takahashi, born in Japan, came to this country and became a resident of California in 1907. Federal laws, based on distinctions of "color and race," . . . have permitted Japanese and certain other non-white racial groups to enter and reside in the country, but have made them ineligible for United States citizenship. The question presented is whether California can, consistently with the Federal Constitution and laws passed pursuant to it, use this federally created racial ineligibility for citizenship as a basis for barring Takahashi from earning his living as a commercial fisherman in the ocean waters off the coast of California.

Prior to 1943 California issued commercial fishing licenses to all qualified persons without regard to alienage or ineligibility to citizenship. From 1915 to 1942, Takahashi, under annual commercial fishing licenses issued by the state, fished in ocean waters off the California coast, apparently both within and without the three-mile coastal belt, and brought his fresh fish ashore for sale. In 1942, while this country was at war with Japan, Takahashi and other California residents of Japanese ancestry were evacuated from the state under military orders. . . . In 1943 during the period of war and evacuation, an amendment to the California Fish and Game Code was adopted prohibiting issuance of a license to any "alien Japanese." . . . In 1945, the state code was again amended by striking out the 1943 provision for fear that it might be "declared unconstitutional" because directed only "against alien Japanese"; the new amendment banned issuance of licenses to any "person ineligible to citizenship," which classification included Japanese. . . . Because of this state provision barring issuance of commercial fishing licenses to persons ineligible for citizenship under federal law, Takahashi, who

---

[2] Reportedly because they themselves were holders of properties covered by restrictive covenants.

met all other state requirements, was denied a license by the California Fish and Game Commission upon his return to California in 1945.

[Takahashi asked and obtained a court order directing the commission to issue him a license. On appeal by the commission the state supreme court reversed this order on the grounds that the state had a proprietary interest in the fish off its shore, and that this interest justified the state in barring from the exploitation of this property aliens in general, and aliens ineligible for citizenship in particular.]

... In *Truax* v. *Raich,* 239 U.S. 33 (1915) [3] ... not deemed controlling by the majority of the California Supreme Court, ... this Court, in upholding Raich's contention that the Arizona law was invalid, declared Raich, having been lawfully admitted into the country under a federal law, had a federal privilege to enter and abide in "any state in the union" and thereafter under the Fourteenth Amendment to enjoy the equal protection of the laws of the state in which he abided; that this privilege to enter in and abide in any state carried with it the "right to work for a living in the common occupations of the community," a denial of which right would make of the Amendment "a barren form of words." ...

However, the Court ... went on to note that it had on occasions sustained state legislation that did not apply alike to citizens and non-citizens, the ground for the distinction being that such laws were necessary to protect special interests either of the state or of the citizens as such. The *Truax* opinion pointed out that the Arizona law, aimed as it was against employment of aliens in all vocations, failed to show a "special public interest with respect to any particular business ... that could possibly be deemed to support the enactment." The Court noted that it had previously upheld various state laws which restricted the privilege of planting oysters in the tidewater rivers of a state to citizens of that state, and which denied to aliens within a state the privilege of possessing a rifle and of shooting game within the state; it also referred to decisions recognizing a state's broad powers, in the absence of overriding treaties, to restrict the devolution of real property to non-aliens.

California now urges, and the state supreme court held, that the California fishing provision here challenged falls within the rationale of the "special public interest" cases distinguished in the

[3] *Supra,* p. 413.

Truax opinion, and thus that the state's ban upon commercial fishing by aliens ineligible to citizenship is valid. . . .

First. The state's contention that its law was passed solely as a fish conservation measure is vigorously denied. The petitioner argues that it was the outgrowth of racial antagonism directed solely against the Japanese, and that for this reason alone it cannot stand. . . . We find it unnecessary to resolve this controversy concerning the motives that prompted enactment of the legislation. . . .

Second. It does not follow, as California seems to argue, that because the United States regulates immigration and naturalization in part on the basis of race and color classifications, a state can adopt one or more of the same classifications to prevent lawfully admitted aliens within its borders from earning a living in the same way that other state inhabitants earn their living. The Federal Government had broad constitutional powers in determining what aliens shall be admitted to the United States, the period they may remain, regulation of their conduct before naturalization. . . . Under the Constitution the states are granted no such powers; they can neither add nor take from the conditions lawfully imposed by Congress upon admission, naturalization and residence of aliens in the United States or the several states. . . .

. . . The Fourteenth Amendment and the laws adopted under its authority . . . embody a general policy that all persons lawfully in this country shall abide "in any state" on an equality of legal privilege with all citizens under non-discriminatory laws.

. . . The state's law here cannot be supported in the employment of this legislative authority because of policies adopted by Congress in the exercise of its power to treat separately and differently with aliens from countries composed of many diverse cultures, races, and colors. For these reasons the power of a state to apply its laws exclusively to its alien inhabitants as a class is confined within narrow limits.

Third. We are unable to find that the "special public interest" on which California relies provides support for this state ban on Takahashi's commercial fishing. . . . California's claim of "special public interest" is that its citizens are the collective owners of fish swimming in the three-mile belt. . . . To whatever extent the fish in the three-mile belt off California may be capable of ownership by California, we think that "ownership" is inadequate to justify California in excluding any or all aliens who are lawful residents of the state from making a living by fishing in the ocean off its shores while permitting all others to do so.

.   .   .   .   .

[Reversed.]

Mr. Justice MURPHY, with whom Mr. Justice RUTLEDGE agrees, concurring.

The opinion of the Court, in which I join, adequately expresses my views as to all but one important aspect of this case. That aspect relates to the fact that Section 990 of the California Fish and Game Code, barring those ineligible to citizenship from securing commercial fishing licenses, is the direct outgrowth of antagonism toward persons of Japanese ancestry. Even the most cursory examination of the background of the statute demonstrates that it was designed solely to discriminate against such persons in a manner inconsistent with the concept of equal protection of the laws. Legislation of that type is not entitled to wear the cloak of constitutionality.

.   .   .   .   .

We need but unbutton the seemingly innocent words of Section 990 to discover beneath them the very negation of all the ideals of the equal protection clause. No more is necessary to warrant a reversal of the judgment below.

Mr. Justice REED, dissenting.

The reasons which lead me to believe that the judgment of the Supreme Court of California should be affirmed may be briefly stated. As fishing rights have been treated traditionally as a natural resource, in the absence of federal regulation, California as a sovereign state has power to regulate the taking of fish in the water bordering its shores. It is, I think, one of the natural resources of the state that may be preserved from exploitation by aliens. The ground for this power in the absence of any exercise of federal authority is California's authority over its fisheries.

.   .   .   .   .

The Federal Government has not pursued a policy of equal treatment of aliens and citizens. Citizens have rights superior to those of aliens in the ownership of land and in exploiting natural resources. Perhaps Congress as a matter of immigration policy may require that states open every door of opportunity in America to all resident aliens, but until Congress so determines as to fisheries, I do not feel that the judicial arm of the Government should require the states to admit all aliens to this privilege.

.   .   .   .   .

. . . A state has power to exclude from enjoyment of its natural resources those who are unwilling or unable to become citizens.

If aliens, as I think they can, may be excluded by a state from fishing privileges, I see no reason why the classification established by California excluding only aliens ineligible to citizenship is prohibited by the Constitution. . . . Whatever we may think of the wisdom of California's statute, we should intervene only when we conclude the state statute passes constitutional limits.

Mr. Justice JACKSON joins in this dissent.

3. SEPARATE BUT EQUAL: JIM CROW AND THE LAW

PLESSY v. FERGUSON
163 U.S. 537 (1896)

[Plessy was one-eighth Negro but appeared white. He occupied a vacant seat in a railway coach for white passengers, to which his ticket otherwise entitled him, on a trip in Louisiana. A state statute imposed a twenty-five dollar fine on persons of Negro blood who would enter train coaches marked for whites. The railroads were required to furnish "equal but separate" railway accommodations for white and colored people. The state courts held the statute valid.]

Mr. Justice BROWN . . . delivered the opinion of the Court.

This case turns upon the constitutionality of an act of the General Assembly of the state of Louisiana, passed in 1890, providing for separate railway carriages for the white and colored races. . . .

The constitutionality of this act is attacked upon the ground that it conflicts both with the Thirteenth Amendment of the Constitution, abolishing slavery, and the Fourteenth Amendment, which prohibits certain restrictive legislation on the part of the states.

1. That it does not conflict with the Thirteenth Amendment, which abolished slavery and involuntary servitude, except as a punishment for crime, is too clear for argument. . . .

2. By the Fourteenth Amendment, all persons born or naturalized in the United States, and subject to the jurisdiction thereof, are made citizens of the United States and of the state wherein they

reside; and the states are forbidden from making or enforcing any law which shall abridge the privileges or immunities of citizens of the United States, or shall deprive any person of life, liberty, or property without due process of law, or deny to any person within their jurisdiction the equal protection of the laws. . . .

The object of the amendment was undoubtedly to enforce the absolute equality of the two races before the law, but in the nature of things it could not have been intended to abolish distinctions based upon color, or to enforce social, as distinguished from political, equality, or a commingling of the two races upon terms unsatisfactory to either. Laws permitting, and even requiring, their separation in places where they are liable to be brought into contact do not necessarily imply the inferiority of either race to the other, and have been generally, if not universally, recognized as within the competency of the state legislatures in the exercise of their police power. The most common instance of this is connected with the establishment of separate schools for white and colored children, which has been held to be a valid exercise of the legislative power even by courts of states where the political rights of the colored race have been longest and most earnestly enforced.

So far, then, as a conflict with the Fourteenth Amendment is concerned, the case reduces itself to the question whether the statute of Louisiana is a reasonable regulation, and with respect to this there must necessarily be a large discretion on the part of the legislature. In determining the question of reasonableness it is at liberty to act with reference to the established usages, customs, and traditions of the people, and with a view to the promotion of their comfort, and the preservation of the public peace and good order. Gauged by this standard, we cannot say that a law which authorizes or even requires the separation of the two races in public conveyances is unreasonable or more obnoxious to the Fourteenth Amendment than the acts of Congress requiring separate schools for colored children in the District of Columbia, the constitutionality of which does not seem to have been questioned, or the corresponding acts of state legislatures.

We consider the underlying fallacy of the plaintiff's argument to consist in the assumption that the enforced separation of the two races stamps the colored race with a badge of inferiority. If this be

so, it is not by reason of anything found in the act, but solely because the colored race chooses to put that construction upon it. The
argument necessarily assumes that if, as has been more than once the
case, and is not unlikely to be so again, the colored race should become the dominant power in the state legislature, and should enact
a law in precisely similar terms, it would thereby relegate the white
race to an inferior position. We imagine that the white race, at least,
would not acquiesce in this assumption. The argument also assumes that social prejudices may be overcome by legislation and that
equal rights cannot be secured to the Negro except by an enforced
commingling of the two races. We cannot accept this proposition.
If the two races are to meet upon terms of social equality, it must
be the result of natural affinities, a mutual appreciation of each
other's merits, and a voluntary consent of individuals. . . . Legislation is powerless to eradicate racial instincts or to abolish distinctions based upon physical differences, and the attempt to do so can
only result in accentuating the difficulties of the present situation.
If the civil and political rights of both races be equal, one cannot be
inferior to the other civilly or politically. If one race be inferior to
the other socially, the Constitution of the United States cannot put
them upon the same plane.

.   .   .   .   .

The judgment of the court below is, therefore,
Affirmed.
Mr. Justice HARLAN, dissenting.

.   .   .   .   .

In respect of civil rights, common to all citizens, the Constitution
of the United States does not, I think, permit any public authority
to know the race of those entitled to be protected in the enjoyment
of such rights. Every true man has pride of race, and under appropriate circumstances when the rights of others, his equals before the
law, are not to be affected, it is his privilege to express such pride
and to take such action based upon it as to him seems proper. But
I deny that any legislative body or judicial tribunal may have regard
to the race of citizens when the civil rights of those citizens are involved. Indeed, such legislation, as that here in question, is inconsistent not only with that equality of rights which pertains to citizen-

ship, national and state, but with the personal liberty enjoyed by everyone within the United States.

.   .   .   .   .

It was said in argument that the statute of Louisiana does not discriminate against either race but prescribes a rule applicable alike to white and colored citizens. But this argument does not meet the difficulty. Everyone knows that the statute in question had its origin in the purpose, not so much to exclude white persons from railroad cars occupied by blacks, as to exclude colored people from coaches occupied by or assigned to white persons. Railroad corporations of Louisiana did not make discrimination among whites in the matter of accommodation for travelers. The thing to accomplish was, under the guise of giving equal accommodation for whites and blacks, to compel the latter to keep to themselves while traveling in railroad passenger coaches. No one would be so wanting in candor as to assert the contrary. The fundamental objection, therefore, to the statute is that it interferes with the personal freedom of citizens. . . . If a white man and a black man choose to occupy the same public conveyance on a public highway, it is their right to do so, and no government, proceeding alone on grounds of race, can prevent it without infringing the personal liberty of each.

.   .   .   .   .

The white race deems itself to be the dominant race in this country. And so it is, in prestige, in achievements, in education, in wealth, and in power. So, I doubt not, it will continue to be for all time, if it remains true to its great heritage and holds fast to the principles of constitutional liberty. But in view of the Constitution, in the eye of the law, there is in this country no superior, dominant, ruling class of citizens. There is no caste here. Our Constitution is color-blind and neither knows nor tolerates classes among citizens. In respect of civil rights, all citizens are equal before the law. The humblest is the peer of the most powerful. The law regards man as man and takes no account of his surroundings or of his color when his civil rights as guaranteed by the supreme law of the land are involved. . . .

.   .   .   .   .

The arbitrary separation of citizens, on the basis of race, while

they are on a public highway, is a badge of servitude wholly inconsistent with the civil freedom and the equality before the law established by the Constitution. It cannot be justified upon any legal
grounds.

If evils will result from the commingling of the two races upon
public highways established for the benefit of all, they will be infinitely less than those that will surely come from state legislation
regulating the enjoyment of civil rights upon the basis of race. We
boast of the freedom enjoyed by our people above all other peoples.
But it is difficult to reconcile that boast with a state of the law which,
practically, puts the brand of servitude and degradation upon a
large class of our fellow-citizens, our equals before the law. The thin
disguise of "equal" accommodations for passengers in railroad coaches
will not mislead anyone, nor atone for the wrong this day done.

. . . . .

MISSOURI ex rel. GAINES v. CANADA
305 U.S. 337 (1938)

Mr. Chief Justice HUGHES delivered the opinion of the Court.

Petitioner Lloyd Gaines, a negro, was refused admission to the
School of Law of the state university of Missouri. Asserting that this
refusal constituted a denial by the state of the equal protection of
the laws in violation of the Fourteenth Amendment of the federal
Constitution, petitioner brought this action for mandamus to compel the curators of the university to admit him. . . .

Petitioner is a citizen of Missouri. In August, 1935, he was graduated with the degree of Bachelor of Arts at the Lincoln University,
an institution maintained by the state of Missouri for the higher
education of negroes. That university has no law school. Upon the
filing of his application for admission to the law school of the University of Missouri, the registrar advised him to communicate with
the president of Lincoln University and the latter directed petitioner's attention to § 9622 of the Revised Statutes of Missouri
(1929), providing as follows:

"Sec. 9622. May arrange for attendance at university of any adjacent state—Tuition fees.—Pending the full development of the
Lincoln University, the board of curators shall have the authority
to arrange for the attendance of negro residents of the state of Missouri at the university of any adjacent state to take any course or to

study any subjects provided for at the state university of Missouri, and which are not taught at the Lincoln University and to pay the reasonable tuition fees for such attendance; provided that whenever the board of curators deem it advisable they shall have the power to open any necessary school or department. Laws 1921, p. 86, § 7."

Petitioner was advised to apply to the state superintendent of schools for aid under that statute. It was admitted on the trial that petitioner's "work and credits at the Lincoln University would qualify him for admission to the School of Law of the University of Missouri if he were found otherwise eligible." He was refused admission upon the ground that it was "contrary to the constitution, laws and public policy of the state to admit a negro as a student in the University of Missouri." It appears that there are schools of law in connection with the state universities of four adjacent states, Kansas, Nebraska, Iowa and Illinois, where non-resident negroes are admitted.

. . . . . .

... We must regard the question whether the provision for the legal education in other states of negroes resident in Missouri is sufficient to satisfy the constitutional requirement of equal protection, as the pivot upon which this case turns.

The state court stresses the advantages that are afforded by the law schools of the adjacent states, Kansas, Nebraska, Iowa and Illinois, which admit non-resident negroes. . . .

We think that these matters are beside the point. The basic consideration is not as to what sort of opportunities other states provide, or whether they are as good as those in Missouri, but as to what opportunities Missouri itself furnishes to white students and denies to negroes solely upon the ground of color. The admissibility of laws separating the races in the enjoyment of privileges afforded by the state rests wholly upon the quality of the privileges which the laws give to the separated groups within the state. The question here is not of a duty of the state to supply legal training, or of the quality of the training which it does supply, but of its duty when it provides such training to furnish it to the residents of the state upon the basis of an equality of right By the operation of the laws of Missouri a privilege has been created for white law students which is denied to negroes by reason of their race. The white resident is afforded legal education within the state; the negro resident having the same qualifications is refused it there and must go outside the state to obtain it. That is a denial of the equality of legal right to the enjoyment of the privilege which the state has set up, and the provision for the payment of tuition fees in another state does not remove the discrimination.

The equal protection of the laws is "a pledge of the protection of equal laws." ... Manifestly, the obligation of the state to give the protection of equal laws can be performed only where its laws operate, that is, within its own jurisdiction. It is there that the equality of legal right must be maintained.... We find it impossible to conclude that what otherwise would be an unconstitutional discrimination, with respect to the legal right to the enjoyment of opportunities within the state, can be justified by requiring resort to opportunities elsewhere. That resort may mitigate the inconvenience of the discrimination but cannot serve to validate it.

Nor can we regard the fact that there is but a limited demand in Missouri for the legal education of negroes as excusing the discrimination in favor of whites....

Here, petitioner's right was a personal one. It was as an individual that he was entitled to the equal protection of the laws, and the state was bound to furnish him within its borders facilities for legal education substantially equal to those which the state there afforded for persons of the white race, whether or not other negroes sought the same opportunity.

.   .   .   .   .

We are of the opinion that ... petitioner was entitled to be admitted to the law school of the state university in the absence of other and proper provision for his legal training within the State....

The judgment of the Supreme Court of Missouri is reversed....

Separate opinion of Mr. Justice McREYNOLDS (joined by Mr. Justice BUTLER)....

The problem presented obviously is a difficult and highly practical one. A fair effort to solve it has been made by offering adequate opportunities for study when sought in good faith. The State should not be unduly hampered through theorization inadequately restrained by experience....

[In *Sipuel* v. *University of Oklahoma*, 332 U.S. 631 (1948), the state sought to bar a woman applicant from the (white) University law school and countered her complaint by the argument that, since legal authority existed in Oklahoma for the establishment of a separate law school for Negroes she should have asked for implementation of that authority rather than for admission to the white law school. The Supreme Court, in a brief unsigned order, held such a promise of future facilities insufficient. "The State," it was said, "must provide . . . [legal education] for her in conformity with the equal protection of the Fourteenth Amendment and provide it as soon as it does for applicants of any other group." Although Justice Rutledge thought that the Court's order meant "that Oklahoma should end the discrimination practiced against petitioner at once . . . not by excluding all students . . . [but] by affording petitioner the advantages of a legal education," the Court declined to interfere when the state court complied with the Court order by decreeing that the University might either admit the Negro applicant or deny admission to all applicants until such time as a separate Negro law school might be opened. *Fisher* v. *Hurst,* 333 U.S. 147 (1948).]

ATTACK ON THE PLESSY RULE

Pressure to break down the wall of segregation in education gained in momentum in the years following World War II. The President's Committee on Civil Rights, in its report *To Secure These Rights,* gave strong impetus to demands for improvement of minority conditions. In 1948, the national platform of the Democratic Party included a committal to remedial action in the field of civil rights. Simultaneously, through Executive Orders and administrative action, the national administration sought to promote racial equality and to break down the segregation pattern. Thus the government filed a brief *amicus curiae* in the *Restrictive Covenant Cases*[4] and in the spring of 1950 the Attorney General and the Solicitor General appeared before the Court to urge the abandonment and disavowal of the "separate-but-equal" doctrine.

The occasion was furnished by a series of three cases which the Court heard as a group. Each of them involved racial segregation in a different pattern of circumstances. Henderson, an employee of the wartime Fair Employment Practices Commission, had been compelled to accept dining car service in a screened-off portion of the car under a company rule which the Interstate Commerce Commission had approved. Sweatt had applied to the University of Texas for admission to its law school. The state authorities sought

4 *Shelley* v. *Kraemer, supra,* p. 432.

to comply with the Court's earlier rulings in such cases by setting up a separate law school. Sweatt contended that this improvised attempt to provide legal equality failed to provide equal opportunity in fact. McLaurin, a highly educated and experienced Negro schoolman, was admitted to the University of Oklahoma for advanced graduate work but was compelled to remain apart and segregated while in attendance.

The issue in all three cases was pursued to its logical conclusion in the briefs of the government and of a volunteer group of legal educators: separation implied inequality; *Plessy* v. *Ferguson* was based on a legal fiction which should be discarded. The Court, while ruling against the segregation practice in all three cases,[5] declined to overturn the precedent but, by its decisions on the facts, raised a strong assumption that nothing short of, at least, approximate equality would in the future satisfy its scrutiny of separate establishments for the two races.

HENDERSON v. UNITED STATES
Brief for the United States, *amicus curiae*[6]

. . . . .

(2) If this Court should conclude that the issues presented by this case cannot be considered without reference to the "separate but equal" doctrine, the Government respectfully urges that, in the half-century which has elapsed since it was first promulgated, the legal and factual assumptions upon which that doctrine rests have been undermined and refuted. The "separate but equal" doctrine should now be overruled and discarded.

The decision in the *Plessy* case appears to rest on two major premises. One is that laws requiring separation of the white and colored races do not imply the inferiority of the colored race. The other is that segregation infringes only "social" rights and that these rights, as distinct from "civil" or "political" rights, are not within the ambit of the equal protection clause of the Fourteenth Amendment.

It is a question of fact what the community at large understands to be the meaning of singling out the members of the colored race

---

[5] *Henderson* v. *United States*, 339 U.S. 816 (1950); *Sweatt* v. *Painter*, 339 U.S. 629 (1950); *McLaurin* v. *Oklahoma State Regents*, 339 U.S. 637 (1950), *infra*, p. 454. All three decisions were unanimous.

[6] Pp. 40–65.

for separation from all other citizens, whether it is in purchasing a bus ticket at the same ticket window, riding on the same street car or railroad coach, or going to the same restaurant, theatre or school. In the *Plessy* case the Court concluded that this minority race is not stigmatized as inferior, as constituting a lower social caste, when law decrees that it shall ride apart, eat apart, or stand in line for tickets apart. We submit that the Court's *a priori* conclusion cannot stand today in the face of a wealth of evidence flatly contradicting it.

We likewise believe that there was error in the second premise of the "separate but equal" doctrine enunciated in the *Plessy* case, namely, that enforced separation of the races affects only "social" rights not within the purview of the Fourteenth Amendment. The Amendment strikes at inequality without qualification. Certainly its language furnishes no basis for the distinction which the Court drew between "social" rights and those which are "civil" or "political." Furthermore, the distinction drawn is, at best, nebulous and largely a matter of emphasis. "In reality it is not possible to isolate a sphere of life and call it 'social.' There is, in fact, a 'social' angle to all relations." [Quoting Myrdal, *An American Dilemma*, vol. I, p. 642.]

It is one thing to define social equality in terms of integration into white social organizations; it is another to define as "social" the right to equality in the use and enjoyment of public facilities. . . .

In the *Plessy* case the Court also said (p. 551) that legislation is "powerless to eradicate" racial prejudice. This observation, even if true, was irrelevant to the constitutional issue before the Court. It might properly have been made before a legislative body considering the merits of a bill to penalize conduct manifesting racial prejudice. But the Court was not called upon to make a judgment of policy as to whether racial prejudice can be eradicated by legislation; the only question was whether a particular statute created, enforced, or supported the denial of a constitutionally protected right. Statutes and ordinances may not in themselves remove racial antagonisms, but it is clear that they cannot constitutionally magnify such antagonisms by giving the sanction of law to what would otherwise be a private, individual act of discrimination. That is the basic vice . . . in this case.

In any event, the Court's observation is, at best, a half-truth. Although legislation cannot "eradicate" racial prejudice, experience has shown that it can create conditions favorable to the gradual disappearance of racial prejudice; or it can, on the other hand, strengthen and enhance it. Civil-rights and antidiscrimination statutes have been shown to have the former effect, and so-called Jim Crow laws the latter. A Commissioner of the New York State Commission Against Discrimination has recently written:

Critics of fair-employment laws used to claim that long-established habits of discrimination could not be changed by legislation. Their argument has been unmistakably answered today. Nearly four years' experience in New York—and similar experience in New Jersey, Massachusetts, Connecticut, Washington, Oregon, New Mexico and Rhode Island, all of which have passed anti-discrimination legislation modeled after the New York law—indicates conclusively that wise legislation creates a climate of opinion in which discrimination tends to disappear.[7]

On the other side of the picture, "Jim Crow" laws, which govern important segments of everyday living, not only indoctrinate both white and colored races with the caste conception, but they solidify the segregation existing outside these laws and give it respectability and institutional fixity. As the Supreme Court of California has pointedly said, the way to eradicate racial tension is not "through the perpetuation by law of the prejudices that give rise to the tension." [*Perez* v. *Sharp*, 32 Calif. 2d 711, 725.] In fields which "Jim Crow" laws do not cover there has been "a slow trend toward a breakdown of segregation"; within the fields of their operation the laws "keep the pattern rigid." [Myrdal, *op. cit.*, vol. I, p. 635.]

.   .   .   .   .

The effects of the segregation to which Negroes are subjected are not confined to those who are colored. They extend also to those who are white, and they bear vitally upon the interests of the Nation as a whole. We submit that the harmful effects to the public interest which have resulted from racial segregation furnish persuasive grounds for rejecting its extension. . . .

---

[7] Simon, *Causes and Cure of Discrimination*, New York Times, May 29, 1949, section 6, p. 10, at p. 35. "Can this technique of eliminating discrimination by rooting out the fears that cause it be applied successfully on a large scale? Our New York experience insists that the answer is an unequivocal 'Yes.' . . . we have changed the entire pattern of employment of the most populous state in the union in less than four years." (*Id.*, p. 36.) See *1948 Report of Progress*, New York State Commission Against Discrimination, pp. 11–12. [Footnote of the original.]

1. *Effect on Negroes*

Segregation is a dominant factor in every aspect of the Negro's life. It limits his physical movements and economic opportunities, and adversely affects his personality and social development. It is much more than jim-crowism in vehicles and public places. It is an ostracism symbolizing inferiority which colors his thoughts and action at almost every moment.

Professional opinion is almost unanimous that segregation has detrimental psychological effects on those segregated. A questionnaire addressed to 849 representative social scientists was answered by 61% of those to whom it was sent. Of those replying, 90.4% believed that enforced segregation has "detrimental psychological effects" on those segregated if "equal facilities" are provided, 2.3% expressed the opposite opinion, and 7.4% did not answer the question or expressed no opinion. Those who elaborated their position with comments (55% of those replying) stressed that segregation induced feelings of inferiority, insecurity, frustration, and persecution, and that it developed, on the one hand, submissiveness, martyrdom, withdrawal tendencies, and fantasy, and on the other hand, aggression.

The resentment and hostility provoked by segregation find various means of psychological "accommodation," various forms of release. Mediocrity is accepted as a standard because of the absence of adequate social rewards or acceptance. Energy and emotion which might be constructively used are lost in the process of adjustment to the "Jim Crow" concept of the Negro's characteristics and his inferior status in society. Psychosomatic disease is induced by the tensions engendered by segregation and other forms of racial segregation.

The extensive study made of Negro troops during the recent war furnished striking example of how racism, of which segregation is the sharpest manifestation, handicaps the Negro. The most important single factor affecting integration of the Negro into Army life was that he had to carry the burden of race prejudice in addition to all of the other problems faced by the white soldier.

For a general discussion of the effects of the caste system, which segregation supports and exemplifies, on Negro personality and behavior, see Myrdal, *An American Dilemma*, vol. 2, pp. 757–767.

2. *Effect on Whites*

Segregation also detrimentally affects the dominant white group.

"Segregation and discrimination have had material and moral effect on whites, too. Booker T. Washington's famous remark, that the white man could not hold the Negro in the gutter without getting in there himself, has been corroborated by many white Southern and Northern observers." Myrdal, *An American Dilemma*, vol. I, pp. 643–644. The white person must adjust himself, consciously or unconsciously, to the hypocrisy of a double standard violating the American creed which he professes to follow. Feelings of guilt are generated and moral values weakened; the basic realities of the racial problem are diverted in the mechanism of segregation:

Those who segregate others soon become frightened, insecure people forced to accept and invent prejudice to justify their actions. They become hypocrites who either close their eyes to stark reality or invent slogans to hide fundamental issues. The master classes, no less than the subjected, become victims of the system.[8]

Segregation and practices allied to it promote the master-race psychology, thus sowing seeds for oppressive individual and collective action.

3. *Effect on the Nation*

Segregation is part of a vicious cycle. It prevents groups from knowing each other. This lack of knowledge engenders distrust and antagonism. They in turn stimulate the demand for sharp cleavage between races and maintenance of a system of segregation. Thus groups within the Nation are kept asunder.

Experience and informed opinion are in agreement that normal contacts between the races diminish prejudice while enforced separation intensifies it. Race relations are improved by living together, working together, serving together, going to school together. The absence of a color line in certain countries goes far to show that racial prejudice is not instinctive or hereditary, but is rather kept alive by man-made barriers such as segregation.

.   .   .   .   .

[The argument proceeds with references to experiences in industry and in the armed forces, quotes baseball player Jackie Robinson to illustrate bitterness engendered by jim-crowism even among deeply loyal Negroes, and shows in what manner racial discrimination embarrasses the international position of the nation.]

[8] Weaver, *The Negro Ghetto*, 270. [Footnote of the original.]

Racial segregation enforced by law hardly comports with the high principles to which, in the international field, we have subscribed. Our position and standing before the critical bar of world opinion are weakened if segregation not only is practiced in this country but also is condoned by federal law.

Mr. Justice Harlan said in his memorable dissent in the *Plessy* case (163 U.S. at 562):

We boast of the freedom enjoyed by our people above all other peoples. But it is difficult to reconcile that boast with a state of the law which, practically, puts the brand of servitude and degredation upon a large class of our fellow-citizens, our equals before the law. The thin disguise of "equal" accommodations for passengers in railroad coaches will not mislead any one, nor atone for the wrong this day done.

Various subterfuges have been employed during the years since the adoption of the Thirteenth and Fourteenth Amendments to evade and nullify the effects of their provisions. The emancipation of an entire race has proved a most complicated task. More than three-quarters of a century has not been enough time within which to break down the barriers surrounding the enslaved, and to bring them to the full dignity and stature of free citizens. Discrimination, political, economic, and social, is still widespread. However, there are indications that the process of education, of lessening the incidence of unreasoned prejudice, lagging for so many years, is increasing in momentum.

The evasions and violations of the Constitution are being gradually eliminated. One handicap is the approval, given in another day and generation, to the proposition that the Constitution could be satisfied and friction removed by the establishment of "separate but equal" facilities. Experience has shown that neither the Constitution, nor the laws enacted under its authority, nor the individuals affected, are given the required respect and status under such an arrangement. "Equal" facilities, if separate, are rarely if ever equal, even in a physical sense. In most situations they have been used to cloak glaring inequalities. And the very idea of separate facilities, or separate rights, is in itself a negation of the full and complete possession of privileges and immunities of citizenship.

So long as the doctrine of the *Plessy* case stands, a barrier erected not by the Constitution but by the courts will continue to work a denial of rights and privileges and immunities antagonistic to the freedoms and liberties on which our institutions and our form of government are founded. "Separate but equal" is a constitutional anachronism which no longer deserves a place in our law. . . .

.   .   .   .   .

McLAURIN v. OKLAHOMA STATE REGENTS
339 U.S. 637 (1950)

Mr. Chief Justice VINSON delivered the opinion of the Court.

In this case, we are faced with the question whether a state may, after admitting a student to graduate instruction in its state university, afford him different treatment from other students solely because of his race. . . .

Appellant is a Negro citizen of Oklahoma. Possessing a Master's degree, he applied for admission to the University of Oklahoma in order to pursue studies and courses leading to a Doctorate in Education. At that time, his application was denied, solely because of his race. The school authorities were required to exclude him by the Oklahoma statutes, 70 Okla. Stat. §§ 455, 456, 457 (1941), which made it a misdemeanor to maintain or operate, teach or attend a school at which both whites and Negroes are enrolled or taught. Appellant filed a complaint requesting injunctive relief, alleging that the action of the school authorities and the statutes upon which their action was based were unconstitutional and deprived him of the equal protection of the laws. Citing our decisions in *State of Missouri ex rel. Gaines v. Canada*, 305 U.S. 337, and *Sipuel v. Board of Regents*, 332 U.S. 631, a . . . District Court held . . . that the State had a constitutional duty to provide him with the education he sought as soon as it provided that education for applicants of any other group. It further held that to the extent the Oklahoma statutes denied him admission they were unconstitutional and void. . . .

Following this decision, the Oklahoma legislature amended these statutes to permit the admission of Negroes to institutions of higher learning attended by white students, in cases where such institutions offered courses not available in the Negro schools. The amendment provided, however, that in such cases the program of instruction "shall be given at such colleges or institutions of higher learning upon a segregated basis." Appellant was thereupon admitted to the University of Oklahoma Graduate School.... [But] he was required to sit apart at a designated desk in an anteroom adjoining the classroom; to sit at a designated desk on the mezzanine floor of the library, but not to use the desks in the regular reading room; and to sit at a designated table and to eat at a different time from the other students in the school cafeteria.

To remove these conditions, appellant ... [asked for an order by] the District Court. That court held that such treatment did not violate the provisions of the Fourteenth Amendment and denied the motion.... This appeal followed.

In the interval between the decision below and the hearing in this Court, the treatment afforded appellant was altered. For some time, the section of the classroom in which appellant sat was surrounded by a rail on which there was a sign stating, "Reserved For Colored," but these have been removed. He is now assigned to a seat in the classroom in a row specified for colored students; he is assigned to a table in the library on the main floor; and he is permitted to eat at the same time in the cafeteria as other students, although here again he is assigned to a special table.

It is said that the separations imposed by the State in this case are in form merely nominal. McLaurin uses the same classroom, library and cafeteria as students of other races; there is no indication that the seats to which he is assigned in these rooms have any disadvantage of location. He may wait in line in the cafeteria and there stand and talk with his fellow students, but while he eats he must remain apart.

The restrictions were obviously imposed in order to comply, as nearly as could be, with the statutory requirements of Oklahoma. But they signify that the State, in administering the facilities it affords for professional and graduate study, sets McLaurin apart from the other students. The result is that appellant is handicapped in his pursuit of effective graduate instruction. Such restrictions impair and inhibit his ability to study, to engage in discussions and exchange views with other students, and, in general, to learn his profession.

Our society grows increasingly complex, and our need for trained leaders increases correspondingly. Appellant's case represents, perhaps, the epitome of that need, for he is attempting to obtain an advanced degree in education, to become, by definition, a leader and trainer of others. Those who will come under his guidance and influence must be directly affected by the education he receives. Their own education and development will necessarily suffer to the extent that his training is unequal to that of his classmates. State-imposed restrictions which produce such inequalities cannot be sustained.

It may be argued that appellant will be in no better position when these restrictions are removed, for he may still be set apart by his fellow students. This we think irrelevant. There is a vast difference—a Constitutional difference—between restrictions imposed by the State which prohibit the intellectual commingling of students, and the refusal of individuals to commingle where the State presents no such bar. *Shelley* v. *Kraemer*, 334 U.S. 1, 13–14. The removal of the State restrictions will not necessarily abate individual and group predilections, prejudices and choices. But at the very least, the State will not be depriving appellant of the opportunity to secure acceptance by his fellow students on his own merits.

We conclude that the conditions under which this appellant is required to receive his education deprive him of his personal and present right to the equal protection of the laws. . . . We hold that under these circumstances the Fourteenth Amendment precludes differences in treatment by the State based upon race. Appellant, having been admitted to a state-supported graduate school, must receive the same treatment at the hands of the State as students of other races. The judgment is reversed.

COMMENT: I[9]

The Supreme Court this past week took a big step toward completing an American revolution that began in 1861 and was supposed to have been, but actually was not, completed with the adoption of the 14th Amendment of our federal Constitution in 1868. That amendment was designed to safeguard the newly acquired rights of the then recently freed Negroes. It was designed to keep them from slipping back into a status of slavery or semi-slavery. The provision that no state shall "deny any person within its jurisdiction the equal protection of the laws" was intended to insure a status of equality to the new Negro citizen.

[9] By Clifton Utley, N.B.C. commentator. The following observations constituted Mr. Utley's scheduled network broadcast on Sunday, June 11, 1950. They are reproduced with his permission.

Naturally the effort to legislate any such drastic change in our country's social customs, even after the stern decision on the battle-field of Civil War, met with profound resistance in parts of our nation.

In the era of disillusionment that marked the turn of the century, the Supreme Court laid down a doctrine that in practice, though not in theory, greatly weakened the force of the 14th Amendment. It was the "separate but equal" doctrine enunciated by the Court in 1896.

It set down the principle that while Negro citizens must be given equal treatment, the constitutional requirement of equality is met even though the Negro is segregated and given separate and distinct facilities of his own. It was this "separate but equal" doctrine that gave legal sanction to the institution popularly known as Jim Crowism—separate schools for Negroes, separate places on trains and in other public transportation, and separation in other matters.

Most leaders of American Negro life have always resented this "separate but equal" doctrine for two reasons. First, the very fact of separation implied to him an invidious distinction, implied that whatever was formally said, he was not considered an equal. This was the more annoying since the American Negro, with keen memory of the institution of slavery and the legally inferior status that went with it, naturally preserved a keen sensitivity toward anything that implied a continuation of that status.

Second, the American Negro resented the "separate but equal" because it was a sham and a pretence. Separate but equal did not in fact mean equality. It meant separate and unequal, or separate and inferior. For it is no secret that where separate schools have existed for whites and Negroes the physical facilities and the instruction has tended to be inferior in Negro schools. The same has tended to be true in matters of public transport and in other things. Train accommodations for Negroes—where separate facilities for Negroes have been maintained—have tended not to be equal to those provided for white patrons.

This past week the Supreme Court struck a severe—I think it is fair to say, a fatal blow—at the "separate but equal" doctrine.

In theory it did not abolish it. But in fact it came so near to doing so that it seems almost certain that in some future decision the Court will once and for all reverse the 1896 doctrine and declare it abolished.

Here are the reasons for thinking that will be the case.

In its decision this past week, the Court dealt with three cases. One concerned the legality of separate dining facilities for Negroes on trains. The other two concernéd special arrangements made for Negro education by the University of Texas and University of Oklahoma.

In the dining car case the Court ruled illegal the requirement, now existing in some states, that Negroes be served in special sections of dining cars. This case, to be sure, turned on a federal statute, and not on the 14th Amendment to the Constitution.

The finding, as I understand it, is this: Even though Negroes are served the same food, at identical prices, and given equally good service by waiters and in other ways, they still are not being accorded equal treatment if they are required to sit in special parts of the dining car to be served, and this is the case, even though whites are also required to sit in special parts of a dining car—namely in the part reserved for white service. Since the law requires equality of dining car service for all, the requirement that Negroes sit in special parts of the dining car is illegal.

The two cases dealing with universities are even more revealing.

In the University of Texas case, Texas had created a special law school for Negroes to avoid admitting Negro students to the University of Texas. This seemed to comply with the traditional concept of the "separate but equal" doctrine. There was a law school for whites. There was another, supported at the taxpayers' expense, for Negroes. Both Negroes and whites could therefore get legal education. But in its decision the Court went behind the fact that the Negro law school was not the equal in quality of educational opportunity offered to the regular and heretofore exclusively white University of Texas law school. Therefore, to comply with the 14th Amendment of the United States Constitution, Texas must admit qualified Negro applicants to the regular University of Texas law school, and be it said to the credit of Texas, that her authorities, without quibbling, have already complied with the Court decision, and without delay admitted the student who brought the case.

The Oklahoma case is still more striking. There Oklahoma had admittedly taken a series of steps that had progressively moved Negro students closer to equality with white students. There Negro students had been admitted to predominantly white universities, but they had been required, at first, to sit in an adjoining room from the classroom. In the library they had been required to sit on a mezzanine floor and, in the cafeteria, they had been required to eat at a different time from the white students.

However, Oklahoma authorities themselves had greatly modified and relaxed these restrictions. Later Negro students were allowed to sit in the same classrooms with whites, but in parts of the classroom specially railed off and reserved for Negroes. In the library, Negroes were allowed to sit on the same floor with other students but at special tables reserved for Negroes, and in the cafeteria they were permitted to eat at the same time with other students, but again, at designated tables.

Obviously, though the degree of separation that continued may have implied an implicit assertion of social superiority on the part of white authorities and students, it did not seriously interfere with the Negroes' ability to receive instruction and get an education.

Yet the Court ruled that there was still some interference with educational equality because—and now I'm quoting the words of Mr. Chief Justice Vinson,—the continuing restrictions "set McLaurin (the Negro student involved in the case) apart" from other students and thus "handicapped" him in efforts to get an education. "Such restrictions," the Chief Justice continued, "impair and inhibit his ability to study, to engage in discussions and exchange views with other students, and in general to learn his profession." So the University of Oklahoma was ordered to discontinue the restrictions, and to permit McLaurin to study on the identical basis that white students study.

Now there are several very interesting aspects to this most important decision, or rather, collection of three decisions.

First, all three were unanimous decisions of the Supreme Court. There was no dissent by any justice.

Second, the Court was specifically asked by Texas to reaffirm the old "separate but equal" doctrine and the Court specifically refused to reaffirm that doctrine. Chief Justice Vinson said specifically that he could not agree that the 1896 doctrine should be reaffirmed. That is important as an indication of what the Court is likely to do in the future. For even if the Court had not wanted to go so far as specifically to reaffirm the "separate but equal" doctrine it could have simply ignored Texas' plea on this point and said nothing about it. But instead Mr. Chief Justice Vinson said that he could not agree that the doctrine should be reaffirmed. That is about as near as the Court can come to overruling the doctrine without actually pronouncing it overruled.

Actually, the Court did not formally overrule the 1896 decision. Its legal grounds for not disposing of the old doctrine one way or the other was that the case could be decided without ruling specifically on the separate but equal finding, and courts traditionally rule on the fewest number of legal points necessary to decide cases. That is, if a case can be decided without ruling on a given point, the Court will usually refuse to rule on the point in question.

But it does seem to me that in the light of this past week's three decisions, the handwriting is writ large on the wall of the future. The Court at this time does not formally overrule the old "separate but equal" doctrine. But its decision does suggest that in practice it will find any specific instance of racial separation does in fact deprive the segregated group of equality, and therefore violates the 14th Amendment of our Constitution.

To put the matter in the fewest possible words, in theory the old "separate but equal" doctrine still stands, but in fact the Court will hold that anything that is separate is not equal, and therefore is not permissible.

The whole experience with the Supreme Court in the past has been that where such a situation exists, the Court, after deciding a certain number of cases, will finally say that it is clear that the distinctions that have been made in a number of cases amount to a ruling that separation is incompatible with equality, and then will completely and formally overrule the old doctrine.

If that is the prospect, why didn't the Supreme Court formally so rule last week?

For two reasons: First, because it was possible to decide the cases at hand without making such a broad decision, and as I mentioned a moment ago, it is traditional in our American legal system to decide the minimum number of legal points necessary to settle the cases at hand.

Beyond that there is the matter of the Court's views on the desired speed of social change.

In theory the members of our Supreme Court are in the way of being sort of legal astronomers. The theory is that the law is all up there in the legal firmament—judges are simply men more qualified and more discerning than others, equipped to explore the legal heavens and draw down those legal principles necessary to decide matters at hand.

Actually, the members of the Supreme Court are, and always have been men living in a current social setting, aware of the problems of life about them, and aware of implications of the decisions they hand down.

The decisions handed down this past week might well have been unenforceable had they been handed down, say, in 1910, because the climate of American opinion at that time was such that the decisions would have been too great a break with the then existing social pattern. Even today these decisions will force breaks with current practices in a number of parts of our nation. But the social pattern has changed since 1910. The relationships between races have changed appreciably. The position of the Negro has improved in many ways. Southern states have installed Negro members on their police forces. There have been some Negro judges both in the south and in the north—thus the break with past tradition caused by these decisions today is not as great as it would have been two or three decades earlier. And thus there is compliance with these decisions. The University of Texas has already complied with the decision in its case.

The clear implication of these decisions is that eventually any racial segregation in any schools will be illegal and in violation of our federal constitution. But obviously a decision that formally overruled the old "separate but equal" doctrine and that made it clear that segregation on the elementary and high school, as well as on the university level, was universally illegal and unconstitutional as of this moment—such a decision now would be a profound shock to the social structure in many parts of the country. Such a decision might even arrest, rather than continue, the social change that has been going on in the relationships between the races.

So the Supreme Court, with its historical knowledge that Rome was not built in a day, does not seek to do everything at once.

It makes a decision, the future implications of which are eloquent and clear, but it leaves the matter for the moment at that point, giving time for the implications to soak in and be better understood by those groups and those parts of our country that will be most affected by them.

Then later, when the nation has fully adjusted to the present decisions, further and more far reaching decisions can perhaps be expected.

I am perfectly aware that this is not the theory of the way in which the United States Supreme Court works.

But anyone who has closely studied our American history will be aware that in fact this is the way it does work.

COMMENT: II[10]

BE IT RESOLVED by the Senate, the House of Representatives concurring, that:

WHEREAS, The recent decisions of the United States Supreme Court involving the public schools of Texas and Oklahoma have placed in danger the entire principle of segregation in our schools and

WHEREAS, We will not submit to the intermingling of white and negro children in our public schools in Alabama contrary to the express provisions of our Constitution and our laws.

NOW, THEREFORE, BE IT RESOLVED by the Senate of Alabama, the House of Representatives concurring, as follows:

We sincerely urge that the federal courts, agencies and employees exercise caution lest the relationship between the races, harmonious in the past, be embittered by the efforts of the federal government to seize power in local matters hitherto reserved to the local governments by the long-recognized principles of local self-government.

We reaffirm our faith in the rights of the states to administer their local affairs including their police power over race relationships and local customs.

We notify our senators and our representatives in the Congress that we expect them to protect us against the continual encroachment of a powerful federal government in breaking down the rights hitherto well recognized of the states and of the local communities in relation to their citizens.

BE IT FURTHER RESOLVED that a copy of this resolution be forwarded to the President of the United States, to the Chief Justice of the Supreme Court and to the Senators and Representatives from Alabama in the Congress.

[10] Joint Resolution adopted by the legislature of Alabama on June 25, 1950.

Personal Liberty for Political Action

1. CITIZENSHIP AND SUFFRAGE

CITIZENSHIP AND NATURALIZATION

The Constitution as originally adopted contains no less than seven references to citizenship without, however, defining the term or clarifying the relationship between state citizenship and national citizenship. The Dred Scott case, *Scott* v. *Sanford*, 19 How. 393 (1857), seemed to declare state citizenship primary and national citizenship subordinate to it.

The adoption of the Fourteenth Amendment in 1868 had the effect of superseding the Supreme Court's interpretation in the Dred Scott case and of making national citizenship primary and paramount. The amendment offered a concise definition of national citizenship, based firmly on the principle of *jus soli* (i.e., the place of birth determines citizenship), and made state citizenship derivative from national citizenship.

Thus citizenship of the United States may be acquired by (1) birth, and (2) naturalization. *Jus soli* operates to confer citizenship on any person born in the United States, i.e., within any of the forty-eight states, the District of Columbia, or an incorporated territory of the United States, except children of persons enjoying diplomatic immunity. Another, and heretofore fortunately academic, exception pertains to children of members of enemy forces occupying parts of the United States (neither foreign occupation troops nor diplomats are "subject to the jurisdiction" of the United States). On the other hand, children of resident aliens acquire

United States citizenship by virtue of birth in this country regardless of possible ineligibility of the parents to attain such citizenship. *United States* v. *Wong Kim Ark,* 169 U.S. 649 (1898). Nor will renunciation of American citizenship by naturalized parents deprive a native-born child of its status as an American citizen by birth. *Perkins* v. *Elg,* 307 U.S. 325 (1939).

The establishment of rules governing the acquisition of citizenship by naturalization is exclusively within the province of Congress. Const., Art. I, sec. 8, cl. 4; *Chirac* v. *Chirac,* 2 Wheat. 259 (1817). Legislation on the subject of naturalization and citizenship has been frequent, often complex and rarely consistent. An attempt at restatement was made in the Nationality Act of 1940 (54 Stat. 1137), but this law, too, has already been subject to extensive modifications. The various legal provisions presently in force may be found collected in Title 8 of the United States Code, 1948 edition. They are implemented by rules and orders of the Commissioner of Immigration and Naturalization and his superior officer, the Attorney General.

Although the judiciary figures importantly in the naturalization procedure, only a relatively small number of cases have reached the Supreme Court. In *United States* v. *Schwimmer,* 279 U.S. 644 (1929), citizenship was denied to a woman pacifist, fifty years of age, because of her refusal to swear that she would bear arms for the United States. A Yale divinity professor who wished to reserve his right to decline military participation in a war of which he might morally disapprove was similarly denied citizenship. *United States* v. *Macintosh,* 283 U.S. 605 (1931).

These cases were overruled, however, following World War II, in *Girouard* v. *United States,* 328 U.S. 61 (1946). Here Girouard, a Canadian and a Seventh Day Adventist, had in 1943 petitioned for naturalization as a United States citizen. In his application accompanying the petition he answered in the negative the question "If necessary, are you willing to take up arms in defense of this country?" and explained that, while he was ready to render noncombatant service, his religious convictions made it impossible for him to bear arms. Nonetheless, the District Court admitted him to citizenship, but the Circuit Court of Appeals, acting on the authority of the *Schwimmer* and *Macintosh* cases, countermanded the order. The Supreme Court, reversing the Court of Appeals, refused to be bound by the earlier cases. Justice Douglas, speaking for the majority, stressed the recognition by Congress of religious objections to combatant service; "the annals of the recent war," said the justice, "show that many whose religious scruples prevented them from bearing arms, nevertheless were unselfish participants in the war effort. Refusal to bear arms is not necessarily a sign of disloyalty or a lack of attachment to our institutions. . . . The effort of war is indivisible; and those whose religious scruples prevent them from killing are no less patriots than those whose special traits or handicaps result in their assignments to duties far behind the fighting front. Each is making the utmost contribution according to his capacity. The fact that his role may be limited by religious convictions rather than by physical characteristics has no necessary bearing on his attachment to his country or on his willingness to support and defend it to his utmost." The *Schwimmer* and *Macintosh* cases (and *United States* v. *Bland,* 283 U.S. 636 [1931]), it was announced, "do not state the correct rule of law."

Chief Justice Stone, himself a vigorous dissenter in the *Macintosh* case, disagreed with the majority on the grounds that "for six successive Congresses, over a period of more than a decade, there were continuously pending before Congress in one form or another proposals to overturn the rulings in the three Supreme Court decisions in question [*Schwimmer, Macintosh* and *Bland*]. Congress declined to adopt these proposals after full hearings. . . . Any doubts would seem to have been dissipated by the reenactment by Congress in 1940 of . . . [the statutory provisions involved in the three cases]. . . . It is not lightly to be assumed that Congress has failed to perform . . . [its duty] and has delegated to this Court the responsibility of giving new content to language deliberately readopted after this Court has construed it. For us to make such an assumption is to discourage, if not to deny, legislative responsibility. By thus adopting and confirming this Court's construction of what Congress had enacted in the Naturalization Act of 1906 Congress gave that construction the same legal significance as though it had written the very words into the Act of 1940. . . . It is not the function of this Court to disregard the will of Congress in the exercise of its constitutional power."

A NOTE ON SUFFRAGE

In the early years after the adoption of the Fourteenth Amendment the Supreme Court had announced that citizenship and the right of suffrage were not synonymous. *Minor* v. *Happersett,* 21 Wall. 162 (1875). But, having met the state's requirements and standards for suffrage, one has a right to have his ballot accepted and properly counted. If the election is for officials of the United States this becomes a federal right which Congress may through appropriate legislation protect. *Ex parte Yarbrough,* 110 U.S. 651 (1884). Largely as a result of this holding, the Southern states, intent upon excluding the Negro vote, began to take recourse to a number of devices which would prevent the compliance by Negroes with the suffrage requirements of the state. A number of these methods of planned disenfranchisement eventually were found to violate the equal protection clause of the United States Constitution. Until quite recently, however, the so-called "white primary" seemed to offer a formula which, while not offensive to the judicial eye, effectively accomplished the purposes of the local legislators. *Smith* v. *Allwright,* extracts from which follow, appears to have spelled the end to this method of disenfranchisement, too. *United States* v. *Classic* paved the way for this decision and establishes an important precedent for federal control of election practices. (Note that, like the naturalization cases, these decisions turn on statutory rather than constitutional interpretation.)

UNITED STATES v. CLASSIC
313 U.S. 299 (1941)

Mr. Justice STONE delivered the opinion of the Court.

Two counts of an indictment found in a federal district court charged that appellees, Commissioners of Elections, conducting a primary election under Louisiana law, to nominate a candidate of the Democratic Party for representative in Congress, willfully altered and falsely counted and certified the ballots of voters cast in the primary election. The questions for decision are whether the right of qualified voters to vote in the Louisiana primary and to have their ballot counted is a right "secured . . . by the Constitution" within the meaning of sections 19 and 20 of the Criminal Code, and whether the acts of appellees charged in the indictment violate those sections. . . .

Section 19 of the Criminal Code condemns as a criminal offense any conspiracy to injure a citizen in the exercise "of any right or privilege secured to him by the Constitution or laws of the United States." Section 20 makes it a penal offense for anyone who, "acting under color of any law" "willfully subjects, or causes to be subjected, any inhabitant of any state ... to the deprivation of any rights, privileges, or immunities secured or protected by the Constitution and laws of the United States." The Government argues that the right of a qualified voter in a Louisiana congressional primary election to have his vote counted as cast is a right secured by Article I, sections 2 and 4 of the Constitution, and that a conspiracy to deprive the citizen of that right is a violation of section 19, and also that the willful action of appellees as state officials, in falsely counting the ballots at the primary election and in falsely certifying the count, deprived qualified voters of that right and of the equal protection of the laws guaranteed by the Fourteenth Amendment, all in violation of section 20 of the Criminal Code.

Article I, section 2 of the Constitution, commands that "The House of Representatives shall be composed of Members chosen every second Year by the People of the several States, and the Electors in each State shall have the Qualifications requisite for Electors of the most numerous Branch of the State Legislature." By section 4 of the same article "The Times, Places and Manner of holding Elections for Senators and Representatives, shall be prescribed in each State by the Legislature thereof; but the Congress may at any time by Law make or alter such Regulations, except as to the Places of chusing Senators." Such right as is secured by the Constitution to qualified voters to choose members of the House of Representatives is thus to be exercised in conformity to the requirements of state law subject to the restrictions prescribed by section 2 and to the authority conferred on Congress by section 4, to regulate the times, places and manner of holding elections for representatives.

We look then to the statutes of Louisiana here involved to ascertain the nature of the right which under the constitutional mandate they define and confer on the voter, and the effect upon its exercise of the acts with which appellees are charged, all with the view to determining, first, whether the right or privilege is one secured by the Constitution of the United States, second, whether the effect under the state statute of appellees' alleged acts is such that they operate to injure or oppress citizens in the exercise of that right within the meaning of section 19 and to deprive inhabitants of the state of that right within the meaning of section 20, and finally, whether sections 19 and 20 respectively are in other respects applicable to the alleged acts of appellees.

Pursuant to the authority given by section 2 of Article I of the Constitution, and subject to the legislative power of Congress under section 4 of Article I, and other pertinent provisions of the Constitution, the states are given, and in fact exercise, a wide discretion in the formulation of a system for the choice by the people of representatives in Congress. In common with many other states, Louisiana has exercised that discretion by setting up machinery for the effective choice of party candidates for representative in Congress by primary elections, and by its laws it eliminates or seriously restricts the candidacy at the general election of all those who are defeated at the primary. All political parties, which are defined as those that have cast at least 5 percent of the total vote at specified preceding elections, are required to nominate their candidates for representative by direct primary elections. Louisiana Act No. 46, Regular Session, 1940, sections 1 and 3. . . .

The right to vote for a representative in Congress at the general election is, as a matter of law, thus restricted to the successful party candidate at the primary, to those not candidates at the primary who file nomination papers, and those whose names may be lawfully written into the ballot by the electors. . . . In fact, as alleged in the indictment, the practical operation of the primary in Louisiana is, and has been since the primary election was established in 1900, to secure the election of the Democratic primary nominee for the Second Congressional District of Louisiana.

Interference with the right to vote in the congressional primary in the Second Congressional District for the choice of Democratic candidate for Congress is thus as a matter of law and in fact an interference with the effective choice of the voters at the only stage of the election procedure when their choice is of significance, since it is at the only stage when such interference could have any practical effect on the ultimate result, the choice of the Congressman to represent the district. The primary in Louisiana is an integral part of the procedure for the popular choice of Congressman. The right of qualified voters to vote at the congressional primary in Louisiana and to have their ballots counted is thus the right to participate in that choice.

We come then to the question whether that right is one secured by the Constitution. Section 2 of Article I commands that Congressmen shall be chosen by the people of the several states by electors, the qualifications of which it prescribed. The right of the people to choose, whatever its appropriate constitutional limitations, where in other respects it is defined, and the mode of its exercise is prescribed by state action in conformity to the Constitution, is a right established and guaranteed by the Constitution and hence is one secured by it to those citizens and inhabitants of the state entitled to exercise the right. . . . While, in a loose sense, the right to vote for representatives in Congress is sometimes spoken of as a right derived from the states, see *Minor* v. *Happersett,* 21 Wall. 162, this statement is true only in the sense that the states are authorized by the Constitution, to legislate on the subject as provided by section 2 of Article I, to the extent that Congress has not restricted state action by the exercise of its powers to regulate elections under section 4 and its more general power under Article I, section 8, clause 18 of the Constitution "To make all Laws which shall be necessary and proper for carrying into Execution the foregoing Powers." See *Ex parte Siebold,* 100 U.S. 371.

Obviously included within the right to choose, secured by the Constitution, is the right of qualified voters within a state to cast their ballots and have them counted at congressional elections. This Court has consistently held that this is a right secured by the Constitution. And since the constitutional command is without restriction or limitation, the right, unlike those guaranteed by the Fourteenth and Fifteenth Amendments, is secured against the action of individuals as well as of the states. . . .

But we are now concerned with the question whether the right to choose at a primary election, a candidate for election as representative, is embraced in the right to choose representatives secured by Article I, section 2. We may assume that the framers of the Constitution in adopting that section, did not have specifically in mind the selection and elimination of candidates for Congress by the direct primary any more than they contemplated the application of the commerce clause to interstate telephone, telegraph and wireless communication which are concededly within it. But in determining whether a provision of the Constitution applies to a new subject matter, it is of little significance that it is one with which the framers were not familiar. For in setting up an enduring framework of government they undertook to carry out for the indefinite future and in all the vicissitudes of the changing affairs of men, those fundamental purposes which the instrument itself discloses. Hence we read its words, not as we read legislative codes which are subject to continuous revision with the changing course of events, but as the revelation of the great purposes which were intended to be achieved by the Constitution as a continuing instrument of government. If we remember that "it is a *constitution* we are expounding," we cannot rightly prefer, of the possible meanings of its words, that which will defeat rather than effectuate the constitutional purpose.

That the only free choice by the people of representatives in Congress, subject only to the restrictions to be found in sections 2 and 4 of Article I and elsewhere in the Constitution, was one of the great purposes of our constitutional scheme of government cannot be doubted. We cannot regard it as any the less the constitutional purpose or its words as any the less guarantying the integrity of that choice when a state, exercising its privilege in the absence of congressional action, changes the mode of choice from a single step, a general election, to two, of which the first is the choice at a primary of those candidates from whom, as a second step, the representative in Congress is to be chosen at the election.

Nor can we say that that choice which the Constitution protects is restricted to the second step because section 4 of Article I, as a means of securing a free choice of representatives by the people, has authorized Congress to regulate the manner of elections, without making any mention of primary elections. For we think that the authority of Congress, given by section 4, includes the authority to regulate primary elections when, as in this case, they are a step in the exercise by the people of their choice of representatives in Congress. . . .

The right to participate in the choice of Representatives for Congress includes, as we have said, the right to cast a ballot and to have it counted at the general election whether for the successful candidate or not. Where the state law has made the primary an integral part of the procedure of choice, the right of the elector to have his ballot counted at the primary is likewise included in the right protected by Article I, section 2. And this right of participation is protected just as is the right to vote at the election, where the primary is by law an integral part of the election machinery, whether the voter exercises his right in a party primary which invariably, sometimes or never determines the ultimate choice of the Representative. Here, even apart from the circumstance that the Louisiana primary is made by law an integral part of the procedure of choice, the right to choose a Representative is in fact controlled by the primary because, as is alleged in the indictment, the choice of candidates at the

Democratic primary determines the choice of the elected Representative. Moreover, we cannot close our eyes to the fact already mentioned that the practical influence of the choice of candidates at the primary may be so great as to affect profoundly the choice at the general election even though there is no effective legal prohibition upon the rejection at the election of the choice made at the primary and may thus operate to deprive the voter of his constitutional right of choice. . . .

Unless the constitutional protection of the integrity of "elections" extends to primary elections, Congress is left powerless to effect the constitutional purpose, and the popular choice of Representatives is stripped of its constitutional protection save only as Congress, by taking over the control of state elections, may exclude from them the influence of the state primaries. Such an expedient would end that state autonomy with respect to elections which the Constitution contemplated that Congress should be free to leave undisturbed, subject only to such minimum regulation as it should find necessary to insure the freedom and integrity of the choice. Words, especially those of a constitution, are not to be read with such stultifying narrowness. The words of section 2 and 4 of Article I, read in the sense which is plainly permissible and in the light of the constitutional purpose, require us to hold that a primary election which involves a necessary step in the choice of candidates for election as Representatives in Congress, and which in the circumstances of this case controls that choice, is an election within the meaning of the constitutional provision and is subject to congressional regulation as to the manner of holding it.

Not only does section 4 of Article I authorize Congress to regulate the manner of holding elections, but by Article I, section 8, clause 18, Congress is given authority "To make all Laws which shall be necessary and proper for carrying into Execution the foregoing Powers, and all other Powers vested by this Constitution in the Government of the United States, or in any Department or Officer thereof." This provision leaves to the Congress the choice of means by which its constitutional powers are to be carried into execution. "Let the end be legitimate, let it be within the scope of the Constitution, and all means which are appropriate, which are plainly adapted to that end, which are not prohibited, but consist with the letter and spirit of the Constitution, are constitutional." *McCulloch* v. *Maryland*, 4 Wheat. 316, 421. That principle has been consistently adhered to and liberally applied, and extends to the congressional power by appropriate legislation to safeguard the right of choice by the people of Representatives in Congress secured by section 2 of Article I.

There remains the question whether sections 19 and 20 are an exercise of the congressional authority applicable to the acts with which appellees are charged in the indictment. Section 19 makes it a crime to conspire to "injure" or "oppress" any citizen "in the free exercise . . . of any right or privilege secured to him by the Constitution."

The suggestion that section 19, concededly applicable to conspiracies to deprive electors of their votes at congressional elections, is not sufficiently specific to be deemed applicable to primary elections, will hardly bear examination. Section 19 speaks neither of elections nor of primaries. In unambiguous language it protects "any right or privilege secured . . . by the Constitution," a phrase which as we have seen extends to the right of the voter to have his vote counted in both the general election and in the primary election, where the latter is a part of the election machinery, as well as to numerous other constitutional rights which are wholly unrelated to the choice of a Representative in Congress.

In the face of the broad language of the statute, we are pointed to no principle of statutory construction and to no significant legislative history which could be thought to sanction our saying that the statute applies any the less to primaries than to elections, where in one as in the other it is the same constitutional right which is infringed. . . . The right to participate through the primary in the choice of Representatives in Congress—a right clearly secured by the Constitution—is within the words and purpose of section 19 in the same manner and to the same extent as the right to vote at the general election. It is no extension of the criminal statute . . . to find a violation of it in a new method of interference with the right which its words protect. For it is the constitutional right, regardless of the method of interference, which is the subject of the statute and which in precise terms it protects from injury and oppression. . . .

If a right secured by the Constitution may be infringed by the corrupt failure to include the vote at a primary in the official count, it is not significant that the primary, like the voting machine, was unknown when section 19 was adopted. Abuse of either may infringe the right and therefore violate section 19. . . .

The right of the voters at the primary to have their votes counted is, as we have stated, a right or privilege secured by the Constitution, and to this section 20 also gives protection. The alleged acts of appellees were committed in the course of their performance of duties under the Louisiana statute requiring them to count the ballots, to record the result of the count, and to certify the result of the election. Misuse of power, possessed by virtue of state law and made possible only because the wrongdoer is clothed with the authority of state law, is action taken "under color of" state law. Here the acts of appellees infringed the constitutional right and deprived the voters of the benefit of it within the meaning of section 20. . . .

Reversed.

Mr. Chief Justice HUGHES took no part in the consideration or decision of this case.

Mr. Justice DOUGLAS (Mr. Justice BLACK and Mr. Justice MURPHY concurring with him), dissented. [They agreed with the majority on the constitutional question of the power of Congress over primaries, but thought the statute under which Classic had been indicted was not sufficiently specific to reach his acts.]

SMITH v. ALLWRIGHT
321 U.S. 649 (1944)

Mr. Justice REED delivered the opinion of the Court.

This writ of certiorari brings here for review a claim for damage in the sum of $5,000 on the part of petitioner, a Negro citizen of the 48th precinct of Harris County, Texas, for the refusal of respondents, election and associate election judges respectively of that precinct, to give petitioner a ballot or to permit him to cast a ballot in the primary election of July 27, 1940, for the nomination of Democratic candidates for the United States Senate and House of Representatives, and Governor and other state officers. The refusal is alleged to have been solely because of the race and color of the proposed voter.

The actions of respondents are said to violate Sections 31 and 43 of Title 8 of the United States Code, 8 U.S.C.A. sections 31 and 43, in that petitioner was deprived of rights secured by Sections 2 and 4 of Article I and the Fourteenth, Fifteenth and Seventeenth Amendments to the United States Constitution. . . .

The State of Texas by its Constitution and statutes provides that every person, if certain other requirements are met which are not here in issue, qualified by residence in the district or county "shall be deemed a qualified elector." Constitution of Texas, Article VI,

Section 2. Primary elections for United States Senators, Congressmen and state officers are provided for by Chapters Twelve and Thirteen of the statutes. Under these chapters, the Democratic Party was required to hold the primary. . . .

The Democratic party on May 24, 1932, in a State Convention adopted the following resolution, which has not since been "amended, abrogated, annulled or avoided":

"Be it resolved that all white citizens of the State of Texas who are qualified to vote under the Constitution and laws of the State shall be eligible to membership in the Democratic party and, as such, entitled to participate in its deliberations." It was by virtue of this resolution that the respondents refused to permit the petitioner to vote.

Texas is free to conduct her elections and limit her electorate as she may deem wise, save only as her action may be affected by the prohibitions of the United States Constitution or in conflict with powers delegated to and exercised by the National Government. The Fourteenth Amendment forbids a state from making or enforcing any law which abridges the privileges or immunities of citizens of the United States and the Fifteenth Amendment specifically interdicts any denial or abridgement by a state of the right of citizens to vote on account of color. Respondents appeared in the District Court and the Circuit Court of Appeals and defended on the ground that the Democratic party of Texas is a voluntary organization with members banded together for the purpose of selecting individuals of the group representing the common political beliefs as candidates in the general election. As such a voluntary organization, it was claimed, the Democratic party is free to select its own membership and limit to whites participation in the party primary. Such action, the answer asserted, does not violate the Fourteenth, Fifteenth or Seventeenth Amendment as officers of government cannot be chosen at primaries and the Amendments are applicable only to general elections where governmental officers are actually elected. Primaries, it is said, are political party affairs, handled by party not governmental officers. . . .

In *Grovey* v. *Townsend,* 295 U.S. 45 (1935), this Court had before it another suit for damages for the refusal in a primary of a county clerk, a Texas officer with only public functions to perform, to furnish petitioner, a Negro, an absentee ballot. The refusal was solely on the ground of race. . . . It was decided that the determination by the state convention of the membership of the Democratic party made a significant change from a determination by the Executive Committee. The former was party action, voluntary in character. The latter was action by authority of the State. The managers of the primary election were therefore declared not to be state officials in such sense that their action was state action. A state convention of a party was said not to be an organ of the state. This Court went on to announce that to deny a vote in a primary was a mere refusal of party membership with which "the state need have no concern," while for a state to deny a vote in a general election on the ground of race or color violated the Constitution. Consequently, there was found no ground for holding that the county clerk's refusal of a ballot because of racial ineligibility for party membership denied the petitioner any right under the Fourteenth or Fifteenth Amendments.

Since *Grovey* v. *Townsend* and prior to the present suit no case from Texas involving primary elections has been before this Court. We did decide, however, *United States* v. *Classic*. We there held that Section 4 of Article I of the Constitution authorized Congress to regulate primary as well as general elections, "where the primary is by law made an integral part of the election machinery." Consequently, in the *Classic* case, we upheld the applicability to frauds in a Louisiana primary of sections 19 and 20 of the Criminal Code, 18 U.S.C.A. sections 51, 52. Thereby corrupt acts of election officers were subjected to Congressional sanctions because that body had power to protect rights of Federal suffrage secured by the Constitution in primary as in general elections. This decision depended, too, on the determination that under the Louisiana statutes the primary was a part of the procedure for choice of Federal officials. By this decision the doubt as to whether or not such primaries were a part of "elections" subject to Federal control . . . was erased. . . . The fusing by the *Classic* case of the primary and general elections into a single instrumentality for choice of officers has a definite bearing on the permissibility under the Constitution of excluding Negroes from primaries. *Classic* bears upon *Grovey* v. *Townsend* not because exclusion of Negroes from primaries is any more or less state action by reason of the unitary character of the electoral process but because the recognition of the place of the primary in the electoral scheme makes clear that state delegation to a party of the power to fix the qualifications of primary elections is delegation of a state function that may make the party's action the action of the state. When *Grovey* v. *Townsend* was written, the Court looked upon the denial of a vote in a primary as a mere refusal by a party of party membership. As the Louisiana statutes for holding primaries are similar to those of Texas, our ruling in *Classic* as to the unitary character of the electoral process calls for a reexamination as to whether or not the exclusion of Negroes from a Texas party primary was state action.

⋯ ⋯ ⋯ ⋯

We think that this statutory system for the selection of party nominees for inclusion on the general election ballot makes the party which is required to follow these legislative directions an agency of the state in so far as it determines the participants in a primary election. The party takes its character as a state agency from the duties imposed upon it by state statutes; the duties do not become matters of private law because they are performed by a political party. The plan of the Texas primary follows substantially that of Louisiana, with the exception that in Louisiana the state pays the cost of the primary while Texas assesses the cost against candidates. In numerous instances, the Texas statutes fix or limit the fees to be charged. Whether paid directly by the state or through state requirements, it is state action which compels. When primaries become a part of the machinery for choosing officials, state and national, as they have here, the same tests to determine the character of discrimination or abridgement should be applied to the primary as are applied to the general election. If the state requires a certain electoral procedure, prescribes a general election ballot made up of party nominees so chosen and limits the choice of the electorate in general elections for state officers, practically speaking, to those whose names appear on such a ballot, it endorses, adopts and enforces the discrimination against Negroes, practiced by a party entrusted by Texas law with the determination of the qualifications of participants in the primary. This is state action within the meaning of the Fifteenth Amendment. . . .

The United States is a constitutional democracy. Its organic law grants to all citizens a right to participate in the choice of elected officials without restriction by any state because of race. This grant to the people of the opportunity for choice is not to be nullified by a state through casting its electoral process in a form which permits a private organization to practice racial discrimination in the election. Constitutional rights would be of little value if they could be thus indirectly denied.

The privilege of membership in a party may be, as this Court said in *Grovey* v. *Townsend,* no concern of a state. But when, as here, that privilege is also the essential qualification for voting in a primary to select nominees for a general election, the state makes the action of the party the action of the state. In reaching this conclusion we are not unmindful of the desirability of continuity of decision in constitutional questions. However, when convinced of former error, this Court has never felt constrained to follow precedent. In constitutional questions, where correction depends upon amendment and not upon legislative action this Court throughout its history has freely exercised its power to re-examine the basis of its constitutional decisions. This has long been accepted practice, and this practice has continued to this day. This is particularly true when the decision believed erroneous is the application of a constitutional principle rather than an interpretation of the Constitution to extract the principle itself. Here we are applying, contrary to the recent decision in *Grovey* v. *Townsend,* the well established principle of the Fifteenth Amendment, forbidding the abridgement by a state of a citizen's right to vote. *Grovey* v. *Townsend* is overruled.

Judgment reversed.

Mr. Justice FRANKFURTER concurs in the result.

Mr. Justice ROBERTS dissented. . . .

[A number of Southern states sought to avoid the results of this decision by repealing all laws pertaining to the primary. This effort to place the effective choice of representatives outside the law was ruled out by the courts. *Chapman* v. *King* [Georgia], 154 Fed. (2d) 460 (1946) ; *Rice* v. *Elmore* [South Carolina], 165 Fed. (2d) 387 (1947). In each instance the Supreme Court denied certiorari, thus by its inaction intimating its approval of the Courts of Appeals' decision. See O. Douglas Weeks, "The White Primary: 1944–1948," 42 *American Political Science Review* 500 (1948), and V. O. Key, *Southern Politics,* pp. 517–522, 619–643, a careful appraisal of Southern reaction to the principal case.]

2. FREEDOM OF EXPRESSION: "CLEAR AND PRESENT DANGER"

SCHENCK v. UNITED STATES
249 U.S. 47 (1919)

Mr. Justice HOLMES delivered the opinion of the Court.

This is an indictment in three counts. The first charges a conspiracy to violate the Espionage Act of June 15, 1917, . . . by causing and attempting to cause insubordination, &c., in the military and naval forces of the United States, and to obstruct the recruiting and enlistment of the United States, when the United States was at war with the German Empire, to-wit, that the defendants wilfully conspired to have printed and circulated to men who had been called and accepted for military service under the Act of May 18, 1917, a document set forth and alleged to be calculated to cause such insubordination and obstruction. The count alleges overt acts in pursuance of the conspiracy, ending in the distribution of the document set forth. . . . [The two other counts alleged violations of statutes by the mailing of the material referred to in the first count.] . . . The defendants were found guilty on all counts. They set up the First Amendment to the Constitution forbidding Congress to make any law abridging the freedom of speech, of the press, and bringing the case here on that ground have argued some other points also of which we must dispose.

It is argued that the evidence, if admissible, was not sufficient to prove that the defendant Schenck was concerned in sending the documents. According to the testimony Schenck said he was general secretary of the Socialist Party and had charge of the Socialist headquarters from which the documents were sent. He identified a book found there as the minutes of the Executive Committee of the party. The book showed a resolution of August 13, 1917, that 15,000 leaflets should be printed on the other side of one of them in use, to be mailed to men who had passed exemption boards, and for distribution. Schenck personally attended to the printing. On August 20 the general secretary's report said, "Obtained new leaflets from printer and started work addressing envelopes," &c.; and there was a resolve that Comrade Schenck be allowed $125 for sending leaflets through the mail. . . . Without going into confirmatory details that were proved, no reasonable man could doubt that the defendant Schenck was largely instrumental in sending the circulars about. . . .

The document in question upon its first printed side recited the first section of the Thirteenth Amendment, said that the idea embodied in it was violated by the Conscription Act and that a conscript is little better than a convict. In impassioned language it intimated that conscription was despotism in its worst form and a monstrous wrong against humanity in the interest of Wall Street's chosen few. It said, "Do not submit to intimidation," but in form at least confined itself to peaceful measures such as a petition for the repeal of the act. The other and later printed side of the sheet was headed "Assert Your Rights." It stated reasons for alleging that any one violated the Constitution when he refused to recognize "your right to assert your opposition to the draft," and went on, "If you do not assert and support your rights, you are helping to deny or disparage rights which it is the solemn duty of all citizens and residents of the United States to retain." It described the arguments on the other side as coming from cunning politicians and a mercenary capitalist press, and even silent consent to the conscription law as helping to support an infamous conspiracy. It denied the power to send our citizens away to foreign shores to shoot up the people of other lands, and added that words could not express the condemnation such cold-blooded ruthlessness deserves, &c., winding up, "You must do your share to maintain, support and uphold the rights of the people of this country." Of course the document would not have been sent unless it had been intended to have some effect, and we do not see what effect it could be expected to have upon persons subject to the draft except to influence them to obstruct the carrying out of it. The defendants too do not deny that the jury might find against them on this point.

But it is said, suppose that that was the tendency of this circular, it is protected by the First Amendment to the Constitution. Two of the strongest expressions are said to be quoted respectively from well-known public men. . . . We admit that in many places and in ordinary times the defendants in saying all that was said in the circular would have been within their constitutional rights. But the character of every act depends upon the circumstances in which it is done. . . . The most stringent protection of free speech would not protect a man in falsely shouting fire in a theatre and causing a panic. It does not even protect a man from an injunction against uttering words that may have all the effect of force. *Gompers* v. *Bucks Stove & Range Co.,* 221 U.S. 418, 439. The question in every case is whether the words used are used in such circumstances and are of such a nature as to create a clear and present danger that they will bring about the substantive evils that Congress has a right to prevent. It is a question of proximity and degree. When a nation is at war many things that might be said in time of peace are such a hindrance to its effort that their utterance will not be endured so long as men fight and that no court could regard them as protected by any constitutional right. It seems to be admitted that if an actual obstruction of the recruiting service were proved, liability for words that produced that effect might be enforced. The statute of 1917 in § 4 punishes conspiracies to obstruct as well as actual obstruction. If the act (speaking, or circulating a paper), its tendency and the intent with which it is done are the same, we perceive no ground for saying that success alone warrants making the act a crime. . . .

Judgments affirmed.

GITLOW v. NEW YORK
268 U.S. 652 (1925)

Mr. Justice SANFORD delivered the opinion of the Court.

Benjamin Gitlow was indicted in the Supreme Court[1] of New York, with three others, for the statutory crime of criminal anarchy. . . .

The contention here is that the statute, by its terms and as applied in this case, is repugnant to the due process clause of the 14th Amendment. Its material provisions are:

"§ 160. Criminal anarchy defined.—Criminal anarchy is the doctrine that organized government should be overthrown by force or violence, or by assassination of the executive head or of any of the executive officials of government, or by any unlawful means. The advocacy of such doctrine by word of mouth or writing is a felony.

"§ 161. Advocacy of criminal anarchy.—Any person who:

"1. By word of mouth or writing advocates, advises or teaches the duty, necessity or propriety of overthrowing or overturning organized government by force or violence, or by assassination of the executive head or of any of the executive officials of government, or by any unlawful means; or,

"2. Prints, publishes, edits, issues or knowingly circulates, sells, distributes or publicly displays any book, paper, document, or written or printed matter in any form, containing or advocating, advising or teaching the doctrine that organized government should be overthrown by force, violence, and unlawful means. . . ,

"Is guilty of a felony and punishable" by imprisonment or fine, or both.

The indictment was in two counts. The first charged that the defendants had advocated, advised, and taught the duty, necessity, and propriety of overthrowing and overturning organized government

---

[1] In New York, the Supreme Court is the name of the trial court; the highest state court is the Court of Appeals.

by force, violence, and unlawful means, by certain writings therein set forth, entitled "The Left Wing Manifesto"; the second, that the defendants had printed, published, and knowingly circulated and distributed a certain paper called "The Revolutionary Age," containing the writings set forth in the first count, advocating, advising, and teaching the doctrine that organized government should be overthrown by force, violence, and unlawful means. . . .

. . . It was admitted that the defendant signed a card subscribing to the Manifesto and Program of the Left Wing, which all applicants were required to sign before being admitted to membership; that he went to different parts of the state to speak to branches of the Socialist party about the principles of the Left Wing, and advocated their adoption; and that he was responsible [as business manager] for the Manifesto as it appeared, that "he knew of the publication, in a general way, and he knew of its publication afterwards, and is responsible for its circulation."

There was no evidence of any effect resulting from the publication and circulation of the Manifesto. . . .

.   .   .   .   .

The statute does not penalize the utterance of publication of abstract "doctrine" or academic discussion having no quality of incitement to any concrete action. It is not aimed against mere historical or philosophical essays. It does not restrain the advocacy of changes in the form of government by constitutional and lawful means. What it prohibits is language advocating, advising or teaching the overthrow of organized government by unlawful means. . . .

.   .   .   .   .

The Manifesto, plainly, is neither the statement of abstract doctrine nor, as suggested by counsel, mere prediction that industrial disturbances and revolutionary mass strikes will result spontaneously in an inevitable process of evolution in the economic system. It advocates and urges in fervent language mass action which shall progressively foment industrial disturbances and through political mass strikes and revolutionary mass action overthrow and destroy organized parliamentary government. It concludes with a call to action in these words: "The proletariat revolution and the Communist reconstruction of society—*the struggle for these*—is now indispensable. . . . The Communist International calls the proletariat of the world to the final struggle!"

This is not the expression of philosophical abstraction, the mere prediction of future events; it is the language of direct incitement. The means advocated for bringing about the destruction of organized parliamentary government, namely, mass industrial revolts usurping the functions of municipal government, political mass strikes directed against the parliamentary state, and revolutionary mass action for its final destruction, necessarily imply the use of force and violence, and in their essential nature are inherently unlawful in a constitutional government of law and order. That the jury were warranted in finding that the Manifesto advocated not merely the abstract doctrine of overthrowing organized government by force, violence and unlawful means, but action to that end, is clear.

For the present purposes we may and do assume that freedom of speech and of the press—which are protected by the First Amendment from abridgement by Congress—are among the fundamental personal rights and "liberties" protected by the due process clause of the Fourteenth Amendment from impairment by the states. . . .

It is a fundamental principle, long established, that the freedom of speech and of the press which is secured by the Constitution, does not confer an absolute right to speak or punish, without responsibility, whatever one may choose, or an unrestricted and unbridled license that gives immunity for every possible use of language and prevents the punishment of those who abuse this freedom. . . .

That a State in the exercise of its police power may punish those who abuse this freedom by utterances inimical to the public welfare, tending to corrupt public morals, incite to crime, or disturb the public peace, is not open to question. . . .

And, for yet more imperative reasons, a State may punish utterances endangering the foundations of organized government and threatening its overthrow by unlawful means. These imperil its own existence as a constitutional State. Freedom of speech and press . . . does not protect disturbances to the public press or the attempt to subvert the government. . . . It does not protect publications prompting the overthrow of government by force; the punishment of those who publish articles which tend to destroy organized society being essential to the security of freedom and the stability of the State. . . . In short this freedom does not deprive a State of the primary and essential right of self-preservation; which so long as human governments endure, they cannot be denied. . . .

By enacting the present statute the State has determined, through its legislative body, that utterances advocating the overthrow of organized government by force, violence and unlawful means, are so inimical to the general welfare and involve such danger of substantive evil that they may be penalized in the exercise of its police power. That determination must be given great weight. . . .

We cannot hold that the present statute is an arbitrary or unreasonable exercise of the police power of the State unwarrantably infringing the freedom of speech or press; and we must and do sustain its constitutionality.

This being so it may be applied to every utterance—not too trivial to be beneath the notice of the law—which is of such a character and used with such intent and purpose as to bring it within the prohibition of the statute. . . . In other words, when the legislative body has determined generally, in the constitutional exercise of its discretion, that utterances of a certain kind involve such danger of substantive evil that they may be punished, the question whether any specific utterance coming within the prohibited class is likely, in and of itself, to bring about the substantive evil, is not open to consideration. It is sufficient that the statute itself be constitutional and that the use of the language comes within its prohibition.

Judgment affirmed.

Mr. Justice HOLMES, dissenting:

Mr. Justice Brandeis and I are of opinion that this judgment should be reversed. The general principle of free speech, it seems to me, must be taken to be included in the Fourteenth Amendment, in view of the scope that has been given to the word "liberty" as there used, although perhaps it may be accepted with a somewhat larger latitude of interpretation than is allowed to Congress by the sweeping language that governs or ought to govern the laws of the United States. If I am right then I think that the criterion sanctioned by the full Court in *Schenck* v. *United States*, 249 U.S. 47, applies:

"The question in every case is whether the words used are used in such circumstances and are of such a nature as to create a clear and present danger that they will bring about the substantive evils that [the state] has a right to prevent."

. . . If what I think the correct test is applied it is manifest that there was no present danger of an attempt to overthrow the government by force on the part of the admittedly small minority who shared the defendant's view. It is said that this manifesto was more than a theory, that it was an incitement. Every idea is an incitement. It offers itself for belief and if believed it is acted on unless some other belief outweighs it or some failure of energy stifles the movement at its birth. The only difference between the expression of an opinion and an incitement in the narrower sense is the speaker's enthusiasm for the result. Eloquence may set fire to reason. But whatever may be thought of the redundant discourse before us it had no chance of starting a present conflagration. If in the long run the beliefs expressed in proletarian dictatorship are destined to be accepted by the dominant forces of the community, the only meaning of free speech is that they should be given their chance and have their way.

. . . . .

NEAR v. MINNESOTA
283 U.S. 697 (1931)

Mr. Chief Justice HUGHES delivered the opinion of the Court.

Chapter 285 of the Session Laws of Minnesota for the year 1925 provides for the abatement, as a public nuisance, of a "malicious, scandalous and defamatory newspaper, magazine or other periodical." Section 1 of the act is as follows:

"Section 1. Any person who, as an individual, or as a member or employee of a firm, or association or organization, or as an officer, director, member or employee of a corporation, shall be engaged in the business of regularly or customarily producing, publishing or circulating, having in possession, selling or giving away

" (a) an obscene, lewd and lascivious newspaper, magazine, or other periodical, or

" (b) a malicious, scandalous and defamatory newspaper, magazine or other periodical,

—is guilty, of a nuisance, and all persons guilty of such nuisance may be enjoined, as hereinafter provided.

"Participation in such business shall constitute a commission of such nuisance and render the participant liable and subject to the proceedings, orders and judgments provided for in this Act. Ownership, in whole or in part, directly or indirectly, of any such periodical, or of any stock or interest in any corporation or organization which owns the same in whole or in part, or which publishes the same, shall constitute such participation.

"In actions brought under (b) above, there shall be available the defense that the truth was published with good motives and for justifiable ends and in such actions the plaintiff shall not have the right to report (sic) to issues or editions of periodicals taking place more than three months before the commencement of the action." . . .

Under this statute (section 1, clause (b)), the county attorney of Hennepin county brought this action [against Near et al.] to enjoin the publication of what was described as a "malicious, scandalous and defamatory newspaper, magazine or other periodical," known as the Saturday Press, published by the defendants in the city of Minneapolis. . . .

Without attempting to summarize the contents of the voluminous exhibits attached to the complaint, we deem it sufficient to say that the articles charged, in substance, that a Jewish gangster was in control of gambling, bootlegging, and racketeering in Minneapolis, and that law-enforcing officers and agencies were not energetically performing their duties. Most of the charges were directed against the chief of police; he was charged with gross neglect of duty, illicit relations with gangsters, and with participation in graft. The county attorney was charged with knowing the existing conditions and with failure to take adequate measures to remedy them. The mayor was accused of inefficiency and dereliction. One member of the grand jury was stated to be in sympathy with the gangsters. A special grand jury and a special prosecutor were demanded to deal with the situation in general, and, in particular, to investigate an attempt to assassinate one Guilford, one of the original defendants, who, it appears from the articles, was shot by gangsters after the first issue of the periodical had been published. There is no question but what the articles made serious accusations against the public officers named and others in connection with the prevalence of crimes and the failure to expose and punish them. . . .

[The state court proceedings are recapitulated in summary. Their ultimate result was that the Supreme Court of the State upheld the constitutionality of the law, and later issued a permanent injunction.]

From the judgment as thus affirmed, the defendant Near appeals to this Court.

This statute, for the suppression as a public nuisance of a newspaper or periodical, is unusual, if not unique, and raises questions of grave importance transcending the local interests involved in the particular action. It is no longer open to doubt that the liberty of the press and of speech is within the liberty safeguarded by the due process clause of the Fourteenth Amendment from invasion by state action. . . . In maintaining this guaranty, the authority of the state to enact laws to promote the health, safety, morals, and general welfare of its people is necessarily admitted. The limits of this sovereign power must always be determined with appropriate regard to the particular subject of its exercise. . . . Liberty of speech and of the press is also not an absolute right, and the state may punish its abuse. . . . Liberty, in each of its phases, has its history and connotation, and, in the present instance, the inquiry is as to the historic conception of the liberty of the press and whether the statute under review violates the essential attributes of that liberty. . . .

First. The statute is not aimed at the redress of individual or private wrongs. Remedies for libel remain available and unaffected. The statute, said the state court (174 Minn. 457), "is not directed at threatened libel but an existing business which, generally speaking, involves more than libel." It is aimed at the distribution of scandalous matter as "detrimental to public morals and to the general welfare," tending "to disturb the peace of the community" and "to provoke assaults and the commission of crime." In order to obtain an injunction to suppress the future publication of the newspaper or periodical, it is not necessary to prove the falsity of the charges that have been made in the publication condemned. In the present action there was no allegation that the publication was "malicious." . . . The judgment in this case proceeded upon the mere proof of publication. The statute permits the defense, not of the truth alone, but only that the truth was published with good motives and for justifiable ends. It is apparent that under the statute the publication is to be regarded as defamatory if it injures reputation, and that it is scandalous if it circulates charges of reprehensible conduct, whether criminal or otherwise, and the publication is thus deemed to invite public reprobation and to constitute a public scandal. The court sharply defined the purpose of the statute, bringing out the precise point, in these words: "There is no constitutional right to publish a fact merely because it is true. It is a matter of common knowledge that prosecutions under the criminal libel statutes do not result in efficient repression or suppression of the evils of scandal. Men who are the victims of such assaults seldom resort to the courts. This is especially true if their sins are exposed and the only question relates to whether it was done with good motive and for justifiable ends.

This law is not for the protection of the person attacked nor to punish the wrongdoer. It is for the protection of the public welfare."

Second. The statute is directed not simply at the circulation of scandalous and defamatory statements with regard to private citizens, but at the continued publication by newspapers and periodicals of charges against public officers of corruption, malfeasance in office, or serious neglect of duty. Such charges by their very nature create a public scandal. They are scandalous and defamatory within the meaning of the statute, which has its normal operation in relation to publications dealing prominently and chiefly with the alleged derelictions of public officers.

Third. The object of the statute is not punishment, in the ordinary sense, but suppression of the offending newspaper or periodical. . . . Under this statute, a publisher of a newspaper or periodical, undertaking to conduct a campaign to expose and to censure official derelictions, and devoting his publication principally to that purpose, must face not simply the possibility of a verdict against him in a suit or prosecution for libel, but a determination that his newspaper or periodical is a public nuisance to be abated, and that this abatement and suppression will follow unless he is prepared with legal evidence to prove the truth of the charges and also to satisfy the court that, in addition to being true, the matter was published with good motives and for justifiable ends.

This suppression is accomplished by enjoining publication, and that restraint is the object and effect of the statute.

Fourth. The statute not only operates to suppress the offending newspaper or periodical, but to put the publisher under an effective censorship. When a newspaper or periodical is found to be "malicious, scandalous and defamatory," and is suppressed as such, resumption of publication is punishable as a contempt of court by fine or imprisonment. Thus, where a newspaper or periodical has been suppressed because of the circulation of charges against public officers of official misconduct, it would seem to be clear that the renewal of the publication of such charges would constitute a contempt, and that the judgment would lay a permanent restraint upon the publisher, to escape which he must satisfy the court as to the character of a new publication. Whether he would be permitted again to publish matter deemed to be derogatory to the same or other public officers would depend on the court's ruling. . . .

The question is whether a statute authorizing such proceedings in restraint of publication is consistent with the conception of the liberty of the press as historically conceived and guaranteed. In determining the extent of the constitutional protection, it has been generally, if not universally, considered that it is the chief purpose of the guaranty to prevent previous restraints upon publication. . . .

.   .   .   .   .

The exceptional nature of its limitations places in a strong light the general conception that liberty of the press, historically considered and taken up by the Federal Constitution, has meant, principally although not exclusively, immunity from previous restraints or censorship. The conception of the liberty of the press in this country had broadened with the exigencies of the colonial period and with the efforts to secure freedom from oppressive administration. That liberty was especially cherished for the immunity it afforded from previous restraint of the publication of censure of public officers and charges of official conduct. . . .

The importance of this immunity has not lessened. While reckless assaults upon public men, and efforts to bring obloquy upon those who are endeavoring faithfully to discharge official duties, exert a baleful influence and deserve the severest condemnation in public opinion, it cannot be said that this abuse is greater, and it is believed to be less, than that which characterized the period in which our institutions took shape. Meanwhile, the administration of government has become more complex, the opportunities for malfeasance and corruption have multiplied, crime has grown to most serious proportions, and the danger of its protection by unfaithful officials and of the impairment of the fundamental security of life and property by criminal alliances and official neglect, emphasize the primary need of a vigilant and courageous press, abused by miscreant purveyors of scandal does not make any the less necessary the immunity of the press from previous restraint in dealing with official misconduct. Subsequent punishment for such abuses as may exist is the appropriate remedy, consistent with constitutional privilege. . . .

.   .   .   .   .

For these reasons we hold the statute, so far as it authorized the proceedings in this action under clause (b) of section 1, to be an infringement of the liberty of the press guaranteed by the Fourteenth

Amendment. We should add that this decision rests upon the operation and effect of the statute, without regard to the question of the truth of the charges contained in the particular periodical. The fact that the public officers named in this case, and those associated with the charges of official dereliction, may be deemed to be impeccable, cannot affect the conclusion that the statute imposes an unconstitutional restraint upon publication.

Judgment reversed.

Mr. Justice BUTLER, dissenting.

The decision of the Court in this case declares Minnesota and every other state powerless to restrain by injunction the business of publishing and circulating among the people malicious, scandalous and defamatory periodicals that in due course of judicial procedure has been adjuged to be a public nuisance. It gives to freedom of the press a meaning and a scope not heretofore recognized and construes "liberty" in the due process clause of the Fourteenth Amendment to put upon the states a Federal restriction that is without precedent. . . .

Mr. Justice VAN DEVANTER, Mr. Justice McREYNOLDS, and Mr. Justice SUTHERLAND concur in this opinion.

3. THE PREFERRED POSITION OF FREE SPEECH

BRIDGES v. CALIFORNIA
TIMES-MIRROR CO. v. SUPERIOR COURT OF CALIFORNIA
314 U.S. 252 (1941)

[The convictions for contempt of court involved in these cases grew out of public criticisms of the court. In each instance, final court action was still pending; in each case political consequences were invoked unless the decision followed a certain course. The court held this to be interference with the administration of justice.]

Mr. Justice BLACK delivered the opinion of the Court.

These two cases, while growing out of different circumstances and concerning different parties, both relate to the scope of our national constitutional policy safeguarding free speech and a free press. All of the petitioners were adjuged guilty and fined for contempt of court by the Superior Court of Los Angeles County. Their conviction rested upon comments pertaining to pending litigation which were published in newspapers. In the Superior Court and later in the California Supreme Court, petitioners challenged the state's action as an abridgment, prohibited by the Federal Constitution, of freedom of speech and of the press, but the Superior Court overruled this contention, and the Supreme Court affirmed. The importance of the constitutional question prompted us to grant certiorari.

[The Court reviews the past application of the "clear and present danger" rule.]

... The likelihood, however great, that a substantive evil will result cannot alone justify a restriction upon freedom of speech or the press. The evil itself must be "substantial," Brandeis, J., concurring in *Whitney* v. *California,* [274 U.S. 357], 374; it must be "serious," *id.,* 376. And even the expression of "legislative preferences or beliefs" cannot transcend minor matters of public inconvenience or annoyance into substantive evils of sufficient weight to warrant the curtailment of liberty of expression. . . .

What finally emerges from the "clear and present danger" cases is a working principle that the substantive evil must be extremely serious and the degree of imminence extremely high before utterances can be punished. Those cases do not purport to mark the furthermost constitutional boundaries of protected expression, nor do we here. They do no more than recognize a minimum compulsion of the Bill of Rights. For the First Amendment does not speak equivocally. It prohibits "any law abridging the freedom of speech or of the press." It must be taken as a command of the broadest scope that explicit language, read in the context of a liberty-loving society, will allow.

Before analyzing the punished utterances and the circumstances surrounding their publication, we must consider an argument which, if valid, would destroy the relevance of the foregoing discussion to this case. In brief, this argument is that the publications here in question belong to a special category marked off by history, a category to which the criteria of constitutional immunity from punishment used where other types of utterances are concerned are not applicable. For, the argument runs, the power of judges to punish by contempt out-of-court publications tending to obstruct the orderly and fair administration of justice in a pending case was deeply rooted in English common law at the time the Constitution was adopted. . . .

. . . No purpose in ratifying the Bill of Rights was clearer than that of securing for the people of the United States much greater freedom

of religion, expression, assembly, and petition than the people of
Great Britain had ever enjoyed. It cannot be denied, for example, that
the religious test oath or the restrictions upon assembly then prevalent in England would have been regarded as measures which the
Constitution prohibited the American Congress from passing. And
since the same unequivocal language is used with respect to freedom
of the press, it signifies a similar enlargement of that concept as well.
Ratified as it was while the memory of many oppressive English restrictions on the enumerated liberties was still fresh, the First Amendment cannot reasonably be taken as approving prevalent English
practices. On the contrary, the only conclusion supported by history
is that the unqualified prohibitions laid down by the framers were
intended to give to liberty of the press, as to the other liberties, the
broadest scope that could be countenanced in an orderly society. . . .

We may appropriately begin our discussion of the judgments below by considering how much, as a practical matter, they would affect
liberty of expression. It must be recognized that public interest is
much more likely to be kindled by a controversial event of the day
than by a generalization, however penetrating, of the historian or
scientist. Since they punish utterances made during the pendency of
a case, the judgments below therefore produce their restrictive results at the precise time when public interest in the matters discussed
would naturally be at its height. Moreover, the ban is likely to fall
not only at a crucial time but upon the most important topics of discussion. Here, for example, labor controversies were the topics of
some of the publications. Experience shows that the more acute labor
controversies are, the more likely it is that in some aspect they will
get into court. It is therefore the controversies that command most
interest that the decisions below would remove from the area of public discussion.

No suggestion can be found in the Constitution that the freedom
there guaranteed for speech and the press bears an inverse ratio to
the timeliness and importance of the ideas seeking expression. Yet,
it would follow as a practical result of the decisions below that anyone who might wish to give public expression to his views on a pending case involving no matter what problem of public interest, just
at the time his audience would be most receptive, would be as effectively discouraged as if a deliberate statutory scheme of censorship had been adopted. Indeed, perhaps more so, because under a
legislative specification of the particular kinds of expressions pro-

hibited and the circumstances under which the prohibitions are to operate, the speaker or publisher might at least have an authoritative guide to the permissible scope of comment, instead of being compelled to act at the peril that judges might find in the utterance a "reasonable tendency" to obstruct justice in a pending case.

This unfocussed threat is, to be sure, limited in time, terminating as it does upon final disposition of the case. But this does not change its censorial quality. An endless series of moratoria on public discussion, even if each were very short, could hardly be dismissed as an insignificant abridgment of freedom of expression. And to assume that each would be short is to overlook the fact that the "pendency" of a case is frequently a matter of months or even years rather than days or weeks.

For these reasons we are convinced that the judgments below result in a curtailment of expression that cannot be dismissed as insignificant. If they can be justified at all, it must be in terms of some serious substantive evil which they are designed to avert. The substantive evil here sought to be averted has been variously described below. It appears to be double: disrespect for the judiciary; and disorderly and unfair administration of justice. The assumption that respect for the judiciary can be won by shielding judges from published criticism wrongly appraises the character of American public opinion. For it is a prized American privilege to speak one's mind, although not always with perfect good taste, on all public institutions. And an enforced silence, however limited, solely in the name of preserving the dignity of the bench, would probably engender resentment, suspicion, and contempt much more than it would enhance respect.

The other evil feared, disorderly and unfair administration of justice, is more plausibly associated with restricting publications which touch upon pending litigation. The very word "trial" connotes decisions on the evidence and arguments properly advanced in open court. Legal trials are not like elections, to be won through the use of the meeting-hall, the radio, and the newspaper. But we cannot start with the assumption that publications of the kind here involved actually do threaten to change the nature of legal trials, and that to preserve judicial impartiality, it is necessary for judges to have a contempt power by which they can close all channels of public expression to all matters which touch upon pending cases. We must therefore turn to the particular utterances here in question and the circumstances of their publication to determine to what extent the substantive evil of unfair administration of justice was a likely consequence, and whether the degree of likelihood was sufficient to justify summary punishment. . . .

Reversed.

Mr. Justice FRANKFURTER, with whom concurred the Chief Justice, Mr. Justice ROBERTS, and Mr. Justice BYRNES, dissenting.

Our whole history repels the view that it is an exercise of one of the civil liberties secured by the Bill of Rights for a leader of a large following or for a powerful metropolitan newspaper to attempt to overawe a judge in a matter immediately pending before him. The view of the majority deprives California of means for securing to its citizens justice according to law—means which, since the Union was founded, have been the possession, hitherto unchallenged, of all the states. This sudden break with the uninterrupted course of constitutional history has no constitutional warrant. To find justification for such deprivation of the historic powers of the states is to misconceive the idea of freedom of thought and speech as guaranteed by the Constitution. . . .

In a series of opinions as uncompromising as any in its history, this Court has settled that the fullest opportunities for free discussion are "implicit in the concept of ordered liberty, and thus, through the Fourteenth Amendment," protected against attempted invasion by the States. *Palko* v. *Connecticut,* 302 U.S. 319, 324, 325. The channels of inquiry and thought must be kept open to new conquests of reason, however odious their expression may be to the prevailing climate of opinion. But liberty "in each of its phases has its history and connotation." Whether a particular state action violates "the essential attributes of that liberty" must be judged in the light of the liberty that is invoked and the curtailment that is challenged. *Near* v. *Minnesota,* 283 U.S. 697, 708. For "the recognition of a privilege does not mean that it is without conditions or exceptions. The social policy that will prevail in many situations may run foul in others of a different social policy, competing for supremacy. It is then the function of a court to mediate between them, assigning so far as possible, a proper value to each, and summoning to its aid all the distinctions and analogies that are the tools of the judicial process." *Clark* v. *United States,* 289 U.S. 1, 13.

Free speech is not so absolute or irrational a conception as to imply paralysis of the means for effective protection of all the freedoms secured by the Bill of Rights. . . . In the cases before us, the claims on behalf of freedom of speech and of the press encounter claims on behalf of liberties no less precious. California asserts her right to do what she had done as a means of safeguarding her system of justice.

The administration of justice by an impartial judiciary has been basic to our conception of freedom ever since Magna Carta. It is the concern not merely of the immediate litigants. Its assurance is everyone's concern, and it is protected by the liberty guaranteed by the Fourteenth Amendment. . . .

A trial is not a "free trade in ideas," nor is the best test of truth in a court room "the power of the thought to get itself accepted in the competition of the Market." . . . A court is a forum with strictly defined limits for discussion. It is circumscribed in the range of its inquiry and in its methods by the Constitution, by laws, and by age-old traditions. Its judges are restrained in their freedom of expression by historic compulsions resting on no other officials of government. They are so circumscribed precisely because judges have in their keeping the enforcement of rights and the protection of liberties which, according to the wisdom of the ages, can only be enforced and protected by observing such methods and traditions.

The dependence of society upon an unswerved judiciary is such a commonplace in the history of freedom that the means by which it is maintained are too frequently taken for granted without heed to the conditions which alone make it possible. . . .

. . . To assure the impartial accomplishment of justice is not an abridgment of freedom of speech or freedom of the press, as these phases of liberty have heretofore been conceived even by the stoutest libertarians. In fact, these liberties themselves depend upon an untrammeled judiciary whose passions are not even unconsciously aroused and whose minds are not distorted by extrajudicial considerations.

. . . Freedom of expression can hardly carry implications that nullify the guarantees of impartial trials. And since courts are the ultimate resorts for vindicating the Bill of Rights, a state may surely authorize appropriate historic means to assure that the process for such vindication be not wrenched from its rational tracks into the more primitive melee of passion and pressure. The need is great that courts be criticized but just as great that they be allowed to do their duty. . . .

Because freedom of public expression alone assures the unfolding of truth, it is indispensable to the democratic process. But even that freedom is not absolute and is not predetermined. By a doctrinaire overstatement of its scope and by giving it an illusory absolute appearance, there is danger of thwarting the free choice and the responsibility of exercising it which are basic to a democratic society. While we are reviewing a judgment of the California Supreme Court and not an act of its legislature or the voice of the people of California formally expressed in its constitution, we are in fact passing judgment on "the power of the State as a whole."

THOMAS v. COLLINS
323 U.S. 516 (1944)

[The state of Texas enacted a law requiring every labor union organizer operating in the state to obtain from the secretary of state an organizer's card before he undertook any solicitation for his union. The prerequisite for the issuance of the card was that the organizer must furnish his name and his union affiliation and display his credentials to the secretary who, thereupon, had to issue the card. There was no discretion in the official to refuse this card once the required data had been produced.

[R. J. Thomas, as president of the United Automobile Workers, C.I.O., went to Texas for the express purpose of creating a test case. He did not obtain a union organizer's card, but at a public meeting he made it a point publicly to invite any nonmembers present to join the union. Previous to the meeting, he had been served with a restraining order and subsequently was cited for contempt for failure to obey the court's command not to address any meeting unless he had registered as a union organizer.]

Mr. Justice RUTLEDGE delivered the opinion of the Court.

The Supreme Court of Texas ... sustained the Act as a valid exercise of the State's police power, taken "for the protection of the general welfare of the public, and particularly the laboring class," with special reference to safeguarding laborers from imposture when approached by an alleged organizer. The provision, it was said, "affects only the right of one to engage in the business as a paid organizer, and not the mere right of an individual to express his views on the merits of the union." ...

The court conceded however that the Act "interferes to a certain extent with the right of the organizer to speak as the paid representative of the union." Nevertheless, it said, "such interferences are not necessarily prohibited by the Constitution. The State under its police power may enact laws which interfere indirectly and to a limited extent with the right of speech or the liberty of the people where they are reasonably, necessary for the protection of the general public." Accordingly, it likened the instant prohibition to various other ones imposed by state or federal legislation upon "the right of one to operate or speak as the agent of another," including securities salesmen, insurance agents, real estate brokers, etc. And various decisions of this Court and others were thought to support the conclusion that the Act "imposes no previous general restraint upon the right of free speech. . . . It merely requires paid organizers to register with the Secretary of State before beginning to operate as such."

.   .   .   .   .   .

The case confronts us again with the duty our system places on this Court to say where the individual's freedom ends and the State's power begins. Choice on that border, now as always delicate, is perhaps more so where the usual presumption supporting legislation is balanced by the preferred place given in our scheme to the great, the indispensable democratic freedoms secured by the First Amendment. That priority gives these liberties a sanctity and a sanction not permitting dubious intrusions. And it is the character of the right, not of the limitation, which determines what standard governs the choice. . . .

For these reasons any attempt to restrict those liberties must be justified by clear public interest, threatened not doubtfully or remotely, but by clear and present danger. The rational connection between the remedy provided and the evil to be curbed, which in other contexts might support legislation against attack on due process grounds, will not suffice. These rights rest on firmer foundation. Accordingly, whatever occasion would restrain orderly discussion and persuasion, at appropriate time and place, must have clear support in public danger, actual or impending. Only the gravest abuses, endangering paramount interests, give occasion for permissible limitation. It is therefore in our tradition to allow the widest room for discussion, the narrowest range for its restriction, particularly when the right is exercised in conjunction with peaceable assembly. It was not

by accident or coincidence that the rights to freedom in speech and
press were coupled in a single guaranty with the rights of the people
peaceably to assemble and to petition for redress of grievances. All
these, though not identical, are inseparable. They are cognate rights,
. . . and therefore are united in the First Article's assurance.

This conjunction of liberties is not peculiar to religious activity
and institutions alone. The First Amendment gives freedom of mind
the same security as freedom of conscience. Great secular causes, with
small ones, are guarded. The grievances for redress of which the right
of petition was insured, and with it the right of assembly, are not
solely religious or political ones. And the rights of free speech and a
free press are not confined to any field of human interest.

The idea is not sound therefore that the First Amendment's safeguards are wholly inapplicable to business or economic activity. And
it does not resolve where the line shall be drawn in a particular case
merely to urge, as Texas does, that an organization for which the
rights of free speech and free assembly are claimed is one "engaged
in business activities" or that the individual who leads it in exercising these rights receives compensation for doing so. Nor, on the other
hand, is the answer given, whether what is done is an exercise of
those rights and the restriction a forbidden impairment, by ignoring
the organization's economic function, because those interests of workingmen are involved or because they have the general liberties of the
citizen, as appellant would do.

These comparisons are at once too simple, too general, and too inaccurate to be determinative. Where the line shall be placed in a
particular application rests, not on such generalities, but on the concrete clash of particular interests and the community's relative evaluation both of them and of how the one will be affected by the specific
restriction, the other by its absence. That judgment in the first instance is for the legislative body. But in our system where the line
can constitutionally be placed presents a question this Court cannot
escape answering independently, whatever the legislative judgment,
in the light of our constitutional tradition. And the answer, under
that tradition, can be affirmative, to support an intrusion upon this
domain, only if grave and impending public danger requires this.

That the State has power to regulate labor unions with a view to
protecting the public interest is, as the Texas court said, hardly to
be doubted. They cannot claim special immunity from regulation.
Such regulation however, whether aimed at fraud or other abuses,

must not trespass upon the domain set apart for free speech and free assembly. This Court has recognized that "in the circumstances of our times the dissemination of information concerning the facts of a labor dispute must be regarded as within that area of free discussion that is guaranteed by the Constitution. . . . Free discussion concerning the conditions in industry and the causes of labor disputes appears to us indispensable to the effective and intelligent use of the processes of popular government to shape the destiny of modern industrial society." *Thornhill* v. *Alabama,* 310 U.S. 88. The right thus to discuss, and inform people concerning, the advantages and disadvantages of unions and joining them is protected not only as part of free speech, but as part of free assembly. The Texas court, in its disposition of the cause, did not give sufficient weight to this consideration, more particularly by its failure to take account of the blanketing effect of the prohibition's present application upon public discussion and also of the bearing of the clear and present danger test in these circumstances.

Thomas went to Texas for one purpose and one only—to make the speech in question. Its whole object was publicly to proclaim the advantage of workers' organization and to persuade workmen to join Local No. 1002 as part of a campaign for members. These also were the sole objects of the meeting. . . . The occasion was clearly protected. The speech was an essential part of the occasion, unless all meaning and purpose were to be taken from it. And the invitations, both general and particular, were parts of the speech, inseparable incidents of the occasion and of all that was said or done.

That there was restriction upon Thomas' right to speak and the rights of the workers to hear what he had to say, there can be no doubt. The threat of the restraining order, backed by the power of contempt, and of arrest for crime, hung over every word. A speaker in such circumstances could avoid the words "solicit," "invite," "join." It would be impossible to avoid the idea. The statute requires no specific formula. It is not contended that only the use of the word "solicit" would violate the prohibition. Without such a limitation, the statute forbids any language which conveys, or reasonably could be found to convey, the meaning of the invitation. That Thomas chose to meet the issue squarely, not to hide in ambiguous phrasing, does not counteract this fact. General words create different and often

particular impressions on different minds. No speaker, however careful, can convey exactly his meaning, or the same meaning, to the
different members of an audience. How one might "laud unionism,"
as the State and the State Supreme Court concede Thomas was free
to do, yet in these circumstances not imply an invitation, is hard to
conceive. This is the nub of the case, which the State fails to meet
because it cannot do so. . . .

. . . The supposedly clear-cut distinction between discussion, lau-
dation, general advocacy, and solicitation puts the speaker in these
circumstances wholly at the mercy of the varied understanding of
his hearers and consequently of whatever inference may be drawn
as to his intent and meaning.

Such a distinction offers no security for free discussion. In these
conditions it blankets with uncertainty whatever may be said. It
compels the speaker to hedge and trim. He must take care in every
word to create no impression that he means, in advocating unionism's most central principle, namely, that workingmen should unite
for collective bargaining, to urge those present to do so. The vice is
not merely that invitation, in the circumstances shown here, is
speech. It is also that its prohibition forbids or restrains discussion
which is not or may not be invitation. The sharp line cannot be drawn
surely or securely. The effort to observe it could not be free speech,
free press, or free assembly, in any sense of free advocacy of principle
or cause. The restriction's effect, as applied, in a very practical sense
was to prohibit Thomas not only to solicit members and member-
ships, but also to speak in advocacy of the cause of trade unionism
in Texas, without having first procured the card. Thomas knew this
and faced the alternatives it presented. When served with the order
he had three choices: (1) to stand on his right and speak freely; (2)
to quit, refusing entirely to speak; (3) to trim, and even thus to risk
the penalty. He chose the first alternative. We think he was within
his rights in doing so.

The assembly was entirely peaceable, and had no other than a
wholly lawful purpose. The statements forbidden were not in themselves unlawful, had no tendency to incite to unlawful action, involved no element of clear and present, grave and immediate danger
to the public welfare. Moreover, the State has shown no justification
for placing restrictions on the use of the word "solicit." We have
here nothing comparable to the case where use of the word "fire" in
a crowded theater creates a clear and present danger which the State

may undertake to avoid or against which it may protect. *Schenck* v. *United States,* 249 U.S. 47. We cannot say that "solicit" in this setting is such a dangerous word. So far as free speech alone is concerned, there can be no ban or restriction or burden placed on the use of such a word except on showing of exceptional circumstances where the public safety, morality or health is involved or some other substantial interest of the community is at stake.

If therefore use of the word or language equivalent in meaning was illegal here, it was so only because the statute and the order forbade the particular speaker to utter it. When legislation or its application can confine labor leaders on such occasions to innocuous and abstract discussion of the virtues of trade unions and so becloud even this with doubt, uncertainty and the risk of penalty, freedom of speech for them will be at an end. A restriction so destructive of the right of public discussion, without greater or more imminent danger to the public interest than existed in this case, is incompatible with the freedoms secured by the First Amendment. . . .

Apart from its "business practice" theory, the State contends that Section 5 is not inconsistent with freedom of speech and assembly, since this is merely a previous identification requirement which, according to the State court's decision, gives the Secretary of State only "ministerial, not discretionary" authority.

How far the State can require previous identification by one who undertakes to exercise the rights secured by the First Amendment has been largely undetermined. . . .

As a matter of principle a requirement of registration in order to make a public speech would seem generally incompatible with an exercise of the rights of free speech and free assembly. Lawful public assemblies, involving no element of grave and immediate danger to an interest the state is entitled to protect, are not instruments of harm which require previous identification of the speakers. And the right either of workmen or of unions under these conditions to assemble and discuss their own affairs is as fully protected by the Constitution as the right of businessmen, farmers, educators, political party members or others to assemble and discuss their affairs and to enlist the support of others.

.   .   .   .   .

. . . If one who solicits support for the cause of labor may be required to register as a condition to the exercise of his right to make a public speech, so may he who seeks to rally support for any social, business, religious or political cause. We think a requirement that one must register before he undertakes to make a public speech to enlist support for a lawful movement is quite incompatible with the requirements of the First Amendment.

The restraint is not small when it is considered what was restrained. The right is a national right, federally guaranteed. There is some modicum of freedom of thought, speech and assembly which all citizens of the Republic may exercise throughout its length and breadth, which no State, nor all together, nor the Nation itself, can prohibit, restrain or impede. If the restraint were smaller than it is, it is from petty tyrannies that large ones take root and grow. This fact can be no more plain than when they are imposed on the most basic rights of all. Seedlings planted in that soil grow great and, growing, break down the foundations of liberty. . . .

The judgment is reversed.

[Mr. Justice ROBERTS dissented in an opinion in which Chief Justice STONE and Justices REED and FRANKFURTER concurred. Justices BLACK and JACKSON wrote concurring opinions.]

KOVACS v. COOPER
336 U.S. 77 (1949)

[In *Thomas* v. *Collins, ante,* Justice Rutledge speaks of the "preferred position" of the freedoms of the First Amendment. The preference alluded to consists in the apparent tendency of the Supreme Court in recent years to reverse the presumption of constitutionality where the First Amendment tends to be affected. That is, whereas normally the Court presumes a state law to be constitutional and its unconstitutionality has to be shown, where free speech, etc., are involved the burden would seem to have been placed on the state now to prove that its attempt at regulation is not bad.

[To be sure, this important shift was not formally announced. A succession of judicial statements, however, has appeared to justify the conclusion. Justice Frankfurter's concurring opinion in *Kovacs* v. *Cooper* is therefore worthy of note, the more so since Justice Rutledge's curt comment on his colleague's expositions would seem to herald the possibility of more emphatic divisions on this point in the future.]

Mr. Justice FRANKFURTER, concurring.

Wise accommodation between liberty and order always has been, and ever will be, indispensable for a democratic society. Insofar as the Constitution commits the duty of making this accommodation to this Court, it demands vigilant judicial self-restraint. . . .

The opinions in this case prompt me to make some additional observations. My brother Reed speaks of "the preferred position of freedom of speech," though, to be sure, he finds that the Trenton ordinance does not disregard it. This is a phrase that has uncritically crept into some recent opinions of this Court. I deem it a mischievous phrase, if it carries the thought, which it may subtly imply, that any law touching communication is infected with presumptive invalidity. It is not the first time in the history of constitutional adjudication that such a doctrinaire attitude has disregarded the admonition most to be observed in exercising the Court's reviewing power over legislation, "that it is *a constitution,* we are expounding," *M'Culloch* v. *Maryland,* 4 Wheat. 316, 407. I say the phrase is mischievous because it radiates a constitutional doctrine without avowing it. . . .

[Judicial statements are quoted and critically analyzed.]

In short, the claim that any legislation is presumptively unconstitutional which touches the field of the First Amendment and the Fourteenth Amendment, insofar as the latter's concept of "liberty" contains what is specifically protected by the First, has never commended itself to a majority of this Court.

Behind the notion sought to be expressed by the formula as to "the preferred position of freedom of speech" lies a relevant consideration in determining whether an enactment relating to the liberties protected by the Due Process Clause of the Fourteenth Amendment is violative of it. In law also, doctrine is illuminated by history. The ideas now governing the constitutional protection of freedom of speech derive essentially from the opinions of Mr. Justice Holmes.

The philosophy of his opinions on that subject arose from a deep awareness of the extent to which sociological conclusions are conditioned by time and circumstance. Because of this awareness Mr. Justice Holmes seldom felt justified in opposing his own opinion to economic views which the legislature embodied in law. But since he also realized that the progress of civilization is to a considerable extent the displacement of error which once held sway as official truth by beliefs which in turn have yielded to other beliefs, for him the right to search for truth was of a different order than some transient economic dogma. And without freedom of expression, thought becomes checked and atrophied. Therefore, in considering what interests are so fundamental as to be enshrined in the Due Process Clause, those liberties of the individual which history has attested as the indispensable conditions of an open as against a closed society come to this Court with a momentum for respect lacking when appeal is made to liberties which derive merely from shifting economic arrangements. Accordingly, Mr. Justice Holmes was far more ready to find legislative invasion where free inquiry was involved than in the debatable area of economics. See my *Mr. Justice Holmes and the Supreme Court, 58 et seq.*

The objection to summarizing this line of thought by the phrase "the preferred position of freedom of speech" is that it expresses a complicated process of constitutional adjudication by a deceptive formula. And it was Mr. Justice Holmes who admonished us that "To rest upon a formula is a slumber that, prolonged, means death." *Collected Legal Papers,* 306. Such a formula makes for mechanical jurisprudence.

Some of the arguments made in this case strikingly illustrate how easy it is to fall into the ways of mechanical jurisprudence through the use of oversimplified formulas. It is argued that the Constitution protects freedom of speech: freedom of speech means the right to communicate, whatever the physical means for so doing; sound trucks are one form of communication; *ergo* that form is entitled to the same protection as any other means of communication, whether by tongue or pen. Such sterile argumentation treats society as though it consisted of bloodless categories. The various forms of modern so-called "mass communications" raise issues that were not implied in the means of communication known or contemplated by Franklin and Jefferson and Madison. Cf. *Associated Press* v. *United States,* 326 U.S. 1. Movies have created problems not presented by the circulation of books, pamphlets, or newspapers, and so the movies have been constitutionally regulated. *Mutual Film Corp.* v. *Industrial Commission,* 236 U.S. 230. Broadcasting in turn has produced its brood of complicated problems hardly to be solved by an easy formula about the preferred position of free speech. See *National Broadcasting Co.* v. *United States,* 319 U.S. 190.

Only a disregard of vital differences between natural speech, even of the loudest spellbinders, and the noise of sound trucks would give sound trucks the constitutional rights accorded to the unaided human voice. Nor is it for this Court to devise the terms on which sound trucks should be allowed to operate, if at all. These are matters for the legislative judgment controlled by public opinion. So long as a legislature does not prescribe what ideas may be noisily expressed and what may not be, nor discriminate among those who would make inroads upon the public peace, it is not for us to supervise the limits the legislature may impose in safeguarding the steadily narrowing opportunities for serenity and reflection. Without such opportunities freedom of thought becomes a mocking phrase, and without freedom of thought there can be no free society.

Mr. Justice RUTLEDGE, dissenting.

. . . I think my brother Frankfurter demonstrates the conclusion opposite to that which he draws, namely, that the First Amendment guaranties of the freedoms of speech, press, assembly and religion occupy preferred position not only in the Bill of Rights but also in the repeated decisions of this Court.

4. POLITICAL LIBERTY AND THE DEFENSE OF DEMOCRACY

TERMINIELLO v. CHICAGO
337 U.S. 1 (1949)

Mr. Justice DOUGLAS delivered the opinion of the Court.

Petitioner after jury trial was found guilty of disorderly conduct in violation of a city ordinance of Chicago and fined. The case grew out of an address he delivered in an auditorium in Chicago under the auspices of the Christian Veterans of America. The meeting commanded considerable public attention. The auditorium was filled to capacity with over eight hundred persons present. Others were turned away. Outside of the auditorium a crowd of about one thousand persons gathered to protest against the meeting. A cordon of policemen was assigned to the meeting to maintain order; but they were not able to prevent several disturbances. The crowd outside was angry and turbulent.

Petitioner in his speech condemned the conduct of the crowd outside and vigorously, if not viciously, criticized various political and racial groups whose activities he denounced as inimical to the nation's welfare.

The trial court charged that "breach of the peace" consists of any "misbehavior which violates the public peace and decorum"; and that the "misbehavior may constitute a breach of the peace if it stirs the public to anger, invites dispute, brings about a condition of unrest, or creates a disturbance, or if it molests the inhabitants in the enjoyment of peace and quiet by arousing alarm." Petitioner did not take exception to that instruction. But he maintained at all times that the ordinance as applied to his conduct violated his right of free speech under the Federal Constitution. The judgment of conviction was affirmed by the Illinois Appellate Court and by the Illinois Supreme Court. The case is here on a petition for certiorari which we granted because of the importance of the question presented.

The vitality of civil and political institutions in our society depends on free discussion. As Chief Justice Hughes wrote in *De Jonge* v. *Oregon,* 299 U.S. 353, 365, it is only through free debate and free exchange of ideas that government remains responsive to the will of the people and peaceful change is effected. The right to speak freely and to promote diversity of ideas and programs is therefore one of the chief distinctions that sets us apart from totalitarian regimes.

Accordingly a function of free speech under our system of government is to invite dispute. It may indeed best serve its high purpose when it induces a condition of unrest, creates dissatisfaction with conditions as they are, or even stirs people to anger. Speech is often provocative and challenging. It may strike at prejudices and preconceptions and have profound unsettling effects as it presses for acceptance of an idea. That is why freedom of speech, though not absolute, is nevertheless protected against censorship or punishment, unless shown likely to produce a clear and present danger of a serious substantive evil that rises far above public inconvenience, annoyance, or unrest. See *Bridges* v. *California,* 314 U.S. 252, 262. There is no room under our Constitution for a more restrictive view. For the alternative would lead to standardization of ideas either by legislatures, courts, or dominant political or community groups.

The ordinance as construed by the trial court seriously invaded this province. It permitted conviction of petitioner if his speech stirred people to anger, invited public dispute, or brought about a condition of unrest. A conviction resting on any of those grounds may not stand.

The statute as construed in the charge to the jury was passed on by the Illinois courts and sustained by them over the objection that as so read it violated the Fourteenth Amendment. The fact that the parties did not dispute its construction makes the adjudication no less ripe for our review. . . . We can only take the statute as the state courts read it. From our point of view it is immaterial whether the state law question as to its meaning was controverted or accepted. The pinch of the statute is in its application. It is that question which the petitioner has brought here. To say therefore that the question on this phase of the case is whether the trial judge gave a wrong charge is wholly to misconceive the issue.

But it is said that throughout the appellate proceedings the Illinois courts assumed that the only conduct punishable and punished under the ordinance was conduct constituting "fighting words." . . . [However,] petitioner was not convicted under a statute so narrowly construed. For all anyone knows he was convicted under the parts of the ordinance (as construed) which, for example, make it an offense merely to invite dispute or to bring about a condition of unrest. We cannot avoid that issue by saying that all Illinois did was to measure petitioner's conduct, not the ordinance, against the Constitution. Petitioner raised both points—that his speech was protected by the Constitution; that the inclusion of his speech within the ordinance was a violation of the Constitution. We would, therefore, strain at technicalities to conclude that the constitutionality of the ordinance as construed and applied to petitioner was not before the Illinois courts. The record makes clear that petitioner at all times challenged the constitutionality of the ordinance as construed and applied to him.

Reversed.

[Chief Justice VINSON and Justice FRANKFURTER wrote dissenting opinions criticizing the majority for deciding the case on a point not raised in the trial court nor in the argument to the Court.]

Mr. Justice JACKSON, dissenting.

The Court reverses this conviction by reiterating generalized approbations of freedom of speech with which, in the abstract, no one will disagree. Doubts as to their applicability are lulled by avoidance of more than passing reference to the circumstances of Terminiello's speech and judging it as if he had spoken to persons as dispassionate as empty benches, or like a modern Demosthenes practicing his Philippics on a lonely seashore.

But the local court that tried Terminiello was not indulging in theory. It was dealing with a riot and with a speech that provoked a hostile mob and incited a friendly one, and threatened violence between the two. When the trial judge instructed the jury that it might find Terminiello guilty of inducing a breach of the peace if his behavior stirred the public to anger, invited dispute, brought about unrest, created a disturbance or molested peace and quiet by arousing alarm, he was not speaking of these as harmless or abstract conditions. He was addressing his words to the concrete behavior and specific consequences disclosed by the evidence. He was saying to the jury, in effect, that if this particular speech added fuel to the situation already so inflamed as to threaten to get beyond police control, it could be punished as inducing a breach of peace. When the light of the evidence not recited by the Court is thrown upon the Court's opinion, it discloses that underneath a little issue of Terminiello and his hundred-dollar fine lurk some of the most far-reaching constitutional questions that can confront a people who value both liberty and order. This Court seems to regard these as enemies of each other and to be of the view that we must forego order to achieve liberty. So it fixes its eyes on a conception of freedom of speech so rigid as to tolerate no concession to society's need for public order.

An old proverb warns us to take heed lest we "walk into a well from looking at the stars." To show why I think the Court is in some danger of doing just that, I must bring these deliberations down to earth by a long recital of facts.

Terminiello, advertised as a Catholic Priest, but revealed at the trial to be under suspension by his Bishop, was brought to Chicago from Birmingham, Alabama, to address a gathering that assembled in response to a call signed by Gerald L. K. Smith, which, among other things said:

"... The same people who hate Father Coughlin hate Father Terminiello. They have persecuted him, hounded him, threatened him, but he has remained unaffected by their anti-Christian campaign against him. You will hear all sorts of reports concerning Father Terminiello. But remember that he is a Priest in good standing and a fearless lover of Christ and America."

The jury may have considered that this call attempted to capitalize the hatreds this man had stirred and foreshadowed, if it did not intend to invite, the kind of demonstration that followed.

Terminiello's own testimony shows the conditions under which he spoke.

.   .   .   .   .

The court below, in addition to this recital [by Terminiello], heard other evidence, that the crowd reached an estimated number of 1,500. Picket lines obstructed and interfered with access to the building. The crowd constituted "a surging, howling mob hurling epithets at those who would enter and tried to tear their clothes off." One young woman's coat was torn off and she had to be assisted into the meeting by policemen. Those inside the hall could hear the loud noises and hear those on the outside yell, "Fascists, Hitlers!" and curse words like "damn Fascists." Bricks were thrown through the windowpanes before and during the speaking. About 28 windows were broken. The street was black with people on both sides for at least a block either way; bottles, stink bombs and brickbats were thrown. Police were unable to control the mob, which kept breaking the windows at the meeting hall, drowning out the speaker's voice at times and breaking in through the back door of the auditorium. About 17 of the group outside were arrested by the police.

Knowing of this environment, Terminiello made a long speech, from the stenographic record of which I omit relatively innocuous passages and add emphasis to what seems especially provocative:

"Father Terminiello: Now, I am going to whisper my greetings to you, Fellow Christians. I will interpret it. I said 'Fellow *Christians*,' and I suppose there are *some of the scum got in by mistake,* so I want to tell a story about *the scum:*

"... And nothing I could say tonight could begin to express the contempt I have for the *slimy scum* that got in by mistake.

"... The subject I want to talk to you tonight about is the attempt *that is going on right outside this hall tonight,* the attempt that is going to *destroy America by revolution....*

"My friends, it is no longer true that it can't happen here. It is happening here, and it only depends upon you, good people, who are here tonight, depends upon all of us together, as Mr. Smith said. The tide is changing, and if you and I turn and run from that tide, we will all be drowned in this tidal wave of Communism which is going over the world.

"... I am not going to talk to you about the menace of Communism, which is already accomplished, in Russia, where from eight to fifteen million people were murdered in cold blood by their own countryman, and millions more through Eastern Europe at the close of the war are being murdered by these murderous Russians, hurt, being raped and sent into slavery. *That is what they want for you, that howling mob outside.*

"I know I was told one time that my winter quarters were ready for me in Siberia. I was told that. Now, I am talking about the fifty-seven varieties that we have in America, and we have fifty-seven varieties of pinks and reds and pastel shades in this country; and all of it can be traced back to the twelve years we spent under the New Deal, because that was the build-up for what is going on in the world today.

. . . . .

"Now, Russia promised us we would *ga* [sic] back to the official newspaper of Russia. Primarily it was back about 1929. They quoted the words of George E. Dimitroff, who at that time was the Executive Secretary of the Communist International. I only quote you this one passage. I could quote thousands of paragraphs for you. Let me quote you: 'The worldwide nature of our program is not mere talk, but on an all embracing *blood-soaked reality.' That is what they want for us, a blood-soaked reality but it was promised to us by the crystal gazers in Washington:* and you know what I mean by the 'crystal gazers,' I presume.

"First of all, we had Queen Eleanor. Mr. Smith said, 'Queen Eleanor is now one of the world's communists.' She is one who said this—imagine, coming from the spouse of the former President of the United States for twelve long years—this is what she said: 'The war is but a step in the revolution. The war is but one step in the revolution, and we know who started the war.'

"Then we have Henry Adolph Wallace, the sixty million job magician. You know we only need fifty-four million jobs in America and everybody would be working. He wants sixty million jobs, because some of the bureaucrats want two jobs apiece. Here he is, what he says about revolution: 'We are in for a profound revolution. Those of us who realize the inevitableness of the revolution, and are anxious that it be *gradual and bloodless* instead of *somewhat bloody. Of course, if necessary, we will have it more bloody.'*

"And then Chief Justice Stone had this to say: 'A way has been found for the effective suppression of speeches and press and religion, despite constitutional guarantee,'—from the Chief Justice, from the Chief Justice of the United States.

"Now, my friends, they are planning another ruse; and if it ever happens to this cou-try [sic], God help America. They are going to try to put into Mr. Edgar Hoover's position a man by the name of *George Swarzwald*. I think even those who were uneducated on so-called sedition charges, that the majority of the individuals in this department, that Christ-like men and women who realize today what is going on in this country, men who are in this audience today, *who want to know the names of those people, before they are outside, they want to know the names if any. Did you hear any tonight that you recognize? Most of them probably are imported. They are imported from Russia, certainly. If you know the names, please send them to me immediately....*

"... Didn't you ever read the Morgenthau plan for the starvation of little babies and pregnant women in Germany? Whatever could a child that is born have to do with Hitler or anyone else at the beginning of the war? Why should every child in Germany today not live to be more than two or three months of age? Because Morgenthau wants it that way, and so did F. D. R.... *You will know who is behind it when I tell you the story* of a doctor in Akron, Ohio. He boasted to a friend of mine within the last few days, while he was in the service of this country as a doctor, he and others of his kind made it a practice—now, this was not only one man—made it a practice to amputate the limbs of every German they came in contact with whenever they could get away with it; so; that they could never carry a gun. Imagine men of that caliber, sworn to serve this beautiful country of ours, *why should we tolerate them?*

"My friends, this moment someone reminded me of the plan to sterilize them. The nurses, they tell me are going to inject diseases in them, syphilis and other diseases in every one that came there all of one race, all non-Christians.

"Now, we are going to get the threats of the people of Argentine, the people of Spain. We have now declared, according to our officials, to have declared Franco to have taken the place of Hitler. *Franco was the savior of what was left of Europe.*

"Now, let me say, I am going to talk about—I almost said, about the Jews. Of course, I would not want to say that. However, I am going to talk about some Jews. I hope that—I am a Christian minister. We must take a Christian attitude. I don't want you to go from this hall with hatred in your heart for any person, for no person....

"Now, this danger which we face—let us call them Zionist Jews if you will, let's call them atheistic, communistic Jews, Jewish or

Zionist Jews, then let us not fear to condemn them. You remember the Apostles when they went into the upper room after the death of the Master, they went in there, after locking the doors; they closed the windows. (At this time there was a very loud noise as if something was being thrown into the building.)

"Don't be disturbed. That happened by the way, while Mr. Gerald Smith was saying 'Our Father who are in heaven;' (just then a rock went through the window.) *Do you wonder they were persecuted in other countries in the world?*

"*You know I have always made a study of the psychology, sociology of mob reaction. It is exemplified out there.* Remember there has to be a leader to that mob. He is not out there. He is probably across the street, looking out the window. There must be certain things, money, other things, in order to have successful mob action; there must be rhythm. There must be some to beat a cadence. Those mobs are chanting; that is the cavemen's chant. They were trained to do it. They were trained this afternoon. They are being led; *there will be violence.*

"That is why I say to you, men don't you do it. Walk out of here dignified. The police will protect you. Put the women on the inside, where there will be no hurt to them. Just walk; don't stop and argue. . . . They want to picket our meetings. They don't want us to picket their meetings. It is the same kind of tolerance, if we said there was a bedbug in bed, 'We don't care for you,' or if we looked under the bed and found a snake and said, 'I am going to be tolerant and leave the snake there.' We will not be tolerant of that mob out there. We are not going to be tolerant any longer.

"We are strong enough. We are not going to be tolerant of their smears any longer. We are going to stand *up and dare them to smear us.*

"So, my friends, since we spent much time tonight trying to quiet the howling mob, I am going to bring my thoughts to a conclusion, and the conclusion is this. We must all be like the Apostles before the coming of the Holy Ghost. We must not lock ourselves in an upper room for fear of the Jews. I speak of the Communistic Zionistic Jew, and those are not American Jews. We don't want them here; we want them to go back where they came from."

. . . . .

Such was the speech. Evidence showed that it stirred the audience not only to cheer and applaud but to expressions of immediate anger, unrest and alarm. One called the speaker a "God damned liar" and was taken out by the police. Another said that "Jews, niggers and Catholics would have to be gotten rid of." One response was, "Yes, the Jews are all killers, murderers. If we don't kill them first, they will kill us." The anti-Jewish stories elicited exclamations of "Oh!" and "Isn't that terrible!" and shouts of "Yes, send the Jews back to Russia," "Kill the Jews," "Dirty kikes," and much more of ugly tenor. This is the specific and concrete kind of anger, unrest and alarm, coupled with that of the mob outside, that the trial court charged the jury might find to be a breach of peace induced by Terminiello. It is difficult to believe that this Court is speaking of the same occasion, but it is the only one involved in this litigation.

Terminiello, of course, disclaims being a fascist. Doubtless many of the indoor audience were not consciously such. His speech, however, followed, with fidelity that is more than coincidental, the pattern of European fascist leaders.

The street mob, on the other hand, included some who deny being communists, but Terminiello testified and offered to prove that the demonstration was communist-organized and communist-led. He offered literature of left-wing organizations calling members to meet and "mobilize" for instruction as pickets and exhorting followers: "All out to fight Fascist Smith."

As this case declares a nation-wide rule that disables local and state authorities from punishing conduct which produces conflicts of this kind, it is unrealistic not to take account of the nature, methods and objectives of the forces involved. This was not an isolated, spontaneous and unintended collision of political, racial, or ideological adversaries. It was a local manifestation of a world-wide and standing conflict between two organized groups of revolutionary fanatics, each of which has imported to this country the strong-arm technique developed in the struggle by which their kind has devastated Europe. Increasingly, American cities have to cope with it. One faction organizes a mass meeting, the other organizes pickets to harass it; each organizes squads to counteract the other's pickets; parade is met with counter-parade. Each of these mass demonstrations has the potentiality, and more than a few the purpose, of disorder and violence. This technique appeals not to reason but to fears and mob spirit; each is a show of force designed to bully adversaries and to overawe the indifferent. We need not resort to speculation as to the purposes for which these tactics are calculated nor as to their consequences. Recent European history demonstrates both.

The present obstacle to mastery of the streets by either radical or reactionary mob movements is not the opposing minority. It is the authority of local governments which represent the free choice of democratic and law-abiding elements, of all shades of opinion but who, whatever their differences, submit them to free elections which register the results of their free discussion. The fascist and communist groups, on the contrary, resort to these terror tactics to confuse, bully and discredit those freely chosen governments. Violent and noisy shows of strength discourage participation of moderates in discussions so fraught with violence and real discussion dries up and disappears. And people lose faith in the democratic process when they see public authority flouted and impotent and begin to think the time has come when they must choose sides in a false and terrible dilemma such as was posed as being at hand by the call for the Terminiello meeting: "Christian Nationalism or World Communism—Which?"

No liberty is made more secure by holding that its abuses are inseparable from its enjoyment. We must not forget that it is the free democratic communities that ask us to trust them to maintain peace with liberty and that the factions engaged in this battle are not interested permanently in either. What would it matter to Terminiello if the police batter up some communists or, on the other hand, if the communists batter up some policemen? Either result makes grist for his mill; either would help promote hysteria and the demand for strong-arm methods in dealing with his adversaries. And what, on the other hand, have the communist agitators to lose from a battle with the police?

This Court has gone far toward accepting the doctrine that civil liberty means the removal of all restraints from these crowds and that all local attempts to maintain order are impairments of the liberty of the citizen. The choice is not between order and liberty. It is between liberty with order and anarchy without either. There is danger that, if the Court does not temper its doctrinaire logic with a little practical wisdom, it will convert the constitutional Bill of Rights into a suicide pact.

I would affirm the conviction.

Mr. Justice BURTON joins in this opinion.[2]

AMERICAN COMMUNICATIONS ASSOCIATION v. DOUDS
339 U.S. 382 (1950)

Mr. Chief Justice VINSON delivered the opinion of the Court.

[The Labor-Management Relations Act of 1947 provides that, before any labor organization may avail itself of the services of the National Labor Relations Board, it must file with the Board an affidavit by each of its officers and the officers of any national or international labor organization of which it is a unit, to the effect that he is not a member of the Communist party and that he does not believe in or is not a member of any organization that believes in or teaches, the overthrow of the United States government by force or by any illegal or unconstitutional means.]

.   .   .   .   .

The constitutional justification for the National Labor Relations Act was the power of Congress to protect interstate commerce by removing obstructions to the free flow of commerce. *National Labor Relations Board* v. *Jones & Laughlin Steel Corp.*, 301 U.S. 1.[3] That Act was designed to remove obstructions caused by strikes and other forms of industrial unrest, which Congress found were attributable to the inequality of bargaining power between unorganized employees and their employers. It did so by strengthening employee groups, by restraining certain employer practices, and by encouraging the processes of collective bargaining.

When the Labor-Management Relations Act was passed twelve

[2] The sweeping holding of the *Terminiello* case appears considerably limited by the recent decision in *Feiner* v. *New York*, 340 U.S. 315 (1951). Irving Feiner was addressing an open-air meeting in Syracuse, New York, inviting the public to attend a Progressive Party rally to be held at a local hotel that evening. His speech contained a number of uncomplimentary references to public officials; he used the term "bum" to describe President Truman, Mayor O'Dwyer of New York, and several others, and called the American Legion a Nazi Gestapo. There was no disturbance but a crowd of about seventy-five had collected when the police ordered him to stop speaking. Upon his refusal he was arrested and charged with violation of a disorderly conduct statute. Following conviction and affirmance by the state courts, Feiner obtained a writ of certiorari from the Supreme Court.

Chief Justice Vinson, speaking for the majority, upheld the conviction, on the grounds that the free speech guarantee did not offer a cloak for incitement to riot. The state courts' approval of the methods of the local police, the Chief Justice added, was entitled to high respect. Justices Black, Douglas, and Minton dissented. "Today's holding," said Mr. Justice Black, "means that, as a practical matter, minority speakers can be silenced in any city. Hereafter, despite the First and Fourteenth Amendment, the policeman's club can take heavy toll of a current administration's public critics."

Notwithstanding the seeming parallelism of the cases, the *Feiner* decision did not undertake to reconcile or to distinguish the earlier *Terminiello* case.

[3] *Supra*, p. 224.

years later, it was the view of Congress that additional impediments to the free flow of commerce made amendments of the original Act desirable. . . .

.   .   .   .   .

One such obstruction, which it was the purpose of § 9 (h) of the Act to remove, was the so-called "political strike." . . . It is sufficient to say that Congress had a great mass of material before it which tended to show that Communists and others proscribed by the statute had infiltrated union organizations not to support and further trade union objectives, including the advocacy of change by democratic methods, but to make them a device by which commerce and industry might be disrupted when the dictates of political policy required such action.

.   .   .   .   .

There can be no doubt that Congress may, under its constitutional power to regulate commerce among the several states, attempt to prevent political strikes and other kinds of direct action designed to burden and interrupt the free flow of commerce. We think it is clear, in addition, that the remedy provided by § 9 (h) bears reasonable relation to the evil which the statute was designed to reach. Congress could rationally find that the Communist Party is not like other political parties in its utilization of positions of union leadership as means by which to bring about strikes and other obstructions of commerce for purposes of political advantage, and that many persons who believe in overthrow of the Government by force and violence are also likely to resort to such tactics when, as officers, they formulate union policy.

.   .   .   .   .

. . . But . . . , in drawing lines on the basis of beliefs and political affiliations, though it may be granted that the proscriptions of the statute bear a reasonable relation to the apprehended evil, Congress has undeniably discouraged the lawful exercise of political freedom as well. . . .

.   .   .   .   .

But the question with which we are here faced is not the same one that Justices Holmes and Brandeis found convenient to consider in terms of clear and present danger. . . . Section 9 (h) . . does not interfere with speech because Congress fears the consequences of speech; it regulates conduct which Congress has determined is carried on by persons who may be identified by their political affiliations and beliefs. The Board does not contend that political strikes, the substantive evil at which § 9 (h) is aimed, are the present or impending products of advocacy of the doctrines of Communism or the expression of belief in overthrow of the government by force. On the contrary, it points out that such strikes are called by persons who, so Congress has found, have the will and the power to do so *without* advocacy or persuasion that seeks acceptance in the competition of the market. Speech may be fought with speech. Falsehoods and fallacies must be exposed, not suppressed, unless there is not sufficient time to avert the evil consequences of noxious doctrine by argument and education. That is the command of the First Amendment. But force may and must be met with force. Section 9 (h) is designed to protect the public not against what Communists and others identified therein advocate or believe, but against what Congress has concluded they have done and are likely to do again.

. . . . . .

[Only six members of the Court participated in this case. Justice Douglas was absent due to illness, Justices Clark and Minton had been too recently appointed to take part. The Chief Justice's opinion had the concurrence of Justices Burton and Reed. Justice Frankfurter wrote a separate opinion in which he agreed with the Chief Justice's reasoning on the issue of the First Amendment but asserted that the provisions of the statute were too vague in parts. Accordingly he would, instead of affirming the decision below, have remanded the case with instructions to enforce only those portions of the law not touching on beliefs and opinions. Justice Jackson likewise disagreed as to the application of the statute to the realm of beliefs and, as to membership in organizations, would rest his affirmance on the marked difference of the Communist Party, in structure and objectives, from the established political parties in this country. Justice Black dissented on the ground that the First Amendment did not permit the suppression of any form of assertion of political belief.

[The issue of Communism in the American political scene is faced squarely only by Justice Jackson in this case. The Court's majority largely evaded it here and numerous other attempts to have the Court rule on the political rights of this (and, by implication, most other) political minority group were frustrated by denials of petitions of certiorari. Meanwhile the government had instituted proceedings against the leaders of the Communist Party in America under the so-called Smith Act and, after a highly publicized and protracted trial, secured convictions of all accused. The Court of Appeals of the Second Circuit affirmed. The defense challenged, among other things, the constitutionality of the Act and the Supreme Court granted certiorari, limiting its scope to the single issue of constitutionality. The decision was announced on June 4, 1951.]

DENNIS v. UNITED STATES
— U.S. — (1951)

Mr. Chief Justice VINSON announced the judgment of the Court and an opinion in which Mr. Justice REED, Mr. Justice BURTON and Mr. Justice MINTON join.

Petitioners were indicted in July, 1948, for violation of the conspiracy provisions of the Smith Act, 54 Stat. 671, 18 U.S.C. (1946 ed.) § 11, during the period of April, 1945, to July, 1948. . . .

Sections 2 and 3 of the Smith Act . . . provide as follows:

"Sec. 2.

"(a) It shall be unlawful for any person—

"(1) to knowingly or wilfully advocate, abet, advise, or teach the duty, necessity, desirability, or propriety of overthrowing or destroying any government in the United States by force or violence, or by the assassination of any officer of such government;

"(2) with intent to cause the overthrow or destruction of any government in the United States, to print, publish, edit, issue, circulate, sell, distribute, or publicly display any written or printed matter advocating, advising, or teaching the duty, necessity, desirability, or propriety of overthrowing or destroying any government in the United States by force or violence;

"(3) to organize or help to organize any society, group, or assembly of persons who teach, advocate, or encourage the overthrow or destruction of any government in the United States by force or violence; or to be or become a member of, or affiliate with, any such society, group, or assembly of persons, knowing the purpose thereof.

"(b) For the purpose of this section, the term 'government in the United States' means the Government of the United States, the government of any State, Territory, or possession of the United States, the government of the District of Columbia, or the government of any political subdivision of them.

"Sec. 3. It shall be unlawful for any person to attempt to commit, or to conspire to commit, any of the acts prohibited by the provisions of . . . this title."

The indictment charged the petitioners with wilfully and know-ingly conspiring (1) to organize as the Communist Party of the United States of America a society, group and assembly of persons who teach and advocate the overthrow and destruction of the Gov-ernment of the United States by force and violence, and (2) know-ingly and wilfully to advocate and teach the duty and necessity of overthrowing and destroying the Government of the United States by force and violence. The indictment further alleges that § 2 of the Smith Act proscribes these acts and that any conspiracy to take such action is a violation of § 3 of the Act.

The trial of the case extended over nine months, six of which were devoted to the taking of evidence, resulting in a record of 16,000 pages. Our limited grant of the writ of certiorari has removed from our consideration any question as to the sufficiency of the evidence to support the jury's determination that petitioners are guilty of the offense charged. Whether on this record petitioners did in fact advo-cate the overthrow of the Government by force and violence is not before us, and we must base any discussion of this point upon the conclusions stated in the opinion of the Court of Appeals, which treated the issue in great detail. That court held that the record in this case amply supports the necessary finding of the jury that peti-tioners, the leaders of the Communist Party in this country, were unwilling to work within our framework of democracy, but intended to initiate a violent revolution whenever the propitious occasion appeared. Petitioners dispute the meaning to be drawn from the evidence, contending that the Marxist-Leninist doctrine they advo-cated taught that force and violence to achieve a Communist form of government in an existing democratic state would be necessary only because the ruling classes of the state would never permit the transformation to be accomplished peacefully, but would use force and violence to defeat any peaceful political and economic gain the Communists could achieve. But the Court of Appeals held that the record supports the following broad conclusions: . . . that the general goal of the [Communist] Party was, during the period in question, to achieve a successful overthrow of the existing order by force and violence.

.   .   .   .   .

The obvious purpose of the statute is to protect existing Govern-ment, not from change by peaceable, lawful and constitutional means, but from change by violence, revolution and terrorism. That it is within the *power* of the Congress to protect the Government of the United States from armed rebellion is a proposition which requires little discussion. Whatever theoretical merit there may be to the argument that there is a "right" to rebellion against dictatorial governments is without force where the existing structure of the government provides for peaceful and orderly change. We reject any principle of governmental helplessness in the face of preparation for revolution, which principle, carried to its logical conclusion, must lead to anarchy. No one could conceive that it is not within the power of Congress to prohibit acts intended to overthrow the Government by force and violence. The question with which we are concerned here is not whether Congress has such *power,* but whether the *means* which it has employed conflict with the First and Fifth Amendments to the Constitution.

One of the bases for the contention that the means which Congress has employed are invalid takes the form of an attack on the face of the statute on the grounds that by its terms it prohibits academic discussion of the merits of Marxism-Leninism, that it stifles ideas and is contrary to all concepts of a free speech and a free press. . . .

The very language of the Smith Act negates the interpretation which petitioners would have us impose on that Act. It is directed at advocacy, not discussion. Thus, the trial judge properly charged the jury that they could not convict if they found that petitioners did "no more than pursue peaceful studies and discussions or teaching and advocacy in the realm of ideas." He further charged that it was not unlawful "to conduct in an American college and university a course explaining the philosophical theories set forth in the books which have been placed in evidence." Such a charge is in strict accord with the statutory language, and illustrates the meaning to be placed on those words. Congress did not intend to eradicate the free discussion of political theories, to destroy the traditional rights of Americans to discuss and evaluate ideas without fear of governmental sanction. Rather Congress was concerned with the very kind of activity in which the evidence showed these petitioners engaged.

But although the statute is not directed at the hypothetical cases which petitioners have conjured, its application in this case has resulted in convictions for the teaching and advocacy of the overthrow of the Government by force and violence, which, even though coupled with the intent to accomplish that overthrow, contains an element of speech. For this reason, we must pay special heed to the demands of the First Amendment marking out the boundaries of speech.

We pointed out in *Douds* [*American Communications Assn.* v. *Douds, supra*] that the basis of the First Amendment is the hypothesis that speech can rebut speech, propaganda will answer propaganda, free debate of ideas will result in the wisest governmental policies. It is for this reason that this Court has recognized the inherent value of free discourse. An analysis of the leading cases in this Court which have involved direct limitations on speech, however, will demonstrate that both the majority of the Court and the dissenters in particular cases have recognized that this is not an unlimited, unqualified right, but that the societal value of speech must, on occasion, be subordinated to other values and considerations.

No important case involving free speech was decided in this Court prior to *Schenck* v. *United States,* 249 U.S. 47 (1919).[4] . . . That case involved a conviction under the Criminal Espionage Act, 40 Stat. 217. The question the Court faced was whether the evidence was sufficient to sustain the conviction. Writing for a unanimous Court, Justice Holmes stated that the "question in every case is whether the words used are used in such circumstances and are of such a nature as to create a clear and present danger that they will bring about the substantive evils that Congress has a right to prevent." 249 U.S. at 52. . . . The phrase bore no connotation that the danger was to be any threat to the safety of the Republic. . . . [The Court shows that in *Schenck* and cases following it, the test of a "clear and present danger" was applied as an evidentiary rule.] The rule we deduce . . . is that where an offense is specified by a statute in nonspeech or nonpress terms, a conviction relying upon speech or press as evidence of violation may be sustained only when the speech or publication created a "clear and present danger" of attempting or accomplishing the prohibited crime, *e.g.,* interference with enlistment [in *Schenck*]. The dissents . . . , in emphasizing the value of speech, were addressed to the argument of the sufficiency of the evidence.

. . . . .

In this case we are squarely presented with the application of the "clear and present danger" test, and must decide what that phrase imports. We first note that many of the cases in which this Court has reversed convictions by use of this or similar tests have been

[4] *Supra,* p. 477.

based on the fact that the interest which the State was attempting to protect was itself too insubstantial to warrant restrictions of speech. In this category we may put such cases as *Schneider* v. *State,* 308 U.S. 147 (1939); *Cantwell* v. *Connecticut,* 310 U.S. 296 (1940); *Martin* v. *Struthers,* 319 U.S. 141 (1943); *West Virginia State Board of Education* v. *Barnette,* 319 U.S. 624 (1943); *Thomas* v. *Collins,* 323 U.S. 516 (1945); *Marsh* v. *Alabama,* 326 U.S. 501 (1946); but cf. *Prince* v. *Massachusetts,* 321 U.S. 158 (1944); *Cox* v. *New Hampshire,* 312 U.S. 569 (1941). Overthrow of the Government by force and violence is certainly a substantial enough interest for the Government to limit speech. Indeed, this is the ultimate value of any society, for if a society cannot protect its very structure from armed internal attack, it must follow that no subordinate value can be protected. If, then, this interest may be protected, the literal problem which is presented is what has been meant by the use of the phrase "clear and present danger" of the utterances bringing about the evil within the power of Congress to punish.

Obviously, the words cannot mean that before the Government may act, it must wait until the *putsch* is about to be executed, the plans have been laid and the signal is awaited. If Government is aware that a group aiming at its overthrow is attempting to indoctrinate its members and to commit them to a course whereby they will strike when the leaders feel the circumstances permit, action by the Government is required. . . . Certainly an attempt to overthrow the Government by force, even though doomed from the outset because of inadequate numbers or power of the revolutionists, is a sufficient evil for Congress to prevent. The damage which such attempts create both physically and politically to a nation makes it impossible to measure the validity in terms of the probability of success, or the immediacy of a successful attempt. . . . We . . . reject, therefore, the contention that success or probability of success is the criterion.

. . . . .

Chief Judge Learned Hand, writing for the majority below, interpreted the phrase as follows: "In each case [courts] must ask whether the gravity of the 'evil,' discounted by its improbability, justifies such invasion of free speech as is necessary to avoid the danger." 183 Fed. (2d) at 212. We adopt this statement of the rule. As articulated by Chief Judge Hand, it is as succinct and inclusive as any other we might devise at this time. It takes into consideration those factors which we deem relevant, and relates their significances. More we cannot expect from words.

Likewise, we are in accord with the court below, which affirmed the trial court's finding that the requisite danger existed. The mere fact that from the period 1945 to 1948 petitioners' activities did not result in an attempt to overthrow the Government by force and violence is of course no answer to the fact that there was a group that was ready to make the attempt. The formation by petitioners of such a highly organized conspiracy, with rigidly disciplined members subject to call when the leaders, these petitioners, felt that the time had come for action, coupled with the inflammable nature of world conditions, similar uprisings in other countries, and the touch-and-go nature of our relations with countries with whom petitioners were in the very least ideologically attuned, convince us that their convictions were justified on this score. And this analysis disposes of the contention that a conspiracy to advocate, as distinguished from the advocacy itself, cannot be constitutionally restrained, because it comprises only the preparation. It is the existence of the conspiracy which creates the danger. . . . If the ingredients of the reaction are present, we cannot bind the Government to wait until the catalyst is added.

·   ·   ·   ·   ·

We hold that §§ 2 (a) (1), 2 (a) (3) and 3 of the Smith Act do not inherently as construed or applied in the instant case, violate the First Amendment. . . . Petitioners intended to overthrow the Government of the United States as speedily as the circumstances would permit. Their conspiracy to organize the Communist Party and to teach and advocate the overthrow of the Government of the United States by force and violence created a "clear and present danger" of an attempt to overthrow the Government by force and violence. They were properly and constitutionally convicted for violation of the Smith Act. The judgments of conviction are

Affirmed.

Mr. Justice CLARK took no part in the consideration or decision of this case. [He had been Attorney General at the time of the institution of the proceedings against the Communist leaders.]

Mr. Justice JACKSON, concurring. [The concurring opinion initially describes the working methods of Communist Party groups as distinguished from the individual anarchists against whom prohibitory statutes were originally directed. It concludes that "overthrow by

force or violence" has become an inadequate way to describe the
dangers presented by Communist plans and methods and that "clear
and present danger" is an equally inappropriate criterion for the
type of problem presented by this case.]

. . . . . .

The "clear and present danger" test was an innovation by Mr.
Justice Holmes in the Schenck case, reiterated and refined by him
and Mr. Justice Brandeis in later cases, all arising before the era of
World War II revealed the subtlety and efficacy of modern revolutionary techniques used by totalitarian parties. In those cases, they
were faced with convictions under so-called criminal syndicalism
statutes aimed at anarchists but which, loosely construed, had been
applied to punish socialism, pacifism, and left-wing ideologies, the
charges often resting on far-fetched inferences which, if true, would
establish only technical or trivial violations. They proposed "clear
and present danger" as a test for the sufficiency of evidence in particular cases.

I would save it, unmodified, for application as a "rule of reason"
in the kind of case for which it was devised. When the issue is crim-
inality of a hotheaded speech on a street corner, or circulation of a
few incendiary pamphlets, or parading by some zealots behind a red
flag, or refusal of a handful of school children to salute our flag, it is
not beyond the capacity of the judicial process to gather, comprehend, and weigh the necessary materials for decision whether it is a
clear and present danger of substantive evil or a harmless letting off
of steam. It is not a prophecy, for the danger in such cases has ma-
tured by the time of the trial or it was never present. The test applies
and has meaning where a conviction is sought to be based on a
speech or writing which does not directly or explicitly advocate
a crime but to which such tendency is sought to be attributed by
construction or by implication from external circumstances. The
formula in such cases favors freedoms that are vital to our society,
and, even if sometimes applied too generously, the consequences
cannot be grave. But its recent expansion has extended, in particular
to Communists, unprecedented immunities. Unless we are to hold
our Government captive in a judge-made verbal trap, we must approach the problem of a well-organized, nation wide conspiracy, such
as I have described, as realistically as our predecessors faced the
trivialities that were being prosecuted until they were checked with
a rule of reason.

I think reason is lacking for applying that test to this case.

If we must decide that this Act and its application are constitutional only if we are convinced that petitioners' conduct creates a "clear and present danger" of violent overthrow, we must appraise imponderables, including international and national phenomena which baffle the best informed foreign offices and our most experienced politicians. We would have to foresee and predict the effectiveness of Communist propaganda, opportunities for infiltration, whether, and when, a time will come that they consider propitious for action, and whether and how fast our existing government will deteriorate. And we would have to speculate as whether an approaching Communist *coup* would not be anticipated by a nationalistic fascist movement. No doctrine can be sound whose application requires us to make a prophecy of that sort in the guise of a legal decision. The judicial process simply is not adequate to a trial of such far-flung issues. The answers given would reflect our own political predilections and nothing more.

The authors of the clear and present danger test never applied it to a case like this, nor would I. If applied as it is proposed here, it means that the Communist plotting is protected during its period of incubation; its preliminary stages of organization and preparation are immune from the law; the Government can move only after imminent action is manifest, when it would, of course, be too late.

[Justice Jackson urges that the case should be approached as one involving conspiracy. "The Constitution does not make conspiracy a civil right." The convictions should be upheld as valid exercises of the power of Congress to protect the Government against conspirators. But Justice Jackson adds his own doubt that the Communist plans could be halted by judicial convictions and prison terms. "Communism will not go to jail with these Communists. No decision by this Court can forestall revolution whenever the existing government fails to command the respect and loyalty of the people and sufficient distress and discontent is allowed to grow up among the masses. . . ."]

Mr. Justice FRANKFURTER, concurring in affirmance of the judgment.

. . . . .

Few questions of comparable import have come before this Court in recent years. The appellants maintain that they have a right to advocate a political theory, so long, at least, as their advocacy does not create an immediate danger of obvious magnitude to the very existence of our present scheme of society. On the other hand, the Government asserts the right to safeguard the security of the Nation by such a measure as the Smith Act. Our judgment is thus solicited on a conflict of interests of the utmost concern to the well-being of the country. This conflict of interests cannot be resolved by a dogmatic preference for one or the other, nor by a sonorous formula which is in fact only a euphemistic disguise for an unresolved conflict. If adjudication is to be a rational process we cannot escape a candid examination of the conflicting claims with full recognition that both are supported by weighty title-deeds.

. . . . .

But how are competing interests to be assessed? Since they are not subject to quantitative ascertainment, the issue necessarily resolves itself into asking, who is to make the adjustment?—who is to balance the relevant factors and ascertain which interest is in the circumstances to prevail? Full responsibility for the choice cannot be given to the courts. Courts are not representative bodies. They are not designed to be a good reflex of a democratic society. Their judgment is best informed, and therefore most dependable, within narrow limits. Their essential quality is detachment, founded on independence. History teaches that the independence of the judiciary is jeopardized when courts become embroiled in the passions of the day and assume primary responsibility in choosing between competing political, economic and social pressures.

Primary responsibility for adjusting the interests which compete in the situation before us of necessity belongs to the Congress. The nature of the power to be exercised by this Court has been delineated in decisions not charged with the emotional appeal of situations such as that now before us. We are to set aside the judgment of those whose duty it is to legislate only if there is no reasonable basis for it. . . . We must scrupulously observe the narrow limits of judicial authority even though self-restraint is alone set over us. Above all we must remember that this Court's power of judicial review is not "an exercise of the powers of a super-legislature."

. . . . .

[The opinion proceeds to examine decisions reached "in more tranquil times" and arrives at these conclusions:]

First.—Free-speech cases are not an exception to the principle that we are not legislators, that direct policy-making is not our province.

How best to reconcile competing interests is the business of legislatures, and the balance they strike is a judgment not to be displaced
by ours, but to be respected unless outside the pale of fair judgment.

. . . . .

Second.—A survey of the relevant decisions indicates that the results which we have reached are on the whole those that would
ensue from careful weighing of conflicting interests. The complex
issues presented by regulation of speech in public places, by picket-
ing, and by legislation prohibiting advocacy of crime have been
resolved by scrutiny of many factors besides the imminence and
gravity of the evil threatened. The matter has been well summarized
by a reflective student of the Court's work. "The truth is that the
clear-and-present danger test is an oversimplified judgment unless it
takes account also of a number of other factors: the relative seriousness of the danger in comparison with the value of the occasion for
speech or political activity; the availability of more moderate controls than those which the state has imposed; and perhaps the specific
intent with which the speech or activity is launched. No matter how
rapidly we utter the phrase 'clear and present danger,' or how closely
we hyphenate the words, they are not a substitute for the weighing
of values. They tend to convey a delusion of certitude when what is
most certain is the complexity of the strands in the web of freedom
which the judge must disentangle." Freund, *On Understanding the
Supreme Court* 27-28.

. . . . .

Third.—Not every type of speech occupies the same position on
the scale of values. . . . It is pertinent to the decision before us to
consider where on the scale of values we have in the past placed the
type of speech now claiming constitutional immunity.

The defendants have been convicted of conspiring to organize a
party of persons who advocate the overthrow of the Government by
force and violence. The jury has found that the object of the conspiracy is advocacy as "a rule or principle of political action," "by
language reasonably and ordinarily calculated to incite persons to
such action," and with the intent to cause the overthrow "as speedily
as circumstances would permit."

On any scale of values which we have hitherto recognized, speech
of this sort ranks low.

. . . . .

[Like Justice Jackson, Justice Frankfurter would uphold the conviction while at the same time avowing his belief that the ultimate preservation of democratic government is to be found not in judicial vindications but in "a persistent, positive translation of the liberating faith into the feelings and thoughts and actions of men and women."]

Mr. Justice BLACK, dissenting.

. . . . .

. . . The opinions for affirmance show that the chief reason for jettisoning the rule [of clear and present danger] is the expressed fear that advocacy of Communist doctrine endangers the safety of the Republic. Undoubtedly, a governmental policy of unfettered communication of ideas does entail dangers. To the Founders of this Nation, however, the benefits derived from free expression were worth the risk. . . .

So long as this Court exercises the power of judicial review of legislation, I cannot agree that the First Amendment permits us to sustain laws suppressing freedom of speech and press on the basis of Congress' or our own notions of mere reasonableness." Such a doctrine waters down the First Amendment so that it amounts to little more than an admonition to Congress. The Amendment as so construed is not likely to protect any but those "safe" and orthodox views which rarely need its protection. . . .

Mr. Justice DOUGLAS, dissenting.

. . . . .

Free speech has occupied an exalted position because of the high service it has given our society. Its protection is essential to the very existence of democracy. The airing of ideas releases pressures which otherwise might become destructive. When ideas compete in the market for acceptance, full and free discussion exposes the false and they gain few adherents. Full and free discussion even of ideas we hate encourages the testing of our own prejudices and preconceptions. Full and free discussion keeps a society from becoming stagnant and unprepared for the stresses and strains that work to tear all civilizations apart.

Full and free discussion has indeed been the first article of our faith. We have founded our political system on it. It has been the safeguard of every religious, political, philosophical, economic, and racial group amongst us. . . . This has been the one single outstanding tenet that has made our institutions the symbol of freedom and equality. We have deemed it more costly to liberty to suppress a despised minority than to let them vent their spleen. We have above all else feared the political censor. We have wanted a land where our people can be exposed to all the diverse creeds and cultures of the world.

There comes a time when even speech loses its constitutional immunity. Speech innocuous one year may at another time fan such destructive flames that it must be halted in the interests of the safety of the Republic. That is the meaning of the clear and present danger test. When conditions are so critical that there will be no time to avoid the evil that the speech threatens, it is time to call a halt. Otherwise, free speech which is the strength of the Nation will be the cause of its destruction.

Yet free speech is the rule, not the exception. The restraint to be constitutional must be based on more than fear, on more than passionate opposition against the speech, on more than a revolted dislike for its content. There must be some immediate injury to society that is likely if speech is allowed. . . .

. . . This record . . . contains no evidence whatsoever showing that the acts charged, *viz.,* the teaching of the Soviet theory of revolution with the hope that it will be realized, have created any clear and present danger to the Nation. The Court, however, rules to the contrary. It says, "The formation by petitioners of such a highly organized conspiracy, with rigidly disciplined members subject to call when the leaders, these petitioners, felt that the time had come for action, coupled with the inflammatory nature of world conditions, similar uprisings in other countries, and the touch-and-go nature of our relations with countries with whom petitioners were in the very least ideologically attuned, convince us that their convictions were justified on this score."

That ruling is in my view not responsive to the issue in the case. We might as well say that the speech of petitioners is outlawed because the Soviet Union and her Red Army are a threat to world peace.

. . . If we are to take judicial notice of the threat of Communism within this nation, it should not be difficult to conclude that *as a political party* they are of little consequence. Communists in this country have never made a respectable showing in any election. I would doubt that there is a village, let alone a city or county or state which the Communists could carry. . . . Communism has been so thoroughly exposed in this country that it has been crippled as a political force. . . . In days of trouble and confusion when bread lines were long, when the unemployed walked the streets, when people were starving, the advocates of a short-cut by revolution might have a chance to gain adherents. But today there are no such conditions. The country is not in despair; the people know Soviet Communism; the doctrine of Soviet revolution is exposed in all its ugliness and the American people want none of it.

How it can be said that there is a clear and present danger that this advocacy will succeed is, therefore, a mystery. . . . On this record no one can say that the petitioners and their converts are in such a strategic position as to have even the slightest chance of achieving their aims.

The First Amendment provides that "Congress shall make no law . . . abridging the freedom of speech." The Constitution provides no exception. This does not mean, however, that the Nation need hold its hand until it is in such weakened condition that there is no time to protect itself from incitement to revolution. Seditious conduct can always be punished. But the command of the First Amendment is so clear that we should not allow Congress to call a halt to free speech except in the extreme case of peril from the speech itself. The First Amendment makes confidence in the common sense of our people and in their maturity of judgment the great postulate of our democracy. Its philosophy is that violence is rarely, if ever, stopped by denying civil liberties to those advocating resort to force. The First Amendment reflects the philosophy of Jefferson "that it is time enough for the rightful purposes of civil government for its officers to interfere when principles break out into overt acts against peace and good order." The political censor has no place in our public debates. Unless and until extreme and necessitous circumstances are shown our aim should be to keep speech unfettered and to allow the processes of law to be invoked only when the provocateurs among us move from speech to action.

Vishinsky wrote in 1948 in *The Law of the Soviet State*, "In our state, naturally there can be no place for freedom of speech, press, and so on for the foes of socialism."

Our concern should be that we accept no such standard for the United States. Our faith should be that our people will never give support to these advocates of revolution, so long as we remain loyal to the purposes for which our Nation was founded.

Liberty of Conscience in a Democracy

1. RELIGIOUS LIBERTY AND PUBLIC POLICY

THE PURITAN BACKGROUND OF THE
FIRST AMENDMENT[1]

By WILLIAM HALLER

The crucial clause in the first provision of the American Bill of Rights as it appears in the First Amendment to the Constitution was, of course, that "Congress shall make no law respecting an establishment of religion, or prohibiting the free exercise thereof." This confirmed existing conditions by making religious liberty the law of the union, and from this, freedom of speech, freedom of the press, the rights of assembly and petition naturally followed.

It is important to note that the principle involved in this legalizing of the unprecedented situation which existed in the thirteen states appears not to have been questioned at the time or even discussed at any length. The Constitution in its primary form failed to affirm toleration not because its authors doubted the principle involved but because they took it for granted. The idea seems not to have occurred to them that one of the functions of the government of the United States might be to establish a church of the United States. As soon, however, as they saw that the affirmation of religious liberty was expedient for winning reluctant states to the union, they promptly affirmed it by amendment. Their object was union, and they found themselves in a situation where no union was possible

---

[1] Reprinted from Conyers Read, editor, *The Constitution Reconsidered*. Copyright 1938 by Columbia University Press.

which did not explicitly authorize the prevalent differences in religious faith and worship and hence in all thought and expression.
Not to establish a church was not enough. The federal government
must definitely establish toleration, must affirm by law the equal
rights of citizens, denominations and states in respect to religion and
must guarantee that each should be protected against all the others
in the exercise of those rights. Toleration, thus established, did not
spring from religious indifference. It sprang from political wisdom
correctly recognizing and allowing for the prime religious conviction common to Americans and bred in them by the very nature of
their religious experience. That conviction was that every citizen
must be expected even on so momentous a concern as religion to
have opinions and beliefs which might or might not be right, but
which it was right for him to express and important for others to hear.

There is little I can say concerning the circumstances that directly
led to the adoption of this provision in the Bill of Rights. There is
also little that I could add to what has been written on the historic
development of the doctrine of toleration. I shall venture, rather, to
offer some general suggestions concerning the causes for the condition of religious life in America which made toleration seem so
natural a necessity to union. This condition, extraordinary at the
time and of the utmost significance for the future of American civilization, arose from two intimately related causes in English life which
came to their fullest fruition in America, namely the disruption of
the historic church and the rise of Puritanism.

Religion, formerly the chief bond of union among the people of
Europe, became in the England of the sixteenth century a principal
occasion for disunion. Religion henceforth reflected not so much the
common brotherhood of Englishmen with all Christians as their division upon various lines as Englishmen. The attempt to reform the
English church which culminated in the great revolution of the
seventeenth century achieved not the reform but the disruption of
the church. The people flew apart into a host of communions, each
professing to hold the one true faith; each excluding, even when not
seeking to persecute, adherents of others; each struggling for existence
if not for complete domination; and each torn by dissension within.
Elizabeth supported the church and repressed its enemies, but only
enough to maintain her own authority, not enough to restore the old
order or forefend the anarchy to come. Every effort of her immediate
successors to do more than she had done to reunite the people under

the church served only to promote civil as well as religious disorder
and to bring ruin on the state. Civil order was reestablished only when
in 1689 the state in effect abandoned responsibility for restoring
religion to its former place and function in society. The government
did not wholly abandon the church, but it acknowledged no responsibility greater than that of maintaining its own authority over all
forms of religion. This it accomplished by compelling all to be not
at one but at peace, proceeding only against such as could plausibly
be argued to be hostile to the political regime. Thus a measure of
toleration was achieved in England by compromise, and toleration
fostered national union while permitting religious disunion to crys-
tallize quietly into the familiar pattern of our own times.

The adoption of the First Amendment signified the recognition
in this country of a similar need in a situation brought on by the same
causes, operating, however, on a simpler and broader scene and scale.
From the point of view of . . . the development of religious life, the
settlement of North America by the English was an incident to the
disruption of the historic English church, an incident rendered momentous by the nature and extent of the country. An enormous area
was ready to be peopled by the religious minorities which sprang
forward to remove themselves one after another into the wilderness.
In England the diaspora of the church remained confined within
definite social and physical limits. In America, they found a continent
to deploy upon. Up to a point, the new society, or rather each par-
ticle into which the old society divided, reduplicated in little the
religious pattern of the old, but with a difference of increasing significance. In each of the new communities, that is, some particular religious denomination was dominant. It had been there from the first
settlement, which soon became in popular consciousness the year one,
the apostolic age, of whatever the local faith might be. There was,
however, no church common to all the new settlements, and the very
idea of the church catholic, which never completely disappeared in
England, became attenuated in America to nothing or practically
nothing. In the typical American community, the local church, so
often and so significantly called the first church, the denomination
comprising the first families and the best people, might be Anglican
in Virginia, but in Plymouth it was Separatist, in Massachusetts Bay
Independent, in Pennsylvania Quaker, in Maryland even Roman
Catholic, all enjoying in the country at large a quite unprecedented
parity of prestige. Thus, freed from traditional checks, the religious

divisions of the English people were leveled, yet at the same time perpetuated and fostered, by dispersion in this country. Even though old jealousies might survive here and there, Anglican Virginia could make good no claim to precedence over Puritan Massachusetts, and Pennsylvania, though Quaker, and Maryland, though Catholic, were under no compulsion to yield to either. Religion was from the start, and has continued in a measure to be, a local affair, representing differences and even conflicts between sectional cultures and interests, but not social or political inequalities.

The typical American community from the beginning also reflected the English pattern of inner division and dissent, again modified by the new conditions. The first church, the dominant communion, never comprised, never pretended to comprise, the whole society. Not all the passengers on the "Mayflower" itself were saints, and Governor Bradford in his chronicle had to begin early to record the strivings of the regenerate with the unregenerate at Plymouth. The members of the first church might deny political rights to the ungodly, might hope to convert them, might drive them out or persecute them, but they always had them on their hands. There was, of course, a good practical reason why this had to be. There was no way really to keep the ungodly out, and besides their presence was needed even in the godliest Utopia to help people the wilderness. Added to that was the fact that it was of the nature of American religious life to breed heterodoxy and disagreement within itself. Added too was the fact that the wilderness offered such a field for the flourishing of dissenters and minorities as had never been before. Someone once asked Hugh Peters what they did with such people in New England. He replied that they put them over the river. The ungodly, that is, had always the frontier whither they might, to be sure, be pursued by the wrath of the godly or where they might be killed by the Indians, but where too they might set up new communities, prosper, perhaps trouble those they left behind and certainly engender fresh dissent among themselves and new exoduses to new lands of promise. Thus each new Jerusalem was always apt to be beset by a Jerusalem still newer. Like Massachusetts, every American community tended to raise up a Rhode Island, a Utah, on its borders, until the saints of the latter days spread to every corner of the continent.

The result of all this has been that American society from its inception was one in which there were churches, in a few instances for a short time churches established by local law, but never at any time in the historic sense the church. Every American religious communion has always had to maintain itself in the midst of competition, hostility, suspicion and indifference. Some when able to do so have resorted to persecution, some from conviction or weakness have not, but it must have been obvious early in our history that the forcible or legal imposition of any one church throughout the country could be accomplished, if at all, only at the expense of the others. What each had most to hope for, therefore, when it came time to form a political union, was the perpetuation of the anarchy to which each owed its present existence. Thanks to the disruption of the English church, thanks to the spacious hospitality of the unpeopled wilderness, religious freedom prevailed even before toleration was acknowledged as a sacred principle to be written into positive law. That it was written into the Bill of Rights gave evidence how completely the authors of that document were aware of the conditions and forces of American life.

.   .   .   .   .   .

MORMONS AND "WITNESSES"

The first major conflict between the principles of religious liberty and legislative notions of public policy involved the polygamous practices of the Mormon Church as originally established. The leading case on the subject was decided in 1878, *Reynolds* v. *United States,* 98 U.S. 145. Here a member of the Mormon Church, who had contracted a polygamous marriage, was tried for violating an Act of Congress making polygamy criminal in the territories of the United States. The defense argued that, since polygamy was enjoined by the teachings of the Mormon Church, the statute conflicted with the First Amendment and was therefore void. The Supreme Court, however, declared that only interference with matters of conscience, dogma, or opinion was forbidden by the First Amendment, and that the government was not denied authority to interfere when religious opinion resulted in overt acts detrimental to the peace and good order of society. This position was reiterated in 1890 in the decision in *Davis* v. *Beason,* 133 U.S. 333, involving a federal statute denying the right to vote to persons engaging in polygamous practices. With these cases, religious liberty appeared effectively confined within the limits of community mores—until a small dissident sect, Jehovah's Witnesses, forced a re-examination of the entire question.

The point at which Jehovah's Witnesses find themselves in almost continuous conflict with temporal authority is their steadfast refusal to submit to any form of regulation in the exercise of their "publishing" activities. They hold that they are commanded by the Scriptures to disseminate, "publish," God's word by house-to-house distribution as well as by street peddling of their interpretations of the Scriptures. The first case considered by the Supreme Court was *Lovell v. Griffin*, 303 U.S. 444 (1938). Here a city ordinance requiring permission from the city manager as a condition precedent to the distribution of any literature or pamphlets within the city was held unconstitutional because no standards were set up to guide the city manager's discretion and he was therefore in a position to exercise an unmitigated and unlimited censorship over the literature to be distributed. Such practice, the Court unanimously declared, violated the liberty guaranteed by the Fourteenth Amendment, which must be considered to embrace within it the principles of freedom of press and religion safeguarded against federal action by the First Amendment. The Court reached the same result in a New Jersey case where the police chief had discretionary authority to deny a license to canvass if, in his judgment, the applicant was not of good character and free from fraud. *Schneider v. Irvinton*, 308 U.S. 147 (1939). And in May, 1940, a Connecticut statute forbidding anyone to solicit for charitable and religious causes without previously satisfying the secretary of the public welfare council that the cause involved was a *bona fide* charitable or religious one, was similarly struck down. *Cantwell v. Connecticut*, 310 U.S. 296 (1940). Increasingly, however, the issues began to narrow and the unanimity of the Court to be shaken. The Flag Salute Cases presented most dramatically the conflict between freedom of conscience and the interests of temporal authority.

THE FIRST FLAG SALUTE DECISION[2]

There are several ways to heaven and men can be as strait about our freedom to choose a way as the Way itself.

Jehovah's Witnesses had been pressing an issue up to the Court and the Court had been ignoring it. Three times in three succeeding years it had dismissed the question whether one of Jehovah's Witnesses could constitutionally be required, contrary to his religious con-

[2] From Charles P. Curtis, Jr., *Lions Under The Throne*, Boston: Houghton Mifflin Co., 1947, pp. 300–321. Reproduced by permission of the author and the publishers.

victions, to salute the flag. The issue had portentous possibilities, like everything which is symbolic. Its significance suddenly struck the Court in the Gobitis case, in 1940.

Lillian Gobitis was thirteen and her brother Walter was twelve when the teacher at the public school which they attended told them that they must join with the other pupils in the salute to the flag with which school opened every morning. They were to say, "I pledge allegiance to my flag, and to the Republic for which it stands; one nation indivisible, with liberty and justice for all." But they were Jehovah's Witnesses, and they had been brought up to believe this was nothing less than idolatry and a breach of the first two Commandments. "Thou shalt have no other gods before me. Thou shalt not make unto thee any graven image. . . . Thou shalt not bow down thyself to them, nor serve them." So Lillian and Walter refused to salute the flag and their father agreed with them and told them not to do it. But he sent them back to school. It was a public school, and attendance was compulsory unless he provided them with a private education. He insisted they had a right to go without breaking the Decalogue. The school insisted they had to salute the flag if they went.

"Some think it the Achilles' heel of democracy that, by its very nature, it cannot foster general agreement on ultimates, and perhaps must foster the contrary," said a recent committee of Harvard professors. Agreeing with them or not, we count on the school as the place where we teach our children their first steps in patriotism. At the same time, we keep religion out of our schools. Now patriotism and religion are made, more or less, out of the same stuff, and they are taught in more or less the same way. There is certain to be trouble when either encroaches on the preserves of the other. Here in the Gobitis case, that is just what happened. Whether it was patriotism which was the intruder on religion, or religion on patriotism, cannot help becoming arguable, one way or the other. However, there was the preliminary question, as there always is, who shall decide the argument? Is Lillian's refusal to salute our flag a good enough reason to make her parents pay for her education? Put yourself on the school board, who consider it their duty to require the salute of all the pupils, all, not only those who volunteer or who are willing or who do not object. Put yourself into the position of the parent who considers his child damned if he salutes the flag, or anything else but Jehovah, and who finds that he must pay for his fears and scruples with a private education. Make believe you are the child, told as she leaves home not to rise and pledge allegiance to her country and sent home by the teacher when she obeys; figure out her feelings, and the feelings of the other children.

"Render unto Caesar the things that are Caesar's and unto God the things that are God's" was not in her Testament. Her God was Jehovah, and what Christ had said did not matter. The Constitution was now called on to decide between Caesar and Jehovah. Or was it between the Gobitis children and their fellow pupils?

On June 3, 1940, Frankfurter wrote the opinion of the Court. Only Stone dissented. The Court declined to hold the regulation unconstitutional.[3]

"A grave responsibility," said Frankfurter, "confronts this Court whenever in course of litigation it must reconcile the conflicting claims of liberty and authority. But when the liberty invoked is liberty of conscience, and the authority is authority to safeguard the nation's fellowship, judicial conscience is put to its severest test. Of such a nature is the present controversy." He stated the facts, and said, "We must decide whether the requirement of participation in such a ceremony, exacted from a child who refuses upon sincere religious grounds, infringes without due process of law the liberty guaranteed by the Fourteenth Amendment." The Fourteenth, mark you.

Frankfurter went on to ask, "When does the constitutional guarantee compel exemption from doing what society thinks necessary for the promotion of some great common end, or from a penalty for conduct which appears dangerous to the general good? To state the problem is to recall the truth that no single principle can answer all of life's complexities. The right to freedom of religious belief, however dissident and however obnoxious to the cherished beliefs of others—even of a majority—is itself the denial of an absolute. But to affirm that the freedom to follow conscience has itself no limits in the life of a society would deny that very plurality of principles which, as a matter of history, underlies protection of religious toleration. Our present task then, as so often the case with courts, is to reconcile two rights in order to prevent either from destroying the other."

But for Stone religious belief was an absolute, not the denial of one. There were limits, yes, even to religious freedom. There were things a man may be made to do, in spite of his most conscientious and profound religious scruples. He could be drafted, and made to

[3] *Minersville School District* v. *Gobitis*, 310 U.S. 586.

fight. So also, Stone agreed, there are things he could be forbidden to do. He could be prevented from disturbing the peace or from offending public morals, though his conscience impelled him to do just that. But these were outward things. Bearing arms or disturbing the peace were conduct which the state either required or forbade for their own sake, and their advantages could be weighted relatively to loss of scruple. But somewhere there was an absolute, and Stone found it in "the higher commandments of God." The very terms of the Bill of Rights, he said, precluded any reconciliation there.

Frankfurter and Stone, and later the others, all treated the issue as if it concerned the relation of the state to the religious freedom of one of the churches. If the salute to the flag offends the religious conscience of the Witnesses, the salute becomes, at least to them, a religious act which the state has forced them to perform. It is a ritual which we regard as political, but which they regard as religious. Now, if the salute is not religious, there is nothing in the Constitution forbidding it. If it is religious, then it constitutes the beginning—*obsta principiis*—of the establishment of a state religion. And the First Amendment, though that was not what the Court was going to apply, forbids the establishment of a state religion quite as explicitly as it protects the free exercise of religion by any church or sect.

This is the way the case struck a friend of mine, and he went on to say that in 1789 there was no danger of the temporal power itself becoming a religion. The fanatics then were men preoccupied with their own plans for eternal salvation and the danger was that one sect by gaining control of the state would try to compel the others to conform, and finally set itself up as the state church. That was the danger which the Constitution had in mind. But with the decay of interest in eternal salvation, when many or most churches became social groups, the religious nature of man turned to the deification of the state. Nationalism became a religion, and the nation became a church. The salute to the flag became an obeisance, so the Witnesses thought, to a new deity, the very image of that new deity. Thus the statute was not so much an interference with religious freedom as the incipient advance of nationalism to become itself an establishment of religion.

Lincoln asked, "Must a government of necessity be too *strong* for the liberties of its people, or too *weak* to maintain its own existence?" Here it is the second alternative. These liberties depend upon government quite as truly as they are endangered by a strong government.

Without government there can be no liberties quite as truly as there are none when the government is too strong. . . . Here in the flag salute case, where Frankfurter quotes this from Lincoln, we have concrete examples of the dilemma. Where would religious liberty be if there was no government strong enough to calm the religious rapacity of the majority? Only an anarchist would hesitate over the answer. Where would freedom of speech rest its head, were there no courts to protect it? The Court is weighing the sanctity of the right against the efficacy of the government that protects any right at all. The Court is engaged in a nice calculus of maximum values of loyalty to the state and an opportunity for devotion to God. . . .

To return to Frankfurter's opinion. "The precise issue, then, for us to decide is whether the legislatures of the various states and the authorities in a thousand counties and school districts of this country are barred from determining the appropriateness of various means to evoke that unifying sentiment without which there can ultimately be no liberties, civil or religious. The influences which help toward a common feeling for the common country are manifold. Some may seem harsh and others no doubt are foolish. Surely, however, the end is legitimate. And the effective means for its attainment are still so uncertain and so unauthenticated by science as to preclude us from putting the widely prevalent belief in flag-saluting beyond the pale of legislative power. It mocks reason and denies our whole history to find in the allowance of a requirement to salute our flag on fitting occasions the seeds of sanction for obeisance to a leader.

"Even were we convinced of the folly of such a measure, such belief would be no proof of its unconstitutionality. For ourselves, we might be tempted to say that the deepest patriotism is best engendered by giving unfettered scope to the most crotchety beliefs. Perhaps it is best, even from the standpoint of those interests which ordinances like the present one under review seek to promote, to give to the least popular sect leave from conformities like those here in issue. But the courtroom is not the arena for debating issues of educational policy. It is not our province to choose among competing considerations in the subtle process of securing loyalty to the traditional ideals of democracy, while respecting at the same time individual idiosyncrasies among a people so diversified in racial origins and religious allegiances. So to hold would in effect make us the school board for the country. That authority has not been given to this Court, nor should we assume it.

"Except where the transgression of constitutional liberty is too plain for argument, personal freedom is best maintained—so long as the remedial channels of the democratic process remain open and unobstructed—when it is ingrained in a people's habits and not enforced against popular policy by the coercion of adjudicated law."

And he concluded, "Judicial review, itself a limitation on popular government, is a fundamental part of our constitutional system. But to the legislature no less than to courts is committed the guardianship of deeply cherished liberties. Where all the effective means of inducing political changes are left free from interference, education in the abandonment of foolish legislation is itself a training in liberty. To fight out the wise use of legislative authority in the forum of public opinion and before legislative assemblies rather than to transfer such a contest to the judicial arena, serves to vindicate the self-confidence of a free people."

REDEMPTION OF RELIGIOUS FREEDOM: *Gobitis* to *Barnette*

Learned and lay commentators alike were quick to register their disapproval of the *Gobitis* decision. The suggestion was voiced that the Court had fallen victim to the sudden crisis hysteria which resulted from the German "blitz" into the Low Countries and France. See Benjamin F. Wright, *The Growth of American Constitutional Law*, pp. 230–231, and, for an attempt to correlate the trends graphically, Francis H. Heller, "A Turning Point for Religious Liberty," 29 *Virginia Law Review* 440, 448 (1943).

While the virtual unanimity of press and profession decried the decision, legislatures and city councils at once availed themselves of the High Court's sanction to enact widespread repressive measures against Jehovah's Witnesses. Informed opinion may have branded such measures as "foolish legislation" but the fruits of the "training in liberty" failed to materialize. It has been suggested that this discrepancy—and hence the shortcoming of the Frankfurter formula—may be attributed to the fact that the urban areas furnish much of the impulses of toleration while Witness activity as well as animosity against them centers mostly in small towns and rural areas. These, however, are the geographic subdivisions which almost everywhere control the state legislature. Heller, *op. cit.*, pp. 453–454.

However, the Court itself soon began to show signs of dissatisfaction with the *Gobitis* rule. Less than a year later, Murphy, Black, and Douglas availed themselves of the opportunity offered by a case involving the constitutionality of a city ordinance imposing a small tax on book peddlers as applied to Jehovah's Witnesses to withdraw their support of the majority opinion of the *Gobitis* case. "Since we joined in the opinion in the Gobitis case," they declared in a brief, separate dissent to *Jones* v. *Opelika*, 316 U.S. 584, at 623–624, "we think this is an appropriate occasion to state that we now believe that it was also wrongly decided. Certainly our democratic form of government, functioning under the historic Bill of Rights, has a high responsibility to accommodate itself to the religious views of minorities, however unpopular and unorthodox these views may be. The First Amendment does not put the right freely to exercise religion in a subordinate position. We fear, however, that the opinions in these and in the *Gobitis* case do exactly that."

Then the appointment of Mr. Justice Rutledge converted the former minority into the Court's majority. Sharply dividing in each instance, the Court proceeded to broaden further the immunity of the Witnesses from the operation of regulatory municipal ordinances. In *Murdock* v. *Pennsylvania*, 319 U.S. 105 (1943), a majority of five invalidated the application to Jehovah's Witnesses of a city ordinance requiring licenses for door-to-door sales. Justice Douglas accepted the Witnesses' contention that their distribution of literature was a religious, not a commercial, venture and likened the license fee to an assessment on a preacher for the privilege of delivering a sermon. "The mere fact that the religious literature is 'sold' by itinerant preachers rather than 'donated' does not transform evangelism into a commercial enterprise. If it did, then the passing of the collection plate in church would make the church service a commercial project. . . . The fact that the ordinance is 'non-discriminatory' is immaterial. The protection afforded by the First Amendment is not so restricted. A license tax certainly does not acquire constitutional validity because it classifies the privileges protected by the First Amendment along with the wares and merchandise of hucksters and peddlers and treats them all alike. Such equality in treatment does not save the ordinance. Freedom of press, freedom of speech, freedom of religion are in a preferred position."

In a case decided the same day, *Martin* v. *Struthers*, 319 U.S. 141, the Court, again dividing 5-4, announced that a municipal ordinance directed against the ringing of door bells, etc., in residential areas of the city could not constitutionally be applied against Jehovah's Witnesses engaged in the distribution of religious material. Said

Justice Black: "While door to door distributors of literature may be either a nuisance or a blind for criminal activities, they may also be useful members of society engaged in the dissemination of ideas in accordance with the best traditions of free discussion. . . . Freedom to distribute information to every citizen wherever he desires to receive it is so clearly vital to the preservation of a free society that, putting aside reasonable police and health regulations of time and manner of distribution, it must be fully preserved. The dangers of distribution can so easily be controlled by traditional legal methods, leaving to each householder the full right to decide whether he will receive strangers as visitors, that stringent prohibition can serve no purpose but that forbidden by the Constitution, the naked restriction of the dissemination of ideas."

Justice Frankfurter disagreed. "The habits and security of life in sparsely settled rural communities, or even in those few cities which a hundred and fifty years ago had a population of a few thousands, cannot be made the basis of judgment for determining the area of allowable self-protection by present-day industrial communities. The lack of privacy and the hazards to peace of mind and body caused by people living not in individual houses but crowded together in large human beehives, as they so widely do, are facts of modern living which cannot be ignored." And again he urged that the Court should not, "however unwillingly, slip into the judgment seat of legislatures."

Justice Jackson saved his objections for a concurring opinion in *Douglas* v. *Jeannette,* a companion case to the *Murdock* case, also decided on May 3, 1943 (319 U. S. 157). And it is only in his opinion that the reverse of the medal is fully presented. Here then Jehovah's Witnesses appear not as a pious and persecuted band of evangelists but as an aggressive, highly organized group, co-ordinated from a national headquarters which annually distributes over eight million items of polemic literature, and which enters "target" communities in well-planned drives, inevitably eschewing to co-operate with the local authorities in even their most reasonable demands and apparently observing the policy of returning in greater strength to any community where their activities have encountered resistance. "Where," asks Justice Jackson, "[do] the Witnesses' rights end and others begin . . . ? . . . Civil government cannot let any group ride rough-shod over others simply because their 'conscience' tells them to do so. . . . We have held [in *Chaplinsky* v. *New Hampshire,* 315

U.S. 568 (1942)] that a Jehovah's Witness may not call a public officer a 'god damned racketeer' and a 'damned Fascist,' because that is to use 'fighting words,' and such are not privileged. How then can the Court today hold it a 'high constitutional privilege' to go to homes, including those of devout Roman Catholics on Palm Sunday morning, and thrust upon them literature calling their church a 'whore' and their faith a 'racket'?"

A few weeks later, however, it was Justice Jackson who spoke for the majority in reversing the *Gobitis* case.

WEST VIRGINIA BOARD OF EDUCATION v. BARNETTE
319 U.S. 624 (1943)

Mr. Justice JACKSON delivered the opinion of the Court.

Following the decision by this Court on June 3, 1940, in *Minersville School District* v. *Gobitis,* 310 U.S. 586, ... the West Virginia legislature amended its statutes to require all schools therein to conduct courses in instruction in history, civics, and in the Constitutions of the United States and of the State "for the purpose of teaching, fostering and perpetuating the ideals, principles and spirit of Americanism, and increasing the knowledge of the organization and machinery of the government." ...

The Board of Education on January 9, 1942, adopted a resolution containing recitals taken largely from the Court's *Gobitis* opinion and ordering that the salute to the flag become "a regular part of the program of activities in the public schools," that all teachers and pupils "shall be required to participate in the salute honoring the Nation represented by the Flag; provided, however, that refusal to salute the Flag be regarded as an Act of insubordination, and shall be dealt with accordingly."

The resolution originally required the "commonly accepted salute to the Flag" which it defined. Objections to the salute as "being too much like Hitler's" were raised by the Parent and Teachers Association, the Boy and Girl Scouts, the Red Cross, and the Federation of Women's Clubs. Some modification appears to have been made in deference to these objections, but no concession was made to Jehovah's Witnesses. What is now required is the "stiff-arm" salute, the saluter to keep the right hand raised with palm turned up while the following is repeated: "I pledge allegiance to the Flag of the United States of America and to the Republic for which it stands; one Nation, indivisible, with liberty and justice for all."

Failure to conform is "insubordination" dealt with by expulsion. Readmission is denied by statute until compliance. Meanwhile the expelled child is "unlawfully absent" and may be proceeded against as a delinquent. His parents or guardians are liable to prosecution, and if convicted are subject to fine not exceeding $50 and jail term not exceeding thirty days.

Appellees, citizens of the United States and of West Virginia, brought suit in the United States District Court for themselves and others similarly situated asking its injunction to restrain enforcement of these laws and regulations against Jehovah's Witnesses. The Witnesses are an unincorporated body teaching that the obligation imposed by law of God is superior to that of laws enacted by temporal government. Their religious beliefs include a literal version of Exodus, Chapter 20, verses 4 and 5, which says: "Thou shalt not make unto thee any graven image, or any likeness of anything that is in heaven above, or that is in the earth beneath, or that is in the water under the earth; thou shalt not bow down thyself to them, nor serve them." They consider that the Flag is an "image" within this command. For this reason they refuse to salute it.

Children of this faith have been expelled from school and are threatened with exclusion for no other cause. Officials threaten to send them to reformatories maintained for criminally inclined juveniles. Parents of such children have been prosecuted and are threatened with prosecutions for causing delinquency. . . .

This case calls upon us to reconsider a precedent decision, as the Court throughout its history often has been required to do. Before turning to the *Gobitis* case, however, it is desirable to notice certain characteristics by which this controversy is distinguished.

The freedom asserted by these appellees does not bring them into collision with rights asserted by any other individual. . . . Nor is there any question in this case that their behavior is peaceable and orderly. The sole conflict is between authority and rights of the individual. The State asserts power to condition access to public education on making a prescribed sign and profession and at the same time to coerce attendance by punishing both parent and child. The latter stand on a right of self-determination in matters that touch individual opinion and personal attitude.

As the present Chief Justice [Stone] said in dissent in the *Gobitis* case, the State may "require teaching by instruction and study of all in our history and in the structure and organization of our government, including the guaranties of civil liberty, which tend to inspire patriotism and love of country." . . . Here, however, we are dealing with a compulsion of students to declare a belief. They are not merely made acquainted with the flag salute so that they may be informed as to what it is or even what it means. The issue here is whether this slow and easily neglected route to aroused loyalties constitutionally may be short-cut by substituting a compulsory salute and slogan. . . .

There is no doubt that, in connection with the pledges, the flag salute is a form of utterance. Symbolism is a primitive but effective way of communicating ideas. The use of an emblem or flag to symbolize some system, idea, institution, or personality, is a short cut from mind to mind. Causes and nations, political parties, lodges and ecclesiastical groups seek to knit the loyalty of their followings to a flag or banner, a color or design. The State announces rank, function, and authority through crowns and maces, uniforms and black robes; the church speaks through the Cross, the Crucifix, the altar and shrine, and clerical raiment. Symbols of State often convey political ideas just as religious symbols come to convey theological ones. Associated with many of these symbols are appropriate gestures of acceptance or respect: a salute, a bowed or bared head, a bended knee. A person gets from a symbol the meaning he puts into it, and what is one man's comfort and inspiration is another's jest and scorn.

Over a decade ago Chief Justice Hughes led this Court in holding that the display of a red flag as a symbol of opposition by peaceful and legal means to organized government was protected by the free speech guaranties of the Constitution. *Stromberg* v. *California*, 283 U.S. 359. Here it is the State that employs a flag as a symbol of adherence to government as presently organized. It requires the individual to communicate by word and sign his acceptance of the political ideas it thus bespeaks. Objection to this form of communication when coerced is an old one, well known to the framers of the Bill of Rights.

It is also to be noted that the compulsory flag salute and pledge requires affirmation of a belief and an attitude of mind. It is not clear whether the regulation contemplates that pupils forego any contrary convictions of their own and become unwilling converts to the prescribed ceremony or whether it will be acceptable if they simulate assent by words without belief and by a gesture barren of meaning. It is now a commonplace that censorship or suppression of expression of opinion is tolerated by our Constitution only when the expression presents a clear and present danger of action of a kind the State is empowered to prevent and punish. It would seem that involuntary affirmation could be commanded only on even more immediate and urgent grounds than silence. But here the power of compulsion is invoked without any allegation that remaining passive during a flag salute ritual creates a clear and present danger that would justify an effort even to muffle expression. To sustain the compulsory flag salute we are required to say that a Bill of Rights which guards the individual's right to speak his own mind, left it open to public authorities to compel him to utter what is not in his mind.

Whether the First Amendment to the Constitution will permit officials to order observance of ritual of this nature does not depend upon whether as a voluntary exercise we would think it to be good, bad or merely innocuous. Any credo of nationalism is likely to include what some disapprove or to omit what others think essential, and to give off different overtones as it takes on different accents or interpretations. If official power exists to coerce acceptance of any patriotic creed, what it shall contain cannot be decided by courts, but must be largely discretionary with the ordaining authority, whose power to prescribe would no doubt include power to amend. Hence validity of the asserted power to force an American citizen publicly to profess any statement of belief or to engage in any ceremony of assent to one, presents questions of power that must be considered independently of any idea we may have as to the utility of the ceremony in question.

Nor does the issue as we see it turn on one's possession of particular religious views or the sincerity with which they are held. While religion supplies appellees' motive for enduring the discomforts of making the issue in this case, many citizens who do not share these religious views hold such a compulsory rite to infringe constitutional liberty of the individual. It is not necessary to inquire whether non-conformist beliefs will exempt from the duty to salute unless we first find power to make the salute a legal duty.

The *Gobitis* decision, however, *assumed,* as did the argument in that case and in this, that power exists in the State to impose the flag salute discipline upon school children in general. The Court only examined and rejected a claim based on religious beliefs of immunity from an unquestioned general rule. The question which underlies the flag salute controversy is whether such a ceremony so touching matters of opinion and political attitude may be imposed upon the individual by official authority under powers committed to any political organization under our Constitution. We examine rather than assume existence of this power and, against this broader definition of issues in this case, reexamine specific grounds assigned for the *Gobitis* decision.

It was said that the flag salute controversy confronted the Court with "the problem which Lincoln cast in memorable dilemma: 'Must a government of necessity be too *strong* for the liberties of its people, or too *weak* to maintain its own existence?'" and that the answer must be in favor of strength. *Minersville School District* v. *Gobitis*.

We think these issues may be examined free of pressure or restraint growing out of such considerations.

It may be doubted whether Mr. Lincoln would have thought that the strength of government to maintain itself would be impressively vindicated by our confirming power of the State to expel a handful of children from school. Such oversimplification, so handy in political debate, often lacks the precision necessary to postulates of judicial reasoning. If validly applied to this problem, the utterance cited would resolve every issue of power in favor of those in authority and would require us to override every liberty thought to weaken or delay execution of their policies.

1. Government of limited power need not be anemic government. Assurance that rights are secure tends to diminish fear and jealousy of strong government, and by making us feel safe to live under it makes for its better support. Without promise of a limiting Bill of Rights it is doubtful if our Constitution could have mustered enough strength to enable its ratification. To enforce those rights today is not to choose weak government over strong government. It is only to adhere as a means of strength to individual freedom of mind in preference to officially disciplined uniformity for which history indicates a disappointing and disastrous end.

The subject now before us exemplifies this principle. Free public education, if faithful to the ideal of secular instruction and political neutrality, will not be partisan or enemy of any class, creed, party, or faction. If it is to impose any ideological discipline, however, each party or denomination must seek to control, or failing that, to weaken the influence of the educational system. Observance of the limitations of the Constitution will not weaken government in the field appropriate for its exercise.

2. It was also considered in the *Gobitis* case that functions of educational officers in States, counties and school districts were such that to interfere with their authority "would in effect make us the school board for the country."

The Fourteenth Amendment, as now applied to the States, protects the citizen against the State itself and all of its creatures—Boards of Education not excepted. . . .

Such Boards are numerous and their territorial jurisdiction often small. But small and local authority may feel less sense of responsibility to the Constitution, and agencies of publicity may be less vigilant in calling it to account. . . . There are village tyrants as well as village Hampdens, but none who acts under color of law is beyond reach of the Constitution.

3. The *Gobitis* opinion reasoned that this is a field "where courts possess no marked and certainly no controlling competence," that it is committed to the legislatures as well as the courts to guard cherished liberties and that it is constitutionally appropriate to "fight out the wise use of legislative authority in the forum of public opinion and before legislative assemblies rather than to transfer such a contest to the judicial arena," since all the "effective means of inducing political changes are left free."

The very purpose of a Bill of Rights was to withdraw certain subjects from the vicissitudes of political controversy, to place them beyond the reach of majorities and officials and to establish them as legal principles to be applied by the courts. One's right to life, liberty, and property, to free speech, a free press, freedom of worship and assembly, and other fundamental rights may not be submitted to vote; they depend on the outcome of no elections.

In weighing arguments of the parties it is important to distinguish between the due process clause of the Fourteenth Amendment as an instrument for transmitting the principles of the First Amendment and those cases in which it is applied for its own sake. The test of legislation which collides with the Fourteenth Amendment, because it also collides with the principles of the First, is much more definite than the test when only the Fourteenth is involved. Much of the vagueness of the due process clause disappears when the specific prohibitions of the First become its standard. The right of a State to regulate, for example, a public utility may well include, so far as the due process test is concerned, power to impose all of the restrictions which a legislature may have a "rational basis" for adopting. But freedoms of speech and of press, of assembly, and of worship may not be infringed on such slender grounds. They are susceptible of restriction only to prevent grave and immediate danger to interests which the State may lawfully protect. It is important to note that while it is the Fourteenth Amendment which bears directly upon the State it is the more specific limiting principles of the First Amendment that finally govern this case.

Nor does our duty to apply the Bill of Rights to assertions of official authority depend upon our possession of marked competence in the field where the invasion of rights occurs. True, the task of translating the majestic generalities of the Bill of Rights, conceived as part of the pattern of liberal government in the eighteenth century, into concrete restraints on officials dealing with the problems of the twentieth century, is one to disturb self-confidence.... But we act in these matters not by authority of our competence but by force of our commissions. We cannot, because of modest estimates of our competence in such specialties as public education, withhold the judgment that history authenticates as the function of this Court when liberty is infringed.

4. Lastly, and this is the very heart of the *Gobitis* opinion, it reasons that "national unity is the basis of national security," that the authorities have "the right to select appropriate means for its attainment," and hence reaches the conclusion that such compulsory measures toward "national unity" are constitutional.... Upon the verity of this assumption depends our answer in this case.

National unity as an end which officials may foster by persuasion and example is not in question. The problem is whether under our Constitution compulsion as here employed is a permissible means for its achievement.

Struggles to coerce uniformity of sentiment in support of some end thought essential to their time and country have been waged by many good as well as by evil men. Nationalism is a relatively recent phenomenon but at other times and places the ends have been racial or territorial security, support of a dynasty or regime, and particular plans for saving souls. As first and moderate methods to attain unity have failed, those bent on its accomplishment must resort to an ever increasing severity.... Those who begin coercive elimination of dissent soon find themselves exterminating dissenters. Compulsory unification of opinion achieves only the unanimity of the graveyard.

It seems trite but necessary to say that the First Amendment to our Constitution was designed to avoid these ends by avoiding these beginnings. There is no mysticism in the American concept of the State or of the nature or origin of its authority. We set up government by consent of the governed, and the Bill of Rights denies those in power any legal opportunity to coerce that consent. Authority here is to be controlled by public opinion, not public opinion by authority.

The case is made difficult not because the principles of its decision are obscure but because the flag involved is our own. Nevertheless, we apply the limitations of the Constitution with no fear that freedom to be intellectually and spiritually diverse or even contrary will disintegrate the social organization. To believe that patriotism will not flourish if patriotic ceremonies are voluntary and spontaneous instead of a compulsory routine is to make an unflattering estimate of the appeal of our institutions to free minds. We can have intellectual individualism and the rich cultural diversities that we owe to exceptional minds only at the price of occasional eccentricity and abnormal attitudes. When they are so harmless to others or to the State as those we deal with here, the price is not too great. But freedom to differ is not limited to things that do not matter much. That would be a mere shadow of freedom. The test of its substance is the right to differ as to things that touch the heart of the existing order.

If there is any fixed star in our constitutional constellation, it is that no official, high or petty, can prescribe what shall be orthodox in politics, nationalism, religion, or other matters of opinion or force citizens to confess by word or act their faith therein. If there are any circumstances which permit an exception, they do not now occur to us.

We think the action of the local authorities in compelling the flag salute and pledge transcends constitutional limitations on their power and invades the sphere of intellect and spirit which it is the purpose of the First Amendment to our Constitution to reserve from all official control.

The decision of this Court in *Minersville School District* v. *Gobitis* ... [is] overruled, and the judgment enjoining enforcement of the West Virginia Regulation is affirmed.

[Justice BLACK, DOUGLAS, and MURPHY concurred.]

Mr. Justice FRANKFURTER, dissenting.

One who belongs to the most vilified and persecuted minority in history is not likely to be insensible to the freedoms guaranteed by our Constitution. Were my purely personal attitude relevant I should wholeheartedly associate myself with the general libertarian views in the Court's opinion, representing as they do the thought and action of a lifetime. But as judges we are neither Jew nor Gentile, neither Catholic nor agnostic. We owe equal attachment to the Constitution and are equally bound by our judicial obligations whether we derive our citizenship from the earliest or the latest immigrants to these shores. As a member of this Court I am not justified in writing my private notions of policy into the Constitution, no matter how deeply I may cherish them or how mischievous I may deem their disregard. The duty of a judge who must decide which of two claims before the Court shall prevail, that of a state to enact and enforce laws within its general competence or that of an individual to refuse obedience because of the demands of his conscience, is not that of the ordinary person. It can never be emphasized too much that one's own opinion about the wisdom or evil of a law should be · excluded altogether when one is doing one's duty on the bench. The only opinion of our own even looking in that direction that is material is our opinion whether legislators could in reason have enacted such a law. . . .

Not so long ago we were admonished that "the only check upon our own exercise of power is our own sense of self-restraint. For the removal of unwise laws from the statute books appeal lies not to the courts but to the ballot and to the processes of democratic government." We have been told that generalities do not decide concrete cases. But the intensity with which a general principle is held may determine a particular issue, and whether we put first things first may decide a specific controversy.

When Mr. Justice Holmes, speaking for the Court, wrote "it must be remembered that legislatures are ultimate guardians of the liberties and welfare of the people in quite as great a degree as the courts," he went to the very essence of our constitutional system and the democratic conception of our society. He did not mean that for only some phases of civil government this Court was not to supplant legislatures and sit in judgment upon the right or wrong of a challenged measure. He was stating the comprehensive judicial duty and role of this Court in our constitutional scheme whenever legislation is sought to be nullified on any ground, namely, that responsibility for legislation lies with legislatures, answerable as they are directly to the people, and this Court's only and very narrow function is to determine whether within the broad grant of authority vested in legislatures they have exercised a judgment for which reasonable justification can be offered.

The reason why from the beginning even the narrow authority to nullify legislation has been viewed with a jealous eye is that it serves to prevent the full play of the democratic process. The fact that it may be an undemocratic aspect of our scheme of government does not call for its rejection or its disuse. But it is the best of reasons, as this Court has frequently recognized, for the greatest caution in its use.

If the function of this Court is to be essentially no different from that of a legislature, if the considerations governing constitutional construction are to be substantially those that underlie legislation, then indeed judges should not have life tenure and they should be made directly responsible to the electorate. There have been many but unsuccessful proposals in the last sixty years to amend the Constitution to that end.

Jefferson's opposition to judicial review has not been accepted by history, but it still serves as an admonition against confusion between judicial and political functions. As a rule of judicial self-restraint, it is still as valid as Lincoln's admonition. For those who pass laws not only are under duty to pass laws. They are also under duty to observe the Constitution. And even though legislation relates to civil liberties, our duty of deference to those who have the responsibility for making the laws is no less relevant or less exacting. . . .

Of course, patriotism cannot be enforced by the flag salute. But neither can the liberal spirit be enforced by judicial invalidation of illiberal legislation. Our constant preoccupation with the constitutionality of legislation rather than with its wisdom tends to preoccupation of the American mind with a false value. The tendency of focusing attention on constitutionality is to make constitutionality synonymous with wisdom, to regard a law as all right if it is constitutional. Such an attitude is a great enemy of liberalism. Particularly in legislation affecting freedom of thought and freedom of speech much which should offend a free-spirited society is constitutional. Reliance for the most precious interests of civilization, therefore, must be found outside of their vindication in courts of law. Only a persistent positive translation of the faith of a free society into the convictions and habits and actions of a community is the ultimate reliance against unabated temptation to fetter the human spirit.

. . . . .

[Mr. Justice ROBERTS and Mr. Justice REED also dissented.]

2. RELIGIOUS LIBERTY AND THE SCHOOLS
HISTORICAL NOTE

The First Amendment to the Constitution embodies not only the guarantee of freedom of religious thought and practice, but also the principle of the separation of church and state. Not until 1947, however, was the import of this prohibition of an "establishment of religion" made a direct issue before the Supreme Court. On previous occasions, conflicts between educational policies of the states and claims of religious groups had been adjudged by reference to constitutional provisions other than the First Amendment's religious clauses. In *Pierce* v. *Society of Sisters*, 268 U.S. 510 (1925), the Court struck down an Oregon statute which would have compelled children to attend the public schools of the state, thus forestalling attendance at private (and parochial) schools. This was interpreted as an attempt to destroy such private schools, hence as a taking of property without due process of law. Leaning on *Meyer* v. *Nebraska,* the Court also declared that parents would be denied the liberty—guaranteed by the Fourteenth Amendment—of directing the upbringing and education of their children.

In *Hamilton* v. *Regents of the University of California*, 293 U.S. 245 (1934), Methodist students at the University of California had been suspended from that institution because of their refusal to participate in the compulsory R.O.T.C. program. They claimed denial of "liberty" under the Fourteenth Amendment but the Supreme Court declined to see the dilemma through their eyes. Their "liberty," the Court found, "undoubtedly" included the right to object to military training because of their religious beliefs; but "California has not drafted or called them to attend the University." Attendance at state institutions of higher learning was thus not viewed as a right but as a privilege which may be conditioned. (Query: In the light of the Supreme Court's change of mind with regard to naturalization of conscientious objectors, and considering also such new approaches to higher education as the G.I. Bill and the report of the President's Committee on Higher Education, does the rule of the *Hamilton* case continue to express public policy?)

EVERSON v. BOARD OF EDUCATION
330 U.S. 1 (1947)

Mr. Justice BLACK delivered the opinion of the Court.

A New Jersey statute authorizes its local school districts to make rules and contracts for the transportation of children to and from schools. The appellee, a township board of education, acting pursuant to this statute, authorized reimbursements to parents of money expended by them for the bus transportation of their children on regular busses operated by the public transportation system. Part of this money was for the payment of transportation of some children in the community to Catholic parochial schools. These church schools give their students, in addition to secular education, regular religious instruction conforming to the religious tenets and modes of worship of the Catholic faith. The superintendent of these schools is a Catholic priest.

The appellant, in his capacity as a district taxpayer, filed suit in a state court challenging the right of the board to reimburse parents of parochial school students. He contended that the statute and the resolution passed pursuant to it violated both the state and federal Constitutions. That court held that the legislature was without power to authorize such payments under the state constitution. . . . The New Jersey Court of Errors and Appeals[4] reversed, holding that neither the statute nor the resolution passed pursuant to it was in conflict with the state constitution or the provisions of the federal constitution in issue. . . .

*   *   *   *   *

The only contention here is that the state statute and the resolution, insofar as they authorized reimbursement to parents of children attending parochial schools, violate the federal Constitution in these two respects, which to some extent overlap. *First.* They authorize the state to take by taxation the private property of some and bestow it upon others, to be used for their own private purposes. This, it is alleged, violates the due process clause of the Fourteenth Amendment. *Second.* The statute and the resolution forced inhabitants to pay taxes to help support and maintain schools which are dedicated

[4] Then the supreme judicial tribunal of the state.

to, and which regularly teach, the Catholic faith. This is alleged to be use of state power to support church schools contrary to the prohibition of the First Amendment which the Fourteenth Amendment made applicable to the states.

First. . . . The New Jersey legislature has decided that a public purpose will be served by using tax-raised funds to pay the bus fares of school children, including those who attend parochial schools. The New Jersey Court of Errors and Appeals has reached the same conclusion. The fact that a state law, passed to satisfy a public need, coincides with the personal desires of the individuals most directly affected is certainly an inadequate reason for us to say that a legislature has erroneously appraised the public need.

Second. The New Jersey law is challenged as a "law respecting the establishment of religion." The First Amendment, as made applicable to the states by the Fourteenth, . . . commands that a state "shall make no law respecting an establishment of religion, or prohibiting the free exercise thereof." . . .These words of the First Amendment reflected in the minds of early Americans a vivid mental picture of conditions and practices which they fervently wished to stamp out in order to preserve liberty for themselves and for their posterity. Doubtless their goal has not been entirely reached; but so far has the nation moved toward it that the expression "law respecting the establishment of religion," probably does not so vividly remind present-day Americans of the evils, fears, and political problems that caused that expression to be written into our Bill of Rights. Whether this New Jersey law is one respecting an "establishment of religion" requires an understanding of the meaning of that language, particularly with respect to the imposition of taxes. . . . Therefore, it is not inappropriate briefly to review the background and environment of the period in which that constitutional language was fashioned and adopted.

[There follows a brief narrative of pre-Revolutionary conditions and of the struggle of the colonists for emancipation from the established Church of England, particularly as exemplified by Jefferson's and Madison's struggle for a religious liberty statute in Virginia. The Court refers to some of its own constructions of that portion of the First Amendment relating to the free exercise of religion, approves a state court's formulation of the inter-relationship of freedom of religious practice and separation of church and state, and concludes that—:]

The "establishment of religion" clause in the First Amendment means at least this: Neither a state nor the federal government can set up a church. Neither can pass laws which aid one religion, aid all religion, or prefer one religion over another. Neither can force nor influence a person to go to or remain away from church against his will or force him to profess a belief or disbelief in any religion. No person can be punished for entertaining or professing religious beliefs or disbeliefs, for church attendance or non-attendance. No tax in any amount, large or small, can be levied to support any religious activities or institutions, whatever they may be called or whatever form they may adopt to teach or practice religion. Neither a state nor the federal government can, openly or secretly, participate in the affairs of any religious organizations or groups or vice versa. In the words of Jefferson, the clause against establishment of religion by law was intended to erect "a wall of separation between Church and State." . . .

We must consider the New Jersey statute in accordance with the foregoing limitations imposed by the First Amendment. But we must not strike that state statute down if it is within the state's constitutional power even though it approaches the verge of that power. . . . New Jersey cannot consistently with the "establishment of religion" clause of the First Amendment contribute tax-raised funds to the support of an institution which teaches the tenets and faith of any church. On the other hand, other language of the amendment commands that New Jersey cannot hamper its citizens in the free exercise of their own religion. Consequently, it cannot exclude individual Catholics, Lutherans, Mohammedans, Baptists, Jews, Methodists, Non-believers, Presbyterians, or the members of any other faith, *because of their faith, or lack of it,* from receiving the benefits of public welfare legislation. . . .

Measured by these standards, we cannot say that the First Amendment prohibits New Jersey from spending tax-raised funds to pay the bus fares of parochial school pupils as a part of a general program under which it pays the fares of pupils attending public and other schools. . . . [The transportation of children to their schools is considered in the same category by the Court as the provision of police protection near school crossings, the availability of fire protection and of sanitary community facilities.] ... Of course, cutting off schurch schools from these services, so separate and so indisputably marked off from the religious function, would make it far more difficult for the schools to operate. But such is obviously not the purpose of the First Amendment. That Amendment requires the state to be a neutral in its relations with groups of religious believers and non-believers; it does not require the state to be their adversary. State power is no more to be used so as to handicap religions than it is to favor them.

This Court has said that parents may, in the discharge of their duty under state compulsory education laws, send their children to a religious rather than a public school if the school meets the secular educational requirements which the state has the power to impose. See *Pierce* v. *Society of Sisters*, 268 U.S. 510. It appears that these parochial schools meet New Jersey's requirements. The state contributes no money to the schools. It does not support them. Its legislation, as applied, does no more than provide a general program to help parents get their children, regardless of their religion, safely and expeditiously to and from accredited schools.

The First Amendment has erected a wall between church and state. That wall must be kept high and impregnable. We could not approve the slightest breach. New Jersey has not breached it here.

Affirmed.

Mr. Justice JACKSON, dissenting.

. . . . .

The Court sustains this legislation by assuming two deviations from the facts of this particular case; first, it assumes a state of facts the record does not support, and secondly, it refuses to consider facts which are inescapable on the record.

. . . . .

The Township of Ewing is not furnishing transportation to the children in any form; it is not operating school busses itself or contracting for their operation; and it is not performing any public service of any kind with this taxpayer's money. All school children are left to ride as ordinary passengers on the regular busses operated by the public transportation system. What the Township does, and what the taxpayer complains of, is at stated intervals to reimburse parents for the fares paid, provided the children attend either public schools or Catholic church schools. This expenditure of tax funds has no possible effect on the . . . child's safety or expedition in transit. As passengers on the public busses they travel as fast and no faster, and are as safe and no safer, since their parents are reimbursed as before.

In addition to thus assuming a type of service that does not exist, the Court also insists that we must close our eyes to a discrimination which does exist. . . . If we are to decide this case on the facts before us, our question is simply this: Is it constitutional to tax this complainant to pay the cost of carrying pupils to church schools of one specified denomination?

Whether the taxpayer constitutionally can be made to contribute aid to parents of students because of their attendance at parochial schools depends upon the nature of those schools and their relation to the church. . . .

[There follow extensive quotations from the Canon Law of the Roman Catholic Church, showing that body's position with regard to the education of children and the maintenance of parochial schools.]

. . . The Roman Catholic Church, counseled by experience in many ages and many lands and with all sorts and conditions of men, takes what, from the viewpoint of its own progress and the success of its mission, is a wise estimate of the importance of education to religion. It does not leave the individual to pick up religion by chance. It relies on early and indelible indoctrination in the faith and order of the Church by the word and example of persons consecrated to the task. . . . Catholic education is the rock on which the whole structure rests, and to render tax aid to its church school is indistinguishable to me from rendering the same aid to the church itself.

. . . If these principles seem harsh in prohibiting aid to Catholic education, it must not be forgotten that it is the same Constitution that alone assures Catholics the right to maintain these schools at all when predominant local sentiment would forbid them. *Pierce* v. *Society of Sisters,* 268 U.S. 510. Nor should I think that those who have done so well without this aid would want to see this separation of church and state broken down. If the state may aid these religious schools, it may therefore regulate them. . . . "It is hardly lack of due process for the government to regulate that which it subsidizes." *Wickard* v. *Filburn*, 317 U.S. 111, 131. . . .

Mr. Justice FRANKFURTER joins in this opinion.

Mr. Justice RUTLEDGE, with whom Mr. Justice FRANKFURTER, Mr. Justice JACKSON and Mr. Justice BURTON agree, dissenting.

. . . .

Not simply an established church, but any law respecting an establishment of religion is forbidden. The Amendment was broadly but not loosely phrased. It is the compact and exact summation of its author's views formed during his long struggle for religious freedom. In Madison's own words characterizing Jefferson's Bill for Establishing Religious Freedom, the guaranty he put in our national charter, like the bill he piloted through the Virginia Assembly, was "a Model of technical precision, and perspicuous brevity." Madison could not have confused "church" and "religion," or "an established church" and "an establishment of religion."

The Amendment's purpose was not to strike merely at the official establishment of a singe sect, creed or religion, outlawing only a formal relation such as had prevailed in England and some of the colonies. Necessarily it was to uproot all such relationships. But the object was broader than separating church and state in this narrow sense. It was to create a complete and permanent separation in the spheres of religious activity and civil authority by comprehensively forbidding every form of public aid or support of religion. In proof the Amendment's wording and history unite with the Court's consistent utterances whenever attention has been fixed directly upon the question.

[There follows an exhaustive account of the history of the First Amendment, stressing Madison's part in the attainment of religious freedom, both in his home state and in the union, and interpreting the concept of separation of church and state by reference to Madison's Remonstrance against the Virginia Assessment Bill of 1785. The text of this document is appended to the dissenting opinion in the reports.]

. . . .

Compulsory attendance upon religious exercises went out early in the process of separating church and state, together with forced observance of religious forms and ceremonies. Test oaths and religious qualification for office followed later. These things none devoted to our great tradition of religious liberty would think of bringing back. Hence today, apart from efforts to inject religious training or exercises and sectarian issues into the public schools, the only serious surviving threat to maintaining that complete and permanent separation of religion and civil power which the First Amendment commands is through use of the taxing power to support religion, religious establishments, or establishments having a religious foundation whatever their form or special religious function.

Does New Jersey's action furnish support for religion by use of the taxing power? Certainly it does, if the test remains undiluted as Jefferson and Madison made it, that money taken by taxation from one is not to be used or given to support another's religious training or belief, or indeed one's own. . . .

The funds here used were raised by taxation. The Court does not dispute, nor could it, that their use does in fact give aid and encouragement to religious instruction. It only concludes that this aid is not "support" in law. But . . . here parents pay money to send their children to parochial schools and funds raised by taxation are used to reimburse them. This not only helps the children to get to school and the parents to send them. It aids them in a substantial way to get the very thing which they are sent to the particular school to secure, namely, religious training and teaching.

.   .   .   .   .

New Jersey's action . . . exactly fits the type of exaction and the kind of evil at which Madison and Jefferson struck. Under the test they framed it cannot be said that the cost of transportation is no part of the cost of education or of the religious instruction given. That it is a substantial and a necessary element is shown by the continuous and increasing demand for the state to assume it. . . .

Our constitutional policy . . . does not deny the value or the necessity for religious training, teaching or observance. Rather it secures their free exercise. But to that end it does deny that the state can undertake or sustain them in any form or degree. For this reason the sphere of religious activity, as distinguished from the secular intellectual liberties, has been given the twofold protection and, as the state cannot forbid, neither can it perform or aid in performing the religious function. The dual prohibition makes that function altogether private. It cannot be made a public one by legislative act. This was the very heart . . . of the Amendment. . . .

By no declaration that a gift of public money to religious uses will promote the general or individual welfare, or the cause of education generally, can legislative bodies overcome the Amendment's bar. . . . Legislatures are free to make, and courts to sustain, appropriations only when it can be found that in fact they do not aid, promote, encourage or sustain religious teaching or observances, be the amount large or small. No such finding has been or could be made in this case. The Amendment has removed this form of promoting the public welfare from legislative and judicial competence to make a public function. It is exclusively a private affair.

.   .   .   .   .

Two drives are constantly in motion to abridge, in the name of education, the complete division of religion and civil authority which our forefathers made. One is to introduce religious education and observances into the public schools. The other, to obtain public funds for the aid and support of various religious schools. . . . In my opinion both avenues were closed by the Constitution. Neither should be opened by this Court. The matter is not one of quantity, to be measured by the amount of money expended. Now as in Madison's day it is one of principle, to keep separate the separate spheres as the First Amendment drew them; to prevent the first experiment upon our liberties; and to keep the question from becoming entangled in corrosive precedents. We should not be less strict to keep strong and untarnished the one side of the shield of religious freedom than we have been of the other.

The judgment should be reversed.

ILLINOIS ex rel. McCOLLUM v. BOARD OF EDUCATION
333 U.S. 203 (1948)

Mr. Justice BLACK delivered the opinion of the Court.

This case relates to the power of a state to utilize its tax-supported public school system in aid of religious instruction insofar as that power may be restricted by the First and Fourteenth Amendments to the Constitution.

The appellant, Vashti McCollum, began this action for mandamus against the Champaign Board of Education in the Circuit Court of Champaign County, Illinois. Her asserted interest was that of a resident and taxpayer of Champaign and of a parent whose child was then enrolled in the Champaign public schools. Illinois has a compulsory education law which, with exceptions, requires parents to send their children, aged seven to sixteen, to its tax-supported public schools where the children are to remain in attendance during the hours when the schools are regularly in session. Parents who violate this law commit a misdemeanor punishable by fine unless the children attend private or parochial schools which meet educational standards fixed by the state. District boards of education are given general supervisory powers over the use of the public school buildings within the school district. . . .

Appellant's petition for mandamus alleged that religious teachers, employed by private religious groups, were permitted to come weekly into the school buildings during the regular hours set apart for secular teaching, and then and there for a period of thirty minutes substitute their religious teaching for the secular education provided under the compulsory education law. The petitioner charged that this joint public-school, religious-group program violated the First and Fourteeenth Amendments to the Constitution of the United States. The prayer of her petition was that the Board of Education be ordered to "adopt and enforce rules and regulations prohibiting all instruction in and teaching of religious education in all public schools in Champaign District Number 71, . . . and in all public school houses and buildings in said district when occupied by public schools."

The board . . . admitted that regular weekly religious instruction was given during school hours to those pupils whose parents consented and that those pupils were released temporarily from their regular secular classes for the limited purpose of attending the religious classes. . . . Much evidence was heard, findings of fact were made, after which the petition for mandamus was denied on the ground that the school's religious instruction program violated neither the federal nor state constitutional provisions invoked by the appellant. On appeal the state supreme court affirmed. . . .

. . . . . .

Although there are disputes between the parties as to various inferences that may or may not be drawn from the evidence concerning the religious program, the following facts are shown by the record without dispute: . . . [In a footnote Justice Black records at this point that appellant had also alleged that in practice certain Protestant groups had obtained an "overshadowing advantage" over other Protestant groups, that the program was voluntary in name only, and that the school superintendent's power to reject religious teachers selected by the religious groups constituted state censorship of religious activities; in the light of the Court's decision, it is noted, it was found unnecessary to enter into these arguments.] In 1940 interested members of the Jewish, Roman Catholic, and a few of the Protestant faiths formed a voluntary association called the Champaign Council of Religious Education. They obtained permission from the Board of Education to offer classes in religious instruction to public school pupils in grades four to nine inclusive. Classes were made up of pupils whose parents signed printed cards requesting that their children be permitted to attend; they were held weekly, thirty minutes for the lower grades, forty-five minutes for the higher. The council employed the religious teachers at no expense to the school authorities, but the instructors were subject to the approval and supervision of the superintendent of schools. The classes were taught in three separate religious groups by Protestant teachers, Catholic priests, and a Jewish rabbi, although for the past several years there have apparently been no classes instructed in the Jewish religion. Classes were conducted in the regular classrooms of the school building. Students who did not choose to take the religious instruction were not released from public school duties; they were required to leave their classrooms and go to some other place in the school building for pursuit of their secular studies. On the other hand, students who were released from secular study for the religious instructions were required to be present at the religious classes. Reports of their presence or absence were to be made to their secular teachers.

The foregoing facts, without reference to others that appear in the record, show the use of tax-supported property for religious instruction and the close cooperation between school authorities and the religious council in promoting religious education. The operation of the state's compulsory education system thus assists and is integrated with the program of religious instruction carried on by separate religious sects. Pupils compelled by law to go to school for secular education are released in part from their legal duty upon the condition that they attend the religious classes. This is beyond all question a utilization of the tax-established and tax-supported public school system to aid religious groups to spread their faith. And it falls squarely under the ban of the First Amendment (made applicable to the States by the Fourteenth) as we interpreted it in *Everson* v. *Board of Education,* 330 U.S. 1. . . .

To hold that a state cannot consistently with the First and Fourteenth Amendments utilize its public school system to aid any or all religious faiths or sects in the dissemination of their doctrines and ideals does not, as counsel urge, manifest a governmental hostility to religion or religious teachings. A manifestation of such hostility would be at war with our national tradition as embodied in the First Amendment's guaranty of the free exercise of religion. For the First Amendment rests upon the premise that both religion and government can best work to achieve their lofty aims if each is left free from the other within its respective sphere. Or, as we said in the *Everson* case, the First Amendment has erected a wall between Church and State which must be kept high and impregnable.

Here not only are the state's tax-supported public schools used for the dissemination of religious doctrines. The state also affords sectarian groups an invaluable aid in that it helps to provide pupils for their religious classes through use of the state's compulsory public school machinery. This is not separation of Church and State.

The cause is reversed and remanded to the state supreme court for proceedings not inconsistent with this opinion.

Mr. Justice FRANKFURTER delivered the following opinion, in which Mr. Justice JACKSON, Mr. Justice RUTLEDGE and Mr. Justice BURTON join (Mr. Justice RUTLEDGE and Mr. Justice BURTON also concurred in the Court's opinion).

We dissented in *Everson* v. *Board of Education,* 330 U.S. 1, because in our view the constitutional principle requiring separation of Church and State compelled invalidation of the ordinance sustained by the majority. Illinois has here authorized the commingling of sectarian with secular instruction in the public schools. The Constitution of the United States forbids this.

This case, in the light of the *Everson* decision, demonstrates anew that the mere formulation of a relevant constitutional principle is the beginning of the solution of a problem, not its answer. This is so because the meaning of a spacious conception like that of the separation of Church from State is unfolded as appeal is made to the principle from case to case. We are all agreed that the First and the Fourteenth Amendments have a secular reach far more penetrating in the conduct of government than merely to forbid an "established church." But agreement, in the abstract, that the First Amendment was designed to erect a "wall of separation between Church and State," does not preclude a clash of views as to what the wall separates. Involved is not only the constitutional principle but the implications of judicial review in its enforcement. Accommodation of legislative freedom and constitutional limitations upon that freedom cannot be achieved by a mere phrase. We cannot illuminatingly apply the "wall-of-separation" metaphor until we have considered the relevant history of religious education in America, the place of the "released time" movement in that history, and its precise manifestation in the case before us.

[There follows an extended discussion of these three points, leading the Justice to the conclusions that (a) "Separation in the field of education . . . was not imposed upon unwilling states by force of superior law," but was "a recognition of the need of a democratic society to educate its children, insofar as the state undertook to do so, in an atmosphere free from pressures in a realm in which pressures are most resisted and where conflicts are most easily and most bitterly engendered"; (b) " 'released time' as a generalized conception, undefined by differentiating particularities, is not an issue for constitutional adjudication. . . . It is only when challenge is made to the share that the public schools have in the execution of a particular 'released time' program that close judicial scrutiny is demanded of the exact relation between the religious instruction and the public educational system in the specific situation before the Court;" and (c) in Champaign, "the momentum of the whole school atmosphere and school planning is presumably put behind religious instruction, precisely in order to secure for the religious instruction such momentum and planning."]

Mr. Justice JACKSON, concurring.

I join in the opinion of Mr. Justice Frankfurter, and concur in the result reached by the Court, but with these reservations: I think it is doubtful whether the facts of this case establish jurisdiction in this Court, but in any event that we should place some bounds on the demands for interference with local schools that we are empowered or willing to entertain. I make these reservations a matter of record in view of the number of litigations likely to be started as a result of this decision.

A federal court may interfere with local school authorities only when they invade either a personal liberty or a property right protected by the federal Constitution. Ordinarily this will come about in either of two ways:

First. When a person is required to submit to some religious rite or instruction or is deprived or threatened with deprivation of his freedom for resisting such unconstitutional requirement. We may then set him free or enjoin such prosecution. Typical of such cases was *West Virginia State Bd. of Edu.* v. *Barnette,* 319 U.S. 624....

Second. Where a complainant is deprived of property by being taxed for unconstitutional purposes, such as directly or indirectly to support a religious establishment. We can protect a taxpayer against such a levy. This was the *Everson* case, 330 U.S. 1, ... as I saw it then and as I see it now....

[The appellant, Justice Jackson argues, cannot claim injury on either count.]

If, however, jurisdiction is found to exist, it is important that we circumscribe our decision with some care. What is asked is not a defensive use of judicial power to set aside a tax levy or reverse a conviction, or to enjoin threats of prosecution or taxation. The relief demanded in this case is the extraordinary writ of mandamus to tell the local Board of Education what it must do.... The plaintiff, as she has every right to be, is an avowed atheist. What she has asked of the courts is that they not only end the "released time" plan but also ban every form of teaching which suggests or recognizes that there is a God. She would ban all teaching of the Scriptures. She especially mentions as an example of invasion of her rights "having pupils learn and recite such statements as 'The Lord is my Shepherd, I shall not want.' " And she objects to teaching that the King James version of the Bible "is called the Christian's Guide Book, the Holy Writ and the Word of God," and many other similar matters. This Court is directing the Illinois courts generally to sustain plaintiff's complaint without exception of any of these grounds of complaints, without discriminating between them and without laying down any standard to define the limits of the effect of our decision.

To me, the sweep and detail of these complaints is a danger signal which warns of the kind of local controversy we will be required to arbitrate if we do not place appropriate limitation on our decision and exact strict compliance with jurisdictional requirements. Authorities list 256 separate and substantial religious bodies to exist in continental United States. Each of them, through the suit of some discontented but unpenalized and untaxed representative, has as good a right as this plaintiff to demand that the courts compel the schools to sift out of their teaching everything inconsistent with its doctrines. If we are to eliminate everything that is objectionable to any of these warring sects or inconsistent with any of their doctrines, we will leave public education in shreds. Nothing but educational confusion and a discrediting of the public school system can result from subjecting it to constant law suits.

While we may and should end such formal and explicit instruction as the Champaign plan and can at all times prohibit teaching of creed and catechism and ceremonial and can forbid forthright proselyting in the schools, I think it remains to be demonstrated whether it is possible, even if desirable, to comply with such demands as plaintiff's completely to isolate and cast out of secular education all that some people may reasonably regard as religious instruction. . . . The fact is that, for good or for ill, nearly everything in our culture worth transmitting, everything which gives meaning to life, is saturated with religious influences, derived from paganism, Judaism, Christianity—both Catholic and Protestant—and other faiths accepted by a large part of the world's peoples. . . .

The task of separating the secular from the religious in education is one of magnitude, intricacy, and delicacy. To lay down a sweeping constitutional doctrine as demanded by complainant and apparently approved by the Court, applicable alike to all school boards of the nation, "to immediately adopt and enforce rules and regulations prohibiting all instruction in and teaching of religious education in all public schools," is to decree a uniform, rigid and, if we are consistent, an unchanging standard for countless school boards representing and serving highly localized groups which not only differ from each other but which themselves from time to time change attitudes. It seems to me that to do so is to allow zeal for our own ideas of what is good in public instruction to induce us to accept the role of a super board of education for every school district in the nation.

· · · · · ·

Mr. Justice REED, dissenting.

. . . I find it difficult to extract from the opinions any conclusion as to what it is in the Champaign plan that is unconstitutional. Is it the use of school buildings for religious instruction; the release of pupils by the schools for religious instruction during school hours;

the so-called assistance by teachers in handing out the request cards to pupils, in keeping lists of them for release and records of their attendance; or the action of the principals in arranging an opportunity for the classes and the appearance of the Council's instructors? None of the reversing opinions say whether the purpose of the Champaign plan for religious instruction during school hours is unconstitutional or whether it is some ingredient used in or omitted from the formula that makes the plan unconstitutional.

. . . From the holding and the language of the opinions I can only deduce that religious instruction of public school children during school hours is prohibited. The history of American education is against such an interpretation of the First Amendment.

.   .   .   .   .

. . . The "wall of separation between Church and State" that Mr. Jefferson built at the University which he founded did not exclude religious education from that school. . . . Mr. Madison's approval of Mr. Jefferson's report as Rector [of the University of Virginia; the report extended an invitation to religious sects to establish facilities near the University] gives, in my opinion, a clearer indication of his views on the constitutionality of religious education in public schools than his general statements on a different subject [the Remonstrance against Religious Assessments relied upon by the dissenting Justices in the *Everson* case].

. . . All churches receive "aid" from government in the form of freedom from taxation. The *Everson* decision itself justified the transportation of children to church schools by New Jersey for safety reasons. It accords with *Cochran* v. *Louisiana State Bd. of Edu.*, 281 U.S. 370, where this Court upheld a free textbook statute of Louisiana against a charge that it aided private schools on the ground that the books were for the education of children, not to aid religious schools. Likewise the National School Lunch Act (Act of June 4, 1946, 60 Stat. 230) aids all school children attending tax exempt schools. . . .

.   .   .   .   .

Cases running into the scores have been in the state courts of last resort that involved religion and the schools. Except where the exercises with religious significance partook of the ceremonial practice of sects or groups, their constitutionality has been generally upheld. . . .

The practices of the federal government offer many examples of this kind of "aid" by the state to religion. The Congress of the United States has a chaplain for each House who daily invokes divine blessings and guidance for the proceedings. The armed forces have commissioned chaplains from early days. They conduct the public services in accordance with the liturgical requirements of their respective faiths, ashore and afloat, employing for the purpose property belonging to the United States and dedicated to the services of religion. Under the Servicemen's Readjustment Act of 1944 ["G.I. Bill"], eligible veterans may receive training at government expense for the ministry in denominational schools. The schools of the District of Columbia have opening exercises which "include a reading from the Bible without note or comment, and the Lord's prayer."

In the United States Naval Academy and the United States Military Academy, schools wholly supported and completely controlled by the federal government, there are a number of religious activities. Chaplains are attached to both schools. Attendance at church services on Sunday is compulsory at both the Military and Naval Academies; . . . both schools since their earliest beginnings have maintained and enforced a pattern of participation in formal worship.

With the general statements in the opinions concerning the constitutional requirement that the nation and the states, by virtue of the First and Fourteenth Amendments, may "make no law respecting an establishment of religion," I am in agreement. But, in the light of the meaning given to those words by the precedents, customs, and practices which I have detailed above, I cannot agree with the Court's conclusion that when pupils compelled by law to go to school for secular education are released from school so as to attend the religious classes, churches are unconstitutionally aided. Whatever may be the wisdom of the arrangement as to the use of the school buildings made with the Champaign Council of Religious Education, it is clear to me that past practice shows such cooperation between the schools and a non-ecclesiastical body is not forbidden by the First Amendment. . . . Devotion to the great principle of religious liberty should not lead us into a rigid interpretation of the constitutional guarantees that conflicts with accepted habits of our people. This is an instance where, for me, the history of past practices is determinative of the meaning of a constitutional clause not a decorous introduction to the study of its text. The judgment should be affirmed.

[The Supreme Court of Albany County, New York, on November 12, 1948, sustained the State Department of Education in granting "released time" periods for school children to receive religious education off school grounds. The suit had been brought by a taxpayer who contended that the practice violated the Supreme Court's ruling in the *McCollum* case.

[Justice Elsworth ruled that the Illinois case and the New York case differ in a number of respects, and that the United States Supreme Court had not intended to hand down a blanket ruling covering the entire subject of released time. He said that in New York school children leave the school area, that the teachers take no part in religious instruction, and that no public funds are spent. The only participation of the public school system in the program of religious instruction is to require the student's parent or guardian to submit a statement asking for the pupil's release for the period of religious instruction, and to demand proof that, when released, the pupil actually attended such instruction. Students not electing to take religious instruction remain in their class rooms "continuing significant educational work." *Lewis* v. *Spalding*, 85 N.Y.S. (2d) 682.

[The *McCollum* decision has given rise to widespread debate and criticism. The Catholic hierarchy, in an official release, charged the Supreme Court with the "establishment of secularism in the schools." New York *Times*, November 21, 1948, Section I, p. 63. Jewish and Protestant groups have also been critical of the result. Legal as well as sociological aspects of the controversy are aired in the several contributions to a symposium "Religion and the State," 14 *Law and Contemporary Problems* 1–159 (1949).]

CHAPTER XIII

Constitutional Limits to Criminal Procedure

1. LAW ENFORCEMENT AND LIBERTY

NEEDS OF SOCIETY AND DEMANDS OF FREEDOM

Scattered from the Fourth to the Eighth Amendment to the Constitution are a number of provisions aiming at the protection of persons accused of crime. In each case the appearance of the protective clause in the Bill of Rights can be traced either to abuses current in England in the seventeenth or eighteenth century or to improvements in the criminal procedure of the mother country so recent in date that it seemed desirable to anchor them in the fundamental law. It is probably not without value to recall that the Star Chamber was of as recent memory with the Founding Fathers as the Civil War or the California gold rush is with our generation. And criminal procedure was only then in the process of transition from the notions of repression and terror to the evolution of a contest that matched disparate strength on an even basis.

Because the procedural guarantees of the Bill of Rights are emphatically the result of contemporary conditions, their utilization and adaptation to twentieth-century needs has been neither uniform nor altogether consistent. This diversity has probably been the principal obstacle in the Court's efforts to relate these several guarantees to the due-process concept of the Fourteenth Amendment. For the history of the procedural guarantees is in itself proof of the unequal weight attached to the several clauses by our society. Rare, for instance, have been the occasions when the guarantee of a speedy trial was invoked (Amendment VI). Does this mean that delays in bringing persons to trial are infrequent, or that they are not considered of sufficient importance to warrant a challenge in court?

The Supreme Court has, as in other fields so here, adjusted itself to the currents of the day. It has read more stringent requirements of assistance by counsel into the Sixth Amendment[1] in recognition of the increasing occurrence of technical criteria in the criminal law. On the other hand, the Court has shown little inclination to insist on a trial by jury, an institution once held sacred but more recently sharply challenged as to its adequacy under modern conditions.[2]

The problem involves, of course, more than mere textual interpretation. Not only do society's notions of criminal justice change but crime itself does not stand still. The highly organized "gangs" of the twentieth century are hardly comparable to the highway bandits of "lawless" eras in our history. The methods of crime, it can easily be observed, have not lagged behind the progress of the machine age. Can nation-wide gambling syndicates be controlled by the means devised to catch chicken thieves? The scope and utility of these means of crime control are circumscribed by the several constitutional guarantees here discussed. Society's interest in law and order makes itself constantly felt, pressing for an interpretation of these guarantees narrow enough so as not to impede the efforts of the police. Opposed to this tendency is the traditional fear of arbitrary officialdom, an aversion which, of course, figured very largely in the minds of the generation of 1776. There is some evidence that in more recent years some elements at least of the police have achieved a position of public esteem which enables them to employ methods normally denied to organs of the state.[3]

The society which thus approves of official efforts to combat and control crime can, of course, hardly be compared with that of the Founding Fathers. "An Englishman's home is his castle," translated into more legal language in the Fourth Amendment, had a different applicability in the days of one-family farm homes than it could be

---

[1] *Johnson* v. *Zerbst,* 304 U.S. 458 (1938).

[2] In *Hawaii* v. *Mankichi,* 190 U.S. 197 (1903), trial by jury was said *not* to be fundamental to our constitutional system. In *Patton* v. *United States,* 281 U.S. 276 (1930), it was held that the right to such a trial could be waived. See Becker, *infra,* for a typical criticism of the jury system.

[3] See, e.g., editorial, "FBI—Outside the Law?" in *The Nation,* vol. 170, p. 99 (1950).

given in our age of apartment-dwelling. Nor should it be overlooked that the range of activities considered criminal has undergone vast expansion and modification. Are the stipulations of the Bill of Rights still adequate under such conditions? Is individual freedom effectively guaranteed by an insistence on indictment by grand jury? Does the citizen still need this protection against servile crown prosecutors —or is he perhaps more in need of safeguards against the "ordeal by slander"?

This section offers a point of departure for the discussion of these conflicts in our society by the inclusion of Professor Becker's criticism of the jury system and of a recent decision on the subject of search warrants. The succeeding section will show the Supreme Court's reluctance to conclude that anything and everything in the Bill of Rights is of such advantageous character that it should prevail in the state as well as in the federal realm. The Court's halfway stand on the extension of the Bill of Rights to the states exemplifies the point made above: that some of these guarantees may no longer serve articulate needs of society nor add to the protection of the individual to a measurable extent.

TRIAL BY JURY IN OUR AGE[4]

Of all our civil liberties, few are more celebrated than the right of a person charged with crime to a trial by a jury of his peers. The right was established in England at a time when it was thought that the neighbors of a man accused of crime would know more about the circumstances of the crime and the persons involved in it than anyone else, and could therefore render a more just judgment. Today the prime qualification for service on a jury is complete ignorance of the circumstances of the crime and of the persons involved in it. Jury trial in criminal cases has become a carefully staged combat between two sets of skilled attorneys, each set primarily concerned, not with establishing the truth about the crime, but with limiting and distorting the evidence in the way best calculated, on the one side to convince the jury that the defendant is guilty, on the other to convince the jury that he is innocent. The function of the judge is to see that the rules of law are observed. The function of the jury is supposed to be to determine the facts. But it is obvious that the

[4] Reprinted from *Freedom and Responsibility in the American Way of Life* by Carl L. Becker, by permission of Alfred A. Knopf, Inc. Copyright 1945 by Alfred A. Knopf, Inc.

ordinary jury is quite incapable of determining the relevant facts elicited in a long and complicated trial, even if they had the full record before them and sufficient time to examine it thoroughly. This is so well understood that in some states judges are now permitted, by their comments on the evidence, to relieve the jury of an impossible task. Where that is not possible, it is scarcely too much to say that the real task of the jury is to guess, with such aid as it can, by questions, induce the judge to give, which set of attorneys has been the most adroit in confusing the witnesses and clouding the issue.

Not that any particular blame attaches to attorneys. No more than other people do they really wish to convict an innocent or discharge a guily defendant. They are prisoners of the system. Better than anyone they know that juries are incapable of performing the function assigned to them. In many states the right to be tried by a jury may now be waived by the defendant, and is rather often so waived. If jury trial works even tolerably well in states where it is compulsory, the chief reason is that by and large the legal profession is composed of men of intelligence and integrity who do the best they can, within the limitations of the system, to prevent a miscarriage of justice. It is the system that is defective; and its fundamental defect is that it proceeds on the assumption that if, within the rules of evidence, the facts are distorted twice but in opposite directions, the truth will emerge and justice will be done.

We are so familiar with trial by jury in criminal cases that it is difficult to look at it objectively. Besides, we have been taught to believe that the administration of justice in English and American courts is the best that has been developed in any society. Taken by and large, that is true. But it still remains true that trial by jury, as a method of determining facts, is antiquated, unscientific, and inherently absurd—so much so that no lawyer, judge, scholar, prescription clerk, cook, or mechanic in a garage would ever think for a moment of employing that method for determining the facts in any situation that concerned him. I am far from suggesting that the judicial process, or any part of it, should be lightly abandoned, or even reformed without the most careful consideration. But certainly in this age, when fact-finding has become very nearly an exact science, some better method could be devised for determining the guilt or innocence of a person accused of crime than one that excludes much relevant evidence, makes far too much of whatever distinction there may be between "direct" and "circumstantial" evidence, and turns the investigation over to two sets of rival attorneys whose professional success depends, not on finding out what happened, but on winning the case.

UNITED STATES v. RABINOWITZ
339 U.S. 56 (1950)

Mr. Justice MINTON delivered the opinion of the Court.

Respondent was convicted of selling and of possessing and concealing forged and altered obligations of the United States with intent to defraud. The question presented here is the reasonableness of a search without a search warrant of a place of business consisting of a one-room office, incident to a valid arrest.

On February 1, 1943, a printer who possessed plates for forging "overprints" on canceled stamps was taken into custody. He disclosed that respondent, a dealer in stamps, was one of the customers to whom he had delivered large numbers of stamps bearing forged overprints.[5] On Saturday, February 6, 1943, with this information concerning respondent and his activities in the hands of Government officers, a postal employee was sent to respondent's place of business to buy stamps bearing overprints. He bought four stamps. On Monday, February 8, the stamps were sent to an expert to determine whether the overprints were genuine. On February 9 the report was received showing the overprints to be forgeries, having been placed upon the stamps after cancellation, and not before as was the Government's practice. On February 11 a further statement was obtained from the printer who had made the overprints. On February 16, 1943, a warrant for the arrest of respondent was obtained.

In 1941 respondent had been convicted and sentenced to three months' imprisonment on a plea of guilty to a two-count indictment charging the alteration of obligations of the United States, that is, of overprinting Government postage stamps, and the possession of a plate from which a similitude of a United States obligation had been printed. Thus, when the warrant for arrest was obtained, the officers had reliable information that respondent was an old offender, that he had sold four forged and altered stamps bearing forged overprints, and that he probably possessed several thousand altered stamps bear-

[5] The stamps involved were genuine postage stamps. At certain times the Government has printed the name of a particular state or possession on stamps prior to post office sale. Canceled stamps bearing these overprints have an unusual value for stamp collectors [Footnote by the Court].

ing forged overprints. While the warrant of arrest was not put in evidence it contained, as a Government witness testified on cross-examination, authority to arrest for more than the sale of the four stamps; it covered all the Government officers' information.[6]

Armed with this valid warrant for arrest, the Government officers, accompanied by two stamp experts, went to respondent's place of business, a one-room office open to the public. The officers thereupon arrested the respondent, and over his objection searched the desk, safe, and file cabinets in the office for about an hour and a half. They found and seized 573 stamps, on which it was later determined that overprints had been forged, along with some other stamps which were subsequently returned to respondent.

Respondent was indicted on two counts. He was charged in count one with selling four forged and altered stamps, knowing they were forged and altered and with the intent that they be passed as genuine. The second count charged that he did keep in his possession and conceal, with intent to defraud, the 573 forged and altered stamps.

Respondent made timely motions for suppression and to strike the evidence pertaining to the 573 stamps, all of which were eventually denied. Respondent was convicted on both counts after trial before a jury in which he offered no evidence. Relying on *Trupiano* v. *United States*, 334 U.S. 699, the Court of Appeals, one judge dissenting, reversed on the ground that since the officers had had time in which to procure a search warrant and had failed to do so the search was illegal, and the evidence therefore should have been excluded. We granted certiorari to determine the validity of the search because of the question's importance in the administration of the law of search and seizure.

Were the 573 stamps, the fruits of this search, admissible in evidence? If legally obtained, these stamps were competent evidence to

---

[6] "Q. Now, when you went to Mr. Rabinowitz's place of business, all you had with you was a warrant to arrest him in connection with the alleged sale of those four stamps; is that correct?

A. And all information contained in the arrest warrant; yes.

Q. I didn't hear the last part of your answer.

A. In our questions a few minutes back, I stated that the four stamps were specifically mentioned in the application for the warrant for arrest, but that there was other information in my possession that was included in that warrant for arrest.

Q. Well, wasn't the warrant of arrest issued solely on the charge that Mr. Rabinowitz had sold four stamps containing false or altered overprints? Wasn't that what the warrant of arrest was issued for?

A. Primarily, yes, but not completely."

[Footnote by the Court.]

show intent under the first count of the indictment, and they were the very things the possession of which was the crime charged in the second count.

The Fourth Amendment provides:

"The right of the people to be secure in their persons, houses, papers, and effects, against unreasonable searches and seizures, shall not be violated, and no warrants shall issue, but upon probable cause, supported by oath or affirmation, and particularly describing the place to be searched, and the persons or things to be seized."

It is unreasonable searches that are prohibited by the Fourth Amendment. *Carroll* v. *United States,* 267 U.S. 132, 147. It was recognized by the framers of the Constitution that there were reasonable searches for which no warrant was required. The right of the "people to be secure in their persons" was certainly of as much concern to the framers of the Constitution as the property of the person. Yet no one questions the right, without a search warrant, to search the person after a valid arrest. The right to search the person incident to arrest always has been recognized in this country and in England. *Weeks* v. *United States,* 232 U.S. 383, 392. Where one had been placed in the custody of the law by valid action of officers, it was not unreasonable to search him.

Of course, a search without warrant incident to an arrest is dependent initially on a valid arrest. Here the officers had a warrant for respondent's arrest which was, as far as can be ascertained, broad enough to cover the crime of possession charged in the second count, and consequently respondent was properly arrested. Even if the warrant of arrest were not sufficient to authorize the arrest for possession of the stamps, the arrest therefore was valid because the officers had probable cause to believe that a felony was being committed in their very presence. *Carroll* v. *United States,* 267 U.S. 132, 156, 157.

The arrest was therefore valid in any event, and respondent's person could be lawfully searched. Could the officers search his desk, safe and file cabinets, all within plain sight of the parties, and all located under respondent's immediate control in his one-room office open to the public?

Decisions of this Court have often recognized that there is a permissible area of search beyond the person proper.

[Certain] cases condemned general exploratory searches, which cannot be undertaken by officers with or without a warrant. In the instant case the search was not general or exploratory for whatever might be turned up. Specificity was the mark of the search and seizure here. There was probable cause to believe that respondent was conducting his business illegally. The search was for stamps over-printed illegally, which were thought upon the most reliable information to be in the possession of and concealed by respondent in the very room where he was arrested, over which room he had immediate control and in which he had been selling such stamps unlawfully. . . . In all the years of our Nation's existence, with special attention to the Prohibition Era, it seems never to have been questioned seriously that a limited search such as here conducted as incident to a lawful arrest was a reasonable search and therefore valid. It has been considered in the same pattern as search of the person after lawful arrest.

What is a reasonable search is not to be determined by any fixed formula. The Constitution does not define what are "unreasonable" searches and, regrettably, in our discipline we have no ready litmus-paper test. The recurring questions of the reasonableness of searches must find resolution in the facts and circumstances of each case. *Go-Bart Importing Co.* v. *United States,* 282 U.S. 344. Reasonableness is in the first instance for the District Court to determine. We think the District Court's conclusion that here the search and seizure were reasonable should be sustained because: 1) the search and seizure were incident to a valid arrest; 2) the place of the search was a business room to which the public, including the officers, was invited; 3) the room was small and under the immediate and complete control of respondent; 4) the search did not extend beyond the room used for unlawful purposes; 5) the possession of the forged and altered stamps was a crime, just as it is a crime to possess burglars' tools, lottery tickets or counterfeit money.

Assuming that the officers had time to procure a search warrant, were they bound to do so? We think not, because the search was otherwise reasonable, as previously concluded. In a recent opinion, *Trupiano* v. *United States,* 334 U.S. 699, this Court first enunciated the requirement that search warrants must be procured when "practicable" in a case of search incident to arrest. On the occasion of the previous suggestion of such a test, *Taylor* v. *United States,* 286 U.S. 1, the Court had been scrupulous to restrict the opinion to the familiar situation there presented. Prohibition agents, having received complaints for about a year, went at 2:30 a.m. to a garage adjacent to a house, flashed a light through a small opening, and then broke in and seized liquor. The Court emphasized that "No one was within the place and there was no reason to think otherwise." *Id., 286 U.S. at 5.* Lest the holding that such a search of an unoccupied building was unreasonable be thought to have broader significance the Court carefully stated in conclusion: "This record does not make it necessary for us to discuss the rule in respect of searches in connection with an arrest. No offender was in the garage; the action of the agents had no immediate connection with an arrest. The purpose was to secure evidence to support some future arrest." *Id. 286 U.S. at 6.*

A rule of thumb requiring that a search warrant always be procured whenever practicable may be appealing from the vantage point of easy administration. But we cannot agree that this requirement should be crystallized into a sine qua non to the reasonableness of a search. It is fallacious to judge events retrospectively and thus to determine, considering the time element alone, that there was time to procure a search warrant. Whether there was time may well be dependent upon considerations other than the ticking off of minutes or hours. The judgment of the officers as to when to close the trap on a criminal committing a crime in their presence or who they have reasonable cause to believe is committing a felony is not determined solely upon whether there was time to procure a search warrant. Some flexibility will be accorded law officers engaged in daily battle with criminals for whose restraint criminal laws are essential.

It is appropriate to note that the Constitution does not say that the right of the people to be secure in their persons should not be violated without a search warrant if it is practicable for the officers to procure one. The mandate of the Fourth Amendment is that the people shall be secure against *unreasonable* searches. It is not disputed that there may be reasonable searches, incident to an arrest, without a search warrant. Upon acceptance of this established rule that some authority to search follows from lawfully taking the person into custody, it becomes apparent that such searches turn upon the reasonableness under all the circumstances and not upon the practicability of procuring a search warrant, for the warrant is not required. To the extent that *Trupiano* v. *United States, 334* U.S. 699, requires a search warrant solely upon the basis of the practicability of procuring it rather than upon the reasonableness of the search after a lawful arrest, that case is overruled. The relevant test is not whether it is reasonable to procure a search warrant, but whether the search was reasonable.

That criterion in turn depends upon the facts and circumstances—the total atmosphere of the case. It is a sufficient precaution that law officers must justify their conduct before courts which have always been, and must be, jealous of the individual's right of privacy within the broad sweep of the Fourth Amendment.

The motion to suppress the evidence was properly denied by the District Court. The judgment of the Court of Appeals is
Reversed.

Mr. Justice DOUGLAS took no part in the consideration or decision of this case.

Mr. Justice BLACK dissenting.

. . . In my judgment it would be wiser judicial policy to adhere to the *Trupiano* rule of evidence, at least long enough to see how it works.

I would affirm the judgment of the Court of Appeals.

Mr. Justice FRANKFURTER, whom Mr. Justice JACKSON joins, dissenting.

The clear-cut issue before us is this: in making a lawful arrest, may arresting officers search without a search warrant not merely the person under arrest of things under his immediate physical control, but the premises where the arrest is made, although there was ample time to secure such a warrant and no danger that the "papers and effects" for which a search warrant could be issued would be despoiled or destroyed?

The old saw that hard cases make bad law has its basis in experience. But petty cases are even more calculated to make bad law. The impact of a sordid little case is apt to obscure the implications of the generalization to which the case gives rise. Only thus can I account for a disregard of the history embedded in the Fourth Amendment, and the great place which belongs to that Amendment in the body of our liberties as recognized and applied by unanimous decisions over a long stretch of the Court's history.

It is a fair summary of history to say that the safeguards of liberty have frequently been forged in controversies involving not very nice people. And so, while we are concerned here with a shabby defrauder, we must deal with his case in the context of what are really the great themes expressed by the Fourth Amendment. A disregard of the historic materials underlying the Amendment does not answer them.

. . . The clue to the meaning and scope of the Fourth Amendment is John Adams' characterization of Otis' argument against search by the police that "American independence was then and there born." 10 Adams, Works 247. One cannot wrench "unreasonable searches" from the text and context and historic content of the Fourth Amendment. It was the answer of the Revolutionary statesmen to the evils of searches without warrants and searches with warrants unrestricted in scope. Both were deemed "unreasonable." Words must be read with the gloss of the experience of those who framed them. Because the experience of the framers of the Bill of Rights was so vivid, they assumed that it would be carried down the stream of history and that their words would receive the significance of the experience to which they were addressed—a significance not to be found in the dictionary. When the Fourth Amendment outlawed "unreasonable searches" and then went on to define the very restricted authority that even a search warrant issued by a magistrate could give, the framers said with all the clarity of the gloss of history that a search is "unreasonable" unless a warrant authorizes it, barring only exceptions justified by absolute necessity. Even a warrant cannot authorize it except when it is issued "upon probable cause . . . and particularly describing the place to be searched, and the persons or things to be seized." With all respect I suggest that it makes a mockery of the Fourth Amendment to sanction search without a search warrant merely because of the legality of an arrest.

What, then, is the exception to the prohibition by the Fourth Amendment of search without a warrant in case of a legal arrest, whether the arrest is on a warrant or based on the historic right of arrest without a warrant if a crime is committed in the presence of the arrester? The exception may in part be a surviving incident of the historic role of "hue and cry" in early Anglo-Saxon law. . . . Its basic roots, however, lie in necessity. What is the necessity? Why is search of the arrested person permitted? For two reasons: first, in order to protect the arresting officer and to deprive the prisoner of potential means of escape, . . . and, secondly, to avoid destruction of evidence by the arrested person. . . . From this it follows that officers may search and seize not only the things physically on the person arrested, but those within his immediate physical control. . . .

Another exception to the constitutional prohibition of unreasonable searches is likewise rooted in necessity. The search without a warrant of moving objects—vehicles and vessels—was sanctioned in *Carroll* v. *United States,* 267 U.S. 132, on the ground that "it is not practicable to secure a warrant because the vehicle can be quickly moved out of the locality or jurisdiction in which the warrant must be sought." 267 U.S. at 153. Furthermore, the limits of the exception were carefully defined in terms of necessity, for the Court added:

"In cases where the securing of a warrant is reasonably practicable, it must be used, and when properly supported by affidavit and issued after judicial approval protects the seizing officer against a suit for damages. In cases where seizure is impossible except without warrant, the seizing officer acts unlawfully and at his peril unless he can show the court probable cause." 267 U.S. at 156.

Even as to moving vehicles, this Court did not lay down an absolute rule dispensing with a search warrant. It limited dispensation to the demands of necessity, where want of time precluded the obtaining of a warrant. The necessity founded on the time factor which guided the Court in the *Carroll* Case cannot justify the search here made of the respondent's premises, for there was ample time to obtain a warrant before the arrest and even on the occasion of the arrest.

It is in this connection that the body of congressional enactments becomes significant, particularly legislation contemporaneous with the adoption of the Bill of Rights. If explicit legislation was deemed necessary to inspect without warrant even vessels and vehicles, and if Congress has been very niggardly in giving authority to search even with a warrant—niggardly both as to the officers who may obtain such warrants and as to strictly defined circumstances under which search is allowed—the attitude disclosed by this impressive legislation bears powerfully on the historic purposes of the Fourth Amendment and the functions that it fulfills in our democracy. It deserves to be recalled that Congress, despite repeated requests by Attorneys General, long refused to make search by warrant generally available as an aid to criminal prosecution. It did not do so until the First World War and even then it did not do so except under conditions most carefully circumscribed.

. . . . .

If the exception of search without a warrant incidental to a legal arrest is extended beyond the person and his physical extension, search throughout the house necessarily follows. I am aware that most differences in the law depend on differences of degree. But differences though of degree must not be capricious; the differences must permit rational classification. If upon arrest you may search beyond the immediate person and the very restricted area that may fairly be deemed part of the person, what rational line can be drawn short of searching as many rooms as arresting officers may deem appropriate for finding "the fruits of the crime"? Is search to be restricted to the room in which the person is arrested but not to another open room into which it leads? Or, take a house or an apartment consisting largely of one big room serving as dining room, living room and bedroom. May search be made in a small room but not in such a large room? If you may search the bedroom part of a large room, why not a bedroom separated from the dining room by a partition? These are not silly hard cases. They put the principle to a test. The right to search an arrested person and to take the stuff on top of the desk at which he sits has a justification of necessity which does not eat away the great principle of the Fourth Amendment. But to assume that this exception of a search incidental to arrest permits a freehanded search without warrant is to subvert the purpose of the Fourth Amendment by making the exception displace the principle. History and the policy which it represents alike admonish against it.

To tear "unreasonable" from the context and history and purpose of the Fourth Amendment in applying the narrow exception of search as an incident to an arrest is to disregard *the* reason to which reference must be made when a question arises under the Fourth Amendment. It is to make the arrest an incident to an unwarranted search instead of a warrantless search an incident to an arrest. The test by which searches and seizures must be judged is whether conduct is consonant with the main aim of the Fourth Amendment. The main aim of the Fourth Amendment is against invasion of the right of privacy as to one's effects and papers without regard to the result of such invasion. The purpose of the Fourth Amendment was to assure that the existence of probable cause as the legal basis for making a search was to be determined by a judicial officer before arrest and not after, subject only to what is necessarily to be excepted from such requirement. The exceptions cannot be enthroned into the rule. The justification for intrusion into a man's privacy was to be determined by a magistrate uninfluenced by what may turn out to be a successful search for papers, the desire to search for which might be the very reason for the Fourth Amendment's prohibition. The framers did not regard judicial authorization as a formal requirement for a piece of paper. They deemed a man's belongings part of his personality and his life. . . .

By the Bill of Rights the founders of this country subordinated police action to legal restraints not in order to convenience the guilty but to protect the innocent. Nor did they provide that only the innocent may appeal to these safeguards. They knew too well that the successful prosecution of the guilty does not require jeopardy to the innocent. The knock at the door under the guise of a warrant of arrest for a venial or spurious offense was not unknown to them. Compare the statement in *Weeks* v. *United States,* 232 U.S. 383, 390, that searches and seizures had been made under general warrants in England "in support of charges, real or imaginary." We have had grim reminders in our day of their experience. Arrest under a warrant for a minor or a trumped-up charge has been familiar practice in the past, is a commonplace in the police state of today, and too well-known in this country. See *Lanzetta* v. *New Jersey,* 306 U.S. 451. The progress is too easy from police action unscrutinized by judicial authorization to the police state. The founders wrote into the Constitution their conviction that law enforcement does not require the easy but dangerous way of letting the police determine when search is called for without prior authorization by a magistrate. They have been vindicated in that conviction. It may safely be asserted that crime is most effectively brought to book when the principles underlying the constitutional restraints upon police action are most scrupulously observed.

It is not as though we are asked to extend a mischievous doctrine that has been shown to hamper law enforcers. We are asked to overrule decisions based on a long course of prior unanimous decisions, drawn from history and legislative experience. . . . For these cases ought not to be allowed to remain as derelicts on the stream of the law, if we overrule *Trupiano.* These are not outmoded decisions eroded by time. Even under normal circumstances, the Court ought not to overrule such a series of decisions where no mischief flowing from them has been made manifest. . . .

2. FEDERAL STANDARDS AND LOCAL COURTS

TWINING v. NEW JERSEY
211 U.S. 78 (1908)

[In a trial before a New Jersey state court, Twining and his co-defendant declined to take the stand nor did they call any witnesses. In accordance with state law the trial judge instructed the jury that they might properly consider this failure to take the stand in their deliberations on the verdict. The defendants were found guilty and sentenced to prison terms on charges of bank fraud.]

Mr. Justice MOODY . . . delivered the opinion of the Court.

In the view we take of the case we do not deem it necessary to consider whether, with respect to the federal question, there is any difference in the situation of the two defendants. It is assumed, in respect of each, that the jury were instructed that they might draw an unfavorable inference against him from his failure to testify, where it was within his power, in denial of the evidence which tended to incriminate him. The law of the State . . . permitted such an inference to be drawn. . . . The general question therefore, is, whether such a law violates the Fourteenth Amendment, either by abridging the privileges or immunities of citizens of the United States, or by depriving persons of their life, liberty or property without due process of law. In order to bring themselves within the protection of the Constitution it is incumbent on the defendants to prove two propositions: first, that the exemption from compulsory self-incrimination is guaranteed by the Federal Constitution against impairment by the States; and, second, if it be so guaranteed, that the exemption was in fact impaired in the case at bar. The first proposition naturally presents itself for earlier consideration. If the right here asserted is not a federal right, that is the end of the case. We have no authority to go further and determine whether the state court has erred in the interpretation and enforcement of its own laws.

The defendants contend, in the first place, that the exemption from self-incrimination is one of the privileges and immunities of citizens of the United States which the Fourteenth Amendment forbids the States to abridge. It is not argued that the defendants are protected by that part of the Fifth Amendment which provides that "no person . . . shall be compelled in any criminal case to be a witness against himself," for it is recognized by counsel that by a long line or decisions the first ten Amendments are not operative on the States. *Barron* v. *Baltimore,* 7 Pet. 243;.... But it is argued that this privilege is one of the fundamental rights of national citizenship, placed under national protection by the Fourteenth Amendment, and it is specifically argued that the "privileges and immunities of citizens of the United States," protected against state action by that Amendment, include those fundamental personal rights which were protected against national action by the first eight Amendments; that this was the intention of the framers of the Fourteenth Amendment, and that this part of it would otherwise have little or no meaning and effect. These arguments are not new to this Court and the answer to them is found in its decisions. The meaning of the phrase "privileges and immunities of citizens of the United States," as used in the Fourteenth Amendment, came under early consideration in the *Slaughter-House Cases,* 16 Wall. 36. . . .

There can be no doubt, so far as the decision in the *Slaughter-House Cases* has determined the question, that the civil rights sometimes described as fundamental and inalienable, which before the war Amendments were enjoyed by state citizenship and protected by state government, were left untouched by this clause of the Fourteenth Amendment. Criticism of this case has never entirely ceased, nor has it ever received universal assent by members of this Court. Undoubtedly, it gave much less effect to the Fourteenth Amendment than some of the public men active in framing it intended, and disappointed many others. On the other hand, if the views of the minority had prevailed it is easy to see how far the authority and independence of the States would have been diminished, by subjecting all their legislative and judicial acts to correction by the legislative and review by the judicial branch of the National Government. But we need not now inquire into the merits of the original dispute. This part at least of the *Slaughter-House Cases* has been steadily adhered to by this Court, so that it was said of it, in a case where the same clause of the amendment was under consideration *(Maxwell* v. *Dow,* 176 U.S. 581, 591), "The opinion upon the matters actually involved and maintained by the judgment in the case has never been doubted or overruled by any judgment of this Court." The distinction between national and state citizenship and their respective privileges there drawn has come to be firmly established. . . . If, then, it be assumed, without deciding the point, that an exemption from compulsory self-incrimination is what is described as a fundamental right belonging to all who live under a free government, and incapable of impairment by legislation or judicial decision, it is, so far as the States are concerned, a fundamental right inherent in state citizenship, and is a privilege or immunity of that citizenship only. Privileges and immunities of citizens of the United States, on the other hand, are only such as arise out of the nature and essential character of the national government, or are specifically granted or secured to all citizens or persons by the Constitution of the United States. . . .

. . . But assuming it to be true that the exemption from self-incrimination is not, as a fundamental right of national citizenship, included in the privileges and immunities of citizens of the United States, counsel insist that, as a right specifically granted or secured by the Federal Constitution, it is included in them. This view is based upon the contention which must now be examined, that the safeguards of personal rights which are enumerated in the first eight Articles of amendment to the Federal Constitution, sometimes called the Federal Bill of Rights, though they were by those Amendments originally secured only against national action, are among the privileges and immunities of citizens of the United States, which this clause of the Fourteenth Amendment protects against state action. . . . The question is no longer open in this Court. The right of trial by jury in civil cases, guaranteed by the Seventh Amendment *(Walker* v. *Sauvinet,* 92 U.S. 90), and the right to bear arms guaranteed by the Second Amendment *(Presser* v. *Illinois,* 116 U.S. 252), have been distinctly held not to be privileges and immunities of the United States guaranteed by the Fourteenth Amendment against abridgment by the States, and in effect the same decision was made in respect of the guarantee against prosecution, except by indictment of a grand jury, contained in the Fifth Amendment *(Hurtado* v. *California,* 110 U.S. 516), and in respect to the right to be confronted with witnesses contained in the Sixth Amendment. *West* v. *Louisiana,* 194 U.S. 258. In *Maxwell* v. *Dow, supra,* where the plaintiff in error had been convicted in a state court of a felony upon information, and by a jury of eight persons, it was held that the indictment, made indispensable by the Fifth Amendment, and the trial by jury guaranteed by the Sixth Amendment were not privileges and immunities of citizens of the United States, as those words were used in the Fourteenth Amendment. . . .

We conclude, therefore, that the exemption from compulsory self-incrimination is not a privilege or immunity of national citizenship guaranteed by this clause of the Fourteenth Amendment against abridgment by the States. . . .

The defendants, however, do not stop here. They appeal to another clause of the Fourteenth Amendment, and insist that the self-incrimination, which they alleged the instruction to the jury compelled, was a denial of due process of law. This contention requires separate consideration, for it is possible that some of the personal rights safeguarded by the first eight Amendments against national action may also be safeguarded against state action, because a denial of them would be a denial of due process of law. *Chicago, Burlington & Quincy Railroad* v. *Chicago*, 166 U.S. 226. If this is so, it is not because those rights are enumerated in the first eight Amendments, but because they are of such a nature that they are included in the conception of due process of law. Few phrases of the law are so elusive of exact apprehension as this. Doubtless the difficulties of ascertaining its connotation have been increased in American jurisprudence, where it has been embodied in constitutions and put to new uses as a limit on legislative power. This Court has always declined to give a comprehensive definition of it, and has preferred that its full meaning should be gradually ascertained by the process of inclusion and exclusion in the course of the decisions of cases as they arise. There are certain general principles well settled, however, which narrow the field of discussion and may serve as helps to correct conclusions. . . .

First. What is due process of law may be ascertained by an examination of those settled usages and modes of proceedings existing in the common and statute law of England before the emigration of our ancestors and shown not to have been unsuited to their civil and political condition by having been acted on by them after the settlement of this country. . . .

Second. It does not follow, however, that a procedure settled in English law at the time of the emigration, and brought to this country and practiced by our ancestors, is an essential element of due process of law. If that were so the procedure of the first half of the seventeenth century would be fastened upon the American jurisprudence like a straightjacket, only to be unloosed by constitutional amendment. . . .

Third. But, consistently with the requirements of due process, no change in ancient procedure can be made which disregards those fundamental principles, to be ascertained from time to time by judicial action, which have relation to process of law and protect the citizen in his private right, and guard him against the arbitrary action of government. . . .

The question under consideration may first be tested by the application of these settled doctrines of this Court. . . . Nothing is more certain, in point of historical fact, than that the practice of compulsory self-incrimination in the courts and elsewhere existed for four hundred years after the granting of Magna Carta, continued throughout the reign of Charles I (though then beginning to be seriously questioned), gained at least some foothold among the early colonists of this country, and was not entirely omitted at trials in England until the eighteenth century.

[The Court surveys the historical background of the subject and concludes that the investigation "does not tend to show that it was then (in 1787) in this country the universal or even general belief that the privilege ranked among the fundamental and inalienable rights of mankind; . . ."]

The decisions of this Court, though they are silent on the precise question before us, ought to be searched to discover if they present any analogies which are helpful in its decision. The essential elements of due process of law, already established by them, are singularly few, though of wide application and deep significance. We are not here concerned with due process in restraining substantive laws, as, for example, that which forbids the taking of private property for public use without compensation. We need notice now only those cases which deal with the principles which must be observed in the trial of criminal and civil causes. Due process requires that the court which assumes to determine the rights of parties shall have jurisdiction, . . . and that there shall be notice and opportunity for hearing given the parties, . . . Subject to these two fundamental conditions, which seem to be universally prescribed in all systems of law established by civilized countries, this Court has up to this time sustained all state laws, statutory or judicially declared, regulating procedure, evidence and methods of trial, and held them to be consistent with due process of law. . . .

It is impossible to reconcile the reasoning of these cases and the rule which governed their decision with the theory that an exemption from compulsory self-incrimination is included in the conception of due process of law. . . .

Even if the historical meaning of due process of law and the decisions of this Court did not exclude the privilege from it, it would be going far to rate it as an immutable principle of justice which is the inalienable possession of every citizen of a free government. Salutary as the principle may seem to the great majority, it cannot be ranked with the right to hearing before condemnation, the immunity from arbitrary power not acting by general laws, and the inviolability of private property. . . .

Judgment affirmed.

Mr. Justice HARLAN, dissenting. . . .

PALKO v. CONNECTICUT
302 U.S. 319 (1938)

Mr. Justice CARDOZO delivered the opinion of the Court.

A statute of Connecticut permitting appeals in criminal cases to be taken by the state is challenged by appellant as an infringement of the Fourteenth Amendment of the Constitution of the United States. Whether the challenge should be upheld is now to be determined.

Appellant was indicted in Fairfield County, Connecticut, for the crime of murder in the first degree. A jury found him guilty of murder in the second degree, and he was sentenced to confinement in the state prison for life. Thereafter the State of Connecticut, with the permission of the judge presiding at the trial, gave notice of appeal to the Supreme Court of Errors. This it did pursuant to an act adopted in 1886. . . . Public Acts 1886, p. 560, now § 6494 of the General Statutes. Upon such appeal, the Supreme Court of Errors reversed the judgment and ordered a new trial. . . . It found that there had been error of law to the prejudice of the state (1) in excluding testimony as to a confession by defendant; (2) in excluding testimony upon cross-examination of defendant to impeach his credibility; and (3) in the instructions to the jury as to the difference between first and second degree murder.

Pursuant to the mandate of the Supreme Court of Errors, defendant was brought to trial again. Before a jury was impaneled, and also at later stages of the case, he made the objection that the effect of the new trial was to place him twice in jeopardy for the same offense, and in so doing to violate the Fourteenth Amendment of the Constitution of the United States. Upon the overruling of the objection the trial proceeded. The jury returned a verdict of murder in the first degree, and the court sentenced the defendant to the punishment of death. The Supreme Court of Errors affirmed. . . . The case is here upon appeal. . . .

1. The execution of the sentence will not deprive appellant of his life without the process of law assured to him by the Fourteenth Amendment of the Federal Constitution.

The argument for appellant is that whatever is forbidden by the Fifth Amendment is forbidden by the Fourteenth also. The Fifth Amendment, which is not directed to the states, but solely to the federal government, creates immunity from double jeopardy. No person shall be "subject for the same offense to be twice put in jeopardy of life or limb." The Fourteenth Amendment ordains, "nor shall any state deprive any person of life, liberty, or property, without due process of law." To retry a defendant, though under one indictment and only one, subjects him, it is said, to double jeopardy in violation of the Fifth Amendment, if the prosecution is one on behalf of the United States. From this the consequence is said to follow that there is a denial of life or liberty without due process of law, if the prosecution is one on behalf of the People of a State. . . .

. . . . . .

We have said that in appellant's view the Fourteenth Amendment is to be taken as embodying the prohibitions of the Fifth. His thesis is even broader. Whatever would be a violation of the original bill of rights (Amendments I to VIII) if done by the federal government is now equally unlawful by force of the Fourteenth Amendment if done by a state. There is no such general rule.

The Fifth Amendment provides, among other things, that no person shall be held to answer for a capital or otherwise infamous crime unless on presentment or indictment of a grand jury. This Court has held that, in prosecutions by a state, presentment or indictment by a grand jury may give way to informations at the instance of a public officer. *Hurtado* v. *California,* 110 U.S. 516; . . . . The Fifth Amendment provides also that no person shall be compelled in any criminal case to be a witness against himself. This Court has said that, in prosecutions by a state, the exemption will fail if the state elects to end it. *Twining* v. *New Jersey,* 211 U.S. 78. . . . The Sixth Amendment calls for a jury trial in criminal cases and the Seventh for a jury trial in civil cases at common law where the value in controversy shall exceed twenty dollars. This Court has ruled that consistently with those amendments trial by jury may be modified by a state or abolished altogether. *Walker* v. *Sauvinet*, 92 U.S. 90; *Maxwell* v. *Dow*, 176 U.S. 581; .... As to the Fourth Amendment, one should refer to *Weeks* v. *United States*, 232 U.S. 383, 398,[7] and as to other provisions of the Sixth, to *West* v. *Louisiana*, 194 U.S. 258.

On the other hand, the due process clause of the Fourteenth Amendment may make it unlawful for a state to abridge by its statutes the freedom of speech which the First Amendment safeguards against encroachment by the Congress, *De Jonge* v. *Oregon*, 299 U.S. 353, 364; *Herndon* v. *Lowry*, 301 U.S. 242, 259; or the like freedom of the press, *Grosjean* v. *American Press Co.*, 297 U.S. 233; *Near* v. *Minnesota*, 283 U.S. 697, 707; or the free exercise of religion, *Hamilton* v. *Regents of University*, 293 U.S. 245, 262; ...; or the right of peaceable assembly, without which speech would be unduly trammeled, *De Jonge* v. *Oregon, supra; Herndon* v. *Lowry, supra;* or the right of one accused of crime to the benefit of counsel. *Powell* v. *Alabama*, 287 U.S. 45.[8] In these and other situations immunities that are valid as against the federal government by force of the specific pledges of particular amendments have been found to be implicit in the concept of ordered liberty, and thus, through the Fourteenth Amendment, become valid as against the states.

The line of division may seem to be wavering and broken if there is a hasty catalogue of the cases on the one side and on the other. Reflection and analysis will induce a different view. There emerges the perception of a rationalizing principle which gives to discrete instances a proper order and coherence. The right to trial by jury and the immunity from prosecution except as the result of an indictment may have value and importance. Even so, they are not of the very essence of a scheme of ordered liberty. To abolish them is not to

---

[7] But note the more recent decision in *Wolf* v. *Colorado*, 338 U.S. 25 (1949), *infra*, p. 604.

[8] In a later, omitted portion of this opinion Cardozo notes that the decision in the *Powell* case "did not turn upon the fact that the benefit of counsel would have been guaranteed to the defendants by the provisions of the Sixth Amendment if they had been prosecuted in a federal court," but that the benefit of counsel was, under the circumstances, held essential to a fair hearing. Beginning with *Betts* v. *Brady*, 316 U.S. 455 (1942), a majority of the Court, against vigorous dissent, have adhered to the rule that the right to counsel is not, as here stated by Cardozo, incorporated into the Fourteenth Amendment. See *Bute* v. *Illinois, ante*, ch. IX. A detailed analysis of the cases may be found in Chapter VI of Francis H. Heller, *The Sixth Amendment to the Constitution of the United States: A Study in Constitutional Development*, Lawrence: University of Kansas Press, 1951.

violate a "principle of justice so rooted in the traditions and conscience of our people as to be ranked as fundamental." . . . Few would be so narrow or provincial as to maintain that a fair and enlightened system of justice would be impossible without them. What is true of jury trials and indictments is true also, as the cases show, of the immunity from compulsory self-incrimination. *Twining* v. *New Jersey, supra.* This too might be lost, and justice will still be done. Indeed, today as in the past there are students of our penal system who look upon the immunity as a mischief rather than a benefit, and who would limit its scope, or destroy it altogether. . . . The exclusion of these immunities and privileges from the privileges and immunities protected against action of the States has not been arbitrary or casual. It has been dictated by a study and appreciation of the meaning, the essential implications, of liberty itself.

We reach a different plane of social and moral values when we pass to the privileges and immunities that have been taken over from the earlier articles of the federal bill of rights and brought within the Fourteenth Amendment by a process of absorption. These in their origin were effective against the federal government alone. If the Fourteenth Amendment has absorbed them, the process of absorption has had its source in the belief that neither liberty, nor justice would exist if they were sacrificed. *Twining* v. *New Jersey, supra,* p. 99. This is true, for illustration, of freedom of thought and speech. Of that freedom one may say that it is the matrix, the indispensable condition, of nearly every other form of freedom. With rare aberrations a pervasive recognition of that truth can be traced in our history, political and legal. So it has come about that the domain of liberty, withdrawn by the Fourteenth Amendment from encroachment by the states, has been enlarged by latter-day judgments to include liberty of mind as well as liberty of action. . . .

Our survey of the cases serves, we think, to justify the statement that the dividing line between them, if not unfaltering throughout its course, has been true for the most part to a unifying principle. On which side of the line the case made out by the appellant has appropriate location must be the next inquiry and the final one. Is that kind of double jeopardy to which the statute has subjected him a hardship so acute and shocking that our polity will not indure it? Does it violate those "fundamental principles of liberty and justice which lie at the base of all our civil and political institutions?". . . The answer surely must be "no." What the answer would have to be if the state were permitted after a trial free from error to try the accused over again or to bring another case against him, we have no occasion to consider. We deal with the statute before us and no other. The state is not attempting to wear the accused out by a multitude of cases with accumulated trials. It asks no more than this that the case against him shall go on until there shall be a trial free from the corrosion of substantial legal error. . . . This is not cruelty at all, nor even vexation in any immoderate degree. If the trial had been in-fected with error adverse to the accused, there might have been review at his instance, and as often as necessary to purge the vicious taint. A reciprocal privilege, subject at all times to the discretion of the presiding judge . . . , has now been granted to the state. There is here no seismic innovation. The edifice of justice stands, in its symmetry, to many, greater than before.

2. The conviction of appellant is not in derogation of any privileges or immunities that belong to him as a citizen of the United States.

There is argument in his behalf that the privileges and immunities clause of the Fourteenth Amendment as well as the due process clause has been flouted by the judgment.

Maxwell v. *Dow, supra,* p. 584, gives all the answer that is neces-sary.

The judgment is affirmed.

Mr. Justice BUTLER dissents.

ADAMSON v. CALIFORNIA
332 U.S. 46 (1947)

Mr. Justice REED delivered the opinion of the Court.

The appellant, Adamson, a citizen of the United States, was con-victed, without recommendation for mercy, by a jury in a Superior Court of the State of California of murder in the first degree. After considering the same objections to the conviction that are pressed here, the sentence of death was affirmed by the Supreme Court of the state. . . . The provisions of California law which were challenged in the state proceedings as invalid under the Fourteenth Amendment to the Federal Constitution . . . permit the failure of a defendant to explain or to deny evidence against him to be commented upon by court and by counsel and to be considered by court and jury. The defendant did not testify. As the trial court gave its instructions and the District Attorney argued the case in accordance with the constitu-tional and statutory provisions [of the state] just referred to, we have for decision the question of their constitutionality in these circumstances under the limitations of § 1 of the Fourteenth Amendment.

The appellant was charged in the information with former convictions for burglary, larceny and robbery and pursuant to § 1025, California Penal Code, answered that he had suffered the previous convictions. This answer barred allusion to these charges of convictions on the trial. Under California's interpretation of § 1025 of the Penal Code and § 2051 of the Code of Civil Procedure, however, if the defendant, after answering affirmatively charges alleging prior convictions, takes the witness stand to deny or explain away other evidence that has been introduced "the commission of these crimes could have been revealed to the jury on cross-examination to impeach his testimony." This forces an accused who is a repeated offender to choose between the risk of having his prior offenses disclosed to the jury or of having it draw harmful inferences from uncontradicted evidence that can only be denied or explained by the defendant.

In the first place, appellant urges that the provision of the Fifth Amendment that no person "shall be compelled in any criminal case to be a witness against himself" is a fundamental national privilege or immunity protected against state abridgment by the Fourteenth Amendment or a privilege or immunity secured, through the Fourteenth Amendment, against deprivation by state action because it is a personal right, enumerated in the federal Bill of Rights.

Secondly, appellant relies upon the due process of law clause of the Fourteenth Amendment to invalidate the provisions of the California law . . . as applied (a) because comment on failure to testify is permitted, (b) because appellant was forced to forego testimony in person because of danger of disclosure of his past convictions through cross-examination and (c) because the presumption of innocence was infringed by the shifting of the burden of proof to appellant in permitting comment on his failure to testify.

We shall assume, but without any intention thereby of ruling upon the issue, that permission by law to the court, counsel and jury to comment upon and consider the failure of defendant "to explain or to deny by his testimony any evidence or facts in the case against him" would infringe defendant's privilege against self-incrimination under the Fifth Amendment if this were a trial in a court of the United States under a similar law. Such an assumption does not determine appellant's rights under the Fourteenth Amendment. It is settled law that the clause of the Fifth Amendment, protecting a person against being compelled to be a witness against himself, is not made effective by the Fourteenth Amendment as a protection against state action on the ground that freedom from testimonial compulsion is a right of national citizenship, or because it is a personal privilege or immunity secured by the Federal Constitution as one of the rights of man that are listed in the Bill of Rights.

The reasoning that leads to those conclusions starts with the unquestioned premise that the Bill of Rights, when adopted, was for the protection of the individual against the federal government and its provisions were inapplicable to similar actions done by the states. *Barron* v. *Baltimore,* 7 Pet. 243, ... With the adoption of the Fourteenth Amendment, it was suggested that the dual citizenship recognized by its first sentence, secured for citizens federal protection for their elemental privileges and immunities of state citizenship. The *Slaughter-House Cases* decided, contrary to the suggestion, that these rights, as privileges and immunities of state citizenship, remained under the sole protection of the state governments. . . . The power to free defendants in state trials from self-incrimination was specifically determined to be beyond the scope of the privileges and immunities clause of the Fourteenth Amendment in *Twining* v. *New Jersey,* 211 U.S. 78, 91–98. . . . After declaring that state and national citizenship coexist in the same person, the Fourteenth Amendment forbids a state from abridging the privileges and immunities of citizens of the United States. As a matter of words, this leaves a state free to abridge,. within the limits of the due process clause, the privileges and immunities flowing from state citizenship. This reading of the Federal Constitution has heretofore found favor with the majority of this Court as a natural and logical interpretation. . . . We reaffirm the conclusion . . . that protection against self-incrimination is not a privilege or immunity of national citizenship.

Appellant secondly contends that if the privilege against self-incrimination is not a right protected by the privileges and immunities clause of the Fourteenth Amendment against state action, this privilege, to its full scope under the Fifth Amendment, inheres in the right to a fair trial. A right to a fair trial is a right admittedly protected by the due process clause of the Fourteenth Amendment. Therefore, appellant argues, the due process clause of the Fourteenth Amendment protects his privilege against self-incrimination. The due process clause of the Fourteenth Amendment, however, does not draw all the rights of the federal Bill of Rights under its protection. That contention was made and rejected in *Palko* v. *Connecticut,* 302 U.S. 319, 323. . . . [That case] held that such provisions of the Bill of Rights as were "implicit in the concept of ordered liberty" became secure from state interference by the clause. But it held nothing more.

. . . For a state to require testimony from an accused is not necessarily a breach of a state's obligation to give a fair trial. Therefore, we must examine the effect of the California law applied in this trial to see whether the comment on failure to testify violates the protection against state action that the due process clause does grant to an accused. The due process clause forbids compulsion to testify by fear of hurt, torture or exhaustion. It forbids any other type of coercion that falls within the scope of due process. California follows Anglo-American legal tradition in excusing defendants in criminal prosecutions from compulsory testimony. . . . That is a matter of legal policy and not because of the requirements of due process under the Fourteenth Amendment. So our inquiry is directed, not at the broad question of the constitutionality of compulsory testimony from the accused under the due process clause, but to the constitutionality of the provision of the California law that permits comment upon his failure to testify. . . .

Generally, comment on the failure of an accused to testify is forbidden in American jurisdictions. This arises from state constitutional or statutory provisions similar in character to the federal provisions. . . . California, however, is one of a few states that permit limited comment upon a defendant's failure to testify. That permission is narrow. The California law . . . authorizes comment by court and counsel upon the "failure of the defendant to explain or to deny by his testimony any evidence or facts in the case against him." This does not involve any presumption, rebuttable or irrebuttable, either of guilt or of the truth of any fact, that is offered in evidence. . . . It allows inferences to be drawn from proven facts. Because of this clause, the court can direct the jury's attention to whatever evidence there may be that a defendant could deny and the prosecution can argue as to inferences that may be drawn from the accused's failure to testify. . . . However sound may be the legislative conclusion that an accused should not be compelled in any criminal case to be a witness against himself, we see no reason why comment should not be made upon his silence. . . .

Appellant sets out the circumstances of this case, however, to show coercion and unfairness in permitting comment. The guilty person was not seen at the place and time of the crime. There was evidence, however, that entrance to the place or room where the crime was committed might have been obtained through a small door. It was freshly broken. Evidence showed that six fingerprints on the door were petitioner's. Certain diamond rings were missing from the deceased's possession. There was evidence that appellant, sometime after the crime, asked an unidentified person whether the latter would be interested in purchasing a diamond ring. As has been stated, the information charged other crimes to appellant and he admitted them. His argument here is that he could not take the stand to deny the evidence against him because he would be subjected to a cross-examination as to former crimes to impeach his veracity and the evidence so produced might well bring about his conviction. Such cross-examination is allowable in California. . . . Therefore, appellant contends the California statute permitting comment denies him due process.

It is true that if comment were forbidden, an accused in this situation could remain silent and avoid evidence of former crimes and comment upon his failure to testify. We are of the view, however, that a state may control such a situation in accordance with its own ideas of the most efficient administration of criminal justice. The purpose of due process is not to protect an accused against a proper conviction but against an unfair conviction. When evidence is before a jury that threatens conviction, it does not seem unfair to require him to choose between leaving the adverse evidence unexplained and subjecting himself to impeachment through disclosure of former crimes. Indeed, this is a dilemma with which any defendant may be faced. If facts, adverse to the defendant, are proven by the prosecution, there may be no way to explain them favorably to the accused except by a witness who may be vulnerable to impeachment on cross-examination. The defendant must then decide whether or not to use such a witness. The fact that the witness may also be the defendant makes the choice more difficult but a denial of due process does not emerge from the circumstances.

. . . . .

We find no other error that gives ground for our intervention in California's administration of criminal justice.

Affirmed.

Mr. Justice FRANKFURTER, concurring.

.   .   .   .   .

For historical reasons a limited immunity from the common duty to testify was written into the Federal Bill of Rights, and I am prepared to agree that, as part of that immunity, comment on the failure of an accused to take the witness stand is forbidden in federal prosecutions. . . . But to suggest that such a limitation can be drawn out of "due process" in its protection of ultimate decency in a civilized society is to suggest that the Due Process Clause fastened fetters of unreason upon the States. . . .

Between the incorporation of the Fourteenth Amendment into the Constitution and the beginning of the present membership of the Court—a period of seventy years—the scope of that Amendment was passed upon by forty-three judges. Of all these judges, only one [Harlan], who may respectfully be called an eccentric exception, ever indicated the belief that the Fourteenth Amendment was a shorthand summary of the first eight Amendments theretofore limiting only the Federal Government, and that due process incorporated those eight Amendments as restrictions upon the powers of the States. Among these judges were not only those who would have to be included among the greatest in the history of the Court, but—it is especially relevant to note—they included those whose services in the cause of human rights and the spirit of freedom are the most conspicuous in our history. It is not invidious to single out Miller, Davis, Bradley, Waite, Matthews, Gray, Fuller, Holmes, Brandeis, Stone and Cardozo (to speak only of the dead) as judges who were alert in safeguarding and promoting the interests of liberty and human dignity through law. But they were also judges mindful of the relation of our federal system to a progressively democratic society and therefore duly regardful of the scope of authority that was left to the States even after the Civil War. And so they did not find that the Fourteenth Amendment, concerned as it was with matters fundamental to the pursuit of justice, fastened upon the States procedural arrangements which, in the language of Mr. Justice Cardozo, only those who are "narrow or provincial" would deem essential to "a fair and enlightened system of Justice." *Palko* v. *Connecticut*, 302 U.S. 319, 325. To suggest that it is inconsistent with a truly free society to begin prosecutions without an indictment, to try petty civil cases without the paraphernalia of a common law jury, to take into consideration that one who has full opportunity to make a defense remains silent is, in de Tocqueville's phrase, to confound the familiar with the necessary.

The short answer to the suggestion that the provision of the Fourteenth Amendment, which ordains "nor shall any State deprive any person of life, liberty, or property, without due process of law," was a way of saying that every State must thereafter initiate prosecutions through indictment by a grand jury, must have a trial by a jury of twelve in criminal cases, and must have trial by such a jury in common law suits where the amount in controversy exceeds twenty dollars, is that it is a strange way of saying it. It would be extraordinarily strange for a Constitution to convey such specific commands in such a roundabout and inexplicit way. After all, an amendment to the Constitution should be read in a " 'sense most obvious to the common understanding at the time of its adoption.' . . . For it was for public adoption that it was proposed." See Mr. Justice Holmes in *Eisner* v. *Macomber*, 252 U.S. 189, 220. Those reading the English language with the meaning which it ordinarily conveys, those conversant with the political and legal history of the concept of due process, those sensitive to the relations of the States to the central government as well as the relation of some of the provisions of the Bill of Rights to the process of justice, would hardly recognize the Fourteenth Amendment as a cover for the various explicit provisions of the first eight Amendments. Some of these are enduring reflections of experience with human nature, while some express the restricted views of Eighteenth-Century England regarding the best methods for the ascertainment of facts. The notion that the Fourteenth Amendment is a covert way of imposing upon the States all the rules which it seemed important to Eighteenth Century statesmen to write into the Federal Amendments, was rejected by judges who were themselves witnesses of the process by which the Fourteenth Amendment became part of the Constitution. Arguments that may now be adduced to prove that the first eight Amendments were concealed within the historic phrasing of the Fourteenth Amendment were not unknown at the time of its adoption. A surer estimate of their bearing was possible for judges at the time than distorting distance is likely to vouchsafe. Any evidence of design or purpose not contemporaneously known could hardly have influenced those who ratified the Amendment. Remarks of a particular proponent of the Amendment, no matter how influential, are not to be deemed part of the Amendment. What was submitted for ratification was his proposal, not his speech. Thus, at the time of the ratification of the Fourteenth Amendment the constitutions of nearly half of the ratifying States did not have the rigorous requirements of the Fifth Amendment for instituting criminal procedings through a grand jury. It could hardly have occurred to these States that by ratifying the Amendment they uprooted their established methods for prosecuting crime and fastened upon themselves a new prosecutorial system.

.   .   .   .   .

It may not be amiss to restate the pervasive function of the Four·teenth Amendment in exacting from the States observance of basic liberties. . . . The Amendment neither comprehends the specific provisions by which the founders deemed it appropriate to restrict the federal government nor is it confined to them. The Due Process Clause of the Fourteenth Amendment has an independent potency, precisely as does the Due Process Clause of the Fifth Amendment in relation to the Federal Government. It ought not to require argument to reject the notion that due process of law meant one thing in the Fifth Amendment and another in the Fourteenth. The Fifth Amendment specifically prohibits prosecution of an "infamous crime" except upon indictment; it forbids double jeopardy; it bars compelling a person to be a witness against himself in any criminal case; it precludes deprivation of "life, liberty, or property, without due process of law." Are Madison and his contemporaries in the framing of the Bill of Rights to be charged with writing into it a meaningless clause? To consider "due process of law" as merely a shorthand statement of other specific clauses in the same amendment is to attribute to the authors and proponents of this Amendment ignorance of, or indifference to, a historic conception which was one of the great instruments in the arsenal of constitutional freedom which the Bill of Rights was to protect and strengthen.

.   .   .   .   .

And so, when, as in a case like the present, a conviction in a State court is here for review under a claim that a right protected by the Due Process Clause of the Fourteenth Amendment has been denied, the issue is not whether an infraction of one of the specific provisions of the first eight Amendments is disclosed by the record. The relevant question is whether the criminal proceedings which resulted in con-

viction deprived the accused of the due process of law to which the
United States Constitution entitled him. Judicial review of that guaranty of the Fourteenth Amendment inescapably imposes upon this
Court an exercise of judgment upon the whole course of the proceedings in order to ascertain whether they offend those canons of decency
and fairness which express the notions of justice of English-speaking
peoples even toward those charged with the most heinous offenses.
These standards of justice are not authoritatively formulated any-
where as though they were prescriptions in a pharmacopoeia. But
neither does the application of the Due Process Clause imply that
judges are wholly at large. The judicial judgment in applying the
Due Process Clause must move within the limits of accepted notions
of justice and is not to be based upon the idiosyncrasies of a merely
personal judgment. The fact that judges among themselves may differ
whether in a particular case a trial offends accepted notions of justice
is not disproof that general rather than idiosyncratic standards are
applied. An important safeguard against such merely individual judgment is an alert deference to the judgment of the State court under
review.

Mr. Justice BLACK, dissenting.

The appellant was tried for murder in a California state court.
He did not take the stand as a witness in his own behalf. The prosecuting attorney, under purported authority of a California statute,
Cal. Penal Code, § 1323, argued to the jury that an inference of guilt
could be drawn because of appellant's failure to deny evidence offered
against him. The appellant's contention in the state court and here
[is] that the statute denies him a right guaranteed by the Federal
Constitution. The argument is that (1) permitting comment upon
his failure to testify has the effect of compelling him to testify so as
to violate that provision of the Bill of Rights contained in the Fifth
Amendment that "No person . . . shall be compelled in any criminal
case to be a witness against himself"; and (2) although this provision
of the Fifth Amendment originally applied only as a restraint upon
federal courts, *Barron* v. *Baltimore,* 7 Pet. 243, the Fourteenth
Amendment was intended to, and did, make the prohibition against
compelled testimony applicable to trials in state courts.

The Court refuses to meet and decide the appellant's first contention. . . . I must consider the case on the same assumption that the
Court does. For the discussion of the second contention turns out to

be a decision which reaches far beyond the relatively narrow issues on which this case might have turned.

This decision reasserts a constitutional theory spelled out in *Twining* v. *New Jersey*, 211 U.S. 78, that this Court is endowed by the Constitution with boundless power under "natural law" periodically to expand and contract constitutional standards to conform to the Court's conception of what at a particular time constitutes "civilized decency" and "fundamental liberty and justice." Invoking this *Twining* rule, the Court concludes that although comment upon testimony in a federal court would violate the Fifth Amendment, identical comment in a state court does not violate today's fashion in civilized decency and fundamentals and is therefore not prohibited by the Federal Constitution as amended.

The *Twining Case* was the first, as it is the only, decision of this Court, which has squarely held that states were free, notwithstanding the Fifth and Fourteenth Amendments, to extort evidence from one accused of crime. I agree that if *Twining* be reaffirmed, the result reached might appropriately follow. But I would not reaffirm the *Twining* decision. I think that decision and the "natural law" theory of the Constitution upon which it relies degrade the constitutional safeguards of the Bill of Rights and simultaneously appropriate for this Court a broad power which we are not authorized by the Constitution to exercise. . . . My reasons for believing that the *Twining* decision should not be revitalized can best be understood by reference to the constitutional, judicial, and general history that preceded and followed the case. That reference must be abbreviated far more than is justified but for the necessary limitations of opinion-writing.

The first ten amendments were proposed and adopted largely because of fear that Government might unduly interfere with prized individual liberties. The people wanted and demanded a Bill of Rights written into their Constitution. The amendments embodying the Bill of Rights were intended to curb all branches of the Federal Government in the fields touched by the amendments—Legislative, Executive, and Judicial. The Fifth, Sixth, and Eighth Amendments were pointedly aimed at confining exercise of power by courts and judges within precise boundaries, particularly in the procedure used for the trial of criminal cases. Past history provided strong reasons for the apprehensions which brought these procedural amendments into being and attest the wisdom of their adoption. For the fears of arbitrary court action sprang largely from the past use of courts in the imposition of criminal punishments to suppress speech, press, and religion. Hence the constitutional limitations of courts' powers were, in the view of the Founders, essential supplements to the First Amendment, which was itself designed to protect the widest scope for all people to believe and to express the most divergent political, religious, and other views.

But these limitations were not expressly imposed upon state court action. In 1833, *Barron* v. *Baltimore,* 7 Pet. 243, was decided by this Court. It specifically held inapplicable to the states that provision of the Fifth Amendment which declares: "nor shall private property be taken for public use, without just compensation." In deciding the particular point raised, the Court there said that it could not hold that the first eight amendments applied to the states. This was the controlling constitutional rule when the Fourteenth Amendment was proposed in 1866.

My study of the historical events that culminated in the Fourteenth Amendment, and the expressions of those who sponsored and favored, as well as those who opposed its submission and passage, persuades me that one of the chief objects that the provisions of the Amendment's first section, separately, and as a whole, were intended to accomplish was to make the Bill of Rights applicable to the states. With full knowledge of the import of the *Barron* decision, the framers and backers of the Fourteenth Amendment proclaimed its purpose to be to overturn the constitutional rule that case had announced. This historical purpose has never received full consideration or exposition in any opinion of this Court interpreting the Amendment.

.   .   .   .   .   .

For this reason, I am attaching to this dissent an appendix which contains a resumé, by no means complete, of the Amendment's history. In my judgment that history conclusively demonstrates that the language of the first section of the Fourteenth Amendment, taken as a whole, was thought by those responsible for its submission to the people, and by those who opposed its submission, sufficiently explicit to guarantee that thereafter no state could deprive its citizens of the privileges and protections of the Bill of Rights. Whether this Court ever will, or whether it now should, in the light of past decisions, give full effect to what the Amendment was intended to accomplish is not necessarily essential to a decision here. However that may be, our prior decisions, including *Twining,* do not prevent our carrying out that purpose, at least to the extent of making applicable to the states, not a mere part, as the Court has, but the full protection of the Fifth Amendment's provision against compelling evidence from an accused to convict him of crime. And I further contend that the "natural law" formula which the Court uses to reach its conclusion in this case should be abandoned as an incongruous excrescence on our Constitution. I believe that formula to be itself a violation of our Constitution, in that it subtly conveys to courts, at the expense of legislatures, ultimate power over public policies in fields where no specific provision of the Constitution limits legislative power. And my belief seems to be in accord with the views expressed by this Court, at least for the first two decades after the Fourteenth Amendment was adopted. [There follows a discussion of the *Slaughter-House Cases* and the subsequent rise of substantive due process.]

. . . . . .

The foregoing constitutional doctrine, judicially created and adopted by expanding the previously accepted meaning of "due process," marked a complete departure from the *Slaughter-House* philosophy of judicial tolerance of state regulation of business activities. Conversely, the new formula contracted the effectiveness of the Fourteenth Amendment as a protection from state infringement of individual liberties enumerated in the Bill of Rights. Thus the Court's second-thought interpretation of the Amendment was an about face from the *Slaughter-House* interpretation and represented a failure to carry out the avowed purpose of the Amendment's sponsors. . . .

The *Twining* decision, rejecting the compelled testimony clause of the Fifth Amendment, and indeed rejecting all the Bill of Rights, is the end product of one phase of this philosophy. At the same time, that decision consolidated the power of the Court assumed in past cases by laying broader foundations for the Court to invalidate state and even federal regulatory legislation. For the *Twining* decision, giving separate consideration to "due process" and "privileges or immunities," went all the way to say that the "privileges or immunities" clause of the Fourteenth Amendment "did not forbid the States to abridge the personal rights enumerated in the first eight Amendments. . . ." *Twining* v. *New Jersey, supra.* And in order to be certain, so far as possible, to leave this Court wholly free to reject all the

Bill of Rights as specific restraints upon state action, the decision declared that even if this Court should decide that the due process clause forbids the states to infringe personal liberties guaranteed by the Bill of Rights, it would do so, not "because those rights are enumerated in the first eight Amendments, but because they are of such a nature that they are included in the conception of due process of law." *Ibid.*

At the same time that the *Twining* decision held that the states need not conform to the specific provisions of the Bill of Rights, it consolidated the power that the Court had assumed under the due process clause by laying even broader foundations for the Court to invalidate state and even federal regulatory legislation. For under the *Twining* formula, which includes non-regard for the first eight amendments, what are "fundamental rights," and in accord with "canons of decency," as the Court said in *Twining,* and today reaffirms, is to be independently "ascertained from time to time by judicial action. . . ." *Id.,* 211 U.S. at 101; "what is due process of law depends on circumstances." *Moyer* v. *Peabody,* 212 U.S. 78, 84. Thus the power of legislatures became what this Court would declare it to be at a particular time independently of the specific guarantees of the Bill of Rights such as the right to freedom of speech, religion and assembly, the right to just compensation for property taken for a public purpose, the right to jury trial or the right to be secure against unreasonable searches and seizures. . . .

Later decisions of this Court have completely undermined that phase of the *Twining* doctrine which broadly precluded reliance on the Bill of Rights to determine what is and what is not a "fundamental" right. . . .

In *Palko* v. *Connecticut,* 302 U.S. 319, a case which involved former jeopardy only, this Court re-examined the path it had traveled in interpreting the Fourteenth Amendment since the *Twining* opinion was written. In *Twining* the Court had declared that none of the rights enumerated in the first eight amendments were protected against state invasion because they were incorporated in the Bill of Rights. But the Court in *Palko, supra* (302 U.S. at 323), answered a contention that all eight applied with the more guarded statement . . . that "there is no such general rule." Implicit in this statement, and in the cases decided in the interim between *Twining* and *Palko* and since, is the understanding that some of the eight amendments do apply by their very terms. Thus the Court said in the *Palko Case* that the Fourteenth Amendment may make it unlawful for a state to abridge by its statutes the "freedom of speech which the First Amendment safeguards against encroachment by the Congress . . . or the like freedom of the press, . . . or the free exercise of religion . . . , or the right of peaceable assembly . . . or the right of one accused of crime to the benefit of counsel. . . . In these and other situations immunities that are valid as against the federal government by force of the specific pledges of particular amendments have been found to be implicit in the concept of ordered liberty, and thus, through the Fourteenth Amendment, become valid as against the states." *Id.,* 302 U.S. at 324, 325. . . .

. . . In a series of cases since *Twining* this Court has held that the Fourteenth Amendment does bar all American courts, state or federal, from convicting people of crime on coerced confessions. *Chambers* v. *Florida,* 309 U.S. 227; *Ashcraft* v. *Tennessee,* 322 U.S. 143, 154, 155, and cases cited. . . . And taking note of these cases, the Court is careful to point out in its decision today that coerced confessions violate the Federal Constitution if secured "by fear of hurt, torture or exhaustion." Nor can a state, according to today's decision, constitutionally compel an accused to testify against himself by "any other type of coercion that falls within the scope of due process." Thus the Court itself destroys or at least drastically curtails the very *Twining* decision it purports to reaffirm. . . .

I cannot consider the Bill of Rights to be an outworn 18th Century "strait jacket" as the *Twining* opinion did. Its provisions may be thought outdated abstractions by some. And it is true that they were designed to meet ancient evils. But they are the same kind of human evils that have emerged from century to century wherever excessive power is sought by the few at the expense of the many. In my judgment the people of no nation can lose their liberty so long as a Bill of Rights like ours survives and its basic purposes are conscientiously interpreted, enforced and respected so as to afford continuous protection against old, as well as new, devices and practices which might thwart those purposes. I fear to see the consequences of the Court's practice of substituting its own concepts of decency and fundamental justice for the language of the Bill of Rights as its point of departure in interpreting and enforcing that Bill of Rights. If the choice must be between the selective process of the *Palko* decision applying some of the Bill of Rights to the States, or the *Twining* rule applying none of them, I would choose the *Palko* selective process. But rather than accept either of these choices, I would follow what I believe was the original purpose of the Fourteenth Amendment—to extend to all the people of the nation the complete protection of the Bill of Rights. To hold that this Court can determine what, if any, provisions of the Bill of Rights will be enforced, and if so to what degree, is to frustrate the great design of a written Constitution.

Conceding the possibility that this Court is now wise enough to improve on the Bill of Rights by substituting natural law concepts for the Bill of Rights, I think the possibility is entirely too speculative to agree to take that course. I would therefore hold in this case that the full protection of the Fifth Amendment's proscription against compelled testimony must be afforded by California. This I would do because of reliance upon the original purpose of the Fourteenth Amendment.

Mr. Justice DOUGLAS joins in this opinion.
[Appendix to Mr. Justice BLACK's opinion omitted.]

Mr. Justice MURPHY, with whom Mr. Justice RUTLEDGE concurs, dissenting.

While in substantial agreement with the views of Mr. Justice Black, I have one reservation and one addition to make.

I agree that the specific guarantees of the Bill of Rights should be carried over intact into the first section of the Fourteenth Amendment. But I am not prepared to say that the latter is entirely and necessarily limited by the Bill of Rights. Occasions may arise where a proceeding falls so far short of conforming to fundamental standards of procedure as to warrant constitutional condemnation in terms of a lack of due process despite the absence of a specific provision in the Bill of Rights.

That point, however, need not be pursued here inasmuch as the Fifth Amendment is explicit in its provision that no person shall be compelled in any criminal case to be a witness against himself. That provision, as Mr. Justice Black demonstrates, is a constituent part of the Fourteenth Amendment.

We are obliged to give effect to the principle of freedom from self-incrimination. That principle is as applicable where the compelled testimony is in the form of silence as where it is composed of oral statements. Accordingly, I would reverse the judgment below.

WOLF v. COLORADO
338 U.S. 25 (1949)

Mr. Justice FRANKFURTER delivered the opinion of the Court.

The precise question for consideration is this: Does a conviction by a State court for a State offense deny the "due process of law" required by the Fourteenth Amendment, solely because evidence that was admitted at the trial was obtained under circumstances which would have rendered it inadmissible in a prosecution for violation of a federal law in a court of the United States because there deemed to be an infraction of the Fourth Amendment as applied in *Weeks* v. *United States,* 232 U.S. 383? The Supreme Court of Colorado has sustained convictions in which such evidence was admitted, . . . and we brought the cases here. . . .

Unlike the specific requirements and restrictions placed by the Bill of Rights (Amendments 1 to 8) upon the administration of criminal justice by federal authority, the Fourteenth Amendment did not subject criminal justice in the States to specific limitations. The notion that the "due process of law" guaranteed by the Fourteenth Amendment is shorthand for the first eight amendments of the Constitution and thereby incorporates them has been rejected by this Court again and again, after impressive consideration. . . . *Adamson* v. *California,* 332 U.S. 46. The issue is closed.

For purposes of ascertaining the restrictions which the Due Process Clause imposed upon the States in the enforcement of their criminal law, we adhere to the views expressed in *Palko* v. *Connecticut,* 302 U.S. 319. . . . That decision speaks to us with the great weight of the authority, particularly in matters of civil liberty, of a Court that included Mr. Chief Justice Hughes, Mr. Justice Brandeis, Mr. Justice Stone and Mr. Justice Cardozo, to speak only of the dead. In rejecting the suggestion that the Due Process Clause incorporated the original Bill of Rights, Mr. Justice Cardozo reaffirmed on behalf of that Court a different but deeper and more pervasive conception of the Due Process Clause. This Clause exacts from the States for the lowliest and the most outcast all that is "implicit in the concept of ordered liberty." 302 U.S. at 325.

The security of one's privacy against arbitrary intrusion by the police—which is at the core of the Fourth Amendment—is basic to a free society. It is therefore implicit in "the concept of ordered liberty" and as such enforceable against the States through the Due Process Clause. The knock at the door, whether by day or by night, as a prelude to a search, without authority of the police, did not need the commentary of recent history to be condemned as inconsistent with the conception of human rights enshrined in the history and the basic constitutional documents of English-speaking peoples.

Accordingly, we have no hesitation in saying that were a State affirmatively to sanction such police incursion into privacy it would run counter to the guaranty of the Fourteenth Amendment. But the ways of enforcing such a basic right raise questions of a different order. How such arbitrary conduct should be checked, what remedies against it should be afforded, the means by which the right should be made effective, are all questions that are not to be so dogmatically answered as to preclude the varying solutions which spring from an allowable range of judgment on issues not susceptible of quantitative solution.

In *Weeks* v. *United States*, 232 U.S. 383, this Court held that in a federal prosecution the Fourth Amendment barred the use of evidence secured through an illegal search and seizure. This ruling was made for the first time in 1914. It was not derived from the explicit requirements of the Fourth Amendment; it was not based on legislation expressing Congressional policy in the enforcement of the Constitution. The decision was a matter of judicial implication. Since then it has been frequently applied and we stoutly adhere to it. But the immediate question is whether the basic right to protection against arbitrary intrusion by the police demands the exclusion of logically relevant evidence obtained by an unreasonable search and seizure because, in a federal prosecution for a federal crime, it would be excluded. As a matter of inherent reason, one would suppose this to be an issue as to which men with complete devotion to the protection of the right of privacy might give different answers. When we find that in fact most of the English-speaking world does not regard as vital to such protection the exclusion of evidence thus obtained, we must hesitate to treat this remedy as an essential ingredient of the right. The contrariety of views of the States is particularly impressive in view of the careful reconsideration which they have given the problem in the light of the *Weeks* decision.

  I. Before the *Weeks* decision 27 States had passed on the admissibility of evidence obtained by unlawful search and seizure.
  (a) Of these, 26 States opposed the *Weeks* doctrine. [Tables of references are compiled in an appendix, here omitted.]
  (b) Of these, 1 State anticipated the *Weeks* doctrine.
 II. Since the *Weeks* decision 47 States all told have passed on the *Weeks* doctrine.
  (a) Of these, 20 passed on it for the first time.
   (1) Of the foregoing States, 6 followed the *Weeks* doctrine.
   (2) Of the foregoing States, 14 rejected the *Weeks* doctrine.
  (b) Of these, 26 States reviewed prior decisions contrary to the *Weeks* doctrine.
   (1) Of these, 10 States have followed *Weeks*, overruling or distinguishing their prior decisions.
   (2) Of these, 16 States adhered to their prior decisions against *Weeks*.
  (c) Of these, 1 State adhered to its prior formulation of the *Weeks* doctrine.
III. As of today 30 States reject the *Weeks* doctrine, 17 States are in agreement with it.
 IV. Of 10 jurisdictions within the United Kingdom and the British British Commonwealth of Nations which have passed on the question, none has held evidence obtained by illegal search and seizure inadmissible.

The jurisdictions which have rejected the *Weeks* doctrine have not left the right to privacy without other means of protection. Indeed, the exclusion of evidence is a remedy which directly serves only to protect those upon whose person or premises something incriminating has been found. We cannot, therefore, regard it as a departure from basic standards to remand such persons, together with those who emerge scatheless from a search, to the remedies of private action and such protection as the internal discipline of the police, under the eyes of an alert public opinion, may afford. Granting that in pratice the exclusion of evidence may be an effective way of deterring unreasonable searches, it is not for this Court to condemn as falling below the minimal standards assured by the Due Process Clause a State's reliance upon other methods which, if consistently enforced, would be equally effective. . . .

We hold, therefore, that in a prosecution in a State court for a State crime the Fourteenth Amendment does not forbid the admission of evidence obtained by an unreasonable search and seizure. ...

Affirmed.

Mr. Justice BLACK, concurring.

In this case petitioner was convicted of a crime in a state court on evidence obtained by a search and seizure conducted in a manner that this Court has held "unreasonable" and therefore in violation of the Fourth Amendment. And under a rule of evidence adopted by the Court evidence so obtained by federal officers cannot be used against defendants in federal courts. For reasons stated in my dissenting opinion in *Adamson* v. *California,* 332 U.S. 46, 68, I agree with the conclusion of the Court that the Fourth Amendment's prohibition of "unreasonable searches and seizures" is enforceable against the states. Consequently I should be for reversal of this case if I thought the Fourth Amendment not only prohibited "unreasonable searches and seizures," but also, of itself, barred the use of evidence so unlawfully obtained. But I agree with what appears to be a plain implication of the Court's opinion that the federal exclusionary rule is not a command of the Fourth Amendment but is a judicially created rule of evidence which Congress might negate. ... This leads me to concur in the Court's judgment of affirmance.

* * * * *

Mr. Justice MURPHY, with whom Mr. Justice RUTLEDGE joins, dissenting.

It is disheartening to find so much that is right in an opinion which seems to me so fundamentally wrong. Of course I agree with the Court that the Fourteenth Amendment prohibits activities which are prescribed by the search and seizure clause of the Fourth Amendment. See my dissenting views, and those of Mr. Justice Black, in *Adamson* v. *California,* 332 U.S. 46, 68, 123. Quite apart from the blanket application of the Bill of Rights to the States, a devotee of democracy would ill suit his name were he to suggest that his home's protection against unlicensed governmental invasion was not "of the very essence of a scheme of ordered liberty." *Palko* v. *Connecticut,* 302 U.S. 319, 325. It is difficult for me to understand how the Court can go this far and yet be unwilling to make the step which can give some meaning to the pronouncements it utters.

Imagination and zeal may invent a dozen methods to give content to the commands of the Fourth Amendment. But this Court is limited to the remedies currently available. It cannot legislate the ideal system. If we would attempt the enforcement of the search and seizure clause in the ordinary case today, we are limited to three devices: judicial exclusion of the illegally obtained evidence; criminal prosecution of violators; and civil action against violators in the action of trespass.

Alternatives are deceptive. Their very statement conveys the impression that one possibiltiy is as effective as the next. In this case their statement is blinding. For there is but one alternative to the rule of exclusion. That is no sanction at all.

. . . . . .

. . . Little need be said concerning the possibilities of criminal prosecution. Self-scrutiny is a lofty ideal, but its exaltation reaches new heights if we expect a District Attorney to prosecute himself or his associates for well-meaning violations of the search and seizure clause during a raid the District Attorney or his associates have ordered. But there is an appealing ring in another alternative. A trespass action for damages is a venerable means of securing reparation for unauthorized invasion of the home. Why not put the old writ to a new use? When the Court cites cases permitting the action, the remedy seems complete.

But what an illusory remedy this is, if by "remedy" we mean a positive deterrent to police and prosecutors tempted to violate the Fourth Amendment. The appealing ring softens when we recall that in a trespass action the measure of damages is simply the extent of the injury to physical property. If the officer searches with care, he can avoid all but nominal damages—a penny, or a dollar. Are punitive damages possible? Perhaps. But a few states permit none, whatever the circumstances. In those that do, the plaintiff must show the real ill will or malice of the defendant, and surely it is not unreasonable to assume that one in honest pursuit of crime bears no malice toward the search victim. If that burden is carried, recovery may yet be defeated by the rule that there must be physical damages before punitive damages may be awarded. In addition, some states limit punitive damages to the actual expenses of litigation. . . . And even if the plaintiff hurdles all the obstacles, and gains a substantial verdict, the individual officer's finances may well make the judgment useless—for the municipality, of course, is not liable without its consent. Is it surprising that there is so little in the books concerning trespass actions for violation of the search and seizure clause?

The conclusion is inescapable that but one remedy exists to deter violations of the search and seizure clause. That is the rule which excludes illegally obtained evidence. Only by exclusion can we impress upon the zealous prosecutor that violation of the Constitution will do him no good. And only when that point is driven home can the prosecutor be expected to emphasize the importance of observing constitutional demands in his instructions to the police.

. . . [Numerous] examples cited to serve to ground an assumption that has motivated this Court since the *Weeks* Case: that this is an area in which judicial action has positive effect upon the breach of law; and that without judicial action, there are simply no effective sanctions presently available.

I cannot believe that we should decide due process questions by simply taking a poll of the rules in various jurisdictions, even if we follow the *Palko* "test." Today's decision will do inestimable harm to the cause of fair police methods in our cities and states. Even more important, perhaps, it must have tragic effect upon public respect for our judiciary. For the Court now allows what is indeed shabby business: lawlessness by officers of the law.

Since the evidence admitted was secured in violation of the Fourth Amendment, the judgment should be reversed.

[Mr. Justice RUTLEDGE and Mr. Justice DOUGLAS agreed in separate dissenting opinions.]

"DUE PROCESS" AND VALUE JUDGMENTS[9]

The decision of a question of importance on grounds of policy is rarely easy. Exercise of judgment is apt to be painful where each alternative has some merit; and men find it natural to seek some clear and impersonal rule to eliminate the harsh necessity of self-reliance in choice. All men tend to look for a philosopher's stone of judgment, for an easier solution, for a resolving formula; and judges, being men, sometimes join in this search. Decorous convention leads us all to reassure ourselves, from time to time, by saying that we are governed by laws and by men. A little wistfully we sometimes speak of "the law" as though it were a complete existing system, adequate

[9] By Arthur E. Sutherland, Jr. From "Due Process and Disestablishment," 62 *Harvard Law Review* 1306 (1949). Reprinted by permission of Professor Sutherland and of the editors of the Harvard Law Review.

to all human needs—as though it had been written ages ago on great hidden tablets by sages wiser because much older than we are; as though it were still existing somewhere; as though if only we could think aright, we could still find it out.

When a judge has to decide a present controversy and consciously to prescribe a future rule for reasons of current policy—where he must say, "By and large, I think this will be the most workable rule, and I so order!" he must often feel uneasy, realizing that his function has become essentially legislative, realizing that no matter how far he seeks he will not find the hidden tablets, for they do not exist. He is more comfortable if he can hide from himself, a little, the nature of the process, if he can look only out of the corner of his eye at the unwelcome truth that when he makes law, he necessarily makes it according to his private predispositions.

The phrase "due process of law," when applied as a criterion of the validity of a substantive enactment, is essentially a convenient verbal cloak hiding that unwelcome truth. When a judge decides that a state statute is invalid for lack of due process, he is saying that to him it appears so unusual and startling, so drastic a change from the customary and the accepted that the federal government must intervene to prevent its enforcement. As all lawyers shrink a little from so frank a statement of this extraordinary jurisdiction, they decorously say instead that the objectionable measure lacks due process of law. The phrase is comforting, for it suggests that somehow "due process of law" briefly describes, to the wise and farsighted, a code of definite, just, and accepted laws, with which the rejected statute is in obvious conflict. But sometimes "due process" begins to look suspiciously vague and we try to find another formula to define its meaning. Unfortunately, because of the infinite variety of man's conflicts of interest, the redefinition always turns out to have contours no less vague. Each new phrase is more satisfying only because for a time it is less familiar. As each in its turn inevitably loses its potency, we find and substitute another.

CHAPTER XIV

✳ ——————————⌢—————————— ✳

✳

War and the Constitution

1. THE CIVIL WAR PRECEDENT

EX PARTE MILLIGAN
4 Wall. 2 (1866)

[Milligan, a "major general" in a "Copperhead" (Confederate sympathizer) organization, was arrested in Indiana in 1864, and tried and sentenced to death by a military commission on a charge of conspiracy. On January 2, 1865, after the proceedings of the military commission had ended, the United States Circuit Court met at Indianapolis and empaneled a grand jury, but neither that nor any other grand jury found any indictment or made any presentment against Milligan. On May 10, 1865, he petitioned the United States Circuit Court for a writ of habeas corpus on the ground that, as he had not been since the beginning of the civil war a resident of any of the states whose citizens were making war on the United States, the military commission had no jurisdiction over him and that he had been deprived of his right to a trial by jury as guaranteed to him by the Constitution of the United States. He therefore asked that he be either turned over to a civil tribunal for trial or discharged from custody altogether.]

Mr. Justice DAVIS delivered the opinion of the Court. . . .

The controlling question in the case is this: Upon the facts stated in Milligan's petition, and the exhibits filed, had the military commission mentioned in its jurisdiction, legally, to try and sentence him? Milligan, not a resident of one of the rebellious States, or a prisoner of war, but a citizen of Indiana for twenty years past, and never in the

616

military or naval service, is, while at his home, arrested by the military power of the United States, imprisoned, and, on certain criminal charges preferred against him, tried, convicted, and sentenced to be hanged by a military commission, organized under the direction of the military commander of the military district of Indiana. Had this tribunal the legal power and authority to try and punish this man?

... If there was law to justify this military trial, it is not our province to interfere; if there was not, it is our duty to declare the nullity of the whole proceedings. The decision of this question does not depend on argument or judicial precedents, numerous and highly illustrative as they are. The precedents inform us of the extent of the struggle to preserve liberty, and to relieve those in civil life from military trials. The founders of our government were familiar with the history of that struggle, and secured in a written Constitution every right which the people had wrested from power during a contest of ages. By that Constitution and the laws authorized by it this question must be determined. The provisions of that instrument on the administration of criminal justice are too plain and direct to leave room for misconstruction or doubt of their true meaning. Those applicable to this case are found in that clause of the original Constitution which says, "That the trial of all crimes, except in case of impeachment, shall be by jury;" and in the fourth, fifth, and sixth articles of the amendments. . . .

Have any of the rights guaranteed by the Constitution been violated in the case of Milligan? and if so, what are they?

Every trial involves the exercise of judicial power; and from what source did the military commission that tried him derive their authority? Certainly no part of the judicial power of the country was conferred on them; because the Constitution expressly vests it "in one supreme court and such inferior courts as the Congress may from time to time ordain and establish," and it is not pretended that the commission was the mandate of the President, because he is controlled by law, and has his appropriate sphere of duty, which is to execute, not to make the laws; and there is "no unwritten criminal code to which resort can be had as a source of jurisdiction."

It can serve no useful purpose to inquire what those laws and usages are, whence they originated, where found, and on whom they operate; they can never be applied to citizens in States which have upheld the authority of the government, and where the courts are open and their process unobstructed. This Court has judicial knowledge that in Indiana the Federal authority was always unopposed, and its courts always open to hear criminal accusations and redress grievances; and no usage of war could sanction a military trial there for any offense whatever of a citizen in civil life, in nowise connected with the military service. Congress could grant no such power; and to the honor of our national legislature be it said, it has never been provoked by the state of the country even to attempt its exercise. One of the plainest constitutional provisions was, therefore, infringed when Milligan was tried by a court not ordained and established by Congress, and not composed of judges appointed during good behavior.

Why was he not delivered to the Circuit Court of Indiana to be proceeded against according to law? . . . The government had no right to conclude that Milligan, if guilty, would not receive in that court merited punishment; for its records disclose that it was constantly engaged in the trial of similar offenses, and was never interrupted in its administration of criminal justice. If it was dangerous, in the distracted condition of affairs, to leave Milligan unrestrained of his liberty, because he "conspired against the government, afforded aid and comfort to rebels, and incited the people to insurrection," the law said, arrest him, confine him closely, render him powerless to do further mischief; and then present his case to the grand jury of the district, with proofs of his guilt, and, if indicted, try him according to the course of the common law. If this had been done, the Constitution would have been vindicated, the law of 1863 enforced, and the securities for personal liberty preserved and defended.

Another guarantee of freedom was broken when Milligan was denied a trial by jury. The sixth amendment affirms that "in all criminal prosecutions the accused shall enjoy the right to a speedy and public trial by an impartial jury,"—language broad enough to embrace all persons and cases; but the fifth, recognizing the necessity of an indictment, or presentment, before anyone can be held to answer for high crimes, "except cases arising in the land or naval forces, or in the militia, when in actual service, in time of war or public danger;" and the framers of the Constitution, doubtless, meant to limit the right of trial by jury, in the sixth amendment, to those persons who were subject to indictment or presentment in the fifth.

The discipline necessary to the efficiency of the army and navy required other and swifter modes of trial than are furnished by the common-law courts; and, in pursuance of the power conferred by the Constitution, Congress has declared the kinds of trial, and the manner in which they shall be conducted, for offenses committed while the party is in the military or naval service. Every one connected with these branches of the public service is amenable to the jurisdiction which Congress has created for their government, and, while thus serving, citizens of States where the courts are open, if charged with crime, are guaranteed the inestimable privilege of trial by jury. . . .

It is claimed that martial law covers with its broad mantle the proceedings of this military commission. The proposition is this: that in a time of war the commander of an armed force (if, in his opinion, the exigencies of the country demand it, and of which he is the judge) has the power, within the lines of his military district, to suspend all civil rights and their remedies, and subject citizens as well as soldiers to the rule of his will; and in the exercise of his lawful authority cannot be restrained, except by his superior officer or the President of the United States.

If this position is sound to the extent claimed, then when war exists, foreign or domestic, and the country is subdivided into military departments for mere convenience, the commander of one of them can, if he chooses, within his limits, on the plea of necessity, with the approval of the Executive, substitute military force for, and to the exclusion of, the laws, and punish all persons, as he thinks right and proper, without fixed or certain rules.

The statement of this proposition shows its importance; for, if true, republican government is a failure, and there is an end of liberty regulated by law. Martial law, established on such a basis, destroys every guarantee of the Constitution, and effectually renders the "military independent of, and superior to, the civil power,"—the attempt to do which by the King of Great Britain was deemed by our fathers such an offense, that they assigned it to the world as one of the causes which impelled them to declare their independence. Civil liberty and this kind of martial law cannot endure together; the antagonism is irreconcilable and, in the conflict, one or other must perish.

But it is insisted that the safety of the country in time of war demands that this broad claim for martial law shall be sustained. If this were true, it could be well said that a country, preserved at the sacrifice of all the cardinal principles of liberty, is not worth the cost of preservation. Happily, it is not so.

It will be borne in mind that this is not a question of the power to proclaim martial law, when war exists in a community and the courts and civil authorities are overthrown. Nor is it a question what rule a military commander, at the head of his army, can impose on States in rebellion to cripple their resources and quell the insurrection. The necessities of the service, during the late Rebellion, required that the loyal States should be placed within the limits of certain military districts and commanders appointed in them; and, it is urged, that this, in a military sense, constituted them the theater of military operations; and, as in this case, Indiana had been and was again threatened with invasion by the enemy, the occasion was furnished to establish martial law. The conclusion does not follow from the premises. If armies were collected in Indiana, they were to be employed in another locality, where the laws were obstructed and the national authority disputed. On her soil there was no hostile foot; if once invaded, that invasion was at an end, and with it all pretext for martial law. Martial law cannot arise from a threatened invasion. The necessity must be actual and present; the invasion real, such as effectually closes the courts and deposes the civil administration. . . .

It follows, from what has been said on this subject, that there are occasions when martial rule can be properly applied. If, in foreign invasion or civil war, the courts are actually closed, and it is impossible to administer criminal justice according to law, then, on the theater of active military operations, where war really prevails, there is a necessity to furnish a substitute for the civil authority, thus overthrown, to preserve the safety of the army and society; and as no power is left but the military, it is allowed to govern by martial rule until the laws can have their free course. As necessity creates the rule, so it limits its duration; for, if this government is continued after the courts are reinstated, it is a gross usurpation of power. Martial rule can never exist where the courts are open, and in the proper and unobstructed exercise of their jurisdiction.

To the third question, then, on which the judges below were opposed in opinion, an answer in the negative must be returned. . . .

THE CHIEF JUSTICE [CHASE] delivered the following opinion:

Four members of the Court . . . unable to concur in some important particulars with the opinion which has just been read, think it their duty to make a separate statement of their views of the whole case. . . .

The opinion . . . as we understand it, asserts not only that the military commission held in Indiana was not authorized by Congress, but that it was not in the power of Congress to authorize it; from which it may be thought to follow that Congress has no power to indemnify the officers who composed the commission against liability in civil courts for acting as members of it. We cannot agree to this. . . . We think that Congress had power, though not exercised, to authorize the military commission which was held in Indiana. . . .

We by no means assert that Congress can establish and apply the laws of war where no war has been declared or exists.

Where peace exists the laws of peace must prevail. What we do maintain is, that when the nation is involved in war, and some portions of the country are invaded, and all are exposed to invasion, it is within the power of Congress to determine in what States or districts such great and imminent public danger exists as justifies the authorization of military tribunals for the trial of crimes and offenses against the discipline or security of the army or against the public safety. . . .

There are under the Constitution three kinds of military jurisdiction: one to be exercised both in peace and war; another to be exercised in time of foreign war without the boundaries of the United States, or in time of rebellion and civil war within States or districts occupied by rebels treated as belligerents; and a third to be exercised in time of invasion or insurrection within the limits of the United States, or during rebellion within the limits of States maintaining adhesion to the national Government, when the public danger requires its exercise. The first of these may be called jurisdiction under MILITARY LAW, and is found in acts of Congress prescribing rules and articles of war, or otherwise providing for the government of the national forces; the second may be distinguished as MILITARY GOVERNMENT, superseding, as far as may be deemed expedient, the local law, and exercised by the military commander under the direction of the President, with the express or implied sanction of Congress; while the third may be denominated MARTIAL LAW proper, and is called into action by Congress, or temporarily, when the action of Congress cannot be invited, and in the case of justifying or excusing peril, by the President, in times of insurrection or invasion, or of civil or foreign war, within districts or localities where ordinary law no longer adequately secures public safety and private rights. . . .

Mr. Justice WAYNE, Mr. Justice SWAYNE, and Mr. Justice MILLER concur with me in these views.

[NOTE: It is important to read the *Milligan Case* in the light of the acute political conditions attending it. At the very beginning of the Civil War, in the case of *Ex parte Merryman,* Fed. Cas. No. 9487 (1861), involving the arrest and imprisonment of Merryman by the

military authorities in occupation of Baltimore, on a charge of giving aid to the enemy, Chief Justice Taney, sitting as a judge of the
Circuit Court, had issued a writ of habeas corpus to the officer in
charge of the prisoner. The military commander refused to obey the
writ, alleging that he was acting under the orders of the President,
who had suspended the writ. The Chief Justice then issued an attachment for contempt; but the marshal who was sent to serve it was
unable to obtain admission to the fort. Thereupon Taney filed an
opinion holding that the suspension of the writ of habeas corpus by
the President was unconstitutional. A copy of the opinion was mailed
to the President, who, however, refused to be influenced by it.

[The decision of the Court in the *Milligan* Case aroused much criticism from the Radical Republicans because of the fact that while the
Court held unanimously that the particular military commission
which tried Milligan was unlawful, the majority went on to hold that
it was not in the power of Congress to authorize the President to
appoint it. The effect of the decision was thus to throw doubt upon
the legality of other military commissions in operation in the Southern States after the war, and at the same time to serve notice upon
Congress that a number of "reconstruction" bills under discussion
would, if passed, meet with a similar fate at the hands of the Supreme
Court. The Radical Republicans answered with a number of proposals for the reorganization of the Court, so as to curb its power to
prevent the operation of the measures under consideration. Thus,
when the Court announced that it would take jurisdiction in the case
of a Southern newspaper editor who, being held under the authority
of one of the Reconstruction Acts, sought to test their validity, Congress passed an act curtailing the Supreme Court's appellate competence in such a manner as to eliminate the pending case. The Court
acquiesced. *Ex parte McCardle,* 6 Wall. 318, 7 Wall. 506.

[These incidents bespeak a marked hesitancy on the part of the
Court to accept without scrutiny the arguments of necessity in time
of war. The *McCardle* case is indeed one of the most emphatic instances of interdepartmental conflict in our history. By contrast, the
judicial record in our more recent wars shows little desire to assert
independence of policy judgment.]

2. CONSTITUTIONAL RIGHTS IN WORLD WAR II
THE "RELOCATION" OF JAPANESE-AMERICANS

Professor Edward S. Corwin has called our wartime treatment of the Japanese-Americans "the most drastic invasion of the rights of citizens of the United States by their own government that has thus far occurred in the history of our nation."[1] In order to appreciate the full import of the so-called "relocation" of the Japanese-Americans from the West Coast it is well to observe the chronological sequence of the events involved. The attack on Pearl Harbor took place on December 7, 1941; almost at once federal agents proceeded to place in custody a number of individuals, mostly enemy aliens, known to them to be dangerous or potentially dangerous to the military security of a nation at war. Not until February 19, 1942, was there any authority given to impose restrictions on other individuals on grounds of military necessity. This was Executive Order No. 9066 by which the President authorized the Secretary of War and appropriate military commanders to prescribe military areas from which any or all persons might be excluded, and within which the rights of other persons to enter, leave, or remain might be subjected to whatever restrictions the Secretary of War or appropriate military commanders might think necessary. On March 2, 1942, the Commanding General of the Western Defense Command (Lt. Gen. DeWitt), acting under this authority, proclaimed the entire Pacific coast area as particularly subject to the danger of military attack and announced that subsequent notices would establish restrictions and exclusions for certain classes of persons within the two "Military Areas" set up by the order.

Meanwhile, doubts having arisen as to the constitutional basis of the Executive Order of February 19, the Secretary of War requested Congress to supplement the President's order by legislative action; accordingly, Congress on March 21, 1942, enacted a statute making it a misdemeanor for any person to enter, remain in, or leave any military zone designated by the President, Secretary of War, or appropriate military commanders, contrary to the restrictions applicable to the zone as prescribed by military authority (56 Stat. 173). Three days later General DeWitt imposed an eight o'clock curfew on German and Italian nationals and all persons of Japanese ancestry, regardless of nationality. On March 27, 1942, on the grounds that eventual removal from the coastal area was necessary to military security, Japanese nationals and Americans of Japanese ancestry were forbidden to leave the Military Area except under future official orders. These exclusion orders were not promulgated until May 9, 1942. Persons affected, more than 112,000 in numbers nearly two-

[1] *Total War and the Constitution,* Alfred A. Knopf, Inc., 1947, p. 91.

thirds of which were native-born American citizens, were then gathered at temporary collecting points and eventually routed to the "relocation centers," operated by a civilian agency with varying skill and success.[2]

Although steps were initiated at once to bring the relocation program to a court test, it was June, 1943, before the first case was decided by the Supreme Court of the United States. Hirabayashi, an American citizen of Japanese descent, had been convicted in a federal court of violating the curfew order and also failing to report at a so-called control center on a specified day. The fact that the two sentences were to run concurrently enabled the Court to limit its decision to a consideration of the validity of the curfew order. With three justices writing separate concurring opinions, the Court unanimously upheld the curfew as a proper wartime measure. *Hirabayashi* v. *United States*, 320 U.S. 81 (1943).

Chief Justice Stone, writing the principal opinion, recited "the facts and circumstances of the particular war-setting" in which the curfew order was adopted—the seriousness of the danger to the West Coast, the peculiar cohesiveness of the Japanese-American population, the dual citizenship held by many of them under Japanese law, the lessons apparently to be deduced from the activities of "fifth columns" in the European Theater of war,—and concluded that, on the basis of these facts, the Court could not declare the conclusions of the responsible military authorities to be without foundation. The federal war power, the Chief Justice urged, must be interpreted broadly enough to permit "necessary war measures." To be sure, discrimination based solely on race was "odious to a free people whose institutions are founded upon the doctrine of equality," yet such discrimination was not forbidden to the federal government. The Fifth Amendment, it was noted, differed from the Fourteenth in that it contained no equal protection clause; and its due process clause could not be considered to have been violated by a classification based on criteria relevant to the situation and the legislative objective. Since the racial factor was not irrelevant in the present instance Congress could justifiably use race as a basis for legislative classification.

---

[2] For a passionate indictment of certain political forces in California held to have been the motivating agencies behind the exclusion program, see Carey McWilliams, *Prejudice: The Story of the Japanese-Americans;* the entire episode is scholarly analyzed by Morton Grodzins in *Americans Betrayed;* and cf. Alexander H. Leighton, *The Governing of Men,* for a social scientist's observations of a relocation center in operation.

In three separate concurring opinions Justices Murphy, Douglas, and Rutledge took exception to the line of reasoning pursued by the majority. Justice Murphy's language was couched in terms that so clearly conveyed his disapproval of the entire program that one is surprised to find him in the end acquiescing in the result of the case. "Distinctions based on color and ancestry," he wrote, "are utterly inconsistent with our traditions and ideals. They are at variance with the traditions for which we are now waging war. We cannot close our eyes to the fact that for centuries the Old World has been torn by racial and religious conflicts and has suffered the worst kind of anguish because of the treatment for different groups. . . ." Specifically he perceived the parallel between our treatment of the Japanese-Americans and the handling of Jews by the enemy in Europe to be "a melancholy resemblance." In spite of this strong language, Murphy, as did the two other concurring justices, chose to uphold the convictions below by more or less veiled allusions to their inability to challenge, in time of war, the judgment of the responsible military leaders.

Abdication to the military met with vigorous dissent, however, when the exclusion program was more squarely presented to the Court in December 1944.[3] This was an appeal from a conviction of a Japanese-American who had remained inside the Military Area in violation of the exclusion order of the Western Defense Command. Justice Black, speaking for a six-man majority, cited the *Hirabayashi* decision as if it had sanctioned the exclusion of this racial group and implied strongly that since military necessity required such action the Constitution allowed it. "When under conditions of modern warfare our shores are threatened by hostile forces, the power to protect must be commensurate with the threatened danger." The victims were advised to comfort themselves with the thought that "hardships are a part of war, and war is an aggregation of hardships."

The brief majority opinion refused to concern itself with the relocation program. The Court declared, contrary to the appellant's contention, that exclusion and relocation were separate matters and the latter was not a necessary consequence of the order under review.

Justice Roberts, dissenting, pointed out that the exclusion order was by no means separable from the entire attempt to relocate this population group. In fact, the appellant had been confronted with a

[3] *Korematsu v. United States*, 323 U.S. 214.

series of orders: one which forbade him to leave the area except under instructions and the other which excluded him and forced him into the relocation channel. This, Justice Roberts rather pointedly stated, was "nothing but a cleverly devised trap to accomplish the real purpose of the military authority, which was to lock him in a concentration camp." The facts, he concluded, constituted "a clear violation of constitutional rights."

Justice Murphy reiterated his opposition to the entire program of exclusion which, he said, "goes over the 'very brink of constitutional power' and falls into the ugly abyss of racism." He was no longer willing to accept the plea of military necessity. On the contrary, he now asserted without equivocation the right of the Court to ascertain for itself whether the decisions of the military leaders were based on reasons of such overwhelming urgency as to outweigh that solicitude for personal freedoms which the Constitution demands. The claim of military necessity, Justice Murphy asserted, "must subject itself to the judicial process of having its reasonableness determined and its conflicts with other interests reconciled." As a test that might be appropriate a reformulation of the "clear and present danger" test was suggested. Applying such criteria, the program of relocation could not be held reasonable. It was not based upon any evidence that Japanese-Americans as a group were less loyal than other Americans, but rather it was the expression of an ill-concealed racialism which presumed that guilt attached to individuals merely by virtue of their ancestry. Such "legalization of racism" could, in the dissenting justice's view, receive no justification under the Constitution.

Justice Jackson, also dissenting, sought to find an answer to the dilemma which separated Justices Black and Murphy. The substance of his argument is the suggestion that necessary wartime actions ought to be justifiable and justified without recourse to the Constitution. He points out, realistically, that "when an area is so beset that it must be put under military control at all, the paramount consideration is that its measures be successful, rather than legal. . . . But if we cannot confine military expedients by the Constitution, neither would I distort the Constitution to approve all that the military may deem expedient." In other words, if the justification of wartime acts of the military would result in a loosening of constitutional guarantees it might be preferable to avow candidly that such military measures were beyond the purview of the Constitution. For "a judicial construction of the due process clause that will sustain this order is a far more subtle blow to liberty than the promulgation of the order itself. A military order, however unconstitutional,[4] is not apt to last longer than the military emergency. Even during that period a succeeding commander may revoke it all. But once a judicial opinion rationalizes such an order to show that it conforms to the Constitution, or rather rationalizes the Constitution to show that the Constitution sanctions such an order, the Court for all time has validated the principle of racial discrimination in criminal procedure and of transplanting American citizens. The principle then lies about like a loaded weapon ready for the hand of any authority that can bring forward a plausible claim of an urgent need. . . ."[5]

The *Korematsu* decision carefully avoided any determination of the constitutionality of the detention program, upholding only the exclusion from the military area. In *Ex parte Endo,* 323 U.S. 283, decided the same day, the Court directed the issuance of a writ of habeas corpus for the release of a young Japanese-American girl whose loyalty the detaining agency itself had established two and a half years earlier. Again, however, the Court's principal opinion merely skirted the problem. Justice Douglas interpreted the act of Congress and the Executive Order preceding it as not having authorized detention. Thus Miss Endo's release was ordered because the subordinate agency enforcing detention possessed no legal authorization, not because a law authorizing detention would have contravened any constitutional principles.

Justices Murphy and Roberts in separate concurring opinions in effect accused the majority of evading the issue. Murphy urged that, regardless of congressional or executive approval, the evacuation program should have received the Court's unconditional condemnation as an "unconstitutional resort to racism." Roberts aimed his criticism primarily at the grounds on which decision of the constitutional issue had been avoided. Congress' well-considered appropriations for the enforcing agency, the President's order setting up the agency and appointing officials to direct that body seemed to Roberts clearly indicative of congressional and executive sanction of the entire detention program. The Court had been "squarely faced" with a constitu-

---

[4] Consistency would have required this reference to read "non-constitutional."

[5] In *Woods* v. *Miller, infra,* Justice Jackson similarly suggests the necessity for clearer demarcation of the limits of the war power. His opinions in the two cases may profitably be read together.

tional issue which, in Roberts' opinion, had been avoided on flimsy technical grounds of doubtful pertinence.

MARTIAL LAW IN HAWAII

The problem underlying the Japanese Exclusion Cases and so assiduously evaded by the Court was essentially the same as that presented by the imposition of martial law in Hawaii: how far ought the judiciary defer to the military in the determination of the propriety of security measures which infringe constitutional rights?

The Territory of Hawaii is governed under the provisions of the Hawaiian Organic Act of April 30, 1900, 31 Stat. 141. Section 5 of this act provides that "the Constitution . . . shall have the same effect within the said Territory as elsewhere in the United States." In Section 67 the governor is enjoined to execute the laws of the United States faithfully and given authority, "in case of rebellion or invasion, or imminent danger thereof, when the public safety requires it," to suspend the privilege of the writ of habeas corpus, or place the Territory, or any part thereof, under martial law.

Invoking this section of the Territory's basic statute, Governor Poindexter on December 7, 1941, proclaimed martial law, suspended the writ of habeas corpus, and conferred on the local army commander all his own powers as governor as well as "all of the powers normally exercised by the judicial officers . . . of this territory . . . during the present emergency and until the danger of invasion is removed." The President approved this transfer of powers two days later and, with minor relaxations, the military ruled Hawaii until October 24, 1944. As a part of its regime the military government set up military courts to try civilians; the sentences of these tribunals were not subject to review in regular courts. Even after partial restoration of civil government in 1943 and the reopening of civilian courts, the writ of habeas corpus continued to be suspended and infractions of military orders by civilians remained within the exclusive province of military courts.

The scope and methods of military rule in Hawaii aroused almost immediate objections.[6] This resistance reached a dramatic climax in the controversy between Lt. Gen. Richardson, the military governor, and federal Judge Metzger, in the course of which Richardson issued

---

[6] See, e.g., J. Garner Anthony, "Martial Law in Hawaii," 30 *California Law Review* 371 (January, 1942).

an order forbidding Metzger to issue any writ of habeas corpus and the judge countered by finding the general in contempt of court and fining him $5000.[7]

When, as a result of this and other civil-military clashes, President Roosevelt lifted the last vestiges of martial law from the islands, two cases designed to test the constitutional validity of the military government in Hawaii were already on the way to the Supreme Court of the United States. Duncan, a shipyard worker, had been found guilty by a military court in 1944 of assault on a sentry at a naval reservation; White, a broker who had been charged with embezzlement prior to the imposition of martial law, had been sentenced to five years' imprisonment by a military tribunal in 1942.

The Court granted certiorari on February 12, 1945, (after the challenged system had been discontinued) and rendered its decision, consolidated to apply to both cases, on February 25, 1946, more than half a year after the cessation of hostilities.

Six of eight justices sitting[8] agreed that the establishment of military tribunals in Hawaii to try civilians was not authorized by law. *Duncan v. Kahanamoku,* 327 U.S. 304 (1946). Justice Black, writing the principal opinion for the majority, based his decision primarily on the terms of the Hawaiian Organic Act and on references to history—though surprisingly *Ex parte Milligan,* which seems to be almost exactly in point, was barely mentioned. Justice Murphy in a concurring opinion urged his brethren to declare unequivocally that "these trials were forbidden by the Bill of Rights of the Constitution of the United States, which applies both in letter and in spirit to Hawaii." In contrast to this appeal to absolutes Chief Justice Stone suggested in another concurring opinion that "there could be circumstances in which public safety requires, and the Constitution permits, substitution of trials by military tribunals for trials in 'civil courts' "; but he found that the record of the present cases, including the testimony of military spokesmen, offered no support for the assumption that "civil courts were unable to function with their usual efficiency at the times these petitioners were tried. . . ."

Justice Burton, speaking for himself and Frankfurter, seems to have aimed his words especially against Stone when he warned against "judging military action too closely by the inapplicable stand-

[7] See Claude McColloch, "Judge Metzger and the Military," 35 *American Bar Association Journal* 365 (1949).

[8] Mr. Justice Jackson was absent in Nuremberg.

ards of judicial, or even military, hindsight." Hawaii, the dissenting
justice reminded the Court, had to be visualized as a battlefield the
peculiar position of which required that all activity be "subordinated
to executive control as the best constitutional safeguard of the civilian as well as the military life." And, with unusual judicial candor,
he invited the Court to ask itself if it would have decided these cases
in the same manner on the dates on which they first arose, in August,
1942, and March, 1944, respectively. "I believe," Burton answered his
own question, "that this Court would not have been justified in granting . . . relief . . . at such times. Also, I believe that this Court might
well have found itself embarrassed had it ordered such relief and then
had attempted to enforce its order in the theater of military operations. . . ."

3. WAR AND THE EFFECTS OF WAR

WOODS v. MILLER

333 U.S. 138 (1948)

Mr. Justice DOUGLAS delivered the opinion of the Court.

The case is here on a direct appeal . . . from a judgment of the
District Court holding unconstitutional Title II of the Housing and
Rent Act of [June 30] 1947. . . .

The District Court was of the view that the authority of Congress
to regulate rents by virtue of the war power (see *Bowles* v. *Willing-
ham*, 321 U.S. 503) ended with the Presidential Proclamation terminating hostilities on December 31, 1946, since that proclamation
inaugurated "peace-in-fact" though it did not mark termination of
the war. It also concluded that even if the war power continues, Congress did not act under it because it did not say so, and only if Congress says so, or enacts provisions so implying, can it be held that
Congress intended to exercise such power. That Congress did not
so intend, said the District Court, follows from the provision that
the Housing Expediter can end controls in any area without regard
to the official termination of the war, and from the fact that the preceding federal rent control laws (which were concededly exercises
of the war power) were neither amended nor extended. The District
Court expressed the further view that rent control is not within the
war power because "the emergency created by the housing shortage
came into existence long before the war." It held that the Act "lacks
in uniformity of application and distinctly constitutes a delegation
of legislative power, not within the grant of Congress" because of the

authorization to the Housing Expediter to lift controls in any area before the Act's expiration. It also held that the Act in effect provides "low rentals for certain groups without taking the property or compensating the owner in any way." . . .

We conclude, in the first place, that the war power sustains this legislation. The Court said in *Hamilton* v. *Kentucky Distilleries & Warehouse Co.*, 251 U.S. 146, 161, that the war power includes the power "to remedy the evils which have arisen from its rise and progress" and continues for the duration of that emergency. Whatever may be the consequences when war is officially terminated, the war power does not necessarily end with the cessation of hostilities. We recently held that it is adequate to support the preservation of rights created by wartime legislation. *Fleming* v. *Mohawk Wrecking & Lumber Co.*, 331 U.S. 111. But it has a broader sweep. In *Hamilton* v. *Kentucky Distilleries & Warehouse Co., supra*, and *Jacob Ruppert, Inc.* v. *Caffey*, 251 U.S. 264, prohibition laws which were enacted after the Armistice in World War I were sustained as exercises of the war power because they conserved manpower and increased efficiency of production in the critical days during the period of demobilization, and helped to husband the supply of grains and cereals depleted by the war effort. . . .

The constitutional validity of the present legislation follows a fortiori from those cases. The legislative history of the present Act makes abundantly clear that there has not yet been eliminated the deficit in housing which in considerable measure was caused by the heavy demobilization of veterans and by the cessation or reduction in residential construction during the period of hostilities due to allocation of building materials to military projects. Since the war effort contributed heavily to that deficit, Congress has the power even after the cessation of hostilities to act to control the forces that a short supply of the needed article created. If that were not true, the Necessary and Proper Clause, Art. 1, Sec. 8, cl. 18, would be drastically limited in its application to the several war powers. . . . The result would be paralyzing. It would render Congress powerless to remedy conditions the creation of which necessarily followed from the mobilization of men and materials for successful prosecution of the war. So to read the Constitution would be to make it self-defeating.

We recognize the force of the argument that the effects of war under modern conditions may be felt in the economy for years and

years, and that if the war power can be used in days of peace to treat
all the wounds which war inflicts on our society, it may not only
swallow up all other powers of Congress but largely obliterate the
Ninth and the Tenth Amendments as well. There are no such implications in today's decision. We deal here with the consequences
of a housing deficit greatly intensified during the period of hostilities
by the war effort. Any power, of course, can be abused. But we cannot assume that Congress is not alert to its constitutional responsibilities. . . .

The question of the constitutionality of the action taken by Congress does not depend on recitals of the power which it undertakes
to exercise. Here it is plain from the legislative history that Congress
was invoking its war power to cope with a current condition of which
the war was a direct and immediate cause. Its judgment on that score
is entitled to the respect granted like legislation enacted pursuant
to the police power. . . .

Reversed.

Mr. Justice FRANKFURTER concurs. . . .

Mr. Justice JACKSON, concurring.

I agree with the result in this case, but the arguments that have
been addressed to us lead me to utter more explicit misgivings about
war powers than the Court has done. The Government asserts no
constitutional basis for this legislation other than this vague, undefined and undefinable "war power."

No one will question that this power is the most dangerous one
to free government in the whole catalogue of powers. It is usually
invoked in haste and excitement when calm legislative consideration
of constitutional limitation is difficult. It is executed in a time of
patriotic fervor that makes moderation unpopular. And, worst of
all, it is interpreted by the Judges under the influence of the same
passions and pressures. Always, as in this case, the Government urges
hasty decision to forestall some emergency or serve some purpose
and pleads that paralysis will result if its claims to power are denied
or their confirmation delayed.

Particularly when the war power is invoked to do things to the
liberties of people, or to their property or economy that only indirectly affect conduct of the war and do not relate to the management
of the war itself, the constitutional basis should be scrutinized with
care.

I think we can hardly deny that the war power is as valid a ground for federal rent control now as it has been at any time. We still are technically in a state of war. I would not be willing to hold that war powers may be indefinitely prolonged merely by keeping legally alive a state of war that had in fact ended. I cannot accept the argument that war powers last as long as the effects and consequences of war for if so they are permanent—as permanent as the war debts. But I find no reason to conclude that we could find fairly that the present state of war is merely technical. We have armies abroad exercising our war power and have made no peace terms with our allies not to mention our enemies. I think the conclusion that the war power has been applicable during the lifetime of this legislation is unavoidable.

CHAPTER XV

Political Issues and Legal Methods

1. DEMOCRACY AND JUDICIAL REVIEW

THE ABSOLUTE REIGN OF LAW[1]

It is easy to understand the attractiveness of judicial review. In the choice of the judiciary as governmental umpire there has seemed to be the possibility of realizing a great dream. A legislature dealing with constitutional limitations tends to treat them from the point of view of expediency and utility. Thus the Constitution, although written, must necessarily exist only as a series of pious political maxims, partaking not infrequently of the nature of New Year's resolutions. Whatever cannot be tested in the ordeal of litigation is not law although it masquerades as such. It is only when John Jones and the government of the United States can stand before a court upon an exact footing of equality and litigate even the most momentous of issues that the Constitution has any reality. It is expected that a court, operating under guarantees of independence and impartiality, will never be tempted to deviate from the letter of the Constitution, which is the letter of the law. Surely it is an inspiring ideal to attempt to assure the stability of government at the same time that the security of the individual is put beyond cavil.

It is true that it is the peculiar virtue of a litigation that it is centered upon the interests of the individuals who are involved. But for that very reason society must come off as best it may. Social issues upon which passions run high when subjected to the judicial proc-

[1] Reprinted from *The Quest for Law* by William Seagle by permission of Alfred A. Knopf, Inc. Copyright 1941 by Alfred A. Knopf, Inc.

ess are bound to become entangled in the strangling meshes of legal techniques and formulae. The legal order is not an order in which purpose reigns supreme. It is not a free order. It exalts stability above change. The life of the law is precedent, and the essence of precedent is the word that binds. Word-fetishism dominates judicial decision, and the cry is for Ten Commandments, Twelve Tables, for something that can be written on tablets, inscribed on stone. The whole legal art is the art of grasping the logical limits of the word. Time and change must be thrust aside. The jurist must be as faithful to the Word as to his wife.

But a constitution can hardly be construed by the same techniques as a grant in a deed. An organic document can set limits to legislation in broad and general terms only. The evils of the "due process" clause are only an illustration of the fatal dilemma which has always beset constitution-makers. If a constitution is too explicit, it ceases to be a constitution, a fundamental law, and becomes a code book. Moreover, since constitutional legislation rapidly assumes a sacrosanct character and becomes, like the law of the Medes and the Persians, unalterable, it is particularly dangerous to enunciate in it much more than general principles. On the other hand, to set more general limits, to create a mere "frame of government," to be terse and epigrammatic rather [than] to indulge in a saving verbosity, is to free the hands of the judges and make them masters rather than servants of the state.

The Supreme Court has frequently been denounced as "lawless." But the charge is beside the point. In the logic of the legal system the Constitution must necessarily mean what the highest tribunal says it means. Hence while the Court may make a decision that is socially vicious, it does not necessarily depart from the Word. In the process of interpretation there is almost always a choice between alternatives, and it is inevitable that the choice of the judges will tend to be in accordance with their economic prejudices. . . .

.   .   .   .   .

It might be supposed that the tremendous strain to which judicial review has been subjected would cause its rapid collapse. But while the injection of legality into the solution of political problems has created a perpetual state of tension, it has also provided means for easing the strain, and preventing the breaking-point from being reached. The advantage of a court in disposing of social and economic issues is that in the judicial forum the conflict of classes is supposed to be reconciled under the highest ideals of objectivity. In Western democracies a judge is as much above suspicion as Caesar's wife. As a railroad or corporation lawyer he may have engaged in sharp or even shady practices, but his past is forgotten as soon as he dons the judicial robe and mounts the bench. The interest which disqualifies a judge is only present interest. The House of Lords, like other upper chambers, long exercised a veto power over legislation, but its power was crudely employed from purely selfish class motives. The Supreme Court, however, speaks its dooms in the name of the impartiality of the law. It can pretend that its hands are tied by the Constitution, which can be changed only by the will of the sovereign people. It is not for a judge, who is a mere delegate of the people, to meddle in matters which do not concern him.

Thus the average man who believes that the law of the Constitution is as simple and definite as any other law, has his wits sadly addled. And his impression that the Constitution can override the personal prejudices of the judges is on occasion substantiated, for judges do intoxicate themselves with precedents to such an extent that they are sometimes taken in themselves. There thus occurs the paradox of conservative justices who seem to be on the liberal side and of liberal justices who seem to be on the conservative side. Chief Justice Taft, who can hardly be called a liberal, was in favor of upholding minimum wage legislation. Justice Holmes betrayed the cause of liberalism on a number of occasions. The liberal justices without exception joined in killing the NRA. Such occurrences as these seem to make all the talk about a liberal or illiberal Supreme Court only another source of confusion. Liberalism is a political doctrine, but it is easy to point out that judicial review is a legal institution. Even frequent dissent does not undermine the belief in the integrity of the Court. Dissent implies at least that there is objective law to be discovered. As long as voices of dissent issue from the vaulted chamber of the Supreme Court itself, the delusive impression is created that the dice are not loaded against the common man.

The halo which surrounds judges makes it possible for them to stand an incredible amount of abuse and vilification. It has always been the privilege of the disappointed litigant to repair to the tavern and curse the judge, for while the individual judge may err, it is assumed that he does so in ignorance, and the integrity of the law itself remains. Thus it has become easy to inculcate an American habit of laying the blame for almost all the ills to which the flesh is heir upon the Supreme Court of the United States, which serves indeed as the national scapegoat. When they have opposed the national will, the . . . justices have been pictured as the ogres of the Constitution while the President and Congress have appeared as the gallant knights battling to save their victims. But only a few Presidents have left reputations of being anything like Supreme Court busters, and their bark always turned out to be worse than their bite. President Taft actually vetoed the first bill admitting Arizona to the Union, on the ground that its constitution would contain a provision for the recall of judicial decisions! A bitter fight was waged against the nomination of Justice Brandeis because of his supposed radicalism. The Supreme Court of the present [the 'thirties] generation has been denounced primarily because of its resistance to labor legislation, but Congress has not been very much better. When it turned out that in the Sherman Anti-Trust Act and the Clayton Act it had sold gold bricks to American labor, it did not enact new legislation, which it might well have done, since the Supreme Court decisions did not turn upon constitutional questions.

The mere fact of the Supreme Court's survival suggests that the myth of interdepartmental war has had only a partial reality, and that the Supreme Court has been able to curb popular aspirations only because it is an integral part of the most adroit political system ever devised to frustrate the popular will. . . .

. . . To subject the decision of momentous political issues to a technique developed to dispose of relatively trivial questions can have only inevitable consequences. Judicial review has been defended in the name of the security of property, yet it has been unable to prevent two of the greatest confiscations in the history of property: the abolition of slavery without compensation, and the destruction of the liquor interests. It has been defended in the name of peace and stability, yet it precipitated one of the bloodiest civil wars in modern history and has kept the country in a constant state of political turmoil and uncertainty. It has been defended in the name of civil liberty, yet the rights of citizens have been trampled underfoot not only in times of war but in peace. The absolute reign of law has often been synonymous with the absolute reign of lawlessness.

TRIAL BY COMBAT: THE PROBLEM TODAY[2]

In times of change, what should be the functions of the Supreme Court? What dangers can this venerable institution guard us against? It is our most important symbol of government. It should be the concrete dramatization of the ideal that there is a power which prevents government action which is arbitrary, capricious, and based on prejudice. It may or may not be that had it developed without the power to declare laws unconstitutional we might have had all the advantages of a flexible government without losing the advantages of a symbol of the law above the king. That question, however, is not worth discussing. We did not develop that way, and the power to declare laws unconstitutional is now inseparable from the prestige and power of the Court. One cannot build up in a day the kind of tradition which surrounds this great institution, and therefore one must accept the institution as one finds it. Sudden changes in its power and function cannot be made, after it has reached its maturity, any more than great branches can be cut off an ancient tree. The practical question, therefore, is not of changing its power, but of how it is to exercise that power.

There is no formula for the exercise of such a power. Yet a judge who recognizes the evanescent nature of any form of social bookkeeping will hesitate to interfere with any exercise of governmental power which is sincere in its purpose and honestly designed as an experiment in social welfare. When the Court stands guard over any legal or economic theory, or over the form of our governmental structure, they are taking a gamble on the continuance of that theory, the outcome of which the Supreme Court cannot be wise enough to predict. The history of the Supreme Court of the United States is spotted with decisions declaring invalid unemployment insurance, income taxes, federal employment agencies, railway pension schemes. None of these decisions has turned back the stream of events. Each of them has only added its quota of confusion.

A Court which recognizes the place of legal and economic theory would be freed from the fear that "an impending moral chaos"[3] could possibly be the result of any conceivable decision which the

2 From Thurman W. Arnold, *The Symbols of Government,* New Haven: Yale University Press, 1935, pp. 195–198. Reproduced by permission of the publishers.

3 Language of Mr. Justice McReynolds, dissenting in the *Gold Clause Cases,* 294 U.S. 240, 381 (1934).

Court could make. He would realize that in times of social change the greatest danger is from intolerance of the ideas of others, and from the neglect of the splendid ideal of a fair trial. Vested property interests will either be strong enough to control the political situation, or so weak that not even the Court can maintain their privileges. But the lowly and oppressed, the fanatical idealists who desire to speak their theories in public without undergoing martyrdom have no protection in the entire system other than the Court. It is here that the Court can take a bold stand without gambling on the future, because the ideal of a fair trial for the oppressed has survived every dictatorship the world has ever known. . . . In the celebration of legal and economic theories the Court should be equipped only with prayer books and collections of familiar quotations. In the protection of those seeking a fair trial it should be armed with a sword which it dared to use with courage. Here is a function for which the grand old ceremony of trial by combat[4] is eminently fitted. It should be used for such purposes rather than as an instrument for hit-or-miss conservative social planning.

THE COURT AND THE POPULAR WILL[5]

. . . What as to juridical matters is the power of the people as expressed through electoral and deliberative processes? And what is the function of the Court? Are there limitations upon the preponderant will and conscience of the people, when deliberatively ascertained? If so, what is then the duty of the Court? Are there rights of persons and of states that are beyond the power of majorities or of all the people to change, while our form of government endures?

To answer these questions it is necessary to understand the philosophy which motivated the founding fathers. They founded this nation upon a system of checks and balances. First there was a balance between the one, the few and the many. They knew that government to be efficient should have an executive head with authority to act where prompt action was required. They knew also that the legislative functions of government required study, deliberation and consultation. The legislative power was therefore vested in representatives of the people. Other powers, however, were reserved to the

---

[4] I.e., the appearance of adversaries before a tribunal.

[5] Editorial in 35 *American Bar Association Journal* 129–131 (1949). Reproduced by permission of the editors.

people themselves, such as the selection of representatives and the determination of questions of broad policy.

The next balance was between departments of government—the executive, legislative and the judicial. Definite restraints were imposed upon the executive and the legislative departments, by providing first that the officers of those departments should be chosen at frequent intervals by the people and next that their acts should be subject to judicial review. An independent judiciary was then established with authority to restrain abuse of power by other agents of government. The judiciary itself was restrained from arbitrary and oppressive power by the strict limitation of its activity to the judicial function. Courts were not authorized to initiate or execute measures. They were empowered merely to determine questions presented in the course of judicial proceedings. With the delivery of judgment the court's power came to an end.

There was a third balance, that between state and national governments. Local self-government was preserved by restricting federal action to such matters of national concern as were entrusted to the national government by the Constitution.

It is therefore apparent that absolute power was not vested in any group or any department. The framers of our Constitution knew that government was necessary. It was therefore their aim to establish an efficient government. History, however, had taught them that it was the tendency of governments to become arbitrary and oppressive, and they attempted to limit this tendency by establishing a Constitution and investing a judiciary with authority to restrain any violation of its provisions.

Our Constitution is based upon a profound understanding of human nature. Every normal individual is subject to two impulses: the impulse to do as he pleases, and the impulse to do as he ought. The one impulse is arbitrary; the other is reasonable. The wisdom of ages has crystallized in the adage that "A wise man does what ought to be done." Man's reason and experience have taught him that there is a higher law which cannot be violated or disregarded with impunity. This has been referred to for centuries as natural law; and it was recognized and acknowledged by the men who drafted the Declaration of Independence and the Constitution. Their intent and their effort was to establish a government which would be free from capricious conduct and regulated wholly by law.

They knew also that the impulse to do as one pleases increases with the increase of power. History revealed to them that those who had opposed arbitrary and oppressive power in others adopted arbitrary and oppressive methods when they in turn became invested with power. When the Parliament of England had won its fight against the absolute sovereignty of the Crown, it in turn assumed absolute parliamentary sovereignty. The revolt of the Colonies was against such assumption of power by Parliament.

The founders of our Government imposed every reasonable restriction upon government to insure the people against despotism—even the despotism of the casual majority or the mob, the political pressures that are confused as the deliberative will of the people. It was the desire of the founders to establish a government which would be motivated by reason, not arbitrary will, and it should be constantly borne in mind that they recognized the danger of arbitrary action no matter by whom exercised. As stated in the *Federalist:*

The accumulation of all powers, legislative, executive and judiciary, in the same hands, whether of one, a few, or many, and whether hereditary, self-appointed, or elective, may justly be pronounced the very definition of tyranny.

Madison, the Father of the Constitution, expressed grave apprehension of the tendency of the popular element to extend the sphere of its activity and draw all power into its "impetuous vortex."

There is a tendency today to pamper and pander to so-called popular will, usually political will or self-interest in ill disguise. History reveals that this tendency leads to the disintegration of government. The people themselves, if they wish to maintain a government that is not of men but of laws, must accept the fact that they and their electoral majorities, no less than the king, are under God and the Law.

Now this consideration of the philosophy and framework of our Government reveals at once the true position and function of the Supreme Court. [Ben W.] Palmer is exactly right when he quotes the statement that "the Court has no reason for its existence if it merely reflects the pressure of the day." Furthermore, the Court would exceed its authority and violate the trust reposed in it if it should attempt to give effect to supposed popular or political opinion against the express provisions of the Constitution, or to attempt to amend the Constitution by interpretation, or to usurp the functions of the legislative department. The people have power to amend the

Constitution, but only in the manner which the Constitution provides. Neither the Court nor the Congress should arrogate to itself the power to amend.

Now it is apparent that if the Supreme Court is to perform its function according to the Constitution, it must be made up of men who are familiar with the history of our jurisprudence and our constitutionalism, and who are impersonal, impartial, courageous, trained in the law and consecrated to judicial service. Partisanship or bias corrupts the judicial office. That is why it is a gross error to appoint partisan judges and why that error cannot be corrected by other partisan appointments from some opposing faction or party. The judges' full allegiance must be to the law, for there is the only true sovereignty.

2. STATESMANSHIP AND JUDICIAL TRADITION
A COURT OF LAW AND ITS ADVANTAGES[6]

The most important historical fact about the Court is that it started its career as a law court for the decision and disposition of law cases. That was what it was set up to do by the Constitution, and that is what it did do. Here history is of the first importance. The Constitution expected its Supreme Court to be a law court, and the debates on the convention show that if the Court was going to nullify legislation it would be expected to do it strictly in line of its judicial duties. What was first proposed, in the Virginia Plan, was a Council of Revision which was to have the veto power instead of the President. This was opposed on the ground that it would give the Justices a double chance to veto an act of Congress, once on grounds of policy in the Council, and again on the grounds of unconstitutionality when the act came before them in a law suit. Gerry added that it was quite foreign to the nature of the office to make them judges of the policy of public measures. Whatever the reason, the convention rejected the proposed Council and gave the veto power to the President alone.

So the Court started as an ordinary law court and it continued to be an ordinary law court for a long time. The Justices sat on the bench, they heard the arguments of counsel, they gave written opinions, just like any court in the ancient tradition of the Common Law. The procedure was, and, of course, still is, the same, writs, declarations, bills in equity, pleadings, judgments, and decrees. . . .

[6] Excerpts from Chapter 7 of Charles P. Curtis' *Lions Under the Thone* (pp. 59–67), reproduced by permission of the author and the publishers, Houghton Mifflin Co.

In the early days about 60 per cent of its business was made up of ordinary law suits between individuals which depended on the ordinary principles of law, either the common law or the special rules that obtain in the three chief fields that had been taken away from the state courts and given to the federal courts, admiralty, bankruptcy, and patents. Anyhow, almost two-thirds of its business was ordinary law suits between individual litigants. And this continued until after the Civil War. In 1875, the proportion was a little less, but not much, 56 per cent. But fifty years later, in 1925, we find a great change. It was only about 15 per cent. Now, in 1945, it would be pretty safe to say that this kind of business had almost completely gone. Thumb your way through one of the recent volumes of the Court's reports, and you will find what Frankfurter and Landis, whose figures I have used, call "a different world of ideas." You find the Court passing on the meaning or the validity of legislation, on the use and abuse of the powers of this or that board or commission, on the right of a state to tax or regulate this or that corporation or union, on the constitutional propriety of this and the other court's handling of some criminal prosecution, on tax matters, on suits against the government. This is a great shift into matters of public concern and public interest. Disappointed litigants often say they will carry their appeal right up to the Supreme Court of the United States, if necessary. They do not get there. For the Court has all but ceased to handle ordinary private litigation.

And yet the Court has never ceased to conduct its business under the guise and with all the tools and procedures of an ordinary law court. We think of it as a law court. In its tradition and procedure it is a law court. Only its business has changed to far transcend ordinary litigation. It would not be true—but a good half truth won't do us any harm—to go back and wonder if the Council of Revision, thrown out of the window by the convention, has not come back down the chimney, and without the President being a member, only the Justices. That is not quite true, but sometimes some of the Justices have acted as if it were true. If the Council of Revision had been included in the Constitution, would it have survived? Democracy elbowed aside the equally undemocratic Electoral College. A Council on which the judges sat and openly and candidly passed on the wisdom of legislation, would that have stood?

Anyhow, it was as a court of law that the Court undertook after the Civil War to exercise its great power over legislation. Not, of course, only because it sat on a bench and wore robes. It had also all the many and great advantages that a court of law possesses in dealing with political and economic questions; and at the same time its disadvantages. The Justices are quite well aware of both.

 . . . .

The judicial tradition makes two quite direct and specific demands upon a court, both so usual that we take them for granted and miss perhaps their efficacy. One is that the case be decided one way or another and as soon as possible. The other is that the judges give written opinions, reasoned statements of what the case is, what they decide and why. Other governmental officials may have to act, and sometimes quickly under the pressure of events. A court is always under the pressure of the tradition, and no other government official is required always to give his reasons. He may or he may not, as he deems best and when it is expected of him, but it is always expected of the Court. A strange inconsistency bids some people deplore criticism of the one governmental body that is required always to offer itself for criticism. . . .

But the requirement of an immediate decision, not contingent on events, is the more important and the more valuable. Not that justice delayed, as the saying is, is justice denied. That is so in private litigation, but in public matters, as in every decision, the advantage of an immediate decision is not so much the disadvantage of delay as the peculiar virtue of being right up against the problem. . . . The pressure of events brings political problems near enough to other departments of the government, meanwhile keeping those that do not call for decision remote enough not to interfere. For the Court it is the traditional duty of deciding the instant case that serves this purpose. Not until a problem is immediate and unavoidable is a man at his best to solve it. . . . The best individual does best under pressure and in a pinch.

 . . . .

These two demands of the judicial tradition work happily together. The Court is faced with a problem which it knows it must now decide, and in its deliberations it knows, too, that it is going to have to give its reasons. A body of men that must explain itself to a public that is going to criticize. The function of the bar on these public questions is sometimes not fully understood. The bar not only aids the Court by arguing the issue before it. The bar is a special set of experts retained by the public at large to read the Court's opinions and expound them to the people. The people not only have a right to criticize the Court. They have professionals to help them do it. It is a double pity when the bar is so eager to defend the Court's prestige that it goes back on its public clients.

. . . . .

THE JURIST'S ART[7]

The art of judgment is of its own kind. Unlike the poet, the historian, or the essayist, the jurist cannot listen to the promptings of his own heart, choose the subject upon which he would write, say as he would all that is in his mind, and follow his interest to a fresh theme. Instead, as a member of a court, his decisions are a mere step in the process of disposing of litigation. He cannot speak until the appropriate cause comes along, he can address himself to the larger issue only so far as a suit at law allows, he must express a partial opinion and wait for a suitable occasion to continue. Even when his concern is with constitutional issues, and in granting or withholding approval to statutes he is declaring public policy, his manner of speech cannot be that of the statesman. His place is in the institution of the judiciary; he is bound by its usages and procedures; he addresses himself, not directly to a social question, but to a matter of policy translated into the language of law; he cannot escape the values, rules, and intellectual ways of the discipline he professes. On the frontier where a changing social necessity impinges upon the established law, the jurist must possess a double competence; he must employ alike legal rule and social fact, and where they clash, as inevitably they will in a developing culture, he must effect the best reconciliation that may lie between them. The judge must become the statesman without ceasing to be the jurist; the quality of his art lies in the skill, the intelligence, and the sincerity with which he manages to serve two masters.

3. LAW AND PROGRESS

THE INHERENT CONSERVATISM OF THE LEGAL PROFESSION[8]

When we study Roman as well as Anglo-American legal history, we find it to be true as a general proposition that the most far-reaching

[7] From the article under the same title by Walton Hamilton in 31 *Columbia Law Review* 1073 (1931), reproduced by permission of the editors.

[8] By Edgar Bodenheimer, in 23 *Indiana Law Journal* 221–235 (1948); reproduced by permission of the editors.

changes and fundamental innovations in the structure and fabric of
the law were brought about, not by the actions of the legal profession,
but by the efforts and acts of men or groups of men outside its ranks.
. . . The torch of law reform and basic innovation was carried by men
or groups wielding political power rather than by professional men
learned in the law. The contributions of the legal profession in promoting and accomplishing momentous changes in the law have been
relatively small. . . . By and large, it can be said that judges and
lawyers, as such and in their capacity as professional men, have rarely
been the primary architects of basic legal change. . . .

. . . . . .

What is the explanation for this conservative and tradition-bound
attitude of the legal profession? It might perhaps be argued that the
customary conservatism of the legal profession finds its explanation
in the fact that the most prominent lawyers, the leaders and spokesmen of the profession, have an emotional attachment to the existing
social and economic order which brought them fame and monetary
reward, and are therefore disinterested in basic social and legal
change which would upset the *status quo*. But this argument does not
furnish a full answer to the problem we are investigating. The medical
profession, too, presents in its most successful representatives a body
of men who have achieved recognition and wealth under the existing
order of things and are generally not in favor of any change. Politically and economically, the American Medical Association is probably just as conservative as the American Bar Association. But there
exists a significant difference. It cannot be said that the medical profession, within the sphere of its own activity, is generally and habitually inclined to oppose changes in medical methods, the introduction
of new therapeutic techniques found to be effective, or the use of new
drugs affording improved methods of treatment. A physician is not
likely to object to the use of a therapeutic technique because 300
years ago some wizard in the profession had rejected it. The legal
profession, on the other hand, is quite prone to maintain the authority of a rule or principle proclaimed 300 years ago on the ground that
it represents the old-established law. Furthermore, radical advances
and innovations in medicine have usually originated within the ranks
of the medical profession and have not, as has happened so frequently
in the history of the law, been imposed from the outside and in the

face of resistance by the profession. The explanation for these differences is to be sought in the fact . . . that, in the sphere of the law, the "yesterday" is to a much greater extent an integral part of the "today" than, for instance, in the domain of medicine.

. . . . .

[Throughout history] . . . the law appears as an institution tending to integrate certain valuable and constructive elements of the past into the fabric of the present, thereby permitting a comparatively unbroken and continuous development of a nation. An intimate study of legal history will also disclose the fact, related to the previous observation, that the law is often an effective device for the neutralization of tensions. Frictions and conflicts of power within as well as between nations can in many cases be resolved or at least alleviated by the law through compromise and adjustment. In this neutralizing process, the treatment of individuals, groups, and nations on the basis of a certain equality plays an important part in the realization of the aims of the law. Just as tensions in the atomic world of nature are neutralized when negative electricity combines with positive electricity of equal charge, thus tensions and frictions in human life tend to become relieved when grave disparities of power are removed and the conflicting forces are brought into a certain state of balance and equilibrium.

Where such an equilibrium has been achieved, the law will strive with all its might to maintain and protect it against disturbances and disruption. This is one of its essential functions. For the neutralization of tensions which the law endeavors to realize would be largely illusory and of little value if the adjustments accomplished by it are of an entirely temporary and fleeting character. . . .

. . . A certain intent of self-perpetuation is inherent in typical creations of a legal character; a law is designed to serve as a general rule of conduct governing an indeterminate number of situations likely to arise in the future. The law-giver means to build a lasting and durable structure; and the greatest monuments of the law are those which have most successfully stood the test of time.

. . . If the law gives up its claim to duration and self-perpetuation and becomes a cluster of *ad hoc* measures, solely designed to meet the exigency of the moment, it is on its way to self-abdication. When the rights and the legal status of individuals and groups in a social system have become insecure, indeterminate, and subject to constant change at short intervals, this is a sign that law has given way to arbitrary power. Social conditions of excessive fluidity and chronic instability are hostile to the idea of law.

. . . If we view the law in this light, if we see in it an attempt to arrest perpetual and chaotic change and to surround certain human relations and institutions with guaranties of permanence and duration, the commonly retrospective and conservative attitude characteristic of the legal profession appears not only as logical but as well-nigh inevitable. The members of the Bench and Bar are not primarily pioneers and engineers of the future. Their functions are those of conservators of certain values of the past which have proved to be worthy of preservation; and the most challenging part of this task is perhaps that of weaving these values intelligently into the texture of the present.

If this is true, we shall not blame the judiciary for making a cautious, sparing, and reluctant use of the instrument of change. We shall understand and, within proper bounds, find justification, for the disinclination of the judges to cast off, suddenly, long-established principles and doctrines, even where basic social changes make us skeptical to their continued application. If the courts have yielded to the forward-moving forces in social development only slightly and gradually, and usually only in cases where a change in social *mores* was so clear that the application of an old rule to new conditions would have been entirely unreasonable, this has been due to reasons inherent in the nature of the law itself.

We find that the functions of the judiciary in the revision and modernization of the law are confined to minor alterations and "repairs," necessary to protect the structure, or parts of it, from disintegration and decay; they do not normally go beyond this type of "maintenance work." For great structural changes the judge must rely on outside assistance. He cannot himself tear down the edifice of the law or substantial parts of it, and replace them with new ones. He is the superintendent of this edifice, charged with the duty of keeping it in a good state of preservation, rather than its architect.

The same is true of the lawyer. He, too, must work with the tools which the past has handed to him, and his chief task is not that of an innovator. The Bench and Bar are not the proper proving ground for reformers and advocates of fundamental social change, whose activities must be confined to the arena of political action where power meets power, and where the dynamic forces of change are beating against the protective harness with which the law surrounds existing interests and institutions.

LAWYERS AS SOCIAL ENGINEERS[9]

Although bench and bar have claimed jurisprudence to be a science, it is "the last in the march of the sciences away from the method of deduction from predetermined conceptions." By their insistence upon the idea of "mechanical jurisprudence"—that the judges do not make but only declare the law and that a decision "must be upon some universal proposition valid in all places and at all times"—lawyers and judges have sought to remove constitutional questions from the field of popular discussion and control. Fortunately, Americans are today [quoting Dean Roscoe Pound] "beginning to learn that judicial decisions are not babies brought by constitutional storks but are born out of the travail of economic circumstance."

To bring the same enlightenment to the legal profession it will happily not be necessary to "kill all the lawyers," as Dick suggested to Jack Cade. Some of the teachers and writers who have been responsible for the education of the public since the turn of the century are also members of a new teaching bar. These men, beginning with Professor James Bradley Thayer of the Harvard Law School, have inculcated in a small but increasing number of law students a skepticism of judicial dogma and a sense of the law as a human institution which is shot through with the vagaries and interest of the human beings controlling it. Assisted by social scientists and philosophers from outside, they have made the leading law school journals organs of criticism and analysis which have awakened the people and the judges to the social and economic bias at the root of judicial decisions. In like manner have they questioned the theory of "benevolent conflict" basic in both laissez faire and the legal process, exposing the tendency of the primitive "trial by verbal combat" to hinder justice by obscuring truth rather than discovering and applying it to social problems. The bar has been a great propaganda machine which has focused on the judiciary a barrage of words, phrases, symbols and creeds rendered weighty by the predominantly verbal nature of legalism. Contentiousness and delay have characterized the process in a day when the normal complexity of human relations is sufficient to

[9] From Benjamin R. Twiss, *Lawyers and the Constitution*, pp. 259–264. Reproduced by permission of the publishers, Princeton University Press.

furnish challenging occupation to any number of enlightened lawyers without the need of perpetuating difficulties as vested interests.

Yet many legal problems are in essence economic or sociological problems, and legal standards alone are likely to be disastrous if applied to large classes of society. While experimental sciences make a point of ascertaining the results of their conclusions, no provision is made in the law for such a method. Nevertheless lawyers invent economic devices and the judges adopt them, with no more justification than the manipulation of the precedents supplied by the lawyers. Fortunately a number of progressive law schools are emphasizing the integration of law with the realities of business, government, and social conditions by relating it continuously to such activities as accounting, administration and industrial relations. Law journals and books are concerned with bringing the law into accord with modern scientific method, and judges are asking the bar to devise better means of determining questions of fact. The increasing use of scientific evidence shows a change from the view that law is self-sufficient to a realization of its function as a social institution, but the rapidity of this change must still depend largely upon the initiative of the lawyers.

Not wholly, however, for the reliance of the Supreme Court upon statistics and other results of economic research in upholding the National Labor Relations Act illustrates the growing influence of governmental administrative agencies upon constitutional law. Whereas precedent, like habit, makes for stability, the administrative process is geared to the dynamic conditions of today, which require a stability more resilient and adaptable to change and complexity than dogmatic attitudes and traditional procedures can provide. Legal formalism leads to the rigid crystallization of administrative practice whose prime requisite is flexibility to meet many variable circumstances equitably and efficiently. Thus the administrator has often to replace the absolute *ought* of legal concepts with the relative *is* of scientific facts or public policy; and when there is a substantial difference of opinion as to the facts involved in a public problem these may not, in a democracy, be what a minority of lawyers, judges, or even scientific experts asserts to be facts, sincerely or otherwise. The process of science, like the law itself, in the field of political questions is exposed to the abuse of bias and interest. Hence the need to have regard for public policy as determined by the understanding of the currently prevailing majority.

The central need is not to obstruct government as baneful. It is to make administration more democratically effective as a protection for the freest possible development of the individual against threats from any quarter. The reconciliation of individual liberty with majority rule is a public problem, for in a complex society liberty is only the result of compromise. Administrative law represents a rational effort to attack this problem on a basis of public organization rather than on the fictitious plane of absolute private rights. By its provision for fact-finding as well as for carrying out public policy it is better adapted than legal procedure to the needs of modern democratic administration. Heretofore the mutually interwoven growth of economic institutions and constitutional doctrines has often been at cross purposes with legislative policy and social fact. Now, as Justice Holmes long advocated, the Supreme Court is manifesting an increasing disposition to accept the aid of legislatures and investigative agencies in determining the structure of our economy. A still more fundamental change in viewpoint toward the judicial process was illustrated by the words of Justice Stone, who said, "The doctrine of *stare decisis,* however appropriate or even necessary at times, has only a limited application in the field of constitutional law."

The lawyers also are needed to help construct channels for social cooperation, to strengthen democracy in legislation, administration, and adjudication. "Law is the frame which contains society, as its banks contain a river," said Brooks Adams, "and if the flow of a river be increased a thousandfold, the banks must be altered to correspond, or there will be a flood overwhelming in proportion to the uncontrollable energy generated." Many recognize the implications of new conditions. There have always been lawyers who have put the public interest before private profit. The Association of the Bar of the City of New York has balanced . . . [servility to private corporate interests] . . . with important public service from time to time. At present it is fighting the movement to impose the rigid formalities of the law on administrative procedure.

Proposed legislation designed thus to hamstring administration, characterized by a senator as "a bill to end unemployment among lawyers," is in reality a flank attack from the camp of laissez faire. It seeks to hinder the effectiveness of the chief new instruments of public regulation of economic enterprise, especially the National Labor Relations Board and the Securities and Exchange Commission. That the leader of the movement is the American Bar Association, supported by the Chamber of Commerce of the United States and the Republican platform of 1940, accords with the old patterns of the relation between law and private capitalism. The accompanying assumption of "authority" to interpret the American spirit as a specially qualified elite is essentially the same as such assertions elsewhere in the world. It therefore behooves the lawyers, unless they wish to lose their position as experts in the structure of society, to reexamine their motives, and to cease insisting upon their divine ordination as a priesthood of legalistic hocus-pocus. Instead, responsibility must be accompanied by humility and dedication to public service.

Individualism as a philosophy and a principle of government is still valid, and the governmental form of individualism is democracy. The true function of the lawyer, then, is to guide the development of popular self-government rather than oppose it; to throw his energy and intelligence as a social engineer into the construction of equitable methods of administration rather than to sabotage cooperative effort with shibboleths and slogans. Law and justice have claimed some of the best intellects history has produced. That these be turned to constructive rather than obstructive efforts is essential to the survival of democracy.

A P P E N D I X

＊ ⌣ ＊

＊

The Constitution of the United States

Preamble

We the People of the United States, in Order to form a more perfect Union, establish Justice, insure domestic Tranquility, provide for the common defence, promote the general Welfare, and secure the Blessings of Liberty to ourselves and our Posterity, do ordain and establish this Constitution for the United States of America.

Article I

Section 1. All legislative Powers herein granted shall be vested in a Congress of the United States, which shall consist of a Senate and House of Representatives.

Section 2. The House of Representatives shall be composed of Members chosen every second Year by the People of the several States, and the Electors in each State shall have the Qualifications requisite for Electors of the most numerous Branch of the State Legislature.

No Person shall be a Representative who shall not have attained to the Age of twenty five Years, and been seven Years a Citizen of the United States, and who shall not, when elected, be an inhabitant of that State in which he shall be chosen.

Representatives and direct Taxes shall be apportioned among the several States which may be included within this Union, according to their respective Numbers, [which shall be determined by adding to the whole Number of free Persons, including those bound to Service for a Term of Years, and excluding Indians not taxed, three fifths of all other Persons.][1] The actual Enumeration shall be made within three Years after the first Meeting of the Congress of the United States, and within every subsequent

[1] Superseded by the Fourteenth Amendment.

Term of ten Years, in such Manner as they shall by law direct. The Number of Representatives shall not exceed one for every thirty Thousand, but each State shall have at Least one Representative; and until such enumeration shall be made, the State of New Hampshire shall be entitled to chuse three, Massachusetts eight, Rhode-Island and Providence Plantations one, Connecticut five, New-York six, New Jersey four, Pennsylvania eight, Delaware one, Maryland six, Virginia ten, North Carolina five, South Carolina five, and Georgia three.

When vacancies happen in the Representation from any State, the Executive Authority thereof shall issue Writs of Election to fill such Vacancies.

The House of Representatives shall chuse their Speaker and other Officers; and shall have the sole Power of Impeachment.

Section 3.   The Senate of the United States shall be composed of two Senators from each State, [chosen by the Legislature thereof,]² for six Years; and each Senator shall have one Vote.

Immediately after they shall be assembled in Consequence of the first Election, they shall be divided as equally as may be into three Classes. The Seats of the Senators of the first Class shall be vacated at the Expiration of the second Year, of the second Class at the Expiration of the fourth Year, and of the third Class at the Expiration of the sixth Year, so that one third may be chosen every second Year; [and if Vacancies happen by Resignation, or otherwise, during the Recess of the Legislature of any State, the Executive thereof may make temporary Appointments until the next Meeting of the Legislature, which shall then fill such Vacancies.]³

No Person shall be a Senator who shall not have attained to the Age of thirty Years, and been nine Years a Citizen of the United States, and who shall not, when elected, be an Inhabitant of that State for which he shall be chosen.

The Vice President of the United States shall be President of the Senate, but shall have no Vote, unless they be equally divided.

The Senate shall chuse their other Officers, and also a President pro tempore, in the Absence of the Vice President, or when he shall exercise the Office of President of the United States.

The Senate shall have the sole Power to try all Impeachments. When sitting for that Purpose, they shall be on Oath or Affirmation. When the President of the United States is tried, the Chief Justice shall preside: and no Person shall be convicted without the Concurrence of two thirds of the Members present.

Judgment in Cases of Impeachment shall not extend further than to removal from Office, and disqualification to hold and enjoy any Office of honor, Trust or Profit under the United States: but the Party convicted

² Superseded by the Seventeenth Amendment.
³ Modified by the Seventeenth Amendment.

shall nevertheless be liable and subject to Indictment, Trial, Judgment and Punishment, according to Law.

Section 4. The Times, Places and Manner of holding Elections for Senators and Representatives, shall be prescribed in each State by the Legislature thereof; but the Congress may at any time by Law make or alter such Regulations, except as to the Places of chusing Senators.

[The Congress shall assemble at least once in every Year, and such Meeting shall be on the first Monday in December, unless they shall by Law appoint a different Day.]⁴

Section 5. Each House shall be the Judge of the Elections, Returns and Qualifications of its own Members, and a Majority of each shall constitute a Quorum to do Business; but a smaller Number may adjourn from day to day, and may be authorized to compel the Attendance of absent Members, in such Manner, and under such Penalties as each House may provide.

Each House may determine the Rules of its Proceedings, punish its Members for disorderly Behaviour, and, with the Concurrence of two thirds, expel a Member.

Each House shall keep a Journal of its Proceedings, and from time to time publish the same, excepting such Parts as may in their Judgment require Secrecy; and the Yeas and Nays of the Members of either House on any question shall, at the Desire of one fifth of those Present, be entered on the Journal.

Neither House, during the Session of Congress, shall, without the Consent of the other, adjourn for more than three days, nor to any other Place than that in which the two Houses shall be sitting.

Section 6. The Senators and Representatives shall receive a Compensation for their Services, to be ascertained by Law, and paid out of the Treasury of the United States. They shall in all Cases, except Treason, Felony and Breach of the Peace, be privileged from Arrest during their Attendance at the Session of their respective Houses, and in going to and returning from the same; and for any Speech or Debate in either House, they shall not be questioned in any other Place.

No Senator or Representative shall, during the Time for which he was elected, be appointed to any civil Office under the Authority of the United States, which shall have been created, or the Emoluments whereof shall have been encreased during such time; and no Person holding any Office under the United States, shall be a Member of either House during his Continuance in Office.

Section 7 All bills for raising Revenue shall originate in the House of Representatives; but the Senate may propose or concur with Amendments as on other Bills.

⁴ Superseded by the Twentieth Amendment.

Every Bill which shall have passed the House of Representatives and the Senate, shall, before it become a Law, be presented to the President of the United States; If he approve he shall sign it, but if not he shall return it, with his Objections to that House in which it shall have originated, who shall enter the Objections at large on their Journal, and proceed to reconsider it. If after such Reconsideration two thirds of that House shall agree to pass the Bill, it shall be sent, together with the Objections, to the other House, by which it shall likewise be reconsidered, and if approved by two thirds of that House, it shall become a Law. But in all such Cases the Votes of both Houses shall be determined by yeas and Nays, and the Names of the Persons voting for and against the Bill shall be entered on the Journal of each House respectively. If any Bill shall not be returned by the President within ten Days (Sundays excepted) after it shall have been presented to him, the Same shall be a Law, in like Manner as if he had signed it, unless the Congress by their Adjournment prevent its Return, in which Case it shall not be a Law.

Every Order, Resolution, or Vote to which the Concurrence of the Senate and House of Representatives may be necessary (except on a question of Adjournment) shall be presented to the President of the United States; and before the Same shall take Effect, shall be approved by him, or being disapproved by him, shall be repassed by two thirds of the Senate and House of Representatives, according to the Rules and Limitations prescribed in the Case of a Bill.

Section 8.   The Congress shall have Power To lay and collect Taxes, Duties, Imposts and Excises, to pay the Debts and provide for the common Defence and general Welfare of the United States; but all Duties, Imposts and Excises shall be uniform throughout the United States;

To borrow Money on the credit of the United States;

To regulate Commerce with foreign Nations, and among the several States, and with the Indian Tribes;

To establish a uniform Rule of Naturalization, and uniform Laws on the subject of Bankruptcies throughout the United States;

To coin Money, regulate the Value thereof, and of foreign Coin, and fix the Standard of Weights and Measures;

To provide for the Punishment of counterfeiting the Securities and current Coin of the United States;

To establish Post Offices and post Roads;

To promote the Progress of Science and useful Arts, by securing for limited Times to Authors and Inventors the exclusive Right to their respective Writings and Discoveries;

To constitute Tribunals inferior to the supreme Court;

To define and punish Piracies and Felonies committed on the high Seas, and Offences against the Law of Nations;

To declare War, grant Letters of Marque and Reprisal, and make Rules concerning Captures on Land and Water;

To raise and support Armies, but no Appropriation of Money to that Use shall be for a longer Term than two Years;

To provide and maintain a Navy;

To make Rules for the Government and Regulation of the land and naval Forces;

To provide for calling forth the Militia to execute the Laws of the Union, suppress Insurrections and repel Invasions;

To provide for organizing, arming, and disciplining, the Militia, and for governing such Part of them as may be employed in the Service of the United States, reserving to the States respectively, the Appointment of the Officers, and the Authority of training the Militia according to the discipline prescribed by Congress;

To exercise exclusive Legislation in all Cases whatsoever, over such District (not exceeding ten Miles square) as may, by Cession of particular States, and the Acceptance of Congress, become the Seat of the Government of the United States, and to exercise like Authority over all Places purchased by the Consent of the Legislature of the State in which the Same shall be, for the Erection of Forts, Magazines, Arsenals, dock-Yards, and other needful Buildings;—And

To make all Laws which shall be necessary and proper for carrying into Execution the foregoing Powers, and all other Powers vested by this Constitution in the Government of the United States, or in any Department or Officer thereof.

Section 9. The Migration or Importation of such Persons as any of the States now existing shall think proper to admit, shall not be prohibited by the Congress prior to the Year one thousand eight hundred and eight, but a Tax or duty may be imposed on such Importation, not exceeding ten dollars for each Person.

The Privilege of the Writ of Habeas Corpus shall not be suspended, unless when in Cases of Rebellion or Invasion the public safety may require it.

No Bill of Attainder or ex post facto Law shall be passed.

No Capitation, or other direct, Tax shall be laid, unless in Proportion to the Census or Enumeration herein before directed to be taken.[1]

No Tax or Duty shall be laid on Articles exported from any State.

No Preference shall be given by any Regulation of Commerce or Revenue to the Ports of one State over those of another; nor shall Vessels bound to, or from, one State, be obliged to enter, clear, or pay Duties in another.

No money shall be drawn from the Treasury, but in Consequence of

[1] Modified by the Sixteenth Amendment.

Appropriations made by Law; and a regular Statement and Account of the Receipts and Expenditures of all public Money shall be published from time to time.

No Title of Nobility shall be granted by the United States: And no Person holding any Office of Profit or Trust under them, shall, without the Consent of the Congress, accept any present, Emolument, Office, or Title, of any kind whatever, from any King, Prince, or foreign State.

Section 10.   No State shall enter into any Treaty, Alliance, or Confederation; grant Letters of Marque and Reprisal; coin Money; emit Bills of Credit; make any Thing but gold and silver Coin a Tender in Payment of Debts; pass any Bill of Attainder, ex post facto Law, or Law impairing the Obligation of Contracts, or grant any Title of Nobility.

No State shall, without the Consent of the Congress, lay any Imposts or Duties on Imports or Exports, except what may be absolutely necessary for executing it's inspection laws; and the net Produce of all Duties and Imposts, laid by any State on Imports or Exports, shall be for the Use of the Treasury of the United States; and all such Laws shall be subject to the Revision, and Control of the Congress.

No State, shall, without the Consent of Congress, lay any Duty of Tonnage, keep Troops, or Ships of War in time of Peace, enter into any Agreement or Compact with another State, or with a foreign Power, or engage in War, unless actually invaded, or in such imminent Danger as will not admit of delay.

Article II.

Section 1.   The executive Power shall be vested in a President of the United States of America. He shall hold his Office during the Term of four Years, and, together with the Vice President, chosen for the same Term, be elected, as follows

Each State shall appoint, in such Manner as the Legislature thereof may direct, a Number of Electors, equal to the whole Number of Senators and Representatives to which the State may be entitled in the Congress: but no Senator or Representative, or Person holding an Office of Trust or Profit under the United States, shall be appointed an Elector.

[The Electors shall meet in their respective States, and vote by Ballot for two Persons, of whom one at least shall not be an Inhabitant of the same State with themselves. And they shall make a List of all the Persons voted for, and the Number of Votes for each; which list they shall sign and certify, and transmit sealed to the Seat of the Government of the United States, directed to the President of the Senate. The President of the Senate shall, in the Presence of the Senate and House of Representatives, open all the Certificates, and the Votes shall then be counted. The person having the greatest Number of Votes shall be the President, if such Number be a Majority of the whole Number of Electors appointed; and if there be more than one who have such Majority, and have an equal Number of Votes, then the House of Representatives shall immediately chuse by Ballot one of them for President; and if no Person have a Majority, then from the five highest on the List the said House shall in like Manner chuse the President. But in chusing the President, the Votes shall be taken by States, the Representation from each State having one Vote; A quorum for this purpose shall consist of a Member or Members from two thirds of the States, and a Majority of all the States shall be necessary to a Choice. In every Case, after the Choice of the President, the Person having the greatest Number of Votes of the Electors shall be the Vice President. But if there should remain two or more who have equal Votes, the Senate chuse from them by Ballot the Vice President.][5]

The Congress may determine the Time of chusing the Electors, and the Day on which they shall give their Votes; which Day shall be the same throughout the United States.

No Person except a natural born Citizen, or a Citizen of the United States, at the time of the Adoption of this Constitution, shall be eligible to the Office of President; neither shall any Person be eligible to that Office who shall not have attained to the Age of thirty five Years, and been fourteen Years a Resident within the United States.

In Case of the Removal of the President from Office, or of his Death, Resignation, or Inability to discharge the Powers and Duties of the said Office, the Same shall devolve on the Vice President, and the Congress may by Law provide for the Case of Removal, Death, Resignation or Inability, both of the President and Vice President, declaring what Officer shall then act as President, and such Officer shall act accordingly, until the Disability be removed, or a President shall be elected.

The President shall, at stated Times receive for his Services, a Compensation, which shall neither be encreased nor diminished during the Period for which he shall have been elected, and he shall not receive within that Period any other Emolument from the United States, or any of them.

Before he enter on the Execution of his Office, he shall take the following Oath or Affirmation:—"I do solemnly swear (or affirm) that I will faithfully execute the Office of President of the United States, and will to the best of my Ability, preserve, protect and defend the Constitution of the United States."

Section 2. The President shall be Commander in Chief of the Army and Navy of the United States, and of the Militia of the several States, when called into the actual Service of the United States; he may require the Opinion, in writing, of the principal Officer in each of the executive Departments, upon any Subject relating to the Duties of their respective

[5] Superseded by the Twelfth Amendment.

Offices, and he shall have Power to grant Reprieves and Pardons for Offences against the United States, except in Cases of Impeachment.

He shall have Power, by and with the Advice and Consent of the Senate, to make Treaties, provided two thirds of the Senators present concur; and he shall nominate, and by and with the Advice and Consent of the Senate, shall appoint Ambassadors, other public Ministers and Consuls, Judges of the supreme Court, and all other Officers of the United States, whose Appointments are not herein otherwise provided for, and which shall be established by Law: but the Congress may by Law vest the Appointment of such inferior Officers, as they think proper, in the President alone, in the Courts of Law, or in the Heads of Departments.

The President shall have Power to fill up all Vacancies that may happen during the Recess of the Senate, by granting Commissions which shall expire at the End of their next Session.

Section 3. He shall from time to time give to the Congress Information of the State of the Union, and recommend to their Consideration such Measures as he shall judge necessary and expedient; he may, on extraordinary Occasions, convene both Houses, or either of them, and in Case of Disagreement between them, with Respect to the Time of Adjournment, he may adjourn them to such Time as he shall think proper; he shall receive Ambassadors and other public Ministers; he shall take Care that the Laws be faithfully executed, and shall Commission all Officers of the United States.

Section 4. The President, Vice President and all civil Officers of the United States, shall be removed from Office on Impeachment for, and Conviction of, Treason, Bribery, or other high Crimes and Misdemeanors.

Article III.

Section 1. The judicial Power of the United States, shall be vested in one supreme Court, and in such inferior Courts as the Congress may from time to time ordain and establish. The Judges, both of the supreme and inferior Courts, shall hold their Offices during good Behaviour, and shall, at stated Times, receive for their Services, a Compensation, which shall not be diminished during their Continuance in Office.

Section 2. The judicial Power shall extend to all Cases, in Law and Equity, arising under this Constitution, the Laws of the United States, and Treaties made, or which shall be made, under their Authority;—to all Cases affecting Ambassadors, other public Ministers and Consuls;—to all Cases of admiralty and maritime Jurisdiction;—to Controversies to which the United States shall be a Party;—to Controversies between two or more States;—between a State and Citizens of another State;6—between Citizens of different States,—between Citizens of the same State claiming Lands

6 Modified by the Eleventh Amendment.

under Grants of different States, and between a State, or the Citizens thereof, and foreign States, Citizens or Subjects.

In all cases affecting Ambassadors, other public Ministers and Consuls, and those in which a State shall be Party, the supreme Court shall have original Jurisdiction. In all the other Cases before mentioned, the supreme Court shall have appellate Jurisdiction, both as to Law and Fact, with such Exceptions, and under such Regulations as the Congress shall make.

The Trial of all Crimes, except in Cases of Impeachment, shall be by Jury; and such Trial shall be held in the State where the said Crimes shall have been committed; but when not committed within any State, the Trial shall be at such Place or Places as the Congress may by Law have directed.

Section 3.　Treason against the United States, shall consist only in levying War against them, or in adhering to their Enemies, giving them Aid and Comfort. No Person shall be convicted of Treason unless on the Testimony of two Witnesses to the same overt Act, or on Confession in open Court.

The Congress shall have Power to declare the Punishment of Treason, but no Attainder of Treason shall work Corruption of Blood, or Forfeiture except during the Life of the Person attainted.

Article IV

Section 1.　Full Faith and Credit shall be given in each State to the public Acts, Records, and judicial Proceedings of every other State. And the Congress may by general Laws prescribe the Manner in which such Acts, Records and Proceedings shall be proved, and the Effect thereof.

Section 2.　The Citizens of each State shall be entitled to all Privileges and Immunities of Citizens in the several States.

A Person charged in any State with Treason, Felony, or other Crime, who shall flee from Justice, and be found in another State, shall on Demand of the executive Authority of the State from which he fled, be delivered up, to be removed to the State having Jurisdiction of the Crime.

No Person held to Service or Labour in one State, under the Laws thereof, escaping into another, shall, in Consequence of any Law or Regulation therein, be discharged from such Service or Labour, but shall be delivered up on Claim of the Party to whom such Service or Labour may be due.

Section 3.　New States may be admitted by the Congress into this Union; but no new State shall be formed or erected within the Jurisdiction of any other State; nor any State be formed by the Junction of two or more States, or Parts of States, without the Consent of the Legislatures of the States concerned as well as of the Congress.

The Congress shall have Power to dispose of and make all needful Rules and Regulations respecting the Territory or other Property belonging to the United States; and nothing in this Constitution shall be so construed as to Prejudice any Claims of the United States, or of any particular State.

Section 4. The United States shall guarantee to every State in this Union a Republican Form of Government, and shall protect each of them against Invasion; and on Application of the Legislature, or of the Executive (when the Legislature cannot be convened) against domestic Violence.

Article V

The Congress, whenever two thirds of both Houses shall deem it necessary, shall propose Amendments to this Constitution, or, on the Application of the Legislatures of two thirds of the several States, shall call a Convention for proposing Amendments, which, in either Case, shall be valid to all Intents and Purposes, as Part of this Constitution, when ratified by the Legislatures of three fourths of the several States, or by Conventions in three fourths thereof, as the one or the other Mode of Ratification may be proposed by the Congress; Provided that no Amendment which may be made prior to the Year One thousand eight hundred and eight shall in any Manner affect the first and fourth Clauses in the Ninth Section of the first Article; and that no State, without its Consent, shall be deprived of it's equal Suffrage in the Senate.

Article VI

All Debts contracted and Engagements entered into, before the Adoption of this Constitution, shall be as valid against the United States under this Constitution, as under the Confederation.

This Constitution, and the Laws of the United States which shall be made in Pursuance thereof; and all Treaties made, or which shall be made, under the Authority of the United States, shall be the supreme Law of the Land; and the Judges in every State shall be bound thereby, any Thing in the Constitution or Laws of any State to the Contrary notwithstanding.

The Senators and Representatives before mentioned, and the Members of the several State Legislatures, and all executive and judicial Officers, both of the United States and of the several States, shall be bound by Oath or Affirmation, to support this Constitution; but no religious Test shall ever be required as a Qualification to any Office or public Trust under the United States.

Article VII

The Ratification of the Conventions of nine States, shall be sufficient for the Establishment of this Constitution between the States so ratifying the Same.

[Signatures omitted.]

ARTICLES in addition to, and Amendment of the Constitution of the United States of America, proposed by Congress, and ratified by the Legislatures of the several States, pursuant to the fifth Article of the original Constitution.

Article I

Congress shall make no law respecting an establishment of religion, or prohibiting the free exercise thereof; or abridging the freedom of speech, or of the press; or the right of the people peaceably to assemble, and to petition the Government for a redress of grievances.

Article II

A well regulated Militia, being necessary to the security of a free State, the right of the people to keep and bear Arms, shall not be infringed.

Article III

No Soldier shall, in time of peace be quartered in any house, without the consent of the Owner, nor in time of war, but in a manner to be prescribed by law.

Article IV

The right of the people to be secure in their persons, houses, papers, and effects, against unreasonable searches and seizures, shall not be violated, and no Warrants shall issue, but upon probable cause, supported by Oath or affirmation, and particularly describing the place to be searched, and the persons or things to be seized.

Article V

No person shall be held to answer for a capital, or otherwise infamous crime, unless on a presentment or indictment of a Grand Jury, except in cases arising in the land or naval forces, or in the Militia, when in actual service in time of War or public danger; nor shall any person be subject for the same offence to be twice put in jeopardy of life or limb; nor shall be compelled in any criminal case to be a witness against himself, nor be deprived of life, liberty, or property, without due process of law; nor shall private property be taken for public use, without just compensation.

Article VI

In all criminal prosecutions, the accused shall enjoy the right to a speedy and public trial, by an impartial jury of the State and district wherein the crime shall have been committed, which district shall have been previously ascertained by law, and to be informed of the nature and cause of the accusation; to be confronted with the witnesses against him;

to have compulsory process for obtaining witnesses in his favor, and to have the Assistance of Counsel for his defence.

Article VII

In Suits at common law, where the value in controversy shall exceed twenty dollars, the right of trial by jury shall be preserved, and no fact tried by a jury, shall be otherwise re-examined in any Court of the United States, than according to the rules of the common law.

Article VIII

Excessive bail shall not be required, nor excessive fines imposed, nor cruel and unusual punishments inflicted.

Article IX

The enumeration in the Constitution, of certain rights, shall not be construed to deny or disparage others retained by the people.

Article X

The powers not delegated to the United States by the Constitution, nor prohibited by it to the States, are reserved to the States respectively, or to the people.

Article XI

The Judicial power of the United States shall not be construed to extend to any suit in law or equity, commenced or prosecuted against one of the United States by Citizens of another State, or by Citizens or Subjects of any Foreign State.

Article XII

The Electors shall meet in their respective states, and vote by ballot for President and Vice-President, one of whom, at least, shall not be an inhabitant of the same state with themselves; they shall name in their ballots the person voted for as President, and in distinct ballots the person voted for as Vice-President, and they shall make distinct lists of all persons voted for as President, and of all persons voted for as Vice-President, and of the number of votes for each, which lists they shall sign and certify, and transmit sealed to the seat of the government of the United States, directed to the President of the Senate;—The President of the Senate shall, in the presence of the Senate and House of Representatives, open all certificates and the votes shall then be counted;—The person having the greatest number of votes for President, shall be the President, if such number be a majority of the whole number of Electors appointed; and if no person have such majority, then from the persons having the highest numbers not exceeding three on the list of those voted for as President, the House of Representatives shall choose immediately, by ballot, the President. But in choosing the President, the votes shall be taken by states, the representation from each state having one vote; a quorum for this purpose shall consist of a member or members from two-thirds of the states, and a majority of all the states shall be necessary to a choice. And if the House of Representatives shall not choose a President whenever the right of choice shall devolve upon them, before the fourth day of March next following, then the Vice-President shall act as President, as in the case of the death or other constitutional disability of the President.— The person having the greatest number of votes as Vice-President, shall be the Vice-President, if such number be a majority of the whole number of Electors appointed, and if no person have a majority, then from the two highest numbers on the list, the Senate shall choose the Vice-President; a quorum for the purpose shall consist of two-thirds of the whole number of Senators, and a majority of the whole number shall be necessary to a choice. But no person constitutionally ineligible to the office of President shall be eligible to that of Vice-President of the United States.

Article XIII

Section 1.   Neither slavery nor involuntary servitude, except as a punishment for crime whereof the party shall have been duly convicted, shall exist within the United States, or any place subject to their jurisdiction.

Section 2.   Congress shall have power to enforce this article by appropriate legislation.

Article XIV

Section 1.   All persons born or naturalized in the United States, and subject to the jurisdiction thereof, are citizens of the United States and of the State wherein they reside. No State shall make or enforce any law which shall abridge the privileges or immunities of citizens of the United States; nor shall any State deprive any person of life, liberty, or property, without due process of law; nor deny to any person within its jurisdiction the equal protection of the laws.

Section 2.   Representatives shall be apportioned among the several States according to their respective numbers, counting the whole number of persons in each State, excluding Indians not taxed. But when the right to vote at any election for the choice of electors for President and Vice President of the United States, Representatives in Congress, the Executive and Judicial officers of a State, or the members of the Legislature thereof, is denied to any of the male inhabitants of such State, being twenty-one years of age, and citizens of the United States, or in any way abridged, except for participation in rebellion, or other crime, the basis of representation therein shall be reduced in the proportion which the number of such male citizens shall bear to the whole number of male citizens twenty-one years of age in such State.

Section 3.   No person shall be a Senator or Representative in Congress, or elector of President and Vice President, or hold any office, civil or military, under the United States, or under any State, who, having previously taken an oath, as a member of Congress, or as an officer of the United States, or as a member of any State legislature, or as an executive or judicial officer of any State, to support the Constitution of the United States. shall have engaged in insurrection or rebellion against the same, or given aid and comfort to the enemies thereof. But Congress may by a vote of two-thirds of each House, remove such disability.

Section 4.   The validity of the public debt of the United States, authorized by law, including debts incurred for payment of pensions and bounties for services in suppressing insurrection or rebellion, shall not be questioned. But neither the United States nor any state shall assume or pay any debt or obligation incurred in aid of insurrection or rebellion against the United States, or any claim for the loss or emancipation of any slave; but all such debts, obligations, and claims shall be held illegal and void.

Section 5.   The Congress shall have power to enforce, by appropriate legislation, the provisions of this article.

Article XV

Section 1.   The right of citizens of the United States to vote shall not be denied or abridged by the United States or by any State on account of race, color, or previous condition of servitude—

Section 2.   The Congress shall have power to enforce this article by appropriate legislation—

Article XVI

The Congress shall have power to lay and collect taxes on incomes, from whatever source derived, without apportionment among the several States, and without regard to any census or enumeration.

Article XVII

The Senate of the United States shall be composed of two Senators from each State, elected by the people thereof, for six years; and each Senator shall have one vote. The electors in each State shall have the qualifications requisite for electors of the most numerous branch of the State legislatures.

When vacancies happen in the representation of any State in the Senate, the executive authority of such State shall issue writs of election to fill such vacancies: *Provided,* That the legislature of any State may empower the executive thereof to make temporary appointments until the people fill the vacancies by election as the legislature may direct.

This amendment shall not be so construed as to affect the election or term of any Senator chosen before it becomes valid as part of the Constitution.

Article XVIII

Section 1. After one year from the ratification of this article the manufacture, sale, or transportation of intoxicating liquors within, the importation thereof into, or the exportation thereof from the United States and all territory subject to the jurisdiction thereof for beverage purposes is hereby prohibited.

Section 2. The Congress and the several States shall have concurrent power to enforce this article by appropriate legislation.

Section 3. This article shall be inoperative unless it shall have been ratified as an amendment to the Constitution by the legislatures of the several States, as provided in the Constitution, within seven years from the date of the submission hereof to the States by the Congress.[7]

Article XIX

The right of citizens of the United States to vote shall not be denied or abridged by the United States or by any State on account of sex.

Congress shall have power to enforce this article by appropriate legislation.

Article XX

Section 1. The terms of the President and Vice President shall end at noon on the 20th day of January, and the terms of Senators and Representatives at noon on the 3d day of January, of the years in which such terms would have ended if this article had not been ratified; and the terms of their successors shall then begin.

Section 2. The Congress shall assemble at least once in every year, and such meeting shall begin at noon on the 3d day of January, unless they shall by law appoint a different day.

Section 3. If, at the time fixed for the beginning of the term of the President, the President elect shall have died, the Vice President elect shall become President. If a President shall not have been chosen before the time fixed for the beginning of his term, or if the President elect shall have failed to qualify, then the Vice President elect shall act as President until a President shall have qualified; and the Congress may by law provide for the case wherein neither a President elect nor a Vice President elect shall have qualified, declaring who shall then act as President, or

[7] Superseded by the Twenty-first Amendment.

the manner in which one who is to act shall be selected, and such person shall act accordingly until a President or Vice President shall have qualified.

Section 4.   The Congress may by law provide for the case of the death of any of the persons from whom the House of Representatives may choose a President whenever the right of choice shall have devolved upon them, and for the case of the death of any of the persons from whom the Senate may choose a Vice President whenever the right of choice shall have devolved upon them.

Section 5.   Sections 1 and 2 shall take effect on the 15th day of October following the ratification of this article.

Section 6.   This article shall be inoperative unless it shall have been ratified as an amendment to the Constitution by the legislatures of three-fourths of the several States within seven years from the date of its submission.

Article XXI

Section 1.   The Eighteenth article of amendment to the Constitution of the United States is hereby repealed.

Section 2.   The transportation or importation into any State, Territory, or possession of the United States for delivery or use therein of intoxicating liquors, in violation of the laws thereof, is hereby prohibited.

Section 3.   This article shall be inoperative unless it shall have been ratified as an amendment to the Constitution by conventions in the several States, as provided in the Constitution, within seven years from the date of the submission hereof to the States by the Congress.

Article XXII

Section 1.   No person shall be elected to the office of the President more than twice, and no person who has held the office of President, or acted as President, for more than two years of a term to which some other person was elected President shall be elected to the office of the President more than once. But this Article shall not apply to any person holding the office of President when this Article was proposed by the Congress, and shall not prevent any person who may be holding the office of President, or acting as President, during the term within which this Article becomes operative from holding the office of President or acting as President during the remainder of such term.

Section 2.   This article shall be inoperative unless it shall have been ratified as an amendment to the Constitution by the legislatures of three-fourths of the several States within seven years from the date of its submission to the States by the Congress.

TABLE OF CASES

(Bold type references are to opinions and case extracts,
all others to citations and text references only.)

I N D E X

683